As Long as Space E

Essays on the Kālacakra Tantra
in Honor of H.H. the Dalai Lama

As Long as Space Endures

Essays on the Kālacakra Tantra in Honor of H.H. the Dalai Lama

Edward A. Arnold
Editor

on behalf of
Namgyal Monastery Institute
of Buddhist Studies

Snow Lion
Boston & London

Snow Lion
An imprint of Shambhala Publications, Inc.
Horticultural Hall
300 Massachusetts Avenue
Boston, Massachusetts 02115
www.shambhala.com

9 8 7 6 5 4 3 2

Printed in the United States of America

♾ This edition is printed on acid-free paper that meets the American National Standards Institute Z39.48 Standard.
♻ Shambhala Publications makes every effort to print on recycled paper. For more information please visit www.shambhala.com.
Distributed in the United States by Random House, Inc., and in Canada by Random House of Canada Ltd

Library of Congress Cataloging-in-Publication Data

As long as space endures: essays on the Kālacakra tantra in honor of H.H. the Dalai Lama / Edward A. Arnold, editor on behalf of Namgyal Monastery Institute of Buddhist Studies.
p. cm.
Includes bibliographical references.
ISBN 978-1-55939-303-4 (hardcover)
ISBN 978-1-55939-330-0 (paperback)
1. Kālacakra (Tantric rite). 2. Tripiṭaka. Sūtrapiṭaka. Tantra. Kālacakratantra—Criticism, interpretation, etc. 3. Yoga—Tantric Buddhism. 4. Tantric Buddhism—China—Tibet. I. Arnold, Edward A., 1969– . II. Bstan-'dzin-rgya-mtsho, Dalai Lama XIV, 1935– .
BQ8921.K34A8 2009
294.3'925—dc22
2008042626

May the wishes of he who has a heart of gems,
Who benefits all with great waves of perfected karma,
Carrying on his courageous shoulders
The burden of the work of countless buddhas,
Be spontaneously fulfilled just so.

And by that power may the heavenly door
Of the auspicious aeon's fulfillment phase
Open onto a springtime revival for beings;
And may there spread to the peaks of the world
Auspicious signs of the enlightenment lore
Flourishing in all times and place.

O Holder of the White Lotus,
May a nectar stream of your transforming powers
Ever mature the might of my heart.
And by my delighting you with the offering
Of living in accordance with the spiritual teachings,
May the seas of bodhisattva deeds reach their goal.

By the power of the blessings of the buddhas and bodhisattvas,
The power of unfailing cause and effect,
And the power of my pure aspirations,
May each and every aim of this prayer
Be easily and quickly fulfilled.

— from *Song Producing Immortality*,
the traditional long-life prayer for His Holiness
the Dalai Lama, written by Ling Rinpoche and
Trijang Rinpoche, translated by Glenn Mullin

It is on behalf of the future of Du Khor Choe Ling, the Land of Kālacakra Study and Practice, the new temple complex of Namgyal Monastery Institute of Buddhist Studies—that it may offer refuge for practitioners and prosper under the ongoing care of His Holiness the Dalai Lama—that this volume is offered to the Great Fourteenth on October 9, 2007, in Ithaca, New York.

Contents

III. Transmission and Transition

Foreword

Reverence to our Guru, (His Holiness the Dalai Lama),
indivisible from Holy Manjughosha
and Primal Buddha Kalachakra,
Please now grant all common and supreme powers!

Reverence to the Primal Buddha, Kalachakra,
Whose Body transcends the subatomic realm,
shining translucent through every aspect,
Whose Speech touches the hearts of all beings
with inexpressible, invincible booming voice,
Whose Mind is the vajra of the great bliss
of the creativity of the undissipated drop,
encompassing all things while sporting
with the aspectless Lover Voidness!

Khedrub Jey (1385–1438), *mKhas Grub Zhal Lung (Kalachakra Sadhana, Salutations)*

I first beheld the color-particle mandala of Kalachakra at 23 in April 1965, during the annual Citra month performance of the Kalachakra practices in the Namgyal Monastery in Dharamsala, Punjab (at that time), India. As I walked around with the jostling crowd and marveled at the glistening vivid colors of the intricate powder-rendered patterns of the measureless mansion and its environs and seed-syllable-represented deities, my own voice, seeming to come from nowhere conscious, startled me by exclaiming in my head in English (that time I was mostly thinking in Tibetan); "If human beings can create something as exquisitely beautiful as that, then surely buddhahood is possible!" Though I might not have expressed it as such then, it was like seeing the genetic template of perfect enlightenment, body, speech, and mind. It awoke me from the subliminal cosmological despair shared with all modernized people, imprisoned within the indoctrinated idea that "life is meaningless, evolution is purposeless, so be resigned to such moments of relief as you can get in whatever way, wherever, whenever." It gave me the hope that my deeper, almost innate determination that true happiness must be possible, this world does have a "happy ending," beyond anything we are allowed to imagine, was in fact realistic. A dream, yes, considering our normal waking state, but a dream that could be realized in life.

The vision of enlightenment elaborated by the Buddha (Shakyamuni Buddha himself, according to Indo-Tibetan traditional scholars; some mystic celestial Shakyamuni Buddha encountered by visionaries in Kashmir fifteen hundred years later, according to modern historicist scholars) as the Wheel of Time buddha emanation and buddha world is among the most extraordinary of human artifacts. Time is usually represented in spiritual traditions, including most forms of Buddhism, as dreadful, destructive, deadly. It is relentless impermanence and cruel death. Krishna in the *Bhagavadgita*, reveals himself to the terrified Arjuna as "Great Time" (*Mahakala*), described as a monster destroyer with countless faces and gaping mouths devouring great streams of beings and worlds that flow into him. Shakespeare has Ulysses say to Achilles, with typically unforgettable profundity, "Time hath my Lord, a wallet at its back, wherein it puts alms for eternity!" (*Troilus and Cressida*). So what is a Buddha doing, creating himself as a "Wheel" (read "Machine") of "Time." How can what is supposed to be wisdom and compassion perfected, the consummation of all that living beings strive for, display itself as a machine of time?

My suggestion is that the buddha-art of the Wheel of Time is the Buddha's solution of the insoluble dilemma of the bodhisattva, the resolution of the double bind she or he catches herself or himself in by undertaking the bodhisattva vow. In this vow, the bodhisattva vows to pursue perfect enlightenment for the sake of all beings, not seeking personal liberation from suffering alone, but only accepting the bliss of release when all beings also receive it. A noble determination, to be sure. His Holiness the Dalai Lama, our precious Guru, mentioning his name here only for a specific purpose, often repeats the verse of Shantideva, that he will stay in the world to help beings as long as space endures, and beings need his or her help.

Yet there have been innumerable buddhas in the past, buddhas free of suffering themselves, active in helping beings, at least some beings. Yet here we are still suffering and suffering. Did they break their vows as bodhisattvas? Did they abandon us to our miserable fates? It would certainly seem so, on the face of it. We cannot deny it.

But wait, we are ignorant, but buddhas are not. Do they know something we do not? Our ignorance causes our suffering. Their wisdom gives them their freedom. "As long as space endures!" "As long as time continues!" Hmmm! Could it be that buddhas go beyond space and time? Does their wisdom see through the intrinsic reality of space and time, realize their voidness of objective existence, thus releasing their universal compassion to reach out through all space and all time?

Certainly, they live beyond life-and-death-duality in a timeless moment and are beyond space because present everywhere. Thus they are *tryadhvajnya, dus gsum mkhyen pa,* conscious of all three times equally. Thus, they have not abandoned us or any living being, they are everywhere and everywhen for our sake, manifesting whatsoever educates whomsoever (*gang la gang 'dul de la de ston pa*), as is said in the famous prayer addressed to Avalokiteshvara, who incarnates in our beloved Teacher.

There are said to be three ways in which a bodhisattva becomes a buddha; like a cowherd, like a boatman, and like a king; each has to do with time, again. Becoming a buddha like a cowherd is to bring all beings to freedom and enlightenment before you do, as a cowherd leads his herd into the pasture before entering it himself. Becoming a buddha like a boatman is to bring beings into freedom at exactly the same time as you enter it, as a boatman and his passengers reach the shore together at the same time. Becoming a buddha like a king is to first become a buddha yourself and then use your buddha powers to bring others into the same freedom as fast and effectively as possible. The first way is said to express the compassionate determination of the bodhisattva; but the last is in fact the practical way to accomplish your aim. How can you liberate others from suffering when you yourself are still caught in it?

The bottom line is that all three ways have to do with time. When through wisdom you break free of the reification of the stream of time and enter the infinite moment, the eternal now, every moment of every being's possible future becomes immediately manifest to you, just as manifest as this particular moment. And yet the future, not being fixed in a concrete fate, can have many possibilities. Beings would perhaps never attain enlightenment completely on their own, if there were not infinite beings already enlightened tirelessly there to help them along the way. Therefore, when you become a buddha, your bodhisattva vow is fulfilled completely since you are present to all beings in all their future moments, not inertly and impassively watching them suffer, but compassionately, actively, totally engaged in seeing to it that they reach their own enlightenment with minimum suffering, optimal speed, total assistance by you in all possible creative manifestations. You accomplish all this instantaneously as far as you can perceive it with your buddha awareness, all the while you remain completely aware that those beings are perceiving themselves caught in the stream of time, evolving laboriously through long lifetimes and lifetimes.

And you can't just pull them instantly, according to how they perceive an instant, into their own buddhahood—they are living beings, delicate and relational—just as you cannot take a sprout from a flower's seed and pull it up into a blossomed flower. It has to grow according to its own causes and conditions of growth. Flowers and beings need **time** to grow, though your compassion, since it makes their suffering as intolerable to you as it is to them, empowers your creativity to accelerate their growth as much as possible.

Your Wheel of Time embodiment, therefore, is your promise to beings that you will remain present with them throughout all time. Your universal compassion turns time itself into an optimal environment for them to evolve optimally toward their own freedom and enlightenment. Your omniscient wisdom destroys time-the-destroyer, which takes away beings' happiness, turning ordinary happiness into the suffering of change. You destroy the space-time of beings' sufferings. Then your universal compassion restructures the space-time that endures and remains real for beings in their ignorance, that ticks away pain by pain for them and holds them in the grip of frustration, and you redesign it for them as a measureless mansion of bliss, a span of evolution, a sporting ground, a playing field of development, and a theater of liberation. And your omniscient wisdom ensures that their evolution beyond ignorance and harmfulness proceeds in the optimal possible way.

So here we are in these times of seemingly endless human violence, confusion, needless destruction of the environment, and even self-destruction of whole societies. We are caught in the poisonous ocean of unrealistic worldviews, especially those of nihilistic science that robs our breath of meaning and our steps of purpose. It is thousands of years past the most recent World Buddha's manifest historical engagement with us, and everything seems to get worse and worse. But who shows up for us? Our Precious Teacher, our Ocean Guru. He constantly and tirelessly renews for us the pledge of Shakyamuni, his exquisite demonstration that he will never abandon any of us to our wretched fate—the art and wisdom of the Kalachakra, the Wheel of Time. He restores and educates and trains the monks of the Namgyal Monastery, the A-team for chasing away unhappiness, that used to, and will definitely soon again, cultivate their wisdom and practice their arts in the Potala Palace in Hlasa in Great Bod ("Lhasa in Tibet" as we inaccurately say it), serving the Dalai Lama incarnations as they keep hope alive on our difficult, "Tolerable" (Sanskrit *Saha*, "Tolerable" as in "barely tolerable"), planet.

So with these heartfelt words of appreciation and encouragement, I welcome this rich volume of learned studies of all sorts of scholars and practitioners of the Kalachakra arts and sciences, assembled by the Namgyal Institute in Ithaca to honor and celebrate His Holiness the Great Fourteenth Dalai Lama of Great Bod especially, and also now the whole world. May it help remove all obstacles from His Holy Person and help Him in whatever slightest way to realize all His deepest wishes for His people and all peoples and beings! May it please not only His Holiness but also all people who are interested in a positive world, a realized Shambhala or Land of Peace, where everyone, no matter what their religion or race or gender or culture, keeping them all and upgrading them all, can live in peace, enjoy their hard-earned human lifetime, and seek its essential potential by educating him- or herself in all the arts of wisdom, kindness, love, and joy!

Sarvamangalam!

Robert A. F. Thurman
(Ari Genyen Tenzin Chotrak)

Tibetan Lunar New Year of the Fire Pig!
Tibetan National Royal Year, 2134
Sunday, February 16, 2007 CE
Woodstock, New York, USA, Turtle Island

Introduction

His Holiness the Dalai Lama has made an indelible impact on the world at large, but this volume has the modest goal of celebrating his contribution, direct and indirect, to the propagation of the tantric Buddhism of Tibet, the Vajrayāna or Diamond Vehicle. More specifically, the volume focuses on the Kālacakra (Wheel of Time) tantric system, which His Holiness has taught widely in the past thirty years, most recently on the 2550th anniversary of the original teaching given at Amarāvatī, in South India. Namgyal Monastery, the Dalai Lama's personal monastery, is the foremost institution of the Kālacakra teachings, being responsible for creating the intricate sand maṇḍala and providing other ritual support at each initiation that His Holiness gives. It is therefore fitting that His Holiness has chosen to name the new facility for Namgyal Monastery Institute of Buddhist Studies *Du Khor Choe Ling,* or Land of Kālacakra Study and Practice. This volume commemorates His Holiness the Dalai Lama's visit to and blessing of this new facility, located in the beautiful Finger Lakes area of Upstate New York.

The Buddhism that flourished in Tibet is an entire worldview involving ethics, logic, epistemology, and metaphysics. In Tibet these provided the basis for the foundational practices which are the steps by which one ascends towards and enters into the Vajrayāna, of which Kālacakra is often considered the pinnacle. The Vajrayāna is known as the sole door to Buddhahood in Tibetan Buddhism, and so the common impulse to bypass the "lower paths" and to engage in only the highest has been problematic since these practices entered Tibet more than a thousand years ago. It remains so now in the West as well. Without adequate preparation in the common paths of the Mahāyāna, the tantric practices are expected to remain off limits. This is why institutions such as Namgyal Monastery Institute of Buddhist Studies have a curriculum which stresses the stages of the path and bodhisattva training instruction. Only with these common practices as a basis can one expect to succeed in the advanced tantric practices.

Kālacakra is the most complex of the Vajrayāna systems. This tantra addresses explicitly in its five chapters the structure of the entire cosmos (outer), human psychophysical constituents (inner), and the processes (other or alternate) by which the outer and inner are purified and which are detailed in three chapters on initiation, sādhana, and wisdom. The Wheel of Time (*cakra* meaning "wheel" and *kāla* "time") refers to this interpenetration of inner and outer realities, which suggests that one's spiritual practice—the purification of the inner—transforms the external world, purifying the outer. Thus the practitioner's role in creating world peace is not simply a passive one but rather a creative process for the benefit of all beings, and clearly this is why His Holiness has emphasized the Kālacakra teachings as Tibetan Buddhism has spread throughout the world.

Holiness' policy has been to give permission for some teachings which had previously been restricted in order to counter popular misunderstandings that some prior publications in the West had caused. His own early work explicating Tsong Khapa's *Great Treatise on Secret Mantra* and on the system of Kālacakra have done much to explain the concepts of tantra. His Holiness has worked with or facilitated the research of many Western scholars who have worked with Tibetan practitioner-scholars to explicate the link between the classic texts and the tradition as it is practiced today. It is this collaborative effort that we celebrate here in Sections I and II, entitled "Translation and Revelation" and "Analysis and Insight," respectively. The Buddha urged his followers not to accept his words without scrutiny and reasoning. This is a value highly prized within the Tibetan tradition. So too, the scholars here do not simply reproduce uncritically claims of the Tibetan tradition.

Further, the living Tibetan Buddhist tradition, at the urging of His Holiness the Dalai Lama, is collaborating with scientists to investigate areas of mutual importance. As with His Holiness' efforts toward interfaith dialogue, his interest in science is for the broader benefit of all humanity, indeed all sentient beings. As he writes in the opening pages of *The Universe in a Single Atom,* His Holiness is concerned to "make the wonderful developments of science into something that offers altruistic and compassionate service for the needs of humanity and the other sentient beings with whom we share this earth" while ensuring that humanity not "be reduced to nothing more than biological machines, the products of pure chance in the random combination of genes, with no purpose other than the biological imperative of reproduction." Thus, Section III, "Transmission and Transition," considers this interface between Buddhism and science and other contemporary issues. We close the volume with teachings from two young Kālacakra scholars affiliated with Namgyal Monastery and, finally, words of instruction from the late master Kirti Tsenshab Rinpoche along with the prayer for his swift return.

With the establishment of Du Khor Choe Ling, and with the support of scholars and practitioners alike, may this Land of Kālacakra become a major center for Kālacakra study and practice in North America. May this volume contribute to the continued development of Kālacakra practice and to its temporary and ultimate goals.

Edward (Ted) Arnold

Acknowledgments

With a work this size that involves so many contributors, those to whom thanks are due may be too many to list. My apologies to anyone I have left out. Foremost of those deserving thanks are the contributors themselves, who have managed to carve some time from their already busy schedules to write or translate for this project. In particular Vesna Wallace, David B. Gray, Thupten Jinpa, and David Reigle have been supportive of the project from its embryonic phase, when it was merely a hare-brained scheme hatched shortly after His Holiness named Namgyal Monastery's new facility *Du Khor Choe Ling.* Also special mention should go to Sofia Stril-Rever for her extraordinary efforts in working with translators to bring her work to an English-speaking audience.

Many kind people at The Foundation for the Preservation of the Mahayana Tradition (FPMT) have assisted with Kirti Tsenshab Rinpoche's material; those not mentioned in that article are Sara Blumenthal, Gyalten Mindrol, and Roger Kunsang, all of whom helped in some way to bring this material to fruition. Special mention must also go to Voula Zarpani, Kirti Tsenshab Rinpoche's translator, who provided kind words and generous assistance during trying times.

Thanks also go to Roger Jackson, John R. Newman, Jeffrey Hopkins, Christian Wedemeyer, Cyrus Stearns, E. Gene Smith, Harunaga Isaacson, and Donald Lopez. All of these great scholars offered words of support for this project even though they could not contribute due to prior commitments. Alan Wallace, a scholar and thinker decades ahead of his time, has been supportive of this and other Namgyal projects for several years, and there is not sufficient space to laud him for his generosity and the impact of his ideas. Thanks are also due to Jay Garfield for many things, especially perhaps his choice of neckties in combating the suffering of suffering, but in this context for allowing use of his article mentioned in the introduction.

Back in Ithaca, among the Finger Lakes and gorges, many people worked in some way to bring this volume to print. Foremost among these is Sidney Piburn, co-founder of both Snow Lion Publications and the North American branch of Namgyal Monastery; he took this farfetched idea, from a person known for farfetched ideas, as worth supporting. Thanks also go to Anne Blackburn, Dan Gold, and Bronwen Bledsoe of Cornell University for their assistance; to Doug and Inez Alfors for proofreading; and to Palden Oshoe for friendship, guidance, and translation. Thanks are due also to the board members of Namgyal Monastery, for their various roles in this and other projects, and to the monks for their instruction.

Joy Paulson, Namgyal Monastery's director of the Kalachakra study group, deserves special thanks for making possible a great number of things, most importantly the editing of the teachings of Geshe Drakpa Gelek and Jhado Rinpoche. This volume could not have come to be without her extraordinary efforts. Assisting Joy in the initial efforts of transcribing and editing was long-time Namgyal student Susan Lytle. Finally deepest thanks go to my wife, Gwen Alphonso, for tolerating the incredibly long hours this project has demanded, beyond the usual demands of my helping to run a Dharma center. She understood the importance of the project and has supported my efforts completely, showing faith in me that I simply did not deserve. I hope I have made her proud.

I hope this volume stands for many years to come both as a resource for scholars and practitioners and a symbol of the important activities of Namgyal Monastery, especially *Du Khor Choe Ling*.

It is a great honor to represent Namgyal Monastery, the personal monastery of His Holiness the Dalai Lama, in publishing this volume. It is also a great honor, quite humbling, to represent in some small way the excellent scholars who have contributed to this volume. Any errors in these pages are entirely my responsibility and do not reflect their talents nor, for that matter, the teaching skills of the monks at Namgyal Monastery Institute of Buddhist Studies!

On behalf of the Namgyal Monastery community and the contributors, this volume is offered to His Holiness the Dalai Lama for his tireless work to bring the important teachings of the Tibetan Buddhist tradition, particularly the Kālacakra system, to the entire world.

Edward (Ted) Arnold
Namgyal Monastery Institute of Buddhist Studies
Ithaca, New York

I.

Translation and Revelation

– 1 –

A Concert of Names of Mañjuśrī

('Jam-dpal mtshan-brjod, Skt. Mañjuśrī-nāmasaṃgīti)
translated from the Tibetan, as clarified by the Sanskrit

Alexander Berzin

Homage to Mañjuśrī in youthful form.

Sixteen Verses on Requesting Instruction

1. Then the glorious Holder of the Vajra,
The most superb tamer of those difficult to tame,
The hero, triumphant over the world's three planes,
The powerful lord of the thunderbolt, ruler of the hidden,

2. With awakened white-lotus eye,
Fully bloomed pink-lotus face,
Brandishing over and again
The supreme vajra with his hand—

3. Together with countless Vajrapāṇis,
With features such as brows furrowed in fury,
Heroes, tamers of those difficult to tame,
Fearsome and heroic in form,

4. Brandishing blazing-tipped vajras in their hands,
Superb in fulfilling the aims of wandering beings,
Through great compassion, discriminating awareness,
And skillful means,

5. Having happy, joyful, and delighted dispositions,
Yet endowed with ferocious bodily forms,
Guardians to further the Buddhas' enlightening influence,
Their bodies bowed—together with them

6. Prostrated to the Guardian, the Vanquishing Master Surpassing All,
The Thusly Gone One, the Fully Enlightened,
And standing in front, his palms pressed together,
Addressed these words:

7. "O Master of the All-Pervasive,
For my benefit, my purpose, from affection toward me,
So that I may obtain
Manifest enlightenment from illusion's net

8. For the welfare and attainment
Of the peerless fruit for all limited beings
Sunk in the swamp of unawareness,
Their minds upset by disturbing emotions,

9. O Fully Enlightened, Vanquishing Master, Guru of Wanderers,
Indicator, Knower of the Great Close Bond and Reality,
Foremost Knower of Powers and Intents,
Elucidate, please,

10. Regarding the enlightening body of deep awareness of the Vanquishing Master,
The Great Crown Protrusion, the Master of Words,
The embodied deep awareness that is self-produced,
The deep awareness being, Mañjuśrī,

11. The superlative *Concert of His Names*,
With profound meaning, with extensive meaning, with great meaning,
Unequaled, and supremely pacifying,
Constructive in the beginning, middle, and end,

12. Which was proclaimed by previous Buddhas,
Will be proclaimed by future ones,
And which the Fully Enlightened of the present
Proclaim over and again,

13. And which, in *The Illusion's Net Great Tantra*,
Was magnificently chanted
By countless delighted great holders of the vajras,
Holders of the hidden mantras.

14. O Guardian, so that I (too) may be a holder
Of the hidden (teachings) of all the Fully Enlightened,
I shall preserve it with steadfast intention
Till my definite deliverance,

15. And shall elucidate it to limited beings,
In accord with their individual intents,
For dispelling disturbing emotions, barring none,
And destroying unawareness, barring none.

16. Having requested the Thusly Gone One with these words,
The lord of the hidden, Vajrapāṇi,
Pressed his palms together
And, bowing his body, stood in front.

Six Verses in Reply

17. Then the Vanquishing Master Surpassing All, Śākyamuni, the Able Sage,
The Fully Enlightened, the Ultimate Biped,
Extending from his mouth
His beautiful tongue, long and wide,

18. Illuminating the world's three planes
And taming the four (*māra*) demonic foes,
And displaying a smile, cleansing
The three worse rebirths for limited beings,

19. And filling the world's three planes
With his sweet Brahmā-voice,
Replied to Vajrapāṇi, the magnificently strong,
The lord of the hidden:

20. "Excellent, O glorious Holder of the Vajra,
(I say) excellent to you, Vajrapāṇi,
You who possess great compassion
For the sake of the welfare of wandering beings.

21. Rise to the occasion to hear from me, now,
A Concert of Names of the enlightening body of deep awareness,
Mañjuśrī, the great aim,
Purifying and eliminating negative force.

22. Because of that, Overlord of the Hidden,
It's excellent that I'm revealing it to you;
(So) listen with single-pointed mind."
"O Vanquishing Master, that's excellent," he replied.

Two Verses of Beholding the Six Buddha-Families

23. Then the Vanquishing Master Surpassing All, Śākyamuni, the Able
Sage,
Beholding in detail the entire family of great hidden mantra:
The family of holders of hidden mantras and of mantras of pure
awareness,
The family of the three,

24. The family of the world and beyond the world,
The family, the great one, illuminating the world,
(That) family supreme, of (*mahāmudrā*) the great seal,
And the great family of the grand crown protrusion,

Three Verses on the Steps of Manifest Enlightenment by Means of Illusion's Net

25. Proclaimed the verse of the Master of Words,
Endowed with the sixfold mantra king,
(Concerning) the nondual source
With a nature of nonarising:

26. "*A ā, i, ī, u, ū, e ai, o au, aṃ aḥ:*
Situated in the heart, I'm deep awareness embodied,
The Buddha of the Buddhas
Occurring in the three times.

27. *Oṃ*—Vajra Sharp,
Cutter of Suffering,
Embodied Discriminating Deep Awareness,
Enlightening Body of Deep Awareness,
Powerful Lord of Speech,
And Ripener of Wandering Beings (Ara-pacana)—homage to you."

Fourteen Verses on the Great Mandala of the Vajra Sphere

28. Like this is the Buddha (Mañjuśrī), the Vanquishing Master Surpassing All,
the Fully Enlightened:
He's born from the syllable *a*,
The foremost of all phonemes, the syllable *a*,
Of great meaning, the syllable that's deepest,

29. The great breath of life, nonarising,
Rid of being uttered in a word,

Foremost cause of everything spoken,
Maker of every word perfectly clear.

30. In his great offering festival, great longing desire's
The provider of joy to limited beings;
In his great offering festival, great anger's
The great foe of all disturbing emotion.

31. In his great offering festival, great naivety's
The dispeller of the naivety of the naïve mind;
In his great offering festival, great fury's
The great foe of great fury.

32. In his great offering festival, great greed's
The dispeller of all greed;
He's the one with great desire, great happiness,
Great joy, and great delight.

33. He's the one with great form, great enlightening body,
Great color, great physique,
Great name, great grandeur,
And a great and extensive maṇḍala circle.

34. He's the great bearer of the sword of discriminating awareness,
The foremost great elephant-hook for disturbing emotions;
He's the one with great renown, great fame,
Great luster, and great illumination.

35. He's the learned one, the bearer of great illusion,
The fulfiller of aims with great illusion,
The delighter with delight through great illusion,
The conjurer of an Indra's net of great illusion.

36. He's the most preeminent master of great generous giving,
The foremost holder of great ethical discipline,
The steadfast holder of great patience,
The courageous one with great perseverance,

37. The one abiding in the absorbed concentration of great mental stability,
The holder of a body of great discriminating awareness,
The one with great strength, great skill in means,
Aspirational prayer, and a sea of deep awareness.

38. He's the immeasurable one, composed of great love,
He's the foremost mind of great compassion,
Great discrimination, great intelligence,
Great skill in means, and great implementation.

39. Endowed with the strength of great extraphysical powers,
He's the one with great might, great speed,
Great extraphysical power, great (lordly) renown,
Great courage of strength.

40. He's the crusher of the great mountain of compulsive existence,
The firm holder of the great vajra;
The one with great fierceness and great ferociousness,
He's the great terrifier of the terrifying.

41. He's the superlative guardian with great pure awareness,
The superlative guru with great hidden mantra;
Stepped up to the Great Vehicle's mode of travel,
He's superlative in the Great Vehicle's mode of travel.

Twenty-five Verses, Less a Quarter, on the Deep Awareness of the Totally Pure Sphere of Reality

42. He's the Buddha (Vairocana), the great illuminator,
The great able sage, having great sagely (stillness);
He's the one produced through great mantra's mode of travel,
And, by identity-nature, he (himself) is great mantra's mode of travel.

43. He has attainment of the ten far-reaching attitudes,
Support of the ten far-reaching attitudes,
The purity of the ten far-reaching attitudes,
The mode of travel of the ten far-reaching attitudes.

44. He's the guardian, the powerful lord of the ten (*bhūmi*) levels of mind,
The one established through the ten (*bhūmi*) levels of mind;
By identity-nature, he's the purified ten sets of knowledge,
And the holder of the purified ten sets of knowledge.

45. He's the one with ten aspects, the ten points as his aim,
Chief of the able sages, the one with ten forces, the master of the
all-pervasive;
He's the fulfiller of the various aims, barring none,
The powerful one with ten aspects, the great one.

46. He's beginningless and, by identity-nature, parted from mental fabrication,
By identity-nature, the accordant state; by identity-nature, the pure one;
He's the speaker of what's actual, with speech of no other,
The one who, just as he speaks, just so does he act.

47. Nondual, the speaker of nonduality,
Settled at the endpoint of what's perfectly so;
With a lion's roar of the lack of a true identity-nature,
He's the frightener of the deer of the deficient extremists.

48. Coursing everywhere, with his coursing meaningful, (never in vain),
He has the speed of the mind of a Thusly Gone One;
He's the conqueror, the full conqueror, with enemies conquered,
A (*cakravartin*) emperor of the universe, one that has great strength.

49. He's the teacher of hosts, the head of hosts,
The (*Gaṇeśa*) lord of hosts, the master of hosts, the powerful one;
He's the one with great strength, the one that's keen (to carry the load),
The one that has the great mode of travel, with no need for travel by another mode.

50. He's the lord of speech, the master of speech, eloquent in speech,
The one with mastery over speech, the one with limitless words,
Having true speech, the speaker of truth,
The one that indicates the four truths.

51. He's irreversible, nonreturning,
The guide for the mode of travel of the self-evolving rhino pratyekas;
Definitely delivered through various (means) of definite deliverance,
He's the singular cause of the great elemental states.

52. He's a (*bhikṣu*) full monk, (an arhat) with enemies destroyed,
Defilements depleted, with desire departed, senses tamed;
Having attained ease of mind, having attained a state of no fear,
He's the one with (elements) cooled down, no longer muddied.

53. Endowed to the full with pure awareness and movement,
He's the Blissfully Gone, superb in his knowledge of the world;
He's the one not grasping for "mine," not grasping for a "me,"
Abiding in the mode of travel of the two truths.

54. He's the one that's standing at the far shore, beyond recurring saṃsāra,
With what needs to be done having been done, settled on dry land,

His cleaving sword of discriminating awareness
Having drawn out the deep awareness of what's unique.

55. He's the hallowed Dharma, the ruler of the Dharma, the shining one,
The superb illuminator of the world;
He's the powerful lord of Dharma, the king of the Dharma,
The one who shows the most excellent pathway of mind.

56. With his aim accomplished, his thought accomplished,
And rid of all conceptual thought,
He's the nonconceptual, inexhaustible sphere,
The superb, imperishable sphere of reality.

57. He's the one possessing positive force, a network of positive force,
And deep awareness, the great source of deep awareness,
Possessing deep awareness, having deep awareness of what exists and what doesn't exist,
The one with the built-up pair of networks networked together.

58. Eternal, the ruler of all, he's the (yogi) yoked to the authentic;
He's stability of mind, the one to be made mentally stable, the master of intelligence,
The one to be individually reflexively known, the immovable one,
The primordial one who's the highest, the one possessing three enlightening bodies.

59. With an identity-nature of five enlightening bodies, he's a Buddha;
With an identity-nature of five types of deep awareness, a master of the all-pervasive,
Having a crown in the identity-nature of the five Buddhas,
Bearing, unhindered, the five enlightening eyes.

60. He's the progenitor of all Buddhas,
The superlative, supreme Buddhas' spiritual son,
The womb giving rise to the existence of discriminating awareness,
The womb of the Dharma, bringing an end to compulsive existence.

61. With a singular innermost essence of firmness, by identity-nature, he's a diamond-strong vajra;
As soon as he's born, he's master of the wandering world.
Arisen from the sky, he's the self-arisen:
The great fire of discriminating deep awareness;

62. The great-light (Vairocana,) Illuminator of All, luminary of deep awareness, illuminating all;

The lamp for the world of the wanderers;
The torch of deep awareness;
The great brilliance, the clear light;

63. Lord of the foremost mantras, king of the pure awareness;
King of the hidden mantras, the one that fulfills the great aim;
He's the great crown protrusion, the wondrous crown protrusion,
The master of space, the one indicating in various ways.

64. He's the foremost one, an enlightening body with the identity-nature of all the Buddhas,
The one with an eye for the joy of the entire wandering world,
The creator of diverse bodily forms,
The great (*ṛśi*) muse, worthy of offerings, worthy of honor.

65. He's the bearer of the three family traits, the possessor of the hidden mantra,
He's the upholder of the great close bond and of the hidden mantra;
He's the most preeminent holder of the three precious gems,
Indicator of the ultimate of the three vehicles of mind.

66. He's the totally triumphant, with an unfailing grappling-rope,
The great apprehender with a vajra grappling-rope,
With a vajra elephant-hook and a great grappling-rope.
Ten Verses, Plus a Quarter, Praising Mirror-like Deep Awareness
He's Vajrabhairava, the terrifying vajra terrifier:

67. Ruler of the furious, six-faced and terrifying,
Six-eyed, six-armed, and full of force,
The skeleton having bared fangs,
Halāhala, with a hundred heads.

68. He's the destroyer of death (*Yamāntaka*), king of the obstructors,
(*Vajravega*) vajra might, the terrifying one;
He's vajra devastation, vajra heart,
Vajra illusion, the great-bellied one.

69. Born from the vajra (womb), he's the vajra lord,
Vajra essence, equal to the sky;
Immovable (*Acalā*), (with matted hair) twisted into a single topknot,
Wearer of garments of moist elephant hide.

70. Great horrific one, shouting "hā hā,"
Creator of terror, shouting "hī hī,"

With enormous laughter, (booming) long laughter,
Vajra laughter, great roar.

71. He's the vajra-minded (*Vajrasattva*), the great-minded (*mahāsattva*),
Vajra king, great bliss;
Vajra fierce, great delight,
Vajra Hūṃkāra, the one shouting "hūṃ."

72. He's the holder of a vajra arrow as his weapon,
The slasher of everything with his vajra sword;
He's the holder of a crossed vajra, possessor of a vajra,
Possessor of a unique vajra, the terminator of battles.

73. His dreadful eyes with vajra flames,
Hair on his head, vajra flames too,
Vajra cascade, great cascade,
Having a hundred eyes, vajra eyes.

74. His body with bristles of vajra hair,
A unique body with vajra hair,
With a growth of nails tipped with vajras,
And tough, (firm) skin, vajras in essence.

75. Holder of a garland of vajras, having glory,
He's adorned with jewelry of vajras,
And has long (booming) laughter "hā hā," with loud sound,
The vajra sound of the six syllables.

76. He's (Mañjughoṣa) with a lovely voice, enormous volume,
A tremendous sound unique in the world's three planes,
A voice resounding to the ends of space,
The best of those possessing a voice.

Forty-two Verses on Individualizing Deep Awareness

77. He's what's perfectly so, the lack of identity-nature, the actual state,
The endpoint of that which is perfectly so, that which isn't a syllable;
He's the proclaimer of voidness, the best of bulls
Bellowing a roar, profound and extensive.

78. He's the conch of Dharma, with a mighty sound,
The gong of Dharma, with a mighty crash,
The one in a state of nonabiding nirvana,
Kettledrum of Dharma in the ten directions.

79. He's the formless one, with an excellent form, the foremost one,
Having varied forms, made from the mind;
He's a glory of appearances in every form,
The bearer of reflections, leaving out none.

80. He's the impervious one, with great (lordly) renown,
The great powerful lord of the world's three planes;
Abiding with a lofty ārya pathway of mind,
He's the one raised on high, the crown banner of Dharma.

81. He's the body of youth unique in the world's three planes,
The stable elder, the ancient one, the master of all that lives;
He's the bearer of the thirty-two bodily signs, the beloved,
Beautiful throughout the world's three planes.

82. He's the teacher of knowledge and good qualities to the world,
The teacher of the world without any fears,
The guardian, the rescuer, trusted throughout the world's three planes,
The refuge, the protector, unsurpassed.

83. The experiencer (of experiences) to the ends of space,
He's the ocean of the deep awareness of the omniscient mind,
The splitter of the eggshell of unawareness,
The tearer of the web of compulsive existence.

84. He's the one with disturbing emotions stilled, without an exception,
The one crossed over the sea of recurring saṃsāra;
He's the wearer of the crown of the deep awareness empowerment,
Bearer of the Fully Enlightened as adornment.

85. He's the one stilled of the suffering of the three kinds of suffering,
The one with an endless ending of the three, having gone to the
liberation of the three;
He's the one definitely freed from all obscurations,
The one who abides in space-like equality.

86. He's the one past the stains of all disturbing emotions,
The one understanding the three times as nontime;
He's the great (nāga) chief for all limited beings,
The crown of those wearing the crown of good qualities.

87. Definitely freed from all (residue) bodies,
He's the one well established in the track of the sky;
Bearer of a great wish-fulfilling gem,
He's master of the all-pervasive, ultimate of all jewels.

88. He's the great and bounteous wish-granting tree,
The superlative great vase of excellence;
The agent fulfilling the aims of all limited beings, the wisher of benefit,
He's the one with parental affection toward limited beings.

89. He's the knower of what's wholesome and what's unwholesome, the knower of timing,
The knower of the close bond, the keeper of the close bond, the master of the all-pervasive;
He's the knower of the faculties of limited beings, the knower of the occasion,
The one skilled in the three (kinds of) liberation.

90. He's the possessor of good qualities, the knower of good qualities, the knower of the Dharma,
The auspicious one, the source of what's auspicious,
He's the auspiciousness of everything auspicious,
The one with the auspicious sign of renown, the famous, constructive one.

91. He's the great breath, the great festival,
The great joy, the great pleasure,
The show of respect, the one showing respect, the prosperous one,
The supremely joyous, the master of fame, the glorious one.

92. Possessor of the best, he's the provider of the best, the most preeminent,
Suitable for refuge, he's the superlative refuge,
The very best foe of the great frightful things,
The eliminator of what's frightful, without an exception.

93. Wearing his hair in a bun, he's the one with a bun of hair,
Wearing his hair in mats, he's the one having matted locks,
He's the one draped with a muñja-grass sacred cord, the one wearing a crown,
The one with five faces, five buns of hair,
And five knotted locks, (each) crowned with a bloom.

94. He's the one maintaining great taming behavior, the one with shaved head,
The one with celibate Brahmā(-like) conduct, the one with superlative taming behavior,
The one with great trials, the one who's completed the trials,
The one who's taken ablution, the foremost, Gautama.

95. He's a brahmin, a Brahmā, the knower of Brahmā,
The possessor of a Brahmā-nirvana attainment;
The liberated one, he's liberation, the one with the body of full liberation,
The fully liberated one, the peaceful one, the state of peace.

96. He's nirvana release, the one with peace, the one released in nirvana,
He's the one most definitely delivered and nearly (brought to an end),
The one who's completed bringing to an end pleasure and pain,
The one with detachment, the one with (residue) body consumed.

97. He's the invincible one, the incomparable one,
The unmanifest one, the one not appearing, the one with no sign that would make him seen,
The unchanging, the all-going, the all-pervasive,
The subtle, the untainted, the seedless.

98. He's the one without a speck of dust, dustless, stainless,
With faults disgorged, the one without sickness;
He's the wide-awake one, by identity-nature, the Fully Enlightened,
The Omniscient One, the superb knower of all.

99. Beyond the nature of partitioning primary consciousness,
He's deep awareness, bearer of the form of nonduality;
He's the one without conceptual thought, spontaneously accomplishing (without any effort),
The one enacting the enlightening deeds of the Buddhas throughout the three times.

100. He's the Buddha, the one without a beginning or end,
The (beginning) primordial Ādibuddha, the one without precedent;
The singular eye of deep awareness, the one with no stains,
Deep awareness embodied, he's the One Thusly Gone.

101. He's the powerful lord of speech, the magnificent speaker,
The supreme being among speakers, the ruler of speakers,
The best of those speaking, the very best one,
The lion of speakers, unconquerable by others.

102. Seeing all around, he's supreme joy itself,
With a garland of brilliance, beautiful to behold;
He's the magnificent light, the blazing one (Viṣṇu, beloved of Śrī,) the curl at the heart,
The illuminator with hands (that are rays) of blazing light.

103. The best of the great physicians, he's the most preeminent one,
The unsurpassed remover of (thorny) pains;
He's the celestial tree of all medications, with none left out,
The great nemesis of the sicknesses of disturbing emotions.

104. He's the beauty mark of the world's three planes, the lovely one,
The glorious one, with a maṇḍala of lunar and zodiac constellation stars;
He's the one extending to the ends of space in the ten directions,
The great ascending of the banner of Dharma.

105. He's the unique extension of an umbrella over the wandering world,
With his maṇḍala circle of love and compassion;
He's the glorious one, the Powerful Lord of the Lotus Dance,
Great master of the all-pervasive, the one with an umbrella of precious gems.

106. He's the great king of all the Buddhas,
Holder of the embodiments of all the Buddhas,
Great yoga of all the Buddhas,
Unique teaching of all the Buddhas.

107. He's the glory of the empowerment of the vajra jewel,
Powerful lord of the sovereigns of all jewels;
Master of all (*Lokeśvaras*) the powerful lords of the world,
He's the sovereign of all (*Vajradharas*) the holders of the vajra.

108. He's the great mind of all Buddhas,
The one that is present in the mind of all Buddhas;
He's the great enlightening body of all Buddhas,
He's the beautiful speech (*Sārasvatī*) of all Buddhas.

109. He's the vajra sun, the great illuminator,
The vajra moon, the stainless light;
He's great desire, the one that begins with nondesire,
Blazing light of various colors.

110. He's the vajra posture of the Fully Enlightened,
The bearer of the Dharma, the concert of the Buddhas;
He's the glorious one, the one that's born from the lotus of the Buddhas,
The keeper of the treasure of omniscient deep awareness.

111. He's the bearer of diverse illusions, he's the king;
He's the bearer of Buddhas' pure awareness mantras, he's the great one;
He's vajra sharp, the great sword,
The supreme syllable, totally pure.

112. He's the Great Vehicle (*Mahāyāna*), the cutter of suffering,
He's the great weapon, Vajra Dharma;
He's (*Jinajik*) the triumph of the triumphant, vajra profound,
He's vajra intelligence, the knower of things and how they exist.

113. He's the perfected state of every far-reaching attitude,
The wearer of all (*bhūmi*) levels of mind as adornment;
He's the lack of a true identity-nature of totally pure existent things,
He's correct deep awareness, the core light of the moon.

114. He's great diligence (applied), *Illusion's Net*,
Sovereign of all tantras, the one that's superb;
He's the possessor of vajra (postures and) seats, without an exception,
He's the bearer of enlightening bodies of deep awareness, without an exception.

115. He's the all-around excellent (*Samanta-bhadra*), he's excellent intelligence,
He's the womb of the earth (*Kṣiti-garbha*), the support of the wandering world;
He's the great womb of all of the Buddhas,
The bearer of a circle of assorted emanations.

116. He's the supreme self-nature of all functional phenomena,
The bearer of the self-nature of all functional phenomena;
He's the nonarising existent, with purposes diverse,
The bearer of the nature of all existent things.

117. Great discriminating awareness in a single moment,
He's the bearer of comprehension of all existent things;
The clear realization of all existent things,
He's the able sage, with foremost intelligence, the endpoint of that which is perfectly so.

118. He's the immovable one, extremely pure, by identity-nature,
The bearer of the purified state of the Perfect, Fully Enlightened Ones;
He's the one having bare cognition of all Buddhas,
The flame of deep awareness, the excellent clear light.
Twenty-four Verses on Equalizing Deep Awareness

119. He's the fulfiller of wished-for aims, he's superb,
The one totally purifying all of the worse rebirth states;
He's the ultimate of all limited beings, the guardian,
The complete liberator of all limited beings.

120. He's the hero in the battle with disturbing emotions, the unique one,
The slayer of the insolent arrogance of the enemy "unawareness";
He's intelligence, bearer of an enamored tone, the one with glory,
Bearer of forms with heroic and disdainful tones.

121. He's the one pounding with a hundred clubs in his hands,
He's the dancer with a pounding-down of his feet;
He's the one with glory, the user of a hundred (user) hands,
The dancer across (the sectors used in) the expanse of the sky.

122. He's the one standing on the surface of the maṇḍala of the earth,
Pressing down on the surface with a single foot;
He's the one standing on the nail of his large toe,
Pressing down on the tip of Brahmā's (egg-like) world.

123. He's the singular item, the item regarding phenomena that's nondual,
He's the deepest (truth) item, (the imperishable powerful lord,) the one that lacks what's fearful;
He's the item with a variety of revealing forms,
The one that has a continuity of mind and of partitioning consciousness.

124. He's joyful awareness of existent things, without an exception,
He's joyful awareness of voidness, the highest intelligence;
The one gone beyond the longing desires, and the likes, of compulsive existence,
He's great joyful awareness regarding the three (planes of) compulsive existence.

125. He's the pure white one—a brilliant white cloud,
With beautiful light—beams of the autumn moon,
With an exquisite (face)—the maṇḍala orb of a (youthful) sun,
With light from his nails—a great (passionate) red.

126. With sapphire-blue hair knotted on top,
And wearing a great sapphire on top of his locks,
He's the glorious one with the radiant luster of a magnificent gem,
Having as jewelry emanations of Buddha.

127. He's the shaker of spheres of hundreds of worlds,
The one with great force with his extra-physical powerful legs;
He's the holder of the great (state of) mindfulness as well as the facts of reality,
He's the ruler of the absorbed concentrations of the four types of mindfulness states.

128. He's the fragrance of the love-blossoms on the branches (leading) to a purified state,
(The cream atop) the ocean of good qualities of the Thusly Gone Ones;
He's the one knowing the mode of travel with the eightfold pathway minds,
The one knowing the pathway mind of the Perfect, Fully Enlightened.

129. He's the one having great adherence to all limited beings,
But without having adherence, like the sky;
He's the one entering the minds of all limited beings,
Having speed in accord with the minds of all limited beings.

130. He's the one with awareness of the powers and objects of all limited beings,
The one who captures the hearts of all limited beings;
He's the one with awareness of the items and reality of the five aggregate factors,
The one who holds the full purity of the five aggregate factors.

131. He's the one standing at the end of every definite deliverance,
The one who's skilled in that which brings every definite deliverance;
He's the one standing on the path for every definite deliverance,
The one who's indicating every definite deliverance.

132. He's the one who's uprooted compulsive existence with its twelvefold links,
The holder of their purification having twelvefold aspects;
Having the aspect of the mode of travel of the fourfold truths,
He's the holder of the realization of the eightfold awareness.

133. He's the points of truth in twelvefold aspects,
The knower of reality in sixteen aspects,
The Fully Enlightened through twenty aspects,
The Enlightened Buddha, the superb knower of all.

134. He's the one making knowable millions
Of enlightening emanation bodies of innumerable Buddhas;
He's the clear realization of everything in a moment,
The knower of the objects of all moments of mind.

135. He's the skillful means of the modes of travel of the various vehicles of mind,
The one who makes knowable the aims of the wandering world;

He's the one who's definitely delivered threefold, through the vehicles of mind,
The one who's established as the fruit of (*Ekayāna*) the single vehicle of mind.

136. He's the identity-nature totally pure of the spheres of disturbing emotions,
He's the depleter of the spheres of karma;
He's the one who has fully crossed over the ocean of currents,
The one who's emerged from the wilderness by means of the yogas.

137. He's the one fully rid of the disturbing emotions, the auxiliary disturbing emotions,
And the general disturbing emotions, together with (all) their habits;
He's discriminating awareness and great compassion as skillful means,
The one fulfilling the aims of the wandering world, meaningfully (without fail).

138. He's the one with objects of all conceptual discernment gotten rid of,
The one with objects of partitioning consciousness brought to a halt;
He's the cognitive object (in reference to) the minds of all limited beings,
The one that abides in the minds of all limited beings.

139. He's the innermost stand of the minds of all limited beings,
The one who's passing as the equality of their minds;
He's the one bringing satisfaction to the minds of all limited beings,
He's the joy of the mind of all limited beings.

140. He's the culminating point of actualization, the one with confusion departed,
He's the one with every mistake dispelled;
He's intelligence not indecisively wavering, the one that is threefold,
The one (fulfilling) everyone's aims, with an identity-nature of three constituents.

141. He's the object (in reference to) the five aggregate factors, the one throughout the three times,
The one that makes things individually knowable in every instant;
He's the one with manifest total enlightenment in an instant,
The bearer of all the Buddhas' self-nature.

142. He's the one with an enlightening body that's incorporeal, the foremost of enlightening bodies,

The one that makes knowable millions of enlightening bodies;
He's the one exhibiting everywhere a variety of forms,
He's the great gem, (*Ratnaketu*) the crowning jewel.

Fifteen Verses on the Accomplishing Deep Awareness

143. He's the one to be realized by all the Fully Enlightened,
He's the purified state of a Buddha, the peerless;
He's the one that isn't a syllable, the one that comes forth from hidden mantra's womb,
The triad of families of great hidden mantra.

144. He's the creator of every significance of hidden mantra,
He's the great creative energy-drop, that which isn't a syllable;
He's the great void, having five syllables,
And the creative-drop void, having six syllables.

145. He's the possessor of all aspects, that which hasn't an aspect,
He's the bearer of the sixteen creative drops, and half of their half;
He's the one without phases, beyond count,
Holder of the peak of the fourth level of mental stability.

146. He's the heightened awareness of the phases of all levels of mental stability,
The knower of the families and castes of absorbed concentration;
He's the one with the enlightening body of absorbed concentration, the foremost of the enlightening bodies,
The ruler of all (*Saṃbhogakāya*) Enlightening Bodies of Full Use.

147. He's the one with a (*Nirmāṇakāya*) Enlightening Body of Emanations, the foremost of the enlightening bodies,
Holder of the lineage of Buddha's emanations;
He's the one issuing forth various emanations in the ten directions,
The one fulfilling the aims of the wandering world, whatever they may be.

148. He's the chief of the deities, the deity over the deities,
The chief of the gods, the overlord of the (devilish) nongods,
The chief of the immortals, the guru of the gods,
The destroyer, and the powerful lord of the destroyers.

149. He's the one with the wilderness of compulsive existence crossed over,
The unique indicator, the guru for the wandering world;
He's renowned throughout the world's ten directions,
The master of generous giving of the Dharma, the great one.

150. Armored with the armor of love,
Coated with a coat-of-mail of compassion,
Wielder of a sword of discriminating awareness and a bow and arrow,
He's the one who finishes the battle against disturbing emotions and unawareness.

151. He's the heroic one, enemy of the (*māra*) demonic forces, subducr of the māras,
The one who brings fear of the four māras to an end;
Defeater of the military forces of all māras,
He's the Fully Enlightened, the leader of the world.

152. He's the one worthy of offerings, worthy of praise, the one for prostration,
Worthy of (being honored) forever in paintings,
Worthy of shows of respect, most worthy of veneration,
Worthy for homage, the highest guru.

153. He's the one traversing the world's three planes in a single stride,
The one striding forth endlessly, just like space;
He's the one with triple knowledge, (proficiency in the sacred,) clean and pure,
Possessor of the six types of heightened awareness and the six types of close mindfulness.

154. He's a bodhisattva, a great-minded (*mahāsattva*),
The one with great extra-physical powers, the one gone beyond the world;
(Situated) at the endpoint of far-reaching discriminating awareness (*prajñāpāramitā*),
He's the one who's come to reality through discriminating awareness.

155. He's the one with all knowledge of self and knowledge of others,
Helpful to all, the foremost person (of all);
He's the one who's gone beyond all comparison,
The superb sovereign of knowing and what's to be known.

156. He's the master of generous giving of Dharma, the most preeminent,
The one who shows the meaning of the fourfold (*mudrā*) seals;
He's the one most fitting to be helped and shown respect by the worldly
And by those traversing the three (pathways of) definite deliverance.

157 He's the purity and glory of the deepest truth,
The portion of excellence of the world's three planes, the great one;

The one bringing all enrichments, the one having glory,
He's Mañjuśrī, (the lovely and glorious,) supreme among those
possessing glory.

Five Verses on the Deep Awareness of the Five Thusly Gone Ones

158. Homage to you, granter of the best (boon), the foremost vajra;
Homage to you, the endpoint of what's perfectly so;
Homage to you, the womb of voidness;
Homage to you, the Buddhas' purified state.

159. Homage to you, the Buddhas' attachment;
Homage to you, the Buddha's desire;
Homage to you, the Buddhas' enjoyment;
Homage to you, the Buddhas' play.

160. Homage to you, the Buddhas' smile;
Homage to you, the Buddhas' (shining) laugh;
Homage to you, the Buddha's speech;
Homage to you, the Buddha's (state of) mind.

161. Homage to you, rising from nontrue existence;
Homage to you, arising from the Buddhas;
Homage to you, rising from space;
Homage to you, arising from deep awareness.

162. Homage to you, illusion's net;
Homage to you, the Buddhas' dancer;
Homage to you, everything for everyone;
Homage to you, enlightening body of deep awareness.

The Mantras

Oṃ sarva dharmā 'bhāva svabhāva,
viśuddhā vajra cakṣu, a ā aṃ aḥ

Oṃ—the total purity of all existents,
By self-nature, nontruly existent,
Through the vajra eye—*a ā aṃ aḥ*

Prakṛti pariśuddhāḥ
sarvadharmā yad uta
sarvatatāagata jñānakāya

mañjuśrī pariśuddhitām
upādāyeti

That which is the completely pure nature
Of all existents takes the form, indeed,
Of the completely purified Mañjuśrī,
The enlightening body of deep awareness
of all Thusly Gone

A aḥ sarvatathāgata hṛdayam
hara hara oṃ hūṃ hrīḥ
bhagavan jñānamūrti
vāgīśvara mahāpaca
sarvadharma gaganāmala
supariśuddha dharmadhātu
jñānagarbha āḥ

A aḥ—the heart of all the Thusly Gone,
Take out, take out—*oṃ hūṃ hrīḥ*
Vanquishing master surpassing all, embodied deep awareness,
Powerful lord of speech, the great one who ripens,
The complete total purity of all the existents, stainless like space,
Womb of deep awareness of the sphere of reality—*āḥ*

Five Verses as an Epilogue

163. Then the glorious Holder of the Vajra,
Joyful and delighted, with palms pressed together,
Bowing to the Guardian, the Vanquishing Master Surpassing All,
The Thusly Gone One, the Fully Enlightened,

164. Together with the other guardians of many (varied) sorts,
Lords of the hidden, Vajrapāṇis,
Kings of the furious,
Loudly proclaimed these words of praise,

165. "We rejoice, O Guardian,
Excellent, excellent, well said.
For us, the great (guardian) aim has (now) been fulfilled,
The attainment of a perfect, full enlightenment state;

166. And for the wandering world also, lacking a guardian,
Wishing for the fruit of complete liberation,

This excellent and pure pathway mind has been shown,
The mode of travel of *Illusion's Net*.

167. This cognitive object indeed of the Buddhas,
Having a profound and extensive broad scope,
The great aim, fulfilling the aims of the wandering world,
Has been expounded by the Perfect, Fully Enlightened One."

A Concert of the Deepest Truth Names of the Vanquishing Master Surpassing All, the Deep Awareness Being Mañjuśrī, expounded by the Vanquishing Master, the Thusly Gone One, Śākyamuni, is hereby completed.

–2–

The Mental Afflictions and the Nature of the Supreme Immutable Wisdom in the *Sekoddeśa* and Its Commentary by Nāropa

Giacomella Orofino

Foreword on the texts

The text translated here is an extract from the *Teaching on the Initiation* (*Sekoddeśa)*, which is one of the most important sources of the Kālacakra tradition and consists of 174 stanzas. According to its literature this is the first text of the Kālacakra to have come down to us and contains the essential nucleus of its doctrines. It is, in fact, considered to be a section of the *Paramādibuddha,* or the *Mūlakālacakratantra*, the root tantra in twelve thousand verses, that was lost in Sanskrit and was not translated into Tibetan.

Tradition has it that the *Paramādibuddha* was first promulgated by Lord Buddha at the request of Sucandra, an emanation of Vajrapāṇi and king of the mythical realm of Śambhala, in the *Dharmadhātumaṇḍala* at Śrīdhānyakaṭaka—a sacred place in the proximity of Amarāvati in the Guntur District of Andra Pradesh in India, regarded in the Kālacakra tradition as the fount of all the Vajrayāna teachings. Sucandra then wrote the twelve thousand verses of the *Mūlatantra* of the *Kālacakra* and returned to Śambhala where he taught and transmitted it. The king was followed by a lineage of kings of Śambhala, all practitioners of the Kālacakra doctrines. The seventh king, Yaśas, was an emanation of Mañjuśrī; he was known as the first Kalkin, or sovereign master, of Śambhala. He wrote the *Śrīkālacakra* or *Laghukālacakra tantra,* an abridged version of the *Paramādibuddha*, traditionally considered to consist of 1,030 stanzas; this text is still extant in Sanskrit and in Tibetan and functions in the tradition as the root tantra. Yaśas's spiritual descendant, Puṇḍarīka, who is considered an emanation of Avalokiteśvara, wrote an extensive commentary to this tantra, the twelve-thousand-line *Vimalaprabhā*.

We have no certainty about the original length of the *Paramādibuddha,* neither are we certain whether it ever existed as an entire text. In the exegetical literature of the early phase of the Kālacakra tradition, however, it is possible to trace numerous other fragments of it independent of the *Sekoddeśa* verses, demonstrating that other sections of the *Mūlakālacakratantra* were circulating in India during the early spread of this religious tradition.

Apart from the first folio kept in the National Archives of Kathmandu, the *Sekoddeśa* was lost in the original Sanskrit version, but very fortunately it is extant in two different Tibetan translations: one by the Kashmiri paṇḍit Somanātha and the Tibetan lotsāva 'Bro Shes rabs grags, and the other by the Nepalese paṇḍit Samantaśrī and the Tibetan lotsāva Rwa Chos rab. The first one is preserved in all the Tibetan Kanjur editions, while the second one, which diverges very much from the first, is preserved in the independent tradition of the Phug brag Kanjur.[1]

According to the *Vimalaprabhā,* the *Paramādhibuddha* was divided in five chapters: Worldly realm, Inner realm, Initiation, Practice, and Gnosis. This division corresponds with that of the *Laghukālacakra.* It is not easy to determine the exact position of the 174 stanzas of the *Sekoddeśa* within the *Paramādibuddha.* The colophon of the first Tibetan translation ('Bro) implies that the *Sekoddeśa,* "the treatise on the performance on the initiation into the fifth chapter's immutable bliss," was extracted from the first chapter on the Worldly realms, so it seems to be a fragment of the first chapter. In the second translation (Rwa), however, this statement is followed by the word "etc.," and in this case the meaning would change and the statement could be interpreted as referring to the entire text of the *Paramādibuddha*, starting from the first chapter. I am quite inclined to think that the second Tibetan translation is more reliable in this case and that the *Sekoddeśa* could be a section of the fifth chapter of the *Paramādibuddha*. This hypothesis is confirmed in the introductory chapter of Kālacakrapāda's commentary (*ṭikā*) to the *Sekoddeśa* where he states that the *Sekoddeśa* was extracted from the fifth chapter of the *Mūlatantra*.[2]

Whatever it might have been, we know that the *Sekoddeśa* was circulating in India as an independent text in the first half of the eleventh century because it drew the attention of many important contemporary religious figures who wrote commentaries on it. Nāropa wrote the most important commentary of this treatise, the *Paramārtasaṃgraha,* which is preserved in both Sanskrit and Tibetan and whose chapter on mental afflictions and the nature of the supreme immutable wisdom is translated below. Other commentaries, still extant in Sanskrit and Tibetan, are a brief commentary (*Ṭippaṇī*) by Sādhuputra Śrīdharānanda and an anonymous commentary, *Pañjikā*. Besides these, two other commentaries are extant only in their Tibetan translations: the *Ṭikā* by Kālacakrapāda mentioned above and a *Ṭippaṇī* by rNam par rgyal ba brjed byang (*Vijayāpāda).

The passage chosen here is taken from Nāropa's commentary to stanzas 129 to 160 of the *Sekoddeśa* and is, in my opinion, quite relevant for understanding the essential Kālacakra teaching on the nature of the mind and ultimate reality. The entire commentary by Nāropa was translated into Italian by Raniero

Gnoli and myself in 1995.[3] Phil Lecso has provided an English translation of it, which I have then revised again, checking it against the Tibetan and Sanskrit texts.[4]

I am very honoured to participate in this publication as a humble tribute to His Holiness the Dalai Lama who has done so much in spreading the Kālacakra teachings in the contemporary world.

The Text

With the following three stanzas the Blessed refutes the mental afflictions:

129. The defilements are not adventitious in the mind,
They do not exist from time immemorial in the mind,
They are not born (elsewhere) except than in the mind,
And they do not reside inexhaustibly in the mind.

130. If the defilements were adventitious,
Then why does the mind first appear without defilements?
And if, on other hand, they have existed from a time immemorial before the mind,
From wherever would they originate?

131. If on the other hand, they were born without the mind,
Then they would be like a flower in the sky;
And if they resided continuously in the mind,
Then they would never be eliminable.

a) First of all, [the defilements] are not able to be adventitious (*āgantuka*) since it would follow, by absurdity, that even a person devoid of passion would be able to become passionate.

b) Nor are they [able to be] prior to the mind, because they would come to lack a cause. The afflictions and so forth are, in fact, a creation of the mind (*cittaviṭhapita*).

c) Nor are they able to be without a cause, because they would then be devoid of causal efficacy "like a flower in the ether."

d) Nor are they, on the other hand, able to be innate with the mind because then they would be indestructible or their becoming less would result in the extinction [of the same mind] just as [occurs when one puts out] a lamp.

Now this concept comes to be explained with the example of copper.

132. In that manner when the impurity in copper comes to be destroyed
Thanks to union with the elixir,
Nor is its essential nature so destroyed,
Which remains in all its purity;

133. Just like that, the defilements of the mind come to be destroyed
Thanks to union with emptiness,
Nor is their nature made of primordial wisdom so destroyed,
Which remains in all its purity.

If this impurity (*mala*) in the copper is adventitious, then at the beginning, the copper would be devoid of stain; on the other hand, if this stain exists from a time immemorial and the existence of the copper is subsequent to it, then from where would this stain ever be born? Then, if [the stain] is born without the copper, then a flower would also be able to be born in the ether. Moreover, if it were inherent, always in the copper, then it would not be able to be removed, not even with the elixir. All these hypotheses are not logically supported, so that the truth is the following: this impurity is born together with the copper and is destroyed by virtue of the elixir. It, in brief, neither precedes the copper, nor succeeds the copper, nor [is it born] independently from it; and therefore the substance of the copper continues to subsist "in all its purity," that is to say, like gold [also after removing the impurities]. [The Blessed] as well demonstrates how all this occurs with respect to the mind, saying, "just like that." "Emptiness" consists of the path of the smoke and so forth; "its nature made of primordial wisdom" is its condition of being able to be personally experienced. Because, as it was said by the venerable Nāgārjuna in the *Praise to the Dharmadhātu*:

The sun and the moon, though immaculate, are covered by the five stains:
clouds, fog, smoke, eclipse (the face of Rāhu), [5] and dust. (18)
In the same manner, the mind's clear luminosity is covered by the five
defilements: desire, spite, laziness, restlessness,[6] and doubt. (19)
As when a filthy garment with multiple stains becomes cleansed and such
by the action of fire,[7] when thrown into the fire, which burns the stains
and not the garment (20)
exactly thus occurs to the mind's clear luminosity polluted by
the stains born from lust: by the fire of primordial wisdom the stains are
burnt, but not
the mind's clear luminosity. (21)
From the Sutras pronounced by the Victorious and
proclaiming emptiness, all of them affirm the elimination of the impurities
(*kleśa*), not the destruction of the elements (*dhātu*). (22)

In that manner, when hidden in the ground, water remains without stain, like that, hidden by impurities, the primordial wisdom remains without stain.[8]

The venerable Āryadeva said the same in the *Sūtaka*:[9]

> Devoid of darkness, [the mind returns] to its clear luminosity in an instant, perfectly pure, generated from a continuous light, characterized by the supreme truth. [It] is known through the eye of primordial wisdom.

And again:

> The primordial wisdom's nature is clear luminosity.

With the stanza that begins with "Just as iron," [the Blessed] says how one who is liberated does not return anymore into transmigration.

134. Just as iron, when penetrated by the elixir,
Does not revert back to the nature of iron,
So the mind, penetrated by bliss,
Does not revert back to the nature of sorrow.

135. There does not exist a greater transgression than the lack of passion,
There does not exist a merit greater than bliss,
Therefore, O King,
You need to apply continuously the mind to immutable bliss.

Misdeed is born from the destruction of passion, as from it aversion is born for the beloved woman; from aversion [comes] obfuscation, and from this, one's own vajra falls, [one develops] a state of continuous mental confusion, and [engages in] activity directed exclusively towards other petty objects, like foods, drinks, and so on. The mind, disillusioned by all this, becomes devoid of bliss and wanders in the six births.[10]

"Misdeed is born from the destruction of passion" because it is generated from the failing of compassion (*karuṇā*). And why is all this? Because aversion derives from it, namely, the destruction of affection (*preman*) for the beloved woman, generated in turn by the failing of benevolence. The verb "is born" is extended to all of the terms of the stanza. "From aversion, obfuscation is born," that is to say, the lack of exhilaration, essentially from the nonexistence of joy (*muditā*). The "state of mental confusion," born from the dissolution of bliss, is generated from the failing of equanimity (*upekṣā*). Therefore, exactly by the nonexistence of the four sublime sentiments, the [lack of passion] is spiritual demerit, certainly not merit.

But [some might ask] what is the authentic source for this assertion when, namely, compassion is characterized by an increase of passion, benevolence by the disappearance of hatred, joy by the dissolution of obfuscation, and equanimity by the immutable bliss? This assertion, we respond, is found in the *Buddhakapāla*:[11]

Compassion is united with the [mutual] glance, benevolence with embrace, joy by contact with the woman, equanimity with the immutable bliss that comes about in union. In such a manner, the one who is united with such yoga, how is he able to be bound by attachment?

"You need to apply" and so forth, due to the meditation of the path.

The [Blessed] now explains how the immutable bliss transcends the paths of the word.

136. A young maiden is unable to describe the bliss of making love
Without [having experienced] the same love.
Having experienced love in her youth, she will know for herself
The [nature of] such great bliss.

137. Analogously, one who has had nothing to do with concentration (*samādhi*),
Is unable to describe the bliss of it;
But, having attained the immutable condition through concentration,
The yogins will know the nature in themselves.

138. Even the omniscient are uncertain regarding
[The true nature of] primordial wisdom which is born from the immutable.
Nevertheless, it is necessary to strive to avoid dispassion
on account of the nonbliss that derives from it in the mind.

Whoever has experienced the bliss of making love in their youth, [that one] has personal awareness of it. [One] "who has had nothing to do with concentration" [is one who is] devoid of the concentration concerning emptiness. In the absence of passion, the mind (*manas*) is devoid of bliss and, because of this deprivation of bliss, it is necessary to strive to avoid dispassion.

[The Blessed] now shows how only emission (*cyuti*) is, by an indirect way, the cause of transmigration:

139. From emission is born dispassion,
From dispassion, suffering is born,
From suffering is born, for humans, the ruin of the elements, and
From ruin, as it was handed down, death.

140. From death, a new existence [arises] from it, again from it [comes] death
And still again, emission.

Thus, for beings, phenomenal existence
Proceeds only from the birth of dispassion, not otherwise.

"Thus": that is to say, the birth of dispassion comes about for beings in the above-mentioned manner. "Not otherwise": if there would not be anymore birth of dispassion by them—those whose birth is caused by emission—then there would not be anymore [birth], not even transmigration, in no other manner. In other words, the cause of it (transmigration) is therefore only emission. Things abiding so, it is therefore useful to avoid passion for emission. Because, as it is said in the *Pañcalakṣabhidhāna*:[12]

> By the arrest of nescience—which is "moved"—one has the arrest of volition; by the arrest of volition, one has the arrest of consciousness; by the arrest of consciousness, one has the arrest of name and form; by the arrest of name and form, one has the arrest of the six bases; by the arrest of the six bases, one has the arrest of contact; by the arrest of contact, one has the arrest of sensation; by the arrest of sensation, one has the arrest of longing; by the arrest of longing, one has the arrest of appropriation; by the arrest of appropriation, one has the arrest of phenomenal existence; by the arrest of phenomenal existence, one has the arrest of birth (*jāti*); and by the arrest of birth, one has the arrest of old age and death. The arrest of the aggregates and of the elements is, by tradition, pacification. In such a manner, by the arrest of the body, one has the arrest of the vital breath; by the arrest of the vital breath, one has the arrest of bodhicitta; by the arrest of bodhicitta, one has the arrest of emission (*cyavana*); by the arrest of the instant of emission, one has, for all corporeal beings, the condition of Buddha. Similarly, by the arrest of the afflictions (*kleśa*), one has the arrest of karma; by the arrest of karma, one has the arrest of suffering; and, by the arrest of suffering, one has the nonbirth of the afflictions; without the birth of the afflictions,[13] one does not produce the birth of karma; without the birth of karma, one does not even produce the birth of suffering; and, without suffering, the yogin, satisfied, will continuously dedicate himself to the benefit of beings.

141. [The yogin] therefore needs to avoid with every effort
The passion for emission,
By which [avoiding it], will attain the immutable bliss,
[Liberating himself] from the bonds of transmigration.

142. Even a lover, because of dispassion,
Will not seek out the *Kāmaśāstra*.[14]
All the more so, will a yogin seek suffering
In the tantra proclaimed by me?

"By which": avoiding, namely, the bliss of emission. With the words "even a lover," [the Blessed] declares that is necessary to strive for immutable bliss. "Suffering" means "characterized by dispassion."

1
43. Taking advantage of the nature of the immutable semen,
[The yogin] will need to realize the supreme immutable.
Once that the support has become the refuge of emission
The supported suffers a lack of passion.

144. This relation of support and supported remains
As long as [the mind] has not attained the immutable [bliss].
Once that [the mind] has attained it,
[The dyad] characterized by support and supported ceases to exist.

Fallen, which is the semen in the support, the supported, namely, bliss, "suffers a lack of passion," by an interruption, so that what is to be realized is the great bliss, resulting from the immobility (*akṣaratvena*) of semen. This relation between the two different realities of support and supported lasts so long as there does not come about a state of fullness at the top of the head. It is accomplished when one has the mind, [immersed] in this fullness, the condition of immutable bliss, then it is not characterized anymore by the [differentiation] into support and supported.[15]

[The Blessed] now describes the state of purity.[16]

145. For one whose body has been born from the immutable (*akṣara*),
And who has arrived at the wheel of the ūrṇā,
Neither the union of the two series of the vowels and consonants,
Nor, O King, [the mantras such as] HŪṂ [and so forth] have any function.[17]

Here by "immutable" [it means] the knowledge of supreme immutable bliss.[18] The body that is born from the immutable is the body that is born from knowledge, constituted by the aggregates, elements, senses, sense organs, and so forth. Then of the one whose body is born from the supreme immutable, one is well able to say that it has arrived at the "wheel of the ūrṇā," namely, the wheel at the forehead. [In other words and] implicitly (*sāmarthyāt*), it comes to signify with that, the sixteenth kalā, which one finds at the top of the head and represents the supported (*ādheya*). For him, the support is neither the moon, itself evolved from the series of vowels, nor the sun, itself evolved from the series of consonants, united together (*sampuñena*),[19] nor the union of the two series of the vowels and consonants in the left and right channels, flowing in the middle channel. Neither is the supported the principal deity of the maṇḍala, itself evolved from the various mantras like HŪṂ and so forth.[20] Instead the truth is this: that for him, the support is the moon and sun, which reside in the lotuses (*varañaka*) at the top of the head and at the jewel, and the supported is the great bliss, which pervades all things.

Because, as it is said in the *Vimalaprabhā*:

Of the Ruler, one foot is resting on the sun of blood [that abides] in the gem of the vajra and the second [foot] on the moon, on the semen [that abides] at the top of the head—to Him, always unbreakable, impenetrable, revered, devoid of the three worlds, I bow.[21]

The "Ruler" (*bhartṛ*) is the adamantine bodhicitta, the venerable Kālacakra.[22] The "foot" (*pāda*) is that, thanks to which a thing is reached (*padyate*) or known, namely to say, the immutable primordial wisdom. "Resting" (*nyastam*) signifies imposed, for the purpose of eliminating nescience. In the "sun of blood" [that abides] in the gem of the vajra, namely, on the level of nirvāṇa without support, which corresponds [in the stanza of the *Nāmasaṃgīti*] to the level of the essence of the earth (*mahīmaṇḍatale*), to the element of primordial wisdom (*jñānadhātu*). The foot which then rests is the right, which is alluded to [in the *Nāmasaṃgīti*] with the expression "occupying the ground with a foot." "In the moon, in the semen that abides at the top of the head" transcends the pleasures of existence, which corresponds [in the stanza of the *Nāmasaṃgīti*] to the expression "he who stands on the nail of the great toe of the foot" and moreover to the element of the consciousness (*vijñānadhātu*), which consists of the initial kalā of desire (*prākkāmakalā*).[23] The foot which then rests is the left [which is alluded to in the *Nāmasaṃgīti* with the expression] "occupying the top of the world of Brahmā." "Always," that is to say, in the three times. Transcending the obstacles of the impurities, it is "unbreakable" by the action of the sword of nescience, of ignorance. Being transcendent, the nature of perception[24] (*vijñāna*) is "impenetrable" on the part of two extremes of the perceptible and the perceiver. Since he is essentially of great bliss, he is "revered," that is to say, [according to the *Nāmasaṃgīti*] resides "in the deserted land, where there is not anymore to accomplish,"[25] namely, in the gem. Transcending the conduct of the world is exactly therefore "devoid of the three worlds"; and from this point of view, "has reached the shore that stands beyond transmigration,"[26] [namely, the top of the head].

The sense of all this is the following. The Blessed to whose lotus feet are bowed by the three worlds, has a wisdom body (*jñānakāya*) made of the six material elements (*dhātu*), that are by nature the six channels, above and below, in a state of arrest. Because the two fortnights, the bright and dark one, which belonging to ordinary existence (*bhāva*) are without obscuration, He, the unique Lord, pervades the full and new moons with his two feet, which, generated from the moon and sun, arrest the paths of transmigration and of nirvāṇa, are essentiated by emptiness and compassion, and are constituted respectively by fifteen moments. I bow to these, his feet.

Various interpretations of the term "akṣara" (immutable)

a) In the [section of the *Vimalaprabhā* called] "The realization supreme immutable/wisdom,"[27] with the word "immutable," it also designates here the wisdom of supreme immutable bliss, [in the sense] of Vajrasattva.

b) With the name of "wisdom of the supreme immutable," it is also called the mantra, which acts as protection for the mind. Because, as it is said in the *Mūlatantra*:

> The mantra is so called because it acts as protection (*trāṇa*) for the body, speech, and mind elements. With the word mantra, one designates the immutable wisdom of emptiness. The mantra, arising from merit (*puṇya*) and wisdom, is constituted of emptiness and compassion.

c) The spiritually supreme awareness is called Prajñāpāramitā and also Mahāmudrā, clear light by its very nature; having the form of innate joy, the natural outflow (*niḥṣyanda*) of the element of the dharma, it consists of a state of perfection. These two mothers of Vajrasattva and of the Buddha[28] are incomprehensible (*agocarau*) to the senses, which are dependently originated and [are only] comprehensible by means of the divine senses. These are generated from the supreme immutable bliss which transcends the nature of atoms and is similar to a magical image in a mirror or to a dream. These are called by the Victorious with the name of the innate body because their nature is immutable.

d) Here, the "immutable" are appearance, sensation, name, volition, and consciousness (*vijñāna*), which, devoid of obstacles, are exactly called the "five immutables," the "five great empties."[29] Similarly, also called the "five immutables" are the earth, water, fire, wind, and ether elements without obstacles. The "six immutables" are the eye, ear, nose, tongue, body, and mind, [they are also] without obstacles, devoid, namely, of the perception of their respective objects. With the name of "six immutables," they are also called appearance, sound, scent, taste, touch, and the dharma, [they are also] without obstacles. These aggregates, elements, and bases, in a state of intimate fusion (*ekasamarasībhūtāni*) [and therefore without obstacles], are the "empty bindu" (*binduśūnya, thig le stong pa*).

e) Then, the same bindu, not being emitted, is called with the name of "supreme immutable."

f) The supreme immutable is also the syllable A. Born from the syllable A, perfectly awakened, generated from wisdom and means, the Vajrasattva, the neutral level, is called with the name of innate body. He is [equally] endowed with knowledge and with the knowable, as cause and result are indivisible [in Him]. That one is Kālacakra, the Blessed, the level of supreme immutable bliss, because, as it is said in the *Nāmasaṃgīti*:

Progenitor of the significance of all mantras,
he is the great bindu, devoid of syllables
with five immutable (syllables) and the greatly void (*mahāśūnya*),
he is voidness in the bindu (*binduśūnya*) with the six immutable (syllables).
(Verse144)

And also in the *Mūlatantra*:

The Element of the Dharma (*Dharmadhātu*), the great immutable, is called with the name of A. It is the adamantine womb/matrix of the Victorious, the cause of body, speech, and mind. That is to say:[30] "The Blessed Buddha, perfectly awakened, is born from the syllable A. The syllable A is the first of all the letters, is endowed with a great significance, is the supreme syllable; it is the great breath, is devoid of birth, is not able to be pronounced by words, is the primary cause of every word, is the clear luminosity in all words."

The adamantine matrix of the bodies of the Victorious is [that principle] from which body, speech, and mind, having the nature of inseparability from three vajras, are born. The place of birth of the Buddhas, who have as qualities sovereignty over all things and so forth, is called with the name of supreme dharmodaya,[31] because by its very nature it is [characterized by] spiritual merit and knowledge.

With these words, it has been summarized the limb of the yoga called concentration (*samādhi*).

The critique of the relation of cause and effect

[The Blessed] now expounds the relation between cause and result, from the point of view of the relative truth, saying:[32]

146. The image, born from emptiness, is the cause, and
Bliss, born from the immutable, is the result.
The cause is sealed by the result and
The result is sealed by the cause.

"The image" characterized by all aspects, born from emptiness, from the sky, is the cause, and "the bliss" born from the immutable semen (*śukra*) is the result.

The cause [consisting, as it is seen, in emptiness], is sealed (*mudrita*) by the result, that is to say, by the bliss devoid of impurity (*anāśrava*). It has the form of bliss—also because by its very nature, it is bliss.

[The result, namely] the bliss devoid of impurity, is sealed by the cause also because it embodies nonconceptual emptiness.[33] [Cause and result therefore are] both characterized by emptiness and compassion, so that the [Blessed] says:

147. Emptiness, which holds the image, is the cause, and
Compassion, which holds the immutable, is the result.
The unity of emptiness and compassion
Is the nonemitted bodhicitta.

The cause is the mind that holds the image, namely, the emptiness with basis (*sālamba*), and the result, [the same mind] that holds the immutable, namely, compassion without basis.[34] Not being separated, the unity of this emptiness and compassion is exactly the bodhicitta which comes to be called with the name of "nonemitted" (*acyuta*), and [no other form of bliss] moved or vibrating, is born from an action mudrā (*karmamudrā*) or from a jñāna mudrā.

148. The image is devoid of nirvāṇa and
The immutable transcends transmigration.
Between these two there is a supreme unity,
Without duality, devoid of eternity and cessation.

This reality is exempt from cessation and from transmigration, so therefore [the Blessed] says how the image is "devoid of nirvāṇa"— [in its form, he means] material—and how the immutable, namely, the great bliss devoid of impurity, "transcends transmigration," characterized by a moved bliss. Between these two realities, the image and the immutable, "there is a supreme unity," the most eminent, "without duality," and this is why [the Blessed] adds "devoid of eternity and of cessation."

To all of this, [the Blessed] now expounds the reason, saying:

149. Because it has as a character, that of origin from nonbeing,
There is not of the image, nonbeing;
And because it has, as a character, that of origin from being,
There is not of the immutable, being.

150. The perfect union of being and nonbeing
Is the vajrayoga, without duality, supreme,
Devoid of form and nonform, complete liberation
Similar to a mirror divination image.

151. The image is not immersed in phenomenal existence,
Nor the immutable in nirvāṇa.
[True reality] is a supreme pacified neutral level,
Mutually embraced by both.

Of the image, consisting of an appearance before one's own mind with all aspects, how is it that there is not nonbeing, that is to say, cessation?[35] "Because it has as a character, that of origin from nonbeing" and because this image, insubstantial emptiness, which is comprehensive of the three worlds and of the three times, arises as individual awareness. Because, as [the Blessed] will say here in the root tantra (*mūlatantra*):

> . . . by virtue of the constant practice on the said image, which originates from space.[36]

And of the immutable, of the bliss devoid of impurity, how is it that there is not being (*bhāva*)? "Because it has as a character, that of origin from being" and because in reality overflows from a being, characterized by the [said] image that appears very clearly. All this [the Blessed] will clarify with the stanza that begins with the words: "Wisdom not born from a cause."[37]

[The phrase "because it has as a character, that of origin from being" is also able to be interpreted otherwise], in this sense: "because the bliss devoid of impurity, different from that of the world, is born from being, consisting [in this case] of the semen directed towards the top, departing from the gem." Being and nonbeing are states so defined. The union, the fusion (*mīlana*) of these two, namely, of emptiness and compassion, essentially of relative truth and of absolute truth, is the adamantine yoga, which in turn is nonduality, called with the name of "two in one" (*yuganaddha*), the immutable. This is the truth.

Because, as it was said by the venerable Āryadeva in the *Sūtaka*:

> That which really exists, this is reality. But that thing is, O Blessed, that which really exists
> and so what does it come to be called? This which is incontrovertible (*avisaṣvādaka*);[38] this is
> reality. And what thing is this that is incontrovertible? The meditative concentration (*samādhi)*
> called with the name of "principle of reality" (*bhūtanaya*). And so what is this meditative
> concentration thus called? The unification of the two truths, such is the above-mentioned
> meditative concentration. And so what are, O Blessed, these two truths? The first is the
> relative truth and the second is the absolute truth.[39]

This is the reason by which [in stanza 150] it comes to say "devoid of form and nonform, complete liberation": In the magical rite of the mirror divination (*pratisenā*),[40] where one sees the appearance of a body in a mirror and so forth, none is present: neither the characters of form, from the moment when there is not a material union of atoms, nor those of nonform, because what one perceives is difficult to be negated. Therefore the image is not "immersed in phenomenal existence," in transmigration, nor is the immutable immersed in nirvāṇa, that is to say, in annihilation. Reality is "mutually embraced by both," "pacified," unalterable (*avikārin*) because it is devoid of the alterations due to the senses. This indeed is essentially of both, is the "neutral level" because of the absence of the two, wisdom and means, taken separately (*kevala*), "supreme," that is to say, the most eminent, because it is different from all things of the world.

But [some will say], seeing that the innate state is born from the Mahāmudrā, it will then be caused and the Mahāmudrā will be the cause of it, so that, things being so, the dyad, cause and result, is by no means surpassed. Not only that, but like the Mahāmudrā, the action mudrā and the jñāna mudrā will also be caused. What difference will there be in fact between them and the Mahāmudrā? [To respond to this objection, the Blessed] says:

152. Wisdom is not born from a cause,
But from the cause of wisdom the result is born
And because wisdom is not born from a cause
From wisdom a cause is not born.[41]

Wisdom, characterized by the image, consists of the knowledge of all aspects and is identified with the emptiness of all the elements. It does not come from a cause, it is not born.[42] In reality therefore, being that the cause (*prakṛti*) is not born, also the result born from it (the cause), that is to say, from wisdom (*prajñāhetūdbhava*), called [in the stanza] with the name of "born from wisdom" (*prajñājāta*), it also, I say, is "not born from a cause," not born from wisdom as [its] cause. And why? Because wisdom is not born in reality from a cause. In fact, seeing that wisdom is not born from a cause, how is it able, I say, [to be] its result, called with the name of born-together (*sahaja*), to be born from a cause? The concept of cause was in fact already refuted earlier.

153. Therefore, the unsurpassable wisdom knowledge,
Is not born from a cause.
The cause and the result are not able to be mutually sealed,
The one by the other.

"Therefore," that is to say, for this reason, the immutable wisdom, which is identified with the knowledge wisdom, "is not born from a cause," and therefore there is not a relation of cause and effect, nor is the cause able to be sealed by the effect nor the effect by the cause "mutually;" nor the cause by the effect nor the effect by the cause.

And why? To this question, [the Blessed] responds, saying:

154. The cause and the result are
Both dependently originated.

The image is sealed by the one and by the other,[43]
Is neither born nor extinguished.

155. Wisdom is completely extinguished and
The supreme immutable is [always] born.
Devoid [of the nature] of cause and result,
They are not sealed the one by the other.

While the cause and the effect are dependently originated and therefore exist from the point of view of relative truth (*saṃvṛti*), [wisdom] transcends the world and is, as such, without beginning and without end. For this reason, the image (*bimba*) is characterized by the one and by the other, is, namely, inseparable from both and is identified with the "two in one" (*yuganaddha*), "is neither born nor extinguished," is, namely, devoid of an origin and of an end. Because, as it is said, "Whether there is birth of the Tathāgata or whether there is not birth of the Tathāgata, the essential nature (*dharmatā*) of the dharma remains equal to itself."[44] Then of this image, inseparable from both, the wisdom part (*prajñābhaga*), because it is always pacified (*ādiśāntatvāt*), is perpetually not born (*nityānutpanna*) and the means (*upāya*) part, because it is an object of personal experience, is always rising [on the horizon], so that also by this there is not between these two either a relation of cause and effect or mutual impression.[45]

Then to prove this mutual nonimpression, [the Blessed] now presents another argument (*yukti*), saying:

156. Here,[46] with regard to this reality, not born and not extinguished,
The vision of the knowable is part of one's own mind and not of another,
By reason of the fact that [one's mind] separates from itself
The [only apparently] external knowable.[47]

An external reality, distinguished from the appearances (*ākāra*) of knowledge is nonexistent, and therefore what is perceived is not other than one's own mind which one projects to the outside, divided [in all the various] appearances of the three worlds. There is no thing other than one's own mind, therefore for the yogin, in that moment[48] there is not, in fact, the false imagination of a division between oneself and other. Because, as it is said in the *Hevajratantra*:

> In that instant, he becomes a single body with the heavens, with the hells, and with the mortals, nor is he in truth obstructed by false conceptualizations [characterized by the] distinction between himself and others.[49]

The expression "by reason of the fact that [one's same mind] separates from itself the [only apparently] external knowable" [refers to the thought] that has separated from itself the external knowable.

With the stanza that begins with the words "that is why" and so forth, it summarizes [what has been said].

157. That is why a thing is absolutely impotent to imprint
Its own character on itself.
Is perhaps a great sword able to cut itself
With the cutting edge of its own blade?

The words "a great sword, is perhaps able to cut" constitute the example.

However [as some will say here], since the Mahāmudrā is not born (*ajāta*), how is it possible a result [arises] from it? From any element whatever that is not born, a result is not perceived on the part of anyone. To respond to this objection, [the Blessed] says:

158. In that manner, when in [sexual] union in a dream, with the daughter of a barren woman,
One is able to experience bliss,
Thus one [experiences bliss] by virtue of the constant practice of the image,
Which is born from the void.

"In [sexual] union, in a dream, with the daughter of a barren woman"— [the daughter who therefore] has never been born—however, "one is able to experience bliss." [Similar to] this is the innate bliss experienced by the yogins, bliss that results exactly (*phalarūpa*) from the constant practice (*sevā*) with the image arising from the sky. This innate bliss is not born from wisdom, from skillful means, or from the [physical] sense organs, but from the Mahāmudrā,[50] devoid of obstacles, similar to the cloudless sky, present in all beings, and is certainly not able to be experienced by the ignorant.[51]

But [some will say][52] that, since it was stated by the Tathāgata that there are not the aggregates, elements, and bases, and also there is not the union of the two [masculine and feminine] organs, and consequently there is not the out-flowing of semen (*acyutavāt*), then the knowledge of wisdom (*prajñājñāna*) cannot be an object of personal experience (*svasaṃvedya*).[53] [Analogously], [everything] always being [merely] a reflection of one's own mind, following [just] this mind, [how] is the yogin ever able to render his mind without obstacles and thus enjoy the wisdom of great immutable? In fact, there does not exist a body constituted of a clustering (*saṃdoha*) of atoms. All this is contrary to logic (*viparīta*), as in the story of Devadatta, who while mounted astride himself, went to the village.

Perhaps some people are able to think like that, in which case our reply is the following. Here, what some destitute (*mūrkha*) people are able to say, that without aggregates, elements, and bases, which are constituted of [material] atoms, the knowledge of wisdom (*prajñājñāna*) is not able to be an object of personal experience by virtue of thought only (*cittamātreṇa*), is not true. And why? Because of the latent impressions of the [same] thought [which] come and go (*āgantuka*). Here, the so-called aggregates, elements, and bases are not other than adventitious mental impressions; owing to this, they make way for the mental impressions of pleasure and of pain and uncertainty to penetrate the mind. If one examines things from the point of view of true reality—it is not by virtue of a terrible offense (*kṣudropadraveṇa*), received by one's body [that ones feels pleasure or pain].

Here, while one dreams, [this, one's] body, constituted by a cluster of material atoms, is lying down, not receiving any [material] offense, because of which pain enters into the mind. Now, it is a fact well known to all that, just by dreaming, one makes manifest another body constituted of mental impressions, devoid of aggregates of [material] atoms. And when this other body is, [for example] brought elsewhere; and while this body is thus brought elsewhere, it receives an offence (*upadrava*) on the part of a thief and so forth and then by way of this offense, pain enters into the mind, by which [whoever so dreams], starts to call out, "Help!" This indeed is truly extraordinary (*mahad adbhutam*), that when without a [true and actual] body and without an actual thief and so forth, one nevertheless [really] ascertains a sensation of pain (*duḥkhajñāna*), [as an] object of personal experience! Analogously, in a dream, thanks to an intense amorous pleasure, bliss is able to enter into the mind. This matter is truly marvelous (*āścarya*), that without a [true and actual] body and without a [true and actual] amorous pleasure, beings nevertheless experience a sensation of bliss in the mind, [as an] object of personal experience! To this knowledge, which is of a limited order (*prādeśika*), not even the scholars themselves succeed in giving a satisfactory explanation. All the more so, ignorant and inexperienced (*mūrkha*) people are certainly not able to satisfactorily distinguish and explain the knowledge of the highest, immutable bliss, complete in all part,[54] transcending the actual mental impressions of transmigration, aroused by the mental impressions belonging to nirvāṇa, the object of personal experience on the part of the yogins.

If one says that wisdom and means are inseparable, this affirmation, from the point of view of true reality, is nevertheless not correct, and therefore [the Blessed] says:

159. There is neither wisdom nor means,
This [being of whom one speaks] is coemergent with wisdom,
Perfectly full of bliss,
And devoid of every sort of obstacle.

160. It is uncontaminated like the sky,
Devoid of the sense organs and of their [relative] objects,
Present, in every part, in all beings,
Unbreakable, devoid of differentiations.

There are not separate categories standing by themselves [as wisdom and means], due to which one can say that bodhicitta is undivided by them. The novice yogins, in fact, are not able to know the [supreme] state. The same term "sahaja" (innate) is referred to this, that is, born together with wisdom mind. [This being] is in possession of a condition "perfectly full of bliss" and as such needs to be considered and explained (*nirṇeya*) as "devoid of every sort of obstacle," constituted by the knowable and by the afflictions such as desire and so forth. The lack of every contact [with the sense organs] such as the hands and so forth, and the absence of a subject and an object of perception, thus makes it "devoid of the sense organs and of their [relative] objects." It is, moreover, all pervading, it knows in every part all of the aspects and therefore is present in every part, in all beings, and in all three times. It transcends the material nature (*dharmatā*) of atoms and by this is exactly "unbreakable" into parts by the knife of nescience (*avidyā*), of nonknowledge; and because it transcends the nature of differentiated knowledge (*vijñāna*), it is not able to be divided into the two extremes (*koñi*) of an object and a subject of perception and is therefore devoid of differentiations.

Endnotes

1. Cf. Orofino 1994b.

2. Cf. Kālacakrapāda, *Sekoddeśaṭikā*: P. vol. 47, 2070, fol. 4b/1.

3. Gnoli, Orofino 1994.

4. The Sanskrit and Tibetan texts have been edited recently, cf. Sferra, Merzagora, 2006.

5. Literally: "the face of Rāhu."

6. According to Conze, the meaning of auddhatya is "excitedness"; see Conze 1961, p. 56. Ruegg (1971, p. 466) translates it as dissipation. In Tibetan the term is rendered as rgod pa, the indomitability of the mind to fall victim to inquietude.

7. Thrown, that is to say, into boiling water.

8. The *Dharmadhātustava* of Nāgārjuna has been studied and analyzed by Ruegg (1971, p. 448.71). The verses quoted are 18-23.

9. The *Sūtaka* corresponds to Āryadeva's *Caryāmelāpakapradīpa*.

10. *Vimalaprabha* I.

11. This tantra is extant only in the Tibetan (P. Vol.3, op.63). Cited from the thirteenth chapter, entitled *Sems rnam par dag pa'i le'u* {*Chapter of the Completely Purified Mind*}, folio 151b, II. 3-4.

12. In Tibetan *Bum phrag lnga mngon par brjod pa*. This title refers to a supposed version of the *Hevajratantra in 500,000 Stanzas*. The passage appears in the *Hevajratantraṭikā (*MS C128, Mf.C14/6 ff., 52a-52b).

13. According to the *Pratītyasamutpādahçdayakārikā* attributed to Nāgārjuna, the twelve moments (*nidāna*) of dependent origination are divided into three groups called afflictions *(kleśa*), karma, and suffering. The first, eighth, and ninth moments are afflictions, the second and the tenth are karma, and the remaining seven are suffering (see Gokhale, 1955, pp. 101 ff.).

14. The meaning seems to be that even a man taken of love will not seek out the *Kāmaśāstra* that teaches the most opportune ways to reach the culmination of erotic experience, because he knows that afterwards dispassion will derive from it, disgust for the beloved woman.

15. Because, as Bu ston explains (705, I, 6), one attains a condition in which all things appear as undifferentiated (*ro mnyam*) and inseparable (*dbyer med*) from the pure state of wisdom.

16. The state of purity (*vaimalyāvasthā*) is the final and most elevated of four states through which the yogin passes in "the subtle yoga."

17. In this stanza, there is a reassertion of the diversity between the yoga of *utpannakrama* and that of *utpattikrama*, that is to say, the yoga of the deity (*devatāyoga*). The various syllables (mantras) such as HŪṂ, PHAṬ, and so forth, from which emanate the different deities, here do not have anymore function. The same concept is elaborated in the LKC V 127. This stanza, provided by Puṇḍarika, begins a long exegesis called the *Paramākṣarajñānasiddhi* ("The demonstration of the knowledge of the supreme immutable") where the principal themes of the Kālacakra are examined.

18. This is the principal explanation of the term "akṣara."

19. Here the Tibetan translation reads differently from the Sanskrit text: (*brten pa yin*, where the Sanskrit reads *nādhāra -brten pa min)*. I have followed the Sanskrit text, according to the general meaning and considering that in the next sentence the Tibetan texts are negative (*rten pa yang ma yin)*.

20. See the *Vimalaprabhā*, I and II: "After my bowing to this Kālacakra, whose body is born from the immutable and who is devoid of the union of ĀLI and KĀLI and of the mantra HŪṂ, PHAṬ, and so forth." In the text of the *Sekoddeśa*, the *na-* before *-iṣyate* also negates ālikālisamāyogaḥ, as indicated in the expression of Nāropa, *nāpi*, which supposes a preceding *na-* is implied.

21. *Vimalaprabhā*, I and II. For the Buddha, the situation is reversed with respect to the ordinary person, in the sense that semen comes to be found at the top of the head and the blood in the vajra, and not the opposite (see the commentary to verse 89 on pp. 129-30).

22. In the commentary to this stanza, Nāropa makes reference to a stanza in the *Nāmasaṃgīti* 122 (IX 4): "He rests on the essence of the earth, occupying the ground with a foot/He stands on the nail of the great toe of the foot, occupying the top of the world of Brahmā." Another stanza in the *Nāmasaṃgīti*, here partially cited, is verse 54 (VI 13): "He has reached the shore that stands beyond transmigration/Resides in the deserted land, where there is not anymore to accomplish." According to the interpretation by Nāropa, the second pāda refers to the gem in the vajra and the first to the uṣṇīṣa.

23. In the first kalā of the bright fortnight, the pratipad (as in Vibhūticandra's *Amṛtakaṇikoddyota*).

24. See *Nāmasaṃgīti* verse 99 (VIII 23): Gone beyond the conditionality of consciousness, he is jñana, bearing the form of nonduality. Devoid of mentation (*nirvikalpa*), spontaneous, he performs the duty of the Buddhas of the three times.

25. Namely, nirvāṇa. See the *Nāmasaṃgīti*, verse 54 (VI 13). Standing at the uttermost limit of saṃsāra, he rests on this terrace, his duty done. Having rejected isolatory knowledge (*kaivalyajñana*), he is the cleaving sword of insight.

26. Ibid.

27. In the fifth chapter of the *Vimalaprabhā*, after stanza 127 of the LKC. In the following lines, Nāropa reproduces, with little variance, the text of Puṇḍarika.

28. Of these two knowledges, both valid (all of the other knowledges are nonknowledge), it is also mentioned in the *Vimalaprabhā* II: "One [of them] is spiritual knowledge, devoid

of differentiated representations, emptiness endowed with all aspects, and the other, the immutable, namely, the knowledge without support, generated from the bliss without stain (*anāśrava*)."

29. In the following lines, Nāropa explains the term "akṣara" on the basis of a famous stanza in the *Nāmasaṃgīti*, 144 (or X 2) cited below, which he interprets following Puṇḍarika, who draws abundantly from it in the commentary to the second stanza of the first chapter of the LKC. According to Puṇḍarika and Nāropa, who follows simplifying it, the five immutables of the great empty are the five aggregates and the five elements, devoid of obstacles. The six immutables of the "empty of bindu" are the six sense organs, devoid of obstacles, namely, the twelve bases *(āyatana)* and so also the six elements (the preceding five plus jñāna) and the six aggregates (the preceding five plus jñāna), devoid, naturally, of obstacles. The "great empty" of the five immutables represents the masculine principle, vajra or kuliśa, the syllable VAṂ, and is essentially of compassion without support (*nirālambakaruṇā*); the "empty of bindu" is the feminine principle, the origin of the elements (*dharmodaya*), the support of the vajra, the syllable E, and is essentially of the emptiness with support (*sālambaśūnyatā*). It is important to rememember that the word *akṣara* in Sanskrit means "immutable" as well as "syllable." In Tibetan it is therefore translated both with *'gyur med* and with *yi ge*, according to its interpretation.

30. This and the following stanza are in reality from the *Nāmasaṃgīti* 28-29 (or V 1-2) inserted into the *Mūlakālacakra*.

31. The dharmodaya, "source of the dharmas"; symbolically the womb is, in Tibetan, chos kun 'byung ba.

32. "Now the Blessed expounds from the point of view of the relative truth, the relation of cause and effect actually of jñāna, nondual and devoid of differentiated representations." (*Tippaṇī*)

33. In other words, the cause, namely, the emptiness, and the result, namely, bliss, are in turn, essentially, one of bliss and the other of the emptiness. It is seen below in stanza 147. The stem *mudr-*, "to seal" or "to characterize," applied to the result and to the cause, also occurs in an analogous sense in the GSU, stanza 78ab: "As they are Impressed/sealed the cause with the result and the result with the cause."

34. If emptiness is not endowed with support, one will fall into nihilism, and if compassion is endowed with support, [one will fall] into materialism.

35. Concerning this image, it is not able to be nonexistent (or cessation), as it is already nonbeing; nor is it able to be existent, positively considered, because the being from which it is born is a simple reflection, of which one is not able to say either that it is or that it is not.

36. *Sekoddeśa*, stanza 158cd (p. 167).

37. *Sekoddeśa*, stanza 152 (p. 164).

38. Noncontrovertible, nondelusive, not subject to contradiction, true, nondeceptive. Also see Nāgārjuna's *Acintyastava* 41 and the *Pramāṇavārttika* of Dharmakīrti.

39. *Caryāmelāpakapradīpa*, II 3-7.

40. On this rite, see Orofino 1994a.

41. "Wisdom is emptiness, endowed with all excellent aspects. The cause is characterized by being, by nonbeing, by both, and by the negation of both. The result is that which exerts itself for the well-being of the world, the state of a Buddha characterized by compassion

without support. Because, as it is said in the *Hevajra in 500,000 Stanzas*: "Emptiness, endowed with all excellent aspects, is the cause from the beginning. Afterwards, one has the result, which consists of compassion without support and exerts itself for the well-being of the world. Therefore, being the cause devoid of actual nature and logically nonexistent, also the result is not born from a cause." (*Tippaṇī*)

42. In this stanza, the expression "prajñāhetor ajātatvāt" is understood by Nāropa as a sort of compound, that is to say, "prajñāya hetor ajātatvāt."

43. The reading of anyonyamudritam in the root text is confirmed either by the comments of Nāropa or from the Tibetan translation. It nevertheless seems that the reading anyonyāmudritam ("is not impressed/sealed either by the one or by the other") would have been more congruous with stanzas 153 and 155. It is nevertheless seen above in stanza 151 (p. 163), anyonyālīgitam or "mutually embraced by both."

44. This citation also appears many times in the Pāli canon: it is seen, for example, in the *Saṃyuttanikāya.*

45. Namely: between one thing that is always extinguished and a thing that always exists, neither is ever able to sustain a relation of cause and effect and so forth.

46. "But if things (*dharma*) are not born nor extinguished, how then is the common experience justified, which is based on knowledge and on the knowable? Therefore here, the Blessed says: [stanza 156]." (*Tippaṇī*)

47. Also see the verse from the *Lankāvatāra Sutra*, verse 489 cited by Kamalaśīla in his *Bhāvanākrama*: "On the outside, material reality does not exist but is one's same mind that appears as external reality."

48. In the moment, namely, of realization.

49. *Hevajratantra*, I 8 53.

50. This is translated expunging *iva* after mahāmudrāsamutpannam. Maintaining *iva,* the translation would be "and is born, so to speak (iva), from the Mahāmudrā."

51. It means "by those who do not know things according to reality."

52. All of the following passage, ending on p. 169 (with "object of personal experience on the part of the yogin") is taken verbatim from the *Vimalaprabhā* V 127.

53. The sense seems to be this: there not being the aggregates and so forth, there is not even able to be the two masculine and feminine sense organs, and from there not being all that, there is not even able to be the out-flowing (*cyuti*) of semen from the uṣṇīṣa as far as to the gem of the vajra. Also see VP V 127.

54. Samantabhadra (Tib. *kun tu bzang po*). This term is also found again in the Tibetan literature of the system of Atiyoga, handed down in the Nyingmapa and Bonpo schools. There it assumes the greatest importance, becoming the symbol of the supreme Buddha, of absolute reality, the immutable, the transcendent of saṃsāra and nirvāṇa.

References

Sanskrit and Tibetan sources

Āryadeva (tantric). *Caryāmelāpakapradīpa* (lost in Sanskrit) in Tibetan: P. vol.61, 2668.

Bu ston. *The Collected Works of Bu-ston*, Part 3 [ga]. Ed. by L. Chandra. New Delhi, 1965.

Guhyasamājatantra. See Y. Matsunaga, 1978.

Kālacakrapāda. *Sekoddeśaṭikā.* Tibetan translation: *dBang mdor bstan pa'i rgya cher 'grel pa* by Somanātha and Shes rab grags in P. vol. 47, 2070.

Kamalaśīla. *Bhāvanākrama.* Ed. by Acarya Gyaltsen Namdol. Bibliotheca Indo-Tibetica 9. Sarnath: Central Institute of Higher Tibetan Studies, 1985.

Mañjuśrīnāmasaṃgīti. See Davidson and Wayman.

Pañjikā, Sekādikoddeśapadaṃ. Ms 363, Mf. A934/8. Kathmandu. Tibetan translation: *dBang mdor bstan pa'i dka' 'grel* by Buston in P. vol. 47, 2071.

Sādhuputra Śrīdharānanda. *Sekoddeśaṭippaṇī.* Ms 10744. Calcutta: Asiatic Society of Bengal. Tibetan translation: *dBang mdor bstan pa'i mdor bshad* by gZhon nu dpal in P. Vol. 47, 2069.

*Vijayāpāda (rNam par rgyal ba brjed byang). *Sekoddeśaṭippaṇī.* English translation. *dBang mdor bstan pa'i brjed byang* by *Dbang blo gros brtan pa* in P. vol. 48, 2104.

Vimalaprabhāṭīkā of Kalkin Śrīpuṇḍarīka on Śrīlaghukālacakratantrarāja. Vol. 1, critically edited and annotated with notes by J. Upadhyaya. Bibliotheca Indo-Tibetica 11. Sarnath: Central Institute of Higher Tibetan Studies, 1986; Vols. 2-3, critically edited and annotated with notes by V. V. Dwivedi and S. S. Bahulkar. Rare Buddhist Text Series 12-13. Sarnath: Central Institute for Higher Tibetan Studies, 1994.

Studies

Carelli, M. 1941. *Sekoddeśaṭīkā of Naḍapāda (Nāropā).* Gaekwad's Oriental Series 90. Baroda.

Conze, E. 1961. *The Large Sutra on Perfected Wisdom*. London: Luzac.

Davidson, R. 1981. "The Litany of Names of Mañjuśrī." In M. Strickmann, ed., *Tantric and Taoist Studies in Honour of R. A. Stein.* Mélanges Chinois et Bouddhiques 20. Bruxelles: Institut Belge des Hautes Études Chinoises, 1-69.

Gnoli, R. and G. Orofino. 1994. *Nāropa, Iniziazione (Kālacakra).* Biblioteca Orientale 1. Milano: Adelphi.

Gokhale, V. V. 1955. "Der Sanscrit Text von Nagarjuna's Pratityasamutpadahrdayakarika." *Studia Indologica, Festschrift für W. Kirfel*. Bonn, pp. 101 ff.

Matsunaga, Y. 1978. *The Guhyasamāja Tantra. A New Critical Edition*. Osaka: Toho Shuppan, inc.

Orofino, G. 1994a. "Mirror Divination. Observations on a Simile Found in the Kālacakra Literature." In *Proceedings of the Sixth Seminar of the International Association for Tibetan Studies, Fagerness 1992.* Oslo: The Institute for Comparative Research in Human Studies, pp. 612-28.

———. 1994b. *Sekoddeśa. A Critical Edition of the Tibetan Translation*. With an appendix by R. Gnoli. Serie Orientale Roma 72. Roma: Istituto Italiano per il Medio ed Estremo Oriente.

Ruegg, D. S. 1971. "Le Dharmadhatustava de Nagarjuna." In *Études Tibetaines dèdièes à la Memoire de Marcelle Lalou.* Paris, pp. 448-71.

Sferra F. and S. Merzagora. 2006. *The Sekoddeśaṭikā by Naropa.* Critical edition of the Sanskrit text by Francesco Sferra and critical edition of the Tibetan translation by Stefania Merzagora. Serie Orientale Roma 99. Roma: L'Istituto Italiano per l'Africa e l'Oriente.

Snellgrove, D. L. 1959. *The Hevajra Tantra, A Critical Study.* Part 1, Introduction and Translation; Part 2, Sanskrit and Tibetan Texts. London Oriental Series 6.

Wayman, A. 1985. *Chanting the Names of Mañjuśrī, The Mañjuśrīnåmasaṃgīti.* Translated, with annotation and introduction. Boston and London: Shambhala.

–3–

The *Sekoddeśaṭippaṇī*
A Brief Commentary on the Summary of the Initiation

Sādhuputraśrīdharānanda

Translated from the Sanskrit into Italian by Raniero Gnoli
Translated from the Italian into English by Phillip Lecso

Editor's Introduction

The translation from the Sanskrit into the Italian of this work is published in *La Rivelazione del Buddha, vol 2, Il Grande Veicolo*, Milan: Arnoldo Mondadori, 2004. The commentary was edited by Gnoli, who has also edited the Sanskrit *Sekoddeśa*, an enormously influential text from which we have quotations of the original Kālacakra text, the *Paramādibuddha.* Only Nāropa's commentary and this commentary survive in their original Sanskrit; a third, anonymous commentary, the *Sekoddeśpañjikā,* is incomplete. Phil Lecso has also translated Nāropa's commentary into English from Giacomella Orofino's Italian translation for the International Kalachakra Network (IKN). It should be noted that Francesco Sferra has recently published a critical edition of the Sanskrit text. The author of this commentary, the *ṭippaṇī*, Sādhuputraśrīdharānanda, was a direct disciple of Anupamarakśita, another important figure in the early Kālacakra transmission and principally known for his work on the six-phased yoga. According to Francesco Sferra in his important recent translation of Anupamarakṣita's treatise on the six-phased yoga, Anupamarakṣita is roughly contemporaneous with, but slightly earlier than, Nāropa. Therefore, the *Sekoddeśaṭippaṇī* is among the earliest treatises in the Kālacakra tradition in India—whether one views the tradition as emerging from the hidden land of Śambhala or as being created in India.[1] Günter Grönbold, in *The Yoga of Six Limbs,* reports that Anupamarakṣita was instructed by Vajrayogini to seek out a teacher and then received instructions on the six-phased yoga (that is, ṣaḍaṅgayoga) directly from Vajradhara, in the form of an ascetic, and that Sādhuputra, who had accompanied his teacher, received instruction in turn.[2] Thus, this brief commentary comes from a valuable source indeed.

Phil Lecso has been an important translator for the IKN, making numerous texts available to the English-speaking practitioners of Kālacakra. As this translation is directed toward practitioners rather than scholars, Phil has not translated many of the technical notes nor those which refer to Nāropa's own commentary; those which are included are important for understanding the material itself. Recently a neuro-muscular disease has caused Phil to discontinue all translation activities, so we are honored to include this, one of his final efforts, here. Phil himself dedicates any merit from this translation effort to his Root Lama, Geshe Wangyal, to his two Root Gurus, His Holiness the Dalai Lama and Jamgon Kongtrul, and to the Kālacakra tradition's growth in the West.

Following the recent trend of allowing access to some otherwise restricted material, we are making this translation available for those who will benefit from it. Please judge yourself and the material wisely, recognizing your own limitations and respecting the text if you find parts of it incomprehensible at this time.

Translation

OṂ Adoration to the Wheel of Time

Praise to that Body (*mūrti*) with which the Omniform Mother, immaculate and empty, and the Lord, full of the sentiment (*rasa*) of peace and devoid of duality, generate the family of the Victorious! Praise to this body, made of peace, purified by union with the innate![3]

Myself bowing to the lotus feet of the master, one writes here, with his favor and by my remembrance, this brief commentary to the *Sekoddeśa*.

While in the great sanctuary of Dhānyakaṭaka, the Blessed, the Lion of the Śākyas, requested by multiple [disciples] who desired to hear the tantras, was teaching the great vehicle of mantras, here King Sucandra, an incarnation of the great bodhisattva Vajrapāṇi, Lord of the Ten Grounds, requested him to teach the great *Paramādibuddhatantra*, composed of twelve thousand stanzas. Such, in fact, is the prophecy of the Blessed:

> The place of awakening is Mahābodhi.[4] The place destined for the teaching of the Vehicle of the Prajñāpāramitā is the great mountain [called] Peak of the Vultures; and the place [destined for the teaching of the] great doctrine of mantras is the sanctuary called Dharmadhātu.[5] According to what was said by the Perfectly Awakened of this world and so forth, such are the places where the Buddhas of the past, present, and future teach.
>
> As to the teaching of the Vaibhāṣika, Sautrāntika, and of the doctrine of the dhāraṇīs, the Victorious have not indicated definite places, but

they [change] according to the inclinations of the beings [taught]. Like that, at the Peak of the Vultures, Maitreya will teach the doctrine of the Prajñāpāramitā and the Buddha, at Dhānyakaṭaka, the pure doctrine of mantras.

On the basis of these words, the teaching of the Mantra Vehicle, on the part of the Blessed, is only able to occur at Dhānyakaṭaka. A great bodhisattva, lord of the ten grounds [as, for example, Vajrapāṇi], or other authors of recited texts are instead able to also extensively teach tantras in other places, according to the propensities of the followers who reside in them.

Sucandra said:

"Sucandra": he is handsome (*su*) and is moon (*candra*), from whence comes the name of Sucandra; the moon of bodhicitta, in fact, attains the state of purity (*vaimalyam*) at the head.

1. The sevenfold initiation, O Instructor, that threefold and so that without superior, explain them to me in short, in order to attain the ordinary accomplishments and that superior [or extraordinary].

"The initiation" and so forth. The initiations of water and so forth are seven, that of the cup and so forth are three [to which it is necessary to add] that "without superior," namely, the great supramundane initiation of the knowledge of wisdom, which is the fourth. These initiations are ordered respectively to the ordinary accomplishments and to that extraordinary. Concerning this, the ordinary accomplishment is determined by the creative meditation on the maṇḍala [which belongs to] discursive [thought] and extends as far as to the lord of the plane/level of the Akaniṣṭha devas.

The higher initiation consists of the attainment of the various grounds, from the first until the twelfth, consisting of the condition of the great Vajradhara, Lord of the Twelve Grounds, and one obtains thanks to the realization of a samādhi that indiscriminately embraces emptiness provided with [all] the excellent aspects and the compassion without support, both in that way [free] of every discursive representation. "In short," namely, in summary.

The Blessed said:

"The Blessed": [the Blessed is called so] because [he is] united to the qualities of sovereignty and so forth and because he defeats (*bhañjanāt*) the four Māras.

2. Listen, O Sucandra, the initiation and its significance, [that] sevenfold, that threefold and that highest, the route of the channels, the control (*āyāma*) [of the vital breath], I will expound them to you in summary.

"The initiation and its significance," namely, the initiation and its purpose. The initiation consists of the action of giving water and so forth and its significance, namely, its end, is that of purifying the body and so forth. "The route of the channels," namely, the route of the two winds of the prāṇa and apāna in the three and three channels, above, in the lalanā, rasanā, and avadhūtī and below in those of excrement, urine, and semen (*śaṇkhinī*). "The route of the channels" is also able to be interpreted optionally as the various arrangement of them in the places [at their destination], because as will be said more later, "such is the route of the channels" and so forth.[6] "The control" consists of the arrest of the flow of the wind in the said channels. The stem *yam-* is used here in the sense of "to cease" (upa + ram) and the term *āyāma* derives from it, with the prefix "ā" and the affix known as "ghañ."[7] "Āyāma" therefore just as well as "āyamana," namely, arrest, which, as it is said in the *Ādibuddha*:[8]

The control of the vital breath is the failing of the two paths and the entry of the prāṇa into the middle channel.

"Listen" and so forth. "But," some will say here, "how does one explain this expression 'I will expound them to you in summary' in a tantra of explanation"? To eliminate this doubt the Blessed, for the purpose of clarifying how each tantra, extensive or concise, is purified by the six points of the summary and so forth, explains one by one the distinctive character of the six parts: the summary and so forth. First of all, the summary and the explanation each have three aspects, so that here it says "the summary" and so forth.

3. The summary, in the tantra, is threefold, and threefold is also the explanation, [in the sense that it has] a thoughtful summary, a great summary, and thoughtful explanation and the other.

4. The summary and the explanation are called by the tantras the recited text; the thoughtful summary and the explanation, the concise commentary (*pañjikā*) that explains the meaning of the words.

5. The great summary and [the great] explanation are the extensive commentary (*ṭīkā*) that indicates all of the import/meaning. These works need to be composed by persons endowed with supernatural powers and not by arid scholars.

With the expression "the other," it alludes to the great explanation. The Blessed now makes a list of the summary and so forth, saying "The summary" and so forth. "The summary and the explanation are called by the tantras the recited (sung) text": the recited text is the correct recitation, on the part of a bodhisattva and so forth, of the [various] Yoga and Yoginī Tantras, purified by the Blessed. Now this recited text is twofold, namely, according to summary or explanation. Concerning this, the recitation on the part of the Blessed of the concise tantra of the Royal Kālacakra in 1,030 stanzas, which is excerpted from the base tantra called the *Paramādibuddha* of twelve thousand stanzas, is the recited text according to summary.

In the same manner, the recitation of the base tantra in twelve thousand stanzas is the recitation according to explanation.

The same thing can be said of the *Samājatantra*, of the *Hevajratantra*, of the *Saṃvaratantra* and so forth, of which one has a recited text according to summary or explanation on the basis of the differentiation of the teaching of concise or extensive tantras.

"The thoughtful summary and the explanation": from the particle "and" one deduces that to the explanation it is necessary to add the specification "thoughtful." "The great summary and the explanation": from the particle "and" one deduces that to the explanation it is necessary to add the specification "great." "By persons endowed with supernatural powers," namely to say, only by great bodhisattvas, lords of the ten grounds. "These works" (*sā*), namely to say, the recited text that is twofold, the concise commentary, and that extensive, which are also themselves twofold. "By [arid] scholars," by those, namely, who have not attained the grounds. Now, the Blessed begins to introduce the tantra with the two stanzas that begin with "thus."

6. Thus, purified by these six points; by the four vajrayogas; by the four awarenesses; by the aggregates, elements, bases, and by the [respective] six families,

7. Purified by the five chapters, dedicated to the structure of the world and so forth, and by the Two Truths, here one has the Primeval Buddha, known with the name of Kālacakra.

"By these six points," namely to say, the summary, the thoughtful summary, the great summary, the explanation, the thoughtful explanation, and the great explanation. "By the four vajrayogas."[9] [It deals here with the] vajrayoga of configuration, of mantras, of dharmas, and of that pure, which destroy the [four states] of wakefulness, dream, deep sleep, and the fourth, and moreover, being essentially of body, speech, mind, and jñāna without obstacles, are materially of the four bodies of creation/formation, enjoyment/use, dharma, and great bliss. "By the four awarenesses," namely, that of a single instant, that of five aspects, that of twenty aspects, and that of the net of māyā. "By the aggregates, elements, bases, and by the [respective] families." The aggregates are six—form, notion, sensation, volition, consciousness, and jñāna—and are respectively purified by Vairocana, Amitābha, Ratnasaṃbhava, Amoghasiddhi, Akṣobhya, and Vajrasattva. The six elements are earth, water, fire, wind, ether, and jñāna and are respectively purified by Locanā, Māmakī, Paṇḍarā, Tārā, Vajradhātvīśvarī, and Prajñāpāramitā.

With the term "bases," it means to include the sense organs, the sense objects, the action senses and their respective actions. Concerning this, the six sense organs are the body, tongue, eyes, nose, ears, and the mind, which are purified by Sarvanivaraṇaviṣkambhin, Lokeśvara, Kṣitigarbha, Khagarbha, Vajrapāṇi, and Samantabhadra. The six sense objects are odors, forms, tastes, tactile sensations, the whole of the dharmas, and sound, which are purified by Gandhavajrā, Rūpavajrā, Rasavajrā, Sparśavajrā, Dharmadhātuvajrā, and Śabdavajrā. The six action senses are the organs of excretion, the feet, hands, speech, the organ of urination, and the divine organ, which are purified by Yamāntaka, Prajñātaka, Padmāntaka, Vighnāntaka, Uṣṇīṣa, and Śumbha. The six actions of the action organs are to speak, to give, to walk, the emission of excrement (stool), that of semen and of urine. They are purified by the wrathful goddesses, called Stambhī, Mānī, Jambhī, Ativīryā, Atinīlā, and Raudrākūṭī.

"By the five chapters," namely to say, of the chapters that deal with the external world, the internal world, initiation, the means of realization, and jñāna.

"Purified," namely, provided (*samanvitam*) with these six points and so forth, here when one has the tantra called the *Ādibuddha*, which, without beginning and without end, devoid of attachment to the two extremes [of eternalism and nihilism], teaches, in their completeness, the two kinds of knowledge, ordinary and extraordinary, purified by the Two Truths, absolute and relative.

Pacified which is the cause (kā), one truly has here the dissolution (la) of the errant mind (ca) from the bonds of transmigration (kra).

It is here "known with the name of Kālacakra."

8. In the beginning, one has the sevenfold initiation that serves to introduce the novice. That threefold is based on the relative truth of the world, and the fourth on the absolute truth.

9. By me, Holder of the Vajra, the teaching of the Dharma is turned depending on two truths, the relative truth of the world and the absolute truth.

With the words "the sevenfold initiation, O King, consists of the water" and so forth, the Blessed now expounds the seven lower initiations.

10. The sevenfold initiation, O King, consists of the water, diadem/crown, ribbon, vajra and adamantine bell, great vow, name, and permission.

11. These initiations purify, two by two, the body, speech, and mind. The permission purifies jñāna. The other [purification comes about] thanks to the purification of the elements.

12. The water purifies the elements, the diadem/crown purifies the aggregates, the ribbon purifies the perfections (*pāramitā*), the vajra and adamantine bell [symbolize] the great motionless.

13. And the uninterrupted speech of the Awakened, and purifies into one the sun and the moon. The vow that does not fail purifies the senses and their objects,

14. The name purifies benevolence and so forth, and the permission purifies the Awakened . . .

Firstly, one has the conferment of the disciplinary rules pertaining to the lay disciples and so forth, and then the giving of the tooth-stick outside of the eastern gateway of the maṇḍala; one then has the casting of the flower onto the vase of victory, characterized by the signs of the five families of the Tathāgatas, and still later, on the basis of the rules set forth in the venerable commentary called the *Vimalaprabhā*, one has "two by two" the initiations of water and so forth, at the eastern, southern, and northern gateways of the maṇḍala, and, at the western gateway, the initiation of permission.

"The other." Thus, one has another purification pertaining to the elements and the aggregates, different from that of the body and so forth. "The vajra and the adamantine bell." Concerning this, the vajra is purified by knowledge of the great motionless and the adamantine bell by the uninterrupted speech of the Buddha. It, in other words, is purified by the inarticulate sound. "Purifies into one the sun and the moon." The gesture of embrace with regard to the vajra and adamantine bell, serves to indicate the indissoluble unity that exists between wisdom and means. "These" and so forth:

> These seven initiations need to be conferred only after having made the maṇḍala.

These seven initiations need to be conferred only in the maṇḍala made of colored particles and not in a maṇḍala made of cloth or another, [as is demonstrated by the fact] that the Blessed does not make mention of this in the tantras.

15. [The three successive initiations are those of the] cup/jar, the initiation of the secret parts, that called by the knowledge through the wisdom [consort] and then again (*punar eva*) that [likewise] called knowledge through the great wisdom.

16. [They are] moved, moved, then vibrating, and the other finally nonvibrating. [Of these], the first three initiations purify respectively body, speech, and mind.

17. The fourth purifies jñāna, [also] purifying body, speech, and mind. The first correspond to a child [who is followed by] the adult and the elder. The fourth is the progenitor/ancestor.

18. Touching the breast of the wisdom [consort], one has a joy [consisting of] a fall of bodhicitta. The one who is consecrated through the breast, [because such joy derives just from the breast] is the child.

19. Sticking [the vajra] into the secret parts [of the wisdom consort for] a long time, one has a joy [consisting of] a fall of bodhicitta. The one who is consecrated through the secret parts, because such a bliss derives just from the secret parts, is the adult.

20. Sticking [the vajra] into the secret parts [of the wisdom consort for] a long time, one has, at the tip of the vajra, a joy made of vibration. The one who is consecrated through knowledge by means of the wisdom [consort], because [he is] just entered [into a state of] vibration [namely, of trembling], is the elder.

21. One then has a joy devoid of vibration that is born from passion towards the Mahāmudrā. The one who is initiated by means of the great wisdom [just] because [he is] immersed into a state devoid of vibration

22. Is called with the name of progenitor/ancestor, parent/genitor of all the Protectors. [As] this [yogin is] without duality, motionless, [he takes] the names of Adamantine Being (*Vajrasattva*), Great Being (*Mahāsattva*), Being of Jñāna (*bodhisattva*),

23. Pledge/Commitment Being (*samayasattva*), the Fourfold Adamantine Yoga and [finally] here of Kālacakra liberator of the yogins.

"Cup/Jar" and so forth. These words of summary are explained more later on, where the Blessed exactly expounds the rite of the bestowal [of the initiation] of the cup/jar with the words "touching the breast of the wisdom" and so forth. "And then again": concerning these words of summary, they are explained more later on where the Blessed, with the words "[from passion towards the] Mahāmudrā" and so forth, explains the initiation of the knowledge of wisdom, which [as is seen] is the fourth and is of an extraordinary nature.

That done, the Blessed, immediately after having hinted at the final result, expounds, with the words "Concerning this reality" and so forth, which is the path that leads to the realization of it.

24. Concerning this [reality, the yogin] will need to put into action the realization with the inconceivable apparitions, namely, the signs of smoke and so forth, images of wisdom, similar to the ether,

25. Transcending being and nonbeing, experiences witnessed by one's own mind, completely devoid of material aggregates [made of] the particles of atoms.

26. [These images are] smoke, mirage, firefly, lamp, blaze/flame, moon, sun, darkness, lightning (*kalā*), the great bindu, the universal image, clear luminosity.

"Concerning this [reality," namely, of the Adamantine Being, who, generated from the great bliss without superior, consists of the intimate fusion of the tetrad body [and so on][10] and transcends every discursive explanation. "Images of wisdom," namely to say, they have the aspect of reflections of wisdom—generated from the wisdom without superior, transcending differentiated thought—namely, indistinct from it, just as the moon and the lunar light. "The signs of smoke" and so forth. In a closed space, the yogin sees there four signs, as far as to the lamp, transcending differentiated thought, thanks to an inconceivable knowledge; the other six signs, from blaze/flame up to the bindu, the yogin sees there in an open space. After that the yogin sees the image that pervades all aspects, transcends discursive thought, like a reflection in a dream. At this point, with the stanza that begins with the words "With the eyes half-closed and half-opened," the Blessed expounds the process of the creative meditation on the universal image.

27. With the eyes half-closed and half-opened, that image which appears in the void, like a dream, nondiscursive, the yogin needs to always meditate upon this image.

28. This meditation on this nonbeing, namely, on this image, is not a meditation for yogins. There is not, of the mind, neither being nor nonbeing, because in the image (*bimbe*), one sees a nondiscursive reality.

"Nondiscursive," namely, nondiscursive at the beginning, in the middle, and at the end. With the stanza that begins with the words "This meditation on this nonbeing," the Blessed demonstrates how this meditation is different from the meditation characterized by a repeated mental application, as the meditation according to true reality is not, by nature, polluted by the impurities of mental constructions and is devoid [as such] of an actual nature. Such is the reason by which it says, "There is not of the mind, neither being nor nonbeing, because in the image, one sees a nondiscursive reality." But, in what manner then does this universal image appear to the yogin? With the words "Like a young maiden," for that reason, the Blessed makes an example:

29. Like a young maiden who sees in a mirror a magical image, not born from a real thing, so also, the true yogin sees in the void a past and future thing.

The magical image (*pratisenā*) one realizes in eight props/supports, namely, in a mirror, sword, [the nail of the] great toe, lamp, moon, sun, water, and in an eye/hole. Here, this refers to a mirror. The magical image [consists of an] imagined [thing] of the operators/agents. The highest meaning is this, that in the same way that a thing appears to a young maiden in a mirror, independent of differentiated representations, as for example a thief, past, present, or future, thus to the yogin there appears in the ether, thanks to the elimination of the dust of every differentiated representation, the universal image, immaculate, devoid of differentiated representations.

This apparition comes to be called elsewhere with the name of the emptiness endowed with all aspects. To this image, it is not necessary to grasp it as a real thing because such [a real thing] it is not, and, to negate this possible attachment, the Blessed produces an example with the words "Concerning it" and so forth.

30. Concerning it (the magical image), being is not a being or a nonbeing, because she has a vision of an empty thing of reality. In spite of the absence of a real thing, something nevertheless appears, like māyā, a dream, or a magical spell.

The being of this magical image is not a being, because what manifests is a thing, by its nature not born, like māyā. But in that manner then, if this jñāna is devoid of every mental construction, how is there able to be a real act of the Buddha [for the benefit of the world]? To dissipate this doubt, the Blessed produces an example with the words "Nevertheless, there is not a real substance" and so forth.

31. Nevertheless, there is not a real substance (*dharmin*), [yet] one sees well that this something (*dharma*) is also born: like the gem of desires, it has the power to fulfill the expectations of infinite beings.

Like the gem of desires, also devoid of mental constructions, performs the benefit of beings, thus no impediment to the Blessed, who is devoid of differentiated representations and possesses infinite qualities, like the ten powers, the [four] faculties and so forth, performs the benefit of all beings. The Blessed with the words "In this magical image" and so forth, now says [that in the same way] this knowing is not deceived and finds correspondence with reality.

32. In this magical image [that appears in the mirror], the young maiden sees [for example] a thief and so forth, [at first] not seen, and the operators going there [after she says] they see him (the thief) **with their ordinary eyes.**

Here, like the young maiden sees in the mirror a thief and so forth, independent from [any] differentiated mental representations, so also ordinary persons, having gone to the place indicated by the young maiden, surprise this thief and so on. The same thing occurs to the true yogin, for whom this vision of the three worlds, independent from [any] differentiated representations, performs the benefit of beings. But is this being that manifests in the form of an object, real or unreal? And it is here that the Blessed, to dissipate this unjustified doubt, says "If" and so forth.

33. If the young maiden sees a real thing, then why does she not see her [own] face [in the mirror]? And if she sees an unreal thing, then why does she not see the horn of a hare?

Now, if what appears is a real thing, then why does not her own face appear to the young maiden, which is exactly present there? Nor is one able to say that what appears is an unreal thing, because what appears to her is not a horn of a hare, which is characterized by an absolute unreality. What it wants to signify is therefore this, that what appears is thus an illusory reality devoid of every relation with mental constructions of being and nonbeing, but that it is, at the same time, endowed with causal efficacy. The Blessed, at this point, to refute the thesis of a vision through the organ of sight and so forth, says, "She does not see" and so forth.

34. She does not see with others' eyes, does not see with her own eyes, but what is seen is a thing not born, just as the son of a virgin.[11]

"With others' eyes," abiding, namely, at the forehead and so forth. She, otherwise, does not see, not even with her own eyes, as they are covered by a blindfold. What it wants to signify is this, that how the dream-like vision, also the vision of things nonconditioned by the error of discursive constructions is not at all unlikely. The Blessed, with the words "but what is seen" and so forth, simply adds an example.

> The yoga is considered [to be] of six limbs, namely retraction, meditation, control of the vital breath, retention, mnemonic application, and concentration.

With the stanza that begins with the words "Concerning this [reality, the yogin]" as far as to the stanza that ends with the words "like the son of a virgin," the Blessed has implicitly expounded the two limbs of the yoga called retraction and meditation, thanks just to the vision of the image which contains all aspects, devoid of differentiated representations.

That done, the Blessed now begins to expound the two limbs called control of the vital breath and retention.

35. Having seen the image, the yogin will then need to perform the control of the vital breath, uninterruptedly, arresting the body, speech, and mind in the three channels, above and below,

36. [in the channels, namely,] that flow by the ways of the moon, sun, and Rāhu above, of excrement, urine, and semen below, [corresponding] to the water, fire, space, earth, wind, and jñāna elements [and] the source [of all the others],

37. In [just] the channels where there is the moon, sun, and the Dark and in those that carry excrement, urine, and semen, pertaining to the two winds of prāṇa and apāna respectively, [they are] channels essentially of body, speech, and mind.

"Having seen the image," namely, the image furnished with all aspects and devoid of differentiated knowing was being seen. "The control of the vital breath," namely, the entry into the channel of Rāhu that abides in the middle, following the cessation of the flow of the vital breath through the two ways of the moon and sun. Retention comes about when one has an arrest of the prāṇa which then flows in the avadhūtī, as it passes through the wheels of the navel and so forth. "In the channels" and so forth, namely, in the channels called lalanā, rasanā, and avadhūtī and in those that conduct excrement, urine, and semen. "Arresting," namely, rendering [them] devoid of obstacles.

With the two stanzas that begin with the words "[in the channels, namely] that flow" and so forth, the Blessed now expounds the nature of the lalanā and so on.

"Source of all the others," as are the place of birth of the elements, notion, and so forth.

"The Darkness," namely, the channel of Rāhu, which abides in the middle.

With the three stanzas that begin with the words "The moon is the body of means," the Blessed now shows how, concerning these [six] channels, there are six families, as wisdom and means they are both divided into three families of body, speech, and mind.

38. The moon is the body of means, the sun is the speech of wisdom, the channel of excrement is the body of wisdom, and the channel of urine is the speech of the omnipervasive (namely of means).

39. Above and below, there are the two channels that respectively carry the darkness and semen, and which pertain to the mind. Regarding means, the mind is the Dark, and regarding wisdom, the mind is the channel that conducts semen.

40. Above and below, these channels, joined with body, speech, and mind, are the six families. They reside in all corporeal beings, as constituent parts of wisdom and of means.

"Of means," that is to say, of the semen element. "Of wisdom," that is to say, of the blood element.

41. The ariṣṭa pertains to the two channels of the body and of speech, because of raging flows above and below. In the two channels "the Dark" and that which carries semen, there are birth, death, and permanence (*sthiti*) [in a state of good health].[12]

42. At the moment of birth, death, and of sexual union, flows the channel that conducts semen. The Dark flows towards the top in the equinox, in the moment of passage of the sun [from one sign to another].

43. In the moments of conjunction with the arising of the ascendant, flows, O King, the wind of the equinox in the middle channel that conducts the "equinoctial" flowing for fifty-six and one-fourth times in inhalation and exhalation.

44-45. In one day and one night, it flows 675 times. The left channel and that of the right thus flow [in one day and one night] for 21,600 times minus the above-mentioned 675. The middle channel flows, in one hundred years, for three years and three fortnights.

46 a. Above, one has the left and right channels, the sun and the moon, corresponding [respectively] to the lalanā, iḍā, to the piṅgalā and to the other.

"Ariṣṭa": it alludes by summary with this word to the ariṣṭa of which it will say more later on. "Of the sun," namely, of the vital breath. "In the moments of conjunction with the arising of the ascendant," namely, at the median point between the lalanā and the rasanā. "The wind of the equinox," namely, the flowing of the prāṇa in the avadhūtī for fifty-six and one-fourth ventilatory actions. These fifty-six and one-fourth ventilatory actions, multiplied by twelve, gives 675 flows in one day and one night. "Minus" minus, that is to say, the above-mentioned 675 flows. "The middle channel flows for three years and three fortnights in one hundred years." The 675 daily ventilatory actions [in the middle channel], multiplied by one hundred years (675 X 36,000), gives the sum of 24,300,000 ventilatory actions pertaining to the middle channel. Subtracting these from the total number of ventilatory actions that flow in one hundred years, which are 777,600,000 (21,600 X 36,000), one obtains 753,300,000 ventilatory actions in one hundred years that belong to the lalanā and rasanā. The 24,300,000 ventilatory actions [of the middle channel] correspond to 1,125 days of breathing (24,300,000 divided by 21,600 = 1,125), that is to say, "Three years (or 1,080 days) and three fortnights (3 X 15 = 45 days)."[13] "Above, one has the left and right channels," namely, above the navel, the left channel is called moon, lalanā, and ióā and the right channel sun, piṅgalā, and "the other," namely, the rasanā.

Now with two and one-half stanzas, the Blessed expounds the purification of these channels of the lalanā and so forth on the part of the families of the Tathāgata, purified by the elements water and so on.

46. b. These two are generated from water and from fire and are considered (mate) **as the Holder of the Lotus and the Holder of the Gem.**

47. Below, one has the two channels that carry excrement and urine, generated from earth and wind. They are respectively the middle channel and that of the left, and are considered as the Holder of the Wheel and the Holder of the Sword.

48. The middle channel above and below that of the right are those of Rāhu and that which conducts semen, generated [respectively] from space and from jñāna, and are considered as the Holder of the Lotus and the Holder of the Vajra.[14]

Concerning this, the Holder of the Lotus and so forth are Amitābha and so on. "The middle channel," namely, downwards, is the channel that carries excrement. "The left channel," downwards, to the base of the vajra, is the channel of urine, which abides just to the left. "The right channel," namely, is the channel, always downwards, which conducts semen. With the second mention of the term "Holder of the Vajra," it means the sixth [Tathāgata], Vajrasattva.

With the following stanza, the Blessed shows how the channels of the moon, sun, and Rāhu, which abide above the navel, carry out as well [below the navel] the functions of conducting excrement and so forth, becoming, as such, the channels of excrement and so forth.

49. In the channel of excrement flows through the way of the moon and that which carries urine through the sun. The channel that carries semen, [active] at birth, death, equinox, and love, flows through Rāhu.

With the stanza that begins with the words "The avadhūtī that abides above the navel" and so forth, the Blessed expounds how the avadhūtī and the channel that conducts semen are also known by other names.

50. The avadhūtī that abides above the navel is also called suṣumnā and "the conductor of darkness" and, below, the channel that conducts semen [also] has another two names: khagamukhā and śaṇkhinī.

With the two stanzas that begin with the words "In the lotus of the navel" and so on, [the Blessed] expounds how the avadhūtī, in exhalation and inhalation, is respectively generated from dissolution and creation/formation and is characterized by the five elements.

51. [Passing] through the lotus of the navel, through the heart, through the throat, through the forehead, and through the lotus at the top of the head, [the avadhūtī] as it makes the earth, water, fire, wind, and space to flow, by way of dissolution,

52. Exiting outside; entering inside, it [then] reenters into earth, by way of creation/formation. From center to center, from the avadhūtī, there is like that coming and going.[15]

With the two stanzas that begin with the words "In the navel" and so on, the Blessed describes the manner in which the śaṇkhinī flows, according to [its three] characters of body, speech, and mind.

53. At the navel, secret parts, and at the lotus of the gem, [the śaṇkhinī] conducts the flowing of body, speech, and mind, exiting outside and entering inside, generated by dissolution and creation.

54. The śaṇkhinī, for all beings, conducts the wind [called] apāna. It, thanks to the bliss of women, conducts semen and, in the menstrual period, blood.

"It," namely, the channel that carries semen. With the stanza that begins with the words "Above, the channels" and so on is expounded how the channels of the lalanā and so forth, which form the six families, [three] parts belong to wisdom and [three] to means, and each embraces a different family.

55. Above, the channels of the right and left and below, that of excrement and that of urine, respectively belong to wisdom and means, and so also [above and below] the currents of blood and semen.

56. [The śaṇkhinī] carrying blood, [takes the name of caṇḍālī] and, carrying semen, [that of] khagamukhā. Above, [the avadhūtī] for women in their period, [is called] ḍombī, and for men, avadhūtī.

"The śaṇkhinī carrying blood" and so on. In women, the śaṇkhinī and the avadhūtī—thanks to the bliss [that comes about] during the flowing of blood—take the name of caṇḍālī and ḍombī. These same names are used metaphorically as well in regard to men, as the birth of the body is not able to come about if [it is] not in close communion with the blood.

With the stanza that begins with the words "The five maṇḍalas [of the aggregates] perception" and so forth is indicated the different flowings of the maṇḍalas of the aggregates, perception and so forth, and of the elements, earth and so forth, in the two nostrils of the left and of the right.

57. The five maṇḍalas [of the aggregates] perception and so forth always flow in the left channel, those [of the elements] earth and so forth in the right channel, and the sixth in the middle.

In other words, the "sixth," or rather, the maṇḍala of jñāna, flows in the middle, in the avadhūtī.

58. In the [twelve] petals of the lotus of the navel, there are therefore sixty maṇḍalas. The ascendants [where they are found are those of] the left and of the right, constituted respectively by Aries and so forth and by Taurus and so forth.

"In the [twelve] petals of the lotus of the navel are sixty maṇḍalas." In one day and one night, [one has the flowing of the wind] through sixty maṇḍalas, constituted by as many grades/degrees; the vital wind transits in each constellation for five maṇḍalas, according to an alternation of odd and even signs, departing respectively from Aries and from Taurus. This signifies that in the navel and in the two nostrils, they succeed as twelve equinoxes and [twelve] constellations.

With the words "At the base" and so forth are expounded the places where the vital wind flows, generated from earth and so forth.

59. The vital wind, as it [flows] at the base, to the left, to the right, above, and in the middle. They thus have for each degree/grade the maṇḍalas of earth and so forth, one-by-one, in the two nostrils.

60. As [in] one nāḍikā,[16] [the vital breath] flows for 360 ventilatory actions and [therefore] in five nāḍikā, [it flows] for 1,800 ventilatory actions.

61. In one day and one night, the ventilatory actions [thus] flow [for] sixty nāḍikā. Such are the maṇḍalas in the body. As the vital breath flows in the center of the petals, then in front [above], to the right, to the left, and elsewhere.

62. The elements, in the left [nostril], begin as a rule from ether and, in the right [nostril] from earth, from the other. In the left [nostril] one has perception (*vijñāna*) and so forth, namely, creation/formation, and in the right, one has earth and so forth, namely, dissolution.

"At the base," namely, at the lower part of the two nostrils. "To the left": namely, at the median region of the channel of the two nostrils. The right and so forth are respectively able to be identified to the outside (lateral), upper, and middle parts [of the two nostrils]. "In the body," departing, namely, from the navel. With the words "In the center of the petals," it shows how the vital breath begins to rise in the left nostril, generated [from the aggregates] perception and so forth. "In front," namely, above. "Elsewhere," namely, at the lower part.[17] With the words "the elements . . . from ether," it states how the elements and the aggregates are dealt with here metaphorically as a single thing, as the aggregates, perception and so forth, are born from the elements, ether and so on. Such is the reason by which it was previously said, "They thus have the maṇḍalas of earth and so forth, in the two nostrils, for each degree/grade." "In the right, from earth, from the other," namely, from the lower part of the right nostril. Here the vital breath begins to rise in the form of the elements, beginning from earth and so forth, and this then is only the initial moment, because, as it is said [in the *Laghukālacakratantra* I 61b.]:

> The region where first arises the sun is the east and the path of the sun is regulated by Mount [Meru].

"But" here some will say, "seeing that in the left nostril the rising vital wind persists at first in the ether (*ākāśe*) how is it never considered as the initial moment?" [To this question, we respond] does not [have a reason for existing], as, it was called the first of the four, indeed [the Blessed, referring to the ether (*tatra*),] has indicated it to be known as front (*pūrve*), the upper part of the nostril. "Phenomenal existence" is namely creation.

At this point with the four stanzas that begin with the words "To the west and to the east," the Blessed shows how earth and wind, fire and water, ether and the jñāna element are mutually constituted by wisdom and means, serving to this end, as a revealing analogy, of the mudrās of propitiation and so forth, which one performs with the thumb, ring finger, and so on.

63. To the west and to the east, one has earth and wind, which are respectively wisdom and means. In fact, through the thumb and the ring finger, in the mouth, one has initiation.

64. To the right and to the left, one has fire and water, mutually wisdom and means. In fact, through the middle and index fingers is born the [mudrā of the] sword.

65. The mudrā from the form of a half-moon is that of the fang/tusk, of the [hooked] knife, of the little finger. The void and the motionless are thus reciprocally wisdom and means, above and below.

66. The union of the [ten] fingers, one with the other, when placed conjoined with the palms of the hand on the head, [symbolizes] the union of the ten maṇḍalas and is [represented] by the mudrā of the vajra with a single point together with the [hooked] knife.

67. The equinox in the middle channel is the cause of creation and dissolution. It is the unity of the aggregates, elements, and of the three vajras [that come about exactly when the vital breath] flows in the middle channel.

Concerning this, the thumb, index, middle, ring, and little fingers are respectively purified by earth, water, fire, wind, and ether and therefore, by means of formation of the [various] mudrās, one has a purification of wisdom and of means. "The motionless" is the jñāna element. "The union of the ten fingers" and so forth symbolizes the unity of the five elements and of the five aggregates. "By a single point," namely, the vajra with a single point.

The expression "Together with the [hooked] knife" serves to make understood [that what one comes to determine is] a reality [that represents the perfect] fusion of the aggregates, elements,[18] and of the three vajras,[19] penetrated/sealed by Vajrasattva together with his wisdom [consort].

Now, by way of a conclusion, the Blessed expounds the characteristics of the control of the vital breath and retention; and exactly with the half-stanza that begins with the words "Thanks to the blockade of the channels of the sun and moon" explains the control of the vital breath and with the half-stanza that begins with the words "Thanks to the blockade of the channel of Rāhu" speaks of retention. With the half-stanza that begins with the words "[Analogously] if there is a release" and so forth, expounds the difficulties which follow in the opposite case.

68. Thanks to the blockade of the channels of the sun and moon, one has the blockade of the channels of excrement and urine. Thanks to the blockade of the channel of Rāhu, below, one blocks the conductor of semen.

69. [Analogously] if there is a release, these three channels, the cause of creation and dissolution, they release. Such is the route of the channels through the three [and three] ways of prāṇa and of apāna.

At this point the Blessed, with the stanza that begins with the words "If in the left channel" and so forth, explains the two ariṣṭa [of sun and moon] mentioned before.

70. If in the left channel or the right, the vital wind flows in an excessive manner for one night or for five, then in three years one has death.

With the two stanzas that begin with the words "In the right channel . . . five" and so forth, the Blessed expounds the characteristics of the ariṣṭa of sun.

71. In the ariṣṭa of sun, to the right, [the vital breath flows] five, ten, fifteen, twenty, twenty-five [days; then] with the increase of one into one, [up to] thirty-three days.

72. Three years, two years, one year, six months, three months, two months, one month, fifteen days, ten days, five days, three days, two days, one day, and the life of corporeal beings if some go.

The sense is the following: When in beings, by an imbalance of the elements, the vital breath flows uninterruptedly for five days and five nights in the right nostril, which persists in the even constellations, then the ariṣṭa of sun that comes about indicates that the years of life remaining are three. Therefore—considering that the ten maṇḍalas flow through the twelve petals of the twelve constellations which abide at the navel—here that [in the first petal, as well as the five days of ariṣṭa] is subtracted from the three years three hundred and thirty days, in which the vital breath has flowed regularly. After that, it passes into the second petal, carrying with itself two years and twenty-five days (or 745 days). In this same petal, in the right nostril, [the ariṣṭa] then flows uninterruptedly for ten days and nights. Then subtracting the three hundred and thirty-five days in which the vital wind has flowed regularly, it passes into the third petal carrying with itself one year, one month, and ten days (or 400 days). In this same petal, the ariṣṭa flows for fifteen days and nights. Then subtracting the one hundred and fifty-five days during which the vital breath has flowed regularly, it passes into the fourth petal, carrying with itself seven months and twenty days (or 230 days). The ariṣṭa flows for twenty days. Then subtracting the two months and two days (or 62 days) during which the vital breath has flowed regularly, it passes into the fifth petal, carrying with itself four months and twenty-eight days (or 148 days). Here, it flows for twenty-five days. Then subtracting one month and two days (or 32 days) during which the vital breath has flowed regularly, it passes into the sixth petal, carrying with itself three months and one day (or 91 days). [In the sixth petal] the ariṣṭa flows for twenty-six days. After again subtracting the two days during which the vital breath has flowed regularly, it passes into the seventh petal, carrying with itself two months and three days (or 63 days). Here the ariṣṭa flows [uninterruptedly] for twenty-seven days. Then in the eighth, ninth, tenth, and eleventh petals, the ariṣṭa flows uninterruptedly for fifteen, ten, five, and three days. In the five petals following from the seventh, the vital wind does not flow anymore in a regular manner. Finally, in the twelfth petal, it flows for two days in the left nostril and for one day in the corolla. [Summarizing,] from the total number of 1,080 days, equal to three years, characterized by the presence of the] ariṣṭa, as they come to be subtracted from the three hundred and thirty-five days and so on, so that in the first of the six petals, as they are abandoned, there are in the beginning five days of ariṣṭa, [in the second, where the vital breath flows for three hundred and forty-five days, {there are} ten days of ariṣṭa and so on]. Except for when, in these five days and so on, the vital breath flows regularly in the other three hundred and thirty days and so on. In the venerable *Ādibuddha*, in conformity with what was said, one has the following stanza of explanation concerning the failing of the days of life by each petal, together with the days of ariṣṭa:

> With reference to the three years of the sun, in the first [petal the wind] abandons three hundred and thirty-five days; then, comprising the ascent [of the ariṣṭa], three hundred forty-five days [in the second petal], one hundred and seventy in the third, then still eighty-two, fifty-seven, twenty-eight, and in the seventh another ascent [of only ariṣṭa]; finally as well all the other days, fifteen and so on, until at the corolla.

[In the *Sekoddeśa*], with the words "[In the period of] three years, two years, one year" and so on, the calculation in months, years of life, and so on is approximate. The precise calculation is, instead, able to be learned from the preceding explanation.

Now, with the stanza and one-half "As with the addition of a single unity" and so on, the Blessed expounds the ariṣṭa of moon.

73. As with the addition of a single unity, the moon, beginning from the root, as it ascends in the left channel for days and months, in the proportion of three days and three months,

74a. By reason of an increase in the days of ariṣṭa and by a diminution of the months . . .

Concerning this, when the vital breath flows uninterruptedly for one day and one night in the left nostril, which persists on the odd constellations, then the ariṣṭa of moon that comes to be determined indicates that the years of life remaining are three. The vital breath then flows regularly, circulating for ten maṇḍalas, for all the first and second months, minus the said days of ariṣṭa. At the entry into the third month, the ariṣṭa flows for two days, after which, the vital breath flows regularly in the third and fourth months, minus the said two days. At the entry into the fifth month, the ariṣṭa then flows for three days, after which, the vital breath flows regularly in the fifth and sixth months, minus the said three days. At this point, of the twelve petals present at the navel, formed by the twelve constellations, the vital breath abandons the first petal. The vital breath then, having abandoned six months of the three years, takes with itself the remaining thirty months and passes into the second petal. At the initial moment of the entry into the seventh, eighth, and ninth months [included in such petal], the ariṣṭa flows as for four, five, and six days. Then subtracting three months minus, of course, the said days of ariṣṭa of each month during which the vital breath has flowed regularly, it passes into the third petal, carrying with itself twenty-seven months. For every three days of ariṣṭa in addition, there are three months fewer, so on the basis of this process, the vital breath, to the end of the seventh petal, abandons it with twenty-one days of ariṣṭa. Concerning this, the vital breath, flowing regularly [in the successive] three months [minus, of course, the twenty-four, twenty-seven, thirty, and thirty-three days of ariṣṭa at the beginning of the entry into the said three months of abandoning] abandons the eighth, ninth, tenth, and eleventh petals.[20]

Of the three days connected with the six months of the first petal and where it does not have flowing of ariṣṭa, the ariṣṭa now flows for two of them in the twelfth petal, in the right nostril, and, for one day, in the corolla. One has, at this point, an interruption of all the winds and the consciousness (*vijñāna*) goes into other forms of existence.

[Such is] the explication of the ariṣṭa of moon.

With the two and one-half stanzas that begin with " . . . At the completion of one hundred years" and so on, he expounds the moment correlated with death in the middle channel.

74b. At the completion of one hundred years, in the middle channel, one has the ascent of death.

75. This ascent of it (death) **to the right and to the left occurs in relation to the even and odd days; [and so also] in relation to the maṇḍalas [which vary according to] the moment of birth [and moreover] after the dissolution** (*vināśanāt*) **of the two parts of right and left.**

76. Or else there will not be death, continuing to subsist the two fortnights, continuing the two channels of the right and left to flow and so also the five maṇḍalas.

After ninety-six years and ten and one-half months connected with the sun and with the moon, the vital breath flows in the left nostril for one day, uninterruptedly pervaded by the time [of death]; after that it flows for one [other] day regularly, circulating for the ten maṇḍalas. Still after, it flows uninterruptedly through the right nostril for two days and still then regularly for two days. In an analogous manner, it flows in the left nostril and in the right—according to the division into odd and even days—for three, four, five, and six days, by which, to the left and to the right, it abandons/vacates the maṇḍalas of ether and of earth.

On the basis of the same process, it then flows for seven, eight, nine, ten, eleven, and twelve days, finally abandoning/vacating the maṇḍalas of wind and water. In the same manner, it flows for thirteen, fourteen, fifteen, sixteen, seventeen, and eighteen days, finally abandoning the maṇḍalas of fire and fire. Then still, it flows for nineteen, twenty, twenty-one, twenty-two, twenty-three, and twenty-four days, finally abandoning the maṇḍalas of water and wind. It then flows for twenty-five, twenty-six, twenty-seven, twenty-eight, twenty-nine, and thirty days, abandoning the maṇḍalas of earth and ether.

After that, it flows for thirty-one, thirty-two, and thirty-three days, finally abandoning the maṇḍala of jñāna. Still after, it flows uninterruptedly for thirty-three days in the right nostril and for one day in the corolla, after which one has the interruption of all the elements. On the basis of the sum of the good and bad days, which amounts to the number of thirty-three, one therefore has 1,122 days. The days, together with the thirty-three, where the vital breath flows uninterruptedly through the right nostril, and by that in the corolla, are therefore in total 1,156.

[This was] the explanation of the moment correlated with death in the middle channel.

With the three stanzas that begin with the words "Knowing the characteristics of the ariṣṭa," the Blessed teaches the manner of cheating/deceiving the ariṣṭa.

Such a teaching needs to be learned from the mouth of the master, and therefore I have not developed it here in detail.

77. Knowing the characteristics of the ariṣṭa, [the yogin] will need to apply the vital breath to the bindu, and having taken as the basis the level of the avadhūtī, will need to realize it meditating upon the supreme motionless.

78. Continuously, [the yogin] will need to maintain the vajra erect, as he [thus] has an interruption of the ways of the sun and moon, because otherwise there is no entry of the prāṇa into the body of the avadhūtī,

79. Nor below the apāna into the śaṇkhinī, by which one has, by its not entering, death. This method of cheating/deceiving the ariṣṭa is accompanied with [various kinds of] joys for the yogins.

Reading the phrase "Is accompanied with [various kinds of] joys" makes one wonder which are these joys, so that the Blessed, responding, explains here in detail.

80. The descent of semen in the lotus of the forehead down from the top of the head is [the first] joy; in the throat and in the heart, one has the highest joy and, still after, the multiform joy.

81. In the navel and in the lotus of the secret parts, one has, in truth, a multiform pleasure. In the adamantine jewel innate in the secret parts, one has the innate joy, not effused.

With the two stanzas that begin with the words "The descent of semen" is indicated, by means of the exposition exactly on the characters of these joys, the limb [of the yoga] called mnemonic application; and, in the middle stanza "[Such is the] nirvana without basis," the limb called concentration.

82. [Such is the] nirvana without basis, the greatly passionate, the motionless, the Lord. The effused bliss, because of the lack of passion, is instead the nirvana endowed with a basis.

"The nirvana without basis," namely, the great bliss of the innate joy, intimately fused with the three vajras, not confined to the forehead and not discharged from the vajra. Immediately after, the Blessed shows, with various stanzas, the particular characters of mnemonic application and concentration.

83. The rising of the moon of semen comes about at the top of the head and the full phase in the lotus of the secret parts. The sixteenth kalā has an abode in the lotus of the jewel, on the point of the vajra.

84. After that, at the arrival of the dark fortnight, one has the period of emission. The sun, [always] by the lack of passion, then arrives at the place of the tuft (*ūrṇa*), where one has the new-moon.

85. The sixteenth kalā of it (the sun) comes about in the lotus at the top of the head and is called with the name of "absence of moon." [It represents], in fact, the extreme disgust for the bliss of passion.

"The rising of the moon of semen" and so on. The meaning is this: here in the external world, the rising moon goes towards three phases of fullness, in the fifth, tenth, and fifteenth [lunar days], on the basis of a gradual increase of the kalā of the lunar days starting from pratipad because, as it was said, "the sixteenth kalā that abides between the end of the bright fortnight and the beginning of the dark, is not a [true and actual] kalā."[21] In an analogous manner, in the inner world, there are three moments of fullness of the moon of bodhicitta, which is born in the head, namely, the fifth, tenth, and fifteenth, which come about in the forehead, heart, and lotus of the secret parts and are in relation with the three joys, initial and so forth. The sixteenth kalā, which abides between the end of passion and the beginning of dispassion, and "has room . . . at the tip of the vajra," is characterized by the nirvāṇa without basis and is called with the name of innate joy.

Because as it is also said in the *Hevajratantra* (II 4, 23):

The moon, constituted by fifteen kalā, is the bodhicitta. It is the great bliss essentially of the fifteen vowels and the yoginis are her parts.

"The sun" is namely, the blood element. "The place of the tuft (*ūrṇa*)" is namely, the lotus of the forehead. "Of it," namely, of the solar blood.

With the stanza that begins "The ambrosia of the moon" and so on, the Blessed shows that, during sexual union, beings meet in an unmistakable situation, as also occurs at the moment of death.

86. The ambrosia of the moon, for all corporeal beings, at the moment of death, goes below, the blood of the sun [goes] above and the consciousness (*vijñāna*) [pertaining to] Rāhu [goes into transmigration] characterized by birth.

"Characterized by birth," because of the karmic impressions. With the two stanzas that begin with the words "For this reason," the Blessed shows [how for Buddhas] exactly the reverse [occurs].

87. For this reason, O King, it is necessary that the lunar ambrosia is made to go towards the top, the blood of the sun towards the bottom, and the consciousness [pertaining to] Rāhu towards the motionless bliss.

88. For all the Buddhas, the phase of greater fullness of the lunar ambrosia comes about in the chignon, and the new-moon of the solar blood in the secret parts. [By their sixteenth] kalā of these two like that in truth at the top of the head and in the jewel.

"Of these two," namely, of the moon of bodhicitta and of the solar blood. This same concept was stated expressly by the Venerable Lokeśvara (Puṇḍarīka), through a stanza of praise:

> Of the Ruler, one foot is supported on the red sun [that abides] in the gem of the vajra,
> the second [foot] on the moon, in the semen [that abides] on the top of the head;
> to Him, always unbreakable, impenetrable, revered, devoid of the three worlds, I bow.[22]

89. This level of the vajra [thus expounded] acts, for the instructor, in an opposite manner [to that] of all corporeal beings. The elements [coming] from this nirvāṇa without basis, they also act in an opposite manner.

"From this nirvāṇa without support," namely, from this immaculate, great bliss, devoid of differentiated representations. "In an opposite manner"—the meaning is that the aggregates, elements, and the bases assume an omniform nature, devoid of obstacles and transcending differentiated thought, on the basis of what was said, when namely "the form and so forth, are different from before."

At this point, with the stanza and one-half that begins "From great bliss [proceed] the mind in the jewel" and so forth, the Blessed expounds how from the Body of Great Bliss, purified by the vajra of jñāna, will manifest, below the navel, the Bodies of the Elements, of Enjoyment/Use and of Creation, purified by mind, speech, and body and joined with means.

90. From great bliss [proceed], the mind in the jewel, speech in the secret parts, and the body in the navel. These three Bodies of the Elements, of Enjoyment/Use, and of Creation radiate [out] from the pure [body].

91. Through means, O King, this radiation [departs] from below and through wisdom, from above. As to her, in the forehead she has the vajra of the body and in the lotuses of the throat, heart, and of the navel,

92. the vajras of speech, mind, and of jñāna, which radiate from the Body of Creation and so forth. The radiation of the elements and of the aggregates, originate [analogously] from the bliss without obstacles.

Concerning this, the expression "Through means," signifies through the bodhicitta, connected with the father. In an analogous manner, with the words "Through wisdom" and so forth, the Blessed expounds how from the Body of Creation, purified by the vajra of body, the Bodies of Enjoyment/Use and so forth will manifest, above the navel, purified by the vajra of speech and so on. "Through wisdom," namely, through the blood element, connected with the mother. This differentiated manifestation [of the Bodies], first from the Innate Body and so on, and here from the Body of Creation and so on, was said in reference respectively to the predominance of the knowledge of the great bliss, constituted by means, namely, from the compassion without support and by that of the knowledge of wisdom, constituted by the emptiness provided with all excellent aspects. Nevertheless, from the point of view of true reality, there is not, as for the bodies and so on, any special differentiation.

93. Thanks to union with the action mudrā, taking as support the jñāna mudrā and by exclusive dedication to the Mahāmudrā, this motionless increases.

With the stanza that begins with the words "Thanks to union with the action mudrā" and so on, the Blessed expounds what is the means for increasing the knowledge of great bliss, devoid of differentiated representations, born from the creative meditation upon the Mahāmudrā. So wishing, one is also to be able to think that this stanza deals with the explanation of the three mudrās and the three respective results. Because as it is said in the *Vimalaprabhā*:[23]

> The result caused by the action mudrā consists of the accomplishments of the World of Desire.
> The result caused by the jñāna mudrā consists of the accomplishments of the World of Form.
> The result caused by the mahāmudrā, [who is identified with the] emptiness devoid of differentiated representations and provided with all excellent aspects, consists of the accomplishment of omniscience, devoid of differentiated representations.
> Such is the reason by which the knowledge of great bliss, devoid of differentiated representations, is not able to be caused by any kind of differentiated representations.

It is thus shown how the two mudrās of action and of jñāna which are not based on great passion, are actually, by exactly this, only a pragmatic and provisional existence but not the ability to generate that knowledge devoid of differentiated representations.

"This motionless," namely, is the knowledge of the great bliss devoid of differentiated representations [characterized by] an intimate fusion of the four Bodies.

"But," some will say here, "what thing is it that ever increases? A thing already increased or a thing not increased? In both cases, one encounters a logical impossibility. In fact, for a thing already increased, the increasing is of no use and for a thing that by nature does not increase [namely, not susceptible to increasing], there is no possibility of becoming such."

With the three and one-half stanzas that begin with the words "Of that which is already grown" and so forth, the Blessed shows how this objection, from the point of view of relative truth, is not valid.

94. Of that which is already grown, there is no growth; of that which is exhausted, there is no exhaustion; of that which has set, there is no setting; of that which has risen, there is no rising,

95. Of that which has ignited, there is no ignition; of that which is covered, there is no covering; of that which is born, there is no being born; of that which is dead, there is no dying,

96. Of that which is liberated, there is no liberation; of that which is not still, there is no mobility; of that which does not exist, there is no nonexistence; of that which exists, there is no existence,

97a. Of that which has moved, there is no movement; of that which is motionless, there is no immobility . . .

But if things abide so, how could birth or extinction be valid? And here the Blessed, responding to this question, says: "Of all dharmas, which are devoid of an actual/own nature . . ."

97b. Of all dharmas, which are devoid of an actual/own nature, birth and thus the end are [simply] a magical spell.

With regard to dharmas, which are devoid of an actual/own nature, birth and extinction are considered as the same, equal to a magical spell (māyā). Thus, thanks to this example of māyā, from the point of view of relative reality, there is not any contradiction. With the words "The beings are not extinguished" and so forth, the Blessed criticizes obstinate adherence to the two theories that support an exclusive being or nonbeing, while [as we know well] all things are not born and not halted.

98. The beings are not extinguished and not born by their own nature. All this universe is devoid of own nature and has as its unique characteristic being and nonbeing.

"And has as its unique characteristic, being and nonbeing." Here, being is any form, and here, nonbeing is the light of emptiness. The whole is united by these two, in the sense that its character, its own/actual nature is unique, that is to say, indistinct from these two. Because as it was said by the Venerable Nāgārjuna:[24]

> Emptiness is not different from being nor without it is there nonbeing,
> so that things, which are born from conditions, were declared by You as empty.

99. Embraced with one's own wisdom [consort], when the bodhicitta comes to find itself in the lotus of the adamantine jewel, the lunar vibration [which then comes about] becomes a meditation devoid of vibration, motionless.

100. In the channels of the body, speech, and mind, one has the meditation of body, speech, and mind. The fusion of the three vajras in the śaṇkhinī is the meditation of jñāna.

101. Concerning the bindu, which, dissolved from the passion for the wisdom [consort], as it descends down from the head, one has the fixation according to reality when it enters into the level/plane of the full [moon].

102. In that manner when the moon, which has risen, as it becomes full by virtue of the kalā and this, its fullness, is [simply] the elimination of the traces [of darkness], because for the moon there is neither damage nor filling,

103. Just like that jñāna, which has risen, as it becomes full by working on the grounds, and this, its fullness, is only the elimination of the traces of the afflictions and so forth, because for jñāna there is neither damage nor filling.

104. By this manner, when the moon, because of the sign of the hare that it bears in the middle, does not remain arrested in the phase of the full moon, so the mind [does not remain arrested] in motionless bliss, because of the character of the latent impressions of ordinary life.

105. The two fortnights, bright and dark, [characterized] by increase and decrease, are well affirmed. [The] full [kalā], instead, which abides in the middle of these, is not stable.

106. When [instead,] the mind attains the awareness in a single instant, it remains immobile in the full phase, namely, in the adamantine jewel, then fills itself of all instants.

107. [The adamantine mind] does not linger in the bright fortnight, does not lead towards that dark. It abides in the middle of the two fortnights, in the full moon, that way [from every] duality.

108. It rises from the top of the head and [the] full [kalā] is in the adamantine jewel. Because of the lack of passion, one has [to the contrary] a decrease of the kalā beginning from the vajra, and by this the fullness [at the top of the head] decreases.

109. For corporeal beings, once more, one has later a rising at the top of the head, once more fullness in the adamantine jewel, [once more] a failing of the kalā because of the lack of passion; one never has however a failing of jñāna.

110. The own/actual nature of it is the highest bliss, and just this is that which comes to be called with the name of full [phase]. All other things, without exception, are caused by creation and dissolution.

111. Just as does the moon with its fortnights and the sun with its two routes, from phenomenal existence proceeds nirvāṇa and from this once more, phenomenal existence.

112. [Instead], when the highest bliss remains immobile in the full phase, it is then made full by all grounds, thanks to the 21,600 ventilatory actions, devoured by the instants of motionless bliss.

113. Devoid of the two fortnights, [this reality] made perfectly full by the grounds, generated from the truth in twelve aspects, endowed with sixteen aspects, motionless.

114. It, full of the grounds, is furnished with twelve aspects, supreme, devoid of duality. This [same] mind then, full of kalā, is endowed with sixteen aspects, motionless,

115. Unique, devoid of duality, supreme truth, unfailing is the mind immersed into the condition of fullness, perfectly full on every side.

116. [This reality] is the great passion that is the beginning of dispassion, the Adamantine Body, the great motionless, perfectly full, not polluted by [impure] traces of the two extremes.

The expression "With one's own wisdom [consort]" refers to the three mudrās of action, jñāna, and Mahāmudrā. Concerning this, the pure substance of the bindu of bodhicitta that is born from discursive meditation with an action mudrā and that of jñāna, and when, residing at the tip of the vajra, is known with the name of vibration (*spanda*), becomes, thanks to a meditation according to reality, devoid of vibration. With the words "In the channels of the body" and so forth, it has shown how the body, speech, and mind will be purified thanks to the respective meditations according to body and so on, in the channels that are the basis of them. Instead, when one has, in the śaṇkhinī, a meditation according to innate jñāna, then comes about here exactly a condition of intimate fusion of the three vajras of body and so on with the innate. "From the head," namely, from the forehead. "In the level/plane of the full moon," namely, in the lotus of the secret parts. "Fixation," namely, consolidation. "According to reality," thanks to a meditation according to true reality, of the Mahāmudrā. "The full [kalā]," namely, the sixteenth kalā, characterized by innate joy. "Filling itself of all the instants," because the successive instants also assume the same nature of the first innate instant, devoid of differentiated knowing, because, as it has been said:

> The one who has seen one thing according to reality, that one has seen according to reality, all things.

"The instant" is characterized here by inhalation and exhalation. Then, when it has arrived at the number of 21,600, it is called with the name of "all the instants." Concerning this, the achievement of every single ground is determined by the arrest of 1,800 instants, which merge intimately with the innate jñāna without signs (*animitta*). The perfect fullness of all instants is determined by the gradual achievement of the twelve grounds. "It," namely to say, this innate knowing, which has, as its own/actual nature, the sixteenth kalā. "A decrease of kalā," namely to say, one has an abandonment of the fifteenth kalā but not of the sixteenth kalā, which only fails at the moment of death. "By this decrease," namely of the blood element.[25] "A failing of jñāna," namely, a failing of the sixteenth kala. "Of it," namely, of the jñāna essentially of innate joy. "All other things," characterized by being and nonbeing, the bright fortnight and the dark fortnight, passion and dispassion. "Devoid of the two fortnights," namely, of passion and dispassion and so forth.

Now the Blessed, with the example that begins with the words "In that manner, when the waters of the rivers," shows how, once entered into the jñāna of the great bliss, all things merge into union with the innate.

117. In that manner, when the waters of the rivers enter into the sea, [they] become equal [with it], so this whole of the forms of existence, enters into the motionless and becomes equal/identical to the same motionless.

118. In that manner, when the whole of the various metals transforms, devoured [by the mercurial elixir], into the elixir and, thanks to the seeds, takes the nature of the same seeds, devoid, at the moment of the result, [of number and] measure;

119. Like that the whole [of the various] forms of existence, devoured by the supreme motionless, becomes the same supreme motionless, which supports/sustains all forms and all aspects.

The novice yogin, having come out from the meditation devoid of differentiated representations, personally experienced by him, says: "I experienced this bliss." Such does not occur for the yogin who has attained the condition of perfect fullness, as he is essentially of a bliss inclusive of all aspects. For the exact purpose of making this understood, the Blessed with the words "Who was bitten" and so on, makes an example with the relative term of comparison.

120. Whoever has been bitten, when the venom reaches a condition of fullness, does not notice the pain in the wound nor elsewhere, nor notices the objects sensible by means of the doorways of the senses;

121. In an analogous manner, when the full kalā has been reached in the mind, [the yogin] does not notice the most real bliss in the adamantine jewel, nor elsewhere, nor notice the objects sensible by means of the doorways of the senses.

Concerning this, the "condition of fullness" is the place at the top of the head.

"The mind" is, namely, the bodhicitta devoid of differentiated representations. "In the full kalā," when, namely, [the yogin] has finally attained a state of perfect fullness of all sixteen kalā through the states of similar derivation and so on.

With the two stanzas that begin with the words "In that manner," the Blessed, making use of the example of an elixir, wants to make understood here how the knowledge born from the Mahāmudrā, devoid of differentiated representations, surpasses in excellence all things, while the meditation with the action mudrā is only a provisional means.

122. In that manner, when the great elixir, although present in only one part of the iron, penetrates to every part all the iron, red-hot from the violent fire,

123. Exactly so the motionless bliss, although present in only one part, penetrates to every part all the mind, red-hot from the fire of desire.

124. In that manner when penetrated of the metals there is not any stain anywhere, like that, of the penetrated mind, there no trace anywhere [of] any [impurity].

125. In that manner when iron transformed into gold becomes without stain thanks to fire, thus the mind repeatedly [red-hot] from the fire of passion becomes without stain.

126. In that manner when, through contact with the great gem, a [simple] stone becomes resplendent, thus through contact with motionless bliss, the mind immerses in fact into bliss.

Having seen that one is not even able to comprehend how the elixir, which is also of a relative nature, is able to penetrate metals and so forth, how will one ever be able to comprehend the power of jñāna, which possesses infinite qualities and is of an absolute nature? The Blessed therefore says: "But why so many words here?"

127. But why so many words here? From the point of view of the relative truth of the world, the power of the elixir is indisputable in regard to the penetration of iron.

128. All the more so, from the point of view of the absolute truth, perhaps the power of jñāna will be disputable in regard to the penetration of the mind [as only] polluted by adventitious stains?

Making understood how the impurities due to the stained condition do not exist by own/actual nature, the Blessed, with the stanza that begins with the words "The stained condition is not in the mind, adventitious," expounds four possible theories, of which, in the two following stanzas that begin with "If" and so forth, show their impossibility. "But" some would be able to object here, "if jñāna unites with emptiness, the possibilities are two, namely, it extinguishes or its nature remains unchanged."[26] In order to remove this doubt, with the two stanzas that begin with the words "In that manner when in the copper," the Blessed, making use of an example and of the term of comparison, underlines the extraordinary nature [of jñāna].

129. The stained condition is not in the mind, [is not] adventitious, does not exist from a time immemorial, [does not exist] before the mind, is not born without the mind, nor resides indestructibly in the mind.

130. If the stained condition is adventitious, then why does the mind first appear without the stained condition? And if, on the other hand, it had existed from time immemorial before the mind, from wherever would it originate?

131. If on the other hand, it had come into existence without the mind, then it would be like a flower in the ether; and if it has resided continuously in the mind, then it would not ever be eliminable.

132. In that manner when the copper's impurities are destroyed thanks to union with the elixir, nor is its essential nature so destroyed, which remains in all its purity;

133. Just like that, the stained condition of the mind is destroyed thanks to union with emptiness, nor is its nature made of jñāna so destroyed, which remains in all its purity.

134. Just as iron, penetrated by elixir, does not revert back to the nature of iron, so the mind, penetrated by bliss, does not revert back to the nature of sorrow.

The meaning is the following. These impurities of the copper are [either] separable or inseparable from it. If they are inseparable, then, becoming less thanks to union with the elixir, the copper would also become less, because it is identical to the impurities. If, on the other hand, the impurities are separable, the copper is not able to be an object of any modification, because between the two things there is no relation/connection. Then, thanks to the elimination of these impurities, as one is not able to say it is either separable or inseparable, one has the manifestation [of an] inconceivable [quantity] of gold. Just like that, thanks to the elimination of the stained condition of jñāna following a union with emptiness, one manifests a knowing inclusive of all aspects, devoid of differentiated representations, similar to a dream, which does not have, as a support, either transmigration or nirvāṇa, residence/seat and shelter of infinite qualities. Because as it was said by the Venerable Saraha:

> The stupid imagine that from the destruction of the imagination derives the destruction of
> the mind. Instead, for persons of intelligence, just by this [destruction] is born something
> that surpasses [the purity] of the sky.

135. There does not exist a greater transgression than the lack of passion, there does not exist a merit greater than bliss, therefore, O King, you need to continuously apply the mind to motionless bliss.

136. A young maiden is unable to describe the bliss of making love without [having experienced] the same love. Having experienced love in youth, she will know for herself [the nature of] such great bliss.

137. Analogously, one who has had nothing to do with concentration, is unable to describe the bliss of it; but, having attained the motionless in concentration, the yogins know the nature for themselves.

138. Even the omniscient are uncertain regarding [the true nature of] jñāna which is born from the motionless. Nevertheless [this is certain]: because of the nonbliss that derives from it in the mind, it is necessary to endeavor to avoid dispassion.

"To the motionless bliss," namely, to the great bliss devoid of differentiated representations. "Dispassion," namely, the instinct that carries one to ordinary passion, the attachment to emission. "It is necessary to strive to avoid"—it is necessary, namely, to avoid putting into practice. But in what manner [is this able to come about], seeing that the continuation and increase of transmigration has [exactly], as its basis, emission, the instinct that carries one to [ordinary] passion?[27] Just for that reason the Blessed says, "From emission" and so on.

139. From emission is born dispassion, from dispassion is born suffering, from suffering is born, for humans, the ruin of the elements, and from ruin, as was handed down, death.

140. From death, a new existence [arises] from it, again from it death and still again emission. Thus, for beings, phenomenal existence proceeds only from the birth of dispassion, not otherwise.

141. [The yogin] then needs to avoid with every effort passion for emission, by which, [avoiding it] will attain the motionless bliss, [liberating himself] from the bonds of transmigration.

If the desire for the bliss of emission is not able to be pursued not even by common persons who seek bliss, all the more so, it will not be able to be sought for by the true yogin; therefore the Blessed says, "Even a lover."[28]

142. Even a lover, because of dispassion, will not seek out the *Kāmaśāstra*. All the more so will a yogin seek out suffering in the tantra proclaimed by me?

Therefore what one needs to strive for is realizing the great bliss of the supreme motionless, devoid of conceptual constructions, which comes about exactly thanks to a union with the motionless bodhicitta, devoid of differentiated representations, and not the conceptual bliss created thanks to the practice of the syllables (*akṣara*) HŪṂ, PHAṬ, and so on. The Blessed therefore says, "Taking advantage of the nature of the motionless semen" and so on.

143. Taking advantage of the nature of the motionless semen, [the yogin] will need to realize the supreme motionless. Once that the support has become a refuge/shelter of emission, the supported suffers a lack of passion.

144. This relation of support and supported remains as long as [the mind] has not attained the motionless [bliss]. Once having attained the motionless, the mind becomes devoid of the characteristics of support and supported.

From an absolute point of view even the division into support and supported is nonexistent, so that the Blessed says, "Once having attained" and so on. With the intent of clarifying how the body that is born from motionless jñāna, devoid of differentiated representations, is not generated from the senses or from the syllable

HŪṂ and so forth, which are created, the Blessed says, "For one whose body is born from the motionless."[29]

145. For one whose body has been born from the motionless (*akṣara*) and who has arrived at the wheel of the ūrṇā (*tuft*), neither the union of the two series of the vowels and consonants, nor, O King, [the mantras such as] HŪṂ [and so on] have any function.

With the words "The image" and so forth, the Blessed now spends time to expound how, as this jñāna without duality is devoid of differentiated representations, one discerns a relation of cause and effect, from the point of view, of course, of relative reality.

146. The image, born from the void, is the cause, and the bliss, born from the motionless, is the result. The cause is impressed/sealed by the result, and the result is impressed/sealed by the cause.

147. Emptiness, which supports the image, is the cause, and compassion, which supports the motionless, is the result. The unity of emptiness and compassion is the nonemitted bodhicitta.

["The image" and so forth, namely] the omniform image born from that which is devoid of own/actual nature.

"Born from the motionless," born, namely, from the knowledge of the omniform mahāmudrā and devoid of differentiated representations. With the words "Emptiness" and so on, the Blessed clarifies the same concept, making use of other words.

With the words "The image is devoid of nirvāṇa" and so on, the Blessed rejects the theories according to which the image of emptiness and the jñāna of the motionless are the one, extinct, and the other, permanent.

148. The image is devoid of nirvāṇa, and the motionless transcends transmigration. Between these two there is a supreme unity, without duality, devoid of eternity and of cessation.

"But, in what manner are they able to avoid these two errors?" To this question, the Blessed responds with the words "Because, it has as a character . . . from nonbeing" and so on.

149. Because it has, as a character, that of birth from nonbeing, there is not of the image, nonbeing; and because it has, as a character, that of birth from being, there is not of the motionless, being.

"Because it has, as a character, that of birth from nonbeing," as, namely, it manifests well [the] omniform [image] that, born from that which is devoid of own/actual nature, is an object of personal experience on the part of the yogins. "Because it has, as a character, that of birth from being," because, namely, it is born from the omniform [image], since that from the beginning is not born.[30] Such is the reason by which the Blessed says, "The perfect union of being and nonbeing" and so on.

150. The perfect union of being and nonbeing is the vajrayoga, without duality, supreme, devoid of form and nonform, similar to a magical image in a mirror.

151. The image is not immersed in phenomenal existence, nor is the motionless [immersed] in nirvāṇa. [True reality] is a neutral plane/level, supreme, pacified, mutually embraced by both.

"Devoid of form and nonform," devoid, namely, of the erroneous ideas of being and nonbeing, permanence and extinction, and so on. With the words "Wisdom" and so forth, the Blessed now expounds the nondual nature [of this reality], without attributing to it the above-mentioned ideas of cause and result.

152. Wisdom not being born from a cause, as well the result born from wisdom, born [namely] from wisdom as the cause, wisdom not being born from a cause, is not born from a cause.

153. Because the knowledge, [namely] the knowledge of wisdom, without higher, is not born from a cause . . .

"Wisdom," namely, the emptiness provided with all excellent aspects. "From a cause," which is able to be characterized by being, nonbeing, by both, or by the nonexistence of both. "The result," namely, the condition of a Buddha, essentially of compassion without support and devoted to performing the welfare of beings. Because as it is said in the *Hevajratantra in Five Hundred Thousand Stanzas*:

> The cause, in the beginning, is emptiness, provided with all excellent aspects, and the result, subsequently, is the compassion without support, devoted to the welfare of the world.[31]

"But then," some will say here, "this relation of cause and effect, is it absolutely inexistent?" The Blessed, responding to this question, says, "The cause" and so on.

154. The cause and the result are both conditionally coproduced. The image is impressed/sealed by one and by the other, is neither born nor extinguished.

155. Wisdom is completely extinguished and the supreme motionless is [always] born. Devoid [of the nature] of cause and of result, they are not impressed/sealed the one by the other.

The meaning is the following. The relation of cause and effect characterized by this, when their components are conditionally coproduced and explained by the examples of māyā and so on, [this relation] only exists from the point of view of relative reality. With the words "The image is impressed/sealed by one and by the other," the Blessed for that reason says how the jñāna of great bliss [in fact] transcends the division into cause and effect, is essentially of wisdom and means, consists of the two-in-one (*yuganaddha*) and is always raised on the horizon. Because as it was said by the Venerable Saraha:[32]

> Hurrah! Hurrah! That King of bliss, unique, devoid of cause, always raised on the horizon for [all] the worlds. In the moment of needing to describe it, the same omniscient one does not know how to find the words!

"But if dharmas are not born and not extinguished, then how does one justify the existence of ordinary life, which takes place on the basis of the two aspects of knowledge and knowable?" To this end, the Blessed says, "The vision of the knowable is part of one's own mind" and so on.

156. Here, the vision of the knowable [as reality] is not born and not extinguished, is not other than [the vision] of one's own mind, by reason of the fact that [it] separated from itself the knowable [only apparently] external.

Knowable reality, just as it appears to us, [is part of one's own mind], which is similar to a dream, not born by its own/actual nature.

Now the Blessed, to refute the theories of the Vijñānavādin,[33] according to whom consciousness is a real thing, says, "That is why a thing is absolutely impotent" and so on.

157. That is why a thing is absolutely impotent to impress/seal the own-character on itself. Is perhaps a great sword able to cut itself with the cutting edge of its own blade?

[In the following stanza] with the words "In that manner when in union in a dream" and so on, he produces a suitable example for the nature of the jñāna of great bliss generated from the [said] omniform image, devoid of differentiated representations.

158. In that manner when in [sexual] union in a dream with the daughter of a sterile woman one is able to feel bliss, so one [feels bliss] by virtue of the constant practice of the said image, which is born from the void.

The meaning is this. A being is able to experience bliss in a dream, from union with the daughter of a sterile woman, a daughter, therefore by her nature, never born. Not unlike the true yogin who experiences uncreated great bliss [characterized by] a state of intimate fusion with the omniform image, devoid of differentiated representations and by its nature never born. With the words "There is neither wisdom nor means," the Blessed now describes the special states of this jñāna of great bliss, devoid of differentiated representations.

159. There is neither wisdom nor means, this reality is innate (literally "born-with") **together with wisdom, perfectly full of bliss, devoid of every sort of obstacle.**

160. It is devoid of obstacles like the ether, devoid of sense organs and of [their relative] objects, present, in every part, of all beings, unbreakable, devoid of divisions.

With the three stanzas that begin with the words "He is the Adamantine Being, self-generated," the Blessed says in summary how this jñāna of great bliss, joined to its greatest degree, of which is mentioned in other tantras, is the object of various names, according to the various propensities of beings. Immediately after this stanza of summary, with the words "The vajra is unbreakable," the Blessed partially explains the cited names.

161. He is the Adamantine Being, Self-Generated, With the Great Aim/Purpose, the Supreme Motionless; he is the Great Being, the Great Passion, One Who Rejoices in All Beings.

162. He is the Bodhisattva, the Great Hatred, Destroyer of the Afflictions, the Great Enemy; he is the Commitment Being, the Great Obfuscation, Destroyer of Obfuscation of the Obfuscated.

163. He is the Adamantine Yoga, of the Great Wrath, the Great Enemy of the Infuriated Demons; he is the Wheel of Time (Kālacakra), the Great Longing/Yearning, Destroyer of the Agitated (or moved) **Longings/Yearnings.**

164. The vajra is unbreakable, and therefore the Blessed has called him here "with the Great Aim." The being [who is] the unity of the three worlds is known with the name of supreme motionless.[34]

165. [The being who] is full of the supreme motionless bliss, perfectly full of [all] the grounds, is the Great Being, the Great Passion, One Who Rejoices in All Beings.

166. That being who abides immobile in awakening is the Bodhisattva, the Great Hatred, the Great Enemy of the Swarm of the Hatreds, namely, the afflictions and so on.[35]

167. The commitment is the devouring, [namely, the] nonemission of the lunar ambrosia, of semen. The Commitment Being owes his name to this and is the Destroyer of the Obfuscation of the Obfuscated.

168. [The Adamantine Yoga] is the unity of all the vajras with wisdom, with the bodies and with the motionlesses. He is endowed with great wrath and is the great enemy of the infuriated Māras.

169. [Kālacakra] through the means of great bliss is not moved, does not ever forget the welfare of beings. He is the liberator of beings, the great longing/yearning, destroyer of the agitated longings/yearnings.

170. These beings, sixfold, are, he says, the [six] families of the aggregates, namely, jñāna, sensation, consciousness, form, volitions, and notions, all in motionless form;

171. Of the elements, namely, jñāna, fire, water, earth, wind, and ether; of the sense organs, namely the mind, eyes, ears, body, nose, and tongue;

172. And so also those of the sense objects, namely, sound, {visible forms,} taste, the element of the dharma, odors, and the tactile sensations. The King of Wrath, furnished with six faces, terrifying, is purified by [these] six families.

The overall meaning is the following. Here are expounded [the figures] of Vajrasattva, the Bodhisattva of the Mahāsattva and of the Samayasattva.[36] They are purified by the vajras of jñāna, mind, speech, and body, devoid of differentiated representations; essentially of the four moments [called] similar derivation, maturation, activity, and purity;[37] formed of the Four Bodies, Innate, of the Elements, Enjoyment/Use, and of Creation/Formation; purified by the four families. In an analogous manner, one has [a group of] six families, purified by jñāna, fire, ether, earth, wind, and water elements, devoid of differentiated representations; formed from the aggregates jñāna, sensation, perception, form, impulses, and notions, purified by Great Egoism/Selfishness, by Great Passion, by Great Hatred, by Great Obfuscation, by Great Wrath, and by Great Longing, rendered pure by the Six Tathāgatas, Vajrasattva, Ratnasaṃbhava, Akṣobhya, Vairocana, Amoghasiddhi, and Amitābha. All tantras of the yogins and yoginis are pervaded by these four or six families. These two differentiations into four or six families are in reality one single item.

173. The body, the organ of the secret parts, and the mind forever constitute the three maṇḍalas. The three vajras [each constituted by] wisdom and means are realized as the Adamantine Being.

174. This [summary of the initiation, valid] means for realizing initiation and the supreme motionless, complete concerning the [instructions] on the channels and on the families, was expounded in summary, Candra.

With the words "The body" and so on, it designates the threefold maṇḍala. "The organ of the secret parts" is the vajra of speech. "Candra" is vocative.

Thanks to the spiritual merit acquired by me from composing the commentary to the *Sekoddeśa*, empower, who transcribes it, to attain the level of the Adamantine Being.

Endnotes

1. Editor's note: Francesco Sferra 2000, *The Ṣaḍaṅgayoga by Anupamarakṣita* (Rome: Istituto Italiano per l'Africa e l'Oriente), p.43.

2. Editor's note: Günter Grönbold 1996, "The Revelation of Ṣaḍaṅgayoga in the Kālacakra-System," in *The Yoga of Six Limbs* (Santa Fe: Spirit of the Sun Publications).

3. The Omniform Mother is emptiness and therefore the spouse of Kālacakra, Viśvamātā (*the Universal Mother*); the Lord (*vibhu*) is compassion. The family of the Victorious is the various Tathāgatas.

4. Bodhigayā or Vajrāsana.

5. At Dhānyakaṭaka. The verse that begins with the words "lokadhātvādisaṃbuddhair" (or saṃbaddhair) is grammatically devoid of sense. One would be able to think of a saṃbaddha, but more likely there is a dropped verse. Our translation is therefore, on the whole, momentary.

6. See stanza 69.

7. In other words, *āyāma* derives from the root *yam* (to subdue, to control), to which is added the prefix intensifier "–ā" and the suffix of action technically called "ghañ."

8. Here the *Laghukālacakratantra* 4 116c.

9. In the commentary to the first stanza of the *Laghukālacakratantra*, Puṇḍarika gives the following explanation: "The innate body, or rather the vajra of jñāna, purified by the liberation through emptiness, 'omniscient,' is called the pure yoga, constituted by wisdom and

means. The body of the elements, the vajra of mind, purified by the emancipation through the absence of character, the 'body of jñāna,' is called the yoga of the dharma, constituted by wisdom and means. The body of enjoyment/use, or rather, the vajra of speech, purified by the emancipation through the absence of taking into consideration, the 'body of the sun,' is called the yoga of the mantra, constituted by wisdom and means. The physical body, the adamantine body, purified by the emancipation through the absence of conditional activity, 'by eyes wide as lotus petals,' is the yoga of configurations, constituted by wisdom and means."

10. Body, speech, mind, and jñāna.

11. In the commentary of Nāropa, he cites the following stanza from the *Samādhirājasūtra* (9.17): "Just like a young maiden, [who] in a dream, sees the birth of a son, and then he dies, and when [he] is born [she] is all happy, and, when [he] is dead, [she is] full of sadness, so you should know that is [the way of] all dharmas."

12. The ariṣṭa, from the stem *riṣ-* , "to abuse" or "to damage/injure" (in Tibetan chi ltas, or literally, "prognostic of death") are, in Indian astrology, the moments of damage/harm, illness, and so forth, and the prognosis of them. The characteristics of the ariṣṭa are described in the *Laghukālacakratantra* (II 61-81) and in numerous other Indian works, like, for example, the *Yogaśāstra* of Hemacandra (fifth chapter). The premonitory signs of death are characterized by the progressive increase in the flowing of the vital breath in only one of the two lateral channels (instead, during regular breathing, the wind flows through both nostrils); the process lasts three years, at the end of which one has the cessation of life. When the wind begins to flow in the left channel (*lalanā*) one then has the beginning of the ariṣṭa of the moon, which carries one to a premature death under the uneven constellations (Aries and so forth). The ariṣṭa of the sun is, instead, characterized by the flow in the right channel (*rasanā*), prognostic of a premature death for [one] born under an even constellation (Taurus and so forth). Instead, the process of natural death—called "death of the central channel"—occurs through the progressive persistence of the vital breath alternating in the left and right channels, and has begun on the fifteenth day of the ninth month of the ninety-sixth year of life. The process lasts three years, two months, and fifteen days, bringing then one to death in the one hundredth year of life.

13. The text of the *ṭippaṇī*, here quite involved, was partially paraphrased by me (Gnoli).

14. Each of the three channels then assumes two functions, respectively above and below the center of the navel (*nābhi*). Nāropa comments: "The left channel that abides above is the moon, lalanā, iḍā, conducts water, and is generated from the Tathāgata Amitābha. The right channel [that abides above] is the sun, piṅgalā, "the other," namely the rasanā, conducts fire, and is generated from the Tathāgata Ratnasaṃbhava. The middle channel that abides below is the channel of excrement, conducts earth, and is generated from Vairocana. The left channel [below] is the channel of urine and is generated from Amoghasiddhi. The middle channel that abides above is the channel of Rāhu, conducts space, and is generated from Akṣobhya. This same channel below is the channel of semen to the right that conducts jñāna and is generated from Vajrasattva. Above, the channel of excrement unifies with the way of the moon, so that they form a single channel. Analogously, the channel of urine is united with the sun. In a similar manner, the channel of semen is active in the four moments of birth and so forth; it unites with Rāhu."

15. During the process of dissolution of life, the wind rises along the central channel passing through the centers of the navel, heart, throat, forehead, and of the top of the head, and as dissolving the earth, water, fire, wind, and space elements, until exiting outside from the

body. Inversely, in the process of the creation/formation of life, the wind enters at the top of the head and descends as far as the center of the navel, concretizing the various elements as wind and so forth until that of earth.

16. A temporal measure corresponding to twenty-four [Western] minutes.

17. The flowing of the maṇḍalas in the two nostrils is commented upon in more detail by Nāropa: "Concerning this, as the vital wind flows to the right in the ascendant (*lagna*) of Taurus and so on, then 'at the base,' namely at the lower part of the [right] nostril, flows for one grade (*daṇḍa*) the maṇḍala of earth. Similarly, in the left part of the nostril, in the nasal channel, one has the maṇḍala of water. 'To the right,' at the right part, one has the maṇḍala of fire and at the upper part, the maṇḍala of wind. In the middle, one has the maṇḍala of space. In such a manner, in the two nostrils, each maṇḍala flows for a degree, so that in the five degrees, the vital breath flows for five maṇḍalas. (. . .) When in the left channel, with Aries and so forth, in the center of the nostril flows the maṇḍala of space, then flows likewise, on the inside, in the wheel at the navel, 'in the center of the petals,' as more will be said later on, 'then in front (above).' Above, one has the maṇḍala of wind, to the right that of fire, to the left that of water, 'and elsewhere' at the lower part, flows the maṇḍala of earth, 'as,' beginning, namely, from there."

18. In the case of the right nostril, the first element that rises is earth and, in the case of the left nostril, ether.

19. Body, speech, and mind.

20. Then on the basis of the same process, becoming less three months of [life] each three days of increase of the ariṣṭa, to the end of the seventh petal, [the vital breath] vacates with twenty-one days of ariṣṭa. Then the vital breath abandons/vacates the eighth, ninth, tenth, and eleventh petals, after having flowed regularly for three months [for each petal], minus the twenty-five, twenty-eight, thirty-one, and thirty-four days of ariṣṭa that flowed respectively at the beginning of each triad of months of abandonment

21. Also in the *Hevajratantra* II 4, 27. "The last one of all must be firmly rejected, for there is no sixteenth phase." (Snellgrove)

22. *Vimalaprabhā* I (twentieth verse of praise in the Homage). Translated by Newman, it reads: "I bow my head to the Master worshipped by the three worlds; one foot on menses-sun in the vajra gem, the second on semen-moon in the uṣṇīṣa. They are always undivided, indivisible, set in desire."

23. I was not able to find this citation in the VP, which is probably an expansion of what Puṇḍarika says.

24. *Catuḥstava*, III 43.

25. The meaning implies the opposite, namely the semen element (śukradhātoḥ).

26. Not seeing that matter, one would here enter into this dilemma with that which is said after. Perhaps read jñānamalasya? (but the reading of the Tibetan suggests jñānasya). Or take malasya as meaning uccheda? The sense would need to be: "If the stained condition of jñāna unites with emptiness, the possibilities are not able to be two, that namely, jñāna extinguishes or remains unchanged."

27. The consequence is not clear to me, neither is excluding that after katham is dropped, something, as for example, katham <viragah samsarakaranam>, namely: "But in what sense [is dispassion the cause of transmigration]? As [I respond] the continuation . . ." and so on.

28. For śrīdharānanda the meaning of stanza 142 thus seems to be: "Even a lover will well consider seeking out the *Kāmaśāstra*, because of dispassion [that derives from the practices taught in it]."

29. The condition of the supreme motionless is therefore born from the motionless (*akṣara*), that is to say, from the immobility of semen and from the relative knowledge by such immobility, and not from the practice of syllables (*akṣara*) as HŪṂ and so on. The term *akṣara* (from the root kṣar "to flow" or "to vibrate") signifies the "absence of vibration" (intending the prefix "–a" as depriving), but it is also able to signify "phoneme a" and more in general, phoneme, syllable (the stem *kṣara*, in fact, assumes the significance of syllable as vibration or acoustic resonance).

30. Concerning the image, one is not able to say that it is nonexistent, because the nonbeing from which it is born is not a true nonbeing; nor on the other hand is one able to say that it exists, because the being from which it is born is not a true being.

31. This stanza appears among those beginning the commentary of Vajragarbha to the *Hevajratantra*. It was probably cited from memory, because in both manuscripts of the work of Vajragarbha, the recurrent variant reading is praṃidhānāt kṛpā paścāt for nirālambakṛpā paścāt. The expression nirālambakṛpā recurs in a successive stanza (nirālambakāruṇā). The meaning is that first it is necessary to realize emptiness for oneself and only afterwards is one able to compassionately put it to use for others. The expression nirālamba, as was explained a few stanzas earlier, stands for sattvadharmanirālamba.

32. This stanza is also cited by Nāropa in his commentary to stanza 103 of the *Sekoddeśa*, in the *Guṇabharaṇī,* and in the *Kriyāsaṃgraha* without mention of the author.

33. The school of the so-called Buddhist idealism, for whom external reality is not other than an expression or projection of the consciousness (cittamātra).

34. The expressions *vajram abhedyam ity āha* and *sattvaṃ tribhavasyaaikatā* also occur in the *Hevajratantra* I 1.4ab and are cited in the *Vimalaprabhā*.

35. This stanza is in the *Hevajratantra* I 1.5.

36. Here the interpretation of Śrīdharānanda is different from that of Nāropa and is apparently in discord with the text of the *Sekoddeśa*, which explicitly speaks of six supramundane beings. Śrīdharānanda isolates the first four from the subsequent two, presenting them in a manner essentially equal and putting them in relation with the various quaternary divisions of body, speech, mind, and jñāna, with the Four Bodies of a Buddha and so on. This quaternary division (precisely into four families or *kula*) is followed by a second interpretation where there are instead presented six families. This second interpretation essentially agrees with the commentary of Nāropa and is, it seems to us, more adherent to the text of the *Sekoddeśa*. The two divisions, into four or six, Śrīdharānanda concludes, are not contradictory and form in reality a single item. A similar concept is elaborated by Puṇḍarika in the *Vimalaprabhā* where he explains that in the Kālacakra one is equally able to distinguish three, four, five, six, or one hundred families.

37. According to the commentary of Kāṇhapāda to the *Hevajratantra* (as reported by Snellgrove) the first moment, "similar derivation" (*niḥsyanda*), is so called because the state to which it alludes, determined by the action mudrā, is similar to that which has determined it (the result is similar to the cause); in the second moment, "maturation" (*vipāka*), the opposite occurs, in the sense that by a limited activity directed towards the jñana mudrā a great result derives; the third moment, "activity" (*puruṣakāra*), refers to the mahāmudrā, which is only able to be attained with a heroic effort (*pauruṣeyasādhyam phalam*); the fourth moment, "purity" (*vaimalya*), consists of the union with the mahāmudrā.

—4—

The *Elucidation of True Reality*: The Kālacakra Commentary by Vajragarbha on the *Tattvapaṭala* of the *Hevajratantra*[1]

Francesco Sferra

Introduction

This is the *editio princeps* and English translation of the *Tattvanirdeśa,* or *Elucidation of True Reality*, the commentary written by Vajragarbha (tenth to eleventh century)—one of the first and most important Kālacakra authors—on the *Tattvapaṭala* of the *Hevajratantra* (i.e., HT 1.5).

The text, the tenth and last chapter of Vajragarbha's *Ṣaṭsāhasrikā* (aka *Hevajratantrapiṇḍārthaṭīkā*), consists of a description from different viewpoints of True Reality, *tattva*, which should not be understood here as a description of reality as it is, but of the state of Buddha as subjectively experienced when attained. This state is described primarily as a different way of experiencing the body and the mind as well as every aspect of reality. Each element (*dhātu*), each aggregate (*skandha*), etc. corresponds to a deity; each gesture, each word, etc. performed by a true yogin is none other than the gesture, the word, etc. of the deity. In this respect we can perhaps speak of a transmutation of the psycho-physical structure of the yogin, who, as is clarified in other texts, attains a "body of knowledge" (*jñānadeha*).[2] Kālacakra, who here is identified with Heruka and Ādibuddha, and is represented

[1] It is a great honour for me to contribute to this volume devoted to such an exemplary and enlightened figure as His Holiness the Dalai Lama.
I would like to thank Edward A. Arnold for having invited me to participate and his kind assistance; the various institutions who very kindly placed manuscript sources at my disposal (NAK, Kaiser Library of Kathmandu, IsIAO, NGMPP, Kashi Prasad Jayaswal Research Institute); Prof. Raniero Gnoli and Prof. Dr. Harunaga Isaacson for having kindly read this paper and their precious suggestions; Susan Ann White for her help with the English text.

[2] Cf. LKCT 4.119 and Dhargyey 1985: 155-157.

iconographically with twenty-four arms, six shoulders, etc., symbolizes all aspects of reality in its purified state, each of which corresponds to a part of his body. Purified reality is not different from ordinary reality, but it is precisely the latter experienced in a universal way: the yogin perceives all things unrelated to "I and mine," namely, devoid of all subjective identification, which is essentially founded on the relationship between space and time. But here space and, particularly, time—on which this system lays considerable emphasis—are completely absorbed and transformed by Kālacakra himself.

The elixir of this alchemical transmutation of reality from an impure to a pure state is the bodhicitta, which is referred to several times in the *Ṣaṭsāhasrikā* (and at times actually with alchemical terminology)[3] and, not by accident, at the beginning of this final chapter. Here the bodhicitta should be understood as both "semen" and "thought of awakening," and therefore as either the vehicle for transmigration or the vehicle for realizing Buddhahood, of which the bodhicitta is the essence itself: it is the object, the means, and also the goal of the practice; it is, among other things, "devoid of beginning and end" and "beneficial in the beginning, in the middle, and in the end," as stated in the opening stanzas of this text (st. 1 is quoted *ex silentio* from the *Samājottara*, st. 38).

In this chapter, as in other parts of the work, there is no explicit reference to yoga, and more particularly the sixfold yoga (*ṣaḍaṅgayoga*) that is so important in this tradition. Nonetheless, unmistakable allusions are made more than once here to that yogic technique—which would later be described in detail in other texts, such as the *Vimalaprabhā* by Puṇḍarīka and the *Ṣaḍaṅgayoga* treatises by Anupamarakṣita—which causes the interruption of emission and the return of the semen (*bodhicitta*) from the secret parts to the crown (cf. stt. 9cd-11), and is the core teaching of the sixfold yoga.

Excluding the introduction and the conclusion, the text—which given its structure could in fact stand alone as a short work independent of the *Ṣaṭsāhasrikā*—can be divided in six parts, each of which is introduced with the word *idānīm* (now).

The introduction contains the opening stanzas (stt. 1-3); a commentary on *Hevajratantra* 1.5.1; two different expositions of "dependent origination" (*pratītyasamutpāda*, stt. 4-15); the description of a virtuous series that starts with the "ten good deeds" (*daśakuśalakarman*), includes "pleasure" (*sukha*), "merit" or "virtue" (*puṇya*), "knowledge" (*jñāna*), and ends with "Buddhahood" (stt. 16-20); and a succinct description of the latter (stt. 21-24). Stanza 20, in particular, describes the attainment of Buddhahood as the interruption of the four states, beginning with the wakeful state. This sequence would later appear in other texts.[4] The first exposition of "dependent origination" (stt. 4-9ab) follows the traditional *pratiloma* treatment of the topic, which appears in several Buddhist works (e.g., *Udāna* 1.2); the second exposition (stt. 12-15) follows the schema of the *Pratītyasamutpādahṛdayakārikā* attributed to Nāgārjuna (*karman* → *kleśa* → *duḥkha*). In Kālacakra texts a similar exposition can be found in a stanza cited by Puṇḍarīka in

[3] Cf. Section Nine, stt. 29-37.

[4] Cf. e.g. SUṬ, ed. p. 73.

his *Paramākṣarajñānasiddhi* as *Laghukālacakratantra* 5.170.[5] This stanza is not actually included in the final redaction of the *Laghukālacakratantra*, which follows a specific Kālacakra interpretation of "dependent origination" where each of its twelve limbs is explained in astronomical terms.[6] Stanza 21 is a quotation *ex silentio* of *Mañjuśrīnāmasaṅgīti* 8.22. Stanza 25, which corresponds to *Bhagavadgītā* 13.13 but is probably a quote *ex silentio* from *Laghusaṃvaratantra*—which, in its turn, incorporates *Bhagavadgītā* 13.13 *ex silentio*[7]—is cited several times in Kālacakra literature[8] and three times by Vajragarbha himself in this text.[9]

The first part includes the commentary on *Hevajratantra* 1.5.2-7, 9-10 and starts with the explanation of the mudrās from a conventional point of view, which are conceived as means for the realization of the state of Buddha. It is worth noting that the author specifies that the mudrās are quoted in their correct order in this text, stating that they are listed in random order in the mūla text. He modifies the original sequence: *jananī, bhaginī, duhitrī, bhāgineyikā, naṭī, rajakī, ḍombī, caṇḍālī,* and *brāhmaṇī*, as follows: *jananī, brāhmaṇī, bhaginī, ḍombī, duhitā, naṭī, bhāgineyikā, rajakī,* and *caṇḍālī*. Other commentators read a slightly different text[10] and do not criticize the original order.[11] It is worth noting that Vajragrabha's sequence does not find a perfect parallel also in some stanzas of the mūlatantra (i.e., the *Ādibuddha*) quoted by Puṇḍarīka in his *Vimalaprabhā* (vol. 2, p. 105). Later in his commentary Vajragarbha describes the correspondence of the mudrās with the Bodhisattvas' consorts (cf. LKCT 5.104-105ab), with cakras, elements, families, and so forth.

jananī	Locanā	[pṛthivī]	tathāgatakulī	brāhmaṇī	nābhi
bhaginī	Māmakī	[toya]	vajrakulī	ḍombī	hṛdaya
duhitṛ	[Pāṇḍarā]	tejas	padmakulī	naṭī	kaṇṭha
bhāgineyikā	[Tāriṇī]	vāyu	karmakulī	rajakī	lalāṭa
bhāryā	Vajradhātvīśvarī	ākāśa	ratnakulī	caṇḍālī	uṣṇīṣa
antajā	[Viśvamātṛ]	jñāna	vajrasattvakulī	[asparśā]	guhya

Next, the twenty-four-armed Heruka is identified with Kālacakra, the Ādibuddha. This is the first such identification in this text and in all other Kālacakra works.[12]

The second part is a commentary on *Hevajratantra* 1.5.8, 11. Stanza 8 has been deliberately omitted from the above commentary on the first part. It deals with the

---

5 PAJS, ed. p. 98, translated in GNOLI 1997: 70-71, and in CICUZZA and SFERRA 1997: 117.

6 Cf. LKCT 1.113-117 and BANERJEE 1971.

7 Cf. *Cakrasaṃvara* 50.26, vol. 2, p. 586.

8 Cf. e.g. VP *ad* LKCT 5.91 (vol. 3, p. 47), AK (p. 43), AKU (p. 138), SU*Pañjikā* (p. 292 [69], cf. also note 6) and *Kalparāja[tantra]*, fol. $39r_{4\text{-}5}$. Harunaga ISAACSON has kindly pointed out to me that this stanza is also quoted in the *Subhāṣitasaṅgraha* (ed. part II, p. $42_{19\text{-}20}$, where it is said to appertain to the *Śrīsaṃvara*). Cf. KVÆRNE 1977: 63-64.

9 See also Section Two (*ad* HT 1.1.1-2) and Section three (*ad* HT 1.1.10cd-11ab).

10 *jananīṃ bhaginīṃ caiva pūjayed yogavit sadā | naṭiṃ ca rajakīṃ vajrīṃ* (*vajrāṃ* in the printed editions) *caṇḍālīṃ brāhmaṇīṃ tathā | prajñopāyavidhānena pūjayet tattvavatsalaḥ ||*.

11 Cf., for instance, *Muktāvalī*, p. 52, and *Yogaratnamālā*, pp. 116-117.

12 Cf. SFERRA 2005: 259.

definition of the term *tathāgata* that is interpreted here in a strictly tantric manner, as it is in later works, such as the *Amṛtakaṇikā* and the *Amṛtakaṇikoddyota*.[13] In this part we find the quotation of *Sekoddeśa* 86-87, one of the first from this celebrated text. The syllable *evaṃ* that—interestingly enough—appears instead of *ekaṃ* in *Hevajratantra* 1.1.10b (commented on in Section Three and quoted here within the commentary) is interpreted as a noun, symbolizing the union between wisdom (*e*) and means (*vaṃ*).[14]

The third part is a commentary on *Hevajratantra* 1.5.12-14ab. It contains an explanation of the six aggregates and a further description of the state of Buddha. Here we have five quotations from the *Mañjuśrīnāmasaṅgīti*.

The fourth part consists in the commentary on *Hevajratantra* 1.5.14cd-15. Here we find the well-known explanation of the word *bhagavān*, which recurs (sometimes with differences) many times in Buddhist and non-Buddhist works, particularly of the Vaiṣṇava tradition.[15]

The fifth part contains the commentary on *Hevajratantra* 1.5.16-18, a slightly modified version of the well-known passage of the *Daśabhūmikasūtra* in which the Blessed One states that all that appertains to the three worlds is only mind (*citta*), and the para-etymological definition of the mudrās.

The sixth part contains a brief commentary on *Hevajratantra* 1.5.19-21, which is immediately followed by the conclusion that makes reference to the root-tantra of the *Hevajratantra*, the *Pañcalakṣahevajra*.

This edition is based on manuscript 128 kept in the Kaiser Library of Kathmandu and listed as C14/6 in the microfilm list of the NGMPP (fols. 51*v*-59*v*). I also used a photographic copy of the aforesaid manuscript made by Giuseppe Tucci and now held by the IsIAO library in Rome.[16] As far as I know this manuscript (henceforth K^k) is the only extant source that contains the text edited and translated here.

This manuscript, in māgadhī script, consists of thirty-three leaves and is incomplete. It begins with *lokācāravivarjita* and finishes with the famous stanza: *ye dharmā hetuprabhavā hetuṃ teṣāṃ tathāgato hy avadat* | *teṣāṃ ca yo nirodha evaṃvādī mahāśramaṇaḥ* ‖ It has probably been written around the end of the twelfth century. Indeed, the copyist, Viśuddhirakṣita, states in the colophon that he worked in Vikramaśīla (*śrīmadvikramaśīlamahāvihāre likhāpitaṃ* {. . .} *viśuddhirakṣitena svārthaṃ parārthaṃ ca* ‖).

I was also able to consult two other sources of the *Ṣaṭsāhasrikā*, which however do not contain the ninth and tenth chapters of the work: one, a manuscript kept in the National Archives of Kathmandu (NAK 3-693, NGMPP A693/11); the other, a manuscript originally belonging to the Ṅor Monastery in Tibet and now probably kept in Lhasa,[17] of which I was only able to study the photographic copy made by Rāhula Sāṅkṛtyāyana in 1934 (of which I was able to make a copy from

13 Cf. AK *ad* NS 1.6 and 6.7; see also AKU, p. 124, and Merzagora *2006: 29.

14 Cf. AK p. 8.

15 For some references, see SUṬ, ed. p. 65, note e; Lal 1989; cf. also *Bhagavadgītābhāṣya ad* 3.37.

16 This photographic copy was taken in June 1954.

17 Cf. Steinkellner 2004.

the negatives kept in Göttingen and Patna, thanks to the good offices of Gustav Roth and Raffaele Torella) and the one made by Giuseppe Tucci on July 21, 1939, and now held by the IsIAO library.

On the basis of all these sources, I prepared my Doctorate thesis (defended in Rome in 1999) that contains the critical edition and English translation of all ten sections of the text,[18] which I have revised through the years and is now forthcoming in the Florence University Press.

The Sanskrit text of the *Ṣaṭsāhasrikā* was translated into Tibetan by Dānaśīla and Seṅ dkar śākya 'od (and revised by several people, among whom Subhūtiśrīśānti). The Qianlong (No. 2310) and sDe dge (No. 1180) editions of the Tibetan translation (henceforth T) were consulted for this paper. Titles in translation are not present in the original text; they have been inserted to assist the reader. Sandhi has been silently standardized.

Translation

Introduction

1. *The bodhicitta is traditionally said to be "devoid of beginning and end," "pacified," "destruction of existence and nonexistence," "all-pervading [Lord]," "undivided from emptiness and compassion."* (GS 18.38)

2-3. *Having bowed with complete devotion to the Jewel of True Reality, which is beneficial in the beginning, in the middle, and in the end,*[1] *[and] which is Great Pleasure, Vajragarbha writes a commentary on the fifth chapter, [a commentary] that teaches the true reality (*tattva*) of the Buddhas in order to benefit all beings, [and] to attain the fruit of the mahāmudrā.*

Commentary on HT 1.5.1

At this point the Blessed One said, "Now we shall illustrate the chapter regarding True Reality (*tattva*)," which opens with [the words]: "According to [their] own nature . . ." (HT 1.5.1) [Their] own nature (*svarūpa*) is the Tathāgata's knowledge, which is self-aware (*svasaṃvedaka*). "By virtue of" this "own nature" (which is free from a perceptible reality, perception, and a perceptive subject, and from the alteration of the eighteen elements) there "does not exist" for the yogins (1) an external "form," (2) a "seeing subject," and (3) a visual consciousness; (4) "sound," (5) "hearer," and (6) audio consciousness; (7) "smell," (8) "smeller," and (9) olfactory consciousness; (10) "taste," (11) "taster," and (12) taste consciousness; (13) "touch," (14) "toucher," and (15) tactile consciousness; (16) element of

[18] The recent edition of the text that has been published by Malati J. Shendge is based only on MS NAK 3-693 and the Ṅor manuscript. It ends in the middle of chapter eight.

the dharmas (*dharmadhātu*), (17) perceptive subject, and (18) mental consciousness. Likewise, the sense-faculties, beginning with the eyes, too do not exist. In this way, by interrupting the [sequence of the dependent origination, starting with] ignorance, the yogin must meditate on the Jewel of True Reality, which is free from alteration by the eighteen elements [listed above]. In the root-tantra [i.e., in the *Pañcalakṣahevajra*] the Blessed One said:

4-9ab. *"Through the 'interruption' of ignorance, which is 'changing' (*kṣara*), there is the 'interruption' of will; through the 'interruption' of will, the 'interruption' of primary awareness; through the 'interruption' of primary awareness, the 'interruption' of name-and-form; through the 'interruption' of name-and-form, the 'interruption' of the sixfold sphere of the senses; through the 'interruption' of the sixfold sphere of the senses, the 'interruption' of contact; through the 'interruption' of contact, the 'interruption' of sensation; through the 'interruption' of sensation, the 'interruption' of craving; through the 'interruption' of craving, the 'interruption' of grasping; through the 'interruption' of grasping, the 'interruption' of becoming; through the 'interruption' of becoming, the 'interruption' of birth; through the 'interruption' of birth, the 'interruption' of old age and death.*

9cd-11. *"The 'interruption' of the aggregates and elements is traditionally conceived as pacification. Thus, through the 'interruption' of the body there is also the 'interruption' of the vital breath; through the 'interruption' of the vital breath, the 'interruption' of the bodhicitta; through the 'interruption' of the bodhicitta, the 'interruption' of the emission (*cyavana*) [of the semen]. All yogins attain Buddhahood through the 'interruption' of the moment of ejaculation.*

12-14. *"Thus, through the 'interruption' of afflictions (*kleśa*) there is the 'interruption' of action (*karman*); through the 'interruption' of action, the 'interruption' of suffering (*duḥkha*). Afflictions no longer arise due to the 'interruption' of suffering. When afflictions no longer arise, the origination of action is interrupted. If the latter does not originate, suffering does not come into existence, and the yogin, being happy and free from suffering, will always be engaged in benefitting beings.*

15. *"Here the mental disposition (*kalpanā*) of beings can be either bad or good. [In any event] from this [mental disposition] comes affliction; from the latter arises action.*

16. *"Suffering arises from action. Therefore, without pleasure, due to the abandonment of the ten good actions (*daśakuśala*),[2] how can happiness occur?*

17. *"When the novice yogins are suffering in their mind [and are] without pleasure, how can they become equipped with spiritual merits (*puṇya*) through deities, mantras, mudrās, and so forth, that are created [for the purpose of the practice]?*

18. *"Without spiritual merits, how can the equipment of knowledge come into being? Without the two, there is no Buddhahood, no supreme condition of Adamantine Being (*vajrasattva*).*

19. *"Without Buddhahood, one cannot [actually] increase one's own welfare and that of others;*[3] *nor can the Pure Body, the Body of the Dharma, the Body of Fruition, and the Body of Transformation manifest.*

20. *"When the tetrad of states (wakeful state, sleeping state, deep-sleeping state, and the fourth state), which are cause and effect, is 'interrupted,' one becomes a Buddha. There is no doubt [concerning this].*

21. *"He [who is a Buddha] is free from passion, pure, immaculate; he has cast off [all] defects; he is free from diseases; he is perfectly awakened, enlightened, omniscient; he is the knower [of all beings], supreme.* (NS 8.22)

22-23. *"Through 'interrupting' effect and cause, the Lords of the Victors (*jinendra*) have a different body, speech, mind, and pleasure; their body (a group of aggregates) is different; their elements (earth, etc.), sense objects and senses are different; their action senses, like the actions they perform, are also different.*

24. *"His hands, feet, etc., are everywhere; his eyes, heads, and mouths are everywhere. Having ears everywhere, he remains in the world enveloping everything."*

Such is the rule of the True Reality [described] in the root-tantra.

Commentary on HT 1.5.2-7, 9-10

Now, to achieve (*sādhana*) this [reality], in the short tantra the mudrās are stated according to the provisional point of view:

*The knower of the yoga (*yogavit*) must always honor, through wisdom and means and the correct application [of each], the mother, the sister, the daughter, the daughter of the sister;*[4] (HT 1.5.2ad)

The word *yoga* means the union of the perceptible and the perceiver; the union of lalanā and rasanā; the union of the caṇḍālī and the semen. [. . .][5] He must honour [the above-mentioned women] through the union of wisdom and means, while remaining chaste and experiencing unchanging pleasure. The mother and so forth exist in relation to the external reality, with regard to a [specific] place and a family.

In the same way, "the knower of the yoga" must honour

the naṭī, the rajakī, the ḍombī, the caṇḍālī, and the brāhmaṇī (HT 1.5.2ef)

through the aforesaid wisdom and means [and] the correct application [of each], always—at all times—through pleasure that is nonemitted (*acyutasukha*).

[Indeed, the above women] must be honoured scrupulously, so that no division arises. (HT 1.5.3ab)

According to the deep meaning, [the word] *division* signifies the emission of the semen; according to the surface meaning, in the external world, it signifies the derision of men. Therefore, the mother, etc., "must be honoured scrupulously" [by the yogin]. Such is the rule of the Blessed One.

Royal courts, etc.,[6] will torment and punish those foolish practitioners who do not conceal their practice.

For the purpose of attaining liberation, the [aforesaid] mudrās are called "five families." (HT 1.5.4ab)

Here [in this stanza], "for the purpose of attaining liberation," the word *mudrā* signifies the families of the five Tathāgatas. "The mudrā," i.e., the avadhūtī, is such since it is marked (*mudryate*) by "this," that is, "the vajra," the bodhicitta.[7]

The mudrās, beginning with the mother, which are listed in the short tantra starting from verse 1.5.1 but in random order, will be quoted here in their correct order. Here, the "mother" belongs to the family of the Tathāgata [Vairocana]; she is the brāhmaṇī, Locanā [earth], and resides in the lotus of the navel. The "sister," Māmakī, is the water element; she belongs to the family of the vajra [Akṣobhya], [resides] in the heart [and] is the ḍombī. The "daughter" is the fire element [Pāṇḍarā]; she belongs to the family of the lotus [Amitābha], she is the nartī [or naṭī and resides] in the throat. The "daughter of the sister" is the wind element; she belongs to the family of the karman [Amoghasiddhi], she is the rajakī [and resides] in the forehead. The "wife" is Vajradhātvīśvarī, the space element, the caṇḍālī; she belongs to the family of the jewel (*ratna*) [Ratnasambhava] [and resides] in the crown. The "last-born woman" (*antajā*) is the element of knowledge; she belongs to the family of Vajrasattva [and resides] in the lotus of the secret parts.

Thus, above the navel,

these, in brief, are known as the family of the five mudrās. (cf. HT 1.5.7cd)

[But if we include the secret parts,] "there are said to be six types of families" (HT 1.5.9a):

1) In the top of the crown there is the family of the space element; in the forehead, the family of the wind element; in the throat, the family of the fire element; in the heart, the family of the water element; in the navel, the family of the earth element; and in the secret parts, the family of the knowledge element.

2) Likewise, we have the element of the dharmas, which is the quality of space; touch, which is the main quality of the wind; taste, which is the main quality of fire; form, which is the main quality of water; odour, which is the main quality of earth; the sound element, which is the main quality of knowledge.[8]

3) Thus, we have [the organs of perception, i.e.] the sense of hearing, the sense of smell, the sense of sight, the sense of taste, the sense of touch, and the sense of mind.

4) [Moreover, we have the organs of action, i.e.] the reproductive organ, the voice organ, the hand, the foot, the anus, and the divine organ.

5) Thus, we have the purification of the mudrās [i.e., the six aggregates].[9]

6) [Moreover, we have the actions:] urinating, evacuating, going, taking, speaking, ejaculating.

In this way, thirty-six families are reduced to six. The thirty-six elements must be known in this way. Thus, there are six kinds of primary awareness, six volitions, six sensations, six notions, six material forms, and six kinds of knowledge.

Thus, the elements and the aggregates amount to seventy-two [principles]. Indeed, these deities are doubled through [the union with] the court of the ḍākinīs. The deities represented in the maṇḍala are thirty-six. The thirty-seventh, Heruka, is united with Vajravārāhī. When he has three families, his court consists of the wheels of the body, speech, and mind.[10] When his court consists of the six wheels, he is doubled. This concept, expounded by the Blessed One here in the *Hevajratantra*, has been hinted at the *Cakrasaṃvara*[*tantra*] with two pādas:

Then, the mantra-user should mutter the court of the ḍākinīs, which is doubled.

On the basis of these words, the [number of] petals, fields, and so on, can [also] be doubled. There are: (1) four holy places (*pīṭha*), (2) four secondary holy places (*upapīṭha*); (3) four fields, (4) four secondary fields; (5) four chandohas, (6) four secondary chandohas; (7) four melāpakas, (8) four secondary melāpakas; (9) four pīlavas, (10) four secondary pīlavas; (11) four cemeteries, (12) four secondary cemeteries.[11] Similarly, we have the twelve Earths.[12] There are four heroines (*vīreśvarī*), with their respective heros, in each of these [Earths].

Thus, there are forty-eight yoginīs in the six wheels.[13] In the wheel of space, there are the eight ḍākinīs of the diamond; in the wheel of wind, the eight ḍākinīs of the sword; in the wheel of fire, the eight ḍākinīs of the jewel; in the wheel of water, the eight ḍākinīs of the lotus; in the wheel of earth, the eight ḍākinīs of the wheel; in the wheel of knowledge, the eight ḍākinīs of the knife. In the gem of the vajra there are eight ḍākinīs that are void; they [each] hold a one-pointed vajra.[14]

In the sixteen cemeteries, there are another sixteen ḍākinīs who are born from the sixteen delights: two are in the ears; two, in the nostrils; two, in the eyes; one, in the tongue and one, in the uvula; two, in the orifice of the crown; two, in the orifice of the anus; two, in the orifice from which urine is emitted; and two, in the orifice from which the semen is emitted. Thus, there are sixteen yoginīs.[15]

In their midst there is Hevajra, the leader, Innate Bliss, embracing Emptiness. He is the Blessed One with twenty-four arms; he is doubled through the court of the six wheels; he presents himself [in different ways], according to specific intervals of time (*kālaviśeṣeṇa*):[16] his body is blue, due to the purification of the year; his feet are white and red, due to the purification of the two semesters; his throats are black, red, and white, due to the purification of the three kālas (a *kāla* is a period of four months beginning with Mārgaśīrṣa). The four yugas consist of three months each, beginning with Makara. [Heruka's] four mouths are black, red, white, and yellow, due to the purification of the aforesaid [periods]. Therefore, there are the six seasons of two months each, beginning with Mārgaśīrṣa. Heruka's six shoulders are blue, red, and white, respectively (three on the left and three on the right). Thus, his twenty-four arms (twelve on the left and twelve on the right) correspond to the twelve months. On each side, four are black, four are red, and four are white. Thus, he has twenty-four hands, which correspond to the fortnights [of a year]. The total number of lunar digits (*tithi*) in a month corresponds to the total number of phalangeal joints in one of his left and right hands.[17] Therefore, the lunar digits of one year correspond to his three hundred and sixty phalangeal joints.[18]

Thus, Heruka, [when he] consists of six families, is known as the Wheel of Time (*kālacakra*) and Primeval Buddha (*ādibuddha*). He has a garland of skulls made with one hundred heads; the Blessed One is said to be the Great Brahmakāpālika due to these severed heads, which represent the hundred schools of the Veda. Thus, he is doubled, [he is united with] the court of the ḍākinīs, he consists of six families. In other tantras he is said to have five families. Therefore:

It has been said that the sixfold families become fivefold through aggregation. Furthermore, they become threefold through differentiation into body, speech, and mind. (HT 1.5.9)

Thus, according to the aforesaid order:

*The name "family" (*kula*) derives from the fact that, through kula the families of the five elements and the five aggregates are enumerated (*kulyate*), i.e., calculated.* (HT 1.5.10)

Such is the rule governing the six, five, and three families.

Commentary on HT 1.5.8, 11

Now, the definition of Tathāgata is given:

*The Glorious One has gone (*gata*) into the tathatā and, exactly in the same way (*tathā*), he has returned (*āgata*). Being united with this wisdom, he is called Tathāgata.* (HT 1.5.8)

Here, "being united with this wisdom," i.e., with emptiness, [or, more precisely,] the image of emptiness, "the Glorious One," the diamond of the bodhicitta, "has gone into the tathatā," namely the lotus of the secret parts (as far as the jewel of the vajra) that corresponds to the apratiṣṭhitanirvāṇa, starting from the crown (the element of space) and descending through the lotuses of the forehead, throat, heart, navel, and secret parts, which correspond to wind, fire, water, earth, and knowledge, according to the principle "He dwelt in the matrixes of the adamantine women."[19] "And, exactly in the same way, he has returned." Just as he has gone down to (*yathā* [. . .] *gata*), he has come up from (*tathā* [. . .] *āgata*) the jewel of the vajra (the element of knowledge), which is in the lotus of the secret parts, through the navel, heart, throat, forehead, and crown, because the semen was directed upwards. Thus, it is proved that he has gone and come back in the same way. He has reached the twelve Earths through the "interruption" of the twelve limbs [of dependent origination]. Just as, from the worldly point of view, he has gone downward from the forehead through the four delights (the [first] delight, the supreme delight, the multiform delight and the innate [delight]); he has gone, from the superior point of view, from the secret parts to the forehead through the four steps of "cause-correspondence" (*niṣyanda*), "ripeness" (*vipāka*), "effort" (*puruṣākara*), and "purity" (*vaimalya*). And [the Blessed One] said:

The "cause-correspondence" is said to be present in the navel; "ripeness," in the wheel of the dharma; "effort," in the [wheel of] fruition; and "purity," in the Great Pleasure.[20]

This is the rule, in accordance with what will be said later. From the worldly point of view, on the basis of the semen directed downwards, the bodhicitta (*jñānacitta*), according to the fifteen kalās (pratipad, etc.), flows into the lotus of the secret parts, where it manifests in the form of the kalā called pūrṇā; similarly, from the superior point of view, on the basis of the semen directed upwards, [the bodhicitta] (drawn from the jewel of the vajra by the force of yoga) ascends from the lotus of the vajra, according to the [fifteen kalās] pratipad, etc., until it reaches the lotus of the forehead, where it manifests in the form of the kalā called pūrṇā, and then continues until it reaches the crown, where it manifests in the form of the sixteenth kalā. Similarly, in the case of those who transmigrate, blood ascends (according to the pratipad, etc., of the black fortnight) from the secret lotus to the crown, where, at the end of the amāvasyā, it manifests as "the absence of kalās," that is, the sixteenth kalā.[21] In the case of those who are awakened, from the superior point of view, the blood descends (according to the various kalās of the black fortnight) from the crown until it reaches the lotus of the secret parts where, at the end of the amāvasyā, it assumes the specific form of the black moon, that is, the sixteenth [kalā].

And thus [the Blessed One] said in the *Ādibuddha*, from the worldly point of view:

For all beings, at the moment of death, the ambrosia of the moon descends [and the blood ascends], the blood of the sun goes upward [and] the conscience of Rāhu goes into transmigration. (SU 86)

And, from the superior point of view:

O King, for this reason the ambrosia of the moon must be made to ascend; the blood of the sun, made to descend; [and] the conscience of Rāhu, made to go into the unchanging pleasure. (SU 87)

Later, the short tantra states:

The bodhicitta is the moon consisting of fifteen digits. [The moon] is the Great Bliss, which possesses the nature of the [fifteen] vowels. The yoginīs are the parts of the moon. (HT 2.4.29)

Such is the rule of the sixteen delights.
Thus, in the chapter on the family, the Blessed One says:

Evaṃ is the cause for correctly generating and maintaining the yoginīs, the capacity [to recite mantras], the general knowledge [of astronomy and so on] and the specific knowledge [of ritual practices], the appropriate source of the yoginīs, the first cause for generating Heruka. (HT 1.1.9-10ab)

The syllable evaṃ *is the Great Pleasure of the Innate Delight, the Supreme Unchanging.*

In the mind devoid of conceptual constructions,

*there is neither a subject who meditates nor a reality that is meditated on; neither a mantra nor a deity. Mantra and deity exist, they are present, in a way that transcends all possible forms of mental elaboration (*niṣprapañca*).* (HT 1.5.11)

[In other words, they manifest] with the very nature of Innate Bliss from which all conceptual constructions and impurities have vanished.[22]

Commentary on HT 1.5.12-14ab

Now, we shall explain the six aggregates, according to the absolute and the conventional points of view, with the stanza beginning with the word "Vairocana" (HT 1.5.12). Here, Vairocana is the leader in the wheel of earth; Akṣobhya, the leader in the wheel of the space; Amitābha, the leader in the wheel of water; Ratnasambhava, the leader in the wheel of fire; Amoghasiddhi, the leader in the wheel of wind; Vajrasattva (*sāttvika*), the leader in the wheel of knowledge. And these—it is said (*ucyate*)—are [also known] respectively as:

Brahmā, Viṣṇu, Śiva, Sarva, Vibuddha, Tattva. (HT 1.5.12cd)

According to the conventional point of view, these are the beings who are characterized by the semen directed downwards, [whereas] according to the absolute point of view, they are the Buddhas that are characterized by the semen directed upwards.

"Since He is release, Buddha is called Brahmā" (HT 1.5.13a): [He is called Brahmā] because He corresponds to the state in which there is no elimination of the excrement element.[23]

"He is called Viṣṇu[24] because of entering" (HT 1.5.13b): since the urine element enters (*viś*) one's body, i.e., it does not flow outside [Him], Buddha is called Viṣṇu.

"He is called Śiva,[25] because He is always beneficial" (HT 1.5.13c): "beneficial" means "upright conduct" (*akhaṇḍaśīla*), [therefore] the Buddha is called Śiva because there is no emission of semen.

"He is called Sarva, because He abides in all things" (HT 1.5.13d). Sarva is Ratnasambhava, the element of blood. As this [element] does not flow [out of Him], there is no suffering. Since there is no suffering, [He corresponds to]

the state that puts an end to pleasure and suffering, the absence of passion, the dissolution of limiting conditions. (NS 8.20cd)

"He abides in all things": the Buddha is called Sarva because He pervades the knowledge of others' minds through divine eyes (*divyacakṣus*).

"He is Vibuddha [i.e., Nonawakened] because of the absence of knowledge"[26] (HT 1.5.14b), [that is to say,] he lacks the [limited] knowledge of the senses (eyes, etc.), [and, as such] he is Amoghasiddhi who corresponds to the flesh. Due to the dissolution of the [flesh], the predispositions (*saṃskāra*) [for the arising] of eyes, and so on, are nonexistent. Due to the absence of the [eyes, etc.], He is Nonawakened.

*Knower of himself, knower of others; he is all, belongs to all; he is the first pudgala; he defies worldly comparison; he is knowable (*jñeya*); he is the lord of knowledge, supreme.* (NS 10.13)

Thus, the Buddha "is Nonawakened because of the absence of [limited] knowledge." Such is the rule.

"He is Tattva [i.e., True Reality], to the extent that He is true bliss" (cf. HT 1.5.14a). True bliss is devoid of passions (*anāśrava*); True Reality is the perfect unity of the four liberations (*śūnyatā, animitta, apraṇihita,* and *anabhisaṃskāra*); it is the support of the supportless compassion, benevolence, sympathetic joy, and equanimity; it consists in wisdom and means; it is known as Buddhahood. Thus, the Buddha, the Blessed One, is

*He who possesses the meaning of the truth that has twelve aspects (*dvādaśākāra*), he who knows the reality of the sixteen aspects, he who possesses perfect knowledge of the twenty aspects, he who is the perfect Buddha, the Knower of the supreme meaning.* (NS 9.15)

Thus, according to the aforesaid order:

There are three families, five families, one single nature [or even] one hundred families.[27]

Thus, in the *Nāmasaṅgīti* [we read]:

King of wrath, six-faced, terrible, six-eyed, six-armed [and] strong: he is a skeleton baring its teeth; in his hundred mouths there is the halāhala poison. (NS 7.1)

And also:

His eyes are like a blazing vajra, his hair is like a blazing vajra; he is Vajrāveśa; he is Mahāveśa; he has a hundred eyes; his eyes are vajras. (NS 7.7)

Such is the rule of the hundred families.

Thus, according to the ordinary point of view and the absolute point of view, True Reality is mundane [and] supramundane, endowed with hindrances [and] devoid of hindrances, endowed with sign [and] devoid of sign, endowed with conceptual constructions [and] devoid of conceptual constructions, endowed with false superimpositions [and] devoid of false superimpositions, endowed with the sense of self (*ahaṅkāra*) [and] devoid of the sense of self, pertaining to beings [and] pertaining to Buddhas, deriving from the dependent origination of the twelve limbs [and] deriving from the cessation of the twelve limbs, and not [only] absolute. Such is the rule of the Buddha, the Blessed One, as stated in all other tantras, which the wise ones must learn.

Commentary on HT 1.5.14cd-15

Now, the deities, etc., are described according to the teaching of the relative point of view, with the words: "[The deity] originates in the body (*dehe sambhavati*)"[28] (HT 1.5.14c), etc. Since ordinary pleasure originates here, in the body, consisting of the five elements, "the word 'deity' has been used" (HT 1.5.14d) by me [i.e., the Buddha].

*The Awakened One possesses happiness (*bhaga*); therefore he is known as the Blessed One (*bhagavān*). It has been said that there are six aspects of happiness, i.e., the virtues starting with lordliness.* (HT 1.5.15ad)

The word "happiness" is traditionally associated with complete sovereignty, knowledge, glory, prosperity, beauty, virtue.

*Alternatively, he is [called] Bhagavān since he destroys (*bhañjanāt*) the Māras, beginning with the Kleśamāra.*[29] (HT 1.5.15ef)[30]

[This is stated] from the absolute point of view. Such is the rule of the means.

Commentary on HT 1.5.16-18

Now wisdom is explained through the words *jananī*, etc. [i.e., stanza 1.5.16]. In this stanza (*iha*) the means is the father, the semen element; wisdom is the mother, the blood element. Empowered by action, the gandharvasattva arises; basic consciousness (*ālayavijñāna*) dies out with death and returns to life in the next birth. This [consciousness] is expressed by the word "universe" (*jagat*). Indeed, the Blessed One said: "O Jinaputras, what pertains to the three worlds is only consciousness."[31] The universe is nothing but this [consciousness]. Wisdom "generates (*janayati*) the universe (*jagat*)," [and] is [therefore] called mother (*jananī*); she corresponds to the blood element (cf. HT 1.5.16ab). In the same way, the means is the semen element.

Wisdom is known as "sister" (*bhaginī*), "since it shows the difference (*vibhāga*)" (cf. HT 1.5.16cd), i.e., [the difference between] hair, skin, flesh, and blood, each of which is a transformation of the [two] elements (*dhātuvikāra*), [blood and semen].[32] Likewise, the means [is called] "brother"; it is the semen element, "as it shows the difference" between the channels, bones, and marrow.

"Wisdom is" known "as 'daughter' (*duhitṛ*), since it extracts (*duhana*) the quality" (cf. HT 1.5.18a). [Here] the word "quality" signifies: word, touch, taste, colour, smell, and the element of dharmas. "Since it extracts" means since it perceives them. In this case, the means (the element of means) corresponds to the son, as it is the activity of the eyes, etc.

Similarly, wisdom is known as the daughter of the sister, as it activates the various kinds of primary awareness with respect to their objects. The means is known as the "son of the brother," as it is the activity of [the various kinds of primary awareness] with respect to its senses, the eyes, etc.

Likewise, wisdom is called wife, because she brings about the pleasure of emission while the means is known as husband: indeed, they are mutually dependent with respect to the pleasure of emission.

Due to the absence of passion, wisdom is called untouchable (*asparśā*)[33] [and] last-born woman (*antajā*), and thus also the means.

Such is the rule of the six mudrās. [This can be summarized as follows:]

As wisdom confuses all elements, it is known as brāhmaṇī; as wisdom colours all elements, it is known as rajakī; as wisdom causes the movement of all elements, it is known as nartakī; as wisdom burns all elements, it is known as caṇḍālī; as wisdom does not touch the elements, it is known as ḍombinī. The means must be understood in the same way, according to the aforesaid five actions.

[To conclude], in the external reality all things manifest in this way; therefore, they are imagined by the heretics on the basis of the Vedas, etc. [But] actually, all women and men, according to their very nature, belong to a single family (*jāti*), mankind. They do not belong to different families. This is stated in all tantras.

Commentary on HT 1.5.19-21

Now, with the words *jalpanam*, etc., the muttering of mantras, etc., is explained according to the nature of [their] verbal roots (*dhātu*). Since, in this world (*iha*), the speech of all beings is the uttering of *āli*s and *kāli*s, i.e., vowels and consonants, the "speech (*jalpana*)" of the true yogins "is said to be recitation [of mantras] (*jāpa*)" (HT 1.5.19a). In the same way, "a footprint could be a maṇḍala," because "the imprint (*malana*)" made on the earth by the [true yogins'] feet "is called maṇḍala" (HT 1.5.19cd). Likewise,

A hand gesture, and thus also a snapping of the fingers, could be a mudrā. (HT 1.5.20ab)

In the same way, the thinking of beings is, for the yogins—due to [their] knowledge of others' minds—an object of concentration, "since this object of concentration is a non[discursive] thinking (*vicintana*)" (HT 1.5.20d), [in other words] since what yogins [truly] concentrate on is a nonthinking (*acintana*).

"The pleasure" that dies out with death and returns to life in the next birth and is experienced in the father during the emission of semen, "is enjoyed" by the male "himself" at sixteen and the female at twelve (cf. HT 1.5.21ab). "The bliss through which death is attained" (cf. HT 1.5.21c), and also the coming into existence and continued existence of transmigrating beings in the transmigration, "is the" same "pleasure" that yogins define as concentration, when it has been made firm at the moment of emission.

Conclusion

All this, briefly, is the essential meaning of each of the chapters [of the root-tantra, which has been drawn] from the middle of each large section [of 100,000 stanzas]

(*lakṣa*) of the *Pañcalakṣahevajra*, which I, Vajragarbha,[34] have imparted in five chapters. The remaining chapters of the short tantra, beginning with the chapter on conduct,[35] must be learnt in detail.

The concise meaning of the first large section is expressed in the chapter on families, in thirty stanzas; the concise meaning of the second large section, in the chapter on mantras, in forty stanzas; the concise meaning of the third large section, in the chapter on deities, in twenty-four stanzas; the concise meaning of the fourth large section, in the chapter on the consecrations, in six stanzas; the concise meaning of the fifth large section, in the chapter on True Reality, in twenty stanzas. Therefore, through this commentary yogins can understand the essential meaning [of the root-tantra that has been summarized in the short tantra] in the hundred and twenty stanzas of the [first] five chapters.[36]

This is the "great exposition" (*mahoddeśa*) [entitled] *Elucidation of True Reality* in the *Ṣaṭsāhasrikā*, a commentary on the *Hevajratantra*. Thus concludes the commentary on the concise meaning of the chapter on True Reality.[37]

Notes to the Translation

1. This concept, which is usually applied to buddhavacana or dhamma, is very common in Buddhist scriptures (e.g., *Dīgha Nikāya* 2.40); it occurs also in other parts of this work, see Section One, st. 50cd (*ādau madhye 'vasāne ca kalyāṇaṃ vacanaṃ mama*), and Section Six (ed. Shendge, p. 40). Cf. also AK *ad* NS 6.5, p. 37.

2. Cf. *Majjhima Nikāya*, vol. 1: 47.

3. See also Section One, stt. 41cd-42 (ed. Shendge, p. 10).

4. On this theme, cf. *Caṇḍamahāroṣaṇatantra* (George 1974: 82); *Tantrāloka* 15.551cd-557ab (Gnoli 1999: 395, note).

5. The meaning of the words *tasmān nivarttitam īśvaravat* is not clear to me. The passage might be corrupt. Here we would expect an explanation of °*vit* at the end of the compound *yogavit*. The Tibetan translation has *de las ṅes par sgrub pa'i dbaṅ phyug daṅ ldan pa ste*, which might suggest the reading *tasmān nirvartiteśvaravān*. This passage has also been quoted by Anaṅgayogin in his *Ḍākinījālasaṃvararahasya*, which, however, is in its turn problematic. I quote it *verbatim* from the edition: *tathā coktaṃ vajragarbheṇa—pūjāvidhir mūlatantroktaḥ yathā—prajñopāyavidhānena pūjayed yogavit sadā | yoga iti caṇḍālīśuklayor aikyam | tasmāt tan nivartate | [ta]m īśvaraṃ tato brahmacaryeṇākṣarasukhena prajñopāyavidhānena pūjayed yogavit sadā sarvasminn eva kāle 'cyutasukheneti* | (p. 4). H. Isaacson has kindly pointed out to me that in the MS of the *Ḍākinījālasaṃvararahasya* kept in the Bodleian Library, Oxford, we find the reading *tasmān nivartitam* instead of *tasmāt tan nivartate | [ta]m*.

6. Namely, those whose duty it is to control the behaviour of society and to administrate law.

7. I have tried to translate literally; one might wonder however whether *anena* is meant to be understood as equivalent here to *anayā*: "*avadhūtī* is called *mudrā* because [something] is sealed by it."

8. These connections are confirmed also by the Tibetan translation. However, in accord with the usual treatment of the subject, we would have expected *śabda* with *ākāśa*, *dharmadhātu* with *jñāna*, *rūpa* with *tejas,* and *rasa* with *udaka*.

9. See below, HT 1.5.10.

10. See below, HT 1.5.9.

11. 12 X 4 = 48.

12. The twelve bhūmis, which correspond with the twelve kinds of place, become forty-eight (four vīras, etc. in each bhūmi). Cf. HT 1.7.10-11. See Snellgrove 1959, vol. 1: 69, note 1.

13. 8 X 6 = 48.

14. These eight ḍākinīs are not included in the total.

15. 48 + 8 + 16 = 72.

16. Vajrapāṇi comments at length on the word *kālaviśeṣeṇa*, which appears in *Cakrasaṃvaratantra* 1.6d. Cf. LTṬ, 4-12 (Cicuzza 1999: 61-119).

17. 3 phalangeal joints X 5 fingers = 15; 15 X 2 hands = 30.

18. 24 hands X 5 fingers = 120; 120 X 3 phalangeal joints = 360 (each month contains 30 *tithi*s).

19. This is the conclusion of the famous *vijahārapada* or *vijahārasthāna*, commented on at length in Section Two (ed. Shendge, pp. 14-16).

20. On these four phases of the sixfold yoga, see *Ṣaḍaṅgayoga*, pp. 33-35.

21. Cf. SU 109.

22. Or "from which all impurities of conceptual constructions have vanished."

23. Brahmā, who is fullness, corresponds to Vairocana.

24. Viṣṇu corresponds to Akṣobhya.

25. Śiva corresponds to Amitābha.

26. Ratnākaraśānti and Kṛṣṇācārya interpret this passage in a different way: "He is completely awakened (*vibuddha*), because of the understanding of the erotic bliss (*rateḥ*)" (cf. *Muktāvalī*, p. 56, and *Yogaratnamālā*, p. 118). On Kṛṣṇācārya, his names and his relation with Ratnākaraśānti, see Isaacson 2001: 458, note 4.

27. See Newman 1987: 401.

28. Like *de*(*he*) *va*(*sati*), this is a para-etymological explanation of the word *deva*: *de*(*he sambha*)*va*(*ti*).

29. Cf. Newman 1987: 271; Gnoli and Orofino 1994: 136-37, note 1.

30. Cf. Lamotte 1944: 115-61.

31. This passage, which comes with slight differences from the *Avataṃsakasūtra*: *Daśabhūmika* 6 (ed. p. 32: *cittamātraṃ bho jinaputrā yaduta traidhātukam*), is quoted in several texts, such as the *Viṃśatikākārikāvṛtti* by Vasubandhu, *ad* st. 1, and the *Muktāvalī* by Ratnākaraśānti (p. 10).

32. Cf. LKCT 2.8d; VP vol. 1: 160.

33. Cf. SU*Pañjikā*, p. 48, line 3.

34. Or, according to the reading *mayā he vajragarbha* [. . .] *deśitaḥ*: "O Vajragarbha, I have explained [. . .]."

35. That is, the chapters 1.6, and so on.

36. 30 (chapter 1) + 40 (chapter 2) + 24 (chapter 3) + 6 (chapter 4) + 20 (chapter 5) = 120.

37. Or, according to the Tibetan translation: "Thus concludes the chapter on True Reality. Here ends the *Śrīhevajrapiṇḍārthaṭīkā.*"

Text

Introduction

anādinidhanaṃ śāntaṃ bhāvābhāvakṣayaṃ vibhum |
śūnyatākaruṇābhinnaṃ bodhicittam iti smṛtam ‖ [1] (= GS 18.38)[a]

ādimadhyāntakalyāṇaṃ tattvaratnaṃ mahāsukham |
praṇipatya sarvabhāvena vajragarbheṇa likhyate ‖ [2]

pañcame paṭale ṭīkā buddhatattvasya deśakī |
hitāya sarvasattvānāṃ mahāmudrāphalāptaye ‖ [3]

Commentary on HT 1.5.1

atra bhagavān āha – **athātas**[1] **tattvapaṭalaṃ vyākhyāsyāmaḥ** | **svarūpeṇe**tyādinā (HT 1.5.1) vitanyate | [b] svarūpaṃ[2] svasaṃvedakaṃ tathāgatajñānam | tena **svarūpeṇa**[3] grāhyagrahaṇagrāhakāṣṭādaśadhātuvikārarahitena yogināṃ bāhya**rūpaṃ nāsti na draṣṭā**[4] na cakṣurvijñānam | evaṃ **na śabdo na** [K[k] 52*r*] **śrotā**[5] na śrotravijñānam | evaṃ **na gandho na ghrātā** na ghrāṇavijñānam | tathā **na raso na rāsako** na jihvāvijñānam | evaṃ **na sparśo na sparṣṭā**[6] na kāyavijñānam | evaṃ[7] na dharmadhātur na grāhako na manovijñānam iti | tathā cakṣurādīny api na santi | evam aṣṭādaśadhātu<vikāra>rahitaṃ[8] tattvaratnaṃ yoginā bhāvanīyam iti, avidyādinirodhena | mūlatantre bhagavān āha[c] –

kṣarāvidyānirodhena saṃskārasya nirodhanam |
saṃskārasya nirodhena vijñānasya nirodhanam ‖ [4]

vijñānasya nirodhena nāmarūpanirodhanam[9] |
nāmarūpanirodhena ṣaḍāyatananirodhanam ‖ [5]

ṣaḍāyatananirodhena sparśasyāpi nirodhanam |
sparśasyāpi nirodhena vedanāyā nirodhanam ‖ [6]

vedanāyā nirodhena tṛṣṇāyāś ca nirodhanam |
tṛṣṇāyāś ca nirodhena upādānanirodhanam ‖ [7]

upādānanirodhena bhavasyāpi nirodhanam |
bhavasyaiva nirodhena jāter api nirodhanam ‖ [8]

jāter api nirodhena jarāmaraṇanirodhanam |
nirodhaḥ skandhadhātūnāṃ sa evopaśamaḥ smṛtaḥ ‖ [9]

evaṃ kāyanirodhena prāṇasyāpi nirodhanam |
prāṇasyāpi niro[K^{k} 52*v*]dhena bodhicittanirodhanam ‖ [10]

bodhicittanirodhena cyavanasya nirodhanam |
cyutikṣaṇanirodhena buddhatvaṃ sarvayoginām[10] ‖ [11]

evaṃ kleśanirodhena karmaṇo <'>pi nirodhanam |
karmaṇaś ca nirodhena duḥkhasyāpi nirodhanam ‖ [12]

duḥkhasyāpi nirodhena kleśotpādo bhaven na saḥ |
kleśotpādaṃ vinotpādaḥ karmaṇo naiva jāyate ‖ [13]

tasyotpādaṃ vinotpādo duḥkhasyāpi na vidyate |
duḥkhaṃ vinā sukhī yogī sattvārthaṃ kurute sadā ‖ [14]

<vi>kalpanātra[11] sattvānām aśubhā vā śubhāpi vā |
kleśa utpadyate tasmāt tasmād dhi karma jāyate ‖ [15]

karmaṇo jāyate duḥkhaṃ sukhaṃ vinā tataḥ punaḥ |
daśakuśalaparityāgāt kutaḥ saukhyaṃ bhaviṣyati ‖ [16]

kuto <'>yaṃ puṇyasambhāro duḥkhacittāt sukhaṃ vinā |
devatāmantramudrādyaiḥ kalpitair bālayoginām ‖ [17]

puṇyaṃ vinā kuto jñānasambhāraḥ samprajāyate |
tābhyāṃ vinā na buddhatvaṃ vajrasattvatvam uttamam ‖ [18]

na ca tena vinā svārthaḥ parārthaḥ sampravartate |
viśuddhadharmasambhoganirmāṇāni[12] sphuranti te ‖ [19]

jāgratsvapnasuṣuptaturyāvasthācatuṣṭayam |[d]
hetuphalaṃ yadā ruddhaṃ tadā buddho na saṃśayaḥ ‖ [20] [K^{k} 53*r*]

arajo virajo vimalo vāntadoṣo nirāmayaḥ |
suprabuddho vibuddhātmā sarvajñaḥ sarvavit paraḥ ‖ [21] (NS 8.22)[e]

anyaḥ[13] kāyo jinendrāṇāṃ phalahetunirodhataḥ |
vāk cittaṃ ca sukhaṃ cānyaḥ[14] <kāya>ḥ skandhasamūhakaḥ || [22]

pṛthivyādidhātavo <'>py anye viṣayā indriyāṇi ca |
karmendriyakriyāś cānyās tathā karmendriyāṇi ca || [23]

sarvataḥpāṇipādādyaṃ[15] sarvato<'>kṣiśiromukham |
sarvataḥśrutimān loke sarvam āvṛtya tiṣṭhati || [24][f]

iti tattvaniyamo mūlatantre ||

Commentary on HT 1.5.2-7, 9-10

idānīm asya sādhanāya saṃvṛtyā mudrā ucyante laghutantre | tadyathā –

jana{nīṃ} bhaginī<ṃ> caiva duhitrī<ṃ> bhāgineyikā<m> |
prajñopāyavidhānena pūjayed yogavit sadā || (HT 1.5.2ad)

yoga iti grāhyagrāhakayor aikyaṃ lalanārasanayor aikyaṃ caṇḍā{lī}śukrayor aikyam | †tasmān nivarttitam īśvaravat†[16] brahmacaryeṇākṣarasukhena prajñopāyasamāpattyā pūjayet | bāhye[17] deśakulavyavahāreṇa jananyādaya iti | tathaiva –

naṭī<ṃ> rajakī<ṃ> tathā ḍombī<ṃ> caṇḍālī<ṃ> brāhmaṇī<ṃ>
[tathā | (HT 1.5.2ef)[g]

yogavid iti | pūrvoktena prajñopāyena vidhānena **pūjayed yogavit**[18] **sadā** sarvasmin kāle 'cyutasu{khena} | [K[k] 53*v*]

sevitavyāḥ[19] **prayatnena yathā**[20] **bhedo na jāyate** | (HT 1.5.3ab)

bhedo nītārthena śukracyavanam | neyārthena bāhye janopahāsaḥ[21] | ato jananyādayaḥ **prayatnena sevitavyā**[22] i{ti bhaga}vato niyamaḥ | yadā prakaṭe **kriyate** sevā tadā rājakulādibhir **duḥkhaṃ** dīyate bālayoginām iti | [h]

mudrāḥ[23] **pañcakulānīti kathyate mokṣahetunā** | (HT 1.5.4ab) iti |

atra mokṣahe{tunā} mudrā nāma pañcatathāgatakulāni | **vajreṇa** bodhicittena **mudryate 'neneti mudrā**vadhūtī | atra **vajram** ityādinā (cf. HT 1.5.5) astavyastenoktā[24] jananyādayo mudrā yathā{kra}meṇa gṛhyante | atra **jananī** tathāgatakulī **brāhmaṇī** locanā nābhikamale | **bhaginī** māmakī <toyadhātur> hṛdaye vajrakulī **ḍombī** | **duhitā** tejodhātuḥ padmakulī **naṭī** {ka}ṇṭhe |

bhāgineyikā vāyudhātuḥ[25] karmakulī **rajakī** lalāṭe | bhāryā vajradhātvīśvary ākāśadhātuś **caṇḍālī** ratnakuly uṣṇīṣe | antajā jñānadhātur vajrasattvakulī guhyaka{ma}le | evaṃ nābhyūrdhvaṃ

pañcamudrākulaṃ hy etat saṅkṣepeṇābhidhīyate || (cf. HT 1.5.7cd)

kulāni ṣaḍvidhāny āhur iti (HT 1.5.9a) | uṣṇīṣa ākāśadhātukulam | lalāṭe vāyudhātukulam | kaṇṭhe tejo{dhā}[K^{k} 54*r*]tukulam | hṛdaya udakadhātukulam | nābhau pṛthivīdhātukulam | guhye jñānadhātukulam |

evam ākāśaguṇo[26] dharmadhātuḥ | vāyuguṇo mukhyaḥ[27] sparśaḥ | tejoguṇo mukhyo rasaḥ | udakaguṇo {mu}khyo[28] rūpaḥ | pṛthivīguṇo mukhyo gandhaḥ | jñāna<dhātu>guṇo[29] mukhyaḥ śabdadhātuḥ |

evaṃ śrotrendriyam | ghrāṇendriyam | cakṣurindriyam | jihvendriyam | kāyendriyam | mana-indriyam |

evaṃ bhagendriyam | vāgindriyam | pāṇīndriyam | pādendriyam | gudendriyam | divyendriyam |

evaṃ mudrāviśuddhiḥ |

<evaṃ> mūtraśrāvaḥ | viṭśrāvaḥ | gatiḥ | ādānam | ālāpaḥ | śukracyutiḥ |

evaṃ ṣaṭtriṃśatkulānāṃ ṣaṭkulāni | evaṃ ṣaṭtriṃśaddhātavo veditavyāḥ | evaṃ ṣaḍvijñānāni | ṣaṭsaṃskārāḥ | ṣaḍvedanāḥ[30] | ṣaṭsañjñāḥ | ṣaḍrūpāṇi[31] | ṣaḍjñānāni |

evaṃ skandhadhātavo[32] dvāsaptatiḥ | tā[33] ca devatā dviguṇā ḍākinījālasaṃvarāt | ṣaṭtriṃśan māṇḍaleyāḥ |

saptatriṃśattamo heruko vajravārāhyā saha | tasya trikulasya[34] kāyavākcittacakrasaṃvaraḥ[35] | dviguṇasya[36] ṣaṭcakrasaṃvaraḥ | [37] atra hevajratantre bhagavatoktaṃ cakrasaṃvare pādadvayena[38] sūcitam –

tato dviguṇaṃ japen[39] mantrī ḍākinījāla[K^{k} 54*v*]saṃvaram | [i]

iti vacanāt | dalakṣetrādikaṃ dviguṇam | catvāri pīṭhāni | catvāry upapīṭhāni | catvāri kṣetrāṇi | catvāry upakṣetrāṇi | catvāri cchandohāni | catvāry upacchandohāni | catvāri melāpakāni | catvāry upamelāpakāni | catvāri pīlavāni | catvāry upapīlavāni | catvāri śmaśān<ān>i | catvāry upaśmaśānāni | evaṃ dvādaśabhūmayaḥ | ekaikasyāś[40] catasro vīreśvaryaḥ savīrāḥ | evam aṣṭacatvāriṃśad yoginyaḥ ṣaṭcakre | ākāśacakre 'ṣṭavajraḍākinyaḥ | vāyucakre 'ṣṭau khaḍgaḍākinyaḥ | tejaścakre 'ṣṭau ratnaḍākinyaḥ | toyacakre 'ṣṭau padmaḍākinyaḥ | pṛthivīcakre 'ṣṭau cakraḍākinyaḥ | jñānacakre 'ṣṭau karttikāḍākinyaḥ | vajramaṇāv aṣṭau śūnyaḍākinya ekaśūkavajradhāriṇyaḥ | anyāḥ[41] ṣoḍaśaśmaśāne ṣoḍaśānandajanitāḥ ṣoḍaśaḍākinyaḥ | śrotradvaye dve | ghrāṇarandhre dve | cakṣurandhre dve | jihvālambikayor dve | uṣṇīṣadvāre dve | gudadvāre dve | mūtradvāre dve | śukracyutidvāre dve | evaṃ ṣoḍaśayoginyaḥ | tāsāṃ madhye nāyakaḥ sahajānandaḥ śūnyatāliṅgito hevajro bhagavān caturviṃśa[K^{k} 55*r*]tibāhur dviguṇaḥ ṣaṭcakrasaṃvarāt[42] kālaviśeṣeṇāvasthitaḥ | varṣaviśuddhyā nīlāṅgaḥ | ayanaviśuddhyā sitaraktacaraṇaḥ | trikālaviśuddhyā kṛṣṇaraktasitakaṇṭhaḥ[43] | mārgaśīrṣādicaturmāsātmakaḥ kālaḥ | makarāditrayamāsātmakāś catvāro yugāḥ | tadviśuddhyā kṛṣṇaraktasitapītacaturmukhaḥ[44] | evaṃ mārgaśīrṣādayo dvimāsātmakāḥ ṣaḍṛtavaḥ | tadviśuddhyā ṣaṭskandhā nīlaraktasitasvabhāvāḥ savyetare | evaṃ catuścaturmāsātmakāḥ savyetare kṛṣṇaraktaśukladvādaśabhujā dvādaśamāseṣu | evaṃ pakṣabhedena caturviṃśati karāḥ | pratyekatriṃśattithibhedena vāmasavyahastāt parvanāḍyaḥ | ṣaṣṭyuttaratriśatāṅgulīparvāṇi[45] varṣatithibhedena[46] |

evaṃ ṣaṭkulātmako herukaḥ kālacakraḥ sa evocyate, ādibuddhaś ceti | asya śatāsyair muṇḍamālā vedaśataśākhāśirobhiś[47] cheditair mahābrahmakāpāliko bhagavān iti dviguṇo ḍākinījālasaṃvaraḥ ṣaṭkulātmakaḥ | anyatantrāntare[48] pañcakulātmakaḥ | ataś ca –

kulāni ṣaḍvidhāny āhuḥ saṅkṣepeṇa tu pañcadhā |
paścāt (*sic*) **trividhaṃ yānti kāyavākcittabhedanaiḥ**[49] || (HT 1.5.9) iti |

evam uktakrameṇa –

kulānāṃ pañcabhūtānāṃ pañca[K[k] 55*v*]**skandhasvarūpiṇām |**
kulyate gaṇyate 'nena[50] **kulam ity abhidhīyate** || (HT 1.5.10)

iti ṣakulapañcakulatrikulaniyamaḥ ||

Commentary on HT 1.5.8, 11

idānīṃ tathāgatalakṣaṇam[51] ucyate |

tathatāyāṃ gataḥ śrīmān āgataś ca tathaiva ca |
anayā prajñayā yuktas tathāgato 'bhidhīyate || (HT 1.5.8) iti |

ih**ānayā prajñayā** śūnyatayā **yuktaḥ** śūnyatābimbena saha **tathatāyāṃ** guhyakamale vajramaṇiparyantam apratiṣṭhitanirvāṇabhūmāv[52] uṣṇīṣād ākāśadhātor lalāṭakaṇṭhahṛnnābhiguhyakamaleṣu vāyutejojalapṛthivījñānadhātusvabhāveṣu[53] vajrayoṣidbhageṣu vihṛtavān iti **śrīmān** bodhicittavajro **gataḥ** | **āgataś ca tathaiva ce**ti (HT 1.5.8b) | yathādhobhāgena gatas tathā vajramaṇer guhyakamale jñānadhātor āgato nābhau hṛdaye kaṇṭhe lalāṭa uṣṇīṣa ūrdhvaretasā | evaṃ yathā gatas tathāgataḥ siddhaḥ | dvādaśāṅganirodhena dvādaśabhūmiprāptaḥ | yathā lokasaṃvṛtyānandaparamānandaviramānandasahajabhedena gato[54] lalāṭād adhaḥ | tathā vivṛtyā niṣyandavipākapuruṣakāravaimalyena guhyāl lalāṭaṃ gataḥ | tathā cāha –

nābhau niṣyandatā proktā vipāko dharmacakrake |
sambho[K[k] 56*r*]ge puruṣakāro[55] vaimalyaṃ tu mahāsukhe ||

iti niyamo vakṣyamāṇe | evaṃ yathā pratipadādipañcadaśakalābhedenoṣṇīṣād[56] guhyakamale pūrṇākalāsvabhāvena gataṃ[57] saṃvṛtyādhoretasā[58] jñānacittam | tathā vajramaṇer uddhṛtaṃ yogabalena guhyakamalād vivṛtyā pratipadādikalābhedena sampūrṇākalāsvabhāvenordhvaretasā lalāṭakamale gatam, uṣṇīṣe ṣoḍaśīkalāsvabhāvena | evaṃ saṃsāriṇāṃ rajodhātuḥ kṛṣṇapratipadādibhedena guhyād uṣṇīṣaṃ gato 'māvāsyante ṣoḍaśīkalāhānibhedena ‖ sa eva buddhānāṃ vivṛtyoṣṇīṣāt kṛṣṇapratipadādikalābhedenāmāvāsyante ṣoḍaśīnaṣṭacandrakalābhedena guhyakamale gataḥ[59] |
tathā cāha saṃvṛtyādibuddhe –

adhaś candrāmṛtaṃ yāti maraṇe sarvadehinām |
ūrdhve sūryarajo rāhuvijñānaṃ bhāvalakṣaṇe[60] ‖ (SU 86)

ataś candrāmṛtasyordhve kartavyaṃ gamanaṃ nṛpa |
adho 'rkarajaso rāhuvijñānasyākṣare sukhe ‖[61] (SU 87)

<iti>[62] vivṛtyā | atra vakṣyamāṇe –

bodhicittaṃ bhavec candraḥ[63] pañcadaśakalātmakaḥ[64] |
ālirūpaṃ mahāsaukhyaṃ yoginyas tasya aṃśakāḥ ‖ (HT 2.4.29)

iti ṣo[K[k] 56*v*]ḍaśānandaniyamaḥ |
tathā kulapaṭale bhagavān āha –

yoginīnāṃ yathānyāyam utpattisthitikāraṇam |
sāmarthyaṃ jñānavijñānaṃ yoginīnāṃ[65] yathodayam ‖ (HT 1.1.9)

prathamaṃ tāvad bhaved evaṃ[66] herukotpattikāraṇam | (HT 1.1.10ab)
sahajānandamahāsaukhyam[67] evaṃkāraṃ mahākṣaram ‖[j] iti[68] |

nirvikalpe manasi

nāsti bhāvako na bhāvyo <'>sti[69] mantraṃ nāsti na devatā |
tiṣṭhete vidyete eva (*sic*)[70] mantradevau ca
[niṣprapañcasvabhāvataḥ ‖ (HT 1.5.11)

tenaiva sahajānandasvabhāvena pratyastamitasakalavikalpakalaṅkarūpeṇa[k] ‖

Commentary on HT 1.5.12-14ab

idānīṃ ṣaṭskandhānāṃ saṃvṛtivivṛtibheda ucyate **vairocane**tyādinā (cf. HT 1.5.12) | {i}ha vairocano bhūmicakre nāyakaḥ | akṣobhya ākāśacakre nāyakaḥ | amitābha udakacakre nāyakaḥ | ratnasambhavas tejaścakre nāyakaḥ |

amoghasiddhir vāyucakre nāyakaḥ[71] | sāttviko jñānacakre nāyakaḥ | [l] te ca yathāsaṅkhyaṃ

brahmā viṣṇuḥ śivaḥ sarvo vibuddhas tattvam ucyate | (HT 1.5.12cd) iti |

saṃvṛtyā sattvā adhoretasaḥ | vivṛtyā buddhā ūrdhvaretasaḥ | **brahmā nirvṛtito**[72] **buddha** iti (HT 1.5.13a) viḍḍhātor asrāvatvāt | **viśanād viṣṇur ucyata** iti (HT 1.5.13b) mūtradhātoḥ svaśarīre viśanād bāhye nirgamābhāvād buddho viṣṇur ucyate | **śivaḥ sadā sukalyāṇād** iti (HT 1.5.13c) kalyāṇam akhaṇḍaśīlam | śukracyavanābhāvād buddhaḥ śiva ucyate | **sarvaḥ sarvātmani sthita** iti (HT 1.5.13d) | sarvo ratnasambhavaḥ sa raktadhātus, tasya cyavanābhāvād duḥkhābhāvaḥ[73] | tadabhāvāt

sukhaduḥkhāntakṛnniṣṭhā vairāgyam upadhikṣayaḥ | (NS 8.20cd)[m] <iti>[74] |

sarvātmani sthita iti | divyacakṣuṣā paracittajñānavyāpakatvād[75] buddhaḥ sarva [K[k] 57*r*] ity ucyate | **vibuddho bodhanād ṛte** (cf. HT 1.5.14b)[76] cakṣurādīndriyabodhaṃ vinā | amoghasiddhir māṃsa<dhātuḥ>[77] | tasya[78] kṣayatvāt saṃskārābhāvaś cakṣurādīnām | tadabhāvād[79] vibuddhaḥ |

ātmavit paravit sarvaḥ sarvīyo hy agrapudgalaḥ |
lokopamām atikrānto jñeyo jñānādhipaḥ[80] paraḥ || (NS 10.13)[n] iti |

vibuddho bodhanād ṛte buddha iti niyamaḥ |
satsukhatvena tattvaṃ syād iti (cf. HT 1.5.14a) | satsukham anāśravaṃ śūnyatānimittāpraṇihitānabhisaṃskāracaturvimokṣaikalolībhūtaṃ karuṇāmaitrīmuditopekṣānirālambasvabhāvenālambitaṃ prajñopāyātmakaṃ tattvaṃ buddhatvam ity ucyate | evaṃ –

dvādaśākārasatyārthaḥ ṣoḍaśākāratattvavit |
viṃśatyākārasambodhir vibuddhaḥ paramārthavit[81] || (NS 9.15)[o]

iti buddho bhagavān | evam uktakrameṇa –

trikulaṃ pañcakulaṃ ca[82] svabhāvaikaṃ śataṃ kulam | [p] iti |

tathā nāmasaṅgītyām[83] –

krodharāṭ ṣaṇmukho bhīmaḥ ṣaṇnetraḥ[84] ṣaḍbhujo balī |
daṃṣṭrākarālaḥ[85] kaṅkālo halāhalaśatānanaḥ[86] || (NS 7.1)[q] iti |

tathā –

vajrajvālākarālākṣo vajrajvālāśiroruhaḥ |
vajrāveśo mahāveśaḥ śatākṣo vajralocanaḥ || (NS 7.7)[r]

iti śatakulaniyamaḥ |
evaṃ saṃvṛtivivṛti[K^k 57*v*]bhedena[87] laukikalokottaraṃ tattvam | sāvaraṇaṃ nirāvaraṇam | sanimittaṃ nirnimittam | savikalpaṃ nirvikalpam | āropitam anāropitam | sāhaṅkāraṃ nirahaṅkāram | sattvānāṃ buddhānām | dvādaśāṅgapratītyotpannaṃ dvādaśāṅganirodhenotpannam[88] | na ca vivṛtam iti sarvatantrāntare niyamo buddhasya bhagavato vidvadbhir veditavyaḥ ‖

Commentary on HT 1.5.14cd-15

idānīṃ punaḥ saṃvṛtidharmeṇa devatādikam ucyate **dehe sambhavatī**tyādinā (cf. HT 1.5.14c) | iha dehe pañcabhūtātmake[89] sambhavati yasmāt saṃvṛtisukhaṃ **tasmād devateti nigadyate** (cf. HT 1.5.14d) mayā |

bhago 'syāstīti buddhasya bhagavān tena[90] **kathyate** |
bhagāni ṣaḍvidhāny āhur aiśvaryādiguṇākhilāḥ ‖ (HT 1.5.15ad)

aiśvaryasya samagrasya jñānasya yaśasaḥ śriyaḥ |
saubhāgyasya[91] guṇasyāsya[92] bhagaśabdaḥ pragīyate ‖[s]

athavā kleśādimārāṇāṃ bhañjanād bhagavān iti | (HT 1.5.15ef)

vivṛtyā | ity upāyaniyamaḥ ‖

Commentary on HT 1.5.16-18

idānīṃ prajñocyate **jananī**tyādinā (cf. HT 1.5.16a) | ihopāyo janakaḥ śukradhātuḥ | prajñā jananī rajodhātuḥ | janyate karmaṇā adhiṣṭhitaṃ gandharvasattvaṃ maraṇāntikam upapattyaṃśikam ālayavijñānam | <tad eva>[93] jagacchabdenocyate | [K^k 58*r*] "vijñānamātraṃ traidhātukaṃ bho jinaputrā" iti bhagavato vacanāt | **jagat** tad eva | jagaj janayatīti prajñā jananī bhaṇyate rajodhātuḥ (cf. HT 1.5.16ab) | evam upāyaḥ śukradhātuḥ | saiva pra{jñā bha}ginī[94] bhaṇyate **vibhāgaṃ darśayed yataḥ**[95] (cf. HT 1.5.16cd) pratyekadhātu<vikāraṃ>[96] lomacarmamāṃsaraktam | evam upāyo bhrātā nāḍyasthimajjā**vibhāgaṃ darśayed yatas** tataḥ śukradhātuḥ | saiva **prajñā guṇasya duhanād duhitā** (cf. HT 1.5.18a) bhaṇyate | guṇaśabdena śabdasparśarasarūpagandhadharmadhātuviṣayāḥ[97] | teṣāṃ **duhanād** grahaṇād iti | evam upāyaḥ putraś cakṣurādīnāṃ pravṛttitvād upāyadhātuḥ | evaṃ bhāgineyikā prajñā viṣaye vijñānānāṃ pravṛttitvāt | upāyo bhrātṛputraś cakṣurādiṣu pravṛttitvād iti | evaṃ cyavanasukhapravṛttitvāt prajñā bhāryā ucyate | upāyo 'pi bhartā ucyate | parasparāpekṣikatvād ubhayoś cyutisaukhyadharmād iti | virāgāt prajñā**sparśā**ntajā ucyate | upāyo 'pīti ṣaṇmudrāniyamaḥ |

mohanāt sarvadhātūnāṃ brāhmaṇīti nigadyate |
rañjanād rajakī prajñā nartakī[98] cañcaladhātutaḥ ||

dahanāc caṇḍālinī [K^{k} 58*v*] khyātāsparśā<d>[99] ḍombinī smṛtā |
evam upāyo 'pi jñeyaḥ[100] pañcakṛtyasvabhāvataḥ ||[t]

evaṃ sarvaṃ bāhye, tasmāt prakalpyate tīrthikair vedādibhiḥ | svabhāvena sarvāḥ striyaḥ sarve puruṣā ekamānuṣajātisambhūtāḥ[101] | teṣām anyakulaṃ nāstīty[102] abhimataṃ sarvatantreṣu ||

Commentary on HT 1.5.19-21

idānīṃ dhātusvabhāvena mantrajāpādikam ucyate **jalpanam** ityādinā (cf. HT 1.5.19) | iha sarvasattvānāṃ **jalpanam ālikālyoḥ** svaravyañjanayor jalpanaṃ yatas tato[103] **jalpanaṃ jāpam ākhyātaṃ**[u] tattvayoginām (HT 1.5.19a) | evaṃ **maṇḍalaṃ** nāma pādayor[104] **lekhaḥ syāt** (cf. HT 1.5.19c) | pādābhyāṃ pṛthivī**malanān maṇḍalam ity ucyate** (HT 1.5.19d) | evaṃ

karasphoṭo bhaven mudrā aṅgulyāmoṭanaṃ tathā[105] | (HT 1.5.20ab)

evaṃ sattvānāṃ yac **cintitaṃ** tad eva **dhyeyaṃ** paracittajñānena yogināṃ iti | <**tad**>[106] **dhyeyaṃ yasmād vicintanam** iti (HT 1.5.20d) | [107] acintanaṃ dhyeyaṃ yoginā<ṃ> yataḥ | **pitari** viṣaye **yat prāptaṃ** maraṇāntikam[108] upapattyaṃśikaṃ sattvena sukhaṃ cyavanāvasthāyāṃ **tad** eva **sukhaṃ** ṣoḍaśavarṣāvadheḥ **svayaṃ bhujyate** puruṣeṇa[109] | striyā dvādaśavarṣāvadher bhujyate (cf. HT 1.5.21ab) | **maraṇaṃ yena sukhene**ha (cf. HT 1.5.21c) saṃsāriṇām utpādaś ca sthitiś ca saṃsāre, **tad** eva **sukhaṃ** cyavanāvasthāy<āṃ>[110] [K^{k} 59*v*[v]] sthirībhūtaṃ yogināṃ **dhyānam ucyate** (cf. HT 1.5.21d) ||

Conclusion

mayā vajragarbheṇedaṃ[111] sarvaṃ saṅkṣepeṇa pañcalakṣād dhevajrāt pratyekalakṣe madhye pratyekapaṭalapiṇḍārtho deśitaḥ pa{ñcapa}ṭaleṣu[112] | ata ūrdhvaṃ caryāpaṭalādikaṃ vistareṇāvaboddhavyam | kulapaṭale (HT 1.1) triṃśacchlokaiḥ piṇḍārthaḥ prathamalakṣāt | catvāriṃśacchlokair mantrapaṭale (HT 1.2) dvi{tī}yalakṣāt | caturviṃśatiślokair[113] devatāpaṭale (HT 1.3) tṛtīyalakṣāt | ṣaṭślokair abhiṣekapaṭale (HT 1.4) caturthalakṣāt | viṃśatiślokais tattvapaṭale (HT 1.5) pañcamalakṣā{t | } evaṃ viṃśatyadhikaśataślokaiḥ piṇḍārthaḥ pañcapaṭaleṣu yogibhir avagantavyo 'nayā ṭīkayā |

iti ṣaṭsāhasrikāyāṃ {heva}jraṭīkāyāṃ tattvanirdeśo mahoddeśaḥ | evaṃ tattvapaṭalapiṇḍārthaṭīkā samāpteti[114] || O ||

Notes to the Text

a. This stanza, which is frequently quoted (e.g., *Kriyāsamuccaya* p. 359, LTṬ p. 48), is commented on by Indrabhūti in chapter 15 of his *Jñānasiddhi*, pp. 134-35). Pāda a has a parallel in *Cittaviśuddhiprakaraṇa* 1a (cf. ed. pp. 15, 55).

b. The following passage (*svarūpaṃ* → *bhāvanīyam ity*) is quoted with slight differences by Nāropā in his SUṬ (ed. p. $175_{11\text{-}17}$; cf. Gnoli and Orofino 1994: 321-22).

c. Stanzas 4-14, which contain some hypermetrical verses (i.e., 5cd, 6ab, 9ab, 16cd), are also quoted with a few differences in the SUṬ (ed. pp. 190-91) where they are introduced with the words *yathā pañcalakṣābhidhāne*.

d. This verse is hypometrical.

e. This stanza is also quoted in Section Two, ed. Shendge, p. 16.

f. On this stanza, see above, Introduction.

g, This stanza is unmetrical in pāda e. See above, Introduction, note 9.

h. Cf. HT 1.5.3cd: *agupte kriyate duḥkhaṃ vyāḍacaurāgnibhūcaraiḥ*.

i. This verse appears with a slightly different wording in the printed edition of the *Cakrasaṃvaratantra*: *vicared dviguṇaṃ mantrī pūjayed* [MS *japed*] *ḍākinījālasaṃvaram* | 2.13ab (p. 32).

j. This verse does not appear in the printed editions of the HT.

k. The passage *nirvikalpe* → *°rūpeṇa* is also quoted in the SUṬ (ed. p. $174_{11\text{-}14}$).

l. The sentence *iha vairocano bhūmicakre* → *jñānacakre nāyakaḥ* is summarized by Vibhūticandra in the following way: *uktaṃ ca vajragarbh<eṇ>a "iha vairocano bhūmicakre nāyakaḥ | akṣobhya ākāśe | amitābha udake | ratnasambhavas tejasi | amoghasiddhir vāyau | vajrasattvo jñānacakre nāyaka" iti* (AKU ed. p. 130; Tokyo University Library, MS 18, fol. 16*r*$_{5\text{-}6}$).

m. Cf. AK pp. 68-69. This stanza is also quoted in the PAJS (p. 78).

n. Cf. AK p. 93. This stanza is also quoted in the PAJS, where it is listed as number 10.16 (p. 78).

o. Cf. AK p. 85.

p. Verse often quoted, cf. VP (vol. 1: 50; vol. 2: 126).

q. Cf. AK p. 49.

r. Cf. AK pp. 51-52.

s. See above, Introduction.

t. Cf. HT 1.5.17-18.

u. Cf. GS 18.74c.

v. K^{k} 59*r* (perhaps originally unwritten), which is almost corrupt and illegible, contains apparently the beginning of another text. The *ductus* reveals the hand of another copyist. It begins with the words: *namo cakrasaṃvarāya* | *divyajñānaṃ kathaṃ tatra*, etc.

Variant Readings

[1] *athātas* K^{k}] *atha* E. [2] *svarūpaṃ* K^{k}] *rūpaṃ* T (*ṅo bo*). [3] *svarūpeṇa* K^{k}] *rūpeṇa* T. [4] T has also *mig med* (= **na cakṣur*). [5] *na śabdo na śrotā* SUṬ (cf. also the

parallelism with the other similar sentences in the passage)] *na śrotā na śabdo* K^{k}. [6] *sparṣṭā* K^{k}] *spraṣṭā* E (ep). [7] *evaṃ* has been later added on the margin in K^{k}. [8] °*vikāra*° SUṬ] *deest* in K^{k} T (ep). [9] °*rūpa*° K^{kpc}] °*rūpasya* K^{kac}. [10] *sarvayoginām* K^{k} T] *sarvadehinām* SUṬ (ep). [11] *vikalpanātra* em. (ISAACSON)] *kalpanātra* K^{kpc}; *kalpanā yatra* (or *kalpanā etra*) K^{kac}; no rendering of *atra* in T; cf. also *Catuḥśataka* 5.5, *Jñānasiddhi* 9.34. [12] °*nirmāṇāni* em.] °*nirmāṇāna* K^{k}. [13] °*anyaḥ* K^{kpc}] *anya* K^{kac}. [14] *cānyaḥ* em.] *cānyad* K^{k}. [15] °*pādādyaṃ* em.] °*pādyādyaṃ* K^{k}. [16] See also Translation, note 5. [17] *bāhye* em.] *bāhya*° K^{k}. [18] *yogavit* K^{k}] **tattvavatsalaḥ* T (*de ñid rig pas*); cf. HT 1.5.2f. [19] *sevitavyāḥ* K^{kpc}] *sevitavyā* K^{kac}. [20] *yathā* K^{kpc}] *yathā bāhya*° K^{kac}. [21] °*hāsaḥ* conj. T (*smod pa*)] °*rāgaḥ* K^{k}. [22] T has here **yoginā* (*rnal 'byor pas*). [23] *mudrāḥ* em.] *mudrā* K^{k}. [24] °*oktā* em.] °*oktaṃ* K^{k}. [25] °*dhātuḥ* K^{kpc}] °*dhātu* K^{kac}. [26] °*guṇo* K^{k}] *°*mukhyaguṇo* T (*gtso bo'i yon tan*). [27] *mukhyaḥ* K^{kpc}] *mukhya*° K^{kac}. [28] *mukhyo* T (*gtso bo ni*). [29] *jñānadhātu*° T (*ye śes kyi khams kyi* [...])] *jñāna*° K^{k}. [30] °*vedanāḥ* K^{kpc}] °*vedanā* K^{kac}. [31] °*rūpāṇi* em.] °*rūpāṇiḥ* K^{k}. [32] *skandhadhātavo* em.] *dhātuskandhadhātavo* K^{k}; **bhūtaskandhadhātavo* T. [33] *tā* conj.] *te* K^{k}. [34] *trikulasya* T (*rigs gsum ste*)] *kulasya* K^{k}. [35] °*citta*° em.] °*cittāṃ* K^{k} ◊ °*saṃvaraṃ* em.] °*saṃvaraṃ* K^{k}. [36] *dviguṇasya* conj.] *dviguṇaṃ* K^{k}. [37] *ṣaṭcakrasaṃvaraḥ* em.] *ṣaṭcakraṃ saṃvaraṃ* K^{k}. [38] *pāda*° em.] *pada*° K^{k}. [39] *japen* K^{k}] **pūjayen* T (*mchod*). [40] *ekaikasyāś* em.] *ekaikasya* K^{k}. [41] *anyāḥ* K^{kpc}] *anyā* K^{kac}. [42] *dviguṇaḥ ṣaṇ*° conj.] *dviguṇaś ca* K^{k}; *deest* in T. [43] °*sita*° em.] °*sitā*° K^{k}. [44] °*pīta*° K^{kpc}] °*pītavaktra*° K^{kac}. [45] °*parvāṇi* conj.] °*parva*° K^{k}. [46] T has here **iti* (*źes pa'o*). [47] °*śirobhiś* T] °*dharmaśirobhiś* K^{k}. [48] °*tantrāntare* em.] °*tantrānte* K^{k}. [49] °*bhedanaiḥ* K^{k}] °*bhedena* E (however, cf. E p. 16, MS A reads °*bhedanaiḥ*). [50] *'nena* em.] *'neneti* K^{k} (*contra metrum*). [51] *tathāgatalakṣaṇaṃ* em.] *tathāgataṃ lakṣaṇaṃ* K^{k}. [52] K^{k} inserts a *daṇḍa*. [53] In T the position of *tejo* (*me*) and *pṛthivī* (*sa*) is inverted; °*dhātu*° *deest*. [54] °*bhedena gato* em.] °*bhedenāgato* K^{k}. [55] *puruṣakāro* em.] *puruṣakāraś ca* K^{k} (*contra metrum*). [56] °*pañca*° K^{kpc}] °*pañcapañca*° K^{kac}. [57] °*bhāvena gataṃ* em.] °*bhāvenāgataṃ* K^{k}. [58] °*retasā* T (*khu bas*)] *cetasā* K^{k}. [59] *gataḥ* em.] *gatāḥ* K^{k}. [60] °*lakṣaṇe* SU (ed. GNOLI) *Kalparājatantra* (fol. 53$r_{2\text{-}3}$)] °*lakṣaṇaṃ* K^{k}. [61] T corresponds to Text A of the edition by OROFINO (p. 82). [62] *iti* T (*źes so*)] *deest* in K^{k}. [63] *candraḥ* K^{k}] *candraṃ* E (p. 64). [64] °*ātmakaḥ* K^{k}] °*ātmakaṃ* E (p. 64). [65] *yoginīnāṃ* K^{k}] *devatānāṃ* E (p. 2) T. [66] *evaṃ* T cf. also K^{k} Section Three] *ekaṃ* E K^{k}. [67] This pāda is hypermetric. [68] *iti* K^{k}] **iti niyamaḥ* T (*źes pa ṅes pa'o*). [69] Pāda a is hypermetric. [70] *tiṣṭhete vidyete eva* K^{k}] *saṃsthitau* E (p. 16). [71] From *nāyaka* till the end of folio 56*v* the *ductus* is different. [72] *nirvṛtito* E (p. 16)] *nivartito* K^{k}. [73] *duḥkhā*° em.] *dukhā*° K^{k}. [74] *iti* T (*źes pa'o*)] *deest* in K^{k}. [75] *sarvavyāpakatvāt* T (*thams cad la* [...]). [76] *bodhanād ṛte* K^{k}] T has the following sentence: *thams cad ces par brjod par bya'o* | *rtogs pa med pas rnam sad do* |. [77] *māṃsadhātuḥ* conj. based on T (*śa'i khams te*)] *māṃsaṃ* K^{k} (ep). [78] *tasya* em.] *tasyā* K^{k}. [79] *tadabhāvād* T (*de med pa'i phyir*)] *tadbhāvād* K^{k}. [80] *jñānādhipaḥ* NS AK] *jñeyādhipaḥ* K^{k}. [81] *paramārthavit* K^{k}] *sarvavit paraḥ* NS AK (ep). [82] *ca* em.] *caiva* K^{k} (*contra metrum*). [83] T has here *brjod par* (**āha*). [84] °*netraḥ* K^{kpc}] °*netra*° K^{kac}. [85] °*karālaḥ* em.] °*karāla*° K^{k}. [86] °*halāhala*° em.] °*halāhalaḥ* K^{k}. [87] *saṃvṛtivivṛti*° em.] *saṃvṛtivivṛtivivṛti*°

K^{k}. [88] °*nirodhena* em.] °*norodhana* K^{kac}. [89] °*ātmake* em.] °*ātmaka* K^{k}. [90] *tena* K^{k}] *iti* E. [91] *saubhāgyasya* em.] *saubhāgasya* K^{k}. [92] *guṇasyāsya* K^{k}] **guṇasyaiva* T (*yon tan ñid*) (ep). [93] *tad eva* T (*de kho na*)] K^{k} is completely erased. [94] *bhaginī* T (*sriṅ mor*). [95] *yataḥ* K^{k} T (*gaṅ phyir*)] *yathā* E (p. 16). [96] *vikāraṃ* is erased in K^{k}. [97] °*dhātu*° K^{k}] *deest* in T. [98] *nartakī* em.] *nartaṭī* K^{k}. [99] T has *reg min phyir*. [100] *'pi jñeyaḥ* T (*kyaṅ śes par bya ste*)] *vijñeyaḥ* K^{k}. [101] °*sambhūtāḥ* em.] °*saṃbhūtāvaḥ* K^{k} (the *visarga* is not clearly readable). [102] *nāstīti* T] *asti* | *iti* K^{k}. [103] *yatas tato* em.] *yatato* K^{k}. [104] The *akṣara yor* of *pādayor* is quite unreadable in K^{k}. [105] *tathā* E (p. 18)] *yataḥ* K^{kpc} T (*gaṅ yin pa*); *yata* K^{kac}. [106] *tad* conj.] *deest* in K^{k}. [107] T has here *bsam bral źes pa*. [108] *maraṇāntikaṃ* em.] *māraṇāntikād dhātur* K^{k}. [109] *puruṣeṇa* K^{k}] *deest* in T. [110] *cyavanāvasthāyāṃ* K^{k}] *deest* in T. [111] *vajragarbheṇa* conj.] *he vajragarbha* K^{k}; *hevajragarbheṇa* T (*kye'i rdo rje'i sñiṅ po bdag gis*). [112] *pañcapaṭaleṣu* T (*le'u lṅa pa rnams su'o*). [113] °*ślokair* K^{k}] *deest* in T. [114] *evaṃ tattvapaṭalapiṇḍārthaṭīkā samāpteti* K^{k}] **evaṃ tattvapaṭalaḥ samāpta iti* ‖ *śrīhevajrapiṇḍārthaṭīkā samāpteti* T (*de ltar de kho na ñid kyi le'u rdzogs so* ‖ *dpal kye'i rdo rje bsdus pa'i don kyi 'grel pa rdzogs so*).

Abbreviations

Sigla

CIHTS	Central Institute for Higher Tibetan Studies
IsIAO	Istituto Italiano per l'Africa e l'Oriente
NAK	National Archives, Kathmandu
NGMPP	Nepal-German Manuscript Preservation Project
SOR	Serie Orientale Roma

ac	*ante correctionem*
conj.	conjecture
deest	omitted/absent in
E	*editio princeps* of the HT
em.	emendation
pc	*post correctionem*
r	*recto*
v	*verso*
T	Tibetan translation
(ep)	equally possible
*	before Sanskrit words means that these have been retranslated from Tibetan
]	separates the accepted reading from the variants
◊	separates the commentary on different lemmas within the same compound
(. . .)	enclose numbers and bibliographical references (not present in the MS)
<. . .>	enclose words or syllables retranslated from Tibetan

[. . .] enclose the pagination (i.e., numbers of folios)
{. . .} enclose parts that are broken in K[k] and that have been retranslated on the basis of T
†. . .† *cruces desperationis*
bold stanzas of the *Hevajratantra, words of the mūla text,* and *pratīka*s

Bibliography

Primary Sources

Amṛtakaṇikā of Raviśrījñāna.
(AK) (1) *Āryamañjuśrīnāmasaṅgīti with Amṛtakaṇikāṭippaṇī by Bhikṣu Raviśrījñāna and Amṛtakaṇikodyotanibandha of Vibhūticandra.* Edited by Banarsi Lal. Bibliotheca Indo-Tibetica 30. Sarnath, Varanasi: CIHTS, 1994.
(2) See also Merzagora *2006.
Amṛtakaṇikoddyota of Vibhūticandra.
(AKU) See *Amṛtakaṇikā.*
Bhagavadgītā.
The Bhagavadgītā with Eleven Commentaries. First Collection. Critically edited and revised by Shastri Gajanana Shambhu Sadhale. Bombay, 1938.
Cakrasaṃvaratantra.
Śrīherukābhidhānam Cakrasaṃvaratantram with the Vivṛti Commentary of Bhavabhaṭṭa. Edited by J. S. Pandey. Rare Buddhist Texts Series 26. 2 vols. Sarnath, Varanasi: CIHTS, 2002.
Caṇḍamahāroṣaṇatantra.
The Caṇḍamahāroṣaṇa Tantra, Chapters I-VIII. Critical edition and English translation by Ch. S. George. American Oriental Series 56. New Haven, Conn.: American Oriental Society, 1974.
Cittaviśuddhiprakaraṇa of Āryadeva.
Cittaviśuddhiprakaraṇa of Āryadeva. Sanskrit and Tibetan Texts. Edited by Prabhubhai Bhikhabhai Patel. Visva-Bharati Studies No. 8. Visva-Bharati, 1949.
Ḍākinījālasaṃvararahasya of Anaṅgayogī.
Ḍākinījālasaṃvararahasya by Anaṅgayogī. Edited by Samdhong Rinpoche and Vrajvallabh Dwivedi. Rare Buddhist Text Series 8. Sarnath, Varanasi: CIHTS, 1990.
Daśabhūmikasūtra.
Daśabhūmikasūtra. Edited by P. L. Vaidya. Buddhist Sanskrit Texts No. 7. Darbhanga, 1967.
Dīgha Nikāya.
The Dīgha Nikāya. Edited by T. W. Rhys Davids and J. E. Carpenter. 3 vols. Oxford: The Pali Text Society, 1889-1911 (reprint 1992-1995).
Guhyādi-Aṣṭasiddhi-Saṃgraha.
Guhyādi-Aṣṭasiddhi-Saṃgraha. Sanskrit and Tibetan text, edited by Samdhong Rinpoche and Vrajvallabh Dwivedi. Rare Buddhist Text Series 1. Sarnath, Varanasi: CIHTS, 1987.

Guhyasamājatantra.
(GS) *The Guhyasamāja Tantra*. A new critical edition by Y. Matsunaga. Osaka: Toho Shuppan, inc., 1978.
Hevajratantra.
(HT) *The Hevajra Tantra: A Critical Study*. Edited by David L. Snellgrove. Part 1, Introduction and Translation; Part 2, Sanskrit and Tibetan Texts. London Oriental Series 6. London: Oxford University Press, 1959.
Hevajraṭippaṇa.
MS preserved on negative at the K. Jayaswal Research Institute, Patna. See Sāṅkṛtyāyana 1935.
Jñānasiddhi of Indrabhūti.
See *Guhyādi-Aṣṭasiddhi-Saṃgraha*: Sanskrit text, pp. 89-157, Tibetan translation, pp. 147-244.
Kalparāja[tantra].
Kalparāja. Roma: IsIAO, MS FGT V/1, 263.
Kriyāsamuccaya.
Kriyā-samuccaya. A Sanskrit Manuscript from Nepal Containing a Collection of Tantric Ritual by Jagaddarpaṇa. Reproduced by Lokesh Chandra. Śata-piṭaka Series, vol. 237. New Delhi: International Academy of Indian Culture, 1977.
Laghukālacakratantra.
(LKCT) (1) Critical edition by B. Banerjee. Bibliotheca Indica. Calcutta: The Asiatic Society, 1985.
(2) Edited by Raghu Vira and Lokesh Chandra in *Kālacakra-Tantra and Other Texts: Part 1*. Śata-piṭaka Series 69. New Delhi: International Academy of Indian Culture, 1966, 53-378.
Laghutantraṭīkā of Vajrapāṇi.
(LTṬ) *The Laghutantraṭīkā by Vajrapāṇi*. Critical edition by Claudio Cicuzza. SOR 86. Roma: IsIAO, 2001.
Majjhima Nikāya.
The Majjhima Nikāya. Edited by V. Trenckner and R. Chalmers. 3 vols. Oxford: The Pali Text Society, 1888-1899 (reprint 1993-1994).
Mañjuśrīnāmasaṅgīti.
(NS) See *Amṛtakaṇikā*.
Muktāvalī of Ratnākaraśānti.
Hevajratantram with Muktāvalī Pañjikā of Mahāpaṇḍitācārya Ratnākaraśānti. Edited by Ram Shankar Tripathi, Thakur Sain Negi. Sarnath, Varanasi: CIHTS, 2001.
Paramākṣarajñānasiddhi of Puṇḍarīka.
(PAJS) See *Vimalaprabhā*, vol. 3, 60-103.
See also Gnoli 1997.
Pratītyasamutpādahṛdayakārikā of Nāgārjuna.
(1) Edited by V. V. Gokhale in *Festschrift für Willibald Kirfel*. Bonn, 1955, pp. 101-106.
(2) Edited by Chr. Lindtner in *Nagarjuniana. Studies in the Writings and Philosophy of Nāgārjuna*. København, 1982, pp. 170-171.
Ṣaḍaṅgayoga of Anupamarakṣita.
The Ṣaḍaṅgayoga by Anupamarakṣita with Raviśrījñāna's Guṇabharaṇīnāmaṣaḍaṅgayogaṭippaṇī. Text and annotated translation by Francesco Sferra. SOR 85. Roma: IsIAO, 2000.

Samājottara.
See *Guhyasamājatantra*, chapter 18.
Ṣaṭsāhasrikā (aka *Hevajratantrapiṇḍārthaṭīkā*) of Vajragarbha.
(HTPṬ) (1) *Ṣaṭ-Sāhasrikā-Hevajraṭīkā.* Critical edition by Malati J. Shendge. Delhi, 2004.
(2) *The* Ṣaṭsāhasrikā *by Vajragarbha. A Commentary on the Condensed Meaning of the* Hevajratantra. Critical edition and translation by Francesco Sferra (forthcoming from Firenze University Press).
Sekoddeśa.
(1) R. Gnoli, "*Sekoddeśaḥ* [Edition of the Sanskrit Text]." In *Dhīḥ. Journal of Rare Buddhist Texts Research Project* 28 (1999), 143-166.
(2) *Sekoddeśa.* Critical edition of the Tibetan translation by Giacomella Orofino. With an appendix by Raniero Gnoli, "On the Sanskrit Text." SOR 72. Roma: Istituto Italiano per il Medio ed Estremo Oriente, 1994.
Sekoddeśapañjikā.
The results of a joint study on the Buddhist Tantric texts, Taisho University. *Annual of the Institute for Comprehensive Studies of Buddhism* 16 (1994), 289-354.
Sekoddeśaṭīkā of Nāropā.
(SUṬ) *The Sekoddeśaṭīkā by Nāropā (Paramārthasaṃgraha).* Critical edition of the Sanskrit text by Francesco Sferra and critical edition of the Tibetan translation by Stefania Merzagora. SOR 99. Roma: IsIAO, 2006. See also Gnoli and Orofino 1994.
Subhāṣitasaṅgraha.
"Subhāṣitasaṅgraha." Edited by Cecil Bendall. In *Le Muséon*, N.S., 4-5 (1903-1904), 375-402; 5-46; 245-74.
Tantrāloka of Abhinavagupta.
The *Tantrāloka of Abhinava Gupta.* With commentary by Rājānaka Jayaratha. Edited by Madhusūdan Kaul Śāstrī. Kashmir Series of Texts and Studies 23, 28, 30, 36, 35, 29, 41, 47, 59, 52, 57 and 58. Bombay and Srinagar, 1918-38.
Udāna.
Udāna. Edited by P. Steinthal. Oxford: The Pali Text Society, 1885 (reprint 1982).
Vimalaprabhā of Puṇḍarīka.
(VP) *Vimalaprabhāṭīkā of Kalkin Śrīpuṇḍarīka on Śrīlaghukālacakratantrarāja by Śrīmañjuśrīyaśas.* Vol. 1, critically edited and annotated with notes by J. Upadhyāya. Bibliotheca Indo-Tibetica Series 11. Sarnath, Varanasi: CIHTS, 1986; Vol. 2, critically edited and annotated with notes by Vrajvallabh Dwivedi and S. S. Bahulkar. Rare Buddhist Text Series 12. Sarnath, Varanasi: CIHTS, 1994; Vol. 3, critically edited and annotated with notes by Vrajvallabh Dwivedi and S. S. Bahulkar. Rare Buddhist Text Series 13. Sarnath, Varanasi: CIHTS, 1994.
Yogaratnamālā of Kāṇha (*alias* Kṛṣṇācārya).
See Snellgrove 1959, vol. 2: 103-59, and Farrow and Menon 1992.

Secondary Sources

Banerjee, Biswanath.
1971. "Pratītyasamutpāda as Viewed by the Kālacakra School." *Journal of the Ganganatha Jha Kendriya Sanskrit Vidyapeetha* 27.3-4 (*Kshetresa Chandra Chattopadhyaya Felicitation Volume*, Pt. 1) 29-33.

Cicuzza, Claudio and Francesco Sferra.

1997. "Brief Notes on the Beginning of the Kālacakra Literature." *Dhīḥ. Journal of Rare Buddhist Texts Research Project* 23: 113-126.

Dhargyey, Geshe Lharampa Ngawang.

1985. *A Commentary on the Kālacakra Tantra*. Translated by Gelong Jhampa Kelsang (Alan Wallace). Dharamsala: Library of Tibetan Works and Archives.

Edgerton, Franklin E.

1970.[2] *Buddhist Hybrid Sanskrit Grammar and Dictionary*. 2 vols. New Delhi: Motilal Banarsidass, [New Haven, 1953[1]].

Farrow, G. W. and I. Menon, trans. and eds.

1992. *The Concealed Essence of the Hevajra Tantra. With the Commentary Yogaratnamālā.* New Delhi: Motilal Banarsidass.

Gnoli, Raniero.

1997. *La realizzazione della conoscenza del Supremo immoto (Paramākṣarajñānasiddhi). Supplemento No. 1 alla Rivista degli Studi Orientali* 70. Roma.

Gnoli, Raniero and Giacomella Orofino.

1994. *Nāropā, Iniziazione (Kālacakra),* a cura di. Biblioteca Orientale 1. Milano: Adelphi.

Isaacson, Harunaga.

2001. "Ratnākaraśānti's *Hevajrasahajasadyoga* (Studies in Ratnākaraśānti's Tantric Works I)." In Raffaele Torella. ed. *Le parole e i marmi. Studi in onore di Raniero Gnoli nel suo 70° compleanno*. SOR 92.1-2. Roma: IsIAO, 457-487.

Kvaerne, Per.

1977. *An Anthology of Buddhist Tantric Songs. A Study of the Caryāgiti*. Oslo.

Lal, Jī.

1989. "bauddha granthoṃ meṃ 'bhagavān' śabda kī vyākhyā." *Dhīḥ. A Review of Rare Buddhist Texts* 7: 67-70.

Lamotte, Étienne.

1944. *Le traité de la grande vertu de sagesse de Nāgārjuna (Mahāprajñāpāramitāśāstra)*. Tome I, Louvain.

Merzagora, Stefania.

*2006. "'The Drop of Ambrosia.' Critical edition and translation of the *Amṛtakaṇikā* by Raviśrījñāna." Ph.D. dissertation, Università degli Studi di Napoli "L'Orientale."

Newman, John R.

1987. "The Outer Wheel of Time: Vajrayāna Buddhist Cosmology in the Kālacakra tantra." Ph.D. dissertation, University of Wisconsin.

Sāṅkṛtyāyana, Rahula.

1935. "Sanskrit Palm-Leaf MSS in Tibet." *The Journal of the Bihar and Orissa Research Society* 21: 21-43.

Sferra, Francesco.

2005. "Constructing the Wheel of Time. Strategies for establishing a tradition." In Federico Squarcini, ed. *Boundaries, Dynamics and Construction of Traditions in South Asia*. Firenze: Firenze University Press and New Delhi: Munshiram Manoharlal, pp. 253-285.

Steinkellner, Ernst.

2004. *A Tale of Leaves. On Sanskrit Manuscripts in Tibet, Their Past and Their Future.* Gonda Lecture, Royal Netherlands Academy of Arts and Sciences, Amsterdam, 2003.

–5–

"Like a Buddha Jewel-Casket Thrown Open": Selected Excerpts from Dge 'dun rgya mtsho's Mtshan yang dag par brjod pa'i rgya cher bshad pa rdo rje'i rnal 'byor gyi de kho na nyid snang bar byed pa'i nyi ma chen po (The Great Sun Illuminating the Reality of Vajra Yoga: An Extensive Explanation of The Ultimate Names of Mañjuśrī)

Laura Harrington

Introduction

Gendun Gyatso (Dge 'dun rgya mtsho) was twenty-seven years old when he composed his Kālacakra-based *Great Sun* commentary to the *Mañjuśrī Nāmasaṃgīti* (Tib. *'jam dpal mtshan brjod*) at the Chogyal Tsentse (Phyogs rgyal mtshan rtse) hermitage in 1503. Fully ordained as a monk from the Drepung ('Bras spungs) Monastery seven years earlier, Gendun Gyatso had just completed an intensive study of Kālacakra treatises under the great master Kaydrub Norzang-gyatso (mKhas-grub Nor-bzang rgya-mtsho) and three years of retreats and pilgrimages in south-western Tibet. The young scholar was conducting a teaching retreat in Yarlung when he wrote the *Great Sun*.

Though he is best known today as the (retroactively designated) Second Dalai Lama, Gendun Gyatso was, at the time of its composition, renowned as one of the most brilliant young monk-scholars of the newly formed Gelug (Dge lugs) tradition. In the subsequent two decades, he would serve as the abbot of the three most influential Dge lugs monasteries in Central Tibet: Tashilhunpo (Bkra shis lhun po), Drepung ('Bras spungs), and Sera (Se ra). He would subsequently found a number of temples and monasteries, most famously the Ganden Pograng (Dga' ldan pho brang) and the Chokhorgyal (Chos 'khor rgyal) Monastery near the Lhama Lhatso Lake (Lha mo' bla mtsho), and would develop a broad network of patrons for the

Gelug school that stretched from the western areas of Ngari, Guge, and Mustang to the borders of Kham in the east.[1]

Gendun Gyatso would also have been renowned as the first formally recognized reincarnated lama, or *tulku* (sprul sku), in Gelug history. The practice of transmitting religious authority on the basis of a reincarnation lineage was, as is well known, first practiced by the Kagyu (Bka' brgyud) tradition in the early thirteenth century and was gradually adopted by virtually all Tibetan Buddhist schools. At the time of Gendun Gyatso's birth, however, it was pointedly absent from the Gelug tradition, which selected its leaders on the basis of their scholarly and spiritual achievement. What circumstances brought the young scholar to such prominence?

Born in Tanak Dorjedan (Rta nags rdo rje gdan) in 1475, Gendun Gyatso had come to maturity in a deeply troubled period in the history of Tsang and the Gelug tradition. Since the early fifteenth century, Tsang had been primarily a Gelug region; the Tashilhunpo Monastery and its core patrons, the Pakmodrupa (Phag mo gru pa) hierarchy, tacitly dominated Tsang's religious *cum* political landscape. By the time of Gendun Gyatso's birth, however, rivalry between the Pakmodrupa and the Rinpungpa (Rin spungs pa) princes had bred sharp sectarian antagonism and political instability in the region. Determined to uproot the Pakmodrupa and establish their own power base in Lhasa, the Rinpungpa had allied themselves with the Karma Kagyu (Karma bka' brgyud) school and in 1480—when Gendun Gyatso was six years old—had sent troops towards Central Tibet. By 1498, these Kagyu allies formally occupied the region of Lhasa, where they took immediate steps to secure their hold by suppressing the Gelugpa centers of Drepung and Sera—bastions of Pakmodrupa supporters.[2] The Gelug recognition of Gendun Gyatso as the reincarnated successor of Gendun Drub (Dge 'dun grub pa), the charismatic founder of the Tashilhunpo Monastery, arguably imparted much-needed prestige to the besieged Gelugpa establishment, though it was not immediately accepted by all his Gelug contemporaries.[3]

These tensions were the backdrop of the years preceding his composition of the *Great Sun*, though we find in it little direct reference to these concerns. His *Autobiography,* however, leaves us in little doubt of the authenticity of his reincarnation status. We learn that in the Year of the Fire Monkey (1475), Gendun Gyatso emerged painlessly from the womb of his mother, Kunga Palmo (Kun dga' dpal mo), the reincarnation of the *dākinī* and consort of Gotsangpa (Rgod tshang pa), a famous Kagyu teacher. His birth was, he notes, accompanied by various signs and auspicious events, including one related to the Kālacakra tradition:

> At the moment of birth, just after my mother dreamed again, a voice said, "Only one son will be born to you. Give him the name 'Sanggye Pel' (Sangs rgyas 'phel). This will be a sign linking him to the Buddha of the past, present, and future." Thus I had this name until my ordination as a monk. Also around this time, my mother dreamt of a large shrine where my father had

engaged excellent painters to paint the Kālacakra *maṇḍala* and just then they finished the final strokes with perfection.[4]

His father, Kunga Gyaltsen (Kun dga' rgyal mtshan), was a well-known Nyingma lama who—as Gendun Gyatso is careful to emphasize—traced his roots back to a chaplain of the Samye Monastery at the time of King Trisong Detsen (Khri srong lde'u btsan). Kunga Gyaltsen was a learned and highly accomplished practitioner and gave his precocious young son initiations and teachings in a wide range of Tantric traditions.[5]

Gendun Gyatso's *Autobiography* tells us that when he was five, he gave indications of remembering his previous birth as Gendun Drub (Dge 'dun grub pa), which brought him recognition by local community members. "I told them quite clearly, according to the memory of my previous life, my mother's name, and my own name Pema Dorje . . . I said this and more . . . At this time in Tanak, it started to be known that the birth of Gendun Drub was in Tanak."[6] This realization was not, apparently, immediately shared by the monastic authorities of Tashilhunpo; it was not until 1485, when he was ten years old, that he was invited to join Tashilhunpo and given some recognition as a *getsul* (dge tshul), "novice," and not until almost a decade later, when he was almost twenty, that he was fully acknowledged as Gendun Drub's successor.

We learn from a later hagiography that the young *tulku* continued in his studies of Tantra and the monastic curriculum of Tashilhunpo over the next half decade. It seems he was not, however, fully accepted as Gendun Drub's successor by all of his monastic *confrères*. In his late teens, therefore, he moved to the Drepung Monastery to continue his studies. His training was rigorous and wide ranging and included a close study of Gyaltseb-je Darma Rinchen's (Rgyal tshab rje dar ma rin chen) treatises on the *Kālacakra Tantra*. On the day of the half moon in the second month of the Hare Year (1495), Gyalwa Gendun Gyatso took on the precepts of a fully ordained monk. He was just twenty years old. Soon thereafter, he traveled to the Olkha Valley where he conducted an intensive study of the *Kālacakra Tantra* and its commentaries with Kaydrub Norzang Gyatso—an accomplished Kālacakra adept who would become one of his primary teachers.[7]

His tutelage unarguably enriched and informed Gendun Gyatso's composition of the *Kālacakra*-centric *Great Sun* commentary three years later. Approximately 160 folios in length, *The Great Sun Illuminating the Reality of Vajra Yoga: An Extensive Explanation of The Recitation of the Names of Mañjuśrī* (*Mtshan yang dag par brjod pa'i rgya cher bshad pa rdo rje'i rnal 'byor gyi de kho na nyid snang bar byed pa'i nyi ma chen po*) is an unsung landmark in Kālacakra literature. Clarifying points of doubt about its Creation Stage practice, explicating *sādhanas* for practical use, articulating the finer points of hermeneutical strategies for Tantric texts—the *Great Sun* exemplifies the breadth of scholarly and spiritual mastery that made Gendun Gyatso so revered a figure in his time. Its core textual focus is, of course, the *Mañjuśrī Nāmasaṃgīti*: a late seventh- or early eighth-century Indian text which is, as its title suggests, comprised of multiple epithets of

Mañjuśrī, the bodhisattva of wisdom. In India from the eighth through the twelfth centuries, the *Mañjuśrī Nāmasaṃgīti* became the focus of cult worship by Indian Buddhist monastics, *tantrikas*, and laypeople alike; it emerged as the subject of twenty-two commentaries and approximately 130 related works. The same may be said of its status in Tibetan culture. Translated into Tibetan in the eleventh century by Rinchen Zangpo (Rin chen bzang po) and revised in the thirteenth century by Lodro Tenpa (bLo gros brtan pa), the hundred-plus *Mañjuśrī Nāmasaṃgīti*-centric works in the Derge (Sde dge) canon underscore its importance. To this day, the *Nāmasaṃgīti* is routinely recited by monks and Tibetan schoolchildren intent on bolstering their memories and academic performance.

Its popularity in Tibet was also linked to its identification with the Kālacakra tradition. The core commentary to the *Kālacakra Tantra*, the *Vimalaprabhā*,[8] cites almost seventy verses from the *Mañjuśrī Nāmasaṃgīti* in order to "explain or substantiate the *Kālacakratantra's* views of Buddhahood and the path of actualizing it."[9] In the segments that follow here, we catch a glimpse of Gendun Gyatso's celebration of the intimacy of the *Kālacakra* with the *Nāmasaṃgīti* and of the tremendous transformative power of enacting their fusion: like "a Buddha jewel-casket thrown open," it is, he tells us, the path that grants the exaltation of Vajradhara in a single lifetime.

Note: My translation from the Tibetan draws from the edition published by the Shes rig dpar khang Tibetan Cultural Printing Press, Dharamsala, 1989. The *Great Sun* is also found in Volume 1 (ja., 141 ff.) of Gendun Gyatso's three-volume collected works (gsung 'bum) in the Potala collection.

Introduction: (1-2b)

I pay homage at all times to the holy Primal Buddha Mañjughoṣa. I bow to the one whose mind, the light rays of a thousand suns of the great wisdom of supreme unchanging great bliss, truly embraces in bliss the maiden of space, the aspectless *dharmadhātu*, liberated from the watery bondage of the incidental defilements, the joyous companion with a wisdom body, the very sun of the true meaning, that glorious king, Mañjuśrī Jñānasattva.

I salute the Śākya lion, the guru of the three states of existence, the Primal Buddha who taught all Tantras with his omnifaceted speech in the immeasurable mansion of the glorious Drepung.[10] As if filled [by a rain of] flowers and robes, his toenail reflects a river of the taintless coiffures of the entire host of deities and *siddhas*—the totally pure retinue of the Abhirati [Heaven]; like the hundred sounds embraced by a net of earth-protectors. I bow to those who commented on the meaning of the Tantra: the Lord of Secrets who compresses all secrets, the two noble ones, the great *siddha* Anupamarakṣita[11] and the glorious Raviśrījñāna,[12] who elucidate the essential meaning. I bow with humility to the glorious Tsong kha pa, the actuality of all Victors, who definitively abandoned errors in regard to the keys of the path of all discourses, particularly the Tantras, and his sons. The

Mañjuśrī Paramārtha Nāma Saṃgīti is the crown [jewel] of all the nondual Tantras, difficult to fathom by even the most intelligent of the Victor's sons. Here, I will explain its intended meaning—the vital point of the path of Vajradhara, Lord of Secrets—according to the way in which it is elucidated by the "Three Bodhisattva Commentaries."[13] From the bottomless and endless ocean of yoga arises a necklace of glistening pearls of reference and reasoning, embracing the throats of the maidens of the directions. This very thing is worthy of delightful joy.

Among however many pronouncements of the doctrine within the two vehicles of cause and effect which, mindful of the stages of his disciples, the Three World guru Buddha Bhagavān composed, the nondual Tantras are the chief, the supreme, the most excellent of the Tantra class. Even among these, the essence of the essence, the chief of the chief is the *Mañjuśrī Nāmasaṃgīti*. Supremely difficult to fathom and to measure, it is the chief amongst all methods of secret mantra which actualize the ultimate essence. This is the doctrine to be set down.

The essential topic of the *Mañjuśrī Nāmasaṃgīti*: (9a-10b)

The chief topic of this very Tantra [the *Mañjuśrī Nāmasaṃgīti*] is the Mañjuśrī Jñānasattva himself of interpretable and definitive meaning and the paths for achieving that. With regard to these, there are two ways of commenting: the Yoga Tantra way and the Unexcelled Yoga Tantra way.

In the first way, the definitive meaning Mañjuśrī Jñānasattva is the nondual intuition of all buddhas. The *Lalitavajra* says: "Here, what is to be expressed is nondual intuition." The interpretable Mañjuśrī Jñānasattva is the arisal for the sake of disciples of that very [intuition] in the form of Mañjuśrī deity wheels.

The Unexcelled Tantra ways of commenting are also of two [types]: the general system and that done in harmony with the *Kālacakra*. In the first of those, there are two types of Mañjuśrī Jñānasattvas: the bliss-void Indivisible and the Two-Reality Indivisible. In general, the Mañjuśrī Jñānasattva is the chief meaning of the fruitional *Evam*. The master Advayavajra comments: "The ones [possessed of] acute, very acute, and extremely acute faculties should strive to go to the essence of that very expression '*evam maya sruta samaya eka.*'"[14] He states that because the Mañjuśrī Jñānasattva will be achieved by realizing the meaning of the fruitional *Evam*, jewel-like individuals with supremely acute faculties should, having understood the meaning of the fruitional *Evam*, strive to generate the path *Evam* in their continuum. They should [strive to] understand the meanings of the *Evam* of the basis and the symbolic *Evam* which induces the *Evam* of the path.

> It is also said that the *Evam* [syllables] illustrate all of the means and wisdom combinations of Unexcelled Yoga's basis, path, and fruition. From that same text: It possesses everything. However many bases and parents enumerated by the 84,000 dharma properties are well taught to be these two

letters. The *E* letter is the mother; *Va* is commonly said to be the father; the *thig le* is the union, which is extremely marvelous.[15]

This is stated therefore in this commentary, which gives as its source the *Devendrā-para-samucca Tantra*. The fruitional *Evam* is of the nature of the nonduality of art and wisdom, whereby the male is means, the female is wisdom, and the nonduality of both is the hermaphroditic being which does not privilege one over the other. That same text says, "The union of male and female is the hermaphrodite." Therefore, "The distinctive individual who enters into that [fruitional *Evam*] is the expression of the *mahāmudrā,* whose nature is the orgasmic bliss. This is certain."

[Clarifying the meaning of] the distinctive individual who enters into the meaning of that fruitional *Evam*: one is the Mañjuśrī Jñānasattva or *Evam* which is the indivisibility of bliss and voidness in the occasion of the fruit; the other one, interpreted by that, is the *Evam* Mañjuśrī Jñānasattva which is the union of the Two Truths: the one thing that is both body and mind, the Enjoyment Body, adorned with signs and marks, which is the sevenfold branches of union, and the *Dharmakāya*, which is bliss-void indivisible.

The definitive meaning Mañjuśrī Jñānasattva as elucidated by the *Kālacakra*-centric "Three Bodhisttava Commentaries" is the aspectless voidness, and the changeless great bliss of experiential uniformity is the natural *Dharmakāya*. The body adorned with signs and marks, which in all aspects has the union in one experiential taste, is the *Rupakāya* in the aspect of union with the *mahāmudrā*. In short, that very thing is the vajra yoga of art and wisdom indivisible, or the definitive meaning fourth initiation. As Avalokiteśvara said in the *Vimalaprabhā* of the *Nāmasaṃgīti*: "What is to be spoken of is the indivisible Ādibuddha. The means of expressing that is to say that. Again, the topic is the Intuition Body. The means of saying that is the mass of these letters."[16] One can understand this in detail from the explanation of the verbal meaning . . .

Brief description of *Mañjuśrī Nāmasaṃgīti* commentaries and their arrangements: (10b-12a)

Generally, the *Mañjuśrī Nāmasaṃgīti* is commented upon as a Yoga Tantra and an Unexcelled Yoga Tantra. Within the first [category], the master Śrī Mañjukīrti wrote a commentary on the *Mañjuśrī Nāmasaṃgīti* which was translated by Rin chen bzang po. There is Sgeg rdor's *Vision of the Meaning of Tantra*, translated by Smṛti and revised by Prajñākuta;[17] the commentary of Someśvara Kīrti Śrī, translated by Ārya Prajñā;[18] *Mañjuśrī Nāmasaṃgīti-vṛtti* translated by Gnyags dzny'a na.[19] Advayavajra wrote the *Vitarka* which was translated by Bsod nams gyan.[20] There is Mañjuśrīmitra's commentary, translated by Rin chen bzang-po;[21] Avadhūti's *GAR,* translated by Chos skyan Bzang po;[22] Avagupta wrote the *Realization of the Essence,* translated by Smṛti; Prajñākīrti wrote a small commentary; Kumarakīrti wrote the *Upadeśa,*[23] and then there are several by Buddhaguhya.

Second, the Unexcelled Yoga category of commentaries are of two kinds: those that elucidate in accordance with the general procedure of Unexcelled Tantra, and those that elucidate in accordance with the *Three Bodhisattava Commentaries*. Among the first [type], there are the commentaries by Vimalamitra;[24] by dGa rab rdo rje;[25] by Śrī Advayavajra; by Prajñāguru;[26] and those of Acarya Advayavajra.[27]

Those that comment from the perspective of the *Kālacakra* in harmony with the *Three Bodhisattva Commentaries* include the Narendrakīrti, translated by Vajrarāja,[28] and the *Essential Abbreviated Mantra Meaning* on the benefits of that commentary by Kālacakrapada,[29] translated by Vajrarāja. Bu ston mentions these two as the basis of doubt. There is Puṇḍarika's *Vimalaprabhā,* translated by Bsod snyoms chen po at Nalenda, the Sa skya monastery.[30] This was not included in Bu ston's *History of Dharma* (*chos 'byung*) index, but it is included in the *bstan 'gyur* of the glorious Ri bo bde chen Monastery and the Rtses thang *bstan'gyur*.[31] Anupamarakṣita wrote *Amṛtabindu-pratyāloka* and Dharmakīrti and rDo rje rgyal mtshan translated it.[32] Raviśrī wrote the *Amṛtakaṇīka*.[33] These are in Bu ston's *History* index, though they are not included by some [others]; these are mentioned only as authoritative commentaries in the Ri bo bde chen Monastery. In addition, there are many *sādhanas* relying on the *Mañjuśrī Nāmasaṃgīti* and many kinds of dharma teachings which offer assorted relevant rituals.

Someone may wonder, "Well then. How do [these commentators] elucidate the import of the *Mañjuśrī Nāmasaṃgīti*?" The Yoga Tantra commentaries, as already explained, taught the Mañjuśrī Jñānasattva of definitive and interpretable meaning to be the arisal of various deity wheels of that very Mañjuśrī, the nondual intuition of all the buddhas. Then, they comment on the *Mañjuśrī Nāmasaṃgīti* as elucidating the arts of achieving that, namely the yogas with and without signs.

Those who elucidate in accordance with the General Unexcelled Yoga way comment, saying: "[The *Mañjuśrī Nāmasaṃgīti*] teaches the bliss-void indivisible Mañjuśrī Jñānasattva and the Two-Reality indivisible Mañjuśrī Jñānasattva, as well as the arts of achieving those, such as the two stages of the path, and so forth." Those who comment in accordance with the *Kālacakra* way teach the Vajra Yoga which is the nonduality of goal and means. Then, they teach the six-branched yoga and so forth as the art of achieving that.

If someone wonders, "Do all those different approaches on how to comment on the *Mañjuśrī Nāmasaṃgīti* abide as the intention of the vajra-words? Or does one make a division, thinking, 'among all those ways of commenting, this one abides as the intention of the *Mañjuśrī Nāmasaṃgīti,* and this one does not.' Which is correct?"

If that is what you're wondering: [I think] the actuality of the *Mañjuśrī Nāmasaṃgīti* is [in harmony with] Unexcelled Tantras, and from among those, the ultimate intent [inheres in] the *Kālacakra*. However, a number of different meanings are taught for each of the vajra-words of the root *Guhyasamāja Tantra,* and there are six different ways of explaining the meanings of each. So, with regard to the authoritative commentaries on the *Mañjuśrī Nāmasaṃgīti*, I think there is no contradiction in asserting that all the different approaches are the meaning of the vajra-words of the *Mañjuśrī Nāmasaṃgīti*.

Why elucidate the *Mañjuśrī Nāmasaṃgīti* in harmony with the *Kālacakra Tantra*: (12b-13a)

Though there are many different perspectives from which to elucidate the intent of the *Mañjuśrī Nāmasaṃgīti*, the ultimate way explains [from the perspective of] the "Three Bodhisattva Commentaries." The heart of the topic of the "Three Bodhisattva Commentaries," which accords with the *Kālacakra,* is vajra yoga itself—means and wisdom indivisible. To explain that clearly, they take that as the chief topic of the *Mañjuśrī Nāmasaṃgīti*. The great *Kālacakra* commentary states: "It is embraced by the *Mañjuśrī Nāmasaṃgīti*, which makes manifest the Vajradhara intuition-body because it is the statement in the *Ādibuddha*."[34] [Here,] "The Vajradhara intuition-body" is the Void Form Body Couple, which has the nature of changeless great bliss; "makes manifest by the *Mañjuśrī Nāmasaṃgīti*" [connotes that it] explains clearly. "Because it is the statement:" here again, having taken that as the chief topic of the *Ādibuddha* which is like that, it is "the statement [of the *Ādibuddha*]. By the method of taking that [vajra yoga] as the chief subject of the *Mañjuśrī Nāmasaṃgīti* and the chief topic of the *Kālacakra,* they are 'embraced.'" Thus it explains clearly.

If one does not understand the meaning of the *Ādibuddha*, one cannot understand the essence-meaning of the *Mañjuśrī Nāmasaṃgīti*. If one does not understand that, one cannot understand the Vajradhara intuition-body as above; and if one does not understand that, one cannot understand the essence of the Mantrayāna path and is separate from the Vajradhara path. Accordingly, one will be unable to eliminate the subtlest instincts of *saṃsāra* and unable to achieve the exaltation of *Kālacakra* which abandons those instincts. From the *Great Commentary* on the sixth summary topic of the "Cosmology Chapter":

> Those who do not understand the *Paramādibuddha* do not understand the *Nāmasaṃgīti.* Those who do not understand the *Nāmasaṃgīti* do not understand the Jñānakāya of Vajradhara. Those who do not understand Jñānakāya of Vajradhara do not understand the Mantrayāna. Those who do not understand the Mantrayāna are thoroughly *samsaric*, separate from the path of Bhagavān Vajradhara. Therefore, noble teachers must teach the *Paramādibuddha,* and those noble disciples who desire liberation should listen.[35]

This explains the need for understanding the *Mañjuśrī Nāmasaṃgīti* in harmony with the *Kālacakra* . . .

The explanation of the setting of the *Mañjuśrī Nāmasaṃgīti*: (13a-14b)

If one were to ask: by which teacher, in what place, to what kind of retinue, at what time, and in what way was it taught? As for the teacher: it was that very Śākya Rāja, possessing the Vajra. When the teacher had taught the method of becoming manifestly enlightened at Vajrāsana, he turned the wheel of the doctrine of general vehicle of perfections, and at Vultures' Peak, he turned the wheel of the *Prajñāpāramitā*. The place is the glorious Drepung Stūpa near the southern part of India at Śrīparvata. Below, [he] emanated the Dharmadhātu-Vagiśvara Maṇḍala, and above, the glorious Great Astronomical Maṇḍala. There in the place of great bliss on the vajra lion throne at the great Dharmadhātu Maṇḍala, he sat—the superlative teacher, the Śākya lion, abiding in the form of the lord of the maṇḍala. The retinue was those [beings] with the good fortune to listen to this Dharmadhātu Tantra. As for the time: in the full moon of the middle spring month of Nakba, he gave the mundane and transcendent initiations for the first time. He taught all the Unexcelled Yoga Tantras, such as the superlative *Mañjuśrī Nāmasaṃgīti* and the *Ādibuddha*. Raviśrī's commentary states:

> Here at the glorious Great Stūpa of [Drepung] Dhānyakaṭaka, the Buddha Bhagavān, the "glorious Śākya Lion," was entreated by *srāvanas* who desired to learn various Tantras. And in the middle spring month, having emanated the glorious Dharmadhātu Maṇḍala, and, above that, the Astrological Maṇḍala, of the Ādibuddha, the Buddha gave initiation to the deities, etc., on that very day. He then taught all the ways of secret mantras, dividing them according to [whether they were] expanded or concise. The Glorious *Ādibuddha* says: "Just as the teacher taught the *Prajñāpāramitā* at Rajrgṛha, so too, he taught the dharma through the modality of secret mantra at the glorious Dhānyakaṭaka." Because it actualized the essence of the ultimate, the *Mañjuśrī Nāmasaṃgīti*, whose depth is difficult to measure, is the main of all mantras.[36]

Likewise, Anupamarakṣita says:

> On the fifteenth [day] of the Citra month, those seeking the meaning of various mundane and transcendent Tantras gathered in the Drepung Stūpa. At that time, for the sake of beings, the teacher emanated the Dharmadhātu-Vagiśvara Maṇḍala at Dhānyakaṭaka. Above that, Vajradhara emanated the Glorious Astronomical Maṇḍala; below, he radiated the Ādibuddha Maṇḍala. He gave initiation to all, such as the gods, and extensively taught the four Tantra classes as well as the essential Tantra—five in all. This is the quintessence.

This also explains that in that place, the Bhagavān taught the four great Tantra classes along with the quintessence, the *Mañjuśrī Nāmasaṃgīti*. The teaching at glorious Dhānyakaṭaka of all of the Unexcelled Tantras is also the intent of the root and commentaries on the *Kālacakra*. It is stated in the supplement chapter of the *Kālacakra*: "The tenfold Mighty One taught the myriad Buddha Tantras in the Dharmadhātu at Glorious Dhānyakaṭaka."

If someone wonders: Who is the collector of the *Mañjuśrī Nāmasaṃgīti*? Generally speaking, Vajrapāṇi is the collector of secret mantra Tantras. In the specific case of the *Mañjuśrī Nāmasaṃgīti* and the *Kālacakra*, the requester and collector was King Sucandra, a [human] emanation of Vajrapāṇi. The *Vimalaprabhā* [commentary] to the *Mañjuśrī Nāmasaṃgīti* states: "Therefore, he is 'Vajrapāṇi Sucandra,' the Lord of Ten Stages, who emerged from the womb of the goddess Suryaprabha Vijaya in the city of Kalapa and the country of Śambhala." Anupamarakṣita [comments on] the meaning of that: "Profound and hard to measure, it cannot be understood by anybody; yet it was taintlessly explained by Sucandra."

The greatness of the *Mañjuśrī Nāmasaṃgīti Tantra* to be explained: (14b-15b)

This *Mañjuśrī Nāmasaṃgīti Tantra* is the chief of all modalities of secret mantra. The great commentary to the *Kālacakra* explains its greatness: "Its very envelopment by the *Mañjuśrī Nāmasaṃgīti* is stated to be the greatness of the *Kālacakra*. One who does not understand the *Mañjuśrī Nāmasaṃgīti* does not understand the Intuition Body of Vajradhara. One who does not understand Vajradhara's Intuition Body does not know the mantra vehicle."[37] Not only that, in the very well-known "Three Bodhisattva Commentaries" [which contain] the full essence of the Unexcelled Vehicle, it is said: "The full essence of the path is definitely made clear by the *Mañjuśrī Nāmasaṃgīti*." In addition, the treatises of the great *siddhas* of India, which elucidate the meaning of the Hiding Tantras, cite the *Mañjuśrī Nāmasaṃgīti* as a source and contain many eulogies to the greatness of the *Mañjuśrī Nāmasaṃgīti*. Speaking as the Lord of all Tantras, this very text itself states that "the Supreme Lord of all Tantras." Moreover, its own Benefit [section] contains various enumerations of praise. The great *siddha* Anupamarakṣita says: "The four Tantra classes, the Essence Tantra, and the Fifth [One] were extensively taught by Vajradhara. This one is the quintessence. It was collected by the *ḍākinīs*, each of whom sealed it in her own place. That is this very quintessence, widely renowned, read a billion [times] for the sake of beings in Jambuling."[38] There are a great many unparalleled praises such as Raviśrī's statement: "It is the chief of all modalities of secret mantra." Accordingly, the essence of all the discourses of the Bhagavān is the mantra collections. And among those that exist within the four classes of Tantras, the nondual Tantras are supreme.

The ultimate essence of all nondual tantras makes clear the intuition body of Vajradhara. Under the influence of the vajra-words of all Tantras, this *Mañjuśrī Nāmasaṃgīti Tantra* is like a Buddha jewel-casket thrown open, for it is the very teaching which makes clear the ultimate profound path that easily grants the exaltation of Vajradhara in one lifetime. It should be understood as the unexcelled of all scriptural statements. From the perspective of learning about and reflecting upon the meaning of Tantra, it is correct to enter it in whatever way possible. It is thus expressly recommended for fortunate [beings].

(19b-20a)

> Wish-fulfilling ocean of nondualistic Tantras which all come from the rain-clouds of Indra, bottomless and endless, which has waves of many explanations of what is unclear, difficult to cross by millions of pretentious scholars, source of precious attainments, look! I alone launched the great boat of analysis to achieve the desired goal of entering wish-fulfillment. In the vermillion ocean, where the rising sun is gently reflected, which makes creepers of the arching eyebrows like unlimited patterns of beauty in all directions, I, having set the eye in the lotus of the face of Mañjuśrī, will illuminate the immutable great bliss which is the nature of that [eye], and which is of one taste with the omnifaceted supreme body, which is the glory of the White Lotus Holder who illuminates things as they are—leading to this point, I will clarify those things . . .

Actual explanation of the meaning of the *Mañjuśrī Nāmasaṃgīti*: (21a-24b)

The entire import of Unexcelled Tantra is condensed in the words of the setting: "This I heard at one time . . ." The *Vajramālā* says: "'This' [*Evam*] is two letters. Their absence at the beginning of a Tantra renders it unacceptable." This quote teaches the necessity of affirming these two letters at the beginning of all Unexcelled Tantras.

If someone should ask: "Given that this Tantra [the *Mañjuśrī Nāmasaṃgīti*] is the chief of all Tantras, how is it that it does not contain such a setting?" It is a small extract from the *Great Sixty-thousand Māyājāla,* wherein the words "*evam maya śrutam,*" etc., do not actually occur at the beginning. However, its meaning is present when one clarifies. Therefore, the equivalent of the quote THEN, VAJRADHARA, THE GLORIOUS, is present in the Indian [Sanskrit] text as *ATHAŚRĪ VAJRADHARA*.

The three letters of that *ATHA ŚRĪ* symbolize all the distinctions of means and wisdom, just as they are symbolized by the two [letters] of *Evam,* which is synonymous with "this" in the quote "This I heard." Accordingly, those three syllables aptly fulfill the meaning of *Evam*. So, the *A* illustrates the meaning of the voidness of aspectless intuition which is characterized by *E*; *THA* illustrates the meaning of the intuition of unchanging great bliss which is characterized by the *Va* letter, and *ŚRĪ* illustrates the meaning of the *anuśvara*, which is the experiential unity of subject and object. Not only that; here *A* indicates the meaning which is characterized by *E*, namely wisdom [as] the Void Form *mahāmudrā*; *Tha* indicates the Mañjuśrī Jñānasattva of multifaceted artistry which is characterized by the letter *Va*; and *Śri* indicates that very meaning of the integration of the art and wisdom pair—the meaning characterized by the *thig le*.

Acarya Raviśrī says:

> Here, by the fact that it designates selflessness; the *A* letter teaches the supreme, omnifaceted voidness; the *Tha* letter teaches the objectless compassion which signifies the nature of Akṣobhya. Those are also mentioned in the *Union of Extreme Faith* by Dgyes pa dor je: "Because those two are nondual, the topic of the utterance *Evam* is the spontaneous joy which is the semen (*gu ba*) which resides at the tip of the jewel. For that, one should say *Atha*."[39]

Similarly, the *Amṛtabindu* teaches: "By adorning the letter *A* which is the melter from Triśakuni with the letter *Tha* of Jālandhara, it explains the source of the doctrine, namely *evam maya*. Just that is what enters into the *yoni* of the vajra-queen."[40]

The seat on which the Teacher sat and taught the dharma is, in some Tantras, referred to as "secret." Similarly, the meaning which is signified by *E* is realm of space, *bhaga*, *dharmottara*, lotus, lion throne, etc. Likewise, the meaning signified by *Va* is called Vajra-possessor, Vajrasattva, Vajrabhairava, Lord Vajra Heruka, Kālacakra, and the Ādibuddha.

In brief, it is explained that *E* is said to signify secret, realm of space, *bhaga, dharmottara*, [and] lotus, while Vajrasattva, teaching the supreme marvel and sitting on the lion throne, is described as *vam*, vajra, Vajrabhairava, Heruka, Śrī Kālacakra, and the Ādibuddha. Here also, it is similarly explained that the signification of the letter *A* is the seat in which the Dharma Teacher sat and taught the Tantra, and *Tha* is the Ādibuddha who taught the dharma while sitting in that [seat], [all of which] is signified by *Va*. This mainly explains the meaning of the fruitional *Evam*.

The wondrous method for explaining in Lokeśvara's *Vimalaprabhā* is as follows: "Therefore, having affirmed *Evam* as the meaning of the *Atha Śrī* as previously explained, initially, virtue is the cause; in the middle, virtue is the path; and at the end, virtue is the fruition." Having explained virtue in reference to the three—beginning, middle, and end—therefore, in the beginning, virtue is the cause. Or, if referred to in the context of the basis: the *A* is the body of the mother whose nature is wisdom, the *Tha* is the body of the father, whose nature is artistry. *Śrī* is composed of the three letters *Śa, ra* and *ī:* As for supplementing the etymological analysis of the first, the *Śa* sound [connotes] *śaśukra*, which is the semen of the father. Supplementing the etymological analysis of the first of the second, the *Ra* sound [connotes] *rakta*, the blood (ovum) of the mother, and the *Ī* which is the *ki gu* serves as *Vam*. As for the etymological analysis of that, Va is *vāyu*, the wind. Those two—the very subtle translucency mind and the vitality wind which is its mount—achieve a human body from entering into the middle of the sperm-ovum mixture of the father and mother. However, having achieved that, it is the meaning of *VAJRA*, "inseparable," for that subtle two-part wind-mind resides inseparably for the life of the body.

As for *DHARA*, it has the meaning either of "grasper" or "holder." These two [wind-mind] are the actual basis for the achievement of the Buddha *Dharmakāya* and *Rupakāya*. Alternately, that "holder" connotes a human being, womb born and endowed with the six elements. This should be called either the support or the basis for complete enlightenment in a single lifetime. This meaning is also in that very text:

> The quote *ATHA ŚRĪ VAJRADHARA* refers to the cause, the path, and the fruition. The *A* of that *ATHA* is the body of the mother, which is of the nature of wisdom, and the *THA* is the body of the father, which is of the nature of means. The *ŚRĪ* functions as three letters: the sound *śaśukra* is the semen of the father; *rakta* the blood (ovum) of the mother, and because *Ī* is *ki-gu*, *Ī* is *Vam*. Because the *VA* is *vāyu*, it is the wind, the ordinary consciousness of the basis of all. Similarly, it is glorious, *ŚRĪ* in Sanskrit, because it achieves a human body. *VAJRA* is adamantine. It resides in the body for as long as there is life and is thus inseparable [from it]. Therefore, it is adamantine. *DHARA* is either dhara as holder or apprehending: therefore the human body of the six elements is established as the wind-mind which is the cause of buddhahood.

Like that, in the context of the basis, either the *EVAM* or the *ATHA ŚRĪ* has the signification of means and wisdom. [These are] the basis-level father and mother, which are the red and white elements of those two. The wind-mind continues through the transition of death and rebirth. Having gone through the transition (i.e., conception, *nying mtsams sbyor wa*) and achieved a human body, it is the wind-mind pair that abides in the body until death. This is the way of training in the context of virtuous actions (lit. "abiding on the path") at the time of the middle.

The *A* signifies the special blazing of the inner fire, the *gtum mo*, at the navel, within the central channel through the power of the winds of the left and right channels (*ro kyang)* being blocked in the central channel during the upwards-moving life-effort (*srog rtsol)*. The *THA* signifies the melting of the white element at the crown by the power of that; the *ŚRĪ* signifies the descent [of the drops] along the path of the central channel [occasioned by] the melting of the *bodhicitta* like that, and the up-and-down movement of the four blisses. *VAJRA* signifies the union of the special bliss from the melting like that with indivisible, immutable voidness. *DHARA* signifies the external retention of the element from the tip of the jewel until the stage of Buddha. Alternately, it is explained as that very indivisible, immutable bliss-voidness grasped until the stage of Buddha. Also, from this very commentary:

> The *A*, because it is achieving the path which is virtuous in the middle, is the blazing intuition from the *gtum mo* at the navel. *THA* is the trickling of the *bodhicitta* from the crown. *ŚRĪ* is glory, the ordered progression of the blisses. *VAJRA*, because indivisible, is bliss and voidness. *DHARA*, because it is grasper, means up to buddha[hood].[41]

In regard to this, the meaning indicated by either *Evam* or *ATHA ŚRĪ* is however many means-wisdom [dyads] are on the occasion of the path: *Evam* of the sex organs which is a way of developing [bliss], existing in the pattern of the kiss [i.e., in union] within the central internal channel complex; the dyad of the *gtum mo* at the navel and the white element at the crown; of the orgasmic bliss which is developed in dependence upon the downward and upward movement of the drops and their object voidness; the dyad of the vajra of the male adept and the lotus of either the *karma-* or *jñānamudrā*; the bliss-void intuition developed in dependence upon that [union of vajra and lotus], and the body of the universal void-form couple; the dyad of vajra and lotus; and the unchanging great bliss which is developed in dependence upon that, and the aspectless voidness which is of one taste with that [bliss].

At the end, if one applies it within the context of the virtue of fruition, having exhausted all bodily substances through 21,600 paths of realizing emptiness by the unchanging bliss, it points to that very circumstance of the twelve stages of blocking the various winds from the twelve "great breath shifts."[42] Therefore, *A* [points to] the ultimate realm of the two purificants of the four liberations, and *THA* [to] that very unchanging great bliss which is experientially uniform with objectless compassion and which, for analytical purposes, exists as the five intuitions. The *ŚRĪ* is glory: it is the ultimate great bliss body of self-interest and the two *Dharmakāyas*, as well as the ultimate all-aspected *Sambhogakāya* of altruistic interest;it is also the *Nirmanakāya*, which is the achievement of four bodies. *VAJRA* is the actual nondifference of the four bodies like that; *DHARA* is either "holding the great intuition of excellent, immutable self-grasping" or "grasper." Like this, from that very text:

> In the end, virtue is the twelfth stage of Buddhahood; *A* is the voidness of the four liberations, the totally purified Dharma realm; *THA* is the five-aspected Buddha-intuitions that are the fulfillment of compassion; *ŚRĪ,* which means glory, is the attainment of the four bodies for the sake of self and others. *VAJRA* is the nondifference of the four bodies. *DHARA* should be called *VAJRADHARA* because it holds the supreme unchanging bliss.[43]

This is spoken in order to illustrate whatever special methods and wisdoms [exist] on the occasion of the fruition.

In short, someone who is born from a human womb and endowed with the six elements is the supreme basis or support for practicing the path. Such a one purifies his continuum through the common path. Having entered into the path of

Kālacakra, he trains himself by the six branches of Creation and Perfection Stage [practice], whereby he attains buddhahood in that very life. All the means and wisdom [dyads] of the basis, path, and fruit [for such a process] are expressed by *ATHA ŚRĪ VAJRADHARA*. It is clarified by ascertaining the statement of Lokeśvara: "In particular, *ATHA ŚRĪ* points to it." As such, the myriad meanings of the topics of the *Mañjuśrī Nāmasaṃgīti* are condensed in the meaning of the first *pāda*: *THEN, VAJRADHARA, THE GLORIOUS*. Therefore, having clarified it in summary as the three letters *A THA ŚRĪ*, seize this explanation, unprecedented in excellence!

Endnotes

1. Gendun Gyatso would ascend the throne of Bkra shis lhun po in 1512, of 'Bras spungs in 1517, and Se ra in 1526. He founded the Dga' ldan pho brang in 1518; it would be his seat for the remainder of his life and the seat of his successors. With the consolidation of power under the Fifth Dalai Lama, its name would be taken over as the formal designation of the Central Tibetan government—a convention that remained true until 1959.

2. In particular, Gelugpa monks were forbidden to participate in the Great Prayer Festival marking the Tibetan New Year—a celebration invented by the Gelug's founder, Tsongkhapa (Tsong kha pa blo bzang grags pa) in 1409, and one which would have convened thousands of Gelugpas in the city center. The Festival would not, in fact, be returned to Gelug leadership until Gendun Gyatso's successful intervention in 1518. For a general overview of this period, see Matthew Kapstein, *The Tibetans* (Oxford: Blackwell Publishers, 2006), 143 ff.

3. For a discussion of this dynamic which focuses more particularly on the history of the Gelug school, see George Dreyfus' essays on the history of 'Bras spungs at: thdl.org/xml/show.php?xml=/collections/cultgeo/mons/drepung/essays/drepung-intro.xml.

4. Cited by Amy Heller, "The Second Dalai Lama, Gendun Gyatso," in Martin Brauen, *The Dalai Lamas: A Visual History* (Chicago: Serindia Publications, 2005), 45.

5. His *Autobiography* notes: "From the time I was five or six, I had already made compositions spontaneously . . . When I started my lessons, I was able to learn to read and write perfectly without studying. At that time, with my father as teacher, I mastered ritual cycles for Cakrasaṃvara, Yamāntaka and special forms for the Four-Armed Mahākāla, Yama, Vaiśravana, Lhamo Makzorma, and Dharmapāla Bektse, too. I also learned the Shangpa amd Dakpo Kagyu teachings of Mahāmudrā, the Zhije system of Padampa, and many other initiations and rituals from my great-grandfather's and grandfather's teachings." See Heller in Brauen, 2005, 49.

6. Heller in Brauen, 48.

7. From Sde srid sangs rgyas rgya mtsho's *Du la la'i gos bzang*, translated by Glenn H. Mullin in De-si Sang-gye Gya-tso's "The Life of the Second Dalai Lama," *The Tibet Journal* 11, no. 3:12-13.

8. Peking 2064, bstan 'gyur, rgyud, Ka-2 1-227a and Kha 2a-297a. Puṇḍarika, *bsDus pa'i rgyud kyi rgyal po dus kyi 'khor lo'i 'grel bshas rtsa ba'i rgyud kyi rjes su 'jug pa stong phrag bcu gnyis pa dri ma med pa'i 'od ces bya ba (Vimalaprabhānāma-mūlatantrānusāriṇī-dvādaśasahāsrikalaghukālacakra-tantrarājaṭīkā)*.

9. Vesna A. Wallace, *The Inner Kālacakratantra: A Buddhist Tantric View of the Individual* (Oxford: Oxford University Press, 2001), 19.

10. This is the Dhānyakaṭaka Stūpa in south India, identified as Amarāvati in the Sattenpalle Tāluka of Guṇṭūr District, Madras. It dates back to at least the second century AD. See footnote 1 of George Roerich, *The Blue Annals: Parts 1 & 2 (Bound in One)* (Delhi: Motilal Banarsidass, 1995), 754. The stūpa is said to have received its name from an event in the lifetime of the Buddha Kanakamuni, when a monk is said to have caused a magic rain of rice to fall for twelve days and thus alleviate a famine. The remaining rice was collected and the Heap of Rice (Dhānyakaṭaka) was used to construct a stūpa.

11. Author of the *Āryamañjuśrīnāmasaṃgīti-amṛtabindu-pradīpālokavṛtti-nāma*. See endnote 30.

12. Author of the *Amṛtakaṇīkanāmāryanāmasaṃgītiṭippaṇi*. See endnote 33.

13. The "Three Bodhisattva Commentaries" are some of the first texts of the Kālacakra literature and constitute commentaries to three Tantras in terms of the Kālacakra path. The *Laghutantraṭīkā* by Vajrapāṇī elucidates the first ten and a half verses of the *Cakrasaṃvara Tantra* (also called *Herukābhidhānatantra)*. The *Hevajratantrapiṇḍārthaṭīkā* by Vajragarbha explores the first five *paṭalas* of the *Hevajra Tantra*, and the *Vimalaprabhā* by Puṇḍarika is an extended commentary on the *Laghukālacakratantra*. Francesco Sferra notes that the success of the Kālacakra in its initial phase is closely linked to the diffusion of these three works, which were also an important source for Nāropa's *Sekoddeśaṭīkā*. See Claudio Cicuzza and Francesco Sferra, "Brief Notes on the Beginning of the Kālacakra Literature," *Dhih: Journal of Rare Buddhist Texts Project* 23:113-14.

14. Peking 2945, 106b.4.

15. Peking 2945, fol. 106b.5-6.

16. Peking 2114, 216a.7-8.

17. Derge 2533, Khu 27b-115b. Sgeg pa'i rdo rje, *'Phugs pa mtshan yan dag par brjod pahi rgya chen hgrel pa mtshan gsang snags kyi don du rnam par lta ba shes bya ba*. Tr. Smṛtijñānakīrti; Rev: Phyag na rdo rje, Klog skya Shes rab brtsegs.

18. Derge 2535, Gu 1b-27a, *Zla-ba grags-pa, Āryamañjuśrīnāmasaṃgītivṛttināma*. Trans. Srimahājana, Phags pa shes rab.

19. Derge 2092, Tshi 1b-38b. Vimalamitra, *Nāmasaṃgītivṛttināmārthaprakāśakaraṇadīpa -nama*. Trans. Gnyags dzny'a na.

20. Derge 2094, Tshi 56b-84b. *Nāmasaṃgītyupasamhāravitarka*. Trans. Śrīvajrabodhi, Bsod-nams rgyal mtshan.

21. Indefinite. This could be the *Nāmasaṃgītivṛtti*, also known as the "Little Commentary," found in Derge 2532, Khu 1b-27b. Alternately it might be the *Āryamañjuśrīnāmasaṃgītiṭī kā,* also known as the "Great Commentary." See Derge 2534, Khu 115b-301a.

22. Derge 2536 Gu 27a-47b. *Āryamañjuśrīnāmasaṃgītivṛtti.* The translator's full name is 'Gar chos kyi bzang po; hence, the text is referred to as the "'Gar."

23. Derge 2539, Gu 118b-145a. *Āryamañjuśrīnāmasaṃgītyupadeśavṛttināma*. Trans. Devarāja, Shes rab bla ma.

24. Derge 2092, Tshi 1b-38b. *Mañjuśrīnāmasaṃgītivṛttināmārthaprakāśakaraṇaḍīpanama.* Trans. Gnyags Jñāna.

25. Derge 2093 Tshi 38b-56b. *Mañjuśrīnāmasaṃgītyarthālokaranama*. Trans. unknown.

26. Derge 2095, Tshi 85a1-92b7. *'Jam dpal gyi snags don rnam gzigs dang ne ba bsdus pahi rnam par rtog ge gnyis kyi don bsdus pa mtshan gyi sgron me*. Trans. unknown.

27. It's not clear why GG mentions Advayavajra twice. However, the texts in question are probably Derge 2098, Tshi 95a-129b, *Āryamañjuśrīnāmasaṃgītiṭīkasārābhisamaya-nāma*. Trans. Prajñāśrījñānakīrti, and Advayavajra's commentary on the Benefits (*anuśamsa*) section, Derge 2094, Tshi 56b-84b, *Nāmasaṃgītyupasaṃhāravitarkanāma*. Trans. Śrīvajrabodhi, Bsod nams rgyal mtshan.

28. Derge 1397, Pha 124a-184b, *Āryamañjuśrīnāmasaṃgītivyākhyāna*. Trans. Abhayavajra and rdo rje rgyal po.

29. Derge 1399, Pha 232b-285b, *Āryamañjuśrīnāmasaṃgīti-anuśaṃsavṛtti*. Trans. Abhaya-vajra, rdo rje rgyal po.

30. Interestingly, the colophon to this text in the Derge edition notes that it was translated at the Tāra temple at Nālanda.

31. The Ri bo che Monastery (the name is usually prefixed with the expression gCung or dPal) was located at the ninety-degree bend of the Gtsang po River, south of Rnam ring in Dbus-Gtsang. The Ttses thang Monastery was based in the town of Rtses thang, located at the head of Tibet's Yarlung Valley, on the south bank of the river.

32. Derge 1396 Pha 96b-124a, *Āryamañjuśrīnāmasaṃgīti-amṛtabindu-pradīpālokavṛtti-nāma*.

33. Derge 1395, Pha 36a-96b, *Amṛtakaṇīkanāmāryanāmasaṃgītiṭippaṇī*. Trans. Norbu dpal ye shes, Nyi ma'i dbang po'i 'od zer, Chos rje dpal.

34. Peking 2064, fol. 17a.1-2.

35. Peking 2064, 52a, 5-8.

36. Peking 2111, 45a, 4-7.

37. Peking 2064, 52a.5ff.

38. Peking 2112, 116a.3-4.

39. Peking 2111, 45b.3-5.

40. Peking 2112, 1450.2. The Kālacakra literature describes twelve sets of cosmic pilgrimage sites in Jambudvīpa, namely *pīṭhas, upapīṭhas, kṣetras, upakṣetras, chandohas, upachandohas, melāpakas, upamelāpakas, veśmas, upaveśmas, śmaśānas*, and *upaśmaśānas*. These sites are also corresponded to the twelve links, the twelve signs of the zodiac, and the twelve bodhisattva-*bhūmis* and are said to reside at the six *cakras* of the human body. Jālandhara—a well-known Śāktata pilgrimage center—is one of the four *pīṭhas* and is identified cosmically with the earth-element maṇḍala and with the *jñānadhātu cakra* at the level of the individual. Triśakuni is one of the four *upakṣetras* and is identified with the water maṇḍala and the earth *cakra*.

41. Peking 2114, fol. 1638, lines 6-7.

42. Twelve months and twelve signs of zodiac correspond to the twelve shifts of breath (pho-ba) of a person in a twenty-four-hour period. Outer Kālacakra analogue is twelve pho-chen in one year, i.e., the twelve months in which the days gradually wax and wane. During half of a person's day, one's breath is predominantly in the right nostril, i.e., the sun channel, and the other half in the left, i.e., the moon channel. In one shift or *pho-ba*, a person takes 1,800 breaths, totaling 21,600 per day. Each of these 12 groups is purified one by one in the Perfection stage.

–6–

Brief Presentation of Channels, Winds, and Drops according to Kālacakra Tradition

Changkya Rölpa Dorjé 1717-1786

Gavin Kilty, translator

Introduction

The *Kālacakratantra* stands apart from other Highest Yoga Tantras. In its description of the vajra body, which is the basis of completion stage practices—the presentation of cakra channels, the winds that move through them, and the vital drops positioned in the vajra body—it differs from that of the *Guhyasamāja*, which epitomizes Highest Yoga Tantra. The path it presents is also at variance in its presentation of the concept of empty form as the basic substantial vehicle for the development of the enlightened body. This is a quite different phenomenon to the illusory body presented by the *Guhyasamāja* and other tantras. Because of this concept of empty form, the Kālacakra does not present the possibility of gaining enlightenment in the intermediate of the bardo state of existence. The resultant enlightened attainment is gained by methods unique to Kālacakra, in which the ordinary body of flesh and blood and the 21,600 winds of karma are alchemically transformed by the six yoga completion stage practices into the final enlightened and empty form Kālacakra.

The *Kālacakratantra* also utilizes in far greater detail than other tantras the observed external cosmos as part of its inner and outer correspondence, which forms its basis of phenomena to be purified. Thus, external planetary movements are replicated in the bodily internal movements of the winds, etc.

Because of these categorical differences it was deemed necessary by past masters of tantra to present the distinguishing features of this tantra separately. The short text translated below is an example.

Within the Kālacakra tradition itself there are differing assertions on the base, path, and result. This text's presentation on the channels, winds, and drops differs a little from those of other authors.

The author

Changkya Rölpa Dorjé was born in 1717 to a nomad family of Mongolian ancestry in northern Tsongkha where people of Tibetan and Chinese stock lived side by side. He was recognized as the third incarnation of the Changya Tulku line. At the feet of many a great master he became learned and practiced in sutra and tantra. He was invited to central Tibet by Kelsang Gyatso, the Seventh Dalai Lama, whose biography he eventually wrote. Having mastered Chinese, Manchu, and Mongolian, he organized the translation of the Kangyur into Mongolian and Manchu. He was honored by Mongolian emperors and invited to Beijing where he built many Tibetan-style monasteries.

His compositions comprise nine volumes and include a famous work on tenets and the wonderful spontaneous poem on understanding emptiness called *Recognizing My Old Mother*. He built Evam Gakyil hermitage in Wutaishan, or Five-Peak Mountain, China in 1767, which was where he died in 1786.

Brief Presentation of Channels, Winds, and Drops according to Kālacakra Tradition

Prostrations to the gurus

The stationary channels

The three main channels—central, left, and right—are located together inside the life channel hosted by the spine and are somewhat closer to its rear than to its front. The upper tips curve forward inside the skull and drop down from the crown to a point midway between the eyebrows. The openings of the left and right channels protrude down to the left and right nostrils. The central or *dhūtı* channel is midway between these two. The lower openings of all three reach as far as the tip of the vajra opening.

The cakras[1] are those of the six families. The space cakra at the crown is green and has four petals.[2] The water cakra at the forehead is white and has four inner petals, eight intermediate and four outer petals, two of which are empty.[3] The fire cakra at the throat is red and has four inner petals, eight intermediate petals, and thirty-two outer petals, of which four are empty. The air cakra in the center of the heart is black and has eight petals. The earth cakra at the navel is yellow and has four inner petals, eight petals outside of that, and sixteen outside of that, of which four are empty petals. Of the remaining twelve, six branch off from the right channel and are named Capricorn, Pisces, Taurus, Cancer, Virgo, Scorpio—the six houses of the sun's northern passage. The other six branch off from the left channel and are named Aquarius, Aries, Gemini, Leo, Libra, Sagittarius—the six houses of the sun's southern passage.[4] Outside of these each of the twelve splits off into five petals to make sixty-four when the four empty petals of the intermediate directions are included. The gnosis cakra at the secret place is blue and has six inner petals, ten intermediate and sixteen outer petals. Therefore, it is said to have thirty-two petals, but this method of counting differs from that of the navel cakra and others where the inner and intermediate petals are not included in the count.

From the center of the navel upwards the *dhūti* central channel is known as the "channel which eliminates" (the other two channels), *avadhūtī,* the Rāhu channel, and the neuter channel. It is black and carries wind. The right channel is known as *rasanā,* the sun channel, and the wisdom channel. It is red and mainly carries blood or menstrual blood. The left channel is known as *lalanā,* the moon channel, and the channel of method. It is white and mainly carries seminal fluid.

Below the navel the continuation of the *dhūti* central channel is known as *śaṅkhinī.* It curves to the right, belongs to the gnosis element, is colored blue, carries seminal fluid, and is also known as the *kālāgni* channel. The continuation of the right channel is known as *piṅgalā.* It curves to the left, is of the air element, black, and carries urine. The continuation of the left channel below the navel is known as *meṣa.* It travels down the middle of the body, is of the earth element, yellow, and carries excrement.

These are called the six upper and lower major channels. The upper three mainly carry the life-sustaining wind and the lower three carry mainly the downwardly expelling wind.

The twelve main channels at the navel each divide up into five, and their continuation spreads throughout the body. Each of these divides up into six channels, and together they form the thirty channel petals on each of the twelve major joints of the arms and legs. These in turn divide to form the 360 channels of the fingers and toes, and so on. In total there are 72,000 channels. All channels originally divide up from the eight channel petals of the heart cakra.

The mobile winds

There are ten main winds: life-sustaining wind, downwardly expelling wind, coexisting wind, upwardly moving wind, pervading wind, *nāga* wind, turtle wind, lizard wind, *devadatta* wind, and *dhanaṃjaya* wind. In this tradition winds are not classified as main and secondary winds.

The coexisting wind and turtle wind flow through the east and southeastern petals of the heart cakra. The upwardly moving wind and the lizard wind flow through the south and southwestern petals. The pervading wind and *devadatta* wind flow through the north and northeastern petals. The *nāga* wind and *dhanaṃjaya* wind flow through the west and northwestern petals of the heart cakra.[5]

The life-sustaining wind is of the space element. The downwardly expelling wind is of the gnosis element. The coexisting wind and turtle wind are of the air element. The upwardly moving wind and lizard wind are of the fire element. The pervading wind and *devadatta* wind are of the water element. The *nāga* wind and *dhanaṃjaya* wind are of the earth element.

From the ten winds of the heart cakra winds flow to the cakras of navel, etc. and to all channels located within the body. Therefore, all winds of the body are permeated by the ten winds of the heart cakra.

According to this tradition the twelve great wind shifts occur as follows.[6] One thousand, seven hundred and forty-three and three-quarter breaths flow uninterruptedly from a particular zodiacal petal of the navel cakra. This is followed by fifty-six and a quarter winds from the central channel. This constitutes one great wind shift. The same process then moves to another navel petal. In this way the great shifts are completed in the twelve zodiacal channels in a single day, resulting in twenty-one thousand, six hundred breaths. If the breaths flowing through the central channel are not counted separately, then in one day the flow of winds in each channel totals eighteen hundred.[7]

On the right the winds flow earth, water, fire, air, space, and earth. On the left they flow space, air, fire, water, earth, and space, constituting six great shifts from each side. The first channel petals in the great shift process are toward the back of the body. The latter channel petals are towards the front of the body.

This process can be illustrated from the time that the shifts begin in the navel channel petals on the right. First one thousand, seven hundred and forty-three and three-quarter earth-maṇḍala breaths flow from the first petal on the right. At this time the same number of earth-maṇḍala breaths flow solely through the right nostril. After that fifty-six and a quarter breaths flow from the central channel. At that time, apart from the quarter breath which when completed in the central pathway does not reach the nostrils, the remaining breaths flow equally through both nostrils. Then without any intervening pause, space-maṇḍala winds of the same quantity as described above flow from the first petal on the left. These flow through the left nostril. This is followed by winds of the same quantity as described above flowing from the central channel and passing equally through both nostrils. Again winds of the water maṇḍala flow from the second channel petal on the right, and so on.

In brief, the cycle of earth, space, water, air, fire, fire again, air, water, space, earth, earth again, and space make up the twelve great shifts. There are six channel petals on each side but only five maṇḍalas. Therefore, there are two earth maṇḍalas on the right and two space maṇḍalas on the left. These are separate channel petals and therefore belong to individual shifts, but it is taught that they are each counted as a single maṇḍala.

Externally, when the sun has completed the six great shifts of its southern passage, it moves on to the six great shifts of its northern passage. Inwardly, however, the process alternates between right and left channel petals as described above.

The twelve channels of the navel each divide up into a further five channels to make sixty lesser channels, through which the maṇḍalas of the minor elements flow. These are known as the maṇḍalas of the lesser shifts or the maṇḍalas of the minor elements. These are described as follows. The earth-maṇḍala wind that flows through the first channel petal during the great shift on the right side has parts corresponding to five elements. These elements flow as follows. Together with the number of earth-maṇḍala winds that flow through the first greater channel on the right as described previously, three hundred and forty-eight and three-quarter minor element earth-maṇḍala winds flow through the first lesser channel. Likewise, a similar number of breaths of water, fire, air, and space flow through the second, third, fourth, and fifth lesser channels, respectively. After that, fifty-six and a quarter gnosis winds flow though the central channel. The same process is repeated with the first channel of the left.

All five lesser channels that branch off from the first great channel on the right are pervaded by the earth maṇḍala in the sense of its being the dominant maṇḍala. A similar correspondence is made with the other groups of lesser channels. All six sets of five lesser channels on the right carry their winds in the dissolution order of earth, water, fire, air, and space. The corresponding sets of channels on the left carry their winds in the creation order of space, air, fire, water, and earth. In this way it can be understood that each great shift of wind at the nostrils carries five minor shifts of wind.

The predominant wind in the upper pathways of the three main channels is the life-sustaining wind. The predominant wind in their lower pathways is the downwardly expelling wind.

Whether it is from the left or right nostril, the earth-maṇḍala wind emerges for twelve finger widths, the water-maṇḍala thirteen finger widths, the fire fourteen, the air fifteen, and the space-maṇḍala wind travels a distance of sixteen finger widths outside the nostrils. When these winds enter the nostrils, the earth-maṇḍala reaches the navel before it returns. The water-maṇḍala stops one finger width before the navel, the fire two finger widths, the air three, and the space-maṇḍala stops four finger widths before the navel and then returns. The flow of the gnosis wind will be the same as the particular maṇḍala winds it follows.

In this tantra the five breath maṇḍalas of the left nostril are known as maṇḍalas of the five aggregates, and the five of the right nostril are known as the maṇḍalas of the five elements. Winds on the left are known as method winds, and those on the right are wisdom winds.

The positioned bodhicitta drops

The center of the forehead cakra carries the body drop that creates the waking state. The throat cakra carries the speech drop creating the dream state. The heart cakra contains the mind drop that creates the deep sleep state. The navel cakra carries the gnosis drop that creates the fourth state.[8] Furthermore, it is taught that the navel, the secret area, the center of the vajra jewel, and the tip of the jewel also carry drops of the waking, dream, deep sleep, and fourth states, respectively.

These drops comprise vital fluid, blood, and wind. In the drops at the throat, navel, and secret area the quantity of red element is greater than that of the white element. At the crown cakra and at the lower end of the central channel in the vajra jewel the quantity of white element is greater than that of the red element. The red element at the navel is the source of all the red element in the body. The white element at the crown is the source of all the white element in the body. At the heart the white and red elements are equal in quantity. The very subtle wind and mind exists in these four drops by way of absorption. The size of a drop is that of a mustard seed.

This brief presentation of channels, winds, and drops according to Kālacakra tradition has been compiled from the teachings of the great master and his disciples and has been set down as a memory aid for its author, Changkya Rölpa Dorjé. The scribe was the monk Lotsawa Ngawang Chöpel, widely learned in many aspects of Dharma.

By this work, may the virtuous and uncontaminated path of the great secret vehicle spread in all directions.

Translated by Gavin Kilty, Devon, England, September 2006

Endnotes

1. Lit. "channel wheels," but "cakra" has now been naturalized into English.

2. The petals too are channels.

3. No winds flow through empty petals.

4. According to Khedrup Norsang Gyatso in his *Ornament of Stainless Light* (Library of Tibetan Classics, vol. 14, Wisdom Publications: Boston, 2004) these two sets of six petals are arranged in the order given, but as listed here the two sets do not represent the zodiacal signs the sun passes through in its northern and southern passages. The signs or houses of the northern passage are, in order: Capricorn, Aquarius, Pisces, Aries, Taurus, Gemini, and of the southern passage Cancer, Leo, Virgo, Libra, Scorpio, and Sagittarius. Therefore, the movement of the airs through these petals to correspond with the sun moving through the signs jumps from one set to the others, from Capricorn to Aquarius, and so on.

5. The locations of the winds as taught here differ considerably from locations as taught in *Ornament of Stainless Light.*

6. A great wind shift or movement occurs within the body about every two hours, corresponding to a new zodiacal ascendant appearing on the horizon also about every two hours.

7. Here "winds" and "breaths" are interchangeable terms.

8. The fourth state is the bliss of orgasm.

II.

Analysis and Insight

—7—

Palden Lhamo: Supreme Guardian Goddess of the Dalai Lamas

Miranda Shaw

Your body blazes like a world's end fire,
Yours is the power of magical creation.
Your dance fills the sky, shaking the three worlds.
Your voice is like a thousand thunderclaps,
Laughing HA! HA! Howling a terrifying HŪM!
Churning the bottom of the ocean to the top of Mount Meru.
BHYOH! Your mind knows everything in essence and in detail;
You never leave the sphere of emptiness, but out of compassion
You tame enemies and obstacles, every method at your command.
I praise you, conquering female with a glorious body, voice, and mind.[1]

Palden Lhamo (*dPal-ldan Lha-mo*) is by any measure a frighteningly fearsome female. Her face displays a smoldering glare, with bared teeth, lashing tongue, and an impaled corpse dangling from her fangs. Her skin of midnight hue glistens with flecks of fat and blood. She sits astride a donkey that carries her fearlessly across seas of blood and gore, amid dense smoke and flames of cremation pyres. Wreathed with snakes, crowned with skulls, she shows her readiness for combat. Her tools of divination make it impossible to conceal misdeeds in her presence. Palden Lhamo brandishes a flaming weapon in one hand and with the other raises a skull bowl brimming with the blood of vanquished enemies. An impregnable castle fashioned of black onyx and corpses held in place by magical incantations, high on a storm-lashed mountain, is the forbidding fortress of this indomitable lady.

It is no wonder that early scholars considered Palden Lhamo to be a "hideous black monster" and "great she-devil," the very portrait of evil.[2] Tibetan Buddhists, however, vest in her a unique ministry and consummate protective powers. For them she serves as the supreme guardian of their nation, their faith, and the Dalai

Lamas. Palden Lhamo, whose name means "Glorious Goddess," is a "transcendent protector" (*'jig rten las 'das pa'i srung ma*), that is, a fully enlightened being, entirely free of malice and selfish intent. She manifests her astonishingly menacing appearance not to frighten the faithful but rather to confound and terrify demonic beings and evildoers who are driven by hatred, anger, and greed to inflict harm on others and increase suffering in the world. Such beings flee in terror at the awesome sight of Palden Lhamo. Giving chase on her intrepid steed, she applies her arsenal of weaponry and magical devices to subdue and transform them, removing the danger they pose to human well-being.

Palden Lhamo is the goddess with the most enduring, historically visible, and deeply personal relationship with the Dalai Lamas. One may wonder why Tibet's sacral rulers might require such a wrathful protector. They are, after all, religious leaders of vast scholarly and spiritual accomplishment, revered for their wisdom, regarded by their followers as living embodiments of Chenrezig, the lord of compassion. The holders of the office have nonetheless been besieged by intrigue and danger. A Dalai Lama was surrounded by all manner of persons who wished to do him harm to advance their own interests. Necromancers, political officials, defenders of the old faith, sectarian rivals, foreign governments, and even traitors in his own circle might unleash curses and spells against him or plot his poisoning, kidnap, or murder. His leadership took root in the treacherous terrain of a medieval feudal kingdom. Buddhist sects vied for regional dominance, backed up by the troops of their warlord patrons. Contending hierarchs raided and seized one another's monastic strongholds. On some occasions, a Dalai Lama had to vacate his abode, put on the run by the soldiers of competing sectarian forces. Demons, too, posed an ever-present threat, whether impelled by their own sinister motives or instigated by the dark arts of his enemies to afflict him with illness, mishap, and other obstacles. The Dalai Lamas required mighty protector deities to combat this array of natural and supernatural threats.

After introducing the form of Palden Lhamo in which the Dalai Lamas envision and propitiate her, I will examine her special relationship with them and her role as their supreme guardian goddess.

Palden Lhamo as Warrior Queen

Palden Lhamo takes numerous iconographic forms in which she appears in varied Tibetan lineage pantheons, meditations, and ritual practices. The epiphanies share many features in common but display different numbers of arms (two or four), handheld attributes, and identifying details of attire and adornment. Palden Lhamo is most commonly dark blue or black, two colors designated by the same Tibetan term (*nag*) and held as symbolically equivalent and largely interchangeable in Tibetan iconography.[3] She also appears in deep red and reddish brown manifestations. Her most prevalent form is known as Magzorma and Magzor Gyalmo, translatable as "Warrior Queen," or "Queen Armed for Combat," with reference to her magical weaponry (*zor*).[4] She is expert in the battle both of demons and of armies. Magzor Gyalmo is a prominent presence in the Tibetan pantheon, serving as a protector of lineages and monasteries across the Buddhist sectarian board and even adopted into Bon.[5] Most importantly for the present essay, Magzor Gyalmo is the form of Palden Lhamo that the First Dalai Lama took as his personal protector and that has remained in place as the guardian of the Dalai Lama lineage.

Magzor Gyalmo is deep blue or black, a coloration associated with wrathfulness and subjugation in Tibetan Buddhist imagery. She holds a vajra-tipped, flaming club in her right hand and skull brimming with blood in her left. The following passage from a Sakya liturgy vividly evokes her ominous appearance and accoutrements:

> Blue-black, with one face and two hands,
> The right hand holding a club topped with a vajra and human head,
> Poised over the brain of a vow-breaker,
> The left holding the skull of an ill-begotten child,
> Filled with blood and magical potions.
> Her face sparkles;
> She gnashes her sharp teeth, munching on a human corpse.
> Her laughter roars like thunder, A! LA! LA!
> Her three bulging eyes glare and flash like lightning,
> Her forehead is furrowed, her auburn hair flies upward.
> Her eyebrows and upper lip blaze like a world's end fire.
> She has . . . a crown of five dried human heads and
> A necklace of fifty freshly severed heads oozing blood.
> Her body is splattered with flecks of fat and drops of blood
> And smeared with cremation ashes
> . . . .
> A pouch of diseases is tied to the reins in front of the saddle,
> And behind is a ball of magical thread.
> A notched tally stick is slung at her waist,
> Along with a red bundle of curses.
> A pair of white and black dice hangs in front;
> Above her head is a canopy of peacock feathers.[6]

Many of these iconographic features are shared by various forms of Palden Lhamo, making them readily recognizable as manifestations of the same goddess. Mythic accounts explain how these bodily traits and implements came into her possession. The narratives of her origins and past lives are too elaborate and varied to recount here.[7] Therefore, I will focus on several key elements of her persona and weaponry in order to clarify how they reflect her character, vocation, and awesome protective powers.

Her appearance itself is part of her arsenal. The source of her astonishingly macabre persona finds varied explanation in her complex legendry. By several accounts she was once the most beautiful female in the universe. The king of demons coveted her as his queen and abducted her to his hellish realm, where she was forced to reign at his side. There she assumed a diabolical appearance and diet of flesh and blood. During her sojourn among the demons she learned many methods of slaughter and acquired her swift steed and tools of magical subjugation. When she finally escaped, she found her way to Śākyamuni Buddha, allied herself with him, and pledged to devote herself to the benefit of humankind. The Buddha affirmed, "You know how to slay demons, evildoers, and malignant spirits. You should become a Dharma-protector. Today I prophesy that henceforth you will be a guardian goddess who has the power to conquer all negative forces and uses it to protect those who follow the Buddhist path. You shall remain in this role until the end of time."[8] At that time, Palden Lhamo was a worldly protector, but through her meritorious deeds in defense of others and deepening insight into reality, she eventually attained enlightenment, becoming a transcendent protector.

As a divine being, Palden Lhamo can assume any bodily form she chooses. She retained her ferocious appearance by choice. Her former beauty had caused her great torment, and her murderous visage would serve her well as an intimidator, terrifier, and destroyer of demons and evildoers. She also retained the powerful possessions she had accrued. Her mount, a seemingly unprepossessing donkey, is the very steed that helped her abscond from the demon kingdom with fiendish minions in hot pursuit, proving its ability to outrun any foe.

The legends describe how Palden Lhamo came away with the flaming sword of the demon king. Magzor Gyalmo, however, holds a club topped with a vajra end-piece and an impaled head. The vajra represents wisdom and truth; it carries the power of indestructibility. She wields her cudgel against "vow-breakers," those who misuse magical rites and spells to harm others. The vajra tip imbues the club with invincibility, while the severed head signals the demise of its victims. The skull cup from which she sups is a *nal thod*, which Robert Beer helpfully characterizes as that of a "misbegotten child," explaining that such skulls have extraordinary ritual potency.[9] The child in this case was conceived during the rape of Palden Lhamo's servant and accomplice, Ramatî, in the demon kingdom. The ladies killed and consumed the ill-conceived offspring, and Rematî gifted the skull to her mistress to use for a bowl. Its presence proclaims Lhamo's thirst for the life-blood of demons. From it she drinks a bloody brew of magical potions that enhances her demon-taming powers.

Palden Magzor's special weaponry includes a ball of colored thread, notched tally stick, bundle of mantric curses, pair of dice, and sack of diseases. She keeps a ball or two of magical thread at the ready for the capture and binding of demons. The notched tally stick (*khram shing*) strapped to her waist or the bridle of her steed is an implement of pre-Buddhist provenance originally used for numerical recordkeeping. The stick lends itself to several uses, such as calculation of the sins and punishments of wrongdoers, the exorcism and destruction of demons, and the counteraction of curses.[10] Lhamo, however, has her own repertory of death-dealing curses, bundled into a small manuscript with reddened edges and bound in red silk. The dice are ancient Tibetan tools of divination, diagnosis, and healing.[11] Used in Buddhism for prognostication, the pair of black and white dice places destiny in Lhamo's hands, to mete out the fate she chooses. The pouch full of diseases reflects her power over illness, which she can use both to inflict sickness and to offer protection from pathogenic spirits.

In sum, her appearance and accoutrements show Magzor Gyalmo to be a formidable protector, consummately equipped for the destruction of demons, counteraction of black magic and evil spells, and conquest of enemy armies. As an enlightened being of nondual wisdom, the goddess recognizes no enemy and perceives the illusory nature of adversarial conflict. She enters the fray on behalf of those who fall prey to profoundly deluded beings that attack and torment others with vicious cruelty, casting themselves as destroyers of life and foes of truth in the drama of worldly existence.

Palden Lhamo and the Dalai Lamas

The Dalai Lamas invoke many divine allies in their meditations and ritual practices, but the primary guardians of their lineage are a pair that has come to be known as the Srung-ma dMar-nag, or "Red and Black Protectors."[12] When the Thirteenth Dalai Lama designed the Tibetan national flag early in the twentieth century, he featured red and black or deep blue lines radiating boldly from the sun-crested snow peak at the center to represent the two deities who have watched over the country's rulers and safeguarded spiritual and secular life in the land of snows.[13] Amy Heller documents how the identity of the red, male protector has shifted over the centuries.[14] The identity of the black, female protector, however, has never been in question. Palden Lhamo, in her Magzor Gyalmo form, was the special guardian of the First Dalai Lama and retained that role for all his successors. Her presence is interwoven through the visionary experiences, ceremonial life, pilgrimages, written works, and incarnational searches of the supreme Tibetan hierarchs. She has appeared in their dreams to deliver crucial messages and manifested in person to intervene at times of danger. To her they entrust their safety and their lives. When the Dalai Lamas speak or write of "Palden Lhamo" or even simply "Lhamo," it is to her they refer, and I follow suit here.

The First Dalai Lama, Gendun Drub (1391-1474), felt a strong personal connection with Palden Lhamo forged during his previous lifetimes. His autobiography records that the goddess appeared to him during his childhood, when he was asleep out of doors with his father and a monk accosted him during the night. Lhamo rode up on her mule, descended from her mount, and drove the monk away with her cudgel. This event impressed on the future lama her personal concern for and nearness to him.[15] Palden Lhamo also manifested before the First Dalai Lama after he took monastic vows at age nineteen and in dreams throughout his life.[16]

Desiring to resume the practices he had performed in his former lives, he traveled to the seat of the Sakya master Bodong to receive initiations and detailed oral instructions in all her rites and meditations. After founding Drepung Monastery, which he made his primary residence, he installed her as its main Dharma protector.[17] When his beloved teacher, Sherab Sengge, passed away, the weeping voice of his tutelary told him something grievous had happened and reassured him that she would follow him to the discovery and protect his followers. This drew him even closer to her and strengthened his devotion.[18] When his second and final major building project was nearing completion, he was pondering what to call the complex when Lhamo spoke to him and provided the name, Tashilhunpo, meaning "Heap of Blessings." When the leader fell ill in 1473 and tried various means of cure in hopes of recovery, he again heard Lhamo weeping and knew that the end of his life drew near, affording him opportunity to give parting instructions before passing away the next day.[19]

The First Dalai Lama's autobiography portrays a remarkably intimate relationship between mortal and goddess, as she remained near to him to counsel, console, and protect. By his own telling, Palden Lhamo became his "unique, chief protector" in a "close bond of mutual commitments," and "she became a unique, close and committed protector" of his lineage.[20]

The Second Dalai Lama, Gendun Gyatso (1475-1542), maintained intensive practice of the goddess. He recited her root mantra a thousand times daily, reaching, according to one of his biographies, a total of ten million recitations. When he was driven by the Karmapa's forces from Tsang to Central Tibet and took residence at Tashilhunpo, he commenced to offer tormas (ritual cakes) to her three times daily, in addition to a morning and evening rite, no doubt calling on her for intercession. During an armed conflict between supporters of the Drikung and Gelug sects, Lhamo caused the ropes of the enemy tents to break and raised a strong wind to carry the tents away, then continued to afflict the forces with mysterious turns of misfortune. Recognizing this miraculous turn of events as her supernatural intervention, Gendun Gyatso journeyed to view her image in his personal monastery, Chokhorgyal (discussed below), where he saw her body rise about six inches above the saddle and she appeared to be moist and fatigued from her exertions. From that time forward, the goddess and the lama "became inseparable as between body and its shadow," and she "appeared to annihilate all obstacles" in his path.[21]

Although the First Dalai Lama established Palden Lhamo as the special protector of his lineage, it was his successor who shaped her official cultus. The Second Dalai Lama penned a history of the goddess and rituals for her invocation.[22] He installed Palden Lhamo as a Dharma protector in monasteries that came under his abbotship and put in place liturgies he authored for her worship, making her practice normative for the Gelug sect.[23] An artist as well as a writer, he is credited with the famed "talking painting" (*gsung-byon-ma sku*) of Magzor Gyalmo that the Dalai Lamas hold as one of their most treasured possessions, serving for them as protective talisman and personal oracle.[24] The Second Dalai Lama also devised a system of dice divination (*sho mo*) under the divine patronage of Palden Magzorma. He formulated the meanings of every possible throw of three dice in answer to queries regarding domestic affairs, property, finances, legal matters, imminent danger, mental health, medical treatment, political and military affairs, business ventures, journeys, and lost objects. His system remains in use today, widely available in an oft-printed and widely circulated text.[25]

The Second Dalai Lama established the main sacred site associated with the goddess, a lake known as Chokhor Gyatso, "Lake of the Victorious Dharma-Wheel," or, more commonly, as Lhamo Latso, "Lhamo's Spirit Lake."[26] About ninety miles southeast of Lhasa, Lhamo's Spirit Lake is the turquoise centerpiece of a landscape of stunning beauty, cradled by three valleys and framed by three mountains. The triangle is associated with femaleness in Indic and Tibetan culture, so the triadic features of the sacred locale convey its feminine nature. Its reputation for association with Palden Lhamo drew Gendun Gyatso to the region in 1509 to investigate. Amy Heller translates his account of his visionary experiences of the goddess while gazing at the water's surface:

> At first it was completely white, a sign produced by the Glorious Goddess. Then proceeding to do a ritual invitation for her, I went east whereupon a sudden snowstorm arose, then the lake turned white as before. Some of the men saw rainbows, some saw a palace with turrets, then the lake became blue like the sky, and from the depths, a square tower grew, and a mountain, becoming increasingly large and frightening. I understood these as magical manifestations of the protector Lhamo . . . we all saw these miraculous sights. It is thus certain that this place is protected by Lhamo. When one sees the infinite ways in which she acts, it defies description.[27]

This experience deepened his devotion to the goddess.[28] The master returned to the area many times, performing Tantric rites that further refined the energies of the landscape and enhanced the visionary properties of the lake. Glenn Mullin observes that the fame of the revelatory powers of the sacred lake has since drawn hundreds of thousands of pilgrims from Tibet and beyond in search of prophecy and guidance and that, among Gendun Gyatso's numerous accomplishments, he is best known for his connection with Lhamo's Spirit Lake.[29]

On the same expedition, the Second Dalai Lama founded a monastery in a valley below the lake. Chokhorgyal Monastery is set in "Flower Meadow" (Metog Thang), so named for its colorful profusion of flowers and blossoming trees. As His Holiness sought a sign of where to build the monastery in this lovely setting, a white dzo appeared and remained motionless at a single spot for many hours, revealing the location.[30] Chokhorgyal and a hermitage nearby remained important for the Dalai Lamas as a place of retreat and practice and as a powerful place to conduct Palden Lhamo rituals. At a distance of four hours by foot from the lake, the monastery afforded a place where the leaders could reside and conduct Lhamo rites when they made pilgrimage to the area. A stone throne for the Dalai Lamas was later erected on a cliff overlook that provides a panoramic view of the lake's surface from a height of about 165 feet. A small temple dedicated to Magzor Gyalmo for the Dalai Lamas' personal use was built on the eastern shore.[31]

The Second Dalai Lama had occasion to call on Palden Lhamo's most potent powers of protection when one of his monasteries came under siege. Glenn Mullin vividly recounts the circumstance and what occurred when the savant journeyed to the sacred lake to appeal to the Warrior Queen for intervention:

> . . . in the autumn of the Fire Bird Year (1537), hostile armies threatened to attack and destroy his monastery at Gyal. As Konchok Kyab puts it, "Evil demons had caused jealousy of the master's great works to arise within the hearts of certain sectarian people. Numerous armies began to move toward Gyal from the east. . . . Many negative signs appeared in the Lake of Visions." The Second Dalai Lama . . . retreated to the Lake of Visions and performed invocations of and prayers to the Dharmapala goddess Palden Lhamo, requesting her to release her spiritual force and restore peace and harmony. A great storm erupted, and the skies were filled with terrible sounds. Palden Lhamo had given them a sign; all would be well. The Biography continues by stating that, as an external condition to fulfilling Palden Lhamo's magical works, King Nangso Donyopa of Droda suddenly swept down from nowhere upon the invading armies and routed them.[32]

This account reveals Gendun Gyatso's profound reliance on his female guardian at a time of direst practical need. Her field of activity is writ large. She thunders and conjures a storm in a vast mountainous setting. She has the power to move armies. Her miraculous provision of military intervention surely affirmed that the leader's confidence in his warrior goddess was well placed.

The Third Dalai Lama, Sonam Gyatso (1543-1588), sustained the close relationship with the protector. His biographer imparts that Palden Lhamo personally transported him to the home of his future mother and purified her womb. He had his first vision of the goddess during infancy, beholding her bearing a sword and skull cup full of jewels.[33] He spent the last day of every month praying and preparing a major torma offering for her and on the following morning made the offering on a terrace by the light of the rising sun. Palden Lhamo appeared in the sky before him and manifested other signs of her presence and blessings. The biographer also records that when "devils" plotted against him, Magzor Gyalmo appeared and destroyed them on the spot, and "this was actually witnessed," suggesting that it was human rather than demonic foes.[34] He placed great importance on Chokhorgyal and consecrated a major image of the goddess there.[35] This homage to his protector further enhanced the monastery as a site for her propitiation.

The Fifth Dalai Lama, Lozang Gyatso (1617-1682), kept reliance on Palden Lhamo in full force. He had ongoing rituals conducted at Chokhorgyal and traveled there regularly to perform them.[36] Like the Second, he left a stamp on the Palden Lhamo cultus. Known as the Great Fifth, it was he who, with the help of his

Mongol patrons, held regional and sectarian strife in check and placed himself at the political helm of a unified Tibet. His sway over the Mongol military consolidated his national influence. Apparently, Palden Lhamo had a hand in his deliverance. Commemoration of her role in victory became part of the New Year festivities in Lhasa. The Dalai Lama and other high officials gathered at the Jokhang to witness a parade of infantry and cavalry costumed in colorful armor, bearing weaponry from centuries past. The "Mongol" soldiers engaged in mock combat with antique swords and guns and sang war songs about Palden Lhamo.[37] This annual ceremony honored the warrior goddess for inspiring the soldiery and supernaturally assisting them in battle when Mongol troops enthroned the Great Fifth and bestowed the title of "Dalai Lama" on his lineage.

The Fifth Dalai Lama proclaimed Magzor Gyalmo to be identical to the supreme goddess of Tibet's pre-Buddhist cosmology, "Grandmother Queen of the Center of the Highest Heaven." The latter figure was the divine ancestress of the royal dynasty of Central Tibet. A resonance in the character of the two deities facilitated this equivalence. The "Grandmother Queen" wore the sun and moon as her ornaments, wielded thunder as her weapon, and was identified with the stormy sky.[38] Magzorma is also adorned with the sun and moon and is a stormy figure, with a thunderous voice and lightning-flash eyes, and a raiser of storms when occasion demands. Lozang Gyatso's equation of the two goddesses may have had political overtones, delivering a unifying yet triumphal message that he had inherited the throne of the theocratic kings before him because the selfsame goddess legitimated his reign.

At the time of his death, Palden Lhamo came to the fore in his final thoughts and parting instructions. His regent, Sangye Gyatso, agonized over whether to keep the leader's passing a secret in order to complete construction of the Potala and to keep Mongolian and Manchurian incursions at bay. The Great Fifth, who died in a seated meditation posture, revived long enough to commend reliance on his "chief Dharma protector" and that of all the Dalai Lamas before him.[39] He imparted that "on less important matters" the regent could follow his own wisdom, but on "momentous decisions" he should "direct all questions to Palden Lhamo" by performing dough ball and other methods of divination in front of the oracular painting."[40] Thus, his final words directed Sangye Gyatso to consult Lhamo regarding major decisions to be made during the interregnum and, by implication, in perpetuity. The regent had images of Lhamo and Begtse placed in Lozang Gyatso's reliquary stupa in the Potala to protect the monument.[41] Remarkably, the official kept the leader's death a secret for fifteen years, keeping the successor in hiding during that period.

The annals of the succeeding Dalai Lamas tell of the ongoing presence of Palden Lhamo in their visions, personal practices, and public ceremonial life. Even the Sixth Dalai Lama, whose assumption of office was significantly delayed, had a vision of Lhamo at age eleven, made pilgrimages to worship her at Chokhorgyal, received a vision from her in the sacred lake, and was delivered from the hands of captors when the goddess appeared, paralyzed them, and raised a storm for his escape.[42] Over the centuries, Dalai Lamas and their ministers have used various means of divination to seek her counsel when faced with weighty decisions. In the practice of dough ball divination (*zan-dbril*, "rolling dough"), sanctioned by the Fifth Dalai Lama on his deathbed, possible answers are written on slips of paper that are pressed into balls of dough and set on an altar in a small bowl, where they remain throughout a lengthy ritual invocation of Palden Lhamo. The bowl is then shaken until one of the dough balls rolls out, revealing her answer.[43] The revered "talking painting" held, and continues to hold, a central role in the divinatory process.

The New Year festivities initiated by the Second Dalai Lama and adopted by his successors opened with offerings to Palden Lhamo at the dawn of the first day. On the third day, the sovereign presided over an incense offering to Lhamo in the Potala and a dough ball divination to forecast the fortunes of the leader, the faith, and the nation during the upcoming year.[44] The military pageant inaugurated by the Fifth Dalai Lama, described above, took place on the twenty-fourth day. Another annual public ritual to secure the long life and good fortunes of the Dalai Lama entailed worship of Palden Lhamo in the Jokhang followed by the elaborate staging of a mock dice divination in which the dice are loaded, so the well-being of the leader is assured.[45]

Chokhorgyal Monastery remained important as a center for the ritual invocation of Palden Lhamo.[46] It also became customary for every incarnation of the Dalai Lama to journey to the sacred lake before he assumed the helm of government in order to foresee the events of his career and manner of his death. He also visited the lakeside Magzor Gyalmo shrine, which he alone may enter, to consult the goddess directly and seek her blessings and receive her prophecies for his upcoming term of leadership.[47]

Lhamo's Spirit Lake played a key role in the discovery of successive incarnations of the Dalai Lama. The search party ventured to the lake for revelations regarding where the leader had been reborn. They first made a retreat at Chokhorgyal Monastery, meditating and invoking Palden Lhamo for an accurate vision. The following account, translated by Glenn Mullin, describes what transpired during the search for the Thirteenth Dalai Lama in 1876:

> At the time of the group's arrival it was the middle of winter and the lake's surface was covered with snow. However, after they had completed their spiritual practices a forceful wind arose and cleaned away the snow, until "the surface of the lake became as clear as a crystal mirror polished a hundred times." Then slowly from within the lake various images began to form. First they saw a farm with neatly kept terraces above to the east. An ancient stupa stood to the northeast . . . . These and many other images came and then faded. The group also saw the shape of the mountains in the area, as well as the nearby villages, grazing lands and meadows . . . . All of this appeared to them "as clearly as though reflected in a mirror, or as though perceived in a crystal ball."[48]

These visions identified the village where the Dalai Lama had been reborn. He was discovered in a hamlet precisely matching the lacustrine scenes.

The present Dalai Lama was found in a similar manner. He relates in his autobiography how the regent journeyed to the sacred lake and on its waters

> . . . clearly saw the Tibetan letters *Ah*, *Ka* and *Ma* float into view. These were followed by the image of a three-storeyed monastery with a turquoise and gold roof and a path running from it to a hill. Finally, he saw a small house with strangely shaped guttering. He was sure that the letter *Ah* referred to Amdo . . . so it was there that the search party was sent.[49]

Again, the vision proved accurate. In Amdo province, Kumbum Monastery, referenced by the letter *Ka*, had a three-tiered turquoise roof, so the search party traveled the surrounding villages looking for the hill and distinctive house seen in the vision, finding at last Tenzin Gyatso's parents' home with gnarled juniper branches on the roof and the fourteenth incarnation of the Dalai Lama, three years old at the time, living within.[50]

The current Dalai Lama has oft stated that Palden Lhamo is his special protector. On the day he was officially recognized as the reincarnation, at age four, a lama pushed through the celebrating throngs and presented the new incarnation with a large red brocade bundle containing the painting of Lhamo by the Second Dalai Lama. On viewing it, the child "was so ecstatic that many of those around him burst into tears."[51] Twenty years later, when he fled from Tibet on horseback, the oracular painting was the only possession he brought with him.[52] Lhamo helped him elude the Chinese soldiers who were on the alert for his flight. Mikel Dunham elicited from firsthand accounts that, just as the leader and his retinue set forth from the Norbulingka on their death-defying journey, the goddess

> . . . made her contribution to the escape: A wind suddenly whipped up outside. A sandstorm enveloped the Vale of Lhasa. . . . According to those who escaped that night, this windstorm and the resultant murky veil were singularly propitious. Who else but Lhamo could have worked such magic?[53]

The sandstorm that enveloped the young leader's escape was blindingly thick, effectively concealing him from patrolling PLA forces. The wind abated precisely as the Dalai Lama and his retinue set across a river on yak skin vessels, calming the current for their safe passage.[54]

Although the Fourteenth Dalai Lama no longer has direct access to the sanctuaries and sacred lake in Tibet, he has the revered painting of Palden Lhamo with him, and he has revived the tradition of the Nechung Oracle in exile. He consults the Nechung trance medium of Dorje Dragden and performs divination in front of the painting on matters of great import, such as the identification of the reincarnations of important lineage masters and issues regarding his own religious life and ritual practices.[55] Services to the goddess are performed at his new monastic seat in Dharamsala, India, and a stupa dedicated to Lhamo has been constructed at the site.

Palden Lhamo emerges in the annals of the Dalai Lamas as a versatile and dynamic figure, providing invaluable foresight, lending guidance when the way forward is unclear, and offering vigorous support when negative powers are arrayed against them. The full story of her roles in their lives and careers has yet to be told and would require extensive research in their voluminous writings and related biographical and historical works. The results would help us better understand the unique relationship of Tibet's special lineage of spiritual and secular leaders with their guardian goddess. That relationship is ongoing, as seen in the Fourteenth Dalai Lama's revelations of the great faith he places in her divinatory counsel.

I close with a prayerful wish that Palden Lhamo and other protector deities will continue to watch over His Holiness and remove obstacles to his long life and Dharma activities, so he may continue to serve the Tibetan people and return to bless the world with his wisdom and compassion for as long as space endures.

Endnotes

1. My translation; *dPal ldan lha mo 'dod pa khams kyi dbang phyug ma'i phyi sgrub kyi gzhung mchog tu zab pa; sGrub thabs kun btus*, vol. 14, fol. 421.6-422.3, 422.5-6, with the refrain represented only once, as the final line.

2. Waddell, *Lhasa and Its Mysteries*, pp. 370-71, among many such judgments.

3. This equivalence of blue and black is seen also in India, as in the case of the goddess Kālī, "Black One," who may be shown as blue or black. Thus, Palden Lhamo's epithet as Mahākālī, "Great Black One," nonetheless leaves open the possibility that she might be conceived and depicted as blue or black.

4. In Tibetan, dMag-zor-ma and dMag-zor rgyal-mo. Her name does not yield easily to literal translation. *dMag* is an adjectival marker of things military; *zor* refers to magical weaponry. I construe this primarily as "magical weaponry of military application," which might apply to their use on behalf of armies or use to defeat armies, while the magical nature of the weaponry suggests its employment against supernatural beings as well. She is invoked in all three capacities, making it difficult to settle on one meaning.

5. See Ladrang Kalsang, *Guardian Deities of Tibet*, pp. 30-31, for a range of lineages with Magzorma as a protector.

6. My translation; *'Dod khams dbang phyug dmag zor rgyal mo'i sgrub thabs gtor chog; sGrub thabs kun btus*, vol. 14, fol. 537.4-538.2.

7. Multiple versions of the legend of Palden Lhamo can be found in Kalsang, *Guardian Deities of Tibet*, pp. 17-25, and in my forthcoming book, *Buddhist Goddesses of Tibet and Nepal*. One origin story is related and analyzed in Shaw, "Transcendent Fury of Palden Lhamo."

8. From the version I collected in oral form from the Sakya lama Khorchag Rinpoche in Kathmandu, Nepal, in the autumn of 1995.

9. Beer, *Encyclopedia of Tibetan Symbols*, pp. 263-64.

10. On the history of the tally stick: Tas, "Tally-stick and Divination Dice," pp. 163-70. On its potential uses: Nebesky-Wojkowitz, *Oracles and Demons of Tibet*, p. 358; Willson and Brauen, eds., *Deities of Tibetan Buddhism*, p. 567.

11. Tas, "Tally-stick and Divination Dice," pp. 170-74.

12. Amy Heller, surveying the history of the duo, reports that this title only came into usage in the twentieth century; "Historic and Iconographic Aspects," pp. 480, 494.

13. Heller, "Historic and Iconographic Aspects," pp. 490-91. For this and further analysis of the flag, see the Office of Tibet, London, official website: http://www.tibet.com/flag.html.

14. This is Heller's primary topic in "Historic and Iconographic Aspects." The main male protector has variously been Begtse, Mahākāla, and Dorje Dragden, who communicates through the Nechung Oracle.

15. Kalsang, *Guardian Deities of Tibet*, pp. 26-27, 29.

16. Heller, "Historic and Iconographic Aspects," p. 486.

17. Kalsang, *Guardian Deities of Tibet*, p. 29.

18. Kalsang, *Guardian Deities of Tibet*, p. 26.

19. Bell, *Religion of Tibet*, pp. 104, 106; recounting these events from a biography, Bell reads *lha-mo* simply as "goddess," not recognizing Lha-mo as a common shorthand designation for Palden Lhamo.

20. Phrases translated from his work by Ladrang Kalsang, *Guardian Deities of Tibet*, pp. 26, 27, 29.

21. Kalsang, *Guardian Deities of Tibet*, p. 27; quotes on pp. 27 and 27-28.

22. Heller, "Historic and Iconographic Aspects," p. 486.

23. Heller, *Tibetan Art*, p. 182; in his system, Begtse was the red male counterpart.

24. Heller, "Historic and Iconographic Aspects," pp. 488-89. The painting was eventually moved from Chokhorgyal to the Potala when the latter became the seat of the hierarchs. Its presence at the Potala is noted during the regnancy of the Seventh Dalai Lama; Heller, op. cit., p. 488.

25. Radha, "Tibet," pp. 17-18. The widely circulated text is a summary by Ngawang Ngodrub of the Second Dalai Lama's treatise on dice divination.

26. In Tibetan, Chos-'khor rgyal-mtsho and Lha-mo bla-mtsho, Lha-mo'i bla-mtsho, or Lha-mo Lung-mtsho.

27. Translation by Amy Heller in *Tibetan Art*, p. 183.

28. Brauen, *Dalai Lamas,* p. 216.

29. Mullin, *Selected Works of the Dalai Lama 2*, 17; see also pp. 199-201 for prophecies of his discovery of the lake.

30. Heller, *Tibetan Art*, p. 183.

31. Dowman, *Power-Places of Central Tibet*, pp. 257, 260-61.

32. Mullin, *Second Dalai Lama,* pp. 103-4.

33. Brauen, *Dalai Lamas,* p. 216, citing the biography by the Fifth Dalai Lama.

34. Ladrang Kalsang, *Guardian Deities of Tibet*, p. 28.

35. Brauen, *Dalai Lamas,* pp. 53, 216.

36. Brauen, *Dalai Lamas,* p. 217.

37. Richardson, *Ceremonies of the Lhasa Year*, pp. 30, 39-41. These battle hymns would make a fascinating study if they have been recorded.

38. Her name in Tibetan, A-phyi gnam-gyi gung-rgyal; Tucci, *Tibetan Painted Scrolls*, p. 719.

39. From the supplement to the Fifth's autobiography by the regent; Kalsang, *Guardian Deities of Tibet*, pp. 28-29.

40. From the description of this event in "Speech Delivered by His Holiness 14th Dalai Lama," p. 15; the specification of dough ball divination is added from the translated excerpt of the regent's text in Kalsang, *Guardian Deities of Tibet*, p. 29.

41. Brauen, *Dalai Lamas,* pp. 217, 225.

42. Heller, "Historic and Iconographic Aspects," p. 488; Aris, *Hidden Treasures and Secret Lives,* pp. 190, 195.

43. The Fourteenth Dalai Lama details his use of this method to determine whether to continue the practice of Shugden; Brauen, *Dalai Lamas,* p. 175.

44. Richardson, *Ceremonies of the Lhasa Year*, pp. 11, 20-21. On the Second Dalai Lama's initiatory role: Brauen, *Dalai Lamas,* p. 216.

45. Richardson, *Ceremonies of the Lhasa Year*, pp. 64-65.

46. Amy Heller gathered references to the Dalai Lamas' activities at Chokhorgyal in "Historic and Iconographic Aspects," pp. 485, 487-90.

47. Bell, *Religion of Tibet*, p. 159. Bell notes a folk belief that the early demise of the Ninth through Twelfth Dalai Lamas may have resulted from some fault in their lakeside propitiation of the goddess but adds the observation, made by a Chinese military officer, that Chinese envoys in Tibet were familiar with the lakeside visit and might take advantage of the popular belief to choose that time to attempt assassination; pp. 159-60.

48. Mullin, *Path of the Bodhisattva Warrior*, p. 24.

49. Gyatso, *Freedom in Exile*, p. 11.

50. Gyatso, *Freedom in Exile*, p. 11.

51. Avedon, *In Exile from the Land of Snows,* p. 10.

52. Tenzin Gyatso, *Freedom in Exile*, p. 138, reports carrying only a rifle as part of his disguise, his eyeglasses, and the painting. He states on pp. 135-36 that, when faced with the heartrending decision of whether to leave his country, he consulted the Nechung Oracle and performed divination (*mo*). Since Dorje Dragden (communicating through the oracle) and Palden Lhamo are the two protectors he consults on all major issues, I deduce that to be the case in this instance as well. They directed him to leave immediately.

53. Dunham, *Buddha's Warriors,* p. 287.

54. Dunham, *Buddha's Warriors,* p. 288.

55. He has reported in various interviews and venues that he consulted the protectors in this manner to confirm the reincarnations of Paltrul Rinpoche and Bodong Rinpoche and to determine whether to continue the practice of Shugden (see note 43 above) and to receive the Phurbu initiation.

Bibliography

Aris, Michael. *Hidden Treasures and Secret Lives: A Study of Pemalingpa (1450-1521) and the Sixth Dalai Lama (1683-1706).* Shimla: Indian Institute of Advanced Study, 1988.

Avedon, John F. *In Exile from the Land of Snows: The Definitive Account of the Dalai Lama and Tibet Since the Chinese Occupation.* 1984. Reprint ed. New York: HarperCollins, 1997.

Beer, Robert. *The Encyclopedia of Tibetan Symbols and Motifs.* London: Serindia Publications, 1999.

Brauen, Martin. *The Dalai Lamas: A Visual History.* Chicago: Serindia Publications, 2005.

Dowman, Keith. *The Power-Places of Central Tibet: The Pilgrim's Guide.* London and New York: Routledge and Kegan Paul, 1988.

Dunham, Mikel. *Buddha's Warriors: The Story of the CIA-Backed Tibetan Freedom Fighters, the Chinese Communist Invasion, and the Ultimate Fall of Tibet.* New York: Penguin, 2004.

Gyatso, Tenzin. *Freedom in Exile: The Autobiography of the Dalai Lama.* New York: HarperCollins, 1990.

Heller, Amy. "Historic and Iconographic Aspects of the Protective Deities Srung-ma dmar-nag." In *Tibetan Studies, Proceedings of the 5th Seminar of the International Association of Tibetan Studies, Narita, 1989*, pp. 479-92. Narita: Naritasan Shinshoji, 1992.

———. *Tibetan Art: Tracing the Development of Spiritual Ideals and Art in Tibet 600-2000 A.D.* Milan: Jaca Book, 1999.

Kalsang, Ladrang. *Guardian Deities of Tibet.* Dharamsala: Little Lhasa Publications, 1996.

Mullin, Glenn H. *Path of the Bodhisattva Warrior: The Life and Teachings of the Thirteenth Dalai Lama.* Ithaca: Snow Lion Publications, 1988.

———. *The Second Dalai Lama: His Life and Teachings.* Ithaca: Snow Lion Publications, 2005.

———. *Selected Works of the Dalai Lama 2: Tantric Yogas of Sister Niguma.* Ithaca: Snow Lion Publications, 1985.

Nebesky-Wojkowitz, Réne de. *Oracles and Demons of Tibet: The Cult and Iconography of the Tibetan Protective Deities.* The Netherlands: Mouton and Co., 1956.

Radha, Lama Chime. "Tibet." In *Oracles and Divination*, ed. by Michael Loewe and Carmen Blacker, pp. 3-37. Boulder: Shambhala, 1981.

Richardson, Hugh. *Ceremonies of the Lhasa Year.* London: Serindia Publications, 1993.

Shaw, Miranda. "The Transcendent Fury of Palden Lhamo: Protector of the Tibetan Faith." *Parabola: Myth, Tradition, and the Search for Meaning* 24, no. 4 (Winter 1999): 40-46.

"Speech Delivered by His Holiness 14th Dalai Lama to the Second Gelug Conference" (Dharamsala, June 12, 2000). Trans. Rabjam Sherab Gyatso. Article posted on http://www.fpmt.org.

Tas, Róna. "Tally-Stick and Divination-Dice in the Iconography of Lha-mo." *Acta Orientalia Academiae Scientiarum Hungaricae* 6 (1956): 163-79.

Tucci, Giuseppe. *Tibetan Painted Scrolls.* 1949. Reprint. Kyoto: Rinsen, 1980.

Waddell, L. Austine. *Lhasa and Its Mysteries: With a Record of the British Tibetan Expedition of 1903-1904.* 1905. Reprint. New York: Dover, 1988.

Willson, Martin, and Martin Brauen, eds. *Deities of Tibetan Buddhism: The Zürich Paintings of the Icons Worthwhile to See (Bris sku mthoõ ba don ldan).* Boston: Wisdom Publications, 2000.

—8—

Oṃ Vākyeda Namaḥ: Mañjuśrī's Mantra and Its Uses

Glenn Wallis

INTRODUCTION

In Chapter Twenty-nine of the *Mañjuśrīmūlakalpa* (henceforth *Mmk*),[1] the Buddha entrusts to the bodhisattva Mañjuśrī a mantra to be used in the dark days when the dharma is in decline. The mantra is *oṃ vākyeda namaḥ.* A pronounced feature of the type of Buddhism promoted in the *Mmk* is the insistence that Buddhist practice accommodate the multiple concerns, both worldly (*laukika*) and ultimate (*lokottara*), that presumably motivate the practitioner. So, here too, the mantra is said to be particularly conducive to three matters of persistent concern in the text, namely, the acquisition of worldly knowledge (*dṛṣṭidharma*), the hindrance of unfortunate rebirths (*durgati*), and the attainment of awakening (*bodhi*). As Matthew Kapstein points out, the mantra, far from being merely a relic of Buddhism's past, "is recited to this day in Tibet, particularly by those wishing to gain the boon of Mañjuśrī's wisdom as an aid to study."[2]

After revealing the mantra, the Buddha gives instructions on rituals to be performed at a caitya containing relics. In fact, the recitation of a mantra *(mantrajapa)* in the *Mmk* is invariably but one element within a larger ritual complex. This complex includes an extended period of preparatory practice (*pūrvaseva* or *puraścaraṇa*), the construction and employment of a painted icon (*paṭa*), and knowledge of the forces of awakening operating in the universe. I will include discussion of these elements in notes to the translation of the text, which I now present.

TRANSLATION

Cosmological setting

Now, the blessed Śākyamuni looked down again on the palace of the śuddhāvāsa heaven and spoke to the princely Mañjuśrī.[3] "This instruction on a ritual employing the painted icon (*paṭa*) is the seventh chapter [*sic*] in your ritual ordinance, Mañjuśrī. Whoever, at this time, in this period at the end of the eon,[4] will practice it, success for that person will certainly be unfailing, fruitful, happiness will arise, happiness will ripen. Success will arise concerning worldly knowledge, leading to the hindrance of all unfortunate rebirths, and leading always to his attainment of awakening."

Bestowal of the mantra

Then, the blessed Śākyamuni spoke the hṛdaya[5] of the princely Mañjuśrī.
Possessing six syllables, by nature releasing one
from the six unfortunate rebirths,
equal to incomparable, inconceivably great power.
Releasing one from the binding fetters of existence,
the tumultuous ocean of every form of existence,
the pain of the three sufferings.

Unbearable for all demons,
an anointment for the entire world.
Invincible against all demons,
completely purifying the path of becoming.

Establishing the teachings of the buddhas,
hindering all obstacles,
applauded by all buddhas,
accomplishing every kind of good fortune.
Superior among all mantras
in the teaching of Mañjughoṣa.

Which mantra is that? It is *oṃ vākyeda namaḥ.*

The preliminary practice

He who subsists on begged alms, greens, and grains, makes the ablution at the three appointed times, and wears the triple robe should recite the syllables one hundred thousand times. He becomes one who has done the preliminary practice.[6]

The paṭa

Then, on a canvas with the outermost fringes left uncut, the noble Mañjuśrī should be painted by an artist who observes the twice-monthly fast. [Mañjuśrī] is situated in the lotus posture teaching the dharma. [Mañjuśrī] is adorned with all of the ornaments, possessing the form of a prince, his outer garment loosened. To his left is the noble Avalokiteśvara, holding a lotus in his hand. On his right is the noble Samantabhadra, who is holding a plume. Above him should be drawn two mālādharas and two vidyādharas coming out of the clouds.[7] Below him is the practitioner (*sādhaka*) holding in his hand an incense vessel. Mountain peaks should be painted all around. At the foot of these are lotus lakes.[8]

The rituals

At a caitya that contains relics, [the practitioner] sets up the paṭa facing east and performs the exalted worship. Lighting lamps of ghee, he consecrates with mantras one thousand and eight flowers of excellent quality one by one. He should throw these at Mañjuśrī's face. He hears the sound of an extremely deep *ḤŪṂ*. The paṭa trembles. By means of the *ḤŪṂ* sound he becomes a king possessing sovereignty over the entire world. When the paṭa trembles, he becomes the superior disputant in all disputations, possessed of knowledge of a single treatise comprising the entire world. Now this is not to be effected; he becomes one who is capable of performing all rituals. This is the first practice.

Throughout the night, he should make oblations of *oilbanum* oil smeared on *khadira* wood charcoal pieces that have been fumigated by aloa wood sticks measuring a half finger's length. At dawn, he sees the noble Mañjuśrī. [Mañjuśrī] grants him a boon, as [the practitioner] wishes, other than one associated with desire.

Burning sandalwood incense continually before the paṭa, he should perform recitation (*japa*) throughout the night. Then [at the end of the night], Mañjuśrī comes into his presence and teaches the profound dharma. [The practitioner] worships him; and, having worshipped him, becomes one who is completely free of, and has power over, illness.

After making a lotus flower ornament out of red sandalwood, mixing together six *angula* long flower stems and red sandalwood, making one thousand mantra consecrations concurrently with one thousand oblations, and placing these on a lotus leaf in front of the paṭa on a full moon day, he should, enclosing this in his hand, perform japa for as long as [the oblation] burns.

In grasping [the paṭa], he assumes the form of a sixteen-year-old, shining in golden resplendence, his glow surpassing that of the sun's, a deva prince. Bowing to all the vidyādharas, he lives for a great eon. And, on the dissolution of his body, he is reborn in Abhirati.

Gathering white *vacā* herbs during a lunar eclipse and cleansing them with the five products of the cow, he wraps them in fig leaves. He should perform japa until it heats up, emits smoke, and burns brightly. He becomes capable of subjecting all people, one who is triumphant in all verbal disputations. As the smoke is rising, he becomes invisible. He lives for thirty thousand years. Radiating, he moves through space, living for a great eon.

Acquiring some ghee from brown, calf-like cows, he sets up a copper vessel with seven fig leaves. He should perform japa until, in this manner, he becomes one who has realized the triple knowledge (*trividhā*). Abounding in that, he becomes in this manner one who moves invisibly through space, retaining the transmitted teachings.

Throwing a flower seed in the face [of the paṭa], he should perform japa when the moon is eclipsed until [the paṭa] is made to quiver. Having wrapped it with the three types of metal and cast it at the face, he becomes one who is rendered invisible. When [the mantra) has been uttered, he is made visible [again].

Casting clove incense at the face, he should recite the mantra six hundred thousand times. He becomes one who subjugates the husband of Yamāla. He who subsists on milk and barley should recite the mantra one hundred thousand times. He becomes a vidyādhara. He who subsists on alms, the sage of the woods, should recite the mantra one hundred thousand times. He becomes one who attains invisibility. He should recite the mantra ten million times. Then Mañjuśrī teaches him the dharma. He becomes a bodhisattva, one who is living his final existence. Through continual recitation of the mantra he becomes one who is exalted in all matters.

Having made an image and covered it with all kinds of fragrances, he offers an oblation. In seven nights, he becomes capable of subduing others at will. He should offer one hundred thousand balls of fragrant resin, each measuring the weight of a jujube fruit kernel, coated with ghee. He obtains a hundred thousand gold coins.

Crossing a river, the seafarer should offer one hundred thousand lotuses. He sees a great treasure equal in value to an abundance of lotuses. He cannot perish. [The practitioner] should offer one thousand and eight white mustard seeds coated with saffron. He becomes a ruler, capable of subduing others at will. He should offer one hundred thousand sesame seeds coated with thickened milk, honey, and ghee. He becomes a great, beneficent, householder.

Erecting a small platform with unclaimed refuse and covering it with scattered flowers, he should recite the mantra one hundred and eight times. Then, he should recite a book of the good teaching. Within a month, he becomes one possessed of superior intelligence. Having made one hundred and eight measurements of yellow pigment, he should fashion a mark on his forehead. He becomes one who is dear to all people. Having made a crown consecrated with seven recitations of the mantra, unassailable among all people. He should offer a garland of *kiri* ten thousand times. He becomes one who is freed from every disease.

Day after day, he should perform japa seven times. He expiates with certainty that which is known as karma. Then, with one hundred and eight recitations of the mantra, at the time of death, he sees the noble Mañjuśrī, completely, face to face.

Endnotes

1. The printed text that forms the basis of this article was prepared by T. Gaṇapati Śāsrtī on the basis of the single known manuscript of the work, discovered near Padmanabhapuram, South India, in 1909. Śāstrī's work was published in three parts in the Trivandrum Sanskrit Series: Part I = no. LXX, 1920; Part II = LXXVI, 1922; Part III = LXXXIV, 1925, Trivandrum. This version was reprinted in a single volume by CBH Publications, Trivandrum,

1992, and recast with superficial changes by P. L. Vaidya, *Mahāyānasūtrasaṃgraha*, Part II, Buddhist Sanskrit Texts, no. 18, Bihar, 1964.

See further: Y. Matsunaga, "On the Date of the *Mañjuśrīmūlakalpa*," in *Tantric and Taoist Studies in Honour of R. A. Stein,* M. Strickmann (ed.), vol. 3, in vol. 22 of *Mélanges Chinois et Bouddhiques,* Brussels (1985): 882-894; G. Wallis, *Mediating the Power of Buddhas: Ritual in the Mañjuśrīmūlakalpa,* Albany, 2002.

2. Matthew Kapstein, "Weaving the World: the Ritual Art of the *Paṭa* in Pāla Buddhism and Its Legacy in Tibet," in *History of Religions*, vol. 34, no. 3 (1995): 241-262.

3. Virtually every chapter of the *Mmk* opens with a scene common to medieval Indian ritual works. Whether Śaiva, Vaiṣṇava, or Buddhist, such works are typically framed by a cosmological setting. The *Mmk* thus begins with the śuddhāvāsa devaputras asking Śākyamuni—who is situated in the sky above the devaputras—to speak on various matters pertaining to awakening. This setting serves two principal, related ends. First, it is a rhetorical strategy legitimizing the teachings that constitute the work; second, it provides the basis for imagining (or viewing) and knowing the universal grounds on which the ritual activity rests. A basic assumption of the *Mmk* is that the power of its rituals is limited by the practitioner's mental darkness concerning this understanding. It is thus one of the functions of the text to disclose to the practitioner the required knowledge. Only when this knowledge is acquired can the elements of cultic practice successfully mediate enlightened power and thereby transform the practitioner into a being of power himself. "Cultic practice," then, clearly includes within its scope a wide range of activities not normally contained in that term. In the *Mmk*, an essential practice that presupposes cultic performance *per se* is that of properly conceptualizing the space that serves as the matrix of the mantracaryā. Significantly, the *Mmk* discloses this space at the very outset. In so doing, the text is arguing that the very foundation of its ritual course is the structure of the cosmos itself. This is the meaning of the lexically complex term *dharma*. The *dharma* (teaching) is the *dharma* (correct, proper) because of the *dharma* (the way things are). The *Mmk*'s teaching is what it is because the cosmos—transfigured by the light of the buddhas—is integral to each of its elements. The opening scene of the *Mmk* evokes for the reader the proper vision of the cosmos.

> Homage to all buddhas and bodhisattvas! Thus have I heard. At one time the Blessed One was dwelling in the vault of sky above the śuddhāvāsa heaven, in the pavilion of the assembly of inconceivably, miraculously, wondrously distributed bodhisattvas. There, the Blessed One spoke to the devaputras, the inhabitants of the śuddhāvāsa. "Hear, O devaputras, about that on which all beings depend: the inconceivable, wondrous, miraculous transformation of the bodhisattva, the [use of the] maṇḍala for superior liberation, purity, contemplation, proper conduct; [hear about] the mantras of that great being, the princely bodhisattva Mañjuśrī, which completely fulfill one's wishes for power, health, and long life. Listen to that and bear it well in mind. I will speak to you."
>
> Then, with hands folded in salutation, those devaputras dwelling in the śuddhāvāsa heaven [requested to be taught]: "Out of compassion for us and for all beings, may the Blessed One, whose mind is benevolent and well disposed, speak about that."
>
> Then, the blessed Śākyamuni, looking down upon the entire dwelling of the śuddhāvāsa, entered into a state of concentration called *destroying through the dispersion of light into the purified sphere of activity*. Immediately upon entering into this state, the Blessed One [issued forth] a ray of light called impelling the bodhisat-

tva in Saḥkusumita. Seeing the brilliant white light, and smiling slightly, he spoke to the group of bodhisattvas: "This, O sons of the conqueror, is my impelling of the light. Come here. Prepare yourselves."

The opening passage of the *Mañjuśrīmūlakalpa* heralds the dispersion of an enlightening power into the world. The emergence of this power is signified by the ray of light emanating from the Buddha. This light is a sign from the Buddha to particular celestial and earthly beings that he is going to teach about "that upon which all beings depend" for their worldly happiness and ultimate liberation. It is also an impelling force causing this host of beings to assemble in his presence. Once they have heard the teaching, this assembly will disperse again to the earthly and celestial regions of the world to serve that teaching—it is for this that they must "prepare" themselves. The ray of light—and the Buddha's smile—is thus a sign that the Buddha has turned his thoughts to our world, "out of compassion for all beings," and will now act to lay the groundwork of a universally applicable teaching: the mantracaryā of the *Mañjuśrīmūlakalpa*.

4. At *Mmk* 7.73.7-18 is a fuller account of "this period at the end of the eon."

> In the future, when the teacher of the world passes away, when the sun lineage of the tathāgata disappears, when every Buddha-field is abandoned by all bodhisattvas, noble hearers, and solitary buddhas; when the receptacle of the world becomes darkened; when the path of the noble ones is severed; when all jewels, gems, mantras, medicines, and knowledge are lost. When, devoid of good people, beings in the world are deprived of light, they will become lazy, desirous of destruction, faithless, divided, surrounded by bad friends, deceitful, deluded, of fraudulent conduct. Hearing this discourse on the teaching, these will be seized by fear. Those who delight in sloth and indolence will not have faith; those seeking pleasure, rejoicing in false doctrines, will not exert themselves. These will produce much nonvirtue; those who discard the true teaching, who descend to the avıci hell, go from terror to greater terror. For the sake of those who are afflicted, subjugating the unsubjugated, in order to give safety to the meek, by means of complete skillfulness in means, O Blessed One, speak about the rules for the painted cloth icon and mantras, if you think the time is right.

This passage can be interpreted in several ways. First, the language of the passage is apocalyptic. The images employed are dramatic, conveying a sense of imminent devastation. It is tempting to claim that something of the social context of the *Mmk* is coming through here. Such language suggests an environment in which a community's established social patterns are being threatened. Chaos and loss might be detected in the first half of the passage in particular. Less drastically, the passage could point to a competitive environment, in which various groups are vying to win adherents and patrons. The apparent fact that the content and style of the Buddhist literature of this period (i.e., from the eighth to the thirteenth centuries) increasingly converged with that of the non-Buddhist sects, such as the Vaiṣṇava Pañcarātrins, might corroborate this suggestion. Unfortunately, too little is known about the date and provenance of the various portions of the *Mmk* to warrant decisive claims about the social conditions surrounding the work. We can more cautiously consider the rhetorical value of this passage. The form of Buddhist practice prescribed in the *Mmk* is not dependent on the monastic communities. The sādhaka is a solitary practitioner, whether monk or layman. As an ācārya, he may teach certain rituals to individual lay people. Other than the initiation rite, there is no indication of communal practice in the *Mmk*. The ability to access the power of the Buddha requires secretive, extra-monastic forms of training and induction. Thus, as opposed to institutional forms of Buddhism, the practice of the *Mmk* is private, lay, and esoteric. In light of this, we might interpret the "[severed] path of the noble ones" as referring not to encroaching Hindu sects, but to the erroneous systems of the Buddhist monastic establishment. It is the monks who have become "lazy, desirous of destruction, faithless, divided, surrounded by bad friends, deceitful, deluded, of fraudulent conduct . . . engaged in sloth and indolence . . . seeking pleasure, rejoicing in false doctrines." Resisting the innovations of the *Mmk*, the establishment monks "produce much nonvirtue [and] discard the true teaching." Whether "the true teaching" of the *Mmk* is being contrasted to non-Buddhist or Buddhist practices, the text is proclaiming the advent of an extraordinary era when traditional practices will have lost their potency. The simplified mantracaryā of the *Mmk* as a whole refines and restructures the universal teaching of the buddhas in the same manner that *Mmk* 7 does for the specific teaching on the cult object. The above passage can thus be read as pointing to the *Mmk's* tendency toward innovative synthesis. Matthew Kapstein (op. cit.) sees in such a tendency a central feature of esoteric Buddhism. He writes of an "apparently paradoxical dimension of esoteric Buddhist doctrine"

> which always claims that, as the world-age steadily degenerates, ever more efficacious means are revealed in the tantras. Though this no doubt served as a rationale for the introduction and gradual acceptance of new tantras and tantric techniques, it may without much interpretive violence be taken to mean that as [the] world becomes a messier place, so that the large-scale order of the Buddhist monastic community can no longer be well maintained, the local, ephemeral and often personal order engendered by high-powered techniques of ritual and yoga perforce become the primary points at which enlightened activity may enter the world.

See also, R. Davidson, *Indian Esoteric Buddhism: A Social History of the Tantric Movement*, New York, 2002.

5. At *Mmk* 2.25.10, there is reference to Mañjuśrī's "class of mantras." This comment is followed by a compendium of the mantras used in the *Mmk* rituals. The first group comprises hṛdaya mantras. Examples of this type are also given at *Mmk* 1.2.20-22, 27-3.9. This section mentions three classes of hṛdaya mantra, namely, the *hṛdaya, paramahṛdaya*, and *upahṛdaya.* Capturing as it does the "heart or essence (*hṛdaya*)" of a being, a hṛdaya mantra functions in the *Mmk* primarily to lead the practitioner into the presence of the being or force that is being invoked by the mantra.

6. The idea that successful ritual performance requires both stringent preparation and continual practice is a commonplace, if often implicit, feature of medieval Indian ritual literature. Throughout the manuals, the simplest ritual gestures are shown to require a considerable groundwork of training and instruction if they are to be effective. From initiation into a cult to its mastery, the practitioner is instructed in a series of interlocking conceptual and technique-oriented practices that aim simultaneously to lead him into the vision of life postulated by the community and to mold him into an ideal type of person. The scope of this ideal is indicated by the term for "practitioner" in this literature, *sādhaka*—one who is able to effect the power of ritual practices and thereby accomplish his, or his benefactors', ends. The term *puraścaraṇa* specifically refers to a series of ritualized activities. Though activities vary from such sect to sect, they generally include such practices as prolonged mantra recitation (*japa*), ablutions (*snāna*), oblations (*homa*), meditation (*dhyāna*), worship (*pūjā*), and alms begging (*bhikṣā*). These practices are carried out under a vow (*vrata*) during an

extended period of training. The execution of the puraścaraṇa follows formal initiation into a cult but precedes the performance of advanced ritual practice; hence, it is literally a preliminary (*puraś*) practice (*caraṇa*). The purpose of the puraścaraṇa is precisely to acquire the expertise deemed necessary for successful practice of advanced rituals (*uttamasādhana*) that are prescribed by a given community. The term is used by both Buddhist and Hindu groups in medieval India. One common characteristic of the diverse groups that fall under these monikers lay in their ritual programs. All placed great emphasis on elements that are generally considered emblematic of a tantric milieu. That is, emphasis was placed on the prerequisite of initiation (*abhiṣeka* or *dikṣa*) by a qualified *guru*, the employment of two- or three-dimensional diagrams (*maṇḍala* or *yantra*) in several categories of rituals—appeasement, possession, attraction, fixation, hostility, destruction, and death—the use of sculpted (*pratimā*) or painted (*paṭa*) images of deities and revered beings in devotional rituals, and the implementation of hand-gestures (*mudrā*) in "sealing" the efficacy established by means of practice. Of paramount importance to these groups' ritual programs, furthermore, is the generative linguistic instrument known as *mantra*. The central role played by the mantra in such groups during this period is reflected in the indigenous terms *mantraśāstra*, *mantracaryā,* and *mantrayāna* as synonymous with both the texts and practices of *tantra*.

See further: H. Brunner, "Le *sādhaka*, personage oblié du Śivaisme du sud," in *Journal Asiatique* 263 (1975): 411-443.

7. See J. Pryzluski, "Les Vidyārāja, contribution à l'histoire de la magie dans les sects Mahāyanistes," *Bulletin de l'École Francaise d'Extrême Orient* 23 (1923): 301-318; P. Prancke, "Becoming a Buddhist Wizard," in D. Lopez (ed.), *Buddhism in Practice*, Princeton (1995): 343-358; R. Davidson, *Indian Esoteric Buddhism: A Social History of the Tantric Movement*, New York, 2002.

8. As the verbal root √*paṭ* (to string together, wrap) implies, a *paṭa* is first of all a piece of cloth formed from raw cotton. The noun *paṭa* thus generally denotes a type of woven cloth used for things such as clothing, screens, and, as in the *Mmk*, canvases for painting. The paṭa, or cult image, is presented in the *Mmk* as being of a single piece with the cosmological image discussed above. The paṭa is thus the area where the Buddha's power manifests in local, concentrated form. In this function, the cult image is held to be a refractive space, reflecting the original domain of awakened power. Thus, the original, cosmic domain is rendered ever present and always available. As mentioned in note 5, a presupposition operating in the *Mmk* is that the darkness of human ignorance obscures this presence and availability. The text remedies this situation by revealing to the practitioner the means by which the Buddha's cosmic assembly may be literally woven into a lively image of tremendous force.

The *Mmk* organizes its presentation of the cult image in terms of three stages undergone by the paṭa. These three stages point to the basic senses of the term as well: canvas, painted image, and animated cult object. Discussing the historical, iconoclastic notion of "icon" (which I am calling "cult image" and "cult object" as more specific terms) as "idol," i.e., as an inherently ineffectual artifact composed of "base matter," Matthew Kapstein offers a helpful insight into this creative process. Kapstein's comments are particularly pertinent here since they are made in regard to what he calls the "world-constructing enterprise" of paṭa creation, specifically in the *Mmk*. Kapstein writes (op. cit):

> In consideration of what is yet unformed, and thus in a crucial sense empty, the construction of value emphatically appears as a matter of intentional practice by human agents within human communities. The art of esoteric Buddhism is appropriate subject matter for our reflections about this, for esoteric Buddhism . . . seems always to

> accentuate the constructedness of human values, with particular attentiveness to the unformed character of the stuff from which those values are constructed, and to the requirement that they be reconstituted continuously in a world of ongoing change.

Long before any image is depicted on the blank canvas, the paṭa is a repository of a complex vision of the world. As the initial space to be fashioned and imprinted with the emblems of the specific value system propagated through the *Mmk*, the raw cotton paṭa is the first step in what Kapstein aptly calls "world-building, in its physical, symbolic, and conceptual dimensions."

The second stage of the paṭa involves the painting of an image on the canvas. The common usage of the term *paṭa* is, in fact, to denote a picture painted on canvas. This applies as well to its cultural and etymological varieties, such as Hindi *pat*, Nepali *paubhā*, Bengali *paṭua*, Tibetan *thangka*, Chinese and Japanese hanging scrolls (Chinese, *zi-thang*), Korean *tangwa*. As the English equivalent to these terms, "painting," might seem to warrant, the paṭa is thus typically discussed within the purview of "painting" or "sacred art." The example of the *Mmk*, however, does not warrant the equation of paṭa with painting. The text does not distinguish between painted image (painting, sacred art) and cult object (icon, relic) categorically. The text is emphatic on this point: what obtains for the whole applies to each minute part. Kapstein alludes to this fact when he mentions the necessity of continuous, repetitive value creation within a single process. In the *Mmk,* a speck of raw cotton, a brilliant image, and a consecrated object are but overlapping moments in a unitary field. The Western idea of "painting," of a work of art, does not allow for this unity.

In his *Bild und Kult* (Munich, 1990), Hans Belting notes the historical shift that gave rise to the notion of "art."

> A history of the image is something other than a history of art. But what does this mean? In its general usage, the term "image" encompasses everything and nothing, as does the term "art." Therefore, let it be said at the outset that by the term "image" . . . is to be understood primarily the figurative depiction, the *imago*. The *imago* presents a person, and, therefore, is treated as a person. In this sense, the *imago* became the preferred object of religious practice. In this regard it was honored as a cult object, and distinguished from the narrative image, or *historia*, which placed before the observer—who simultaneously read a corresponding text—the sacred history.
>
> "Art" . . . presupposes the crises of the ancient image and its new valorization as art work in the Renaissance . . . While the old type of images were destroyed during the phase of iconoclasm, images of the new type were appearing in art collections. From that point on, it becomes possible to speak of an *epoch of art* [in distinction to the previous "*epoch of the image*"] (p. 9).

Although paṭas, thangkas, hanging scrolls, etc., now appear in art collections around the world, their intended use and function (past and present) are best perceived when they are viewed as images, in the sense of *imago*—animated presentations.

As a visual presentation, the paṭa of the *Mmk* serves several purposes. By its specific use of color and figurative expression and form it communicates to the practitioner the attitude required of him toward both the parts and the whole. In the largest paṭa, for example, Mañjuśrī is painted a soft, muted red, his expression gentle; Yamāntaka is dark and ferocious-looking; the whole is backgrounded by a calming, deep blue sky with soft, billowing white clouds. These features instill an attitude of reverence, and they are instructive of the appropriateness of that attitude. In fact, the practitioner himself is depicted in the paṭa reverentially making an offering to the assembly, stressing this didactic feature.

This depiction points to an additional purpose of the visual form. Belting mentions the *historia*, the narrative image of the "sacred history," and distinguishes this from the *imago*, the image as cult object. In the *Mmk*, the presentation of the "sacred history" is an aspect indistinguishable from the cult object *per se*. As *historia*, the paṭa presents a vital moment in the *Mmk's* history. It does this in both senses of the term "present." As an image it makes present to the imagination of the practitioner the scene of a primordial event in both the history of the Buddha's teaching and the history of salvation. In this way, it serves as a catalyst to an imaginative remembrance of that pivotal moment. As an image, then, the cult object is a refractive space. But what it reflects is a *real* domain of power, one that is conceived as being fluid, unbound by time and space, and thus unfolding continuously. In this way, the cult object transforms the imagination "into a spiritual organ of making present." While it is itself a form of imaginative experience, it is one whose primary function is to make present an otherwise obscured reality.

The image, then, does not serve merely as an instrument of communal memory. The scene presented on the paṭa is of the continuous unfolding in the present of a past event. We might consider this past as having occurred in "mythic" space and time, or as being "sacred history," if these terms are meant to refer to the fact that all traditions creatively interpret and use "history," statically conceived. In any case, the image on the paṭa merges this past with the present. The sādhaka, as mentioned above, is to be painted in a gesture of worship on the paṭa itself, thereby situating him within the history of revelation. Furthermore, external to the painting, in a bodily act of devotion or ritualized coercion, he contemplates the image of revealed power presented by means of the paṭa. This points to both a highly synchronic conception of past and present and to the immediacy of mundane and transcendent space.

With this idea of the merging of past and present events by means of the image, the notion of the paṭa as an instrument of liveliness and efficacy is introduced. The interpretive translation of the term *paṭa* as "animated cult image" is useful in this respect. Through correct ritualized production, the paṭa becomes permeated by the power of the Buddha. As such, the paṭa was believed to possess miracle-producing properties often associated with buddhas. For example, proper ritual employment of the paṭa enabled the adept to traverse great distances of space rapidly, overcome the force of time, heal sickness, produce food during a famine, and converse with gods and enlightened beings. Most importantly perhaps, it assured the practitioner of the attainment of buddhahood. Throughout the history of Buddhist cultic life, other objects have played this role. Relics, statues, architectural monuments, books, remembrance, and visualization have, at various times and in various places, been believed to render present the otherwise inaccessible power that accompanies a living Buddha.

See further: M. Lalou, *Iconographie des Étoffes Peintes (Paṭa) dans le Mañjuśrīmūlakalpa*, Paris, 1930; A. MacDonald, *Le Mandala du Mañjuśrīmūlakalpa*, Paris, 1962; M-T. de Mallmann, *Étude iconographique sur Mañjuśrī*, Paris, 1964; V. Mair, *Painting and Performance: Chinese Picture Recitation and Its Indian Genesis*, Honolulu, 1988; Matthew Kapstein, "Weaving the World: the Ritual Art of the *Paṭa* in Pāla Buddhism and Its Legacy in Tibet," in *History of Religions*, vol. 34, no. 3 (1995): 241-262; G. Wallis, *Mediating the Power of Buddhas: Ritual in the Mañjuśrīmūlakalpa*, Albany, 2002.

–9–

The Body as a Text and the Text as the Body: A View from the *Kālacakratantra's* Perspective

Vesna A. Wallace

Introduction

When contemporary geneticists study the body, they look at it as a genetic text and strive to read it as an intelligible blueprint for how the body is formed and maintained. In this sense, for geneticists, a malleable genetic text serves as a metaphor of the body. The holders of the Kālacakra tradition in India saw the body in a similar way. They viewed it as a tantric text, consisting of mantras and letters that provide a blueprint of the mind-body complex, its operations, its habitual propensities, and its potentialities for transformation. They devised their own method of interpreting, editing, and changing that text in order to transmute the ordinary body characterized by afflictions into the blissful body of empty form.

One can say that, in the context of the Kālacakra tradition, a tantra is also interpreted as a metaphor for the body, since the tantric text and its discourse are themselves treated as blueprints of the individual's mind and body. However, a tantric text is also understood as representational of the body of ultimate reality, manifesting in a literary form, as a literary reproduction of Vajrasattva, the Buddha's gnosis of bliss.

In this paper, I will discuss both—the Indian Buddhist interpretation of the *Kālacakratantra* discourse as the body, and the interpretations of the body as the Kālacakra tantric text having a performative function. These two interpretations can be equally relevant for our understanding of the concepts of tantra and the tantric body. I surmise that these two interpretations could also have broader implications for contemporary theories in literary and cultural studies, as they extend the existing notions of the text, its function, and the role of the reader.

In the context of Indian tantric Buddhism, the concept of the body as a sacred text is evoked in various definitions of the term *tantra* and is elaborated within the Buddhist tantric discourse on the body and tantric practice.

The Buddhist tantric concept of the body as a Dharma discourse or as a sacred text has its precursors in earlier Buddhist literature. In the early Pāli sources, its antecedents can be recognized in the Buddhist definitions of Dharma, contained in discussions pertaining to the Buddha's discourse on Dharma. In the *Ariyapariyesanā* sutta of the *Majjhimanikāya*, I. 167, Dhamma is defined as dependent origination (paṭiccasamuppāda), which is synonymous with saṃsāra, the condition of a sentient being, and it is also defined as nibbāna. The Mahāhatthipadopama-sutta (MN, 2001, p. 282) further states that one who sees dependent origination sees Dhamma, and one who sees Dhamma sees dependent origination. In the Pāli suttas, the Buddha himself is identified with Dhamma due to his insight into dependent origination. Therefore, one of the epithets of the Buddha in the Pāli suttas is dhamma-bhūta ("one who has become Dhamma"); and the Buddha is quoted as saying: "He who sees the Dhamma sees me, and he who sees me sees the Dhamma."[1] This early Buddhist interpretation of Dharma suggests that by gaining transformative insight into a Dharma-discourse, one becomes the embodiment of Dharma. It further shows that in the context of early Buddhism, a saṃsāric individual who fully grasps a Dharma-discourse with both of its aspects—saṃsāric and nirvāṇic—becomes transformed into its nirvāṇic aspect. Thus, there is nothing outside the Dharma itself that is being transformed, and there is nothing outside the Dharma that brings about a transformation. This interpretation can be also supported by a statement given in the commentary on the *Paṭisambhidā-maggā*, which interprets the phrase "dhamma-cakka" as Dharma being a weapon (*paharaṇa-cakka*) by means of which mental afflictions (*kleśa*) are destroyed.[2] This understanding of Dharma as a three-faceted phenomenon, consisting of the basis, means, and the result of a transformative insight, is echoed in the later Buddhist views of Mahāyāna sūtras and in the Buddhist tantric interpretations of the term *tantra*.

In the subsequent Mahāyāna literature, a Mahāyāna sūtra, sometimes referred to as a Dharma text, is seen as a textual embodiment of all the good qualities of Buddhahood. Therefore, one is told that by listening, memorizing, reciting, or copying a Mahāyāna sūtra, one will acquire those good qualities and see the Buddhas.[3] Similarly, the *Saddharmapuṇḍarika* asserts that by reading, copying, mastering, and teaching this text to others, one attains the pure and perfect body, which reflects the triple universe with all the Buddhas and Bodhisattvas in it.[4] Moreover, it is stated in the *Lalitavistara* that the house in which this Dharma text is found is the dwelling place of the Tathāgatas, and one who masters it will be like the imperishable ocean.[5] Statements like these indicate that also in the context of Mahāyāna, by mastering a Dharma discourse, which is a container of all virtues and the means of attaining the virtues, one becomes a living Dharma text, instilled with virtue and worthy of reverence.

In Indian Buddhist tantric sources, the term *tantra* is frequently defined as a "connected discourse."[6] In the *Amṛtakaṇikā*, one reads the following:

> A tantra is called a "connected discourse." Saṃsāra is considered a tantra.
> A tantra is called a "secret mystery." The higher is called a "tantra."[7]

Thus, like the early Buddhist definition of Dharma, here a tantric discourse has saṃsāra and nirvāṇa as its two interconnected aspects.

According to other Buddhist definitions of this term, this "connected discourse" is said to have three aspects, namely: the cause (hetu), result (phala), and method (upāya) leading to the result. Although in various Buddhist tantric texts, interpretations of these three mutually related aspects of a tantric discourse differ slightly, they equally suggest that the individual may be viewed as a tantra with all of its facets. According to the *Yogaratnamālā* commentary on the *Hevajratantra* (1959, p. 105), the causal aspect of a tantra is sentient beings (*sattva*) who are the members of the vajra-family. The *Hevajrapañjikā-muktāvali*, which is another commentary on the *Hevajratantra*, presents the causal tantra as a causal Hevajra (*hetu-hevajra*), which it identifies as a genealogical line (*gotra*) and as a vajra-family.[8] In the *Guhyasamājatantra* (Ch.18, vv. 34-35), the causal aspect is the nature (*prakṛti*), which is the cause of a form, or appearance (*ākṛti*).[9] In the *Guṇavatiṭikā*, a commentary on the *Mahāmāyātantra*, (1992, pp. 2-3), it is the beginningless and endless mind of sentient beings, which is luminous by nature (*prakṛtiprabhāsvara*) and the cause of spiritual awakening.[10]

As for the method aspect of a tantra, in all the aforementioned texts, it is described as a means of transforming a tantra's causal aspect into its resultant form. As will be demonstrated later in this paper, the method aspect of a tantra is an embodied practice; it is a performative facet of an embodied tantric text.

Furthermore, the resultant form of a tantra, which is reality (*tattva*), or the gnosis of supreme and imperishable bliss, is declared to have its origin and place in the body. In the *Amṛtakaṭikā*, the gnosis of sublime bliss (*mahā-sukha-jñāna*) is referred to as a sublime tantra (*mahā-tantra*) and as a sublime mantra (*mahā-mantra*).[11] In this and other Buddhist tantric texts, the identification of a mantra with the gnosis of sublime bliss is justified on the basis that the mantra secures protection (*trāṇa*) of the mind (*manas*) through the regulation of prāṇas, while innate bliss is the source of the origination of all mantras and their accomplishments.[12] In the *Vimalaprabhā* commentary on the *Kālacakratantra*, Ch. 4, v.7, the state of supreme, indestructible bliss (*paramākṣarasukha*) is identified with the syllable *a*, which, as the first syllable of the Sanskrit alphabet, stands for the dharma-source (*dharmodaya*) and for the vajra-womb of all the Buddhas. As such, it is seen as the fundamental cause of all expressions, as the birthplace of all mantras.[13] In light of this view, the individual syllables that constitute a tantric discourse are declared to be of the nature of a mantra;[14] and the mantra is said to be in the body. Thus, a tantra, which is identified with mantra on this ground, is a text that is encoded in the individual's body in the form of mantric syllables.

Here too, then, that which is being transformed on the tantric path is not something outside the tantra itself, but rather one aspect of a tantra is transformed into its other aspect by means of yet another aspect of a tantric discourse. This suggests that a tantra as a text that is encoded in a human body is malleable and therefore can be altered. It is an embodied tantric text that can be changed not through an external agency but through its own internal workings. As will be shown later, only the inner workings of an embodied tantric text, or its own self-manipulation, leads to its transformation.

A Perspective from the Indian Kālacakra Tradition

In the *Sekoddeśa*, the following is said with regard to the *Ādibuddhatantra*:[14]

> Thus, the *Ādibuddha* [*tantra*], denoting the *Kālacakra*, is purified by means of the six points (*koti*),[15] four *vajra-yogas*,[16] four perfect awakenings, six families of the psychophysical aggregates (*skandha*), elements (*dhātu*), and sense-bases (*āyatana*), five chapters known as "Cosmos," and so on, and by means of the two truths.[17, 18]

These two verses clearly suggest that the *Kālacakratrantra* text, which is purified by its content and structure, should be understood not only as a mere discourse on the Kālacakra, but also as the Ādibuddha himself. Sādhuputra and Nāropā, commenting on these two verses in the *Sekoddeśaṭippaṇī* and *Sekoddeśaṭīkā* respectively, point to the *Ādibuddhatantra* as the Ādibuddha Kālacakra himself. For Sādhuputra, the *Ādibuddhatantra* is "without beginning or end, devoid of adherence to the two doctrinal positions, and imparting the complete mundane and supramundane knowledge."[19] Referencing the verse cited in the *Vimalaprabhā*, Vol. 1, 1986, p. 43, which gives the Kālacakra tradition's etymological explanation of the phrase "*kālacakra*" and reads:

> *kākārāt kāraṇe śānte lakārat layo 'tra vai*
> *cakārāc calacittasya krakārāt kramabandhanaiḥ*

Sādhuputra identifies the *Ādibuddhatantra* with the resultant aspect of the *tantra*, the Buddha Kālacakra. Nāropā does the same by explaining the *Vimalaprabhā*'s above-cited expostion of the term "*kālacakra*" in the following way. With regard to the syllable *kā*, he asserts, "The cause (*kāraṇa*), called the body of *bodhicitta*, is peaceful and free from conceptualizations (*vikalpa*) on account of the destruction of the waking state; and it is a Nirmāṇakāya owing to the cessation of the drop of the body (*kāya-bindu*) in the *lalāṭa*." With regard to the syllable *la*, he says: "When it is so, a dissolution (*laya*) of *prāṇa*, which is of the nature of the destruction of the dreaming state, is a Saṃbhogakāya owing to the cessation of the drop of the speech (*vāg-bindu*) in the throat." With respect to the syllable *ca*, he states: "A motion (*cala*) that moves toward the sense-objects such as sound and the like in the waking and dreaming states is the mind that is of the nature of [seminal] emission (*cyuti*), overcome by darkness, and acquired through a transformation of the eighteen bodily constituents. Its binding is a removal of darkness, a destruction of the dreamless state owing to the cessation of the drop of the mind (*citta-bindu*) in the heart, a Dharmakāya." Lastly, with regard to the syllable *kra*, he comments:

"A sequential process (*krama*) is an emission of the drops of the body and so on. A binding of that [emission] is a destruction of the fourth state by means of innate bliss. Owing to the cessation of the drop of gnosis (*jñāna-bindu*) of perishable [bliss], it is a Sahajakāya. Thus [Kālacakra] consists of the four bodies."[20]

Moreover, since Kālacakra is said to be a unity (*ekatva*) of the knowledge of indestructible bliss, referred to by the term "time" (*kāla*), and of the object of knowledge, or the world characterized by endless beings of the three realms, referred to by the term "wheel" (*cakra*),[21] the *Kālacakratantra* with which he is identified, is to be seen not only as a representation of the Buddha Kālacakra's mind but also as the representation of the body of sentient beings. Nāropā supports this interpretation with the verse from the *Kālacakratantra* (1994, Ch. 5, v. 56), which identifies all sentient beings within the six realms of existence with a *cakra*, referred to in the same text as the body of the Buddha.[22]

In the *Kālacakratantra* and in the *Vimalaprabhā*, a *tantra* is also identified with the body of the individual, as a sublime *mantra* and as a tantric discourse and its subject matter. One reads in the *Vimalaprabhā*[23] that the original *Ādibuddhatantra*, which consists of 1,620 deities, is the *nāḍīs* in the body. From that root-*tantra* emerged the *Kālacakratantra* in accordance with the classification of the *nāḍīs* of the heart-*cakra*. According to the Kālacakra tradition, the number of *nāḍīs* in the body is 72,000. It is worth noting that this number of bodily *nāḍīs* corresponds to the number obtained by adding the 12,000 lines of the *Kālacakratantra* to the 60,000 lines of the *Vimalaprabhā* commentary.[24] Since the significance of the number of lines in these two texts has not been discussed by their authors, it is not clear whether or not the authors or redactors of these texts wrote the aforementioned numbers of lines with the intention to correlate them to the number of the *nāḍīs* in the body.

One is further informed in the *Vimalaprabhā* that not only the *Ādibuddhatantra* but also all other tantras are contained in the body. In some places, it is said that the yogini-tantras are present in female bodies, and the yoga-tantras are in male bodies;[17] and in other places it is asserted that both of these classes of tantras are in a single body. The body is presented as a collection of the kings of tantras (tantra-rāja)—namely, the threefold *Māyājālatantra* and the sixfold *Samājatantra*.[18] The origination of the two mentioned tantra-rājas within the body is described as a process of their gradual composition. The expansion of the number of their emerging sections is understood to accord with the development of a child from the moment of its conception to the age of sixteen. Thus, the three phases of the *Māyājālatantra's* composition in the body take place in the following way. With the arising of the five psychophysical aggregates (*skandha*), five elements (*bhūtas*), eight bodily constituents (*dhātu*), twelve sense-bases (*āyatana*), six faculties of action (*karmendriya*), four cakras, and three doṣas—vāta, pitta, and kapha—the *Māyājāla* emerges as a text having forty-two parts, or sections. With the development of the uṣṇiṣa and secret (*guhya*) cakras, it expands into a text with forty-five sections; and with the arising of the mental afflictions (*kleśa*) of attachment, aversion, delusion, and pride it becomes a complete text consisting of forty-nine sections.[19] The process of the composition of the *Samājatantra* in the body is also understood to accord with the development of a human being from the initial embryonic state to a sixteen-year-old person. With the arising of the psychophysical aggregates and elements of the fetus, the *Samājatantra* emerges as a text that has nine sections. Upon the origination of the four cakras, it has thirteen sections; and with the arising of the sense-faculties (*indriya*) and sense-objects (*viṣaya*), it extends into a text with twenty-five sections. Afterwards, with the emergence of the faculties of action, the secret cakra, and uṣṇiṣa, it has thirty-two sections; and with the arising of the divine faculty (*divyendriya*) and bliss (*sukha*), it becomes a complete text with thirty-four sections.

Furthermore, according to the *Kālacakratantra* tradition, one becomes the Buddha Mañjuvajra by knowing the manner in which the *Ādibuddha* and all other tantras that are included in the *Ādibuddhatantra* are present in the body.[20] Here too then, right insight into one's own body as a tantric text and its subject matter is a requisite for spiritual transformation. One should know the tantras that are present in the body by their respective classes of consonants, which are the letters of a mantra. Here, like in other anuttara-yoga-tantras, a tantric body is constructed on a specific linguistic model, on the taxonomic order of syllables. This suggests that Indian Buddhists considered linguistic structures of the embodied tantric texts to be important and powerful. Consonants are referred to as the presiding deities of the nāḍis and the lords (*nātha*) of the cakras.

For example:

1.

In the joint of the left shoulder and upper arm are gutturals with short vowels of space, etc. in inverted order.

In the joint of the right shoulder and upper arm are gutturals with long vowels of gnosis.

In the joint of the left upper arm and forearm are palatals with short vowels of space, etc.

In the joint of the right upper arm and forearm are palatals with long vowels of gnosis, etc.

In the joint of the left hand and forearm are retroflex consonants with six short vowels of space, etc.

In the right joint of the left hand and forearm are retroflex consonants with long vowels of gnosis, etc.

In the joint of the right hip and thigh are labials with six long vowels of gnosis, etc.

In the joint of the left hip and thigh are labials with six short vowels of space, etc.

In the joint of the right knee and thigh are dentals with six long vowels of gnosis, etc.

In the joint of the left knee and thigh are dentals with six short vowels of space, etc.

In the joint of the right foot and shin are sibilants with six long vowels of gnosis, etc.
In the joint of the left foot and shin are sibilants with six short vowels of space, etc. in the inverted order.
Thus, every single class of consonants, making up thirty syllables, is in the twelve cakras, which have thirty spokes—in the action (karma) cakras and in the activity (kriyā) cakras.
2.
In every joint of the right thumb are gutturals with six long vowels of gnosis, etc.
In the joint of the lower knuckle of the thumb are six nāḍis, or gutturals with six long vowels of gnosis, etc.
In the joint of the right forefinger is the syllable *kha*.
The syllable *ga* is in the middle finger.
The syllable *gha* is in the joint of the right ring finger.
The syllable *ṅga* with six long vowels of gnosis, etc. is in the joint of the right little finger.
The syllable *ṅga* with six short vowels of space, etc. is in the joint of the lower knuckle of the left little finger.
The syllable *gha* with six short vowels of space, etc. is in the joint of the left forefinger.
The syllable *ga* with six short vowels of space, etc. is in the left middle finger.
The syllable *kha* with six short vowels of space, etc. is in the left ring finger.
The syllable *ka* with six short vowels of space, etc. is in the left thumb.

The six classes of consonants—ka, ca, ṭa, pa, ta, sa—make up thirty consonants due to their respective fivefold divisions.[21] These thirty consonants, together with ha, ya, ra, la, va, and kṣa, are considered to be the lords of the thirty-six bodily cakras. Each class of the six consonants is further divided into thirty-six syllables, in accordance with the accompanying short and long vowels, guṇas, and vṛddhis. These thirty-six syllables of each consonantal class are declared to be the lords of the cakras in thirty-six tantras in the body, namely, in the ka-vajra-tantra, kha-vajra-tantra, and so on.[22] Thus, each class of consonants with its thirty-six syllables is itself a tantra.[23] This implies that each nāḍicakra is an individual tantra. These diverse individual tantras are linked together, forming a single, all-inclusive tantra—namely, the *Ādibuddhatantra*, or the *Kālacakratantra*. Among these multiple tantras, not a single tantra exists independently of other tantras. The numerous tantras in the body are linked together by their common pervader (*vyāpaka*), which is the mind (*citta*), or gnosis (*jñāna*). Perhaps this presentation of the interconnection of the multiple tantras in the body could be interpreted as a unique *Kālacakratantra's* theory of intertextuality, one that pertains to the embodied texts.

The aforementioned thirty-six consonants are also identified as the six psychophysical aggregates, six elements, six faculties of action and their activities, sense-faculties, sense-objects, and the like.[24] Thus, every bodily constituent is to be known as an individual tantric text, and the body is to be seen as a multi-volumed tantra. These individual tantric texts in the body, represented by the groups of thirty-six syllables, are also identified as the yoga (method) and yogini (wisdom) tantras.[25]

However, due to being a corporeal text, this inclusive tantra in the body is characterized by finitude, as it is subject to destruction. It carries the meaning of ordinary, conventional reality, which must be transcended. For this reason, this corporeal and provisional tantra is in need of transformation into the definitive text. Its transformation requires a certain kind of translation, a transition from presentation to reality. Its transition from a finite text with a provisional meaning to a transcendent text with a definitive meaning is a process of transformation from the conceptually constructed text to the nonconceptual text. This transition of a text from one state of being to another involves a rewriting of personal history. In this process of rewriting, the old signs must be reinterpreted and subsequently replaced by new signs needed for capturing reality. The signs that express the unitary and partless reality are deemed as nonconceptual signs; and thus, although functioning as signs, ultimately they are not signs at all.

It is the earlier-mentioned, third aspect of a tantra, known as the method, or sādhana, that provides the new encoding necessary for such transition. In the course of the sādhana, or the stage of generation practice, the earlier-discussed groups of thirty-six consonants of various tantras are mentally dissolved. The embodied tantric text is disintegrated. Upon this disintegration, a new tantra is generated, the thirty-six consonants are encoded in a new form—in the form of a deity-maṇḍala—and their new meaning is produced. The consonants are transformed into the textual body of mantric deities (*mantra-devatā*). By being generated with new meanings into the new textual form, the consonants undergo a gradual transformation in the same six-phased sequence in which they initially had emerged from the time of the individual's conception till the age of sixteen. Upon their regeneration in the new form with new meaning, they continue to undergo further metamorphosis in the six main cakras (uṣṇiṣa, heart, lalāṭa, and guhya) brought by the intervention of different sets of vowels.[26] The vowels are the six types of wisdom (*prajñā*), or the pure psychophysical aggregates, elements, and the like. Spliced on the top of the consonants, which carry the meaning of compassion in relation to the vowels, they take possession of the consonants. In the context of the *Kālacakratantra* practice, this process of altering the embodied text, carried out through the "splicing" of the completely different classes of sounds—namely, the consonants and vowels—is called "sealing," or "printing" (*mudraṇa*) of the revised text of the body, speech, and mind. In this phase too, the redacted consonants, or the revised yoga and yogini tantras, in the body are mutually linked by the mind (*citta*), or the pervading gnosis (*jñāna*), which is their presiding deity (*nāyaka*).

However, the embodied tantric discourse that is redacted in this way is still a provisional and conceptually constructed text, which is said to be a fabrication of the individual's own mind.[27] Although in this new form it continues to be a complete and coherent unit, it is still structured as a composition of the mutually connected but disparate parts. Consequently, a further redaction is needed for its complete alteration, the redaction that will amalgamate the mutually differing parts of the text in a novel way. A subsequent phase of revision entails the mutual assimilation of the different classes of consonants that have been earlier sealed by their respective vowels. In Buddhist tantric jargon, this is referred to as an "embracing of a different family" (*para-kula-liṅgana*). It is a preparatory phase for the actual merging of the body's yoga and yogini tantras into each other, forming a unitary text, devoid of diverse parts. It is followed by a further redaction by means of which the embodied text becomes a partless and nondual text, in which all the letters of the nāḍi-prāṇas are unified into the single word *evaṃ*. The word *evaṃ* is said not to be a term, or a conceptual sign, because it is the union of wisdom and method. *E* is a syllable *a,* or emptiness, the space-element, in the locative case; and *vaṃ* is gnosis, sublime bliss, which arises from and abides in emptiness, or space. Thus, the multi-syllable text is reduced to a two-syllable text, which is neither a yoga nor yogini tantra.

In the final phase of revision, the embodied text is completely transformed with the incineration of all of its letters by the fire of the same gnosis that previously linked them together. Following the model of the six-phased composition, dissolution, and reconstruction of the text's two earlier forms—phenomenal and conceptual—the process of its incineration is also carried out in six consecutive phases. This new text, which is devoid of parts and signs (*nimitta*), is said to have a unique nonconceptual form, characterized by nonpronounceable consonants and vowels. It is reduced to the single syllable *a*. As such, it is likened to formless, nonembodied (*arūpa*) space and is characterized as inexplicable (*anirdeśya*) and ungrounded (*apratiṣṭha*) in anything.[28]

On account of being reduced to the single letter, it transcends the subject-object duality and is thereby self-cognizant in the sense that it is an indivisible union of the discourse, its subject matter, and the author. In contrast, the embodied, conceptual text, consisting of many letters, exists as an object of knowledge in relation to the reader as its subject. Furthermore, the embodied, conceptual text, which is composed of a complex set of systems, exists in dialectical relationship with other sets outside its boundaries; whereas, the nonembodied and nonconceptual text is seen as free from controversial relations due to being nonlocalized. Although the disembodied tantric text is not characterized by form, it is said not to be characterized by formlessness either, since it exists in the vowel *a*, which is its empty form.[29]

The discussed revisional methods and their results suggest that a tantric text is always productive of what it denotes. Arising from the syllable *a*, the source of all expressions and gnosis in the body, a sublime tantra takes on various phenomenal forms. In order to elucidate the mundane and transcendent truths and paths, it takes on the form of a book, consisting of mantra symbols and characterized by articulation. It also assumes the form of the text embodied in a human figure, consisting of the nāḍis, psychophysical aggregates, and the like. Due to sharing a common source (*yoni*), these two phenomenal forms of a sublime tantra—the book and the body—are fundamentally nondual. In this regard, they are not just mere metaphors of each other, but two different manifestations of the same reality. A reader of a tantra who knows this truth knows that he is not a mere consumer of the text but also its producer. He knows that it is his mind alone that links all the letters together into a single text and gives it different meanings until it finally absorbs them into its own gnosis, from which they initially arose. By knowing himself to be all of these—the text itself, its author and revisionist, and its subject matter—one becomes liberated from the mind's ideation and spiritual ignorance. One's impermanent body, subject to illness, aging, and disease becomes altered into the blissful body of gnosis.

Although all of the anuttara-yoga-tantras agree that a single-syllable text of the gnosis of sublime and imperishable bliss is fundamentally the same in all sentient beings, they offer different transcriptions for it. For example, in the *Hevajratantra*,[30] it is transcribed as the syllable *he*, standing for Hevajra, in the Kālacakra tradition as the syllable *kā*, or Kālacakra, and so on. Its different transcriptions are determined by differing forms in which it may appear and not by any other factors. Thus, in the context of the anuttara-yoga-tantras, just as the evolution of the physical body corresponds to the creation of a canonical tantra, so the closing of the physical body corresponds to the closing of the canonical tantric text. In the case of the *Kālacakratantra*, which is the latest Indian Buddhist tantra, the closing of the body intimates the closing of Indian tantric tradition. The implications of these notions are intriguing. One of the implications that is significant for the Indian Buddhist tantric tradition is that a canonical tantric text and the body, which are ultimately nondual and function as a vehicle to spiritual awakening, are like a raft that is discarded when its purpose is accomplished. In that respect, a canonical tantric text and the body are to be understood as the Vajrayāna itself.

Moreover, while being closed and cast aside in the case of the individual who has reached his final goal, a canonical tantra continues to be open and functional for those who have not yet reached spiritual awakening. Thus, being simultaneously closed for one person and open for another, a tantric text calls for diverse hermeneutical approaches.

Vimalaprabhāṭikā of Kalkin Śripuṇḍarika on Śrilaghukālacakratantrarāja by Śrimañjuśriyaśas. Vol. 2. 1994. Edited by Vrajavallabh Dwivedi and S. S. Bahulkar. Rare Buddhist Texts Series, vol. 12. Sarnath, Varanasi: Central Institute of Higher Tibetan Studies.

Vimalaprabhāṭikā of Kalkin Śripuṇḍarika on Śrilaghukālacakratantrarāja by Śrimañjuśriyaśas. Vol. 3. 1994. Edited by Vrajavallabh Dwivedi and S. S. Bahulkar. Rare Buddhist Texts Series, vol. 13. Sarnath, Varanasi: Central Institute of Higher Tibetan Studies.

Endnotes

1. *Saṃyuta Nikāya*, III.

2. *Paṭisambhidamaggā Aṭṭhakathā* cited in the *Encyclopaedia of Buddhism*, 1979-1989, vol. 4, 371-372.

3. The *Ugraparipṛcchāsūtra*, 2003, ch. 7, pp. 319-320.

4. *Saddharma-puṇḍarika* or *The Lotus of the Good Law*, 1963, ch.18, pp. 349-353.

5. *Lalitavistara Sūtra*, 1983, vol. 2, 673-674.

6. See the *Guhyasamājatantra*, 1965, ch. 18, v. 34, the *Mahāmāyātantram* with *Guṇavatiṭikā*, 1992, p. 2, *Amṛtakaṇikā* commentary on the *Mañjuśrināmasaṃgiti*, 1994, p. 200, the *Yogaratnamālā*, 1959, p. 105: tantraṃ prabandham, tantram iti prabandhaḥ.

7. The *Amṛtakaṇikā* commentary on the *Mañjuśrināmasaṃgiti*, v. 13, 1994, p. 9: tantraṃ prabandham ākhyātaṃ saṃsāraṃ tantram iṣyate/ tantraṃ guhyaṃ rahasayākhyātam uttaraṃ tantram ucyate//

8. Cf. the *Hevajrapañjikā-muktāvali*, 2001, p. 9: "A tantra is a connected discourse (*prabandha*). It is of three kinds: the causal tantra (*hetu-tantra*), the resultant tantra (*phala-tantra*), and the method tantra (*upāya-tantra*). Therefore, Hevajra is also of three kinds: causal Hevajra, resultant Hevajra, and the method Hevajra. A cause (*hetu*), a genetic line (*gotra*), and a family (*kula*) are synonyms. Here, a vajra-family itself is called a 'causal Hevajra' and a 'causal tantra' due to being a receptacle of virtues that have the sublime compassion (*mahā-karuṇā*) and wisdom (*prajñā*) as their essential part. Why is it Hevajra? Because Hevajra is the cause. Why is it a connected discourse? Due to the multitude of sentient beings who belong to the vajra-family and due to the power of causal Hevajra, the state of the sublime Vajradhara, which is attainable through the long-term practice of the method Hevajra, is called a 'resultant Hevajra' and a 'resultant tantra.'"

9. prabandhaṃ tantram ākhyātaṃ tat prabandhaṃ tridhā bhavet/
ādhāraḥ prakṛtiś caiva asaṃhāryaprabhedataḥ//
prakṛtiś cākṛter hetur asaṃhāryaphalaṃ tathā/
ādhāras tadupāyaś ca tribhis tantrārthasaṃgrahaḥ//

10. tantram iti prabhandham/ trividhaṃ tantraṃ—hetutantraṃ phalatantram upāyatantraṃ ca/ tatra prakṛtiprabhāsvaram anādinidhanaṃ cittaṃ bodhicittam/ sa hetus tadbijam/ kasya bijam/ bodheḥ/

11. The *Amṛtakaṇikā*, 1994, pp. 9, 21.

12. The *Amṛtakaṇikā*, 1994, p. 200, the *Vimalaprabhā* commentary on the *Kālacakratantra*, ch. 4, v. 7, ch.1, v. 1. Cf. the *Hevajrapañjikā-muktāvali*, 2001, p. 29: "It is a mantra due to protecting the world from cogitating on reality." (tattvārthamananāj jagat trāṇāc ca mantraḥ.)

13. The *Mañjuśrināmasaṃgiti*, vv. 28-29, cited in the *Vimalaprabhā* commentary on the *Kālacakratantra*, ch. 1, v. 3. Cf. the *Hevajrapañjikā-muktāvali*, 2001, p. 24: A mantra itself is reality (*tattva*), the letter a, and so on. Gnosis itself is reality, free from mental elaborations (*niṣprapañca*) and unexcelled (*anuttara*) gnosis of bliss (*sukha-jñāna*).

14. The *Vimalaprabhā* commentary on the *Kālacakratantra*, ch. 4.

15. The *Vimalaprabhā* commentary on the *Kālacakratantra*, ch. 2, vv. 56-57.

16. According the *Vimalaprabhā* commentary on the *Kālacakratantra*, these two texts are traditionally considered to consist of sixty thousand lines and twelve thousand lines, respectively.

17. The *Vimalaprabhā* commentary on the *Kālacakratantra*, ch. 2, v. 53.

18. The *Vimalaprabhā* commentary on the *Kālacakratantra*, ch. 2, v. 55.

19. The *Vimalaprabhā* commentary on the *Kālacakratantra*, ch. 2, v. 52.

20. The *Vimalaprabhā* commentary on the *Kālacakratantra*, ch. 2, vv. 56-57.

21. According to the *Vimalaprabhā* commentary on the *Kālacakratantra*, ch. 1., v. 1, the six classes of consonants with their individual fivefold divisions are:

ka kha ga gha ṅga
ca cha ja jha ña
ṭa ṭha ḍa ḍha ṇa
pa pha ba bha ma
ta tha da dha na
sa ḥpa ṣa ḥka

The vowels are listed as these: a ā i i u ū ṛ ṝ ḷ ḹ aṃ aḥ e ai ar ār o au al āl ha hā ya yā ra rā va vā la lā

22. The *Vimalaprabhā* commentary on the *Kālacakratantra*, ch. 5, vv. 7-8.

23. The *Vimalaprabhā* commentary on the *Kālacakratantra*, ch. 5, v. 9: kha-vajrādikaṃ tantram ucyata eka vyañjānātmakaṃ ṣaṇtriṃśan-mātrā-bhinnam iti.

24. The *Vimalaprabhā* commentary on the *Kālacakratantra*, ch. 5, v. 10.

25. The *Vimalaprabhā* commentary on the *Kālacakratantra*, ch. 5, v. 9.

26. The *Vimalaprabhā* commentary on the *Kālacakratantra*, ch. 5, v. 10:

A, i, u, ṛ, ḷ, aṃ—or Akṣobhya, Amoghasiddhi, Amitābha, Vairocana, Ratneśa, and Vajrasattva—for the transformation of the body.

ḷ, u, ṛ, i, a, for the speech, or prāṇa
oṃ, āh, hūṃ for the mind (*citta*)
a for gnosis (jñāna).

27. The *Vimalaprabhā* commentary on the *Kālacakratantra*, ch. 1, v. 1.

28. The *Sekoddeśaṭikā* of Naḍapāda, 1941, pp. 57-58.

29. The *Vimalaprabhā* commentary on the *Kālacakratantra*, ch. 1, v. 1.

30. See the *Hevajratantra*, 2001, ch. 1, v. 7, and the *Hevajrapañjikā-muktāvali*, 2001, p. 9.

Bibliography

Āryamañjuśrināmasaṃgīti with Amṛtakaṇikā-ṭippaṇī by Bhikṣu Raviśrijñāna and Aṛṭakaṇikodyota-nibandha of Vibhūticandra. 1994. Edited by Banarsi Lal. Bibliotheca Indo-Tibetica, vol. 30. Sarnath, Varanasi: Central Institute of Higher Tibetan Studies.

Cicuzza, Claudio. 2001. *The Laghutantraṭikā by Vajrapāṇi*. Serie Orientale Roma, vol. 86. Rome: Instituto per il Medio ed Estremo Oriente.

Damdinsüren, C. 1981. "A Commentary on the Kālacakra of Wheel of Time," in *The Tibet Journal* 6, no. 1 (1981): 43-49.

Encyclopaedia of Buddhism, vol. 4. 1979-1989. Edited by Jotiya Dhirasekera and W. G. Weeraratne. Sri Lanka: The Government of Sri Lanka.

Gnoli, Raniero, ed. 1997. "La Sekoddeśaṭippaṇī di Sādhuputra Śrīdharānanda: Il Testo Sanscrito." In *Rivista degli Studi Orientali*. Vol. 70, fasc. 1-2 (1996): 115-145. Rome: Universita di Roma "La Sapienza," Dipartimento di Studi Orientali.

Guhyasamāja Tantra or Tathāgataguyhaka. 1965. Edited by S. Bagchi. Buddhist Sanskrit Texts, No. 9. Darbhanga: The Mithila Institute.

Guhyasamāja Tantra. 1978. Edited by Yukei Matsunaga. Osaka: Toho Shuppan Inc.

Hammar, Urban. 2005. "Studies in the Kālacakra Tantra: A History of the Kālacakra in Tibet and a Study of the Concept of Ādibuddha, the Fourth Body of the Buddha and the Supreme Unchanging." Ph.D. dissertation, Stockholm University.

Hevajratantram with Muktāvali Pañjikā of Mahāpaṇditācārya Ratnākaraśānti. 2001. Edited by Ram Shankar Tripathi and Thakur Sain Negi. Bibliotheca Indo-Tibetica Series, vol. 18. Sarnath, Varanasi: Central Institute of Higher Tibetan Studies.

Khedrup Norsang Gyatso. 2004. *Ornament of Stainless Light: An Exposition of the Kālacakra Tantra*. Translated by Gavin Kilty. Boston: Wisdom Publications.

The Lalitavistara Sūtra: The Voice of the Buddha, The Beauty and Compassion, vols. 1-2. 1983. Translated into English from French by Gwendolyn Bays. Berkeley: Dharma Publishing.

Mahāmāyātantram with Guṇavati by Ratnākaraśānti. 1992. Edited by Samdhong Rinpoche and Vrajavallabh Dwivedi. Rare Buddhist Text Series, vol. 10. Sarnath, Varanasi: Central Institute of Higher Tibetan Studies.

The Middle Discourses of the Buddha: A Translation of the Majjhima Nikāya. 2001. Translated by Bhikkhu Ñāṇamoli and Bhikkhu Bodhi. Boston: Wisdom Publications.

Nattier, Jan. 2003. *A Few Good Men: The Bodhisattva Path according to The Inquiry of Ugra (Ugraparipṛcchā)*. Studies in Buddhist Traditions. Honolulu: University of Hawai'i Press.

Paṭisambhidāmagga Aṭṭhakathā (Saddharmappakāsini), vols.1-3. 1933-1947. Edited by C. V. Joshi. London: Pali Text Society.

Saddharma-Puṇḍarika or the Lotus of the True Law. 1963. Translated by H. Kern. The Sacred Books of the East, vol. 21. New York: Dover Publications, Inc.

Sekoddeśaṭikā of Naḍapāda (Nāropa): Being a Commentary of the Sekoddeśa Section of the Kālacakra Tantra. 1941. Edited by Mario E. Carelli. Baroda: Oriental Institute.

Vimalaprabhāṭikā of Kalkin Śripuṇḍarika on Śrilaghukālacakratantrarāja by Śrimañjuśriyaśas. Vol. 1. 1986. Edited by Jagannatha Upadhyaya. Bibliotheca Indo-Tibetica Series, No. 11. Sarnath, Varanasi: Central Institute of Higher Tibetan Studies.

Vimalaprabhāṭikā of Kalkin Śripuṇḍarika on Śrilaghukālacakratantrarāja by Śrimañjuśriyaśas. Vol. 2. 1994. Edited by Vrajavallabh Dwivedi and S. S. Bahulkar. Rare Buddhist Texts Series, vol. 12. Sarnath, Varanasi: Central Institute of Higher Tibetan Studies.

Vimalaprabhāṭikā of Kalkin Śripuṇḍarika on Śrilaghukālacakratantrarāja by Śrimañjuśriyaśas. Vol. 3. 1994. Edited by Vrajavallabh Dwivedi and S. S. Bahulkar. Rare Buddhist Texts Series, vol. 13. Sarnath, Varanasi: Central Institute of Higher Tibetan Studies.

Yogaratnamālā. 1976. In *The Hevajra Tantra: A Critical Study. Part 2*. Edited and translated by D. L. Snellgrove. London Oriental Series, vol. 6. London: Oxford University Press.

–10–

The Influence of the Kālacakra: Vajrapāṇi on Consort Meditation

David B. Gray

The *Kālacakratantra* was the last of the major Buddhist tantras to be composed in India.[1] As such, it benefited from the rich legacy of Indian tantric Buddhist scholarship, and it is thus, naturally, one of the most complex and sophisticated of the tantric traditions. But its adherents were also faced with the serious challenge of establishing its legitimacy and disseminating it within a Buddhist world replete with practice traditions. Judging by its popularity in Tibet, there is no doubt that this project was ultimately successful. And this success is partly attributable to the early advocates who composed the influential series of commentaries known as the "bodhisattva" commentaries, so named because their authorship was attributed to three bodhisattvas. These works significantly advanced the prestige and influence of the Kālacakra tradition and helped establish it as an influential tantric tradition.

The best known among these is the *Vimalaprabhāṭīkā*,[2] attributed to Puṇḍarīka, who was believed to be an emanation of the bodhisattva Avalokiteśvara. It was by far the most influential commentary on the *Laghukālacakratantra*.[3] The remaining two are audacious attempts by advocates of the Kālacakra tradition to compose commentaries on other major tantras. One of these texts, the *Hevajrapiṇḍārthaṭīkā*,[4] a commentary on the *Hevajra Tantra*, was attributed to Vajragarbha, the bodhisattva interlocutor of the *Hevajra Tantra*.[5] The third, the *Laghutantraṭīkā*,[6] a commentary on the *Cakrasamvara Tantra*, was attributed to Vajrapāṇi, likewise considered by many to be the bodhisattva interlocutor of the *Cakrasamvara*.[7] While it is possible that these texts were authored by persons so named, it seems very likely that the attribution of authorship to the bodhisattvas who play central roles in the origin myths of these respective traditions represents an aggressive attempt to assert legitimacy, undertaken by the audacious and confident advocates of this new tantric tradition.[8]

A peculiar feature of both commentaries, and one that may have somewhat limited their influence, is the fact that they are both incomplete, commenting on only portions of the tantras. The *Hevajrapiṇḍārthaṭīkā* comments on the first one hundred and twenty stanzas of the *Hevajra Tantra*. Vajrapāṇi's commentary is particularly unusual in that it, on the surface, comments on only a small fraction of the text, namely, the first ten and a half verses of chapter one. The Tibetan tradition accounted for this by claiming that the works are incomplete and that significant portions of them were lost on account of warfare.[9] However, this story is almost certainly not true. In the case of the *Cakrasamvara Tantra*, the first chapter, on which Vajrapāṇi focused, is traditionally considered to be an abstract of the contents of the text. From the very modest basis of the text's first ten and a half verses, Vajrapāṇi commented upon a substantial range of very important topics. Vajrapāṇi concludes his text with an assertion that this is exactly what he was doing, confirming that the text is not incomplete.[10]

Despite the fact that neither of these commentaries is exhaustive, they achieved great fame in Tibet. Taken as a whole, the "bodhisattva" commentaries are sophisticated works of tantric exegesis, and their attribution to great bodhisattvas certainly added to their prestige. Advocates of the Kālacakra tradition, such as Bu-ston, were particularly fond of these works. Tsongkhapa, however, took a more balanced approach. Reacting, perhaps, to Bu-ston's exuberance,[11] Tsongkhapa warned the readers of his commentary on the *Cakrasamvara Tantra* against excessive dependence on the "bodhisattva" commentaries. He cleverly did this by referring to Vajrapāṇi's explanation of the sources on which one should rely in order to understand cryptic tantras such as the *Cakrasamvara*: "Furthermore, due to its abundance of adamantine expressions,[12] learned ones desiring liberation should know it by means of the instruction of the holy guru, what is said in other tantras, and the commentaries written by the bodhisattvas."[13] In other words, the "bodhisattva" commentaries are one source, but not the only source, that should be taken into account by those seeking to understand the tantra.[14]

Vajragarbha's and Vajrapāṇi's works represent attempts by Indian advocates of the Kālacakra tradition to expand the commentarial system of this tradition to other tantras. The justification for this approach is the simple and elegant idea that this tantra, and presumably all others, should be understood in the context of "what is said in other tantras." As Vajrapāṇi states later in the text, "one should understand [this] tantra by means of other tantras, since the Tathāgata stated them."[15] This is a refreshingly nonpartisan approach, one designed to counteract the perhaps natural tendency of advocates of a given tantric tradition to downplay works from a different tradition. In other words, if one accepts the claim that the tantras are spoken by the Buddhas, that they are buddhavacana, then there is no basis for accepting some and rejecting others. But this argument also provides the basis for applying the Kālacakra tradition's interpretive framework to this and other tantras.

Following the *Vimalaprabhā*, Vajrapāṇi's commentary is the next best known and best preserved of the bodhisattva commentaries.[16] This may in part reflect the popularity of the *Cakrasamvara Tantra* itself, as evidenced by the thirteen commentaries on this text preserved in the Kanjur.[17] But the relative success of Vajrapāṇi's commentary over Vajragarbha's may also be due to the relative vulnerability of the *Cakrasamvara Tantra* to this sort of external commentarial appropriation. The *Hevajra Tantra* may have been far less vulnerable to this sort of activity. This is because the Hevajra tradition gave rise to a very influential commentarial system, namely the "fury fire" (*caṇḍālī*) and the four joys/ four moments system of perfection stage meditation.[18] Having its own influential system of perfection stage practice, it was almost certainly less susceptible to the application of an external system.

The *Cakrasamvara Tantra*, however, was far more vulnerable to this sort of approach. The *Cakrasamvara Tantra* lacked a convincing system of perfecting stage practice, a fact that, paradoxically, may have contributed to its popularity, as this permitted the application of various other systems. While at least three distinct systems of perfecting stage practice were developed within the Cakrasamvara tradition,[19] none of them achieved universal acceptance. As a result, many of its commentators drew upon the systems devised for other tantras, especially the "five-stage" system of the Guhyasamāja tradition, as well as the Hevajra four-stage system.[20] The *Cakrasamvara Tantra* was thus particularly open to the ambitious commentarial project of the "bodhisattva" commentators.

Vajrapāṇi's commentary is particularly interesting for two reasons. First, as a work of considerable length, it is capable of shedding light on the history of late tenth- and early eleventh- century Indian esoteric Buddhism. Secondly, it is a truly ambitious work and tackles, in a fascinating manner, some of the most controversial issues debated by Indian tantric Buddhists at this time.

Regarding the first point, an interesting feature of Vajrapāṇi's commentary is his frequent quotations from the lost ur-tantras, such as the twenty-five-thousand-stanza *Guhyasamāja Tantra* or the *Paramādibuddha Tantra*, the legendary source of the Kālacakra tradition.[21] Given the fact that, by the tenth century, it had become de rigueur to claim that the root tantras of the various tantric traditions derive from massive ur-texts, a skeptic might be inclined to suspect that they never existed. Quoting from these texts might be seen as a clever strategy for supporting one's arguments, via the use of unverifiable quotations from authoritative sources. While such skepticism may very well be warranted, it is important to note that it is certainly possible that some of these texts did exist, particularly the relatively modest ones claimed by Vajrapāṇi, such as a twenty-five-thousand-stanza *Guhyasamāja Mūlatantra*, or a twelve-thousand-stanza *Paramādibuddhatantra*. While these root texts have not survived, it is certainly possible that texts of these size existed during Vajrapāṇi's time.[22] Their existence is far more plausible than the texts of hundred of thousands or even millions of stanzas claimed by some other traditions.[23]

Indeed, given the fact that the Kālacakra tradition appears to originate in far northern India in the late tenth century, just as this region was subject to the depredations of Mahmud of Ghazni and his successors,[24] it is certainly plausible that a significant number of the texts available to Vajrapāṇi may not have survived to be translated by the Tibetans who would soon descend upon northern India in search of Buddhist scriptures.

The influence of Vajrapāṇi's work was likely heightened by his willingness to confront one of the most controversial issues facing Indian Buddhists at this time.

This was the status of the sexual practices in the tantras. The *Cakrasamvara Tantra* provided an excellent opportunity for this sort of exegesis, as it is a text that treats this topic in a confounding fashion, both blunt and ambiguous. That is, while the tantra contains numerous erotic passages strongly suggesting sexual practices, few details about these practices are related in the text itself. The interpretation of these passages thus became a controversial issue.[25]

This topic had two facets. The first is the status of the controversial second and third consecrations in the Unexcelled Yogatantras, which, if practiced as literally described in texts such as this one, apparently require sexual union with a consort. A second and closely related issue was whether or not perfecting stage practice required sexual union with a physical consort, or karmamudrā. While the tantra itself does not present any unambiguous descriptions of perfecting stage practice, it does treat at some length the consecration process, focusing particularly on the second "secret" (*guhyābhiṣeka*) and third "Consort-gnosis" (*prajñājñānābhiṣeka*) consecrations, which involve sexual practices as described in the tantra itself.[26]

This provoked controversy because it gave the impression that sexual activity was required for full participation in what was then consider the "highest" tantric system by many Buddhists. This threatened the status of the monks, traditionally the authority figures of Buddhist communities. They were presented with the choice of preserving their vow of celibacy or fully engaging in the "highest" practices. Faced with this dilemma, it appears that some monks made the decision to engage in these practices and thereby violated their monastic vows. This is strongly suggested by Atīśa, who, writing during the early eleventh century in his *Bodhipāthapradīpa*, urges his fellow monks to refrain from this as follows:

> Due to the specific prohibition in the *Ādibuddhamahātantra*,[27] the secret and consort[-gnosis] consecrations should not be received by the celibate. If these consecrations are taken, since those who live celibately and ascetically would be engaging in what is prohibited to them, their ascetic vows would be broken, and they would incur the downfalls which defeat the observant. And as they would certainly fall into the evil destinies, [for them] there would be no success.[28]

It seems that Vajrapāṇi would agree with Atīśa. In his discussion of this issue, Vajrapāṇi focuses on the question of practice with consort (*mudrā*).[29] In so doing, he addresses in some detail practice with an actual physical consort (*karmamudrā*) as well as practice with a visualized consort (*jñānamudrā*). For him, both of these contrived practices are inferior to practice with the "great consort" (*mahāmudrā*), a term which can, in this context, refer to the female consort or deity and the "absolute truth as realized through her," as David Snellgrove has noted.[30]

Vajrapāṇi broaches this topic in the context of commenting on the second half of the seventh verse of the text, which reads as follows: "with an inwardly focused mind, give rise to (or, meditate upon)[31] the achievement of pleasure" (antargatena manasā kāmasiddhiṃ tu bhāvayet).[32] His commentary occurs as follows:

> Now, the meditation on Mahāmudrā will be explained by means of [the text] "with an inwardly focused mind" (antaragatena manasā) and so forth. Here in the method of mantra, in the tantras of wisdom and expedience, this adamantine expression can be realized in other tantras by means of the different [systems of] symbolic language. The first member of the compound in [the text] "with an inwardly focused mind" is an adamantine expression in the *Twenty-five Thousand* [*Verse*] *Śrī Samāja*, [in which] the Blessed Lord Buddha stated: "One who is [sitting in] the adamantine lotus posture should observe the mind that has gone within the jewel (cittaṃ maṇyantargatam), so that it reaches the state of purity, filled with the bliss of emission and so forth." Likewise, "Placing the penis (*liṅga*) in the vulva (*bhaga*), seminal essence (*bodhicitta*)[33] should not be emitted. One should meditate on the Buddha's image as the triple realm in its entirety."
>
> One should understand their meaning by taking these two verses, which are adamantine speech, together. It is expressed in half a verse in this tantra. It is said that it is the seminal essence that is going within the adamantine jewel. With a mind that is inwardly focused, i.e., with unejaculated seminal essence, one meditates on the Buddha's image, which has the characteristics of the triple realm, in union with a physical consort (*karmamudrā*) or visualized consort (*jñānamudrā*). The yogī should meditate on the triple realm—which is characterized by the desire, form, and formless realms, which is the nature of things animate and inanimate, and which is endowed with the perfection of all forms——in its entirety.[34]

Here Vajrapāṇi presents the sexual practices in a rather noneuphemistic fashion, making it clear that they can be practiced with a physical or visualized partner. For Vajrapāṇi, however, the erotic passages in the text are "adamantine expressions," in need of careful elucidation. In his view, these passages ultimately point toward the noncontrived practice of mahāmudrā, the "great consort" in the sense of buddhajñāna, the gnosis of awakening, personified in divine female form as Prajñāpāramitā. In his view, the text employs erotic language simply because this is a characteristic feature of the yoginī or prajñā tantras. He continues his commentary as follows:

> Now, since Prajñāpāramitā is endowed with the perfection of all forms, the Blessed Lord stated in this Tantra that she is the "achievement of pleasure," because it is a Wisdom Tantra. The yogī "should meditate upon" this "achievement of pleasure." Here "pleasure" refers to Vajrasattva of great passion, great aim, the supreme imperishable,[35] and "achievement" is the great consort (*mahāmudrā*) Prajñāpāramitā, endowed with all perfect forms. Moreover, his passion is nonconceptual great compassion, and the achievement is the conceptual great emptiness, as they are [conceived in] the self-awareness of the yogīs. In the achievement of the physical and visualized consorts, there is the supreme achievement. "For the sake of Buddhahood,

> one should meditate on her, namely, the great consort (*mahāmudrā*), who is the achievement of pleasure [in which] all is known, all forms are known, the path is known, the forms of the path are known, and who is the heir[36] to the Buddha qualities such as the ten powers and the four fearlessnesses, and so forth." This is the determination of the Tathāgata [stated] in other tantras. One should understand [this] tantra by means of other tantras, since the Tathāgata stated them.[37]

He then goes into greater depth describing this meditation practice, which he divides into two stages, "prior image meditation" (*pūrvabimbabhāvanā*) and "subsequent image meditation," which appear to be visualization practices associated with perfecting stage meditation. He describes them as follows:

> Now, this meditation has two aspects, prior image meditation and subsequent image meditation. Prior image meditation is meditation on the signs of smoke, etc.,[38] the ultimate image. When the image is seen, one places the penis in the vulva, then there is the meditation on the subsequent image, the supreme imperishable, for the sake of increasing of bliss. Moreover, in order to produce great bliss, one should then abandon the physical or visualized consort and meditate on the great consort. Regarding the prohibition on meditation with a physical or visualized consort, the Blessed Lord stated [the following] in the *Paramādibuddha* [*Tantra*] *in Twelve Thousand* [*Stanzas*]: "Having abandoned the physical consort and set aside the imagined consort, meditate upon the great consort through the yoga of the supreme imperishable." With respect to the first action, the prior meditation, [it also states]: "Unceasing supreme bliss is obtained in the vulva (*yoni*) as long as the yogī does not emit seminal essence. One should always visualize oneself as the Buddha image, endowed with a blissful form, as long as one keeps one's semen stabilized." This adamantine expression should be understood in the context of consecration.[39]

While Vajrapāṇi treats the sexual practices, whether real or imagined, he clearly does not see these practices as the "highest" teaching, but rather, at best, as preliminaries to the practice that he does see as supreme, namely meditation on mahāmudrā. He then addresses the crucial issue of the status of the controversial second and third consecrations and their relation to the enigmatic "fourth" consecration, in which esoteric knowledge of the tradition is revealed to the initiate:

> With respect to this, it truly is the case that the Blessed Lord, in this King of Tantras that has the nature of wisdom and expedience, taught, as a conventional truth and for the sake of those of childish intellect, the [third] Consort-gnosis [consecration] of perishable bliss produced from the union of the two organs, and arising through passion with a physical consort. This was [not taught] as an ultimate truth. Why is that? It is because of the state-

ment of the Blessed Lord that it is the fourth [consecration] that is thus [i.e., taught as an ultimate truth].[40]

Vajrapāṇi then addresses the argument made by "childish people," namely that the fourth consecration depends upon the third, that the "third is the cause, and the fourth is the fruit."[41] He rejects these arguments, and this rejection is consonant with his privileging of mahāmudrā meditation over the forms of meditation employing a real or imagined consort. In other words, in both cases he does not wish to admit the dependence of the disembodied, inner realizations upon outer, physical practices, presumably because doing so would lend authority to practices that, by Vajrapāṇi's time, were quite controversial.

Vajrapāṇi's position was an intermediate one in the ongoing process of the reinterpretation of these tantras. While Vajrapāṇi problematicizes the sexual practices, he does not clearly and unambiguously prohibit their practice (by all or for monks specifically), as Atīśa would do within a few decades. This work thus contributed to the ongoing movement in tantric Buddhism away from external, body-oriented practices and toward internal contemplative practices. A corresponding and closely related trend was the movement away from the performance of transgressive ritual practices and toward the performance of rituals employing symbolic substitutes for the ritual elements associated with sexuality or violence. Hence the second and third consecrations, as publicly practiced by Tibetans, no longer involve overt sexuality, but rather purely symbolic elements.[42]

In conclusion, while Vajrapāṇi's commentary may have made a relatively modest contribution to the study of the *Cakrasamvara Tantra*, it appears to be an extremely valuable work insofar as it sheds light on the development of Indian tantric Buddhism. It illuminates the problematic reception of the transgressive Unexcelled Yoga Tantras within monastic Buddhist communities in northern India. It also provides tantalizing hints of how the traditions associated with these tantras was transformed, via the application of creative commentary, during the crucial ninth- through eleventh-century period, between the time of their initial composition in India and their transmission to Tibet.

Endnotes

1. The *Kālacakratantra* and its associated literature has been dated to the late tenth and early eleventh centuries. Regarding this issue, see John Newman, "The Epoch of the Kālacakra," *Indo-Iranian Journal* 41 (1998): 319-49. In comparison, the *Guhyasamāja Tantra* was composed by the late seventh or early eighth centuries, and the *Hevajra* and *Cakrasamvara Tantra*s are datable to the late eighth or early ninth centuries. Regarding the dating of these works, see the introduction to my *The Cakrasamvara Tantra: A Study and Annotated Translation* (New York: American Institute of Buddhist Studies/Columbia University Press, 2007).

2. This is now a very well-known work. The Sanskrit text has been edited and published (*Vimalaprabhāṭīkā of Kalki Śrī Puṇḍarīka on Śrī Laghukālacakra-tantrarāja,* vol. 1, J.

Upadhyāya, ed. [Sarnath: Central Institute of Higher Tibetan Studies, 1986], and vol. 2, V. Dwivedi and S. S. Bahulakar, eds. [Sarnath: Central Institute of Higher Tibetan Studies, 1994]). It is also preserved in Tibetan translation (To. 1347).

3. Regarding Puṇḍarīka and the significance of the *Vimalaprabhā,* see Vesna Wallace, *The Inner Kālacakratantra* (New York: Oxford University Press, 2001), p. 3.

4. To my knowledge, the Sanskrit manuscripts of this work have not survived. This work is preserved in Tibetan translation (To. 1180).

5. The text of the *Hevajra Tantra* itself makes it clear that Vajragarbha was the Buddha's interlocutor. See, for example, the opening of the text, *kalpa* 1, ch. 1, vv. 2-13, translated in David Snellgrove, *The Hevajra Tantra: A Critical Study* (London: Oxford University Press, 1959), vol. 1, 47-49, and edition in vol. 2, 2-5.

6. The Sanskrit for this text has been edited by Claudio Cicuzza in his *The Laghutantraṭīkā* (Serie Orientale Roma, vol. 86, Roma: Istituto Italiano per l'Africa e l'Oriente, 2001). There is also a Tibetan translation (To. 1402).

7. Unlike the *Hevajra Tantra,* the *Cakrasamvara Tantra* (CS) contains only traces of dialogue, with no indication of the identity of the text's interlocutor. This identity thus became the object of debate among CS commentators. The influential commentator Kambala argued that the interlocutor was Vajrapāṇi (To. 1401, D fol. 4b). However, Bhavabhaṭṭa argued that the interlocutor was Vajravārāhī and relegated Vajrapāṇi to the position of the tantra's compiler (To. 1403, D fol. 41a). Interestingly, Vajrapāṇi qua author of the Kālacakra-inspired CS commentary humbly attributed this influential position to Vajravārāhī, in agreement with Bhavabhaṭṭa. See D fol. 79a, and Cicuzza, *Laghutantraṭīkā,* 44.

8. The Tibetan tradition held that there was a person of this name who was the author of a text on Mahāmudrā and who, according to the *Blue Annals,* was born in 1017 CE. The author of the Kālacakra- inspired CS commentary is clearly very interested in the topic of Mahāmudra, so these works may have been composed by the same individual. Cicuzza, however, argues that this commentary belongs to the early phase of Kālacakra exegesis and was most likely composed between 967 and 1026 CE, when most of the other early Kālacakra texts were composed, making it highly unlikely that the author of this text was born in 1017 CE. See Cicuzza, *Laghutantraṭīkā,* 25-26.

9. For a summary of this story see Cicuzza, *Laghutantraṭīkā,* 24. For the full account see George Roerich, trans., *The Blue Annals by gZhon-nu dPal* (2nd ed., Delhi: Motilal Banarsidass, 1976), 762-763.

10. See Cicuzza, *Laghutantraṭīkā,* 24, for a translation of Vajrapāṇi's concluding remarks.

11. Bu-ston composed a lengthy and influential commentary on the CS, the *rgyud sde spyi'i rnam par gzhag pa rgyud sde rin po che'i mdzes rgyan zhes bya ba,* in *The Collected Works of Bu-ston,* Lokesh Chandra, ed. (New Delhi: International Academy of Indian Culture, 1966), vol. ba, 1-610. Tsongkhapa, in composing his commentary on the CS, followed Bu-ston's work closely. As a result, Bu-ston is the most frequent object of Tsongkhapa's criticism.

12. "Adamantine expressions" (*vajrapada*) are the instances of symbolic speech found in the tantras, which require detailed explanation.

13. Trans. from the text in Cicuzza, *Laghutantraṭīkā,* 52, and D fol. 82b-83a.

14. For Tsongkhapa's comments, see his *bde mchog bsdus pa'i rgyud kyi rgya cher bshad pa sbas pa'i don kun gsal ba,* in the *rJe yab sras gsung 'bum*, bKra-shis Lhun-po ed. (repr. Delhi: Ngawang Gelek Demo, 1980), vol. nya, fol. 13b-14a.

15. My translation from the Sanskrit in Cicuzza, *Laghutantraṭīkā,* 124, and the Tibetan at To. 1402, D fol. 124b. The larger passage containing this text is translated below.

16. The fact that this work was preserved in Nepal and Vajragarbha's commentary apparently was not, *may* indicate that Vajrapāṇi's work was more popular.

17. These include the commentaries of Kambala (To. 1401), Vajrapāṇi (To. 1402), Bhavabhaṭṭa (To. 1403), Durjayacandra (To. 1404), Bhavyakīrti (To. 1405), Jayabhadra (To. 1406), Devagupta (To. 1407), Vīravajra (To. 1408), Tathāgatarakṣita (To. 1409), *Śāśvatavajra (*rtag pa'i rdo rje*) (To. 1410), Sumatikīrti (To. 1411), Vīravajra (To. 1412), and Indrabhūti (To. 1413). Eleven of these treat the entire Tantra; Vajrapāṇi's is an extended commentary based on the first ten and a half verses, and Sumatikīrti's is a short summation and analysis of the Tantra's contents. Among these, Sanskrit texts have survived for three of them—Vajrapāṇi's, Bhavabhaṭṭa's, and Jayabhadra's. See section 1.3 of Gray, *The Cakrasamvara Tantra,* for a discussion of these works.

18. Regarding this system see Per Kvaerne, "On the Concept of Sahaja in Indian Buddhist Tantric Literature," *Temenos* 11 (1975): 88-135.

19. I refer to the systems attributed to the mahāsiddhas Lūipa, Ghaṇṭapa, and Kāṇha and outlined in Lūipa's *Śrībhagavad-abhisamaya* (To. 1427), Ghaṇṭapa's *Śrīcakrasamvara-pañcakrama* (To. 1433), and Kāṇha's *Ālicatuṣṭaya* (To. 1451).

20. Regarding the Guhyasamāja system, see Daniel Cozort, *Highest Yoga Tantra* (Ithaca, NY: Snow Lion Publications, 1986). For examples of CS commentators employing the concepts derived from these other systems, see the notes to my translation in Gray, *The Cakrasamvara Tantra.*

21. Regarding this text, see John Newman, "The *Paramādibuddha* (The Kālacakra *mūlatantra*) and its Relation to the Early Kālacakra Literature," *Indo-Iranian Journal* 30 (1987): 93-102.

22. The *Paramādibuddha* is, in fact, the most plausible of the legendary *mūlatantras,* not only because of its relatively modest size, but also because it is the best attested. A number of early Kālacakra texts quote from it, and a significant portion is preserved in Nāropa's *Sekoddeśaṭīkā,* which purports to comment on the chapter on consecration in this text. Regarding this see Giacomella Orofino, *Sekoddeśa: A Critical Edition of the Tibetan Translations* (Roma: Istituto Italiano per il Medio ed Estremo Oriente, 1994).

23. For example, the *Abhidhāna,* the legendary Cakrasamvara root text, supposedly consisted of one hundred thousand or more stanzas. Regarding this see Gray, *The Cakrasamvara Tantra,* 28-35.

24. Regarding the impact of the Buddhist-Muslim encounter in northern India on the Kālacakra tradition, see John Newman, "Islam in the Kālacakra Tantra," *Journal of the International Association of Buddhist Studies* 21.2 (1998): 311-71.

25. Regarding the sexual practices described in the CS, see David Gray, *The Cakrasamvara Tantra,* 103-131. See also David Gray, "Disclosing the Empty Secret: Textuality and Embodiment in the *Cakrasamvara Tantra,*" *Numen* 52.4 (2005): 417-44.

26. For an introduction to the consecrations, see David Snellgrove, *Indo-Tibetan Buddhism* (London: Serindia Publications, 1987), 213–77.

27. In her discussion of this passage, Vesna Wallace points out that there is no clear passage in the *Laghukālacakra Tantra* or the *Vimalaprabhā* supporting Atīśa's claim. On the other hand, there are passages in the *Paramādibuddha Tantra* and the *Vimalaprabhā* that

contradict him, and describe monks and wandering ascetics receiving these consecrations and being offered consorts for the practice of sexual yoga. (See *The Inner Kālacakratantra*, p. 124.) This is certainly the case, but it is fascinating that Vajrapāṇi, as we shall see below, quotes a verse from the *Paramādibuddha* that addresses the related issue of consort practice.

28. Atīśa, *Bodhipāthapradīpa*, To. 3947, D fols. 240b–241a.

29. The term *mudrā* has many meanings, such as seal, stamp, gesture, and consort. In the context of tantric passages such as Vajrapāṇi's below, I feel that "consort" is the best translation of this term. Regarding this see Jan Gonda, "Mudrā," *Studies in the History of Religions* 12 (1972): 21–31.

30. See David Snellgrove, *Indo-Tibetan Buddhism*, 265–69.

31. The Sanskrit *bhāvayet* could be translated as "should give rise to" or "should meditate upon." In the context of the root text, I use the former, following the Tibetan translation *bya.* However, the Tibetan translation of Vajrapāṇi's text translates it as "should meditate upon," *bsgom par bya.*

32. CS 1.7cd—my translation from my forthcoming edition.

33. While I normally translate *bodhicitta* as "spirit of awakening," I translate it as seminal essence in contexts such as this, when it is used as a euphemism for male or female reproductive fluids.

34. My translation from the Sanskrit in Cicuzza, *Laghutantraṭīkā,* 123, and the Tibetan at To. 1402, D fol. 123b-124a.

35. Here and below I translate the Sanskrit *paramākṣaraḥ* following the Tibetan *mchog tu mi 'gyur ba.* This might also be translated as "the supreme syllable," and in some contexts this compound refers to the syllable *oṃ.*

36. This translates the Sanskrit, *dāyakī,* rather than the Tibetan, *ster bar byed pa mo,* "she who bestows."

37. My translation from the Sanskrit in Cicuzza, *Laghutantraṭīkā,* 123-24, and the Tibetan at To. 1402, D fol. 124a,b.

38. I presume that *dhūmādinimitta* refers to the eight signs seen during the dying process and visualized in some traditions of perfecting stage meditation. Regarding these signs see Robert Thurman, *The Tibetan Book of the Dead* (New York: Bantam Books, 1994), 42.

39. My translation from the Sanskrit in Cicuzza, *Laghutantraṭīkā,* 124, and the Tibetan at To. 1402, D fol. 124b-25a.

40. My translation from the Sanskrit in Cicuzza, *Laghutantraṭīkā,* 124, and the Tibetan at To. 1402, D fol. 125a.

41. See Cicuzza, *Laghutantraṭīkā,* 124, and the Tibetan at To. 1402, D fol. 125a.

42. I refer, for example, to the red and white food substances employed in the second consecration as a substitute for female and male sexual fluids.

–11–

The Concept of Ādibuddha in the *Kālacakratantra*

Urban Hammar

The *ādibuddha* (dang-po sangs-rgyas) is a concept which has been the object of much controversy and misunderstanding in the history of research on the Kālacakra and other tantras where it has been mentioned. The word in Sanskrit is composed of *ādi-* and *Buddha*: *ādi-* means the first or the original, and consequently the ādibuddha means the first, or the original, Buddha. It can be a purely temporal concept, saying that it is the Buddha which came first in time. It can also mean the original Buddha-concept which can stand for the Buddha-principle which was at the origin of everything. It can also mean the Buddha-principle corresponding to the void/śūnyatā. In Tibetan the translation is always *dang-po sangs-rgyas*, which means literally "the first Buddha."

Below I will provide a short review of how the concept and related concepts are used in the Kālacakra literature. This article is mainly based on my doctoral dissertation from 2005.[1] But it is necessary to begin with a brief account of how the concept has been treated in occidental research.

The first short article on the ādibuddha concept was written by Csoma de Körös in 1833. He mentioned the ādibuddha in the context of quoting a text from the Tibetan historian Padma dkar-po, but the verse was originally from the *Vimalaprabhā*. "He that does not know the chief first Buddha (Ādibuddha), knows not the circle of time (Kālacakra)."[2] It probably only alluded to the Kālacakra root-text, *Paramādibuddha*.

B. H. Hodgson published an account of the ādibuddha concept that seemed as though it would have great importance.[3] He presented the ādibuddha as a sort of creator god that stood above and beyond the four tathāgatas (or jinas). The study was based on Nepalese material, especially the *Svāyambhū Purāṇa*, which was written in the tenth century and followed the model of the Hindu purāṇas. This aiśvarika system of Nepal cherished the idea of an ādibuddha that was at the origin of the five jinas and had its origin in the Void (śūnyatā). Western (Christian) scholars here found an idea which could be interpreted as monotheistic. Later studies by

Gellner have shown that the Nepalese concept is more polytheistic and does not correspond to the semitic monotheistic concept of god.[4]

The most important contribution to the study of the ādibuddha in the *Kālacakratantra* was made by Grönbold in his article in 1992. He studied the different places where *ādibuddha* can be found in the Kālacakra texts and determined that it could mean different things in these texts. It can be purely temporal and often stand merely as the name of the Kālacakra texts; it can be found in an enumeration of Buddhas and bodhisattvas, without any specific meaning; and finally it can stand as a personification of the highest principle, which also implies that it can stand for the impersonal concepts of śūnya (the void), tathatā (suchness), mahāsukha (the great bliss). Grönbold also studied some of the Tibetan works on the Kālacakra and concluded that, in terms of the three-body system, the ādibuddha has a position superior to the dharmakāya concept. In some texts it is obvious that the ādibuddha actually represents the fourth body, which is most frequently called svābhāvikakāya.[5]

The latest study has been made by Wallace in her recent work on the second chapter of the Kālacakra texts. Wallace notes that the ādibuddha concept in the *Kālacakratantra* is primarily related to the corresponding concept in the *Mañjuśrīnāmasaṃgīti*. The ādibuddha is called the primordial Buddha because he was the first to obtain buddhahood by means of the unchanging bliss characterized by perfect awakening in a single moment. In the *Vimalaprabhā ādi* means "without beginning or end" and "without origination and cessation." Wallace stresses that in the Kālacakra tradition this refers to the "innate gnosis" (sahaja-jñāna) that pervades the minds of all sentient beings and is the basis for both saṃsāra and nirvāṇa. When the tantra speaks of the ādibuddha as the one who first attained perfect enlightenment by means of unchanging bliss, it is referring to the actual realization of one's own innate gnosis. Wallace concludes that the ādibuddha refers to the ultimate nature of one's own mind and to the one who has realized that innate nature by purificatory practices.[6] Her conclusions seem to be perfectly coherent, but I will here try to make some complementary observations which point to other interpretations of the ādibuddha concept.

Ādibuddha in the *Kālacakratantra*

The basic texts

I have studied the basic Kālacakra texts to find the concept of the ādibuddha and how it is expressed. The texts are as follows:

1. The *Paramādibuddha* is the lost root-tantra text, which according to the Kālacakra tradition contained twelve thousand verses and now only can be found as a small fragment in the Sekoddeśa[7] and through scattered citations in other texts, especially the *Vimalaprabhā* commentary. The text is supposed to have been written by the king Sucandra of Śambhala who requested the Buddha's preaching

of the text. Consequently, it was supposedly written during the lifetime of Buddha Śākyamuni, perhaps in the later part of his life,

2. The *Paramādibuddhoddhṛta Śrī Kālacakra-nāma-tantra-rāja* (the laghutantra), (KCT or *Śrī Kālacakra*) contains 1,048 verses and is the extant basic text of the *Kālacakratantra*. For the Sanskrit I have used mainly the *Vimalaprabhā* editions from the Central Institute of Higher Tibetan Studies in Varanasi edited by Samdhong Rinpoche, where the KCT is included. The Tibetan translations are in Tohoku 362 and 1346 and Peking 4. This text is supposed to have been written as an abbreviation of the *Paramādibuddha* by a successor of Sucandra as king of Śambhala called Mañjuśrī-Yaśas. This text, together with the *Vimalaprabhā* commentary, definitely appeared in India at the beginning of the eleventh century and is now the extant surviving basic Kālacakra text. The dating of the text is uncertain, but the references to Islam, Muhammad, and Mecca, and the fact that Muslims are the enemies (mlecchas), indicate a date after or during the Muslim invasions of India, beginning towards the end of the tenth century.

3. The *Vimalaprabhā* commentary (VP) in twelve thousand lines. This is the great commentary on the KCT and the *Paramādibuddha* which has always been transmitted together with the KCT; it is considered of the same value as the laghutantra. The Sanskrit editions are from Varanasi, *Vimalaprabhāṭīkā,* vol. 1 1986, vol. 2 1994, and vol. 3 1994. Tibetan translations are in Tohoku 845 and 1347 and Peking 2064. The *Vimalaprabhā* was written by Puṇḍarika, a later king of Śambhala. There is also said to have existed a root-*Vimalaprabhā* of sixty thousand lines.[8]

These texts have now been translated into English in great part. John Newman translated the first chapter of the KCT, verses 1-27 and 128-170 together with the *Vimalaprabhā*. Banerjee translated the whole of the KCT into German, but not the *Vimalaprabhā*. Wallace translated the whole of the second chapter together with the VP commentary, and a translation of chapter four is coming. Andresen translated chapter three only of the KCT without the commentary. Hartzell has translated the greater part of chapter five in his lengthy doctoral dissertation. Finally, Stril-Rever has translated the whole of the second chapter into French.[9]

The concept of ādibuddha and paramādibuddha as found in the basic texts *Śrī Kālacakra-tantra-rāja* and *Vimalaprabhāṭīkā*

I have gone through the *Śrī Kālacakra* and *Vimalaprabhā* looking for *ādibuddha* and *paramādibuddha* as well as concepts related to them. There are five chapters, but most quotations occur in the first chapter. Actually the word *ādibuddha* is mentioned only seven times in the whole laghutantra (KCT). There are not many places where the words *ādibuddha* or *paramādibuddha* are found, but the content of these concepts can be found in many other ways. They are related, for example, to the concepts of the fourth body of the Buddha, the sahajakāya, and also to the concept of the supreme unchanging/indestructible which is treated in the fifth chapter. Also, for example, the word *jinapati* (master of jinas), which is related to the ādibuddha concept, is mentioned forty-two times in chapters three to five of the laghutantra (KCT). The most common use of the word *ādibuddha* in the Kālacakra texts is in referring to the very texts themselves. The basic root-tantra of the Kālacakra teachings is called the *Ādibuddha* or the *Paramādibuddha*. In other contexts also both designations are given.

In the *Vimalaprabhā* commentary to the basic text there are elaborated the basic ideas of a philosophical ādibuddha concept. Ādibuddha is given the following qualifications in two of the introductory verses to the text:[10]

• Omniscience (sarvajñā), or the knowledge body (jñānakāya): this qualification is given at several places in the Kālacakra texts and can sometimes be regarded as another designation of the fourth body of the Buddha, normally given the name of sahajakāya (the innate body) in the Kālacakra texts.

• Progenitor of the Buddhas: it is not clear which Buddhas are intended, but normally these should be the five jinas, or as in the Kālacakra, the six jinas, as the number "six" is very important in this tantra.

In these verses the concept of paramādibuddha is also said to be uncreated and without end. This is of course one of the fundamental ideas in Buddhism, that one must transcend the changing world; therefore, this may be a way of expressing the concepts of nirvāṇa or śūnyatā. Paramādibuddha is also said to be equipped with three bodies, which corresponds to the three-kāya system. There is the complication that there seems to be the system of four bodies in the Kālacakra literature, but actually the fourth body seems to correspond to the concept of ādibuddha/paramādibuddha. "Knowing the three times, past, present, and future" is another designation of the paramādibuddha, who is consequently beyond time. Another designation of the ādibuddha is nonduality (advaya), which indicates that the concept is beyond the wisdom/means duality (prajñā/upāya). He is also known as the wisdom body (jñānakāya) which can be seen as the fourth body of the Buddha; this qualification is given in several places in the texts. The ādibuddha is further designated as the supreme of the four bodies, the sahajakāya (the innate body), which is the transcendent level of existence. In these same verses the ādibuddha is also said to be the master of jinas (jinapati), and he is consequently at the origin of the five jinas—Akṣobhya, Amitābha, Amoghasiddhi, Ratnasambhava, and, at the maṇḍala's center, Vairocana/Kālacakra. The sixth jina, usually called Vajrasattva, is mentioned many times. Slightly later it is written that Viśvamāta, the female counterpart of Kālacakra, is the progenitor of the Buddhas and of Kālacakra that he is arisen from the unchanging (paramākṣara).[11] All these indicate that the concept of ādibuddha is beyond time and existence, but also that it can have several meanings within the same text.

Another interesting qualification of the ādibuddha is that it is defined as without family/connection/parts/relation. The variant translations depend on the Sanskrit word *niranvaya*, which is problematic. The Sanskrit word *anvaya* can be interpreted as following: succession, connection, logical connection of cause and effect, descendent, lineage, or family; *nir-* is a negation of that word and consequently the concept means "without causal connection, connection, family, etc."[12] In Tibetan it has been translated as rgyu-med, "without cause," in the *Mañjuśrīnāmasaṃgīti*, but in the *Kālacakratantra* it is translated as rigs-med, "without family or retinue." In the *Kālacakratantra* this word is found in many places in connection with the ādibuddha or paramādibuddha. The first is in the beginning of the *Vimalaprabhā* where it is said that the ādibuddha is without parts (niranvaya) and a little later where the paramādibuddha is also said to be without parts.[13] The use of this qualification of the ādibuddha strongly indicates that it is nondual and also without connection with other levels of existence. Actually this designation of the ādibuddha is already found in the *Mañjuśrīnāmasaṃgīti*, the first text where the ādibuddha is mentioned and defined. There it is written that the bodhisattva Mañjuśrī is the ādibuddha without causal connection, and this is to say that the ādibuddha is beyond the world of causality.[14]

Later in the *Vimalaprabhā* it is stated that the paramādibuddha is indivisible and undivided.[15] Later still the word *niranvaya* is analyzed in the text itself, where it is said that *anvaya* is the dharma which consists of wisdom and means, and then that is negated by *nir-* in *niranvaya*. Consequently this means that the concept of niranvaya is completely unified and without duality, and is also indicated as unchanging bliss.[16] Then, in a commentary on the first verse of the laghutantra it is written that the ādibuddha is without beginning or end and also again without connection. The ādibuddha is consequently eternal but not a creator of the world. He is also unchanging bliss.[17]

In another place in the *Vimalaprabhā,* again commenting on the first verse of the KCT, there is this interesting elaboration: "The oneness of these two minds [the yogin's own mind and the knowledge mind of unchanging bliss], consisting of wisdom and method, the vajrayoga, the great aim, the supreme unchanging (*paramākṣara*), the ādibuddha without connection (*niranvaya*), Bhagavān Kālacakra, is renowned in all the various tantras as Vajrasattva."[18] This seems to be a way of relating many ideas together without defining them explicitly and placing them all under the name/concept of Vajrasattva. There is a tendency to regard these various concepts as being unchanging/imperishable, using the word *paramākṣara* which is composed of *parama-*, the supreme, and *akṣara-*, the imperishable or unchanging. This tendency can be found in Mahāyāna Buddhism in many other texts, as has been very well remarked by Jens Braarvig in his work analyzing the concept of the indestructible in the *Akṣayamatinirdeśasūtra*. He states that this idea of something eternal or imperishable became widely accepted in Mahāyāna Buddhism when the concepts of ālayavijñāna and tathāgatagarbha were elaborated in Yogācāra Buddhism.[19]

In the second chapter of the KCT and the VP an example of how the word ādibuddha signifies the Kālacakra maṇḍala can be found. The maṇḍala normally hosts 722 divinities which all have different roles in the context of the KCT, but here there are 1,620 divinities in the maṇḍala. It is explained that this is the maṇḍala of the root-tantra *Paramādibuddha*, now lost. That changed in the abbreviated

Kālacakra maṇḍala where only 722 deities are arranged in the maṇḍala; these figures are based on calculations of the reckoning of time in hours, days, etc.[20]

Verse 92 in the second chapter of both the KCT and the VP contains interesting information: ". . . so he, Bhagavān the unique teacher, is not one who is a creator. He is the omniscient ādibuddha, revered by the three worlds, Kālacakri, not Cakri, at the root of whose foot-lotus Brahmā, Viṣṇu, and Rudra have found refuge. Kālacakra, who is the jina-producer, who is without qualities, who is without mental constructions (nirvikalpa), to him I pay homage."

It is stated in Bu-ston's commentary to the VP that the ādibuddha has attained the fourth body of the Buddha, the sahajakāya, and later also possesses Buddha's other three bodies. Also, direct correspondence is made between Kālacakra and the ādibuddha: they have the same characteristics. Finally it is said that this is the precept of a śūnyatā-vādin, that is, someone who honors śūnyatā/the void as the ultimate goal.[21]

The consequences of these quotations are that Bhagavān/Ādibuddha is not a creator, but he is omniscient and producer of the jinas. He is also the same as Kālacakra and the master of the three great Hindu gods, which supports the theory of why the Kālacakra appeared around year 1000 when Muslim armies were entering India: the Kālacakra could have been an effort to try to unite the Indian peoples against the invading Muslims.[22]

Verse II: 92 is the first time in the KCT, and its commentary in the VP, that something more substantial is said about the ādibuddha; it is here more than merely a name, as the quotation above shows. He is also equated with Kālacakra, which makes the understanding of the Kālacakra deity figure easier—Kālacakra is therefore definitely a deity of the ādibuddha type, like Samantabhadra and Vairocana. It is of course impossible to give the concept of ādibuddha a gender, but I use the male gender here, following convention. When not in union with his female consort, Viśvamāta, Kālacakra himself contains the two principles of wisdom and means and consequently is the union of these two concepts. It is also important that Puṇḍarika, the author of the *Vimalaprabhā*, claims here to be a śūnyatā-vādin, that is, an adherent of the Mādhyamika school of Buddhism. Other aspects of the teachings, however, show perhaps even more influence from the Yogacārā school.

The next mention of the ādibuddha is in chapter five of the KCT and the VP. Puṇḍarika states: "I will explain the characteristics of the four bodies of the Buddha as Mañjuvajra extracted them from the ādibuddha without causal connection/family."[23] This is another place where the term *niranvaya* has a special role. If interpreted as meaning "without logical connection of cause and effect," then it means that the ādibuddha is a deity outside of the world of cause and effect and without connection with normal existence. From this cosmic principle Mañjuvajra drew out the four bodies of the Buddha. Another possible, more prosaic meaning is that Puṇḍarika simply intends that Mañjuśrī-Yaśas, the author of the laghutantra, drew out the characteristics of the four bodies from the root-tantra text called the *Ādibuddha*, which is still not found. The latter interpretation is the more probable, but why then would the text be qualified with *niranvaya*? This does not seem to make much sense and is one of the disputed places in the Kālacakra texts.

The last place where the word *ādibuddha* is mentioned is in KCT V: 256: ". . . even though you [Mañjuśrī] are born from all the jinas, so were you in the beginning [Bu-ston: 'because you have been transformed into the wisdom body (jñānakaya) of all the Tathāgatas you are the ādibuddha'] the ādibuddha."[24] I have included this interesting remark from Bu-ston's commentary here because there is no *Vimalaprabhā* commentary on these last verses and because Bu-ston's commentaries are basic for the interpretation of Kālacakra when the Fourteenth Dalai Lama gives his Kālacakra initiations.

Ādibuddha in this verse seems to be a contradictory concept because it is stated that Mañjuśrī is, in the beginning, the ādibuddha but is also the son of the jinas. Bu-ston comments that Mañjuśrī is the wisdom body of the Tathāgatas/jinas and therefore is the ādibuddha. One conclusion that can be drawn from this is that the ādibuddha seems to be an independent concept meaning approximately "the first Buddha" or the wisdom body/fourth body of the Buddha.

Preliminary conclusions

What then can we understand about the ādibuddha from analyzing the two basic Kālacakra texts, KCT and VP? In the KCT the most important characteristics are that he is not one who acts; he is omniscient (*sarvajñā*); he is progenitor of the best of jinas (*jinavarajananam*); he is without qualities (*nirguṇa*); he is without mental constructions (*nirvikalpa*); he is master of jinas (*jinapati*); and he is ruler of the three worlds. In the *Vimalaprabhā* these characteristics and the following ones can be found: he is unchanging bliss (*akṣarasukha*); he is progenitor of the buddhas (*jinajanaka*); he is nondual (*advaya*); he is beginningless and endless; he is nondual wisdom and means; he is the first to obtain buddhahood; and he is without parts/connection.

Consequently, it is possible to discern in these texts a number of qualifications of the ādibuddha which fit quite well with general ādibuddha theories, especially in that the ādibuddha brings forth the jinas and is without beginning or end. Consequently, it can be stated that the ādibuddha is described as an entity in these two texts, but it is not possible to find one ādibuddha deity described in the concrete way as Hogdson attempted. What are described more concretely are aspects or emanations such as Kālacakra, Akṣobhya, Viśvamāta, Vajrasattva, and Vajradhara. In the Indo-Tibetan iconography one can recognize an aspect of the ādibuddha in that they all have their arms crossed over the chest with vajra and bell in their hands. Another possible conclusion is that the whole description of the different aspects of the ādibuddha is a positive way to describe śūnyatā (the void) according to Madhyamaka Buddhism.

Still another way of interpreting the concept of the ādibuddha is as a designation of the concept of tathāgatagarbha, the notion that there exists a permanent

Buddha-seed (*garbha*) in all beings and whose discovery results in buddhahood. Ruegg has studied this subject in detail and states about the tathāgatagarbha that it is "characterized as permanent (*nitya*), immutable (*dhruva*), blissful (*sukha*) and eternal (*śāśvata*), and sometimes we are even told that it is Ātman."[25] These epithets correspond well with the ones given to the concept of the ādibuddha in the KCT and the VP. In the *Mahāparinirvāṇasūtra* the concept of tathāgata indicates the ideas of being permanent, blissful, void, without marks, and very pure (*viśuddha*).[26] These concepts are found as designations of the ādibuddha in the KCT/VP. In his analysis Ruegg concludes that the concept is not identical to the brahmanical ātman, but that it is founded on a distinct theory which may neutralize and cancel both the ātmavada and the anātmavāda. Perhaps there is a common stock of experiences which are described by both Buddhists and Hindus.[27] This idea about the tathāgatagarbha has recently been studied further by Stearns in his work on Dol-po-pa.[28] Dol-po-pa states that the ādibuddha is to be compared to "indestructible self-arisen gnosis," probably corresponding to the phrase "acintya-sahaja-jñāna" in Sanskrit.[29]

Despite these seeming contradictions, it seems that there exists some consistent idea of the ādibuddha in the KCT and VP. The problem is that it is almost impossible to find a systematic explication of the idea. As will be shown later, more possibilities for interpretation appear when examining the theory of the four bodies of the Buddha (the fourth body is sahajakāya or śuddhakāya) and the whole complex of ideas concerning the concept of the supreme unchanging, supreme unchanging gnosis, or supreme unchanging bliss (*paramākṣara*). The concept of something unmanifest which manifests itself in some way to shape the world as we see it is known in other branches of Indian philosophy. In Sāṃkhya philosophy there are some similarities, with its discussion of the root-base (*mūla-prakṛti, pradhāna*) which is the unmanifest (*avyakta*) that becomes manifest (*vyakta*).

The fourth body of the Buddha and the ādibuddha concept

The concept of "kāyas," bodies of the Buddha, came to be elaborated in the Mahāyāna. Often the tradition holds that there exist three so-called bodies (*kāya*), dharmakāya, sambhogakāya, and nirmāṇakāya, but in some texts a fourth body is introduced, especially in the *Abhisamayālaṃkara* of the Yogācāra tradition. This controversy has been analyzed by John Makransky: Vimuktisena's view holds that there are only three bodies, with the fourth body, the svābhāvikakāya, a kind of essence of the other three; the other line of interpretation, Haribhadra's, counts four bodies, with the svābhāvikakāya an essence body, unconditioned and related to the tathāgatagarbha, the Buddha-seed as found in all beings.[30] In the *Vimalaprabhā*, a connection is made to Haribhadra's interpretation of the *Abhisamayālaṃkāra* and is taken as an argument for the theory of the four bodies presented in the *Kālacakratantra*.[31] In this context the fourth body is named sahajakāya and is given some of the same characteristics as the ādibuddha, such as omniscience.[32]

The fourth body in the *Kālacakra* is variously called sahajakāya (the simultaneously arisen body), śuddhakāya (the pure body), and svābhāvikakāya (the essence body). I have not seen the term *śuddhakāya* in other contexts, and in these texts it seems to mean the fourth body of the Buddha. There is an interesting place in the second chapter of the KCT and VP where śuddhakāya is described at the microcosmic level of the birth of a child. The śuddhakāya represents the moment when the child has been conceived in the womb but is still without characteristics, unmanifested, and in unity. The moment of birth when the child comes into existence is on the dharmakāya level.[33] In general in the Kālacakra there are the different levels of macrocosmos, the external world, and microcosmos, the human body, and there are correspondences between what happens in the two worlds. In the human body the śuddhakāya is on the unmanifest level, while in the outer cosmos it can be compared to the Ādibuddha concept which is on the unmanifest level.

In the second chapter, which treats the human body, this theme is continued by correlating the four bodies to the six cakras of the human body. Principally the fourth body, sahajakāya, is situated in the head cakras, in the forehead or crown-cakras. In the fifth chapter of the KCT and the VP there is a subchapter discussing the four bodies of the Buddha, KCT V: 89-126. The *Vimalaprabhā* comments: ". . . the sahajakāya is not prajñā and is not even upāya; it is the sahajatanu of the Buddhas . . . Thus, from the sahajatanu's (*tanu* means form or body and thus equates to *kāya*) being accomplished for the sake of itself, and being accomplished for the sake of others, became the dharmakāya, the sleep being ended. And that one [the dharmakāya] has as its very nature prajñā and upāya . . . Thus, sahaja [-kāya] is one, and there are four separate kinds, this very one [Bu-ston: sahajakāya], the dharma [-kāya], the sambhoga [-kāya], and the nirmāṇa [-kāya]."[34] It is interesting that here it is said that the sahajatanu is transformed into perfection for the benefit of itself, as this is another confirmation of the transcendence of the concept. It is beyond this world and said to be in a sort of sleeping state—waking up from this sleep, it becomes the dharmakāya. Having become the dharmakāya, it can be of perfect benefit for others. This is another indication that the sahajakāya is beyond the world of appearances. This kind of "body" is presented as being transcendental but on other levels is manifested as dharmakāya and the other "bodies" which become more and more active in the world. This kind of principle is very similar to the way the ādibuddha is presented in other places in the tantra, and this fourth body of the Buddha may be another way of presenting the principle of the ādibuddha.

A disciple of Tsong-kha-pa's disciple mKhas-grub-rje, Zhang-zhung Chos-dbang-grags-pa, wrote an important commentary on the *Kālacakratantra*. It is part of the collected works of mKhas-grub-rje.[35] He adds interesting explanations regarding the nature of the four bodies of the Buddha, and these together with the material from the Kālacakra texts themselves are the basis of the following scheme of the relation between the four bodies and the concept of ādibuddha:

- Sahajakāya exists by itself, and the great bliss (mahāsukha)-side and the void (śūnya)-side are united in the sahajakāya as the water is with the wet. It can be seen as another way of denominating the content of the concept of ādibuddha.

• Sahajakāya has a mind-side with the concept of mahāsukha and mahāsukhakāya and a body-side with the void-form body (śūnya-rūpa-kāya). On the mahāsukha-side is also the svābhāvika-kāya and prajña (wisdom), and on the body-side is upāya (means).

• Dharmakāya comes into existence when the sahajakāya is turning into benefit for others. It comes into existence from a state of sleep. Dharmakāya divides into jñāna (knowledge) and vijñāna (discriminative knowledge).

• Sambhogakāya then emerges when sound comes into existence. This level is when sound begins to be transferred to living beings.

• Nirmāṇakāya is the gross level where the teachings for maturing the living beings can be done.

This analysis by Zhang-zhung Chos-dbang-grags-pa corresponds well with verse 89 of the *Śrī Kālacakra-tantra-rāja* and its commentary in the *Vimalaprabhā*. The original level of sahajakāya can be compared directly to the concept of ādibuddha, and we may conclude after this brief investigation that there are lines of development in the ādibuddha concept in connection with the svābhāvikakāya (self-existent body) system of the four Buddha-bodies. Already in the *Abhisamayālaṃkara*, and especially in the commentary to this text by Haribhadra, one can find information on the svābhāvikakāya that points forward to the concept of śuddhakāya (the pure body) which is found in the main Kālacakra texts. As yet I have not seen in any literature that the fourth body should be named śuddhakāya as in the Kālacakra texts, but Haribhadra writes about the fourth body which is pure (*viśuddha*). Thus there is a link to the Kālacakra texts, from the developed concept of svābhāvikakāya to the ādibuddha concept. The sahajakāya is here also said to be beyond the duality of prajñā (wisdom) and upāya (means) and can consequently be seen as being on the level of the ādibuddha principle.

Paramākṣara: the supreme unchanging/immutable and its relation to the ādibuddha concept and the fourth body of the Buddha

Beginning with KCT V: 127, there is a subchapter called the *Paramākṣara-jñāna-siddhi* ("The supreme unchanging perfection of knowledge") which addresses the concept of the supreme unchanging/immutable/indestructible. It has by far the most extensive commentary in the *Vimalaprabhā* of all the verses in the *Śrī Kālacakra-tantra-rāja*. The word *paramākṣara* can be analyzed as *parama- a-kṣara*. *Parama-* means "supreme," *kṣara-* means "melting away, perishable," and *a-* is the negation of that which melts away—thus the translation is "unchanging or immutable or indestructible." There is, for example, a mention of the supreme unchanging in the *Vimalaprabhā* commentary to KCT V: 127: "Therefore, from the sahajakāya produced from that which is unchanging, there is a perceiving of the dharmas that assume the form of syllables . . ."[36] This supports the analysis of the fourth body of the Buddha in connection with the ādibuddha, for it is said that the sahajakāya is produced from the unchanging/immutable. This could mean that the level of the unchanging is above the level of the fourth body and nearing the ādibuddha concept. Later in the text there is a mention of the imperishable knowledge (*jñāna*) of the supreme unchanging bliss of the vajrin (the one possessing the vajra). That there exists an imperishable knowledge which is also unchanging indicates that the concept of ādibuddha is very close to this theory of the supreme unchanging.

The word *bindu* (drop, point) has an important place in the verse KCT V: 127. There it is described as that which has created all aspects, and in the next line the supreme master of jinas (*paramajinapati*) is mentioned.[37] Later the imperishable bindu is called the supreme unchanging (*paramākṣara*) and therefore could be interpreted as the unchanging point which is imperishable from one life to another, being an imperishable principle in the human body.[38] In that way it approaches the ādibuddha principle which is beginningless, endless, and imperishable. It could be a relation between micro- and macrocosmos. A summary of the places where the supreme unchanging (*paramākṣara*) is mentioned provides interesting information.

• There is the transcendent level where there is the supreme unchanging/imperishable (*paramākṣara*) which contains the imperishable bindu (point). On that level is also the moment of imperishability where there is no transmigration; the supreme unchanging has passed beyond the dharmas of indivisible particles. It is also the cause which has consumed all the obscurities.

• The first level of manifestation emerges as sahajakāya and Vajrasattva (the essence of means and wisdom), the most perfect Buddha, the bindu of all beings, jinapati, the Buddha-essence which is nonexistence and is attached to the knowledge of the completely pure supreme unchanging bliss.

• The next level of manifestation is Kālacakra/Viśvamāta, the supreme unchanging bliss. Bu-ston comments that the knowledge of the supreme unchanging bliss is the own nature of knowledge characterized by time.[39]

A clarification of the meaning of the supreme unchanging bliss can be found near the end of the *Vimalaprabhā* commentary on KCT V: 127. There information on the relationship between the six-limbed yoga (*ṣaḍaṅga-yoga*), which is the essence of the practice of Kālacakra, and the concept of the supreme unchanging is given. The experience of the supreme unchanging bliss in the sixth limb of that yoga is related with the retention of the semen.[40] This has to do with the ultimate goal of this yoga, which is to stop all motion and to stop time (*kāla*). When one has reached that goal, one will experience the great bliss, which in this context is the same as the supreme unchanging bliss.

Final comments

Clearly it is not an easy task to define the doctrine of ādibuddha in the Kālacakra texts. A comparatively simple solution is to hold that ādibuddha is just another way of describing the tathāgatagarbha concept, which means that there is the Buddha-seed present in all sentient beings. In that case, it is another way of saying that one must strive to obtain the state of Buddhahood. It can also be a positive way of describing the void (*śūnyatā*) which is ever present.

Despite the above-mentioned arguments, it is still possible to state that there is a coherent concept of a transcendent "ādibuddha" who was the first Buddha or in some way at the origin of everything, though not a creator. The fourth body of the Buddha, sahajakāya or śuddhakāya, is a sort of primordial manifestation in the world. Of course the fourth body has many other connotations on the individual level, but on the cosmological level it is connected with the origin of the five jinas. The concept of the supreme unchanging bliss, paramākṣara-sukha, may be regarded as a qualification of the fourth body. The supreme unchanging then should represent the bindu that is without beginning or end in beings.

The ādibuddha concept is qualified by various epithets, as has been shown: omniscient, without qualities, master of jinas, without mental constructions, unchanging or indestructible, unchanging bliss (*akṣarasukha*), nondual, progenitor of the Buddhas, simultaneously arisen master of jinas, beyond origination and dissolution, nondual wisdom and means, pure yoga (*śuddhayoga*), without causal connection (*niranvaya*), supreme (*parama*), the one who first (*ādi*) obtained Buddhahood, without beginning in time, without termination, indivisible vajrayoga, endless Buddha, and the supreme unchanging (*paramākṣara*). All these qualifications are strong evidence of there existing a concept of something transcending the apparent world, and this transcendent concept could be called the "ādibuddha." Actually, these qualifications can also be applied to other deities or principles, though the true importance is that there exists such a concept.

As found in KCT V: 127, there also exists the concept of bindu which can be compared to the ādibuddha concept of the individual level. The bindu stands for the indestructible or unchanging in the heart cakra of the human body, which is described in a similar way as the ādibuddha. Consequently, the concept of ādibuddha has both a macrocosmic and microcosmic interpretation. The fourth body of the Buddha—known as the sahajakāya, śuddhakāya, and svābhāvikakāya—can also be associated with pure, unchanging mind which transcends everything, sahajakāya being beyond wisdom and means (*prajñā* and *upāya*). Finally, the concept of the knowledge (*jñāna*) of the supreme unchanging bliss, paramākṣarasukha jñāna, can be compared to the transcendent concept of something unchanging or indestructible, describing the final state of bliss attainable.

Abbreviations

KCT - *Śrī Kālacakra-tantra-rāja*, the laghutantra
VP - *Vimalaprabhā-ṭīkā*
Toh. - A Complete Catalogue of the Tibetan Buddhist Canons, Tohoku Catalogue
P - The Tibetan Tripitaka. Peking edition

Endnotes

1. See Hammar 2005: 88-201.

2. Csoma de Körös 1833: 58-59. Vimalaprabhā I.6 in VP vol. 1, 1986: 52; Hammar 2005: 88-89.

3. Hodgson, B. H. 1874.

4. Gellner, David 1989: 7-19; Hammar 2005: 88.

5. Grönbold 1992: 128-131.

6. Wallace 2001: 17-18; Hammar 2005: 94-95.

7. The Sanskrit text has not been found, but an analysis has been made by R. Gnoli in Orofino 1994, which also contains an edition of the Tibetan text (Peking 7, Tohoku 365).

8. Vimalaprabhā I.1 in VP vol. 1, 1986: 3, lines 17-20.

9. Newman 1987, Banerjee 1958, Wallace 1995 and 2001, Andresen 1997, Hartzell 1997, and Stril-Rever 2000.

10. The Vimalaprabhā commentary, chapter I, subchapter 1, in VP vol. 1, 1986: 1, lines 3 and 11; Hammar 2005: 99-102.

11. Vimalaprabhā I.1 in VP vol. 1, 1986: 2, lines 19 and 21; Hammar 2005: 103.

12. Monier-Williams 1976 (1899): 46.

13. Vimalaprabhā I.2 in VP vol. 1, 1986: 12, line 24; 15, line 3; Hammar 2005: 106-107.

14. Mañjuśrī-nāma-saṃgīti, verse 100, Tohoku no. 360; trans. in Davidson 1981: 30; Hammar 2005: 76-77.

15. Vimalaprabhā I.2. in VP vol. 1, 1986: 16, line 26; Hammar 2005: 108.

16. Vimalaprabhā I.2. in VP vol. 1, 1986: 17, line 9; Hammar 2005: 108-109.

17. Vimalaprabhā I.4 in VP vol. 1, 1986: 32, lines 16-21; Hammar 2005: 112-113.

18. Vimalaprabhā I.5 in VP vol. 1, 1986: 42, line 22; 43, line 3; Hammar 2005: 115-116.

19. Braarvig 1993: vol. 2, lviii-lxiv.

20. Vimalaprabhā II.3 in VP vol. 1, 1986: 188, lines 5-14; Hammar 2005: 118-120.

21. Vimalaprabhā II.3 in VP vol. 1, 1986: 219, lines 18-28; Hammar 2005: 122-124.

22. This has been underlined already by B. Bhattacharya 1958: 109, Banerjee 1959: 50-51, and lately by Newman, among other places, in a paper given at Stockholm University on May 26, 2005.

23. Vimalaprabhā V.2 in VP vol. 3, 1994: 45, line 14; an introduction to KCT V: 89.

24. Vimalaprabhā V.4 in VP vol. 3, 1994: 153; Tibetan: Bu-ston 1965a: 295, line 7, to 296, line 4; Hammar 2005: 134-135.

25. Ruegg 1992: 19.

26. Ruegg 1992: 22; Ruegg 1973: 123-124.

27. Ruegg 1992: 54-55.

28. Stearns 1999: 238-239, notes 30-32.

29. Stearns 1999: 118.

30. Hammar 2005: 143-144.

31. Vimalaprabhā I.5 in VP vol. 1, 1986: 43, lines 5-6; Hammar 2005: 146.

32. Vimalaprabhā I.5 in VP vol. 1, 1986: 45, line 20; Hammar 2005: 147.

33. KCT II: 16 and 17; Vimalaprabhā II.1 in VP vol. 1, 1986: 164; Hammar 2005: 148-151.

34. Vimalaprabhā V.2 in VP vol. 3, 1994: 45-46; Hammar 2005: 160-164.

35. Zhang-zhung Chos-dbang-grags-pa 290: 7 to 293: 1; Hammar 2005: 164-168.

36. Vimalaprabhā V.3 in VP vol. 3, 1994: 60, line 4; Hammar 2005: 175-177.

37. Vimalaprabhā V.3 in VP vol. 3, 1994: 60, lines 7-10; Hammar 2005: 175.

38. Vimalaprabhā V.3 in VP vol. 3, 1994: 61, lines 3-4; Hammar 2005: 179-180; Dhargyey 1985: 91.

39. Vimalaprabhā V.3 in VP vol. 3, 1994: 62, line 16; Bu-ston 1965c: 107, lines 1-3.

40, Vimalaprabhā V.3 in VP vol. 3, 1994: 102, lines 23-33; Hammar 2005: 199-200.

Bibliography

Sources in Sanskrit and Tibetan.

Āryamañjuśrīnāmasaṃgīti and Amṛtakanikā-ṭippaṇī by Bhikṣu Raviśrījñāna and Amṛtakaṇikodyota-nibandha of Vibhūticandra. 1994. Edited by Banarsi Lal. Sarnath, Varanasi: Central Institute of Higher Tibetan Studies.

Haribhadra. 1932-1935. *Abhisamayālaṃkāra-āloka.* Edited by U. Wogihara. Tokyo.

Śrī Kālacakratantra-rāja. 1985. Edited by Biswanath Banerjee. Calcutta.

The Tibetan Tripitaka. Peking edition (P). Kept in the library of Otani University. Reprinted under the supervision of Otani University, Kyoto. Edited by D. T. Suzuki. Catalogue and Index (1 vol.). Tokyo 1962. (Reprint Kyoto 1985).

Vimalaprabhāṭīkā of Kalkin Śrī Puṇḍarika on Śrīlaghukālacakratantrarāja by Śrī Mañjuśrīyaśas. Vol. 1. 1986. Edited and annotated with notes by Jagannatha Upadhyaya. Bibliotheca Indo-Tibetica Series 11. Sarnath, Varanasi: Central Institute of Higher Tibetan Studies.

Vimalaprabhāṭīkā of Kalkin Śrī Puṇḍarika on Śrīlaghukālacakratantrarāja by Śrī Mañjuśrīyaśas. Vol. 2. 1994. Edited by Samdhong Rinpoche. Rare Buddhist Texts Series 12. Sarnath, Varanasi: Central Institute of Higher Tibetan Studies.

Vimalaprabhāṭīkā of Kalkin Śrī Puṇḍarika on Śrīlaghukālacakratantrarāja by Śrī Mañjuśrīyaśas. Vol. 3. 1994. Edited by Samdhong Rinpoche. Rare Buddhist Texts Series 13. Sarnath, Varanasi: Central Institute of Higher Tibetan Studies.

Zhang-zhung Chos-dbang-grags-pa. 1983. "Nges mdzad pa'I 'grel chen dri med 'od kyi rgya cher bshad pa de kho na nyid snang bar byed pa las ye shes kyi le'u'i 'grel bshad la". [This is the commentary on the fifth chapter of the Vimalaprabhā by Zhang-zhung Chos-dbang-grags-pa.] In *The Collected Works of Mkhas-grub dge-legs dpal.* Vol.5. Gedan Sungrab Minyam Gyunphel Series 120. New Delhi, 161-626.

Sources in other languages

Andresen, Jensine. 1997. "Kālacakra: Textual and Ritual Perspectives." Ph.D. dissertation, Harvard University.

Bandyopadhyaya, Biswanath. 1952. "A Note on the Kalacakratantra and Its Commentary." *Journal of the Asiatic Society of Bengal* 18 (1952): 71-76.

Banerjee, Biswanath. 1959. "Über das Lokadhātu Paṭala. 1. Kapitel des Laghu-Kālacakratantra-rāja." Ph.D. dissertation, Universität München.

Bhattacharyya, Benoytosh. 1958. *The Indian Buddhist Iconography*. Calcutta.

Braarvig, Jens. 1993. *The Akṣayamatinirdeśasūtra*. Vol. 1, *Edition of extant manuscripts with an index*. Vol. 2, *The Tradition of Imperishability in Buddhist Thought*. Oslo.

A Complete Catalogue of the Tibetan Buddhist Canons (Bkha'-'gyur and Bstan-'gyur). 1934. Derge edition. Edited by Hakaju Ui, Munetada Suzuki, Yensho Kanakura, and Tokan Tada. Tokyo. (Tohoku Catalogue).

Csoma de Körös, Alexander. 1833. "Note on the origin of the Kála-Chakra and Adi-Buddha Systems." *Journal of the Asiatic Society of Bengal* 2 (1833). Reprint in *Journal of the Asiatic Society of Bengal* 28 (1986): 108-111.

Davidson, Ronald M. 1981. "The Litany of Names of Mañjuśrī." Text and Translation of the Mañjuśrīnāmasaṃgīti. *Mélanges Chinois et Bouddhiques* 20 (1981): 1-69.

Dhargyey, Geshe Ngawang. 1985. *A Commentary on the Kālacakra Tantra*. Dharamsala: Library of Tibetan Works and Archives.

Gellner, David N. 1989. "Hodgson's blind alley? On the so-called schools of Nepalese Buddhism." *Journal of the International Association of Buddhist Studies* 12 (1989): 7-19.

Grönbold, Günther. 1992. "Zwei Ādibuddha-Texte." *Sanskrit-Texte aus dem Buddhistischen Kanon: Neuentdeckungen und Neueditionen 2.* Bearbeitet von Jens-Uwe Hartmann, Claus Wille, Claus Vogel, Günther Grönbold. Sanskrit-Wörterbuch der buddhistischen Texte aus den Turfan-Funden. Beiheft 4. Göttingen: 111-161.

Hammar, Urban. 2005. "Studies in the Kālacakra Tantra: A History of the Kālacakra Tantra in Tibet and a Study of the Concept of Ādibuddha, the Fourth Body of the Buddha and the Supreme Unchanging." Ph.D. dissertation, Stockholm University.

Hartzell, James Francis. 1997. "Tantric Yoga: A Study of the Vedic Precursors, Historical Evolution, Literatures, Cultures, Doctrinal and Practices of the 11th Kaśmirī Śaivite and Buddhist Unexcelled Tantric Yogas." Ph.D. dissertation, Columbia University.

Hodgson, Brian H. 1874. "Notes of the Adi Buddha and of seven mortal Buddhas." *Essays of the languages, literature and religion of Nepal and Tibet.* London: 115-120. Reprint New Delhi 1972: 83-88.

La Vallée Poussin, Louis de. 1908. "Ādibuddha." *Encyclopaedia of Religion and Ethics,* vol.1. Edinburgh, 93b-100b.

Lessing, Ferdinand and Alex Wayman, translators. 1968. *Mkhas grub rje's Fundamentals of the Buddhist Tantras.* The Hague.

Makransky, John. 1997. *Buddhahood Embodied: Sources of Controversy in India and Tibet.* New York.

Newman, John. 1987. "The Outer Wheel of Time: Vajrayāna Buddhist Cosmology in the Kālacakra Tantra." Ph.D. dissertation, University of Wisconsin.

———. 2000. "Vajrayoga in the Kālacakra Tantra." In *Tantra in Practice,* edited by David Gordon White. Princeton: Princeton University Press, 587-594.

Orofino, Giacomella. 1994. *Sekoddeśa: A Critical Edition of the Tibetan Translation.* With an appendix by Raniero Gnoli on the Sanskrit text. Serie Orientale Roma 72. Roma: Istituto Italiano per il Medio ed Estremo Oriente.

Ruegg, David Seyfort. 1992. *Buddha-nature, Mind and the Problem of Gradualism in Comparative Perspective: On the Transmission and Reception of Buddhism in India and Tibet.* New Delhi.

Stearns, Cyrus R. 1999. *The Buddha from Dolpo.A Study of the Life and Thought of the Tibetan Master Dolpopa Sherab Gyaltsen.* New York: State University of New York.

Stril-Rever, Sofia. 2000. *Tantra de Kālachakra. Le Livre du Corps subtil.* Paris.

The Nyingma Edition of the sDe-dge bKa'-'gyur and bsTan-'gyur. Research Catalogue and Bibliography, vol.1-8. Vol. 1, Comparative Tables of Editions, 1-93. Vol. 8, Sanskrit Manuscripts, Pāli Texts, Bibliography, Indexes, 1-193.

Wallace, Vesna A. 1995. "The Inner Kālacakratantra: A Buddhist Tantric View of the Individual." Ph.D. dissertation, University of California, Berkeley.

Wallace, Vesna A. 2001. *The Inner Kālacakratantra: A Buddhist Tantric View of the Individual.* New York: Oxford University Press.

– 12 –

A Lineage History of Vajrayoga and Tantric Zhentong from the Jonang Kālacakra Practice Tradition

Michael R. Sheehy

According to Tibetan tradition, a year after his awakening, encompassed by constellations during the full moon night of spring, on a vajra lion-throne in a cavern that was expanded to miraculously enormous proportions within the Śrī Dhānyakaṭaka Stūpa in South India, Śākyamuni Buddha displayed the Wondrous Lunar Mansion maṇḍala, emanated as the resplendent Kālacakra deity, and revealed the *Kālacakratantra* or *Wheel of Time Continuum* to King Sucandra of Śambhala and an astronomic assembly of both human and nonhuman beings.[1] This legendary account and its subsequent impact on the life of Vajrayāna Buddhism has reverberated indefinitely throughout the historical consciousness of the Kālacakra traditions, remaining a resonating force within the memories of today's Kālacakra masters.

In narrating their history—oral and written, collective and personal, experienced and imagined—the tantric Buddhist traditions, as all living traditions, bring what is most valued and remembered about their past into the present. As the Kālacakra traditions communicate their histories, they recount a genealogical line from their apical ancestor, the historical Buddha himself in the fifth century BC, on to the kings and kalkī of the mythically impressive yet geographically elusive domain of Śambhala, down through their ancient Indian ancestors, on to the reception and elaboration of the tantra by their later Tibetan successors, up to now.[2]

A History of Vajrayoga and Tantric Zhentong

As the last great tantra to appear from the Vajrayāna scene in India, the *Kālacakratantra* had an ineffable effect on shaping tantric Buddhist thought and practice in Tibet. Seeking to define autonomy during the new translation period, emerging Tibetan traditions identified themselves with different aspects of Indic Buddhist praxis and assimilated distinct bodies of yogic knowledge from the tantras, as these texts made their way into the Tibetan language. With numerous streams of transmission, and a great deal of cross-fertilization among them from the eleventh century onwards, whispered instructions on the Kālacakra's sixfold vajrayoga completion stage practices and the oral histories of their inheritors began to be recorded in Tibet during the thirteenth century.

Although there was a variety of Kālacakra traditions that came from India into Tibet from the eleventh through the thirteenth centuries, including the transmission lines (*brgyud rim*) from Lotsāwa Gyijo Dawè Ödzer, Ma Gewè Lodrö, Azha Jakarteg, Kyungpo Chöton, Rwa Chörab, and Tsami Sangyè Drak, the Jonang have inherited and sustained the Dro tradition (*'bro lugs*) as transmitted sequentially from Dro Lotsāwa and the Kashmiri paṇḍita Somanātha.[3] The Dro tradition along with the lineal descent from Rwa Lotsāwa known as the "Rwa tradition" (*rwa lugs*) constitute the two major existing lines of Kālacakra transmission up to the present.[4]

Since the Tibetan yogi Kunpang Thukje Tsöndru's (1243-1313) synthesis of seventeen different transmission lineages of the Kālacakra sixfold *vajrayoga*, the Jonang have largely identified themselves with this distinctive tantric system.[5] From its ancient antecedents up to its contemporary exemplars, the Jonang tradition specializes in this unique tantra, its gnoseological and cosmological thought, and the complex ritual life associated with this esoteric Buddhist literature. In particular, the Jonang Kālacakra tradition places emphasis on its inheritance of the path of vajrayoga (*rdo rje'i rnal 'byor*)—the Kālacakra completion process (Skt. *sampannakrama*, Tib. *rdzogs rim*) yoga that is composed of six ancillary phases (Skt. *ṣaḍaṅgayoga*, Tib. *sbyor ba yan lag drug*)—and the tantric *zhentong* (*sngags gi gzhan stong*) view of mind and reality according to the meditative system of the Great Madhyamaka.[6]

What follows is a brief history of the transmission lineage according to the Jonang Dro Kālacakra practice tradition of vajrayoga and tantric zhentong. This article is based upon my translation of excerpts from the Tibetan text, *Lamp of the Moon: A History of the Jonang Tradition* by the modern Jonang scholar from Dzamthang Tsangwa Monastery, Khenpo Ngawang Lodrö Drakpa (1920-75).[7] With few exceptions, Khenpo Lodrak's abbreviated accounts of the early lineage masters repeat almost verbatim from the accounts recorded by the seventeenth-century Jonang lineage-holder and Buddhist historian Jetsun Tāranātha (1575-1635) in his *History of the Kālacakratantra*.[8] Recounting the hagiographies of these siddhas—the tantric yogins and yoginīs who have animated this lineage—these chroniclers of their tradition narrate to us the generations of descent as they are received by living Jonang Kālacakra masters.

Origins of the *Kālacakratantra*

As this story continues, King Sucandra returned to Śambhala after his sojourn to the Śrī Dhānyakaṭaka Stūpa in South India. While in Śambhala, it is said that he wrote down the original verses taught by the Buddha, entitled the *Paramādibuddhatantra,* and began teaching the tantra throughout the kingdom. This root tantra was then transmitted on through the line of six successors to Kalkī Yaśas, an emanation of Mañjuśri who composed the condensed version of the tantra, entitled the *Laghu-kālacakra-tantra-rāja,* or the *Royal Abridged Wheel of Time Continuum.*[9] Kalkī Yaśas' son, Kalkī Puṇḍarīka, later wrote the *Vimalaprabhā,* or *Stainless Light,* explanatory commentary on the abbreviated tantra.

From Kalkī Yaśas onwards, the disparate social castes of Śambhala are said to have been united by initiation into the *Kālacakratantra,* and the successive inheritors of the kingdom of Śambhala were given the title "kalkī" to signify their single caste or tantric lineage.[10] According to tradition, the eleventh emperor in this regal line was Kalkī Aja, the kalkī who traveled to India in order to transmit the tantra back to its native land.[11]

Then, circa the early eleventh century AD, as a young man named Jamyang Dorje was walking along a path in India, he had a vision of his meditation deity Mañjuśri.[12] The bodhisattva prophesized for him to travel northward, and as Jamyang Dorje proceeded along his path to the north, he encountered the kalkī Aja. The kalkī then apparently bestowed the Kālacakra empowerment upon him, initiating him as the first Indian master in this line of esoteric transmission.

After six months meditating on the profound sixfold vajrayoga of the Kālacakra completion process, Jamyang Dorje is said to have transported to Śambhala via his supernatural powers. In the kingdom, the tradition maintains, he met Kalkī Aja in person and received further instructions on the *Kālacakratantra*, the *Trilogy of Commentaries by Bodhisattvas,* and several other unexcelled yoga tantras.[13] Memorizing most of these texts and carrying a few selected volumes with him, Jamyang Dorje is said to have returned to India where he became known as "Kālacakrapāda the Elder."

While in India, before dissolving his physical body into rainbow light (*'ja' lus*), the tradition continues, Kālacakrapāda the Elder passed the tantra and its commentary on to his disciple, the learned Śrībhadra, or "Kālacakrapāda the Younger."[14] An accomplished adept, Kālacakrapāda the Younger was known for his unhindered supernormal talent for clairvoyance, and it was during his time that the Kālacakra became popularized in India.

Kālacakrapāda the Younger's son was Bodhibhadra, proprietor of the Nālendra estate, who was also known as "Nālendrapa."[15] Though he was renowned for performing each of the four kinds of karmic activity, Nālendrapa's accomplishments are attributed to his yogic practice of mobilizing his vital winds (Skt. *prāṇayoga,* Tib. *rlung gi rnal 'byor*).[16]

At this time in Kashmir, Nālendrapa's primary disciple, the young and intelligent scholar Somanātha, was receiving his brahmin education. Later, Somanātha traveled to Central India where he received the *Kālacakratantra* from Nālendrapa. After meditating upon the profound meaning of the Kālacakra and associated unexcelled tantras, Somanātha is said to have perfected the yoga of retaining his life force (*srog 'dzin*) and was able to paralyze menacing thieves by merely pointing his finger at them. The Kashmiri paṇḍita Somanātha eventually traveled to Tibet on three occasions and taught on many topics, including Candrakīrti's *Radiant Lamp*, Nāgārjuna's *Six Collections of Reasoning,* and Asaṅga's *Five Treatises on the Stages*—however, he is most celebrated for transmitting the Kālacakra.[17]

Tibetan Forefathers of the Jonang

Signifying the reception of the tantra in Tibet, and the historical convergence of Indian and Tibetan Kālacakra scholarship, Dro Lotsāwa Sherab Drakpa translated the tantra and its commentary, the *Vimalaprabhā,* into Tibetan with Paṇḍita Somanātha in the late eleventh century.[18] Dro Lotsāwa, along with his fellow disciples Lama Lhajè Gompa and Lama Droton Namseg all inherited the complete empowerment and textual authorizations, and each was given extensive guidance instructions on the sixfold vajrayoga of the Kālacakra completion process from their root teacher, Paṇḍita Somanātha.[19]

The mahāsiddha Yumo Mikyö Dorje (b. 1027) was also the recipient of related instructions on the practice of vajrayoga from Paṇḍita Somanātha, and for a period of five years he stayed in the Khong region of southern Tibet where he received the entire tantric transmissions and instructions from Lama Droton Namseg.[20] Later, Yumowa resided in the region of Üyug where he composed several texts on Kālacakra practice, many of which are considered by the tradition to be among the earliest Tibetan works to articulate a tantric zhentong view.[21]

Yumowa's son Dharmeśvara was considered a prodigy who, by the time he had reached the age of twenty, had memorized all of the guidance instructions possessed by the mahāsiddhas, the great tantric adepts. Following this line of ancestry, Dharmeśvara's three children each inherited the tantric tradition of their grandfather, father, and the lineage masters who had preceded them. Dharmeśvara's eldest son, Namkha Ödzer, was learned in both sūtra and tantra, and was the author of numerous works including the *Garland of Radiance*.[22] His sister, Machik Tulku Jobum, is known to have retained every word of the *Vimalaprabhā* commentary on the *Kālacakratantra*, and after meditating on her father's instructions on the sixfold vajrayoga, she is said to have perfected the ten signs of inner radiance in a day.[23] After practicing for seven more days, she then is said to have dissolved the vital winds into her central channel and was able to accomplish extraordinarily beneficial feats. Machik Tulku Jobum's brother, Semo Chewa Namkha Gyaltsen, was renowned as an adept whose intellectual brilliance and depth of meditative experience were attributed to his extensive practice of the vajrayoga path. He received the *Vimalaprabhā* from Namkha Ödzer, and both the *Commentary That Briefly Teaches the Empowerment* along with the *Lotus Endowed* commentary that elucidates the difficult points in the *Kālachakratantra* from his sister.[24] During the latter period of his life, he established Semochè Monastery in the Ölung region of Central Tibet.

In accord with a prophetic utterance from Mañjuśri, Jamyang Sarma Sherab Ödzer received the Kālachakra empowerment from Semo Chewa.[25] A dedicated student and teacher, it is said, Jamyang Sarma remained in an ever-increasing state of learning and teaching throughout his life. Then, from the time of Jamyang Sarma onwards, the precepts and personal instructions on the Kālacakra completion stage practices in the Dro lineage are considered to have been kept extremely strict.

Jamyang Sarma's primary disciple was Kunkhyen Chöku Ödzer (1214-92) whom he entrusted with the entire instructions and empowerment of the tantra. In fact, the history of the tradition conveys that while the pristine wisdom (Skt. *jñāna*, Tib. *ye shes*) empowerment of the Kālacakra was being bestowed by Jamyang Sarma, Chöku Ödzer perceived his vajra master as a wisdom deity, and in just half a day, pristine wisdom infused his mind indefinitely. Chöku Ödzer was also famous for being able to recite every syllable of the *Guhyasamājatantra* in Sanskrit, and it is said that every time he fell asleep, he would sink into an altered state of clear light where he would be performing tantric visualizations and recitations while simultaneously teaching other people.[26]

Early Jonang Lineage Masters

Up until this point, from the early eleventh to the late thirteenth century, the Dro Kālacakra tradition had passed through generations of succession in a lineal current parallel to the other major and minor transmission lines that were simultaneously codefining the transplantation of this distinct tantric system into Tibet. Relayed from guru to disciple, across cultures and bloodline relations, this transmission lineage that had come to be identified with its first Tibetan inheritor—the translator Dro Lotsāwa Sherab Drakpa—would soon be linked with another tradition altogether.

Having received the Rwa tradition at an early age, and the empowerment, textual authorizations, and oral explanations according to the Dro tradition from his master Chöku Ödzer, Kunpang Thukje Tsöndru came to be a central figure in the Tibetan assimilation of the Kālacakra transmissions.[27] Trained as a ritual master for Jamyang Sarma's monastic seat at Kyang Dur and a prodigy of the Sakya and Ngar monastic complexes in Central Tibet, Kunpang-pa collected, practiced, and integrated seventeen variant instruction lineages of the Kālacakra's sixfold vajrayoga.[28]

While in the meditation cave of Sè Karchung, Kunpang-pa thought to condense the essence of the *Kālacakratantra*, and as he invoked the masters of the lineage, it is said that each of the kalkī of Śambhala appeared at once within the cave to instruct him. Soon afterwards, the principal female protector deity of Jomonang, Jomo Nagmen Gyalmo, visited Kunpang-pa at Sè Karchung cave and requested that he come to the valley of Jomonang to reside. Three years later, Kunpang-pa arrived in the place called "Jomonang" in South Central Tibet, and since his arrival, the tradition of meditation practice and philosophical thinking that flourished in that site has been known as "Jonang."[29]

Fulfilling a prophecy, Kunpang-pa settled in Khachö Dedan, the "Bliss-Infused Enjoyment of Space" meditation cave at Jonang where, it is maintained, he had a vision of the Kālacakra deity, composed a complete root text and commentary on the essential tantra, and put into writing the oral transmission lineage (*snyan brgyud*) of the guidance instructions on the sixfold vajrayoga practices. During this time in retreat at Jonang, Kunpang-pa emphasized through his writings that the sixfold vajrayoga was the supreme method for actualizing the coalescence of bliss and emptiness as described within the Great Madhyamaka tantric zhentong tradition, and that this was the main point of meditation practice.[30] These literary works composed by Kunpang Thukje Tsöndru were among the earliest extensive instruction manuals (*khrid yig*) on the sixfold vajrayoga of the Kālacakra in Tibet, and were the texts that initiated the newfound Jonang tradition's scholastic and contemplative commitment to this tantra.[31] Throughout his lifetime, Kunpang-pa taught the *Vimalaprabhā* commentary on the tantra, and he taught the essential *Kālacakratantra* twice a year while living at Jonang.

From the time they met, Changsem Gyalwa Yeshe (1257-1320) is said to have had incredible confidence in his teacher Kunpang-pa. He learned many of the sūtras and tantras from him, and when Changsem Chenpo was guided in the practice of the sixfold vajrayoga by Kunpang-pa, radical experiences of realization are said to have arisen within him. At the request of his master, Changsem Chenpo traveled to Kunpang-pa's residence at Jonang, where his teacher then asked him to maintain the ever-increasing activities of the meditation retreat hermitages of Jonang and to assume the role of his lineage heir (*brgyud 'dzin*).

After eight years of overseeing the monastic seat at Jonang, Changsem Chenpo appointed another one of Kunpang-pa's main disciples, Khetsun Yöntan Gyatso (1260-1327), as his own heir to Jonang. Along with Changsem Chenpo, Yöntan Gyatso received guidance instructions on the profound path of vajrayoga and explanations on the tantras from Kunpang Thukje Tsöndru while residing at Jonang. For seven years, from 1320 to the fall of 1326, Yöntan Gyatso facilitated the activities at Jonang until he entrusted leadership to his own disciple, the fourth successor to the throne at Jonang.

Dolpopa and His Dharma Heirs

In 1322, a year after his initial visit to Jonang, Kunkhyen Dolpopa Sherab Gyaltsen (1292-1361) returned from pilgrimage in Central Tibet to request the full empowerment and transmissions of the Dro Kālacakra tradition along with the oral instructions on the sixfold vajrayoga completion stage practices from the throneholder of Jonang, Yöntan Gyatso.[32] By this time, Dolpopa had already spent a decade studying at Sakya Monastery and had toured the most prestigious monastic complexes of Central Tibet, learning both sūtra and tantra from some of the greatest masters of his time. In particular, he had received the empowerment and transmissions of the Rwa Kālacakra tradition, extensive teachings on the sixfold vajrayoga and the *Vimalaprabhā,* as well as transmission for sūtra zhentong from his primary Sakya teacher, Kyiton Jamyang Drakpa Gyaltsen.[33]

Having had a dream the night before Dolpopa's arrival in which Kalkī Puṇḍarika of Śambhala raised a victory-banner at Jonang, Khetsun Yöntan Gyatso proceeded to bestow on Dolpopa the entirety of tantric initiations and instructions on the esoteric completion stage yogas.[34] Yöntan Gyatso then encouraged the young yogi to enter into a solitary retreat at Khachö Dedan cave where Kunpang-pa had lived years before. Dolpopa asked his teacher Yöntan Gyatso to guide him through the practice of each yoga carefully, and Dolpopa gradually progressed through the yoga of withdrawal (Skt. *pratyāhāra*, Tib. *so sor sdud pa*), the yoga of meditative concentration (*dhyāna*, *bsam gtan*) and the yoga of harnessing one's life force (Skt. *prāṇāyāma*, Tib. *srog rtsol*), mastering these first three of the sixfold vajrayoga.[35] At this time, while staying in Khachö Dedan meditation cave at Jonang, Dolpopa began to turn his intellectual understanding of the sixfold vajrayoga into experiences born from meditation, and as a result he had his first realizations of zhentong.

Enthroned the year before Yöntan Gyatso's passing, Dolpopa assumed leadership at Jonang in 1326. From 1330 to 1333, while constructing the Great Stūpa of Jonang—the largest physical embodiment of enlightenment in Tibet—Dolpopa began formulating his realizations and meditative experiences. Built to replicate the stūpa of the Wondrous Lunar Mansion as described within the *Vimalaprabhā*, the Great Stūpa of Jonang served as an inspiration for Dolpopa's syncretization of the *Kālacakratantra* with his realization of zhentong, as derived from his vajrayoga practice. Dolpopa's contemplative understandings coalesced, and he began to systematize his elucidations on zhentong within the cosmological context of the tantra as presented in the *Vimalaprabhā*.[36] These teachings eventually crystallized in his masterpiece, *Mountain Dharma: Ocean of Definitive Meaning* where Dolpopa clarifies how his codifications are definitive in meaning (Skt. *nītārtha*, Tib. *nges don*), in contrast to teachings that remain provisional in meaning (Skt. *neyārtha*, Tib. *drang don*).[37]

Then in 1334, Dolpopa requested his disciples Lotsāwa Lodrö Pal (1299-1353) and Sazang Mati Panchen (1294-1376) to prepare a new translation of the *Kālacakratantra* along with its commentary, the *Vimalaprabhā*.[38] Serving as the textual basis for Dolpopa's teachings, these Jonang translations were conducted under the care of Dolpopa himself in order to explicate the texts' hidden definitive meaning. Dolpopa then composed a topical outline (*sa bcad*) along with his own commentary in the form of annotations (*mchan 'grel*) on the *Vimalaprabhā* that emphasized zhentong as a view implicit within the tantra and its commentary.

To complement Dolpopa's annotations and to elaborate on crucial points within the tantra and *Vimalaprabhā* that his teacher did not emphasize, one of Dolpopa's closest disciples, Choglè Namgyal (1306-86), composed his own annotated commentary.[39] Choglè initially had traveled to Jonang as a young man with the wish to examine the zhentong system as it was being taught by Dolpopa. When he arrived at Jonang, Choglè met Dolpopa circumambulating the Great Stupa and asked the master if he would teach zhentong. For the next seven days, Dolpopa instructed Choglè Namgyal on zhentong in his private residence. Choglè later returned to Jonang where he received the Kālacakra empowerment and transmissions on the sixfold vajrayoga from Dolpopa, and from that time onwards he lived in retreat at Jonang or at Kunpang-pa's Sè Karchung cave when he was not presiding as a ritual master in Ngamring.[40] In 1354, with the passing of the abbot Lotsāwa Lodrö Pal, Dolpopa appointed Choglè as the throne-holder of Jonang.[41]

Another one of Dolpopa's fourteen major disciples, Nyawon Kunga Pal (1285-1379), met his teacher Dolpopa on numerous occasions as a child at Sakya.[42] He then went on to study the sūtras and tantras closely with Dolpopa, mastering the Buddhist sciences of psychology and phenomenology and receiving the entirety of the Dro Kālacakra transmissions. Nyawon also remained close to Choglè Namgyal throughout his lifetime and sought council from Choglè regarding his most extraordinary experiences in meditation.

Later Jonang Lineage Masters

Nyawon Kunga Pal's disciple and successor in this tantric transmission lineage was the mahāsiddha Kunga Lodrö.[43] Considered an incarnation of Dolpopa's contemporary, the great Tibetan Kālacakra master Butön Rinchen Drup (1290-1364), Kunga Lodrö received elaborate explanations on the Kālacakra from Nyawon in addition to his studies on the *Prajñāpāramitā* literature. Kunga Lodrö then went on to instruct Jamyang Konchog Zangpo in the profound meaning of the tantra and its associated contemplative techniques. His heir, Namkha Chökyong, was known for his deep comprehension of zhentong and for his dedicated practice of the sixfold vajrayoga.[44] The lineage then passed on to Namkha Palzang, who was trained as a youth in what was known as the "northern Kālacakra tradition." Then, it is said that once he heard the guidance instructions on the sixfold vajrayoga according to the Jonang tradition from Namkha Chökyong, experiences of realization immediately arose within him.[45]

Continuing on from Namkha Palzang, this tradition was transferred to Lochen Ratnabhadra. An adept rich in meditative experiences, Ratnabhadra composed several instruction manuals on the sixfold vajrayoga completion stage practices. The direct recipient of this transmission from Ratnabhadra was the enigmatic figure Kunga Dolchok (1507-66).[46] A major holder of the three main tantric practice lineages of the Sakya Lamdrè, the six teachings of Niguma according to the Shangpa Kagyü, and the vajrayoga path of the Kālacakra as sustained by the Jonang, Kung Dolchok was one of the early contributors to a pluralistic orientation (*ris med*) regarding the diversity of Tibetan religious and intellectual traditions.[47]

This lineage then passed on through Losal Gyatso Dejè and Khadrup Namtsö until it was inherited by Jetsun Tāranātha, a successor to Kunga Dolchok's reincarnation line and the last great abbot of the Jonang in U-Tsang, Central Tibet.[48] As the throne-holder at Jonang as well as a lineage-holder of the Kadam, Zhalu, Sakya, Shangpa Kagyü, and Kamtsang Kagyü, Tāranātha was a foremost expert on the tantras of the new translation traditions (*gsar bsgyur*).[49] He received the Kālacakra transmissions according to the Dro tradition from his teacher Kunga Palzang at Jonang, and then he received the full empowerment, textual authorizations, and explanations on the sixfold vajrayoga according to the Jonang, as well as the transmissions according to Butön's Zhalu Kālacakra tradition, from Kunga Dolchok's disciple Kenchen Lunrig Gyatso.[50]

Tāranātha is said to have had frequent visions of Dolpopa Sherab Gyaltsen and to have visited Śambhala during his dreamtime where he would meet with the kalkī Śrīpāla.[51] Inspired by these visionary experiences, Tāranātha was one of the most prolific authors on zhentong and the Kālacakra, second only to Dolpopa. Among his collected writings, thirty-two works are solely dedicated to various topics concerning the Kālacakra. These works range from his *History of the Kālacakratantra* to precise directions on how to prepare for a tantric feast (*tshogs mchod*), clarifications on tantric precepts (*sdom pa*), methods for meditation practice (*sgrub thabs*), and ritual techniques (*cho ga*) for performing the Kālacakra empowerment and associated ceremonies. Eleven of these works are dedicated to explaining the path of vajrayoga through precise introductions (*ngo sprod*), guidance instructions (*man ngag*), and responses to critical inquiries (*dri lan*). Included in his works on the Kālacakra are his texts *Meaningful to Behold* and its supplement (*lhan thabs*), which remain the standard Jonang instruction manuals for intensive meditation retreat on the sixfold vajrayoga.[52]

In 1615, Tāranātha established Takten Damchö Ling Monastery on the lip of Jomonang Valley, about an hour's walk from the Great Stūpa. Takten Damchö Ling was then the center of Jonang activity with a large Buddhist studies college, meditation retreat facilities, a printing press, and sixteen temples. At that time, there were thousands of yogis and scholars who lived in the vicinity of Takten Damchö Ling Monastery and the mountain hermitages (*ri khrod*) that surround the stūpa. Then, in the year 1650, fifteen years after Tāranātha's passing, the Fifth Dalai Lama, Ngawang Lozang Gyatso (1617-82), backed by the Mongol army, forcefully prohibited the Jonang study curriculum throughout Central and western Tibet and instituted a Geluk study center (*bshad grwa*) at Takten Damchö Ling.[53] By 1658, Takten Damchö Ling was officially converted into a Geluk monastery, sequestering the Jonang.

The Jonang in Amdo

In accord with a prophecy ascribed to Kunkhyen Dolpopa, one of Choglè Namgyal's disciples, Ratnaśrī (1350-1435), established Chöjè Monastery in the Dzamthang region of Amdo in the year 1425.[54] Here, under the imperial patronage of the Ming Court of China and outside the political and military influence of the central Tibetan government in Lhasa, the Jonang had already begun to make their home in the vast countryside of the far northeastern domain of Tibet.

For 225 years prior to their persecution in Central Tibet, the transmission lineages of zhentong and the Kālacakra according to the Jonang continued without interruption far from headquarters at Takten Damchö Ling. During these formative years, from the mid-fifteenth to the late seventeenth century, the Jonang in Amdo were busy building new monasteries, meditation retreat facilities, and institutes for Buddhist learning, all in constant exchange with their contemporaries in U-Tsang.

In fact, Tāranātha's close disciple Lodrö Namgyal (1618-83) traveled to Dzamthang from Takten Damchö Ling, where he lived and taught for twelve years. Before his departure from Takten Damchö Ling, Lodrö Namgyal received instructions on the sixfold vajrayoga from Tāranātha as well as the full Kālacakra transmissions from Tāranātha's disciple and successor to the throne, Kunga Rinchen Gyatso.[55] Then in 1658, the year that Takten Damchö Ling was officially converted, Lodrö Namgyal bestowed the full Kālacakra empowerment and explanations of the tantra during the inauguration ceremony of Tsangwa Monastery in Dzamthang—the central seat of the Jonang today.[56]

Lodrö Namgyal's nephew, disciple, and successor to the throne at Dzamthang Tsangwa Monastery was Ngawang Thinley (1657-1723). Raised in the care of his paternal uncle, Ngawang Thinley received the Kālacakra transmissions along with in-depth explanations of the generation and completion stages of tantric practice from him. Born in U-Tsang, Ngawang Thinley spent much of his life traveling back and forth between Central and eastern Tibet, and it was not until the time of his disciple Ngawang Tenzin Namgyal (1691-1738) that the throne-holders at Tsangwa Monastery were native to Amdo.

By the eighteenth century the Jonang had consolidated their monastic complexes in and around the Dzamthang, Golok, Gyarong, and Ngawa regions. The great monastery of Tsangwa in Dzamthang had begun to branch out into its affiliate monasteries (*dgon lag*), and independent monasteries such as Droggi, Swe, and Yarthang had established themselves and their own distinct lines of esoteric transmission for the sixfold vajrayoga. The Jonang had survived, and their vital teachings on zhentong and the Kālacakra were thriving.

Following Ngawang Tenzin Namgyal, there were six Kālacakra lineage heirs in the line of the vajra masters at Dzamthang Tsangwa Monastery before Ngawang Chöpel Gyatso's and Ngawang Chökyi Phakpa's primary disciple, Bamda Thubtan Gelek Gyatso (1844-1904).[57] Born in "Bamda," close to Tsangwa Monastery in the Dzamthang Valley, Bamda Lama was recognized as a prodigy and educated within his own Jonang tradition at Dzamthang until he was a young man.[58] Bamda later traveled to the Derge district of Kham in eastern Tibet where he found himself immersed in the midst of the Rimè eclecticism and studied closely with Jamgön Kongtrul (1813-99) and Dzogchen Patrul Rinpoche (1808-87).

Returning to Dzamthang, Bamda received extensive training in the Jonang Kālacakra tantric system. In particular, he studied intensively both Choglè Namgyal's and Lochen Ratnabhadra's manuals on the sixfold vajrayoga, the details concerning the specific yogic techniques and postures (*'khrul 'khor*), and the entire cycle of ancillary practices involved in the completion process. His comprehension and depth of experience in these complex subjects are clearly reflected in his own writings, the most famous being his text, *The Stages of Meditation*.[59]

As one of the most widely recognized Kālacakra masters from the Jonang tradition—overshadowed only by Dolpopa and Tāranātha—Bamda's tantric and nontantric writings continue to serve as core sources for the contemporary Jonang scholastic and meditation practice curriculums. Among his most prominent disciples was Tsoknyi Gyatso (1880-1940), an expert on Kālacakra symbolism and the maṇḍala, whose influence on the previous generation of Jonang Kālacakra adepts is felt through to today's exemplars.[60]

Tradition, Transmission, and Transition

By recounting the lives of its masters, the tantric Buddhist traditions in general and the Jonang Kālacakra practice tradition in particular, suggest that something more than remembrance is brought from the past into the present: that there is esoteric transmission occurring. As these narratives draw from the larger genre of Tibetan historiography, we can concede that the survival of these traditions is due to their own self-preservation of passing memories through the generations. Yet, the question lingers: "Is there something about the nature of the Buddhist tantric traditions that is amenable to more than remembering—is there also the reexperiencing?" With this in mind, we may wish to consider to what extent tantric knowledge is living, and to what extent tantric practices keep this knowledge alive?

As participants or as mere bystanders in this multigenerational happening, we are invited to wonder how these tantric adepts made their transitions in order to keep this tantric knowledge vibrant; how they maneuvered through the cultures, among the languages, and between the interfaces of their time; how these yogis and yoginīs transferred their spiritual authority, navigated their life-worlds, represented their identities, and transmitted their private experiences; how these masters—at once historic and surreal—have become legends; how these mystical figures of the past have been imagined, and how imagining them defines us?

(Endnotes)

1. For encouraging and informing my studies of the Jonang, I would like to thank my teacher Khenpo Kunga Sherab Saljè Rinpoche, Jigmè Dorje Rinpoche, Tulku Kunga Zangpo, Steven Goodman, Gene Smith, and, in particular, Cyrus Stearns for making helpful suggestions to this article.

2. For a record, Tā ra nā tha, *Dpal* and *Dus*; Ruegg (1971), 3.

3. Tā ra nā tha, *Rdo rje*, 145-54.

4. Roerich (1976), 755-56.

5. These seventeen six-fold vajrayoga traditions are from: (1) Lotsāwa Gyi jo Zla ba'i 'Od zer; (2) Lotsāwa Rma dge ba'i Blo gros; (3) Khrom Lotsāwa Padma 'Od zer; (4) Bla ma Nag po Mngon shes can; (5) Kha che PaN chen Zla ba Dgon po [Kashmiri paṇḍita Somanātha]; (6) Rwa Lotsāwa Chos rab; (7) Tsa mi Lotsāwa Sangs rgyas Grags; (8) Amoghavajra to Ras chung Rdo rje Grags pa; (9-11) Rga lo and Tsa mi; (12-13) Kashmiri paṇḍita Śākyaśrī; (14-15) Paṇḍita Vibhūticandra; (16) Paṇḍita Nyi dbang Srung ba to Chags Lotsāwa Chos rje Dpal; (17) Man lung Gu ru, Tā ra nā tha, *Rdo rje*, 146-47.

6. Buddhist tantric traditions generally define authentic transmission (*brgyud*) according to: (1) textual authorization (*lung*); (2) empowerment (*dbang*); (3) instruction (*khrid*). "Tantric zhentong" (esoteric extrinsic emptiness) here refers to a view or contemplative understanding that is associated with the practice of the sixfold yoga (*sbyor drug*) completion process of the Kālacakra, in accord with Buddhist tantric literature and the *Kālacakratantra* in particular. The Great Madhyamaka system of sūtra zhentong (*mdo'i gzhan stong*) was transmitted in a parallel continuum until Dol po pa's synthesis of the sūtra and tantra systems. For a record of the sūtra zhentong lineage, Tā ra nā tha, *Zab mo*. The sixfold vajrayoga of the Kālacakra completion stage are: (1) withdrawal (Skt. *pratyāhāra*, Tib. *so sor sdud pa*); (2) meditative concentration (Skt. *dhyāna*, Tib. *bsam gtan*); (3) harnessing life force (Skt. *prāṇāyāma*, Tib. *srog rtsol*); (4) retention (Skt. *dhāraṇā*, Tib. *'dzin pa*); (5) recollection (Skt. *anusmṛti*, Tib. *rjes dran*); (6) meditative absorption (Skt. *samādhi*, Tib. *ting nge 'dzin*). On the sixfold yoga, Stearns (1999), 99-100; Grönbold (1996), 19-33; Newman (2000), 587-94; Henning's article in this volume.

7. Ngag dbang (1992); Kapstein (1993), 1-12. My translation of the *Jo nang Chos 'byung* is in progress.

8. Tā ra nā tha, *Dpal*; Fendell (1997); Templeman (1981).

9. Transmission in Śambhala: (1) Dharma King Sucandra (*Chos rgyal Zla ba Bzang po*); (2) Dharma King Sureśvara [Deveśvara] (*Chos rgyal Lha dbang*); (3) Dharma King Tejī (*Chos rgyal Gzi brjid can*); (4) Dharma King Somadaṭṭa (*Chos rgyal Zla bas byin*); (5) Dharma King Sureśvara (*Chos rgyal Lha'i dbang phyug*); (6) Dharma King Viśvamurti (*Chos rgyal Sna tshogs gzugs*); (7) Dharma King Surśāna (*Chos rgyal Lha'i dbang ldan*). The eighth successor in this line was Yaśas, the first kalkī (*rigs ldan*) of Śambhala.

10. For more on the term "kalkī," Wallace (2001), 115-16.

11. The transmission lineage in Śambhala continues: (8) Kalkī Yaśas (*Rigs ldan Grags pa*); (9) Kalkī Puṇḍarika (*Rigs ldan Padma dkar po*); (10) Kalkī Bhadra (*Rigs ldan Bzang po*); (11) Kalkī Vijaya (*Rigs ldan Rnam rgyal*); (12) Kalkī Sumitra (*Rigs ldan Bshes gnyen Bzang po*); (13) Kalkī Raktapāṇi (*Rigs ldan Phyag dmar*); (14) Kalkī Viṣṇugupta (*Rigs ldan Khyab 'jug Sbas pa*); (15) Kalkī Sūryakīrti (*Rigs ldan Nyi ma Grags pa*); (16) Kalkī Subhadra (*Rigs ldan Shin tu Bzang po*); (17) Kalkī Samudravijaya (*Rigs ldan Rgya mtsho Rnam rgyal*); (18) Kalkī Aja (*Rigs ldan Rgyal dka'*).

12. Ngag dbang (1992), 17.

13. The *Sems 'grel skor gsum* (*Trilogy of Commentaries*) are: (1) *Vimalaprabhā* commentary on the *Kālacakratantra* by Kalkī Puṇḍarīka; (2) *Hevajrapiṇḍārthaṭīkā*

commentary on the *Hevajratantra* by Vajragarbha; (3) *Lakṣābhidhanād-uddhṛta-laghutantra-piṇḍārthavivaraṇa* commentary on the *Cakrasaṃvaratantra* by Vajrapāṇi.

14. Ngag dbang (1992), 17.

15. Newman suggests Kālacakrapāda and Nālendrapa to be the same figure, the famed Nāropa of Nālandā, Newman (1985), 70-71; Fendell (1997), 5-6 and 44, n. 144; Roerich (1976), 758.

16. Four activities (*las bzhi*): (1) pacification (*zhi*); (2) enrichment (*rgyas*); (3) subjugation (*dbang*); (4) wrath (*drag*).

17. Candrakirti's *Radiant Lamp* (Skt. *Pradīpodyotana*, Tib. *Sgron gsal*), Nāgārjuna's *Six Collections of Reasoning* (*Rigs tshogs drug*): (1) *Root Treatise on Wisdom* (Skt. *Prajñāmūla*, Tib. *Rtsa ba shes rab*); (2) *Elegantly Woven Scripture* (Skt. *Vaidalya-sūtra*, Tib. *Zhib mo rnam 'thag*); (3) *Reversing the Roots of the Mind* (Skt. *Vigrahavyāvartanī*, Tib. *Rtsad ldog*); (4) *Seventy Stanzas on Emptiness* (Skt. *Śūnyatāśaptati*, Tib. *Stong nyid bdun cu pa*); (5) *Sixty Stanzas on Reasoning* (Skt. *Yukiṣaṣṭikā*, Tib. *Rigs pa drug cu ba*); (6) *Precious Garland* (Skt. *Ratnāvalī*, Tib. *Rin chen phreng ba*), and Asaṅga's *Five Treatises on the Stages* (*Sa sde lnga*): (1) *Stages of Yogic Practice* (Skt. *Yogācārya-bhūmi*, Tib. *Rnal 'byor spyod pa'i sa*); (2) *Compendium of Ascertainments* (Skt. *Nirṇaya-saṃgraha*, Tib. *Gtan la phab pa'i bsdu ba*); (3) *Compendium of Grounds* (Skt. *Vastu-saṃgraha*, Tib. *Gzhi bsdu ba*); (4) *Compendium of Enumerations* (Skt. *Paryāya-saṃgraha*, Tib. *Rnam grangs bsdu ba*); (5) *Compendium of Detailed Explanations* (Skt. *Vivaraṇasaṃgraha*, Tib. *Rnam par bshad pa'i bsdu ba*).

18. Davidson (2005), 281.

19. Ngag dbang (1992), 17-18. Bla ma Sgro ston Gnam brtsegs received instructions on the sixfold vajrayoga from Bla ma Lha rje Sgo pa first, then later from Somanātha, Byang sems (2004), 29-30.

20. Mkhan po Blo grags writes that Yu mo ba was born during the first year of the sixty-year Tibetan calendar cycle (*rab byung dang po'i dus su byon*), Ngag dbang (1992), 18; Stearns (1999), 199-200, n. 10.

21. Mkhan po Blo grags writes, "[Yu mo ba] formulated the system of tantric zhentong," Ngag dbang (1992), 18. At present, we have access to a limited number of Yu mo ba's surviving works and are therefore unable to make an accurate assessment of his views. Among these surviving works are his *Gsal sgron skor bzhi* (*Fourfold Cycle of Illuminated Lamps*) which do not mention the term, "*gzhan stong*." However, these four short texts present ideas resembling those of Dol po pa's. With this in mind, I would like to suggest that a distinction be made between the employment of the actual technical term, "*gzhan stong,*" and the articulation of sentiments reflecting a view that can be characterized as "*gzhan stong*," for there are surely a range of nuanced understandings for both the term and its intended meaning that deserve further investigation, Yu mo ba (1983); Stearns (1999), 43-5 and 199-200, n. 10; Ruegg (1963), 80.

22. *'Od zer phreng ba.*

23. Ngag dbang (1992), 18.

24. *Dbang mdor bstan bka'* [dka'] *'grel padma can*; these are the *Sekkodeśa* (*Dbang mdor bstan*) and *Padmini* (*Padma can*) commentaries, listed in the Kālacakra section of the Bka' 'gyur and Bstan 'gyur.

25. Ngag dbang (1992), 18.

26. Ngag dbang (1992), 18.

27. Mkhan po Blo grags writes, "From his [Kun mkhyen Chos sku 'Od zer's] disciple Kun spangs Thugs rje Brtson 'grus, up until the great Jonang master [Dol po pa Shes rab Rgyal mtshan], transmission of the view and practice of the great secret tantric Zhentong Madhyamaka flowed like the course of a river," Ngag dbang (1992), 18.

28. Ngag dbang (1992), 21; Stearns (1996), 147-48, n. 71.

29. The place Jomonang (*jo mo nang*) or Jonang (*jo nang*) is generally referred to as "Richö Chenmo" (*Ri khrod Chen mo*), or "The Great Mountain Hermitage." This is a valley with extensive meditation caves (*sgrub phug*) and mountain hermitages (*ri khrod*) that serve as residences (*gzims khang*) for yogis. This was the monastic seat of the Jonang (*jo nang gi gdan sa*) from the time of Kun spangs pa. See also, Ruegg (1963), 90-91.

30. Ngag dbang (1992), 22.

31. Mkhan po Blo grags writes, "These were the earliest extensive instruction manuals on the sixfold yoga in Tibet," Ngag dbang (1992), 21. On Kun spangs pa's writings, Kun spangs, *Dpal*; Stearns (1996), 147-49.

32. Mkhan po Blo grags writes, "The cycle of the Kālacakra teachings from the time of the kalkī of Śambhala, on through the dissemination of these systems in the noble land of India, until the great Jonang master of these teachings [Dol po pa Shes rab Rgyal mtshan] appeared in this world—did nothing more than repeat the sayings of the Rwa and Dro lineages without clarifying our own tradition. Nevertheless, during the latter period of his life, Dol po pa engaged in the intended meaning of the tantra and its commentary, the consummation of our [Jonang] tradition," Ngag dbang (1992), 97.

33. Skyi ston 'Jam dbyangs studied the Kālacakra under Rong pa Shes rab Seng ge (1251-1315) and is listed by Tāranātha as Dol po pa's primary teacher for sūtra zhentong, Tā ra nā tha, *Zab mo*, 6; Stearns (1999), 13-14; Roerich (1976), 756.

34. Dol po pa was considered by his contemporaries to have been an emanation of Kalkī Puṇḍarika, Ngag dbang (1992), 541-42; Stearns (1999), 17 and 180, n. 32.

35. Stearns (1999), 18.

36. Kapstein (2000), 106-16; Stearns (1999), 79-81.

37. Dol po pa, *Ri chos*; Hopkins (2006), 5-8.

38. Stearns (1999), 24-27.

39. Ngag dbang (1992), 37-38; Phyogs las, *Jo nang*. This text was recently acquired by the Jonang Foundation. Phyogs las Rnam rgyal's commentary in the form of annotations (*mchan 'grel*) places less emphasis on zhentong than Dol po pa's work. Another one of Dol po pa's primary disciples, Sa bzang Ma ti Pan chen, wrote an interlinear commentary to reconcile the differences in these two works.

40. Phyogs las Rnam rgyal studied with Bu ston Rin chen Grup, Ngag dbang (1992), 37; Ruegg (1963), 76.

41. Dol po pa appointed Lotsāwa Blo gros Dpal as his successor to Jonang—he served as the throne-holder for seventeen years, and Phyogs las Rnam rgyal then served for six years.

42. Ngag dbang (1992), 38. Nya dbon Kun dga' Dpal also studied with the Kālacakra master Bu ston Rin chen Grup. Nya dbon Kun dga' Dpal and Phyogs las Rnam rgyal were teachers to Tsong kha pa Blo bzang Grags pa (1357-1419), founder of the Dge lugs tradition.

43. Ngag dbang (1992), 39.

44. Nam mkha' Chos skyong also taught Sgo rum Kun dga' Legs pa (1477-1544), who held the throne at Jonang and was a teacher of Nam mkha' Dpal bzang, Stearns (1999), 64 and 208, n. 80.

45. Mkhan po Blo grags writes, "He [Nam mkha' Dpal bzang] became learned in what was referred to as 'the northern Kālacakra tradition' (*dus 'khor byang lugs*) as it was taught by Shangs ston, a disciple of the great master from Lhun sdings. However, at an earlier time, because he had received the guidance instructions (*man ngag*) on the sixfold yoga according to the Jonang tradition from Rgyal ba Nam mkha' [Nam mkha' Chos skyong], incredible experiences and realizations were born within him," Ngag dbang (1992), 40. Fendell identifies the great master (*bdag chen*) as Bdag chen Rnam rgyal Grags pa, Fendell (1997), 72, n. 253.

46. Mkhan po Blo grags writes, "In particular, he [Kun dga' Grol mchog] received the complete teaching cycle of the Kālacakra transmissions as it came from Nam mkha' Dpal bzang via Lochen Ratnabhadra," Ngag dbang (1992), 50.

47. The six teachings of Niguma (*ni gu chos drug*) as transmitted through the Shangs pa Bka' brgyud are held within the Jonang to the present day. Jonang authors including Tāranātha and 'Ba' mda' Dge legs have composed works on these teachings. Smith (2001), 55-56 provides a list of this transmission lineage. Kun dga' Grol mchog's eclecticism is best exemplified within his work, *Jo nang khrid brgya,* or *Grol mchog khrid brgya* (*The One-Hundred-and-Eight Instructions*), a compilation of essential Tibetan Buddhist teachings. This text was included by Kong sprul in the last volume of his *Gdams ngag Mdzod*.

48. Another figure in the lineage at this point is Mkhan chen Lung rigs Rgya mtsho who received the empowerment, oral transmissions, and guidance instructions on the *Kālacakratantra* from Kun dga' Grol mchog, Ngag dbang (1992), 41.

49. Ngag dbang (1992), 55.

50. Mkhan po Blo grags writes, "Mkhan chen Lung rigs Rgya mtsho bestowed [upon Tāranātha] the empowerment, explanation of the tantra, and guidance instructions on the sixfold yoga, comprising the transmission of ultimate blessings—and by putting these into practice, [Tāranātha] had heightened experiences and realizations. These were the instructions according to the Jonang tradition (*jo lugs*) as it came from Kun dga' Grol mchog, and then the instructions according to Bu ston's tradition (*bu lugs*) were given to him quickly," Ngag dbang (1992), 55.

51. Ngag dbang (1992), 56.

52. Tā ra nā tha, *Zab lam* and *Rdo rje*.

53. Stearns (1999), 70-71; Fendell (1997), 27-30.

54. Ngag dbang (1992), 61-62.

55. Ngag dbang (1992), 67-68. Kun dga' Rin chen Rgya mtsho's disciple 'Brog dge Kun dga' Dpal bzang was also a disciple of Blo gros Rnam rgyal, and he established Jonang 'Brog dge Monastery in Ngawa, Ngag dbang (1992), 521-53.

56. Ngag dbang (1992), 68; Jo nang mdza' mthun (2005), 53.

57. These successors at 'Dzam thang Gtsang ba Monastery were: Mkas btsun Dar rgyas, Kun bzang 'Phrin las Rnam rgyal, Nus ldan Lhun grub Rgya mtsho, Dkon mchog 'Jigs med Rnam rgyal, Ngag dbang Chos 'phel, Ngag dbang Chos kyi 'Phags pa, Ngag dbang (1992), 75-76.

58. Ngag dbang (1992), 412-24; Kapstein (2001), 306-13.

59. 'Ba' mda', *Dpal*.

60. Tshogs gnyis Rgya mtsho passed the Kālacakra lineage on to Mkhan po Ngag dbang Blo gros Grags pa; his disciple was Ngag dbang Yon tan Bzang po (1928-2002).

Bibliography

Tibetan Sources

'Ba' mda' thub bstan dge legs rgya mtsho. *Dpal dus kyi 'khor lo'i rdzogs rim sbyor ba yan lag drug gi sgom rim grub pa'i lam bzang sku bzhi'i rgyal sar bsgrod pa'i shing rta*. In *'Ba' mda' gsung 'bum*, 15, 1-259. 'Dzam thang.

Byang sems rgyal ba ye shes (2004). *Dpal ldan dus kyi 'khor lo jo nang pa'i lugs kyi bla ma brgyud pa'i rnam thar*. Beijing: Mi rigs dpe skrun khang.

Dol po pa shes rab rgyal mtshan. *Ri chos nges don rgya mtsho*. In *Kun mkhyen chen po'i gsung 'bum*, 3, 189-741. 'Dzam thang.

Jo nang mdza' mthun lo rgyus phyogs srig tshogs (2005). *Jo nang ba'i gdan rabs mdor bsdus drang srong rgan po'i zhal lung*. Beijing: Mi rigs dpe skrun khang.

Kun spangs thugs rje brtson 'grus (1972). *Dpal dus kyi 'khor lo'i rnal 'byor yan lag drug gi 'grel pa snying po bsdus pa*. In *Gdams ngag mdzod*, 'Jam mgon kong sprul blo gros mtha' yas (ed.), 10, 15-24. Delhi: N. Lungtok and N. Gyaltsan.

Ngag dbang blos gros grags pa (1992). *Jo nang chos 'byung zla ba'i sgron me*. Qinghai: Nationalities Press (*krung go'i bod kyi shes rig dpe skrun khang*).

Phyogs las rnam rgyal. *Jo nang phyogs las rnam rgyal gyis mchan gyis gsal bar mdzad pa'i bsdus pa'i rgyud kyi rgyal po dus kyi 'khor lo'i rgyas 'grel rtsa ba'i rgyud kyi rjes su 'jug pa stong phrag bcu gnyis dri ma med pa'i 'od*, 1-5. Unpublished Manuscript.

Tā ra nā tha. *Dpal dus kyi 'khor lo'i chos bskor gyi byung khungs nyer mkho*. In *Kun mkhyen rje btsun tā ra nā tha'i gsung 'bum*, 179-219. 'Dzam thang.

———. *Zab lam rdo rje'i rnal 'byor gyi 'khrid yig mthong ba don ldan*. In *Kun mkhyen rje btsun tā ra nā tha'i gsung 'bum*, 3-121. 'Dzam thang.

———. *Rdo rje'i rnal 'byor gyi 'khrid yig mthong don ldan gyi lhan thabs 'od brgya 'bar ba*. In *Kun mkhyen rje btsun tā ra nā tha'i gsung 'bum*, 123-381. 'Dzam thang.

———. *Dus kyi 'khor lo'i brgyud 'debs*, 177-83. In *Kun mkhyen rje btsun tā ra nā tha'i gsung 'bum*, 'Dzam thang.

———. *Zab mo gzhan stong dbu ma'i brgyud 'debs*. In *Kun mkhyen rje btsun tā ra nā tha'i gsung 'bum*, 3-8. 'Dzam thang.

Yu mo mi bskyod rdo rje (1983). *Gsal sgron skor bzhi*. Gangtok: S. Gyaltsen and L. Dawa.

Western Sources

Davidson, Ronald M. (2005). *Tibetan Renaissance: Tantric Buddhism in the Rebirth of Tibetan Culture*. New York: Columbia University Press.

Fendell, Ramsey P. (1997). "Tāranātha's *Dpal dus khyi 'khor lo'i chos bskor gyi byung khungs nyer mkho* and its Relation to the Jo-nang-pa School of Tibetan Buddhism." M.A. Thesis. Indiana University: Department of Central Eurasian Studies.

Grönbold, Günter (1996). *The Yoga of Six Limbs: An Introduction to the History of Ṣaḍaṅgayoga*. Robert L. Hütwohl (trans.). Santa Fe: Spirit of the Sun Publications.

Hopkins, Jeffrey (trans.) (2006). *Mountain Doctrine: Tibet's Fundamental Treatise on Other-Emptiness and the Buddha-Matrix*. Ithaca: Snow Lion Publications.

Kapstein, Matthew T. (1993). "Introduction." In *Contributions to the Study of Jo-nang-pa History, Iconography and Doctrine: Selected Writings of 'Dzam-thang Mkhan-po Blo-gros-grags-pa*, 1-2, 1-12. Xylographic Prints from 'Dzam-thang and Rnga-ba, collected by Dr. Matthew Kapstein and Dr. Gyurme Dorje. Dharamsala: Library of Tibetan Works and Archives.

——— (2000). *The Tibetan Assimilation of Buddhism: Conversion, Contestation, and Memory*. Oxford: Oxford University Press.

——— (2001). "From Kun-mkhyen Dol-po-pa to 'Ba'-mda' Dge-legs: Three Jo-nang-pa Masters on the Interpretation of the *Prajñāpāramitā*." In *Reasons Traces: Identity and Interpretation in Indian and Tibetan Buddhist Thought*, 301-16. Boston: Wisdom Publications.

Newman, John R. (1985). "A Brief History of the Kalachakra." In *The Wheel of Time: The Kalachakra in Context*, Geshe Lhundub Sopa, Roger Jackson Jackson, and John Newman (eds.), 51-90. Madison: Deer Park Books.

——— (2000). "Vajrayoga in the Kālacakra Tantra." In *Tantra in Practice*, David Gordon White (ed.), 587-94. Princeton: Princeton University Press.

Roerich, George N. (trans.) (1976). *The Blue Annals*. Delhi: Motilal Banarsidass Publishers.

Ruegg, David Seyfort (1963). "The Jo naṅ pas: A School of Buddhist Ontologists According to the Grub mtha' šel gyi me loṅ." *Journal of the American Oriental Society*, 83, 73-91.

——— (1971). "Forward to Tāranātha's Life of the Buddha and His Histories of the Kālacakra and Tārātantra." In *Tāranātha's Jo nang Mdzad Brgya*, N. G. Demo (ed), 1-3. New Delhi: Gadan Sungrab Minyam Gyunphel Series, 20.

Smith, Gene E. (2001). "The Shangs pa Bka' brgyud Tradition." In *Among Tibetan Texts: History and Literature of the Himalayan Plateau*, 53-57. Boston: Wisdom Publications.

Stearns, Cyrus (1996). "The Life and Tibetan Legacy of the Indian Mahāpaṇḍita Vibhūticandra." *Journal of the International Association of Buddhist Studies*, 19, 1.

——— (1999). *The Buddha from Dolpo: A Study of the Life and Thought of the Tibetan Master Dolpopa Sherab Gyaltsan*. New York: State University of New York Press.

Templeman, David (1981). "Tāranātha the Historian." *Tibet Journal*, 17, 1, 41-46.

Wallace, Vesna A. (2001). *The Inner Kālachakra: A Buddhist Tantric View of the Individual*. Oxford: Oxford University Press.

–13–

The Six Vajra-Yogas of Kālacakra

Edward Henning

The six yogas are the perfection process (Skt. *utpannakrama,* Tib. *rdzogs rim*) meditations of the Kālacakra cycle and are often described as embodying the meaning of all the various generation and perfection processes of the different tantras and of being the pinnacle (*yang rtse*) of all Buddhist yānas.

As Günther Grönbold (Grönbold 1996) has pointed out, the classification of a system of yoga into six components (*ṣaḍaṅgayoga*, and more famously eight, *aṣṭāṅgayoga*) is very old, dating back to the time of the Upaniṣads. It should come as no surprise that the Buddhist system that is considered to be the ultimate expression of Vajrayāna practice should be styled in this way. The six yogas of Kālacakra share names with five of the components in the most common systems in early India, but their meditation practices are very different. These practices, the vajra-yoga of six components (*rdo rje'i rnal 'byor yan lag drug*), are mainly described in the Kālacakra cycle, but there is also mention of them in both the Guhyasamāja and Hevajra literature.

A work such as this is not an appropriate place in which to describe any details of such practices, and so in the following pages I shall explain something of the structure and theory of the six yogas as preserved in the Jonang tradition, relying mainly on the writings of Tāranātha and Banda Gelek (*'ba' mda' dge legs*). But first, a little history.

The Kālacakra system appeared in India around the beginning of the eleventh century CE and continued to be developed in India until the early thirteenth century when the Muslim invasions of Magadha and Bengal destroyed the main monastic universities, leaving only pockets of Buddhism remaining.

Among the many Indian Kālacakra practitioners who specialised in the six yogas, certain individuals stand out. The foremost of these is Anupamarakṣita. He was probably born late in the first half of the eleventh century, and two important texts by him on the six yogas survive in their Tibetan translations. Also surviving are two commentaries to these works by Raviśrījñāna, who lived about a century later. In terms of a simple word count, these four works of the Anupamarakṣita tradition account for just over half of the original Indian six-yoga material that survives in Tibetan translation today.

A generation or so after Raviśrījñāna, around the end of the twelfth century, these teachings passed through Vibhūticandra, the abbot of the famous Tham Bahī in Kathmandu, the monastery founded by Atiśa, another Kālacakra practitioner. Vibhūti also received a direct transmission from the siddha Śabari, and played a central role in the translation and transmission of these teachings into Tibet.

The next most important tradition comes from the two teachers having the title Kālacakrapāda. Kālacakrapāda the Elder was almost certainly the person who introduced Kālacakra into India, and the Younger was probably the famous teacher Nāropa (956-1040), of Nālandā (see Newman 1987 for a useful discussion of this subject). Vibhūticandra was also involved in the translation and transmission of the Kālacakrapāda six-yoga teachings, but more importantly, these teachings passed through the Kashmiri Somanātha, who travelled to Magadha to meet the two Kālacakrapādas. He later travelled extensively in Tibet, teaching Kālacakra and helping with the work of translation, particularly with the famous translator Dro (*'bro lo tsā ba shes rab grags*).

These are just the leading figures known to us today, but there were many others. The Kālacakra system attracted a great deal of attention from Tibetans: the tantra itself was translated into Tibetan by at least twenty different translators, and the tantra and the various other Kālacakra texts found their way into Tibet by a great variety of routes. Naturally, there were many variations in these different traditions of the six yogas that entered Tibet, and the most important work on collating all of this in Tibet was performed by Kunpang Thuje Tsondru (*kun spang thugs rje brtson 'grus*, 1243-1313).

He identified and learned seventeen distinct traditions of the six yogas, and the great strength of the Jonang six-yoga tradition is that it preserves this great body of learning and experience in a single coherent system. The main instruction text by Tāranātha (Katodo) defines the system as consisting of fifty-three discrete meditation practices, with which are combined a total of 108 physical exercises, described most fully by Banda Gelek (6ykrab). Throughout these relevant instructions texts there are many comments indicating the origin of the various instructions, in the traditions originally identified by Thuje Tsondru.

The following, adapted from Tāranātha (Kayolt), is a brief list of the traditions gathered by Thuje Tsondru—many of these are simply identified by the name of the relevant translator or early teacher.

1. The instructions coming from the translator Jijo (*gyi jo zla ba'i 'od zer*), who is reputed to have been the first translator of the Kālacakra Tantra.

2. The translator Magewai Lodro (*lo tsa ba rma dge ba'i blo gros*).

3. The translator Trom, Pema Weuzer (*khrom lo tsa ba padma 'od zer*).

4. The tradition from Atiśa, which he learned from a teacher named as the "Intuitive black teacher" (*bla ma nag po mngon shes can*). This is possibly Rāhulaguhyavajra, the master of the vihāra at Black Mountain, near Rājgṛiha.

5. The Dro tradition coming from the Kashmiri Pandit Somanātha.

6. The Rwa tradition, the teachings that Samantaśrī taught to the translator Rwa Chorab (*rwa chos rab*). These two, the Dro and Rwa traditions, are generally considered to be the most important in Tibet.

7. The "Yoga garland" tradition, from the translator Tsami, Sangye Drak (*tsa mi lo tsa ba sangs rgyas grags*).

8. The tradition that Rechung Dorje Drakpa received from Amoghavajra.

9, 10, & 11. Three traditions from the translator Galo (*rga lo*), including one which is derived from the Hevajra cycle and one from the Guhyasamāja. The other, a Kālacakra system, was obtained from the translator Tsami, but as their methods of explaining the instructions are quite different these are counted separately.

12 & 13. Two traditions from the Kashmiri Pandit Śākyaśrī (1127-1225). One of these concerned the Hevajra system and its six-yoga instructions as composed by Nāropa, and was passed to Chal translator, Chozang (*dpyal lo chos bzang*). The other was the tradition passed to Sakya Panchen, known as the "oral tradition of the six vajra words."

14 & 15. Two traditions that passed through Vibhūticandra. The first is the long lineage from Anupamarakṣita that Vibhūti heard from Ratnarakṣita. The second is the short lineage that Vibhūti received from Śabari when the latter visited him at Tham Bahī.

16. The tradition that Chag translator, Choje Pal (*chag lo tsa ba chos rje dpal*, 1197-1264), heard from the Nepali Pandit Nyiwang Sungwa (*paṇ chen nyi dbang srung ba*).

17. The tradition of instructions of Rāhulaśrībhadra, which passed through Manlung Guru (*man lungs gu ru*).

Thuje Tsondru is also famous for having founded Jonang Monastery, and the tradition that developed as a result became known as the Jonang tradition. They have always specialised in the practices of Kālacakra, and the structure of the six-yoga practices found today in the Jonang tradition is very much as was originally described by Thuje Tsondru.

Structure of the six yogas

Before going into any detail of the theory of the six yogas, it would be useful first to describe something of their overall structure and the nature of the practices they entail. I find it more useful to refer to each of the yogas by their Sanskrit names, but in the following initial list I also give English translations after their Tibetan names:

1. Pratyāhara (*so sor sdud pa*)—withdrawal

2. Dhyāna (*bsam gtan*)—mental focus

3. Prāṇāyāma (*srog rtsol*)—wind control

4. Dharāṇā (*'dzin pa,*)—retention

5. Anusmṛiti (*rjes dran*)—consummation

6. Samādhi (*ting nge 'dzin*)—absorption

1. The first yoga, pratyāhara, is a nonconceptual meditation, completely free from any mental activity. Mostly performed in complete darkness, this practice is a very powerful method for developing a meditation of great peace, together with an unshakeable presence of mind, or mindfulness. Once this has been properly developed, and a certain degree of genuine nonconceptual awareness has arisen, images start to appear to the mind, completely naturally and without prompting. These are known as empty-forms (Tib. *stong gzugs*, Skt. *śūnyabimba*), because they are not external and are clearly empty of any independent existence. They are natural manifestations from the mind. These empty-forms are classified into ten different types, known as the ten signs (*rtags bcu*).

These ten signs are very important within the Kālacakra system; in fact, the eight goddesses immediately surrounding Kālacakra in the maṇḍala have the names of eight of the signs, the other two being considered inherent in Kālacakra's consort, Viśvamātā. The signs are listed in the *Kālacakratantra* (chapter five, v. 115): "Out of emptiness one comes to see smoke, mirages, pure and spotless fire-flies, lamps, and, Blazings (yellow blazing, kālāgni) and the moon (white blazing) and sun (red blazing), vajra (black blazing, rāhu), ultimate flashes, and drops."

The practice of pratyāhara is divided into two parts: night-yoga, which is performed in complete darkness, and day-yoga, performed in a wide open, desolate place, in view of a large expanse of sky. The first four signs in the above quotation are those associated with night-yoga, and the other six are day-yoga. The names in brackets are alternative names to those originally given in the tantra.

In his excellent discussion of these (Bg6yspyi), Banda Gelek makes the point that the names of the signs are not intended to describe the forms of the images that will appear, rather the manner of their appearance. For example, the sign of smoke could well take the form of the image of a building or person, but the image will be smoky in form, flowing, floating upwards, "like newly formed rain clouds".

Similarly, the mirage-like sign could take the same form of a building or person, but would shimmer like flowing water or "drizzling rain blown about by the wind". Banda Gelek gives similar but more extensive descriptions of all of these signs and associates each of them with the dissolution into the central channel of the winds of the five elements in the right and left channels.

Tāranātha makes (Kayolt) an interesting comment on the nature of these signs: "The word sign here should not be understood just as a sign of the path, but a sign of the nature of reality. For example, if you are travelling a long way at night and see in the distance a real light, this is a sign that when you reach the light it will be able to warm you up and remove the feeling of cold. Similarly, an empty-form should be understood as a genuine expression of reality and a sign of the existence of that reality, tathāgatagarbha, and a sign of the quick realisation of enlightenment."

Another point worth mentioning about pratyāhara is that this type of practice is said to have its origins in the Prajñāpāramitā. Many writers, including Anupamarakṣita, give the following quotation from the eight-thousand-line Prajñāpāramitā:

> The king of gods, Sakra, said to Subhuti, the Elder: "Holy Subhuti, if someone wishes to practise this perfection of wisdom, what should he practise, and in what manner should he practise?"
>
> Subhuti the Elder said to the king of gods, Sakra: "Kaushika, someone wishing to practise this perfection of wisdom should practise with the sky. Kaushika, someone wishing to practise this perfection of wisdom should learn the practice in a roofless place."

This is considered to be the origin of the day-yoga practice, performed in an open place.

2. In the second yoga, dhyāna, one settles the mind one-pointedly on these empty-forms. Most importantly, the mind focuses on the equality and inseparable nature of mind and forms. There are several steps in this process of coming to perceive these empty-forms, understand them, and control them.

These first two aspects to the practice have the effect of calming the motion of the action-winds through the right and left rasanā (*ro ma*) and lalanā (*rkyang ma*) channels, developing the ability in the next practices to bring the winds into the central channel.

3. In prāṇāyāma, one combines the prāṇa (*srog rlung*) and apāna (*thur sel gyi rlung*) winds into one entity in the central channel, through suppressing the movements in the rasanā and lalanā channels. This is mainly accomplished by means of vajra-repetition (*rdo rje'i bzlas pa*) meditations, observing the coming and going of the breath, and other breath-manipulation exercises.

4. Dharāṇā is concerned with the winds in the central channel that in prāṇāyāma originated from the ten aspects of the right and left winds. Here, these prāṇa and apāna winds that have been combined into one entity are made stable by means of breathing exercises, particularly various types of flask-breathing (*bum can rlung*), and are merged into the indestructible drops in the central channel. This is the dissolution, or fading, of the coming and going of the winds—their dissolution back into the drops from which they originated.

5. In anusmṛiti the practitioner's body is substituted by the mahāmūdrā of empty-form. This means that the practitioner's body is naturally perceived as appearing as Kālacakra in union with the consort, Viśvamātā. When the practice is performed properly, it should appear naturally as an empty form and not as a contrived image.

Naturally, relative beginners practising anusmṛiti may well need to imagine themselves in the form of Kālacakra in union with the consort, but when the ability has been more fully developed, the experience will be more one of observing oneself as the deity, an empty-form, rather than a contrived "visualisation". The process of developing this ability starts with the practice of pratyāhara, allowing empty-forms to arise spontaneously in non-conceptual meditation. Any attempt at any form of contrived visualisation would be completely to miss the point.

Through the union of the male and female divine empty-forms, based on the blazing-melting of the white and red elements of the practitioner's physical body, one repeatedly cultivates and perfects the four joys (*dga' ba bzhi*) in both progression and regression. This refers to the movement of the red and white elements up and down the central channel, and this increases the experience of bliss and also the experience of empty-form—one perceives more of them. Having brought the movement of the winds under control, the practitioner now starts to practise with the drops and winds and the forces that operate between them. This mainly entails tummo (*gtum mo*) meditation and similar practices.

6. With the sixth yoga, samādhi, the sexual desire of the empty-form of the personal deity is transformed to create unchanging bliss. That desire is transformed into great bliss and compassion towards all beings. This has the nature of both method and understanding, and is free from subject and object. This is explained as the equality of empty-form and bliss. As the emptiness aspect of the practice has now been well developed through the earlier yogas, the emphasis now fully falls on the development of great bliss.

The structure here is straightforward, and the six yogas are clearly arranged into three pairs: pratyāhara and dhyāna are yogas of the channels, and by means of these practices the channels are purified, enabling control to be developed later over the winds. With prāṇāyāma and dharāṇā the movements of the winds are reduced to nothing—the winds being returned to the drops from which they originate. Finally, anusmṛiti and samādhi are yogas of the drops.

Other classifications of the yogas are given, and one or two of these will be described later. It is worth pointing out here that a full description of the six yogas would normally include a six-fold breakdown of each one, derived from the tradition of Kālacakrapāda. For each yoga, this would be the meaning of the name of the yoga, time for the practice, the characteristics of the practice, the confirmation, i.e., signs of success in the practice, the type of purification achieved by the practice, and the final result of the practice. Space does not permit more than a mention of these here.

One point that should immediately be clear from the short description above is that there is a natural causal process through the six yogas, with each yoga building on what has previously been developed and creating the ability to perform the following yogas. This causal structure is much more obvious with these six yogas than with the famous six dharmas of Nāropa (*nā ro chos drug*, often misleadingly translated as the six yogas of Nāropa). Although the first of the six dharmas, tummo, is clearly the basis for the other practices, the causal relationship between the others is not clear. With the six yogas, that relationship is essential.

Terminology of the yogas

In the following I shall give a very brief description of the theory of the six yogas based on the long discussion of this given by Tāranātha (Kazuju). I shall basically be picking out some of the key, and to my mind most interesting, points that he makes.

There are several terms that need to be introduced before describing this theory, and these largely represent the particular Kālacakra view on the nature of existence and the means to achieve enlightenment.

We have already come across the channels (*rtsa*, nāḍī), winds (*rlung*, vāyu), and drops (*thig le*, bindu), often translated as seed; I find "drop" more meaningful in the context of a meditation practice; this best represents how they are imagined. It might well be better simply to use the equivalent Sanskrit term *bindu*; the word "potential" is also often useful here. These three form the so-called vajra-body (*rdo rje'i lus*, vajrakāya), representing the structures, processes, and potentials that constitute our physical and mental existence. The main channels are three in number: the central channel (green, sometimes blue) and the right and left—rasanā (red) and lalanā (white). These are considered as running parallel through the centre of the body, towards the back, near the spine.

The three channels extend below the navel area but with different colours. Underneath the navel the central channel is known as the śaṃkhinī (*dung can ma*) and is coloured blue. The lower extension of the rasanā is black; it bends to the left, joining with the śaṃkhinī to reach the genitals. The lower extension of the lalanā is yellow and bends to the right and back, extending to reach the anus.

Groups of minor channels branch off from the central channel at six centres, at the level of the crown, forehead, throat, heart, navel, and genitals. These are associated respectively with the elements of space, water, fire, wind, earth, and awareness.

The numbers of channels in each of the six centres, and their colours, are as follows:

Crown	4				green
Forehead	4	8	16		white
Throat	4	8	32		red
Heart	4	8			black
Navel	4	8	12	60 or 64	yellow
Genitals	6	10	16		blue

With the four main centres, four minor channels branch off from the central channel and then subdivide to give the total numbers given above. Therefore, for the throat centre, four channels branch from the central channel; these each subdivide into two to give eight, and then again each into four to give thirty-two. The minor channels of the centres are curved like the spokes of an umbrella, with those of the crown, forehead, and throat curving downwards, and the others curving upwards (Tāranātha does not actually mention the genital centre here, but it seems safe to assume that its channels curve upwards).

There are also secondary centres associated with the twelve main joints: at the shoulders, elbows and wrists, and hips, knees and ankles, and other more minor ones.

The winds move through the various channels and are of ten main types, in two sets of five, each associated with the elements. The ten winds are:

prāṇa (*srog*)	- space
samāna (*mnyam gnas*)	- wind
udāna (*gyen rgyu*)	- fire
vyāna (*khyab byed*)	- water
apāna (*thur sel*)	- earth
nāga (*klu*)	- awareness
kūrma (*rus sbal*)	- wind
kṛikara (*rtsangs pa*)	- fire
devadatta (*lhas byin*)	- water
dhanañjaya (*nor rgyal*)	- earth

Sometimes the element associations of nāgavāyu and apānavāyu are reversed. The following list describes the main locations of these ten winds and something of their functions.

1. Prāṇavāyu: in the central channel, above the navel, and in the upper channels of the heart; it maintains life and identity and creates many thoughts; if damaged, the concentration is broken, resulting in a lack of consciousness, craziness, and ultimately death.

2. Samānavāyu: in the channels on the front side of the heart; preserves the heat in the belly, maintains the separation of nutrients and waste in food, passing

nutrients through the body and expelling waste downwards; if damaged, stomach illnesses result.

3. Udānavāyu: in the south-east (east is towards the front of the body) channel; controls speech, taste, drinking, eating, spittle, vomiting; if damaged, fever and upper (body) ailments result.

4. Vyānavāyu: exists throughout the body; combines with the power of the rasanā channel; in the joints it enables stretching and contraction of the limbs; if damaged causes paralysis, palsy.

5. Apānavāyu: in the central channel, below the navel, and the channels starting on the lower side of the heart; controls emission and retention of faeces, urine, and drop; if damaged, cold and lower ailments result. Tāranātha makes the point that this wind and prāṇavāyu are material winds.

6. Nāgavāyu: in the south-west channel; regulates eyesight, fatness, belching.

7. Kūrmavāyu: in the rear channel(s); regulates extension and contraction of the limbs.

8. Kṛikaravāyu: in the north-west channel; controls anger, distraction, intoxication.

9. Devadattavāyu: in the left channel; controls yawning and creates ailments of the winds.

10. Dhanañjayavāyu: in the north-east channel; earth ailments result. This wind remains in the body for a long time, even after death. This is presumably a reference to processes such as the growth of hair and fingernails that do indeed continue after death.

These are the primary locations for the winds, but they also permeate all channels in the body. Prāṇavāyu moves upwards with great strength, but does not do so downwards. However, there is some minor mixing with apānavāyu, and for this reason it moves a little downwards. Similarly, apānavāya moves downwards, not upwards, with great strength, but due to some mixing with prāṇavāyu it moves upwards. Samānavāyu is mainly concentrated in the belly, maintaining heat (digestion), but to some extent permeates the whole of the body. And similarly for the others.

The drops are generally classified into two types: the conventional consciousness drop and the ultimate awareness drop. The latter is identical with ultimate reality, the buddha-nature or tathāgatagarbha, which eternally exists as unelaborated, unchanging great bliss. The purification, or realisation, of this is the goal of all practice.

From the point of view of conventional drop, there are two primary drops which are the basis for the generation of all drops. Below the navel exists the essence of blood, the "inner sun", chief of all red elements and source of warmth and heat, active tummo. Above the crown exists the essence of semen, the "inner moon" or "conventional spring", chief of all white elements, the indestructible letter "haṃ", the nature of loosening bliss.

As these two are the basis for all other drops, they are described as having the nature of the syllables "e vaṃ".

Arisen from these are four drops located in the middle of the four main centres. At the forehead is the water-drop, the nature of moon, body. At the throat is the fire-drop, the nature of sun, speech. At the heart is the wind-drop, the nature of rāhu, mind. At the navel is the earth-drop, the nature of kālāgni, awareness.

The body-drop creates the errors of the waking state, the speech-drop the errors of the dream state, the mind-drop the errors of the deep sleep state, and the awareness-drop creates the errors of the fourth state—this latter is usually considered to be the experience of orgasm, but including some other experiences as well. These four drops are therefore described as being the potential for the various aspects of experience, categorised by the four states.

On the path, these drops are the basis for the experience of the four joys, and when by means of the path the four conventional drops are transformed into the ultimate drop of reality, one attains the four kāyas: respectively, the nirmāṇakāya (*sprul pa'i sku*), saṃbhogakāya (*longs spyod rdzogs pa'i sku*), dharmakāya, (*chos kyi sku*), and sahajakāya (*lhan cig skyes pa'i sku*).

Considered to be inherent in these four are the space-element drop at the crown and the awareness-element drop at the genitals. This give a total of six drops, and these last two are considered to be in essence the same as the two primary drops mentioned earlier. It is also sometimes described that the awareness-drop is inherent in the other five.

Finally on terminology, Kālacakra uses three terms that are not found in other Buddhist literature, but are taken from the Hindu Sāmkhya system. These are the three qualities (Tib. *yon tan gsum*, Skt. *triguṇa*): gloom (Tib. *mun pa*, Skt. *tamas*), passion (Tib. *rdul*, Skt. *rajas*), and goodness (Tib. *snying stobs*, Skt. *sattva*). Other terminology will be introduced as necessary.

Theory of the yogas

The following will be a very reduced summary of the detailed theory of the six yogas as described by Tāranātha (Kazuju). The point of practices such as the six yogas is to transform the practitioner's experience: to achieve, as Tāranātha puts it, ultimate liberation, which he describes as "the direct knowledge of the nature and state of all things". He continues: "The path is the method to remove the errors that obscure that true nature. Once the direct knowledge of this nature has been achieved, one will never deviate from the path."

His theory describes the state of things as we find them, the state of saṃsāra, or cyclic existence, the nature of which is suffering. Key to this discussion is the fact that the causes of saṃsāra can be removed, the path being the methods used to this purpose and the final result being liberation from that suffering, nirvāṇa.

This basic idea is summed up by the concept of the three tantras (*rgyud gsum*), and on this point Tāranātha quotes the main Buddhist definition of the word *tantra*, from the *Guhyasamājatantra*:

"Tantra is called continuity, and this tantra is classified into three aspects: ground, together with its nature, and inalienableness. Nature is the basic cause, ground is called the method, and inalienableness is the result. The meaning of tantra is contained in these three."

The terminology used in recent years has changed a little from that original quote, but this is clearly referring to ground (the state of things as we find them), path, and goal.

Tāranātha points out that this in fact reflects the structure of the *Kālacakratantra* itself, although it also has its own classification of outer, inner, and other. The tantra is divided into five chapters, the first of which describes outer Kālacakra, the physical worlds. The second describes inner Kālacakra, the body with the channels, winds, and drops. These two constitute the ground. The last three chapters are other Kālacakra, dealing with the empowerment, practices, and finally awareness. These describe the path and goal.

Outer and inner are known as the causal-tantra/continuum; other is both the method-tantra and the result-tantra. All things are contained in these three, which together describe the nature of reality.

The word *tantra*, continuity, is used to indicate the fact that these three are essentially inseparable. Individuals experience the various phenomena of cyclic existence, the path, and the final goal of liberation, but these are not different realities, but different experiences of one reality.

The essence of causal tantra is known by many different names, such as the radiant light Ādibuddha, perfect enlightenment, or tathāgatagarbha, buddha-nature. This is simply the basic nature of mind, which has the characteristic of originally coincident bliss and emptiness.

Mind is described as being of two types: saṃsāra-mind and nirvāṇa-mind. There are many other pairs of words used to express the same distinction: conventional and absolute mind, mind and nature of mind, etc.

Conventional saṃsāra-mind refers to mind afflicted with the incidental defilements of the eight consciousnesses, the fifty-one mental events, and so on. This experience is described by such concepts as the four states of waking. From the point of view of these four states, the causal continuum, the radiant light nature itself has no components or subdivisions, but it exists as the essence of the four potentials or drops when afflicted by the incidental defilements. And, when the defilements are removed by the path, those same four potentials are the causal continuum for the four kāyas, or the four vajras—the body-vajra, speech-vajra, etc.

Looked at in this way, the ground and result are indistinguishable, and so these four drops are the four kāyas. But because all the experiences of beings flow from these drops, they are included within the causal continuum; and because they are the basis for the four activities of enlightenment, they are included within the result-continuum. A similar argument could be made regarding the method-continuum.

This basic nature of reality is both the ultimate cause and the ultimate result, and there is no such thing as cause or result. However, from the point of view of ordinary beings, we talk in causal terms.

The word "incidental" that qualifies the defilements is important here. The basic nature of mind is the essence of the experiences of both saṃsāra and nirvāṇa, and it is merely the presence of these defilements that creates that distinction. The defilements are incidental because there is nothing essential in the difference between saṃsāra and nirvāṇa. The defilements are empty of inherent existence.

Tāranātha continues this discussion by pointing out that there are other pairs of terms with the same distinction. For example, ultimate reality is referred to as the "five letters of great emptiness" because it is the essence of the five elements and the causal continuum which is the nature of the five awarenesses. The word "great" here does not imply that emptiness—the mere absence of inherent existence—is great, but indicates that emptiness itself is awareness.

Similarly, ultimate reality is referred to as the "six unchanging empty potentials" because it is the essence of the six skandhas and the six elements and the causal continuum of the six types of buddhas and their six consorts. The potentials are said here to be empty because the potential of great bliss is free from all artifices of subject and object.

In the same way, ultimate reality is the essence of the twelve links of dependent origination (*rten 'brel bcu gnyis*) and also the essence of the twelve changes of (inner) winds, and it is the causal continuum of the dharmakāya awareness that perceives the twelve realities (*bden don bcu gnyis*).

There are many analogies given for the process of removing the incidental defilements, and the following should serve as a summary. Copper possesses a certain colour, lustre, and other qualities, but when it is in the form of ore, these are not observed because of the presence of other elements and impurities. However, once those impurities have been removed by the right process, pure copper results, together with its qualities of lustre, colour, and so forth. The copper has not been changed and its qualities not newly created—simply the impurities have been removed.

The creation of saṃsāra

Tāranātha now starts to get into more detail and describes how ultimate reality, the radiant nature of mind, base awareness, indestructible drop, etc., exists as the essence of the four drops and eight qualities, and that from these arise the incidental defilements which appear to be merged with it and which are the essence of base consciousness, which is sometimes referred to as the "great primary mis-perception".

Specifically, there are the dispositions and so forth of the four states. The presence of these gives rise to all the appearances and thoughts of the four states and the eight qualities of gloom, passion, and goodness, together with sounds, sensations, tastes, forms, and smells. From these arise the skandhas, elements, senses, actions, and so forth.

That base awareness is said to have as its mount the so-called awareness wind, which is essentially identical with it. The mount of the primary mis-perception is the subtle winds.

From this root mis-perception arise two things that have the characteristic of wind: the joyous wind which generates the fourth state, and the connate wind which creates the states of waking, dream, and deep sleep.

It is not the case that from this mis-perception physical winds are created, but rather that these "winds" have the nature of wind in that they create the thought (structures) of the four states. From these arise the ten winds described earlier; from these the winds of the twelve ascendants; these create the senses apprehending the five objects; following on from this are mental consciousness and the self-centred emotional mind, and from these two aspects of mind grows all the limitless range of thoughts.

Furthermore, this awareness is the essence of the three: white element, red element, and wind. For this reason, the primary mis-perception exists in the manner of defilements of these three, and so exists as the subtle nature of the white, red, and wind and gives rise to more coarse potentials.

As the dispositions of the four states associated with the four drops are only awareness, they do not exist in particular parts of the body. However, from the activity of the channels, winds, and drops of the forehead, the dispositions of the waking state are activated and give rise to all appearances, perceptions, and thoughts when awake.

Similarly, dream comes from those of the throat, deep sleep from the heart, and from the navel are activated the dispositions of the fourth state, to give rise to the appearances, perceptions, and thought of sexual desire. In this way the four centres, the four vajras, and the four states are associated together.

As we have seen, the primary consciousness exists like a drop, as the dispositions of the white, red, and winds. From this point of view, the power of the winds (gloom, from the three qualities) causes thoughts, which have the nature of delusion. The red element, the disposition of passion, causes the characteristics of desire, and goodness, the disposition of the white element, causes the characteristics of the bliss that is associated with sexual loosening and emission.

This primary mis-perception causes the movements of the winds and the generation of thoughts, and it has the power to create the sixteen joys of the bliss of emission and the coarse twelve links. As potential, these coarse states do not exist, but the subtle characteristics of winds, thoughts, joys, and links do exist.

From the association of this primary mis-perception and the coarse body there specifically arises the experience of saṃsāra of the desire realm. Apart from a difference of degree of grossness with the form realm and formless realm, it is basically the same for them.

Furthermore, the activation of the power of winds arising from the dispositions of the white, red, and wind causes the movements of the winds of the twelve changes (the changes of the twelve ascendants, associated with changes within the body). This activity stirs the red aspect and causes it to blaze; this causes the white aspect to melt completely.

The movements of the winds, the blazing of the red aspect, and the melting of the white aspect in general cause the creation of all the variety of thoughts, and, propelled by previous actions, other potentials are activated. As a result there arise all the appearances of self and others of the animate and inanimate worlds, and the various emotional defilements that drive actions are created.

Then again, with the increase of these emotions together with the winds, one accumulates the actions that in the future propel one to rebirth. These actions are of two kinds: the first is a normal (neutral) action which mainly creates the world in which other births will occur, and the second type which creates each being's individual body, possessions, and so forth. The animate and inanimate worlds that are created in this way are included within the skandhas, elements, and senses.

At this point Tāranātha gives a brief description of the manner in which saṃsāra is created that could, like many of these descriptions, be read as something of a time-line, but that is not the intention here. These are not descriptions of some kind of initial process that happened in the distant past that creates our current condition, but an on-going process, one that is always happening. In the previous section mention was made of just such a process: the interaction between the red and white elements, driven by the winds. This process is contemplated in a pure form during tummo and associated practices, as a means of controlling and purifying the processes that create saṃsāra. The following description is closely related to this.

The source of saṃsāra is taken here to be (attachment to) the bliss of emission; one could possibly say attachment to life itself. In this way, mis-perception is the beginningless disposition of desire. Once that desire is activated, there is then change regarding the object of that desire, and this change leads to separation from the original object of desire, and from that develops anger. The nature of anger is mindlessness, and mindlessness is delusion. In this way mis-perception has the nature of the three main emotional defilements of desire, anger, and delusion.

Tāranātha summarises the manner of the development of saṃsāra in the following way:

> From the mind of the disposition of the bliss of emission arise semen, drop, and wind. From these three arise this present body, speech, and mind. And from the appearance of the channels, winds, and drops of this body, speech, and mind arise all the various appearances of the outer physical world.
>
> From the combination of the basic cause of the power of the inner dispositions manifesting semen, drop, and wind, together with the objects of the external physical world and one's own body, emotions are generated and one accumulates actions that propel one towards other births. The initial emotional dispositions are energised and create in the future a variety of emotions. In this way all those wandering round in circles (saṃsāra) create

from emotions arising in their own minds the experience of saṃsāra entailing all kinds of suffering.

Nobody else creates the sufferings of saṃsāra; it is like a silk worm bound up in its own cocoon.

The reversibility of saṃsāra

The point should be clear that the creation of saṃsāra is reversible because the error that creates it is not inherently existent. The wandering of beings in saṃsāra is real enough, but is not truly established and is simply an error concerning that which is not real. This error is just a thought-construct, and that thought is created by the power of the dispositions and the movements of the action-winds.

It is necessary to apply an antidote to all this, and that is non-conceptual awareness which will suppress the action-winds. Then, through this non-conceptual awareness perceiving reality directly, one eliminates the disposition of changing bliss. With the action-winds stopped, the white and red aspects subside and the processes of the sixteen blisses of emission and the twelve links come to a stop.

This brings to an end the stream of previous activity, emotions, and sufferings; and having overcome thought-constructs, these will not arise again, and the origination of existence through actions and emotions is exhausted.

Just the mere collapse of this cycle of apparent but not truly existent error is liberation.

At this point Tāranātha quotes the Kālacakra commentary, the *Vimalaprabhā*: "For this reason, that which is called Māra is the stain of dispositions of the saṃsāric mind of beings; that which is called Buddha is mind free from the dispositions of the saṃsāric mind." This expresses the fact that conventional individual beings are merely the stream of consciousness and the infinite elements of saṃsāra, as in them eternally exists ultimate enlightened awareness.

The yogas as antidote

Before going into more detail with regard to the individual yogas, Tāranātha discusses the nature of the path of the yogas as a whole, the profound path of vajra-yoga.

As the nature of the reality of the ground is of union, so the nature of the awareness of the result is also of union. For this reason the method or path that should bring about the realisation of that result should be one of union, because it is in the normal nature of things that the result is compatible with the cause. For this reason this profound path of vajra-yoga is the path of union.

But what is referred to here by union? It is the union of the awareness of unchanging great bliss and the body of emptiness possessed of all positive characteristics. This is the same as the union of great compassion and emptiness, or the union of illusory body and radiant light.

In this context, great compassion, radiant light, and unchanging bliss mean the same, normally understood as method (Tib. *thabs*, Skt. *upāya*) and explained as conventional reality. Emptiness, illusory body, and body of all positive characteristics also mean the same, and are normally understood as understanding (Tib. *shes rab*, Skt. *prajñā*) and explained as ultimate reality.

As this great bliss is able to overcome the suffering of self and others, it is called great compassion, because that which completely protects from suffering has the characteristic of compassion. But this is not just a matter of applying the name "compassion," as this great bliss does in fact create an attitude of love towards all beings.

Another term that is used in this context is "non-conceptual compassion." This refers to the eradication of the appearances of subject and object, and of it not going beyond the seal of non-elaboration.

Also, regarding the body of all positive characteristics, this is an awareness free from all elaborations of subject and object. But, having stopped all appearances of subject and object, this does not mean that there will be no appearances at all. Free from elaboration, the retinue of the maṇḍala and so forth and all the positive characteristics of saṃsāra and nirvāṇa will appear, but are not called conventional appearances or erroneous appearances; they are awareness appearance, appearance of reality, and so forth.

But why is great bliss referred to here as conventional reality? It is not actually conventional reality, but is referred to as such here because its development depends on methods that utilise the conventional loosening-bliss.

The word "union" is also applied to the union of cause and result, and with regard to this, Tāranātha quotes the *Sekoddeśa*: "From emptiness flow images, from unchanging comes the result of bliss; the cause is sealed by the result, and the result sealed by the cause." Seal carries here the meaning of non-dual, or union.

The point is that the two are essentially the same. However, as far as the nature of reality is concerned, there is no actual cause and result by way of anything that creates anything or is itself created.

However, the nature of all causes is empty-form, and the nature of all results is unchanging bliss. Because from the emptiness of one's own essence there arises bliss, the cause and result are similar; and although they are essentially indistinguishable, in order to realise them, the first five yogas are concerned with the development of the perception of emptiness, while the last, samādhi, is concerned with great bliss.

As it combines these two aspects of bliss and emptiness, the path of vajra-yoga is called the path of great union.

The six yogas are classified in several ways, and Tāranātha in fact gives a list of twelve classifications. Four of these are worth mentioning here.

The four drops: pratyāhāra and dhyāna remove obscurations from the body-drop, prāṇāyāma and dhāraṇā from the speech-drop, anusmṛiti from the mind-drop, and samādhi from the awareness-drop.

The four states: pratyāhāra and dhyāna purify the waking state, prāṇāyāma and dharāṇā the dream state, the anusmṛiti the state of deep sleep, and the samādhi the fourth state.

Concerning the appearance of empty forms purifying the waking state, the purification is by means of similarity to the clear appearance of various images (as in the waking state).

Regarding the purification of dream by stopping the winds, as the obscurations of subtle appearances such as those of dreams, the intermediate state, and so forth are caused by the agitation of the winds; the purification is by means of stopping the movements of the winds.

The purification of deep sleep by the connate melting bliss in anusmṛiti occurs through similarity with the non-conceptual dissolving of the winds.

Samādhi purifies the fourth state by overcoming the drop (potential) that brings about change.

Four aspects of approach-accomplishment (Tib. *bsnyen sgrub*, Skt. *sevāsādhana*): the processes of pratyāhara and dhyāna are approach because they lay the foundation for the body of awareness. The processes of prāṇāyāma and dharāṇā are close approach because they lay the foundation for the path of the speech-vajra. The process of anusmṛiti is accomplishment, because it lays the foundation for the path of the mind-vajra, being the special method for the immediate development of unchanging bliss. The process of samādhi is great accomplishment, because it develops in particular the awareness-vajra but in general achieves the realisations of all four vajras.

Tāranātha gives a simple analogy to illustrate the meaning of these four aspects of approach-accomplishment: to come close to the ultimate realisation is approach, such as, for example, considering a journey to a town. Close approach means coming closer to realisation, like making preparations for the journey. Accomplishment refers to the beginning of the development of the causes that bring about the special result, like actually setting out on the journey. Great accomplishment has the meaning of developing the result without obstacle, like entering the gate of the town.

The four yogas: pratyāhāra and dhyāna are the yoga of form, as they generate images; prāṇāyāma and dharāṇā are the yoga of mantra, as they purify the winds; anusmṛti is the yoga of dharma as it develops bliss through focusing on all characteristics (emptiness); as from this develops the realisation of ultimate non-conceptual emptiness, samādhi is the yoga of purity. Also, the four yogas can have the names of the four kāyas as they develop the realisation of the kāyas.

Functioning of the yogas

Going into more detail regarding the six yogas, Tāranātha explains how they each have two aspects.

With pratyāhara, the night-yoga binds the rasanā channel, and the day-yoga binds the lalanā channel. With dhyāna, the practice of eliminating the perception of the empty-forms as objects purifies the lalanā channel, and the practice of eliminating elaborating conceptual clinging to the empty-forms purifies the rasanā channel. Of these two yogas, pratyāhara is mainly concerned with mind, as here the solar elements are purifying the lunar elements. In dhyāna, as the lunar elements are purifying the solar, the emphasis is mainly with body. With pratyāhara, the bliss of focusing the attention in space which is the lunar element is in union with the solar element, the empty-forms. In dharāṇā, the lunar and solar elements are the uncontrived attitude of mind and the arising of empty-forms.

With prāṇāyāma there are six upper and lower channels (right, left, and centre, above and below the navel). Suppressing the right and left upper winds and combining them with the lower central wind in the śaṃkhinī (*dung can ma*) purifies the rasanā channel, the path of the sun; stopping the right and left lower winds and combining them with the upper central wind in the avadhūtī (central channel) purifies the lalanā channel, the path of the moon. The order in which these occur is not specified, but in general the upper winds are stopped first, and after all ten winds have been halted they become combined into one entity. The lunar and solar elements are the mastering, respectively, of the prāṇa and apāna winds.

With dharāṇā there are also two stages. Contemplating in a regressive direction from the navel to the crown mainly arrests the solar elements, and contemplating in a progressive direction from the crown to the navel purifies the lunar elements. With these two yogas, prāṇāyāma is mainly concerned with mind, and dharāṇā with body. The lunar element is the dissolution of the winds into the drops and the solar element the blazing of tummo.

The two stages of anusmṛiti depend on one's ability. When one is unable to induce the full four joys with the mahāmūdrā of empty-form, then practising mainly with the blazing of tummo purifies the lunar elements. Then, once the ability to induce the full four joys has been developed, practising mainly with the bodhicitta, the basis for unchanging melting bliss, one purifies the solar elements.

With samādhi, arresting the five elements at the five centres from the genitals to the forehead (upwards) purifies the solar elements, and arresting the five skandhas at the five centres from the crown centre (downwards) purifies the lunar elements. The five elements are classified as understanding and the five skandhas as method. Of these two yogas, anusmṛiti is mainly associated with mind, and samādhi with body. The lunar element is the body of empty-form and the solar element the unchanging melting bliss.

This two-fold classification concerns the order in which the particular qualities are developed in the individual performing the practice. The way in which the practice is performed should be in the manner of the union of method and understanding. The lunar and solar elements are, respectively, the cessation of the movements (activities) of the white and red elements.

Pratyāhāra is free from mental activity, but it is not simply a state in which thoughts have been stopped. Without any artificiality, by engaging with that reality which is the pure awareness that is naturally free from mental activity, incidental thoughts are reduced, and one spontaneously comes to rests in pure awareness.

Both day- and night-yoga are important as it is necessary to purify the defilements associated with both the method and understanding aspects, in particular to purify the dispositions regarding birth and death. Also, the night-yoga makes it particularly easy to develop empty-forms, and by having practised that, one then develops with the day-yoga a more rounded skill in the practice.

The experience of empty-forms is stabilised with the practice of dhyāna, and this stability in the practice means that the empty-forms cannot be stopped.

There are five aspects to the development of dhyāna: with the aspect of understanding the forms are simply observed; with perception they are recognised; with analysis they are understood for what they are; with joy one develops attachment to the forms; and, with unwavering bliss, one identifies the forms with mind.

Prāṇāyāma is a method for reverting the two types of impure winds, with the characteristics of sun and moon, into awareness winds. This awareness wind is in essence the same as empty-form mahāmudrā, but the practitioner has not previously perceived the empty-forms as being the essence of the winds.

By focusing on these empty-forms one applies the methods of flask-breathing and so forth gradually to restrict the movements of the solar and lunar winds. These solar and lunar winds are the obstacles that prevent the perception of the true nature of the winds, and as these are gradually reduced and dissolved one develops a real experience of the nature of empty-form.

In dharāṇā, the "ultimate drop" exists as the empty-form mahāmūdrā and has the nature of great bliss. From the nature of this blissful reality arises the process of all incidental appearances, which exists as the essence of the physical drop in the navel centre of the conventional channels and centres. This is the basis for all the subtle and coarse winds, and they originated from there. From wherever they originated, so there will they be returned.

So, dharāṇā is the method for coercing these subtle and coarse winds back into the physical drops, so that which originally created the structure of life appears as the drop of great bliss.

When the meditation is done properly, and the prāṇa and apāna winds have been combined into one entity, then this enables the "cheating of death". This is because one gains the ability to fill all the six centres and even the centres in the fingers and toes of the hands and feet with the prāṇa (life) wind. Through the power of the ten winds dissolving into the drop, the sufferings of old age and illness are removed, and through perceiving the nature of the emotional defilements, one is not enslaved by those defilements.

Anusmṛiti represents something of a culmination of the processes of the previous four yogas. With pratyāhāra, the rasanā and lalanā are partially bound, and one starts to experience empty-forms for the first time. With dhyāna, this is developed further and the right and left channels are bound more strongly and the appearance of empty-forms increases by an order of magnitude. Whereas in pratyāhāra there was nothing more than a subtle feeling of bliss, the multiplication of the empty-forms causes experiences of joy and bliss to take hold.

Through prāṇāyāma the movements of the winds in the right and left channels are gradually brought to a halt, the appearance of empty-forms multiplies a hundredfold, and the experience of bliss increases with the merging of the prāṇa and apāna winds. With dharāṇā the winds dissolve into the six drops and tummo blazes, beginning the experience of melting bliss. The empty-forms now increase a hundred- or a thousand-fold.

With anusmṛti these empty-forms are increasingly stabilised and now appear together with, or combined with, melting bliss. It is this process of cumulative development on the path that gives this yoga its name of consummation. The word anusmṛti would normally translate as recollection, but in this context that does not seem to have sufficient strength. Consummation also usefully carries something of the sense of working with the sexual dispositions, the disposition of the melting bliss.

The focus of attention in anusmṛti and samādhi is essentially the same, and so an explanation of anusmṛti is also an explanation of samādhi. However, the process of anusmṛti is intended to develop the unchanging drop, but in that practice that has not been achieved. In samādhi, it has been achieved, and the practice builds from there.

Association of the yogas with the creation of saṃsāra

It should now be clear how the purification process of the yogas proceeds, with the winds being calmed, returned to the central channel, and dissolved back into the drops. Then the process of interaction between the winds and drops is purified in the perspective of emptiness with the last two yogas.

Finally, I shall return to the process of the creation of saṃsāṛa from a slightly different point of view and show how the purification of this aligns with the characteristics of the yogas. One source for this is the commentary by Jamgon Kongtrul (Zabnang) to the *Profound Inner Meaning* (*zab mo nang gi don*) by the Third Karmapa, Rangjung Dorje; this is a text that is largely based on Kālacakra theory. Another source is the tantra commentary, the *Vimalaprabhā* (Vimala), and I am also leaning heavily on the discussion of the creation of saṃsāṛa by Herbert Guenther (Guenther 1972), also based on the *Profound Inner Meaning*.

The starting point of the creation of saṃsāra is the radiant light, base awareness. Of the winds of the six elements, this is the awareness-wind and of the six skandhas, the skandha of awareness.

From this the first split into subject and object occurs, giving a sense of separation and space. This is the space-wind, and base consciousness, the skandha of consciousness. This is the root of the emotional defilement of aversion.

Mind becomes fascinated by this apparent existence of external objects and reacts to their appearance. This is the wind-wind, the skandha of response, and the root of the emotional defilement of desire.

The process deepens, and mind becomes immersed in the increasing mass of apparent external objects. This is the fire-wind, the skandha of sensation, and the root of the emotional defilement of delusion.

Mind now tries to make sense of the situation that has developed by means of conceptual thought, by applying characteristics to objects, and so forth, and thereby developing a false sanity. This is the water-wind, the skandha of interpretation.

Finally, all of this becomes fixed, with rigid views and responses. This is the earth-wind, the skandha of form. Individuals then act on the basis of these fixed wrong views that have developed, and the wheel of saṃsāra relentlessly turns.

The order given here of the development of the winds and skandhas is as follows, with the buddhas, which are the purified forms of the skandhas, also given:

Awareness	Awareness	Vajrasattva
Space	Consciousness	Akṣobhya
Wind	Response	Amoghasiddhi
Fire	Sensation	Ratnasambhava
Water	Interpretation	Amitabha
Earth	Form	Vairocaṇa

The function of the six yogas is to purify this process:

1. Pratyāhāra develops the appearance of signs, empty-forms. This purifies the awareness skandha, the result being the realisation of the buddha Vajrasattva.

2. In dhyāna the appearance of those signs is stabilised, and they are perceived correctly. This purifies the skandha of consciousness, the result being the buddha Akṣobhya.

3. In prāṇāyāma one brings the right and left action-winds together. This purifies the skandha of response, resulting in the buddha Amoghasiddhi.

4. In dharāṇā one retains the prāṇa wind, dissolving it into the seeds. This purifies the skandha of sensation, resulting in the buddha Ratnasaṃbhava.

5. In anusmṛti one purifies the instances of desire in the central channel. This purifies the skandha of interpretation, resulting in the buddha Amitabha.

6. With the yoga of samādhi, one brings to a stop the activity of all the winds. This purifies the skandha of form, resulting in the buddha Vairocana.

A similar description could be made with the elements and their purified forms, the goddesses that are the consorts of the buddhas.

References

English materials

Grönbold, Günther. 1996. *The Yoga of Six Limbs: An Introduction to the History of Ṣaḍaṅgayoga*. New Mexico: Spirit of the Sun Publications.

Guenther, Herbert V. 1972. *The Tantric View of Life*. Shambhala, The Clear Light Series.

Newman, John. 1987. "The Outer Wheel of Time: Vajrayana Buddhist Cosmology in the Kalacakra Tantra." Ph.D. dissertation, University of Wisconsin.

Tibetan texts

6ykrab: dus 'khor rdzogs rim sbyor ba yan lag drug gi 'khrul 'khor gyi sdom 'grel ba dang bcas pa rab tu gsal bar bshad pa grub pa'i dgongs rgyan, 'ba' mda' dge legs.

Bg6yspyi: dpal dus kyi 'khor lo'i rdzogs rim sbyor ba yan lag drug gi spyi don legs par bshad pa rdo rje bdud rtsi'i chu gter, 'ba' mda' dge legs.

Katodo: zab lam rdo rje'i rnal 'byor gyi 'khrid yig mthong ba don ldan, Tāranātha.

Kayolt: rdo rje'i rnal 'byor gyi 'khrid yig mthong ba don ldan gyi lhan thabs 'od brgya 'bar ba, Tāranātha.

Kazuju: zab lam rdo rje'i rnal 'byor gyi rnam par bshad pa rgyas par bstan pa zung 'jug rab tu gsal ba chen po, Tāranātha.

Vimala: bsdus pa'i rgyud kyi rgyal po dus kyi 'khor lo'i 'grel bshad rtsa ba'i rgyud kyi rjes su 'jug pa stong phrag bcu pa bcu gnyis pa dri ma med pa'i 'od, rigs ldan padma dkar po.

Zabnang: rnal 'byor bla na med pa'i rgyud sde rgya mtsho'i snying po bsdus pa zab mo nang gi don nyung ngu'i tshig gis rnam par 'grol ba zab don snang byed, 'jam mgon kong sprul.

–14–

Compassionate Aspirations and Their Fulfillment: Dol-po-pa's *A Prayer for Birth in Sukhāvatī*

Georgios T. Halkias

Prelude to the Field

Hundreds of years after the death of Buddha Śākyamuni, the traditional founder of orthodox lineages of Buddhism,[1] a rich body of soteriological doctrines grouped under the penumbra of Mahāyāna Buddhism originated in North India and spread to Central and South Asia, China, Tibet, Korea, and Japan. Mahāyāna, or the vehicle of the Bodhisattvas (Skt. *Bodhisattvayāna*), is a distinct vehicle which accords with early Buddhist doctrines of liberation in the realization of no Self (Skt. *anātman*), but places heavy emphasis on the spiritual training of individuals who strive after supreme awakening—bodhisattvas who aspire to attain the spiritual refinement of Buddha Śākyamuni, endeavouring to reach one day, just like Him, unsurpassable and perfect *bodhi* (Skt. *anuttarā samyaksaṃbodhī*). For this purpose, bodhisattvas cultivate a set of perfections (Skt. *pāramitā*) while attributing great spiritual worth in the generation and recognition of extensive and unprejudiced compassion.

In the Mahāyāna sūtras, we read accounts of this overwhelming compassion turning into a sacred resolve, an aspiring pledge that qualifies a bodhisattva's awakening to be inseparable, cognitively and emotively, from the liberation of all visible and invisible species of suffering sentience. This awakening is said to be coextensive with the perfection of a wisdom-awareness that transcends concepts, ideas, and theoretical proliferations (Skt. *prajñāpāramitā*), and draws from an experiential understanding that there exist no predestined substances, agents, or reasons in a causal universe that mirrors links between points of reference and the unfolding of events. In this respect, a bodhisattva fashions a life beneficial for others while training to recognize that all "physical and mental worlds" experienced by "self and other" are devoid of inherent designations. All phenomena are said to arise and cease as experiences and perceptions according to the dynamics of dependent coorigination (Skt. *pratītyasamutpāda*), an interpretive frame that holds instructive and symbolic power over notions such as self and other, bodhisattva and buddha, confusion and clarity, compassionate prayers and their fulfilment, and so forth.

Arguably the most ubiquitous and controversial North Indian doctrinal and ritual expression of the bodhisattva vow is what has come to be uniquely identified in East Asia as Pure Land Buddhism.[2] For the most part, the Buddhism of pure-lands has come to be synonymous with the cult of Buddha Amitābha, a tradition that preserves a collection of doctrines and contemplative practices centered around Sukhāvatī—a pure-land portrayed as an after-death destination and the redeeming outcome of the bodhisattva's vows. According to the Large and Small *Sukhāvatīvyūha* sūtras, the core texts of the Indo-Tibetan Amitābha tradition,[3] Sukhāvatī (*bDe-ba can*) stands for a spiritual field of possibilities and actualities molded by the aspirations of Dharmākara, the great bodhisattva. His unsurpassable compassion for all sentient beings culminates, hagiographically, in the activities of the Buddha of Infinite Luminosity whose universal aspirations find expression and meaning in his buddha-field (Skt. *buddhakṣetra;* Tib. *zhing-khams*), a grand goal that resonates doctrinally with the rhetoric of Mahāyāna soteriology.

The conception of buddha-fields exercised considerable influence in the history of Mahāyāna thought,[4] without strictly belonging to Mahāyāna, for a number of references can be found within the varied contents of the *Mahāvastu*, a text of the Lokottaravādin sect.[5] Nevertheless, as shown by Kloetzli, while the Sarvāstivādin sect recognized the existence of only a single buddhakṣetra, "a full and dramatic use of the buddhakṣetra is reserved for the Mahāyāna" (1983: 6). Here we find countless buddha-fields populating our physical and mental landscapes, extending in all directions as outcomes and destinations of previous ennobling aspirations. The most prominent and influential of all Mahāyāna buddha-fields, known throughout East Asia and Tibet, is a luminous field of bliss: Sukhāvatī, the pure-land of Buddha Amitābha cosmologically located in the West.

Texts and Origins of Sukhāvatī in Tibet

According to traditional accounts, the importation of Buddhism and the concomitant translation of Buddhist literature into Tibetan commenced during the times of the first religious king (Skt. *dharmarāja*) Srong-btsan-sgam-po (617-649/50) and continued until the seventeenth century.[6] With the imperial patronage of Buddhist monasticism from the eighth century onwards, a number of registers of Buddhist and non-Buddhist works[7] in Tibetan translation were compiled and maintained across monastic communities and royal depositories. The growing political role of a Tibetan monastic community (Dargyay 1991) and the need for a systematic and standardized exposition of Buddhist doctrines eventually led to the official sponsorship of authoritative catalogues (*dkar-chag*), which represent a revised selection mainly of Sanskrit and Chinese Buddhist literature translated into Tibetan, as well as related works authored by Tibetans (Muge Samten 2005: 3-31).

The two main sūtras, dedicated exclusively to Buddha Amitābha and his buddha-field Sukhāvatī, are known in East Asia as the Small and Large *Sukhāvatīvyūha* sūtras. They were composed in North-Western India during the Kuṣāna Empire (50-250 CE) amid a vibrant climate of cultural pluralism, commercial dynamism, and religious syncretism between the East and the West (Fujita 1996: 10-11)—with Buddhism acting as a common factor among the different trading peoples of the Silk Road whose diverse religions included Christianity, Hinduism, Islam, Zoroastrianism, and Manichaeism. According to Akamatsu, the earliest Tibetan translation of the Small *Sukhāvatīvyūha-sūtra* is text Pelliot No. 758 from the Chinese translation of a Sanskrit original by Kumārajīva (Ducor 1988: 110). Tibetan translations of the Sanskrit *Sukhāvatīvyūha-sūtra* (*bDe ba can gyi bkod pa'i mdo*) and *Amitābhavyūha-sūtra* (*'Od dpag med kyi bkod pa'i mdo*) are included in the first proto-canonical catalogues of Buddhist texts edited, registered, and deposited in the royal treasure houses (*dkor mdzod*) of the Tibetan Empire. The official reception of these sūtras, and by extension Sukhāvatī doctrines and practices, is in fact reflected in their being listed in two extant catalogues, the *dkar-chag lDan dkar ma*, a register from the fortress of lDan-dkar, and the *dkar-chag 'Phang thang ma*, a catalogue from the palace of 'Phang-thang.[8] Consulting these registers, later Tibetan Buddhist scholars embraced Sukhāvatī doctrines as buddhavacana (the speech of the Buddha) and included the *Sukhāvatīvyūha* sūtras in their canonical collections of the bKa'-'gyur. In addition to the canonical sūtras, we find a good number of indigenous Tibetan compositions and aspirational prayers to Sukhāvatī and related dhāraṇī written during the times of the Tibetan occupation of Dunhuang (Halkias 2006: 37-41).

Just as the writing, recitation, and reproduction of aspirational prayers may have reinforced the devotional aspects of Sukhāvatī worship, the recitations of dhāraṇī and employment of Vajrayāna "methods of attainment" (*sgrub-thabs*) came to represent more efficacious components of pure-land religiosity in Tibet. In fact, the diverse number of texts dedicated to the realization of Sukhāvatī form a distinct genre in Tibetan literature known as the *bDe-smon.*[9]

Throughout the centuries, the dGe-lugs, bKa'-brgyud, rNying-ma, Sa-skya, and Jo-nang Tibetan Buddhist orders produced evocative prayers and elaborate commentaries exclusively devoted to the understanding and practice of Sukhāvatī. The spiritual yearning to reach and/or behold Amitābha's pure-land carried on ever more forcefully into the hands of Tibetan tantric adepts employing the expedient means of Vajrayāna to secure birth in Sukhāvatī in one lifetime. A good number of distinct, yet mutually reinforcing practices that draw inspiration and legitimation from the sūtras and tantras can be classified as belonging to the *bDe-smon* genre of Tibetan literature.

In Tibet, aspirational prayers (*smon-lam*) often formed the basis for longer commentaries (*'grel-ba*) composed either by the authors of the prayers or by other Tibetan scholars. Just as *bde-ba can gyi smon-lam* prayers reflected a zealous devotion and yearning for Amitābha's pure-land, the commentarial tradition drew doctrinal legitimation primarily from the Large and Small *Sukhāvatīvyūha* sūtras. Here we find summaries of the essential points of contemplation and practice arranged in progressive fashion (*lam-rim*), with divisions and subdivisions of the main topics under discussion. In this respect, most Tibetan commentaries on Sukhāvatī are similar to the extent that they systematically prescribe a complete path for Mahāyāna liberation defined in the context of securing birth in Amitābha's pure-land.

The contents of the commentaries reflect their authors' familiarity with a range of Mahāyāna sūtras. From among their many references derived from the sūtras, Dharmākara's nineteenth vow[10] from the Large *Sukhāvatīvyūha-sūtra* (henceforth *Lv*) has been of recurrent importance:

> Subduer, if, when I attain enlightenment, whatever sentient beings may hear my name, directing their minds for the purpose of birth in buddha-fields, in countless and immeasurable buddha-fields, totally dedicating their roots of virtues, and ten (times) generating (this) thought, until they should be born in these buddha-fields, except for sentient beings who commit heinous crimes and who have become obscured by the defilement of abandoning the excellent dharma, may I not awaken to fully manifested, complete, and perfect enlightenment.[11]

Most Tibetan scholars are in agreement about their understanding of one key passage from the *Lv* where four causes are recounted for securing birth in Sukhāvatī. The passage in question, unanimously quoted and known to all Buddhist commentators, is a short excerpt from Śakyamuni's sermon to Ānanda:

> Ānanda, any sentient being who recollects the Tathāgata and his aspects, generates immeasurable roots of virtue, fosters the mind of enlightenment, completely dedicates [his merits for that cause], and prays to be born in the Land [of Bliss], when the time of death nears he will face the Tathagāta, Arhat, perfectly enlightened Amitābha, surrounded by a gathering of monks.[12]

Although authors of the commentarial tradition may differ in what they consider to be among the four most important causes for realizing Sukhāvatī, they all concur that the recitation of aspirational prayers, that is, the cultivation of the wish to take birth in Amitābha's buddha-field, is only one of the causes for attaining his exalted land. Other prerequisites for securing birth in his budda-field include: the remembrance of Amitābha and his qualities (Skt. *buddha-anusmṛti*), that is, visualization of his aspects and those of his pure-land; the accumulation of vast merit; and the dedication of such merit with a mind set on enlightenment.

The recitation of the *Seven-Limb Prayer,* incorporated as part of a Mahāyāna text widely used in Tibetan tantric rituals, the *Bhadracaryā-praṇidhāna-rāja* (*'Phags pa bzang po spyod pa'i smon lam gyi rgyal po;* D: 1095), is in fact sufficient for fulfilling the accumulation of vast roots of merit and meeting the second cause of birth in Amitābha's buddha-field. The well-known *Seven-Limb Prayer* may be summarized in the following four verses:

> May whatever little virtue I have gained
> From prostrating, offering, confessing,
> Rejoicing, requesting, and beseeching,
> Be dedicated so that all may attain perfect enlightenment.[13]

The *Bhadracaryā-praṇidhāna-rāja,* also known as *Samantabhadra's Prayer*, is especially invoked by Tibetan proponents of Sukhāvatī for containing two seminal references to Buddha Amitābha. The first one, quoted in full in the *Anthology of Aspiration Prayers* (DM1), is a prayer to be born in Sukhāvatī and thereafter, receive from Buddha Amitābha the prophetic confirmation of future enlightenment (*lung bstan-pa*):

> In that fine and joyful *maṇḍala* of the Buddhas,
> May I be reborn from an excellent and truly beautiful lotus,
> And the Buddha Amitābha himself foretell my own enlightenment.
>
> After my prediction, with countless emanations and the strength of my mind, may I benefit many beings in all directions.[14]

The second reference recommends that the merit, accrued through the recitation of the *Bhadracaryā-praṇidhāna-rāja*, be dedicated to reaching Amitābha's pure-land:

> Through the boundless excellent merit gained by so dedicating this *Aspiration to Noble Deeds*, may the countless beings, immersed in the torrent of suffering,
> Reach the supreme realm of Amitābha.[15]

In Tibet, the tradition of Sukhāvatī never formulated itself into an exclusive religious or sectarian movement. As compared with East Asia, where the cult of Sukhāvatī became influential for supplying a "monastic and autonomous source of religious authority" (Amstutz 1998: 45), in Tibet, it met with broad acceptance and enthusiasm by the monastic establishments and siddha movements as evidenced by a prolific outburst of indigenous commentarial, devotional, and ritual literature (Halkias 2006). Moreover, the Tibetan fascination with Sukhāvatī extended well into the Vajrayāna tactics of Buddhist soteriology. This is evident in the popular development of the mind-transference technique (*'pho-ba*) that entails a creative visualization of the Land of Bliss, wherein practitioners train to transfer their subtle consciousness utilizing breath and the subliminal energies of their vajra bodies (*rdo-rje lus*). The reason why the Tibetans, though keen to embrace and innovate upon Sukhāvatī rituals, never formulated their understanding into a distinct ritual and soteriological tradition, is perhaps that they inherited a "language of buddha-fields" as part and parcel of a wide doctrinal range of Indo-Mahāyāna teachings, and, while being eclectic in their approach to Buddhism, they did not construct Buddhist orders around Mahāyāna texts in the way the Japanese did.

The Jo-nang-pa Lineage

Faith and devotion in Amitābha's pure-land is not lacking in the writings of one of the sharpest religious thinkers of fourteenth-century Tibet and one of the most controversial Buddhist scholars the tradition has ever known. Versed in a wide range of Buddhist subjects, Dol-po-pa shes-rab rgyal-mtshan (1292-1362), also known as the "Buddha of Dol-po" (*Dol-po sangs-rgyas*), is said to have composed at least 174 treatises (Kapstein 1992: 16). He is best known for his controversial and stunning contributions to the philosophical interpretation of Indian Mahāyāna Buddhism.

As noted by Stearns in his introduction to the life and teachings of Dol-po-pa, "contradictory descriptions of emptiness (Skt. *śūnyatā;* Tib. *stong-pa-nyid*)" in the Indian Mahāyāna scriptures and commentaries culminated in "one of the major sources of tension in the interpretation of late Indian Buddhism as it was received in Tibet" (2001: 1). The concern with these issues "seems to have reached a point of critical mass" in fourteenth-century Tibet as seen in the scholarly contributions of the Third Karma-pa, Rang-'byung rdo-rje (1284-1339), Bu-ston rin-chen (1290-1364),[16] Long-chen rab-'byams (1308-1364), and 'Ba'-ra-ba rgyal-mtshan (1310-1391). Stearns explains that Dol-po-pa sought to reconcile the Yogācāra notion of "an enlightened eternal essence," or buddha-nature (Skt. *tathāgatagarbha; bde bzhin gshegs pa'i snying po*), present in every sentient being, with an earlier Madhyamaka emphasis "on the lack of an enduring essence in sentient beings" to which it stood in "marked contrast" (ibid). Envisioning a Yogācāra-Madhyamaka philosophical synthesis, Dol-po-pa's greatest contribution lies in his reformulation of absolute reality, or "buddha-nature," as gzhan-stong, that is, empty of "other phenomena" but not empty "in itself."

Despite the scriptural polemics launched predominantly by the adherents of the dGe-lugs and Sa-skya orders, with the eventual sealing of Jo-nang-pa scriptures and prohibition of their reproduction during the reign of the Fifth Dalai Lama,[17] the gZhan-stong-pa interpretation found adherents in the Sa-skya, bKa'-brgyud, and rNying-ma schools and was championed by such major Tibetan thinkers as gSer-mdog Paṇ-chen Śākya mchog-ldan (1428–1507), Tāranātha (1575-1634),[18] and 'Ba'-mda' thub-bstan dge-legs rgya-mtsho (1844-1904).[19] In the nineteenth century, it became the philosophical underpinning for the nonsectarian movement founded by 'Jam-mgon kong-sprul (1813-1899). Only the dGe-lugs-pa order rejected the Jo-nang doctrines completely and unanimously, against which Tsong-kha-pa is known to have composed *The Essential Correct Explanation of Intentional and Definitive Meaning (Drang nges legs bshad snying po)*, a later work that expounds his stance on Indian sources written largely as a response to Jo-nang-pa hermeneutics.[20]

Dol-po-pa shes-rab rgyal-mtshan (1292-1362)

Dol-po-pa's birthplace was sPu-mdo in the Dol-po region of modern-day Nepal.[21] Already as a young boy he was versed in the rNying-ma tantras connected with the cult of the Vajrakilāya, and over time he pursued advanced Buddhist studies with the Sa-skya-pa scholars and soon came to master a range of scholastic Buddhist subjects such as the *Prajñāpāramitā* sūtras, the manuals of "logical reasoning" (*pramāṇa*), *Abhidharmakośa*, *Madhyamaka*, *Vinaya*, and so forth (Stearns 2002: 12; Kapstein 1992: 9). The teachings he received from the Sa-skya he would teach throughout the last half of his life to support his controversial ontology of the tathāgatagarbha's unchanging nature. Among them, the *Kālacakratantra* he received from Rong-pa Shes-rab seng-ge (1251-1315) is important, especially for its doctrine of the *ādibuddha* (Ruegg 1963: 4). According to the Jo-nang tradition, he is the sixteenth lineage holder of the gZhan-stong sūtra lineage and the eighteenth holder of the gZhan-stong Kālacakra lineage, and, known to have outwitted many great scholars in debate, he was credited with the title "omniscient." In all, he composed eighteen commentaries on the *Kālacakratantra* while some of his other works include: the *Bodhisattva Trilogy* (*Sems 'grel skor gsum*); the ten *Sūtras on the Buddha-nature* (*Snying po'i mdo*); the five *Sūtras of Definitive Meaning* (*Nges don mdo*); and the five treatises of Maitreya (*Byams chos*) (Stearns 2002: 13-14).

Dol-po-pa traveled to many monasteries in Utsang province, giving teachings, debating, and practising meditation, especially the "perfection stage" (*rdzogs-rim*) of the *Kālacakratantra*, known as the "six-branch yoga" (*sbyor-ba yan-lag drug-pa*), which he considered to be the most efficacious yogic means for the vital "karmic winds" (*las-rlung*) to be drawn into the central channel of the subtle body and thereby to be transformed into the "vital wisdom winds" (*ye-shes-rlung*) that serve as the support for nonconceptual *gnosis* (Stearns 2002: 99-100). During his retreats he is said to have "experienced a number of visions, both of pure lands and specific tantric deities," and that he beheld "the pure land of Shambhala, the source of Kālacakra teachings," while "on another occasion claimed to have gone there by visionary means" (ibid: 28). His personal connection with Sukhāvatī is perhaps revealed in his premonitory words in 1361 when he announced to his senior disciples that he was not going to be bothered with Tibet's cold weather anymore when he would reach Sukhāvatī, where it is warm (ibid: 36). His affinity with Amitābha's field of aspirations is not surprising, for it is recorded that, during "his visit to the monastery of Gsang phu, he also directly beheld the pure land of Sukhāvatī and composed a praise of it" (ibid).[22]

Among his writings on Sukhāvatī, we find: the *Prayer for Birth in Sukhāvatī* (*bDe ba can du skye ba 'dzin pa'i smon lam; gSung-'Bum*, vol. 1, kha, 680-84; DM1: 172-175); the *Praise and Aspiration to the Sukhāvatī Field* (*Kun mkhyen chen po mdzad pa'i bde ba can gyi zhing gi bstod smon;* DM1: 176-181); and a Commentary to the Large *Sukhāvatīvūha-sūtra* entitled *The Expedient Means for Oneself and Others to Attain Birth in Sukhāvatī* (*Rang gzhan bde ba can du skye ba'i thabs mchog ces bya ba bde ba can gyi mdo'i spyi don ba; gSung-'Bum*, vol.

1, kha, 91-103; *'Dzam-thang*, vol. 7: 877-91). Kapstein mentions that Dol-po-pa had "a special interest in the sūtras" and that he composed an "interesting text extracted from the *Adhyāśayasaṃcodana sūtra* concerning the relationship between the tenfold cultivation of *bodhicitta* and the conditions for attaining Sukhāvatī" (2004: 29). As noted in the works of other Tibetan religious exegetes, Dol-po-pa's devotion for Amitābha's pure-land was tempered by his scholastic training in the interpretation of sūtras and their commentaries. His own commentary to the Large *Sukhāvatīvyūha-sūtra* aims at setting the record straight concerning claims that birth to Sukhāvatī may be secured through grace alone. For Dol-po-pa, as for other scholars after him, prayer is necessary, but it is not a sufficient condition for such an accomplishment:

> [that] it is not enough to have prayed, but that one must also have parted far from the (five) deeds bringing immediate retribution and from the rejection of the doctrine, and have engendered the enlightened attitude tenfold—it says thus that (rebirth in Sukhāvatī) will not be achieved by prayer alone. And it is because it exemplifies a temporally displaced intention only inasmuch as the intention is directed to prayer alone (that is to say, prayer is taken as the sole relevant factor, the rebirth in Sukhāvatī may be many lifetimes removed) (ibid: 30).

Both the short *Prayer for Birth in Sukhāvatī* translated here and the somewhat longer *Praise and Aspiration for the Sukhāvatī Field* are evidently inspired by detailed descriptions of the Land of Bliss that abound in the Large *Sukhāvatīvyūha-sūtra*. The *Prayer for Birth in Sukhāvatī* is said to have been composed in accordance with a vision of Sukhāvatī had by Dol-po-pa in the residence of rNgog Lo-tsā-ba in the morning of the fifteenth day of the Saga month of the Tibetan lunar calendar.[23]

A Prayer for Birth in Sukhāvatī, by Dol-po-pa shes-rab rgyal-mtshan

I

Homage to Lokeśvara! I prostrate to the *Unsurpassable Subduer*, the *One who has Passed Beyond*, the *Foe Destroyer*, the *Fully and Perfectly Enlightened Buddha*, the one of boundless life and wisdom called the *King of Majestic Brilliance*.

II

As prophesied by Buddha Amitāyus who grants the siddhi of longevity and immortality for [the benefit of] all those migrating beings inflicted by birth, aging, sickness and death, I too shall say this prayer of aspiration from previous lives: *Whichever beings in this world-system hear my name, may they arrive in my field, without turning back for even a single lifetime*.

III

As written in the *Sukhāvatī-sūtra*, through your unsurpassed power and wish to lead beings, I too shall go for refuge to Buddha Amitāyus. Having discarded my physical body, may I take birth in the Land of Bliss.

IV

Through the power of completing unlimited prayers, whose qualities like strings of beads are praised by all the Buddhas of the ten directions, may I spontaneously arise in Sukhāvatī.

V

May I spontaneously arise in Sukhāvatī, where Amitābha, the *Leader of Men,* dwells, Avalokiteśvara, the powerful one [Vajrapāṇi], and many other countless Buddhas and Bodhisattvas.

VI

May I spontaneously arise in Sukhāvatī, a precious land as smooth as the palms of our hands, encircled by golden lattices and filled with many marvelous lotuses.

VII

May I spontaneously arise in Sukhāvatī, where from the top of each lotus limitless light-rays radiate, emanations of the Buddhas of the ten directions spreading from all places.

VIII

May I spontaneously arise in Sukhāvatī, where trees of all varieties are made of seven precious substances appearing colourful and in good form, delightful to behold, pervaded in all directions by pleasant sounds.

IX

May I spontaneously arise in Sukhāvatī, where many kinds of flocks of birds are manifestations of the Sugata, producing melodious sounds and praises, recalling the Protector of all [beings].

X

May I spontaneously arise in Sukhāvatī, where delightful streams endowed with sweet fragrance sing constant praises of the qualities of the Subduer.

XI

May I spontaneously arise in Sukhāvatī, where gods and humans with golden complexion, attired in beautiful clothes and decked with ornaments, enjoy immeasurable bliss in the practice of the dharma.

XII

May I spontaneously arise in Sukhāvatī, where nourishment, clothing, bedding, medicine, monastic robes, and jewelled mansions manifest the moment one wishes them.

XIII

May I spontaneously arise in Sukhāvatī, where material offerings, such as canopies and banners, and whatever one desires, appear instantly through the power of the aspirations of the Protector.

XIV

May I spontaneously arise in Sukhāvatī, where one attains supernormal powers, such as clairvoyance, clairaudience, retrocognition, and superior intelligence.

XV

May I spontaneously arise in Sukhāvatī and directly discern, at the moment of death, the prophesy granted by ninety-nine million and a thousand rejoicing Buddhas extending their hands in salutation.

XVI

May I spontaneously arise in Sukhāvatī when I and all others are about to die, and Amitābha, the *Leader of Beings* and *King of Dharma*, along with hundreds of ordained monks appear lovingly before me and encircle me.

XVII

Having seen the Protector and his retinue, may there spring to my mind the highest joy, and with no loss of awareness, may I spontaneously arise in Sukhāvatī.

XVIII

May these aspirational prayers be fulfilled through the blessings of Avalokiteśvara, *King of the World*, through powerful prayers to the source of all phenomena, the great force of Amitābha's blessings, the power of whatever merit has been accumulated by all beings, the blessings of the Mahāmudrā of Clear Light, and the blessings of the truth of the Three Jewels. No sooner have I discarded this impure body, may I spontaneously arise in Sukhāvatī, and soon after being born there, may I complete the ten levels and engender emanations in all directions to serve others.

Transliteration of Tibetan Text

[DM1: 172] na mo lo ke sva rā ya / bcom ldan de bzhin gshegs pa dgra bcom pa / yang dag rdzogs pa'i sangs rgyas bla na med / tshe dang ye shes dpag med rnam nges pa / gzi brjid rgyal po'i zhabs la phyag 'tshal lo / skye rga na 'chi'i nyam thag 'gro ba la / 'chi med tshe yi dngos grub stsol mdzad pa / sangs rgyas tshe dpag med pas lung bstan pa / ngas ni sngon tshe smon lam 'di btab po / sems can gang gis nga yi ming thos pa'i / 'jig rten khams na gnas pa'i sems can rnams / de dag nga yi zhing du [173] lhags nas kyang / skye ba gcig la phyir mi ldog par 'gyur / 'dren pa khyod kyi mthu dang smon lam mchog / bde ldan zhing bkod mdo nas gsungs pa bzhin / bdag kyang tshe dpag med la skyabs su mchi / lus 'di bor nas skye ba len par shog / smon lam mtha' yas yongs su rdzogs pa'i mthus / phyogs bcur bzhugs pa'i sangs rgyas thams cad kyis / yon tan bsngags pa'i phreng pa brjod pa'i zhing / bde ba can du rdzus te skye bar shog / rkang gnyis gtso bo 'od dpag med pa dang / spyan ras gzigs dbang mthu chen thob la sogs / sangs rgyas byang sems dpag med bzhugs pa'i zhing / bde ba can du rdzus te skye bar shog/ lag mthil ltar mnyam rin chen sa gzhi ni / thams cad gser gyi dra bas khyab gyur cing / ngo mtshar padma mang pos gang ba'i zhing / bde ba can du rdzus te skye bar shog / padma re re'i rtse mo thams cad las / dpag med 'od 'phro 'od zer thams cad kyis / bde gshegs sprul pa phyogs bcur 'gyed pa'i zhing / bde ba can du rdzus te skye bar shog / ljon shing sna tshogs rin chen bdun las grub / kha dog dbyibs legs mdzes shing blta na sdug / snyan pa'i sgra dbyangs phyogs bcur sgrogs pa'i zhing / bde ba can du rdzus te [174] skye bar shog / bya tshogs rnam mang bde gshegs sprul pa'i bya / sna tshogs skad snyan snyan par sgrog byed cing / kun gyi mgon po rdzes su dran pa'i zhing / bde ba can du rdzus te skye bar shog / chu klung nyams dga' dri mchog rnams dang ldan / rgyal ba'i yon tan dpag med sgra tshogs kun / rtag par rgyun mi 'chad par sgrogs pa'i zhing / bde ba can du rdzus te skye bar shog / gser gi mdog can lha mi thams cad kyang / sna tshogs gos gyon rin chen rgyan gyis spras / dam chos dga' bde dpag med spyod pa'i zhing / bde ba can du rdzus te skye bar shog / zas dang gos dang mal cha sman rnams dang / chos gos lhung bzed rin chen khang pa sogs / yid la bsam ma thag tu 'byung ba'i zhing / bde ba can du rdzus te skye bar shog / gdugs dang rgyal mtshan la sogs mchod pa'i rdzas / yid la bsam ma thag tu ci 'dod kun / mgon po'i smon lam stobs las 'byung ba'i zhing / lha yi mig dang lha yi rna ba dang / tshe rabs dran dang blo gros mkhas mchog sogs / rdzu 'phrul stobs rnams thob par 'gyur ba'i zhing / bde ba can du rdzus te skye bar shog / 'chi ba'i tshe na sangs rgyas bye ba phrag / dgu bcu [175] rtsa dgus mngon sum lung ston cing / sangs rgyas stong gis dgyes pa'i phyag rkyong nas / bde ba can du rdzus te skye bar shog / bdag dang sems can 'chi ba'i dus kyi tshe / 'dren mchog chos kyi rgyal po 'od dpag med / dge slong brgya phrag tshogs kyis yongs bskor nas / brtse bas bdag gi mdun du 'byon gyur cig / mgon po 'khor bcas bdag gis mthong nas kyang / sems la dga' bde dpag med skye ba dang / dran pa ma nyams skad cig de nyid la / bde ba can du rdzus te skye bar shog / 'jig rten dbang phyug rgyal po'i byin rlabs dang / chos kyi 'byung gnas smon lam mthu stobs dang / 'od dpag med pa'i byin rlabs chen po'i mthu / dge ba gang bsags kun gyi nus mthu dang / 'od gsal phyag rgya chen po'i byin rlabs dang / dkon mchog gsum gyi bden pa'i byin rlabs kyis / smon lam 'di dag ji bzhin 'grub par shog / mi gtsang lus 'di bor bar gyur ma thag / bde ba can du rdzus te skye bar shog / skyes ma thag tu sa bcu rab rdzogs te / sprul pas phyogs bcur gzhan don byed par shog / ces pa 'di yang dol po pa shes rab rgyal mtshan dpal bzang pos bkod pa'o.

Endnotes

1. In this context, "orthodox" Buddhism refers to Buddhist lineages that historically trace their religious beginnings to Śākyamuni Buddha as contrasted to "heterodox" lineages whose origins claim to go back to a source other than Śākyamuni, as in the case of the *Purified* and *Awakened* (*sangs-rgyas*) Miwo Sherab of the Tibetan Bon order.

2. Technically speaking, even though we may adopt the term "pure-land," as is commonly the case in English scholarship, in the Sanskrit texts and Tibetan translations Sukhāvatī is clearly referred to as either the field of a buddha (*sangs-rgyas kyi zhing*), or a world-system (*'jig-rten-gyi khams*). This being said, the term "pure-land" (*rnam-dag zhing*) does occur in later Tibetan scholarship, as for example in Tsong-kha-pa's *Praise to the Protector Amitābha: Opening the Door to the Excellent Pure-Lands.* Similarly, in Mi-pham's *Sun-like Instructions of a Sage* we find the term (*zhing-dag-pa*) as well as the occasional laudatory epithets of Sukhāvatī, such as a "Buddha-field of the Noble Ones" (*'phags-pa'i-zhing-khams*) (Halkias 2006: 86-97; 108-127). We should bear in mind that the term "Pure Land Buddhism" was specially coined to embrace historically specific trends in East Asian Buddhism, and, for the purpose of not excluding other pure-land traditions, I have employed Nattier's designation "Buddhism of pure-lands" (2000). A Buddhism of pure-lands serves to reinforce an historical observation, namely, that within a common Mahāyāna soteriology we can speak of scripturally distinct traditions and unique developments of pure-land worship (e.g., Tibetan vs. Japanese) and of other well-known pure-land cults besides Sukhāvatī (e.g., Maitreya's heaven that reached its popular peak in the seventh century in China).

3. East Asian adherents of Amitābha's pure-land promote three sūtras as their fundamental scriptures: the longer and shorter versions of the *Sukhāvatīvyūha-sūtra*, and a later text, whose reconstructed Sanskrit title is *Amitāyurdhyāna,* or *Amitāyurbuddhānusmṛti-sūtra* (Ch. *Kuan-Wu-liang-shou-ching;* Jpn. *Kammuryōju-kyō*). The latter is extant only in one Chinese version attributed to the Central Asian master Kālayaśas (424 CE). For a detailed discussion on the origins, legitimation, and contents of this text, see Fujita's "The Textual Origins of the *Kuan Wu-liang-shou ching:* A Canonical Scripture of Pure Land Buddhism," and "The Kuan-wu-liang-shu Fo-ching: its Origins and Literary Criticism" by Pas.

4. For an old but seminal study on the background and early use of buddha-fields, see Rowell 1935 and 1937.

5. References to the buddha-fields in the *Mahāvastu* can be found in: vol. 2, 9, 276, 283, 298, 299, 302, 304, 318, 326, 342; and in vol. 3, 135, 262, 265, 337, 340; see Jones 1949.

6. Although informative Tibetan encounters with Buddhism prior to the seventh century cannot be ruled out, most sources admit that Srong-btsan-sgam-po's minister, Thon-mi Sambhoṭa, devised the Tibetan script and rendered the first translations of Buddhist texts

into Tibetan (Skilling 1997: 87-89). For evidence of a small, but steady, number of literary transmissions to Tibet beyond the thirteenth century, see Shastri 2002.

7. For a discussion of secular texts in the Tibetan Tripiṭaka, see Roesler 2002; Ruegg 1995: 95-147; Pathak 1974.

8. The *lDan dkar ma* lists the Large *Sukhāvatīvyūha-sūtra* under the title *'Od dpag med kyi bkod pa* and records its size as 3 *bam-po* and 900 *śloka* long. It is found under the section *Mahāyāna Sūtras of the Ratnakūṭa Class* (§III, 29). The *'Phang thang ma* lists it under the name *De bzhin gshegs pa 'Od dpag med kyi zhing gi bkod pa* and records its size as 3 *bam-po* long, listing it under the section *Mahāsūtras by Size* (§IV, 89). The Small *Sukhāvatīvyūha-sūtra* is listed in the *lDan dkar ma* with the title *bDe ba can gyi bkod pa*, 136 *śloka* long, in the section *Miscellaneous Mahāyāna Sūtras Less Than One Bam-po* (§VI, 196). The *'Phang thang ma* records it under the same title and size in the section *Small Sūtras Less Than One Bam-po* (§V, 188). For introductions and text-number references to the *lDan dkar ma* and the *'Phang thang ma,* see Lalou (1953) and Halkias (2004), respectively.

9. The term *bDe-smon* is an abbreviation of "*bde-ba can gyi smon-lam,*" or aspiration prayers dedicated for birth in the Land of Bliss. In the introduction to *Tibetan Literature: Studies in Genre*, Cabezón and Jackson write that "there appears to be no Tibetan term that conveys exactly the sense that 'genre' does in the West. There are, of course, 'typology' words, such as *rigs* ('kind'), *sde* ('class'), or *rnam pa* ('aspect'), but none of these seems to be used consistently to refer to an abstract notion of literary type in the way that 'genre' does. Nevertheless, even in the absence of a specific terminological equivalent for 'genre,' we can infer with some certainty that Tibetans were concerned with issues like those of genre-theorists in the West, simply from the fact that—virtually from the beginning of their literary tradition—they have had to organize the increasingly numerous texts that make up the written corpus. To organize is, by definition, to classify, and to classify requires at least the implicit identification of types, hence of 'genres'" (1996: 20-21). For the sake of our discussion, the *bDe-smon* genre encompasses a distinct genus of religious literature that has as its common theme Sukhāvatī and which reflects a shared aspiration to reach it. Texts of this genre may include dedications, praises, commentaries, Vajrayāna rituals, and methods of attaining Amitābha's pure-land.

10. Dharmākara's vows differ both in number and content as between the various editions of the Large *Sukhāvatīvyūha*—with the Tibetan edition being a relatively late formulation that features forty-nine vows. The Sanskrit text lists forty-seven vows and the Chinese recensions have either twenty-four, thirty-six, or forty-eight vows (Fujita 1996: 16). For a comparative table of the Sanskrit and Chinese (Saṃghavarman) versions of the vows, see Gómez 1996: 264-65. The so-called eighteenth vow, based on the translation attributed to Saṃghavarman, has been doctrinally the most important for the Shin-shū sect in Japan (Nakamura 1987: 205).

11. The Tibetan text reads: *bcom ldan 'das gal te bdag byang chub thob pa'i tshe / sangs rgyas kyi zhing grangs ma mchis pa dpag tu ma mchis pa dag na / sems can gang dag gis bdag gi ming thos nas / sangs rgyas kyi zhing der skye bar bgyi ba'i slad du sems gtong zhing / dge ba'i rtsa ba rnams kyang yongs su bsngo bar bgyid na / mtshams ma mchis par bgyid pa dang / dam pa'i chos spong ba'i sgrib pas bsgribs pa'i sems can rnams ma gtogs par de dag tha na sems bskyed pa'i 'gyur ba bcus sangs rgyas kyi zhing der skye bar ma gyur pa de srid du bdag bla med pa yang dag par rdzogs pa'i byang chub mngon par rdzogs par 'tshang rgya bar mi bgyi'o* (Q: Vol. 22, 3.8.113).

12. The Tibetan text reads: *kun dga' bo sems can gang dag kha cig de bzhin gshegs pa de rnam pas yang dang yang yid la byed pa dang dge ba'i rtsa ba mang po dpag tu med pa bskyed pa dang / byang chub tu sems yongs 'jig rten gyi khams der skye bar smon lam 'debs pa de dag 'chi ba'i dus nye bar gnas pa na / de bzhin gshegs pa dgra bcom pa yang dag par rdzogs pa'i sangs rgyas 'od dpag med dge slong gi tshogs du mas yongs su bsgor zhing mdun gyis bltas nas bzhugs par 'gyur de* (Q: Vol. 22, 5.9.119).

13. The Tibetan text reads: *phyag 'tshal ba dang mchod cing bshags pa dang / rjes su yi rang bskul zhing gsol ba yi / dge ba cung zad bdag gis ci bsags pa / thams cad bdag gis byang chub phyir bsngo'o* (*'Phags pa bzang po spyod pa'i smon lam gyi rgyal po;* 2000: folio 7).

14. The Tibetan text reads: *rgyal ba'i dkyil 'khor bzang zhing dga' ba der / padmo dam pa shin tu mdzes las skyes / snang ba mtha' yas rgyal bas mngon sum du / lung bstan pa yang bdag gis der thob shog / der ni bdag gis lung bstan rab thob nas / sprul ba mang po bye ba phrag brgya yis / blo yi stobs kyi phyogs su rnams su yang / sems can rnams la phan pa mang po bgyis shog* (DM1: 150).

15. The Tibetan text reads: *bzang po spyod pa'i smon lam bsngos pa yis / bsod nams dam pa mtha' yas gang thob des / 'gro ba sdug bsngal chu bor bying ba rnams / 'od dpag med pa'i gnas rab thob par shog* (*'Phags pa bzang po spyod pa'i smon lam gyi rgyal po;* 2000: folio 23).

16. For a discussion of Bu-ston's philosophical stance against Dol-po-pa's views, see Ruegg's detailed introduction and translation of Bu-ston's *mDzes rgyan,* the first Tibetan treatise to deal with a critical study of the canonical texts and the theory of the *tathāgatagarbha* (1973).

17. See Smith (2001: 250) and Kapstein (1997: 462). There have been a series of recent moves by His Holiness the Fourteenth Dalai Lama, to compensate for the calamities of the past. In 1998, he offered his own monastery in Shimla (Takten Phuntsok Ling) to the Jonang order, and in 2002 he visited Phuntsok Ling, imparting the *Jonang Kunga Dolchog* teachings to all the monks and the Shimla community. Evocative stands the prayer he composed for the propagation of the Jonang teachings on November 23, 2001, in Dharamsala at the behest of Khenpo Ngawang Dorje and other Jo-nang followers (Ngawang Dorje 2004). It remains to be seen, if the request of Jo-nang-pas to officially register their tradition with the Tibetan government-in-exile will be approved in the near future.

18. For a list of Jo-nang transmission holders, see Smith (2001: 56). Tāranātha (alias, Kun-dga' snying-po), the last great representative of the Jo-nang order, is well known for his *History of Buddhism in India*. Although in his history he makes no reference to the cult of Amitābha in India, he authored a short aspirational prayer for Sukhāvatī entitled *bDe smon* (DM1: 211-13).

19. According to Kapstein, the rNying-ma/Jo-nang eclectic 'Ba'-mda' dge-legs, played an important role in contemporary Jo-nang-pa monastic education, for he is "one of the three authors whose works form the primary basis for the curriculum, the other two, of course, being Dol-po-pa and Tāranātha" (1997: 463). In his *Collected Works* we find several works on Sukhāvatī, such as: the *bDe ba can gyi rgyu tshogs nyams su len tshul* (Vol. 15, Ba-pa: 3 folios); the *bDe smon bsdus pa* (Vol. 19, Dza-pa: 1 folio); the *bDe ba can gyi smon lam 'dod dgu 'byung ba'i ljon shing zhes pa dang Mtshan ldan bla ma rin po che Ngag dbang chos 'dzin dpal bzang po'i gsol 'debs* (Vol. 19, Dza-pa: 1 folio); and a Sukhāvatī *sādhana* entitled *bDe chen zhing sgrub kyi dmigs rim bde chen lam bzang* (Vol.16, Ma-pa: 16 folios).

20. For a philosophical exposition of the Jo-nang doctrines, see Ruegg 1963; for their critique by the dGe-lugs-pa, see Tauscher 1995. For seminal contributions to the tathāgatagarbha theory by one of the leading experts in the field, see Ruegg 1969, 1973, and 1989.

21. The following biographical information on Dol-po-pa's life and works is primarily drawn from Kapstein 1992 and Stearns 2002.

22. For Stearns, this inspired praise to Sukhāvatī is recorded in the 'Dzam-thang edition and is not found in the *Collected Works* of Dol-po-pa (2002: 189, n. 87). Kapstein locates it in vol. 7: 891-96 (2004: 47, n. 51).

23. The colophon reads: *ces pa 'di ni sa ga zla ba'i tshes bco lnga'i snga dro la zhing khams bde ba can nye bar gzigs nas tshu la ji lta ba bzhin bstod pa ni / chos rdze kun mkhyen jo nang ba chen po shes rab rgyal mtshan dpal bzang po nas rngog lo tsā ba'i gzim khang du mdzad pa'o / 'di la brtson pas phyi ma la bde ba can du skye bar the tshom med do* (DM: 181).

Bibliography

Primary

Abbreviations

D sDe-rge Edition of the Kanjur.
DM1 *bDe smon phyogs bsgrigs.* 1994. Volume 1. Si-khron: mi rigs dpe skrun khang.
Q Peking Edition of the Kanjur.

Other

Dol-po-pa shes-rab rgyal-mtshan. *'Dzam thang Edition of the Collected Works (Gsung-'bum) of Kun mkhyen Dol po pa Shes rab rgyal mtshan.* 1992-1993. Collected and presented by M. Kapstein. Delhi: Shedrub Books.

______. *Kun mkhyen Dol po pa'i gsung 'bum.* 1984. Reproduced from eye-copies of prints from the rGyal-rtse rdzong blocks preserved at Kyi-chu Monastery in Paro, Bhutan. Reprinted in Delhi.

'Phags pa bzang po spyod pa'i smon lam gyi rgyal po. 2000. *Bhadracaryā-praṅidhāna-rāja.* New Zealand: Dhargye Buddhist Centre.

Secondary

Amstutz, G. 1998. "The Politics of Pure Land Buddhism." *Numen*, 45/1: 69-96.

Cabezón, J. and R. Jackson 1996. *Tibetan Literature: Studies in Genre.* Ithaca: Snow Lion Publications.

Dargyay, E. K. 1991. "Sangha and State in Imperial Tibet." In *Tibetan History and Language: Studies Dedicated to Uray Géza on his Seventieth Birthday*, ed. E. Steinkellner. Wien: Universität Wien, 111-129.

Ducor, J. 1988. *Le Sûtra d'Amida prêché par le Buddha.* Schweizer Asiatische Studien/Études asiatiques suisses, monograph, vol. 29. Bern: Peter Lang.

Fujita, K. 1996. "Pure Land Buddhism in India." Translated by Taitetsu Unno. In *The Pure Land Tradition: History and Development*, ed. J. Foard et al. University of California, Berkeley: Institute of Buddhist Studies, 2-41.

______. 1990. "The Textual Origins of the *Kuan Wu-liang-shou ching:* A Canonical Scripture of Pure Land Buddhism." In *Chinese Buddhist Apocrypha,* ed. R. E. Buswell. Hawaii: University of Hawaii Press, 149-173.

Gómez, L. 1996. *The Land of Bliss: The Paradise of the Buddha of Measureless Light.* Hawaii: University of Hawaii Press.

Halkias, T. G. 2006. "Transferring to the Land of Bliss: Among Sukhāvatī Texts and Practices." D.Phil. Thesis. University of Oxford.

______. 2004. "Tibetan Buddhism Registered: An Imperial Catalogue from the Palace Temple of 'Phang-thang." *Eastern Buddhist,* 36, 1 and 2: 46-105.

Jones, J. 1949. *The Mahāvastu.* Vols. 1-3. London: Luzac and Company.

Kapstein, Matthew. 2004. "Pure Land Buddhism in Tibet? From Sukhāvatī to the Field of Great Bliss." In *Approaching the Land of Bliss: Religious Praxis in the Cult of Amitābha,* ed. R. Payne and K. Tanaka. Honolulu: University of Hawaii Press, 1-16.

______. 1997. "From Kun-mkhyen Dol-po-pa to 'Ba'-mda' Dge-legs: Three Jo-nang-pa Masters on the Interpretation of the Prajñāpāramitā." *Proceedings of the Seventhth Seminar of the International Association for Tibetan Studies*, Graz 1995, ed. E. Steinkellner et al. Wien: Verlag der Österreichischen Akademie dern Wissenschaften, 457-475.

______. 1992. Introduction to *The 'Dzam-Thang edition of the Collected Works of Kun-mkhyen Dol-po-pa shes-rab rgyal-mtshan*. Delhi: Shedrub Books.

Kloetzli, R. 1983. *Buddhist Cosmology: Science and Theology in the Images of Motion and Light.* Delhi: Motilal Banarsidass.

Lalou, M. 1953. "Les textes bouddhiques au temps du roi Khri-sroṅ-lde-bcan. Contribution à la bibliographie du Kanjur et du Tanjur." *Journal Asiatique*, 241: 313-353.

Muge Samten. 2005. *A History of Traditional Fields of Learning* (*Bod du rig gnas tshul mdor bsdus bshad pa*). Trans. Sangye Tandar Naga. Dharamsala: Library of Tibetan Works and Archives.

Nakamura, H. 1987. *Indian Buddhism: A Survey with Bibliographical Notes*. Delhi: Motilal Banarsidass.

Nattier, J. 2000. "The Realm of Akṣobhya: A Missing Piece in the History of Pure Land Buddhism." *Journal of the International Association of Buddhist Studies*, 23/1: 71-103.

Ngawang Dorje. 2004. *Jo nang rdzogs ldan smon lam lam chen mo 'dzam gling phan bde'i gru char*. New York: Dorje Ling Buddhist Center.

Pathak, S. K. 1974. *The Indian Nītiśāstras in Tibet*. Delhi: Motilal Banarsidass.

Pas, J. 1977. "The Kuan-wu-liang-shu Fo-ching: its Origins and Literary Criticism." In *Buddhist Thought and Asian Civilization*, ed. L. Kawamura and K. Scott. California: Dharma Publishing, 182-194.

Roesler, U. 2002. "The Great Indian Epics in the Version of Dmar ston Chos kyi rgyal po." In *Religion and Secular Culture in Tibet, Proceedings of the Ninth Seminar of the International Association of Tibetan Studies*, ed. H. Blezer. Leiden: Brill, 431-451.

Rowell, T. 1935. "The background and early use of the Buddha-Kṣetra concept, chapters 2-3." *Eastern Buddhist,* 6/4: 379-431.

______. 1937. "The background and early use of the Buddha-Kṣetra concept, chapter 4." *Eastern Buddhist,* 7/2: 132-176.

Ruegg, D. S. 1995. *Ordre Spirituel et Ordre Temporel Dans la Pensée Bouddhique de l'Inde et du Tibet.* Paris: Collège de France.

______. 1989. *Buddha-nature, Mind and the Problem of Gradualism in a Comparative Perspective: On the Transmission and Reception of Buddhism in India and Tibet.* London: School of Oriental and African Studies.

______. 1973. "La Traité du Tathāgatagarbha de Bu ston Rin chen grub. Traduction du *De bžin gśegs pa'i sñin po gsal źin mdzes par byed pa'i rgyan.*" Paris: *Publications de l'École Française d'Extrême-Orient,* vol. 88: 12 -162.

______. 1969. "La Théorie du *Tathāgatagarbha* et du *Gotra*. Études sur la Sotériologie et la Gnoséologie du Bouddhisme." Paris: *Publications de l'École Française d'Extrême-Orient,* vol. 70: 531.

______. 1963. "The Jo naṅ pas: A School of Buddhist Ontologists according to the Grub mtha' śel gyi me loṅ." *Journal of the American Oriental Society* 83: 73–91.

Shastri Lobsang 2002. "Activities of Indian paṇḍitas in Tibet from the 14th to the 17th century." In *Tibet, Past and Present, Proceedings of the Ninth Seminar of the International Association for Tibetan Studies,* eds. H. Blezer and A. Zadoks. Leiden: Brill, 129-146.

Skilling, P. 1997. "From bKa' bstan bcos to bKa' 'gyur and bsTan 'gyur." In *Transmission of the Tibetan Canon*, ed. H. Eimer. Wien: Österreichische Akademie Der Wissenschaften, 87-111.

Smith, G. 2001. *Among Tibetan Texts: History and Literature of the Himalayan Plateau.* Boston: Wisdom Publications.

Stearns, C. 2002. *The Buddha from Dolpo: A Study of the Life and Thought of the Tibetan Master Dolpopa Sherab Gyaltsen.* 1999. Reprint. Delhi: Motilal Banarsidass.

Tauscher, H. 1995. *Die Lehre von den Zwei Wirklichkeiten in Tsoṅ kha pas Madhyamaka-Werken.* Wiener Studien zur Tibetologie und Buddhismiskunde 36. Vienna: Universität Wien.

–15–

Medicine and Astrology in the Healing Arts of the *Kālacakratantra*

Vesna A. Wallace

The Kālacakra tantric system concerns itself with the ways in which the nature, structure, and functioning of celestial bodies correlate with and influence the human body. The *Kālacakratantra*'s elaborate system of correspondences between the individual and the cosmos is based on several fundamental postulates which one cannot ignore when addressing the issue of the convergence of astro-science and medicine in Indian esoteric Buddhism. Its first fundamental premise is that the individual and the cosmos are of the nature of time. The second one is that the cosmos and the individual are equally supported by karmic winds and composed of the same atomic particles that make up the elements of earth, fire, water, wind, space, and gnosis. These two primary postulates elucidate the ways in which the Kālacakra tradition understands how the configurations and events in the celestial sphere influence human psychophysiology.

The Concept of Science in the *Kālacakratantra*

A textual study of the *Kālacakratantra* reveals that when Brahmanic formal education in eleventh-century India was exclusively theological and disdainful of technical knowledge,[1] north-Indian Buddhist monastic education incorporated training in nontheological skills that required knowledge of medicine, alchemy, mathematics, artisanship, and even weaponry.[2] The sharp split between theological and scientific education, which impaired the Brahmanic educational system of that time, was absent in Buddhist monastic education due to the prevailing Buddhist tantric view that theological knowledge and technical and scientific learning are not only compatible but also complementary.[3] The *Kālacakratantra* with its diverse and well-integrated topics best attests to that fact.

The topics of the *Kālacakratantra's* first two chapters—called respectively "The Universe" and "The Individual"—directly pertain to the investigation of the universe as macrocosm and individual as its microcosm. The *Kālacakratantra's* inquiry into the nature of the external world and the individual as two facets of conventional reality—the external (*bāhya*) and internal (*adhyātma*)—utilizes the knowledge of the various branches of Buddhist science. Disciplines analogous to cosmology, astronomy, astrometry, chronometry, embryology, physiology, psychophysiology, anatomy, medical therapeutics, pharmacology, alchemy, botany, psychology, and philosophy are either directly or indirectly incorporated into the first two chapters of the *Kālacakratantra.* For tantric Buddhist adepts, those diverse scientific disciplines provide a systematic analysis of the natural world, conventionally viewed as an object of purification, and humans' place and interactions in that world. Thorough understanding of the structures and functions of conventional reality is considered to be indispensable for the realization of ultimate reality (*paramārtha-satya*) which is Buddhahood. On the basis of the analysis of the *Kālacakratantra,* one may infer that there are two main reasons for that. First, conventional reality marks a starting point from which a tantric adept ventures into tantric practices; and secondly, a thorough knowledge of the ways in which conventional reality operates induces the insight into the nature of conventional reality, which is not fundamentally different from the nature of ultimate reality. The *Kalacakratantra's* identification of conventional reality with the ultimate is related to the ontological views of emptiness (*śūnyatā)* of the Madhyamikas, who equate emptiness with the ultimate nature of dependent origination *(pratītyasamutpāda*).

Since the time of Śākyamuni, Buddhists' investigation of the world has been based on their understanding of nature as a causal system governed by discernible causal laws. This same theoretical basis of investigation also permeates the discussions of the universe and the individual in the first two chapters of the *Kālacakratantra.* Analysis of those chapters indicates that the primary goal of the tantric Buddhist investigation of the natural world is to discover the causal factors operating within the universe as macrocosm and within the individual as microcosm. The secondary goal is to demonstrate the correspondence of the universe to the individual by identifying the properties of the external physical universe in the body of the individual.[4] This goal reflects the *Kālacakratantra*'s intent that its very presentation of the Buddhist scientific truths be nondual, that is, without drawing an absolute distinction between the subject and object. The tertiary objective of the Buddhist tantric scientific investigation is to ascertain the properties of the universe and the individual as the mere appearances invoked by the power of the individuals' karmic imprints. Finally, the ultimate aim is to see things as they are *(yathā-bhūta)* by means of acquiring direct knowledge of the nature of reality. Seeing things as they are means perceiving the illusory nature of conventional reality and realizing the nonduality of conventional and ultimate realities. The nature of this nonduality is that conventional reality, although manifesting as the physical world, has the form of emptiness *(śūnyatā-rūpinī),* and emptiness has the form of conventional reality *(saṃvṛti-rūpinī).*[5]

The realization of the fundamental nonduality of the conventional and ultimate realities and the contemplative path to that realization are the chief topics of the other three chapters of the *Kālacakratantra,* called, respectively, "The Initiations," "Sadhana," and "Primordial Wisdom." A careful analysis of those three chapters indicates that the Buddhist Tantric contemplative path of actualizing Buddhahood is structured on two theoretical grounds. One is a theory that the universe is contained within the body of the individual as demonstrated by the diverse disciplines of Buddhist natural sciences; and the second theoretical ground is that the natural world as we experience it and explain it through scientific analysis is already nirvāṇa but needs to be recognized as such.

Thus, in the context of Buddhist tantric soteriology, the proper understanding of the conventional world that is the object of purification, the genuine practice of the Buddhist tantric path that is the means of purification, and the authentic actualization of Buddhahood that is the result of purification, are directly contingent upon adequate knowledge of the Buddhist natural and social sciences.

The concept of science in the *Kālacakratantra* is indicated by the Sanskrit word *vidyā,* also meaning "knowledge." Already in some of the early Buddhist expositions on vidyā, the term signifies more than knowledge regarding the Four Noble Truths. In the *Nettipakaraṇa,*[6] the definition of vidyā includes such concepts as investigation *(vicaya),* scrutiny or observation *(upaparikkhā),* and correct views or theories (*sammādiṭṭhi).* Thus, from early times, Indian Buddhists have recognized the relevance of rational and empirical methods in their studies of the natural world and human thought and relations. However, just as the Western concepts of religion and philosophy do not clearly apply to Buddhism as a whole, so the Western concept of science *does not directly correspond* to the phenomenon of Buddhist science. There are several critical reasons for that. Namely, Buddhist science is characterized by widely known and used contemplative and introspective methods[7] of scientific investigation, its application of extrasensory perception as one of the means of scientific verification, the difficulty of demonstrating the knowledge acquired by contemplative means, and by its goal of progress towards, not unprecedented knowledge, but knowledge previously acquired by Buddha Śākyamuni and other Buddhist contemplatives. Nevertheless, I feel that the term *science* is justified here for several reasons. First, in Buddhist science there are working hypotheses that are tested by means of experience and are capable, in principle, of being refuted experientially. Moreover, the conclusions drawn from experience are formulated as rational theories that are internally consistent and make intelligible a wide range of phenomena.

A careful study of the *Kālacakratantra* reveals that the scope of science in tantric Buddhism includes not only a wide range of natural sciences but cognitive sciences as well. Those diverse branches of Buddhist science present systematized knowledge of the nature and composition of the natural world and of humans' place and interactions in that world. Adequate knowledge of the Buddhist scientific disciplines and their practical application in an integrated form on the tantric Buddhist path are viewed as highly relevant for one's spiritual maturation and liberation. For that reason, that knowledge and its practical application should be acquired and cultivated by the *Kālacakratantra's* adepts for the sake of liberation and also for the sake of temporary well-being. Thus, within the Kālacakra system, all of the aspects of the natural world become legitimate fields of Buddhists' scientific investigation, and knowledge of them becomes a significant component of the Buddhist dharma as the body of verifiable truths.[8]

The *Kālacakratantra* also demonstrates the ways in which the natural sciences become integrated with cognitive and social sciences on that Buddhist tantric path. Disciplines that are presently classified as history, philosophy, fine arts, and psychology are presented in the *Kālacakratantra* alongside astronomy, cosmology, physics, medicine, biology, pharmaceutics, and alchemy (or chemistry) and are jointly utilized in the varied modes of the *Kālacakratantra* practice. The integration of different sciences on this Buddhist tantric path is facilitated by the earlier-mentioned tantric view of the nonduality of the individual and the individual's environment. That particular view implies that all psychophysiological processes of the individual correspond to the physical and socio-historical processes occurring in the individual's environment. For example, the passage of days, seasons, and years corresponds to the passage of prāṇas in the human body; and the individual's spiritual battle with his or her own mental distortions has its external aspect in the religious war of Kalkī with the King of Barbarians in the land of Mecca, and so forth.[9] Thus, one may say that in tantric Buddhism, the content of the Buddhist natural sciences becomes analogous to the content of contemporary cognitive sciences.

In all of the above-mentioned disciplines of Buddhist tantric science, the verification of the Buddhist scientific truths appears to be based on the following four means: namely, sensory perceptions, mental perceptions, extrasensory perceptions, and inference. Since the earliest times, extrasensory perceptions have been regarded in the Buddhist tradition as valid means of scientific verification. In its last two chapters, the *Kālacakratantra* presents rational psychological and physiological conditions for bringing about extrasensory perceptions. The verification of Buddhist scientific truths concerning the relative nature of the world, as expressed in natural causal laws, is based on all the aforementioned means of verification. Correspondingly, knowledge of relative scientific truths is viewed in this tantric system as perceptual and conceptual and as a provisional knowledge of the world as it appears to the dualistic, biased mind. The verification of absolute scientific truth regarding the ultimate nature of the world, as expressed in emptiness (*śūnyatā*), is presented as a form of nondualistic contemplative perception. Knowledge of absolute truth, however, is described as the nonconceptual *(avikalpita),* unmediated knowledge of all things in which the distinction between the perceiver and the perceived no longer appears.[10]

An important common feature of the aforementioned disciplines of Buddhist tantric science is their individual syncretism that permeates their theories and modes of their practical application. The syncretistic nature of Buddhist tantric science, as evidenced in the *Kālacakratantra,* stems from the Buddhist tantric view of the commonality of the Buddhists' and heterodox groups' *(tīrthika)* teachings concerning the conventionally existent phenomena. The *Kālacakratantra* contends that there is no distinction between the Buddhists and heterodox groups with regard to the manner in which conventional reality appears. That view of the commonality of the Buddhists' and heterodox groups' approaches to conventional reality justified the Buddhist tantric incorporation of specific ideas from other Indian religious and scientific systems[11] and resulted in the syncretism of Buddhist tantric science. By amalgamating the ideas characteristic of non-Buddhist systems into its own theoretical framework, the *Kālacakratantra* attempts to accomplish two objectives: namely, to facilitate its modeling of conventional reality and to convert heterodox groups. In this way, the Buddhist tantric proselytizing efforts significantly contributed to the complex nature of most of the Buddhist tantric scientific disciplines.

However, the syncretism of Buddhist tantric medicine appears less related to those efforts. It stems chiefly from the Buddhist tantric distinctive emphasis on the favorable effects of physical health on one's spiritual development.

The Characteristics of Buddhist Tantric Medicine in the *Kālacakratantra*

On the grounds that the achievements of supernormal abilities and liberation are contingent upon proper bodily functioning, the preservation of one's health is given great importance in the *Kālacakratantra.* Since its earliest stages, the Buddhist tradition has been concerned with medical knowledge and its practical application as supplementary systems of Buddhist learning and religious practice. The favorable effects of physical health on one's spiritual development are already indicated in the earliest Buddhist Pāli literature. As recorded in the *Majjhimanikaya,*[12] Buddha Śākyamuni himself saw health as the individual's finest possession and pointed out the difficulty of reaching enlightenment with an impaired body. For that reason, understanding of the human body and knowledge of maintaining and restoring health have been given soteriological significance in all of Indian Buddhism. However, it is within the context of tantric Buddhism that the preservation of one's health becomes of paramount importance. The *Kālacakratantra*[13] mentions an explicit reason for that, namely, that without health or a body, it is impossible to achieve mundane and supramundane *siddhis.* Consequently, in the *Kālacakratantra* and in other Highest Yoga Tantras *(anuttara yoga-tantra)* as well, Buddhist medicine has been regarded as a major facet of Buddhist Dharma.

The earliest records of Buddhist theoretical and practical approaches to medicine are already found in the Pāli *Tipiṭaka.* Those records reveal that the early Buddhists' understanding of human anatomy and physiology was generally in accord with that of classical Āyurveda, whose basic contents were already formed and well known throughout the Indian subcontinent. The early Buddhist *materia medica* was also similar to that of the Āyurveda. Nevertheless, in the early Buddhist records, the knowledge of illnesses and medicinal substances is frequently presented in a less systematic manner and on a more popular level than in the later Āyurvedic texts and later Buddhist medical treatises. Also, the Āyurvedic concept of vital energies (*prāṇa*) as a support of life is only mentioned in the Buddhist Pāli Canon and is not yet developed and medically utilized as it is in the *Kālacakratantra.*

By the time of Mahāyāna Buddhism in India, a rational system of classical Āyurvedic medicine was in general use among the Buddhists, and it strongly influenced the scientific framework of later Buddhist medicine.[14] Several medical treatises, such as *Yogaśataka,*[15] *Jīvasūtra, Avabheśśajakalpa, Āryarājanāmavaṭikā,* and *Āryamūlakoṣamahauṣadhāvalī,*[16] which the Buddhist tradition ascribes to Nāgārjuna, contain systematized knowledge concerning selected collections of medicinal formulas, discussions of physiological aspects of diseases, and medical treatments that are concordant with Āyurveda.

Moreover, the disciplines of alchemy and magic developed alongside the traditional and empirico-rational system of Buddhist medicine. According to a tradition no later than the seventh century CE, those disciplines were already in practice by the time of Nāgārjuna. Nāgārjuna is mentioned by Hsüan-tsang as an accomplished alchemist; and the *Rasaratnākara* and the *Kakṣapuṭa*[17] have been traditionally attributed to Nāgārjuna as his writings on alchemy and magic, respectively. The Mahāyāna Buddhist tradition considered Āyurvedic medicine, alchemy, and magic as separate but complementary branches of knowledge. It resorted to alchemical preparations, recitation of mantras, and drawing of maṇḍalas as supplementary methods of healing.

However, Buddhist tantric medical treatises as well as the *Kālacakratantra* integrate classical Āyurvedic medicine, alchemy, and magic even more strongly into a unique and comprehensive system of Buddhist tantric medicine. The broad scope of the tantric medical system, evidenced in the *Kālacakratantra,* also encompasses knowledge of preparing incenses and perfumes used for worshipping buddhas and bodhisattvas during healing rites. The *Vimalaprabhā* commentary[18] on the *Kālacakratantra* indicates that the *Kālacakratantra's* instructions on preparing incenses and perfumes are based on information contained in the specialized treatises on the preparation of perfumes and incenses *(gandha-śāstra).* Thus, the manuals on preparing perfumes and incenses form a significant supplementary branch of Buddhist tantric medical literature.

As in the earlier Buddhist medical systems, so in Buddhist tantric medicine one may find distinctions between magico-religious treatments and rational therapeutics based on induction from observation.

In Buddhist tantric medicine, the determination of a medical treatment is frequently contingent upon determining the nature of a disease. Illnesses induced by malevolent spirits (*bhūta*), also known as nonhuman diseases, and snakebites are commonly treated by means of religious healing rites and incantations.[19] Incantations are also implemented as the protective, or preventive, methods of counteracting the evil intentions of nonhuman entities.[20] The *Kālacakratantra*[21] mentions diverse types of evil spirits and malicious siddhas who are to be appeased with the building of a specific maṇḍala outside the village, or under the tree, in a cemetery, in a temple, or at the confluence of rivers, with offerings of delicacies, incenses, perfumes, flowers, candles, praises, and invocations (*mantra*). The yakṣas, grahas, rākṣasas, piśācas, śakinīs, evil nāgas who delight in human blood, ḍakinīs, rūpikās, vampire-ghouls feeding in cemeteries *(kumbhāṇḍa),* protectors of fields *(kṣetrapāla),* gaṇapatis, hungry ghosts *(preta),* goblins, the lords of ḍakinīs who are accompanied by epilepsy, and siddhas are all considered to be powerful entities that may cause both illnesses and supreme well-being. Therefore, the worship of them is seen as indispensable for the patient's safe recovery. However, the *Kālacakratantra*[22] warns against the pacification of malevolent spirits when symptoms of irrevocable death appear,[23] and it gives two reasons for this caution. The first is that religious healing rites are ineffective in such a case; and the second reason is that this situation may create temptation for the tantric healer to perform the rites simply for the sake of his own material gain, while knowing that they will be of no benefit to the patient.

Tantric healing rites also entail the drawing of yantras, the initiation of a patient in the maṇḍala, and ablutions. For example, the yantra consisting of thirty-four numbers that are placed in their respective sections within the yantra is to be shown to a pregnant woman when her womb stiffens at the time of childbirth.[24] Those afflicted by grahas are to be bathed with five ambrosias *(amṛta),* namely, water, milk, sour milk, ghee, honey, molasses, and fragrant water that are contained within the seven unbaked vessels.[25]

At times, certain herbal medications, empowered by mantras, are administered to those possessed by malevolent spirits in order to alleviate the symptoms of afflictions. For instance, in the case of a pregnant woman's sharp uterine pains caused by malevolent entities, the pregnant woman is to be given pounded *kuṣṭha, uśīra*[26]*, kaseru* grass, *tagara,*[27] blue water-lily *(keśara),* and a filament of a lotus with cold water, after they have been consecrated by mantras and vajras.[28]

Thus, the boundaries between magico-religious and empirico-rational treatments become far less noticeable in Buddhist tantric medicine than in its precedents. For instance, in tantric rites of healing the afflictions caused by nonhuman entities, the magico-religious and empiricio-rational approaches clearly concur. The empirico-rational approach involves the diagnosis of a disease based upon the observation of its symptoms and the occasions for their occurrence; it establishes the causes of affliction, and determines the treatment according to those causes. For example, symptoms such as a convulsion of the body, sharp pains in the eyes, the face, arms, and legs becoming yellow, the color of urine being distinctively yellow, fever, vomiting, emaciation, and possible fainting are described as the symptoms characteristic of the children's disease caused by the possession of cruel spirits and treatable by a ritual oblation of the child in the maṇḍala.[29] In this way, the empirico-rational approach essentially underlies the magico-religious healing rites.

Furthermore, the treatments of other ailments provoked by the disequilibrium of the three humors—namely, wind *(vāta),* bile *(pitta),* and phlegm *(kapha)*—or by external actions, poor hygiene, inadequate diet, and other factors predominantly follow an empirico-rational approach. For example, the application of slightly warmed *akṣobhya* in the mouth is administered in the case of the infection of the mouth; the anointing of the neck with *karkoṭī,*[30] *lāṅgalī,*[31] and *indrī*[32] is applied in the case of the inflammation of the glands of the neck, and so forth.[33] Nevertheless, meditation, visualization of tantric deities, and the recitation of mantras, which are the common healing factors in magico-religious healing rituals, often accompany the administering of medicaments in empirico-rational therapeutics. For example, in the case of the malignant boils in the throat, one abiding in *samādhi* should annihilate strong pains in the following way: together with *prāṇayāma* one visualizes in the heart-cakra Viśvamātā as having the appearance of the stainless moon, with the hands in the wish-granting posture holding a lotus, situated on the lotus-seat in the *vajra* posture, and having one face and two arms.[34]

Tantric medicinal mantras that are mentioned in the *Kālacakratantra* can be classified into three main categories: protective mantras, supplicatory mantras such as *"oṃ phre* Viśvamātā, eliminate, eliminate vajra-like sharp and stringent pains, bring on my forbearance, bring on *svāhā,"*[35] and consecratory mantras such as *"oṃ āḥ huṃ* take away, take away pains in the womb of such and such a person *svāhā."*[36] In many instances, one mantra can perform more than one function. For example, in treatments of malignant diseases accompanied by fever and pain in the joints, the mantra *oṃ phre vajra* simultaneously empowers medicinal herbal ingredients and protects the patient's bodily cakras.[37]

Thus, a recitation of protective and supplicatory mantras that induce a physiological change by directly influencing the patient's prāṇas can be regarded as an empirico-rational treatment. The *Kālacakratantra's* definition of prāṇa as the deity of mantra[38] and its view of the individual's *vajras,* or capacities, of body, speech, mind, and primordial wisdom as the source *(yoni)* of mantras[39] indicate a close and reciprocal influence between the mantras and the individual's mind and body. In light of this view, one may infer that in the context of Buddhist tantric medicine, a recitation of mantra can be utilized as a medicinal treatment of both the mind[40] and the body.

As its rational methods of cure, Buddhist tantric medicine utilizes the techniques of haṭha-*yoga,* particularly the practices of *prāṇayāma* and different yogic postures (*āsana*). For instance, in the *Kālacakratantra,* the vajra posture *(vajrāsana)*[41] is recommended for the elimination of backache, the head-stand posture *(śīrṣāsana)* for the cure of a disease induced by a disorder of phlegm, and the vase technique *(kumbhaka)* of prāṇayāma is recommended for the alleviation of abdominal ailments, leprosy, etc. In case of leprosy,[42] the patient is advised to practice the vase technique of prāṇayāma for a period of six months, during which the patient should not emit semen while having sexual intercourse. The *Kālacakratantra*[43] also cautions that one should practice prāṇayāma only until heat in the heart or pain in the head occurs. If one continues to practice prāṇayāma after those symptoms occur, prāṇa reaches congealment in the navel-cakra, or if unrestrained, it causes death by violently splitting the crown cakra and leaving the body.

Sometimes, especially in the cases of the malignant diseases, prāṇayāma is recommended as a therapy alternative to the application of medicaments. It is chiefly recommended to the experienced Buddhist tantric yogis who are capable of developing deep concentration *(samādhi)* and who do not always have access to appropriate medication. For instance, to yogis suffering from the malignant disease of the throat[44] which is accompanied by fever, pains in the joints of the arms and legs, and headache, the following practice of prāṇayāma is recommended: having entered a house that has no windows, a yogi should let his arms hang down towards the feet, that is, as far as the thighs, and should practice the vase *(kumbhaka)* technique of prāṇayāma for as long as he does not fall on the ground and for as long as his fever does not drop down.[45]

The most prevalent empirico-rational therapeutics of Buddhist tantric medicine encountered in the *Kālacakratantra* are dietary therapy, hydrotherapy, treatments carried out by means of nasal inhalation and oral consumption of drugs, fumigation, and anointing. For example, anything bitter, when combined with three myrobalans *(kaṭuka),*[46] obliterates a disorder of phlegm, therefore goat's milk combined with the three myrobalans is recommended to those suffering from a phlegm-disorder. Sweet and astringent substances eliminate a disorder of bile, hence buffalo-cow's milk is administered to those suffering from such a disorder. Camel's milk is administered to those suffering from a disorder of wind, because camel's milk, when combined with rock salt *(saindhava),* becomes an alkaline fluid *(kṣārāmbu)* that removes a wind-disorder. A nasal inhalation of the *akṣobhya* plant or a nasal inhalation of water in the morning is prescribed as a cure for headache.[47] In the case of boils, pustules, etc., fumigation with ghee and sea-salt that are wrapped in a cloth and anointing with the sap of *arka*[48] are suggested as an effective therapy.[49] In the case of the infections of the ear and eye, the application of warm urine in the ear and of cold urine in the eye is recommended. In the case of sunstroke, the oral ingestion of a decoction containing the equal portion of *dhātrī,* coriander, and powder of tamarind leaves for three nights is recommended as an effective cure.

Those types of empirico-rational treatments best illustrate the classical Āyurvedic and early Buddhist medical heritage in Buddhist tantric medicine. Its materia medica is also similar to that of Āyurveda and early Buddhist medicine. In addition to herbal and other remedial substances well known from Āyurveda and earlier Buddhist medical treatises, the *Kālacakratantra* mentions medicinal substances that are not specified in Āyurvedic texts nor in earlier Buddhist medical works. It is possible, however, that those medicinal substances are known in Āyurvedic and earlier Buddhist texts by different names, since the *Kālacakratantra* occasionally designates the medicinal herbs by their regional folk names, such as "lion's urine" (*siṃhamūtra*), "son's hair" *(putrakeśa),*[50] etc., instead of by their generally accepted names.

Indian tantric Buddhists, concerned with the preservation of the body, expanded the already existent science of rejuvenation and longevity and structured it as an additional branch of Buddhist tantric medicine. On the grounds that Buddhist monastic schools of the eleventh-century India attracted the scholars from other countries such as China, Persia, and so forth, one may suspect that tantric Buddhist methods of rejuvenation were influenced to some degree by the Taoists' methods of the prolongation of life. Tantric Buddhists composed numerous tantric works dealing exclusively with the diverse methods of rejuvenation and prolongation of life, which involve the arts of extracting rejuvenating essences and the knowledge of performing rituals ensuring long life.[51] In its exposition of Buddhist tantric medicine, the *Kālacakratantra* indicates the following individual methods of rejuvenation: the meditation *(dhyāna)* that involves the bringing of prāṇas into the middle channel *(madhyamā),* the practices of prāṇayāma, the ingestion of the five combined ambrosias *(amṛta),*[52] the ingestion of life-giving essences extracted from herbs and foods, and the ingestion of elixirs produced by means of complex alchemical processes. For example, the vase technique *(kumbhaka)* of prāṇayāma accompanied by the retaining of regenerative fluids in sexual union, which was mentioned earlier with regard to the elimination of leprosy, is also seen as having a rejuvenating efficacy. It is said that if practiced for two years, it eradicates old age and all of its symptoms. Also, the nasal inhalation of menstrual blood and the honey of black bees *(keśarājikā),* accompanied with meditation, is suggested as a six-month therapy of rejuvenation.

The *Kālacakratantra* also discusses the intricate procedures of preparing tonics, elixirs, and gold, also called external elixirs *(bāhyarasāyana)* and regarded by Buddhist tantric tradition as nutrients inducing the attainment of a divine body *(divya-deha)* free of wrinkles and gray hair.

Thus, with respect to the Buddhist tantric therapeutics, one may draw the following conclusions. Buddhist tantric therapeutics establishes four aims, namely, to prevent and cure disease, to secure longevity, and to bring forth liberation. The first three goals are of a temporal nature. They are not mere ends in themselves, but ancillary to the actualization of the ultimate goal which is enlightenment. In order to actualize its goals, Buddhist tantric therapeutics utilizes the syncretized knowledge and practices of Tantric yoga, *haṭha yoga,* Āyurveda, folk medicine, religious esoteric rites of healing and exorcism, the science of distillation, and alchemy in its distinctive Buddhist tantric medical theory and practice. Thus, the immediate objective of the syncretism of the Buddhist tantric medicine is to utilize all available medical knowledge and to provide all possible means of cure and disease-prevention in order to facilitate one's liberation. However, the syncretism of the Buddhist tantric medicine should not be understood as a *reconciliation* of disparate views and practices but rather as their *synthesis.* The *Kālacakratantra* does not attempt to reinterpret diverse medical theories and practices, it pragmatically juxtaposes them.

The *Kālacakratantra's* medical therapeutics rest on several theoretical grounds that are characteristic of Buddhist tantric medicine as a whole. The primary theoretical basis of *Kālacakratantra* medicine is tantric Buddhist soteriology that focuses on the intimate relationship among the mind, body, and liberation. On that foundation rests the *Kālacakratantra's* principal medical theory of the predominant effects of prāṇas on one's mental, physical, and spiritual condition. To that theory the *Kālacakratantra* adds the theoretical framework of secular Āyurvedic medicine, which operates on the presumption that good health is maintained by the equilibrium of the three humors: wind, phlegm, and bile. The fourth element of this theoretical context is the principles of haṭha yoga, which are based on the view of a causal relationship among the bodily postures, breathing exercises, and mental and physical health. Finally, the last theoretical ground of the Buddhist tantric medical therapeutics is the premises of folk medicine and occult beliefs concerning bewitchment and spirit possession, according to which spirits can possess and thereby influence the individual's mental and physical states.

Moreover, the theoretical syncretism of *Kālacakratantra* medicine induces a wide variety of medical treatments. Among the aforementioned medical treatments, the tantric yogic practices of manipulating the prāṇas and retaining regenerative fluids are believed to most directly effect the accomplishments of medical and soteriological ends. Thus, according to the *Kālacakratantra,* the yogic methods of actualizing supernormal powers *(siddhi)* are a part of the Buddhist tantric medical theory and practice. The tantric yogic practices of manipulating the flows of vital energies (*prāṇa*) and retaining regenerative fluids during sexual intercourse are given a dual purpose: spiritual and medicinal. When practiced by yogis endowed with good health, the tantric yogic practices induce spiritual powers and liberation. To those facing premature death, that is, death prior to the age of one hundred, and to those suffering from various diseases such as abdominal ailments,[53] asthma, cough, eye-diseases, poisoning, dysuria, and leprosy, they serve as preventive and curative therapeutics. For example, when the signs of untimely death occur, the following yogic practices are to be sequentially performed. The first is the obstruction of the vital energies (*prāṇa*) in the left and right channels (*nāḍī*); the immediately following phase entails the bringing of those energies into the central channel *(madhyamā)* and making them circulate there for a day; the third phase involves the filling of one's arms, legs, and fingers with vital energies *(prāṇa);* and the final phase involves the visualization of the buddhas' six female consorts with their hands in the protection mudra and standing within one's own six cakras. In the case of the abdominal and other aforementioned diseases, one is advised to contract the wind of apāna from below the navel and the wind of prāṇa from above. In this way, those two winds collide and cause a strong digestive fire to arise and spread throughout the entire body. It is said that after a month of practicing this yoga, one averts the maladies of liver, spleen, hemorrhoids, asthma, headache, cough, etc.[54]

Lastly, the syncretism of the *Kālacakratantra's* medical theory reduced the boundaries between magico-religious and empirico-rational therapeutics. The concurrence of magico-religious and empirico-rational treatments in individual cases was invariably used for two purposes: simultaneously to alleviate the symptoms of the disease and to eliminate the cause of the disease.

These multiple aims and means of cure in *Kālacakratantra* medicine required the incorporation of different sciences as additional branches of medicine, particularly astrology, as we see below. For example, the science of preparing perfumes and incenses, the science of extracting elixirs from foods and herbs, the science of alchemy, etc., became supplementary fields of medical study. In this way, the syncretism of the Buddhist tantric medical theory and practice broadened the scope of Indian Buddhist medicine as a whole, and it extended the Buddhist tantric framework of theory and practice.

Astro-Science in the *Kālacakratantra*

From the early Vedic period until now, knowledge of celestial bodies has played an important part in the healing arts of South Asian civilization. The names of constellations and planets that are well known in the classical Indian astronomy can be traced to the earliest Indian medical record, the *Atharva Veda*, in which the negative and positive influences of constellations and planets on one's well-being are already acknowledged.[55] Likewise, the earliest references to the importance of the concurrence of some healing rites with particular astrological conjunctions, which is well recognized by subsequent Āyurvedic and tantric medical traditions,[56] is already contained in the Vedic literature, specifically in the *Atharva Veda Saṃhitā*.[57] Already in the *Atharva Veda* one finds the earliest indications to time (*kāla*) as an efficient factor that links together the cosmos and the individual on the grounds that it is time that creates and governs heavenly spheres and living beings. According to the *Atharva Veda*, just as due to the efficacy of time, the sun shines, wind blows, and the earth revolves, so are the individual's mind, breath, and functioning of sense-faculties established by the power of time.[58] This Atharva Vedic view is one of the earliest antecedents to the later taxonomies of correspondences between the cosmos and the individual, which are given in the subsequent Brahmaṇic literature and in much later Hindu and Buddhist tantras. These and other ancient allusions to the relation between the individual and the cosmos through the efficacy of time, eventually developed into full-fledged theories concerning definite relationships between the circulation of the humors (*tri-doṣa*) and vital energies (*prāṇas*) in the body and the positioning of constellations and movement of planets. These theories became an essential part of Buddhist tantric medicine, as shown above, which fully integrates the fields of medical and pharmaceutical knowledge with astronomy and astrology.

Throughout the history of Buddhist Mahāyāna monastic learning in India, astronomy and astrology were treated as ancillary to medicine. The records of the two renowned Chinese pilgrims in India, Xuanzang (seventh century) and Yijing (seventh to eighth centuries), inform us that astronomy along with medicine was a part of the curriculum at the famous Buddhist university of Nālanda. Hence, it is not surprising to see that in the Kālacakra tradition, the integral application of astronomical and medical knowledge is recognized as facilitative to the flourishing of human potential and attainment of well-being with regard to one's mundane and spiritual pursuits.

The analysis of the *Kālacakratantra* reveals that this tradition inherited the geocentric astronomy of classical India, which considers the earth as the center around which all other celestial bodies orbit in a horizontal line. In contrast to the ancient Greek system, which uses a tropical zodiac,[59] in this astro-system the pole star *dhruva* is considered as a point of relative fixity. The *Kālacakratantra*'s astro-system also shares some common features with those of ancient Greek and classical Indian astronomy, particularly with regard to the twelvefold division of the zodiac. Its astronomy combines Buddhist cosmology with disciplines that are analogous to astrometry and chronometry. As we have already seen, the *Kālacakratantra* tradition combines the diverse branches of classical Buddhist medicine with alchemy, religious healing rites, and yogic and contemplative practices. This syncretistic character of the *Kālacakratantra*'s astronomy and medicine indicates that the concepts of astronomy and medicine within this tradition should be understood as the broad categories that include a wide array of Buddhist scientific and religious views and practices. Thus, they may not thoroughly correlate to the classical Western notions of medicine and astronomy.

Time is considered here to be the all-pervasive force that is inherent to and embodied in the individual and in the cosmos. Therefore, the individual and the cosmos are seen as two closely related mechanisms of time that perfectly correlate to each other in terms of their structures and modes of operation. As such, they are two aspects of embodied temporality. The individual is the aspect of time that is measured by the number of inhalations and exhalations that take place in the course of a day and night when the vital energies (*prāṇa*) circulate through the twelve subtle channels (*nāḍı*) in the navel cakra,[60] or in the internal zodiac. The cosmos, on the other hand, is the aspect of time that is characterized by the passage of days, months, and years, which is determined by the movement of the sun through the twelve houses of the external zodiac. Thus, time is conceptualized and measured as internal and external. The orbiting of the sun through the twelve houses in the course of a year correlates with the daily passage of vital energies through the twelve subtle channels of the internal zodiac. When the positioning of the twenty-seven constellations and ten planets along the zodiacal belt conform to the flow of vital energies in the twelve channels in the navel cakra, they promote physical and mental health. But when they are in disharmony, the configuration of planets in the celestial sphere has a pernicious effect on one's health and general well-being. This close connection between the external and internal zodiacs is based on the earlier-mentioned premise that the celestial sphere (*gola*), which holds the constellations and planets, is of the nature of wind, which is nondifferentiated from the wind of vital energies that supports a human body. These two types of winds support their respective spheres by holding and transmitting the elements of earth, water, fire, wind, space, and gnosis.

Each of the twelve houses of the external zodiac is said to be of the nature of one of the six elements, which determines its dominant characteristics. Thus, Capricorn is of the nature of the space-element, Aquarius of the nature of the wind-element, Pisces of the fire-element, Aries of the water-element, Taurus of the earth-element, and Gemini of the gnosis-element. The remaining six signs, Cancer, Leo, and so on, are also of the nature of the aforementioned elements, but in the inverted order. Thus, Cancer is of the nature of the gnosis-element, Leo of the earth-element,

Virgo of the water-element, Libra of the fire-element, Scorpio of the wind-element, and Sagittarius of the space-element. The planets are also of the nature of the elements, particularly of the nature of the elements of their birth houses, in which they appeared at the beginning of the cosmos.[61] However, planets occupy the houses other than those in which they were born. Adding their own characteristics to those of the houses they govern, they create new combinations of features.

Furthermore, in accordance with the division into twelve houses, planet earth is divided into twelve sections dominated by their corresponding constellations in the sky.[62] Thus, the earth can be seen as a terrestrial reflection of the celestial zodiac. As the sun orbits the earth along the zodiacal belt in its northward and southward passages, it sequentially orbits the twelve sections of the earth, exerting its influence on these sections in accordance with its different degrees of intensity.

The six types of elemental particles, which determine the specific characteristics of the solar houses, their dominating planets, and the twelve sections of the earth, also produce corresponding properties in the plants, metals, minerals, and gems used for medicinal purposes. The elementary particles determine the colors and tastes of these medicinal substances used to counteract imbalances in the elements of the body. For example, the earth-element, which is solidity, produces the color yellow and a salty taste. Substances dominated by this element are used for the elimination of sharp, acute pains, like those of colic, rheumatism, and the like, which are characterized by an excess and disturbance of the wind-element. Being of the nature of solidity, the earth-element calms the bodily wind-element, which is of the nature of mobility. Similarly, substances of the nature of the water-element that are characterized by the color white and a sweet taste are used for balancing the fire-element in the body, for the removal of toxins that aggravate the fire-element, and so on. Substances dominated by the fire-element and characterized by the color red and a hot taste counteract disturbances of the earth-element in the body and diseases caused by spirit possession. Substances of the nature of the wind-element are characterized by the color black and a pungent taste. They counteract disturbances of the water-element and conditions such as stiffness and paralysis. The space and gnosis elements, which produce blue and green colors and give bitter and sour tastes, respectively, facilitate the removal of a wide range of diseases caused by imbalances of various elements.[63] The elemental nature and medicinal qualities of the natural substances are contingent upon the time of year and season in which certain medicinal plants grow and upon the geographical areas in which particular medicinal substances are found. The time of year and geographical areas, in turn, accord with the nature of particular constellations, planetary positions, and the time of their influence on specific regions of the earth. According to the Kālacakra tradition, due to the efficacy of the aforementioned six elements there are two sets of six months and six seasons,[64] which make up a solar year. Each set of three seasons consisting of six solar months is characterized by the qualities of sattva (luminosity, intelligibility), rajas (activity, passion), and tamas (darkness, inertia), which are inherent in the elements.[65] These three qualities are also inherent in diverse natural substances, with one of them being the most dominant quality. Similarly, each of the six seasons, which consists of two months, is divided into five periods due the nature of these five elements—space, wind, fire, water, and earth.[66]

With regard to the human body, the six elements are carried by the vital energies in the channels that spread from the twelve zodiacal houses in the navel during the development of the fetus and that make up the mind-body complex. According to this Buddhist system, three hundred and sixty solar days, thirty lunar days (*tithi*), sixteen digits (*kalā*) of the moon, and other divisions of time have their individual correlates in the various channels of the vital energies that carry the previously mentioned elements in the body. The vital energies in the body become disturbed by these elements, which constitute the three main bodily humors (*doṣa*)—wind (*vāta*), bile (*pitta*), and phlegm (*kapha*),[67] which correspond to the three previously mentioned qualities of sattva, rajas, and tamas. In consequence, the disturbed vital energies give rise to physical and mental disorders that can lead to death. In contrast, the equilibrium of the elements of the three humors keeps the vital energies in balance and maintains good health. For as long as vital energies circulate through the twelve houses of the internal zodiac in the course of a day and night, the individual's life is preserved. But when vital energies begin to uninterruptedly circulate in a single left channel, that is, in a single uneven zodiacal house, for a day and night, for a fortnight, or for a month, then premature death becomes imminent within a year, a half year, or three months, respectively.[68]

According to the Kālacakra tradition, the optimal lifespan of the individual is one hundred years. In the course of one hundred years, the bodily elements undergo a process of maturation that lasts ninety-six years and ten-and-a-half months. For the first thirty-two years and three-and-a-half months, vital energies in the body are dominated with the quality of sattva. For the next thirty-two years and three-and-a-half months, the vital energies are dominated by the quality of rajas; and for the last thirty-two years and three-and-a-half months, the vital energies are dominated by the quality of tamas. In the course of the remaining three years, three fortnights, and three days, vital energies gradually cease circulating, as the houses of the internal zodiac begin to collapse. In this way, vital energies leave the bodily elements, causing their sequential dissolution that results in death. This division of the human lifespan of ninety-six years and ten-and-a-half months corresponds to the length of time it takes eight planets altogether to move through the circle and a half of twenty-seven constellations (*nakṣatra*).[69]

According to this astronomical system, constellations, which are by themselves stationary, are positioned within their individual houses that move from the east to the west. Each constellation is divided into four quarters, and nine such quarters make up one house (*lagna*). Every zodiacal house has two-and-a-quarter constellations. In contrast to constellations, the eight out of ten planets[70] that rise above the stars move from the west to the east[71] in an incremental motion within their respective houses. The moon, Mercury, Venus, and Ketu, which originally arose on the left side of the celestial sphere, are considered auspicious planets that exert pacifying and soothing influences. In contrast, the sun, Mars, Jupiter, and Saturn, which arose on the right side of the celestial sphere, are regarded as inauspicious planets, exerting the wrathful and disturbing influences.[72] The auspicious planets orbit on the left, or on the northward passage, of the sun, passing on the left of the inauspicious planets; and the inauspicious ones orbit on the right, or on the southward passage, of the sun, passing on the right of the auspicious planets. Thus, in terms of the place of their origin and path of orbiting,[73] they are each other's natural enemies. Mercury, born in Scorpio, and Mars, born in Leo, are each other's enemies. Likewise, Jupiter, born in Virgo, and Venus, born in Gemini, are each other's enemy, and so are Saturn, born at the end of Sagittarius, and Ketu, also born in Sagittarius. The planets that are each other's natural enemies come into conflict when one of them enters the constellation in which its enemy was born.[74] They also come into conflict when any of these planets enters the zodiacal house that is governed by the planet that is the enemy.[75] When planets come into mutual conflict, they impede the patient's recovery and negatively interfere with healing rites. When they stay within their own fields of domain or enter the domains of the planets that are not their natural enemies, their zodiacal houses (*rāśi*) do not obstruct medical treatment and the patient's recovery. Instead, they bring about desirable results to the rites of healing.

Just as planets take hold and govern certain zodiacal houses as their respective fields in the celestial sphere, they also preside over the elements carried by the vital energies that circulate through the left and right sides of the body.[76] Thus, on the left and right respectively, Rāhu and Kālāgni preside over the space-element; the moon and sun preside over the wind-element; Mercury and Mars preside over the fire-element; Venus and Jupiter preside over the water-element; and Ketu and Saturn preside over the earth-element. The passing of the elements of space, wind, fire, water, and earth through the uneven zodiacal signs—Aries, Gemini, Leo, Libra, and Sagittarius—correlates with the passing of the corresponding five elements through the left nostril. The passing of these elements in the inverted order—beginning with the earth-element and ending with the space-element—through the even zodiacal signs, namely, Taurus, Cancer, Virgo, Scorpio, and Capricorn, correlates with the passing of the corresponding five elements through the right nostril. The left and right paths of the elements, circulating in the celestial sphere and in the body, accord with the sequence of the origination and dissolution of the cosmos and the individual.[77] Therefore, the planets that preside over the five elements passing on the left are auspicious planets, and those that preside over the elements passing on the right are inauspicious planets.

Furthermore, as the moon transits through the six houses of the zodiac in the north—Aries, Gemini, Leo, Libra, Sagittarius, and Aquarius—for six months, the element of semen, which is considered the internal moon, circulates in the left channel for six months. Likewise, in accordance with the sun's passing through the six houses of the zodiac in the south—Taurus, Cancer, Virgo, Scorpio, Capricorn, and Pisces—the element of uterine blood, or the internal sun, is in the right channel for six months. Just as it takes thirty solar and lunar days for the sun and the moon, respectively, to pass from one house to another, so it takes the five elements thirty days altogether to pass through the four main directions and the center of a single house, or a petal, within the internal zodiac, or the navel cakra. It takes six days for each element to pass through a single petal, or zodiacal house. When one multiplies six days with the five elements, one gets thirty days. When the movement of the elements and planets in the celestial sphere or in the body diverges from these set paths, the winds that uphold the celestial sphere and that support the body become agitated, damaging one's physical and mental health. Therefore, in order to keep them on their set paths or to restore their disrupted motion, this Buddhist astro-medical system prescribes various yogic exercises that involve different bodily postures and breathing techniques that are designed for this purpose.

However, since one's body is a revolving mechanism of time, all physical and mental ailments are ultimately brought into existence by the power of time that is of the nature of death. From the moment of inception in the womb, time in the form of lunar days, which at certain times are malefic, assembles in the joints, knuckles, and other parts of the body due to the efficacy of the elements, and it seizes one in its merciless grip.[78] The fifteen lunar days of a lunar fortnight are obtained by the five sets of three lunar days, which are in accordance with the fivefold classification of the elements, multiplied by the three—sattva, rajas, and tamas.[79]

Accordingly, the five sets of three lunar days are said to be of the nature of the elements of space, wind, fire, water, and earth.[80] Thus, everything that is of the nature of the perishable elements is ultimately of the nature of time, or death.

The Kālacakra tradition utilized its classification of all astral phenomena in terms of the elements not only in its medical therapeutics but also in its system of astrological predictions. For example, when a person whose name begins with the letter *a*, which is of the nature of the space-element, becomes sick or wounded on the first day of a lunar month (*nandā*), which is also of the nature of the space-element, if that lunar day is in conjunction with a particular solar day and constellation, e.g., when it is in conjunction with Tuesday (the third day of a week) and the *kṛttikā* constellation, then that person will die.[81] However, if this lunar day coincides with Sunday, a sick or an injured person will be in pain but will not die.[82] Moreover, when a person whose name has the letter *i*, which is of the nature of the wind-element as its second letter, becomes ill or wounded on the second lunar day (*bhadrā*), which is also of the nature of the wind-element, if that lunar day is in conjunction with a particular solar day and constellation, e.g., if it coincides with Wednesday (the fourth day of a week) and the *māgha* constellation, then that person will die. But this will not be the case when this lunar day coincides with Monday. When a person whose name has the letter *ṛ*, which is of the nature of the fire-element as its third letter, becomes sick or wounded on the third lunar day (*jayā*), which is also of the nature of the fire-element, if that lunar day is in conjunction with a particular solar day and constellation, then that person will die. The same applies when a person whose name has the letter *u*, which is of the nature of the water-element as its fourth letter, becomes ill or wounded on the fourth lunar day (*riktā*), if that lunar day is in conjunction with a particular solar day and constellation. For instance, if it coincides with Thursday (the sixth day of a week) and the *aśleṣā* constellation, then that person will die. Similarly, when a person whose name has the letter *l*, which is of the nature of the earth-element as its fifth letter, becomes sick on the fifth lunar day (*pūrṇā*), which is also of the nature of the earth-element, if that lunar day is in conjunction with a particular solar day and constellation. For example, if it coincides with Saturday (the seventh day of a week) and the *bhāraṇı* constellation, that person will die.

In this tradition, astrological predictions that are based on the classification of the elements can be also carried out by utilizing the internal, or bodily, astral system. In the astrological predictions that are related to the internal astral system, the entirely auspicious and inauspicious outcomes depend on whether or not the five elements and the planets that preside over their respective elements move in the right (inauspicious) or in the left (auspicious) channels of vital energies. For instance, if at the time of illness, the space-element, which is presided over by the internal planet Kālāgni, arises in the right channel, then the sick person will die. If the wind-element, which is presided over by the internal sun, arises in the right channel, the sick person will be in distress. If the fire-element, which is presided over by the internal Mars, arises in the right channel, sores will manifest. If the wind-element, which is presided over by the internal Jupiter, arises in the right channel, there will be comfort; and if the earth-element, which is presided over by the internal Saturn, arises in the right channel, the condition will remain the same.[83]

In addition to these two types of predictions, there are other astro-medical predictions within this tantric system that appear not to be closely related to the classification and interaction of the elements. Some predictions seem to be based on whether or not the parts of the constellation that follows the constellation of the patient's birth are even or uneven in numbers. The prediction is carried out in the following way. The twenty-seven constellations are divided into three groups, each consisting of nine constellations. The first constellation within each group of nine constellations is always the constellation of the patient's birth. If the inauspicious planets meet with the moon in the uneven part (*pada*)[84] of the constellation that comes after the nine constellations, the patient will die. If they meet in the even pada, the patient will recover.[85]

While incorporating the astrological predictions into its practical framework, the Kālacakra tradition provides a system of practices designed for counteracting negative predictions, thus making it clear that astrological predictions should not be interpreted in a fatalistic manner. Likewise, although this esoteric tradition acknowledges the pragmatic value of astrological predictions, it emphasizes that ultimately it is the person's previously accumulated karma that determines whether or not any celestial events will have auspicious or inauspicious influences on the person's well-being. It points out that ultimately it is one's own karma that determines one's physical and mental conditions and one's lifespan. The following verses from the root tantra illustrate this point.

vārasthitiś ca nakṣatra˙ yoga¯ karaṇam eva ca/
lagna˙ krūragrahaiś caitat kalyāṇa˙ puṇyakāriṇām//

ekakṣa˚aprasūtānā˙ jātakānā˙ pṛthak pṛthak/
phala˙ naikaphala˙ teśā˙ svasvakarmopabhogata¯//

sa˙grāme vanadāhe ca kaivartājjālabandhane/
maraṇa˙ yaugapadyena bahavo y›nti dehina¯//

puṇeynāyurbala˙ vırya˙ ṛddhi¯ saubhāgyarūpatā/
pāpenāyu¯kśayo vıryarddhihāniś ca dehinām//

The solar and lunar days, constellations, *yogas*,[86] halves of the lunar months (*karaṇa*), zodiacal houses (*lagna*), and inauspicious planets (*krūra-graha*) are auspicious to those who engage in virtue.

Those who are born at exactly the same moment have their own respective results [of karma]. Their various [karmic] results accord with the experiences of their individual actions.

Numerous embodied beings simultaneously die in war, in forest fires, and in fishermen's nets.

Long life, strength, vitality, vigor, and good fortune are due to virtue. The disruption of living beings' lives and the loss of their vitality and vigor are due to sin.[87]

Thus, with regard to illness and recovery, the Kālacakra tradition presents two levels of causality that correlate with each other. While the individual's karma is the inner and fundamental cause of illness and recovery, the celestial events that correlate with the karma and the events in the internal zodiac are its outer indicators. In conformity with these two levels of causality, this tantric system offers two types of practices that are auxiliary to each other—namely, the Buddhist tantric methods designed for the purification of karma and the astro-medical practices that support those methods. In conclusion, one may say that although Buddhist tantric astro-medicine is primarily concerned with the immediate causes and outcomes of illness, its main purpose is to point out when and by whom the purificatory practices are to be performed for medical reasons.

Endnotes

1. See Romila Thapar, *A History of India,* vol. 1 (London: Penguin Books, 1966), 253-54.

2. The verses 128-47 of the first chapter of the *Kālacakratantra* give a detailed instruction on building the different types of weapons that should be used by the Kalkī's army in the final battle with Barbarians in the land of Mecca.

3. This view of theological knowledge and scientific learning as complementary is dominant in the Vajrayāna, whereas in the Sūtrayāna they are simply compatible rather than complementary.

4. This is not characteristic of the *Kālacakratantra* only. Much earlier medical treatises of Āyurveda, such as the *Suśrutasaṃhitā* (first to second centuries CE) and the *Caraksaṃhitā*

(ca. fourth century CE), assert that the five elements which are present in the body, namely, earth, water, fire, wind, and space, form the entire universe.

5. See Jagannātha Upādhyāya's edition of the *Vimalaprabhā* commentary on the *Śrīlaghu kālacakratantrarāja,* Bibliotheca Indo-Tibetica Series, no. 11 (Sarnath: Central Institute of Higher Tibetan Studies, 1986), 43.

6. The *Nettipakaraṇa* (London: Pāli Text Society, 1962), [76].

7. If one asks, "How is introspection scientific in the context of Buddhism?" an answer would be that just as physical phenomena are to be studied scientifically as far as possible by means of direct observation, so also are first-person mental phenomena; and introspection is widely recognized in Buddhism as the sole means of observing one's own conscious states.

8. Already in the early Buddhist Pāli literature, the Buddhist dhamma was referred to as the verifiable teaching (ehipassika).

9. Jagannātha Upādhyāya, ed., *Śrīlaghukālacakratantrarāja,* Bibliotheca Indo-Tibetica Series, no. 11 (Sarnath: Central Institute of Higher Tibetan Studies, 1986), ch.2, vv. 48-50, reads:

> Within one's own body, Cakrī is one who has the vajra; the eminent lords of gods are the twelve restrained limbs; Kalkī is the right knowledge; the elephants, horses, chariots, and servants are the [four] Immeasurables; Rudra's name is Pratyeka [Buddhas]; Hanūmān is Śrāvakas; a vicious king of Barbarians is the vice of living beings; and Kṛnamati, a bestower of suffering, is a nonvirtue.
>
> Aśvatthāma is spiritual ignorance; the entire host of demons is the four classes of Māras; its destruction in the battle is the annihilation of the fear of saṃsāra; the glorious victory is a path to liberation; the teaching of Dharma on Mt. Kailāśa is the removal of the fear of saṃsāra. The earth is full of substances. Brahmā and Sureśa, sons of the teacher of thirteen men, are in the rear and in the front [of the army, respectively].
>
> Mañjuśrī, the glorious protector of people and the conqueror of the three worlds, is splendid blood and bodhicitta. The offsprings on the diverse earth, beginning with Brahmā in the rear, etc., are many pure Buddhas. Thus, a battle with the king of Barbarians is indeed within the body of living beings. However, the battle with Barbarians, fought outside in the kingdom of Mecca, is not an illusory experience.

10. See Upādhyāya, *Śrīlaghukālacakratantrarāja,* ch. 2, v. 96 with the *Vimalaprabhā* commentary.

11. The *Kālacakratantra* incorporates the ideas characteristic of the Sāṃkhya philosophical system, and at least on one occasion, it brings in ideas derived from the Jaina world-view.

12. David W. Evans, trans., *The Discourses of Gotama Buddha: Middle Collection* (London: Janus Publishing Company, 1992), "With Māgandiya," "Major Discourse on the Destruction of Craving."

13. Upādhyāya, *Śrīlaghukālacakratantrarāja*, ch. 2, v. 107, lines a-b read, "Firstly, a mantrī should preserve the entire body of the Jina for the sake of siddhis. In the absence of the body, neither a siddhi nor supreme bliss is attained in this life."

14. For more information see Kenneth G. Zysk, *Asceticism and Healing in Ancient India: Medicine in the Buddhist Monastery* (New York, Oxford: Oxford University Press, 1991) and *Encyclopaedia of Buddhism,* s.v. "Āyurveda," by Jean Filliozat.

15. According to the *Encyclopaedia of Buddhism*, s.v. "Āyurveda," by Jean Filliozat, 478, some Indian manuscripts ascribe the *Yogaśataka* to Vararuci instead of Nāgārjuna.

16. These five Buddhist medical treatises are included among the twenty-two Āyurvedic works that are incorporated in the Tibetan Tengyur, where they are ascribed to Nāgārjuna. Apart from the *Yogaśataka,* the Sanskrit originals of the other four treatises are lost.

17. According to the *Encyclopaedia of Buddhism*, s.v. "Āyurveda," by Jean Filliozat, 478, an alternative attribution of the *Kakṣapuṭa,* or the *Kacchapuṭa,* is to Nityanāthasiddha.

18. See the *Vimalaprabhā* commentary on Upādhyāya, *Śrīlaghukālacakratantrarāja,* ch. 2, v. 141.

19. Cf. Śantideva, *Śikṣāsamuccaya,* ed. P. L. Vaidya, Buddhist Sanskrit Texts, no. 11 (Darbhanga: The Mithila Institute of Post-graduate Studies and Research in Sanskrit Learning, 1961), 77-78, where Śantideva advises bodhisattvas to counteract diseases with the recitation of mantras in addition to the usage of medications and water and in addition to the offerings of flowers to the image of the Buddha.

20. Cf. Maurice Walshe, trans., *Thus Have I Heard: The Long Discourses of the Buddha: Dīgha Nikāya:* "Aṭānāṭiya Sutta: The Aṭānāṭā Protective Verses," (London: Wisdom Publications, 1987), 471-78; H. Oldenberg, ed., *Vinayapiṭaka,* vol. 4 (London: Pāli Text Society, 1879-83). Cf. Śantideva, *Śikṣāsamuccaya,* ed. P. L. Vaidya, Buddhist Sanskrit Texts, no. 11 (Darbhanga: The Mithila Institute of Post-graduate Studies and Research in Sanskrit Learning, 1961), 77, where Śantideva cites the mantras set forth in the *Trisamayarāja* as the mantras to be used for the protection of bodhisattvas against Māras and other evil entities.

21. Upādhyāya, *Śrīlaghukālacakratantrarāja*, ch. 2, vs. 154-60.

22. Ibid., ch. 2, vs. 152-53.

23. According to ibid., ch. 2, v. 153, the symptoms of irrevocable death, which cannot be warded off by gods, men, or nāgas, are the following: the entire body becomes white, very subtle boils appear, the neck is bent together with the body, blood drips into the mouth, sexual organ, or the rectum.

24. Ibid., ch. 2, v. 146 with the *Vimalaprabhā* commentary.

25. Ibid., v. 159.

26. The fragrant root of *Andropogon Muricatus*.

27. *Valeriana jatamansi.*

28. See Upādhyāya, *Śrīlaghukālacakratantrarāja,* ch. 2, v. 149 with the *Vimalaprabhā* commentary.

29. Ibid., ch.2, v. 152.

30. Name of a plant with a bitter root.

31. Methonia Superba.

32. *Cucumis Colocynthis*, a wild bitter gourd.

33. See Upādhyāya, *Śrīlaghukālacakratantrarāja,* ch. 2, vs. 124, 126-27.

34. The *Vimalaprabhā* commentary on ibid., ch. 2, v. 128.

35. Ibid., v. 130: "*oṃ phre Viśvamāte vajra-kaṇṭakān nāśaya nāśaya mama śāntiṃ kuru* kuru svāhā."

36. Ibid., v. 149: "oṃ āḥ huṃ amukāyā garbhaśūlaṃ hara hara svāhā."

37. Ibid., v. 129.

38. See the *Vimalaprabhā* commentary on the *Śrīlaghukālacakratantrarāja,* eds. Vajravallabha Dvivedī and S. S. Bahulakara. Bibliotheca Indo-Tibetica Series, no. 12 (Sarnath, Varanasi: Central Institute of Higher Tibetan Studies, 1994) ch. 4, v. 109.

39. Ibid., v. 56.

40. See ibid., ch. 3, v. 1, where mantra is defined as primordial wisdom (*jñāna)* on the grounds that it protects the mind.

41. Ibid., ch. 2, v. 112 describes the vajra posture in the following way: "The vajra posture entails the left leg on the right thigh, and the right leg on the left thigh. Those two legs have the vajra-connection with the arms being on the top. The right foot is held by the left hand, and the left foot is held by the right hand."

42. The Sanskrit word *kuṣtharoga*, or "leprosy," is a general term for the eighteen types of leprosy. Neither the *Kālacakratantra* nor the *Vimalaprabhā* specifies whether the term *kuṣtharoga* here refers to all of the eighteen types of leprosy or to a specific type of it.

43. Upādhyāya, *Śrīlaghukālacakratantrarāja,* ch. 2, v. 114.

44. Bu ston (p.471) in his annotation indicates the appearance of boils in the throat as a symptom of malignant disease of the throat.

45. See Upādhyāya, *Śrīlaghukālacakratantrarāja,* ch. 2, v. 128 with the *Vimalaprabhā* commentary.

46. Three *kaṭukas* are three spices, namely, black and long peppers and dry ginger.

47. See Upādhyāya, *Śrīlaghukālacakratantrarāja,* ch. 2, v. 124.

48. *Arka* is a tropical and subtropical milky plant that grows in the dry, plain areas. It is also known as *Calotropis gigantean,* linn, or the milky weed plant.

49. See Upādhyāya, *Śrīlaghukālacakratantrarāja,* ch. 2, v. 114.

50. The *Vimalaprabhā* commentary on ibid., ch. 2, v. 135.

51. See the *Āyuṣparirakṣānāma,* which is preserved in Tibetan translation under the title *Tshe bsgrub pa'I gdams ngag ces bya ba* and is included in the Tantra commentary (*rgyud 'grel)* section of the *Tengyur* (Peking edition of the *Tibetan Tripiṭaka,* edited by D. T. Suzuki, vol. 69, no. 3236. Tokyo-Kyoto: Tibetan Tripiṭaka Research Foundation, 1955-1961); the *Āyuḥsādhana,* which is extant only in the Tibetan translation under the title *Tshe sgrub pa'i thabs* and occurs in the Tantra commentary section of the *Tengyur* (Peking edition of the *Tibetan Tripiṭaka,* edited by D. T. Suzuki, vol. 86, no. 4863. Tokyo-Kyoto:Tibetan Tripiṭaka Research Foundation, 1955-1961); the *Āyurbuddhāsmuṛti,* which is also extant only in its Tibetan translation under the title *'Phags pa sngas rgyas rjes su dran pa* and is included in the Tantra commentary section of the *Tengyur* (P. Cordier, ed., *Catalogue du Fonds Tibétain,* vol. 2, 371, no. 4); the *Āyurvardhanīvidhi* which is attributed to Candragomin and is preserved only in Tibetan translation under the title *Tshe 'phel ba'i cho ga* in the Tantra commentary section of the *Tengyur (Tōhoku-Teikoku-Daigaku Hōbun-gakubu Tibet-Daizōkyō-So-Mokuroku,* 1932, no. 3666).

52. According to Upādhyāya, *Śrīlaghukālacakratantrarāja,* ch. 2, v. 125 and the *Vimalaprabhā* commentary, the five internal amṛtas (feces, urine, semen, blood, marrow), when combined with the equal portions of the five external *amrtas* (sulfur, nectar from black bees, talc, quicksilver, and three myrobalans), soaked for seven days, dried in the heat, and

ingested with ghee and honey every day for up to six months, have a life-giving power because they release energy, acid, oil, and salt.

53. According to ibid., ch. 2, v. 111 and the *Vimalaprabhā* commentary, the maladies of liver, spleen, and hemorrhoids are considered as abdominal ailments.

54. See the *Vimalaprabhā* commentary on ibid., ch. 2, v. 11.

55. The *Atharva Veda*, Book IX, Hymn 7; Book XIX, Hymns 7-9.

56. The *Suṣruta Saṃhitā*, 4.29: "Rejuvenation through Soma."

57. K. G. Zysk, *Medicine in the Veda: Religious Healing in the Veda*, 1996, pp. 9, 22.

58. The *Atharva Veda*, Book XIX, Hymns 53-54.

59. In the tropical zodiac, used in ancient Greece, when the sun is at the vernal equinox in the northern hemisphere, its position is referred to as the zero degrees Aries, regardless of where the actual Aries is in the sky.

60. The number of those inhalations and exhalations is said to be 21,600.

61. According to the *Kālacakratantra*, 1994, ch. 5, v. 191, and the *Vimalaprabhā*, the individual birth signs of the planets are as follows: the moon is in Aries, Venus is in Gemini, the sun is in Cancer, Mars is in Leo, Jupiter is in Virgo, Rāhu is in Libra, Mercury is in Scorpio, Saturn is in Sagittarius, and so on. Ketu is at the limit of it. Likewise, Āgasti is in Aquarius, and the polar star is in Taurus.

62. The *Kālacakratantra*, 1986, ch. 1, v. 75, and the *Vimalaprabhā*.

63. The *Kālacakratantra*, 1994, ch. 5, vv. 185-87, ch. 2, v. 126, and the *Vimalaprabhā*.

64. The six seasons are: spring (*vasanta*), hot season (*grıṣma*), rainy season (*varṣās*), autumn (*śarad*), winter (*hemanta*), and cool season (*śiśira*).

65. According to the classical Āyurveda, *sattva* is the quality of the wind-elements, *rajas* is the quality of the fire-elements, and *tamas* is the quality of the earth-element.

66. The *Kālacakratantra*, 1994, ch. 5, v. 138, and the *Vimalaprabhā* commentary.

67. *Vāta* is related to the movement in the body, and it consists of the wind and space elements. *Pitta* is related to digestion and metabolism, and it consists of the fire and water elements; and *kapha* is related to lubrication and bodily structure, and it consists of the earth and water elements.

68. The *Kālacakratantra*, 1986, ch. 2, v. 61, and the *Vimalaprabhā* commentary.

69. The *Kālacakratantra*, 1986, ch. 1, v. 65, mentions these eight planets: the moon, the sun, Mars, Jupiter, Venus, Mercury, Saturn, and Ketu.

70. The ten planets are enumerated in the Kālacakra astronomy as the sun, moon, Mars, Mercury, Jupiter, Venus, Saturn, Ketu, Rāhu, and Kālāgni. Rāhu and Ketu are listed as planets although they are mere mathematical points on the zodiac.

71. This means that a planet that is in Aries will proceed to Taurus and not to Gemini, etc.

72. The *Kālacakratantra*, 1986, ch. 1, v. 50, ch. 5, v. 113, and the *Vimalaprabhā* commentary.

73. The moon was born in Aries, the sun in Cancer, Venus in Gemini, and Rāhu in Libra.

74. See the *Kālacakratantra*, 1986, ch. 1, v. 51, and the *Vimalaprabhā* commentary. Venus was born in the Punarvasu constellation, Mars in Māgha, Jupiter in Hastā, Mercury in Anurādhā, Saturn in Mūla, and Ketu in Uttarāṣāḍhā.

75. See the *Kālacakratantra*, 1986, ch. 1, v. 51, ch. 5, v. 140, and the *Vimalaprabhā* commentary. Mars governs Aries and Scorpio, Mercury governs Gemini and Virgo, Jupiter governs Sagittarius and Pisces, Venus governs Taurus and Libra, Saturn governs Capricorn and Aquarius, Ketu governs Cancer, and the sun governs Leo.

76. The *Kālacakratantra*, 1986, ch. 2, v. 40, and the *Vimalaprabhā* commentary.

77. The *Kālacakratantra*, 1986, ch. 1, v. 8, ch. 2, v. 61, ch. 5, v. 134, and the *Vimalaprabhā* commentary.

78. The *Kālacakratantra*, 1986, ch. 2, v. 143, and the *Vimalaprabhā* commentary.

79. The *Kālacakratantra*, 1986, ch. 1, v. 8, and the *Vimalaprabhā* commentary.

80. One lunar month (*tithi*) is the interval of time from one new moon day to the next.

81. See the *Kālacakratantra*, 1986, ch. 1, vv. 95-97, and the *Vimalaprabhā* commentary.

82. The *Kālacakratantra*, 1986, ch. 1, v. 97, and the *Vimalaprabhā* commentary.

83. The *Kālacarkatantra*, 1986, ch. 1, vv. 103, 105, and the *Vimalaprabhā* commentary. Rāhu, moon, Mercury, Venus, and Ketu are the auspicious planets that preside over the elements of space, wind, fire, water, and earth, respectively; and Kālāgni, sun, Mars, Saturn, and Jupiter are the inauspicious planets that preside over the elements of space, wind, fire, water, and earth.

84. Every constellation (*nakṣatra*) has four parts (*padas*), thus there are altogether 108 *padas* of the twenty-seven constellations.

85. The *Kālacakratantra*, ch. 1, v. 112, and the *Vimalaprabhā* commentary.

86. *Yoga* is the period in which the combined longitudinal motion of the sun and the moon equals one constellation (*nakṣatra*).

87. This citation from the root-*tantra* is given in the *Vimalaprabhā* commentary on the *Kālacakratantra*, 1986, ch. 1, v. 36. See also the *Vimalaprabhā* commentary on the *Kālacakratarantra*, 1986, ch. 1, v. 111.

– 16 –

Sanskrit Mantras in the Kālacakra Sādhana

David Reigle

While the Tibetan lotsawas of old translated even Sanskrit names in their renowned translations of the Buddhist canonical texts, they left Sanskrit mantras untranslated. This is because the power of mantras is believed to derive from their sounds, sounds that could not be altered if this power was to remain intact. Thus we find that the mantras in the Kālacakra sādhana, like in all sādhanas, are in Sanskrit, not in Tibetan.

Yet it is just here that, because of how foreign these sounds are, errors are most likely to creep in. Indeed we find that, over the centuries, the pronunciation of these sounds has altered, and, due to unfamiliarity with the words, even the spellings have been subject to scribal errors. One of the clearest examples of altered pronunciation may be seen in the case of the famous Vajrasattva mantra, widely used on its own for purification, and found as an integral part of many sādhanas, including most of the fuller versions of the Kālacakra sādhana.

The hundred-syllable Vajrasattva mantra as now pronounced may be seen in recent books on Tibetan Buddhism where it is given phonetically. From these, we see that the word Vajrasattva has become Benzar sato,[1] Benzar satto,[2] or Bedzra sato.[3] These transformations of its pronunciation are largely due to its being pronounced as in modern Tibetan. We see the same thing in English, where Vajrasattva is pronounced as if it is an English word. But it is a Sanskrit word, and as such, the first syllable of Vajra should rhyme with "judge," and the first syllable of sattva should rhyme with "hut." If the early Tibetan translators gave such importance to preserving the Sanskrit sounds, we should make an attempt to pronounce them correctly.[4]

Then there is the question of meaning. The great majority of Sanskrit mantras have clear meanings that were meant to be understood.[5] Their meanings form an important part of the sādhanas in which they are used, making what is happening there more comprehensible. For example, at the beginning of the full-length Kālacakra sādhana is this mantra:[6]

> oṃ āḥ hūṃ hoḥ haṃ kṣaḥ prajñôpāyâtmaka-kāya-vāk-citta-jñānâdhipate
> mama kāya-vāk-citta-jñāna-vajraṃ vajrâmṛta-svabhavaṃ kuru kuru skandha-
> dhātv-āyatanâdikaṃ niḥsvabhāvaṃ svāhā

It was introduced with the phrase, "the mantra words purifying body, speech, mind, and primordial wisdom (*jñāna*) are: . . ."[7] Leaving aside the untranslatable syllables, the straightforward grammatical meaning of this mantra is:

> oṃ āḥ hūṃ hoḥ haṃ kṣaḥ; O overlord of body, speech, mind, and primordial wisdom, consisting of wisdom and means! my vajra of body, speech, mind, and primordial wisdom, into the nature of vajra immortality, transform! transform! Aggregates, elements, sense-spheres, and the rest, are without inherent existence; svāhā!

This meaning would have been fully understood by the Indians who first used these mantras. But when translating the sādhanas in which they are found into Tibetan, the meaning had to be sacrificed for the sake of preserving the all-important sounds. When we know the meaning, the often-seen mantra that comes shortly thereafter becomes much more comprehensible:[8]

> oṃ svabhāva-śuddhāḥ sarva-dharmāḥ svabhāva-śuddho 'ham
> oṃ; Naturally pure are all things; naturally pure am I.

It will therefore be of considerable usefulness to have English translations of the Sanskrit mantras included in the translations of the sādhanas. One can then do the prescribed meditations with greater understanding of what is occurring.

The Kālacakra sādhana from which I am drawing for the mantras discussed here is the full-length *Śrī Kālacakra Sādhana* by Sādhuputra, the only known Kālacakra sādhana to survive in the original Sanskrit.[9] It consists of lengthy direct extracts from the *Vimala-prabhā*, "Immaculate Light,"[10] the great commentary on the *Kālacakra Tantra* written by King Puṇḍarīka of Śambhala. These were compiled and arranged by Sādhuputra, with brief connecting paragraphs condensed from the *Vimalaprabhā*. So most of this Kālacakra sādhana, except the middle section that names all the deities of the Kālacakra maṇḍala in metrical verses, is actually by Puṇḍarīka, the author of the *Vimalaprabhā*, rather than by Sādhuputra. As such, it could hardly be more authoritative. Besides this, it has the advantage that it cannot be considered sectarian, since it was written in India, before the various orders of Tibetan Buddhism came into existence. It would therefore be the sādhana of choice as the most original form of the Kālacakra sādhana.

The Kālacakra sādhana has many elements in common with other Buddhist sādhanas, including a number of mantras. When we see elements in one sādhana after another, we know that these must be of basic importance. It will repay our time to try to understand these as fully as we can. Basic to all sādhanas of the highest yoga tantra class, such as Kālacakra, are the ideas of "clear appearance" and "divine pride." Since these sādhanas consist of the visualization of oneself as a divine being (*devatā*), in a divine residence (*maṇḍala*), the "clear appearance" part is self-explanatory. One must make these visualizations appear to the mind as clearly as possible. The "divine pride" part means that you identify so fully with the divine being or deity you are visualizing that you feel a "sense of self" (*ahaṃkāra*) as that deity. So the idea of divine pride is literally "sense of self as the deity" (*devatâhaṃkāra*).[11] Like almost everything else in these sādhanas, including the visualizations from seed-syllables, this is done through the use of mantras. Thus, for example, early in the *Śrī Kālacakra Sādhana* we are instructed as follows: "Then [assert] the sense of self [as a divine form or deity, i.e., 'divine pride,' with this mantra]":[12]

oṃ sarva-tathāgata-vajra-kāya-svabhāvâtmako 'ham
oṃ; I consist of the nature of the vajra body of all the Tathāgatas.

Again, we see that the meaning of these mantras is crucial to performing the sādhana with full consciousness of what is happening. Most of the mantras that are used to assert or affirm divine pride end with the phrase, *svabhāvâtmako 'ham*, "I (*aham*) consist of (*ātmaka*) the nature of (*svabhāva*) . . ." Sometimes they only end with *aham*, "I." Both of these kinds may be seen at the conclusion of the "circle of protection" (*rakṣā-cakra*) in the *Śrī Kālacakra Sādhana*. All but the shorter Kālacakra sādhanas begin by generating a "circle of protection" within which the visualizations will take place. The *Śrī Kālacakra Sādhana* has a very extensive circle of protection, making up nearly a third of the sādhana. At its conclusion, one commands the ten wrathful protectors to take their places in the ten directions. To do this, one must first generate the divine pride, the sense or conviction of self as the lord and commander of the wrathful protectors, with the following mantra. This is a particularly clear example:[13]

oṃ hūṃ krodhêndro 'haṃ krodhānām ājñā-dāyakaḥ svāhā
oṃ hūṃ; Lord of the wrathful protectors am I, giver of commands to the wrathful protectors, svāhā!

Once again we see the necessity of understanding the meaning of these mantras. Then, after commanding each of the ten wrathful protectors to their places with an individual mantra, one completes the circle of protection portion of the sādhana by asserting and affirming the divine pride or conviction of self as the entire circle of protection, with this mantra:[14]

sarva-tathāgata-rakṣācakra-svabhāvâtmako 'ham
I consist of the nature of the circle of protection of all the Tathāgatas.

Besides clear appearance and divine pride, there are three even more universal elements of Buddhist sādhanas. These are found at the beginning of virtually all sādhanas. First is refuge, then is generating bodhicitta, and last is dissolving everything into emptiness. At that point the visualizations of the particular sādhana actually begin. For the first of these a formula is often used. It is not a mantra, but can be recited like a mantra. It is:

buddhaṃ śaraṇaṃ gacchāmi
dharmaṃ śaraṇaṃ gacchāmi
saṅghaṃ śaraṇaṃ gacchāmi

I go for refuge to the Buddha (the enlightened one).
I go for refuge to the dharma (the Buddhist teachings).
I go for refuge to the saṅgha (the Buddhist community).

Although "refuge" has become the accepted translation of the word *śaraṇa*, it here has more the sense of "guidance,"[15] and has also been translated as "safe direction."[16] The refuge formula cited above is so well known that it is not usually spelled out in the sādhanas, which often just instruct the practitioner to go for refuge. They sometimes give alternative versions of the refuge formula, as is the case in the *Śrī Kālacakra Sādhana*.[17]

For generating bodhicitta, the thought or determination to lead all living beings to enlightenment, and thereby free them from suffering, the various sādhanas sometimes give different verses to recite.[18] As with the refuge formula, the verses used for this are not mantras. Again, because it is so widely done, the sādhanas often just tell the practitioner to generate bodhicitta, without spelling out how to do this. The *Śrī Kālacakra Sādhana* just tells us to recall the three roots (of virtue, or wholesome roots), the first of which is generating bodhicitta.[19] Interestingly, the third of these is abandoning the sense of I and mine. Here, the same word is used that is used in the idea of divine pride, *ahaṃkāra*, "sense of self," or "sense of I." So we first abandon the sense of I in regard to our personal selves, and then affirm it in regard to the divine forms as which we visualize ourselves.

Then, to dissolve everything into emptiness in preparation for beginning the visualizations of the particular sādhana, these sādhanas frequently use the so-called emptiness mantra.[20]

oṃ śūnyatā-jñāna-vajra-svabhāvâtmako 'ham
oṃ; I consist of the nature of the primordial wisdom vajra of emptiness.

We immediately recognize the characteristic phrase used for asserting and affirming divine pride. The idea here is that, even though we may in fact have only a conceptual understanding of emptiness, while doing this meditation we are to act as if we have a full and direct realization of emptiness. We are to really believe that we see everything as empty. Then we can begin the particular visualizations of our sādhana in the proper manner. But what is the "primordial wisdom vajra"?

In these texts, the word "vajra," literally, "diamond," refers to the ultimate nature of something. This ultimate nature, like a diamond, is "indivisible" (*abhedya*).[21] Our body, our speech, and our mind each have an ultimate or vajra nature, which is that of a Buddha, and so does primordial wisdom.[22] Primordial wisdom is *jñāna*, distinguished from wisdom, *prajñā*, which it includes.[23] It is the pure nondual knowledge where there is no distinction between the knower and the known, because all is empty. The primordial wisdom vajra is the overall vajra that includes the other three, the body vajra, speech vajra, and mind vajra. This vajra is therefore the ultimate or vajra nature of the universe; and this is why we identify with it in order to dissolve everything into emptiness. The vajra of primordial wisdom is described in the *Jñāna-siddhi* by Indra-bhūti in these beautiful verses:[24]

46. It is not burnt by a conflagration, nor is it made wet by water.
It is not cut by a sharp weapon, even with much effort.
47. Like space, it is without support, [all-]pervasive, and devoid of distinguishing characteristics. This is the highest truth, the unsurpassed vajra [or ultimate] primordial wisdom.

In the *Śrī Kālacakra Sādhana* the emptiness mantra occurs as the first of a group of four such mantras on the four doors of liberation, namely, emptiness (*śūnyatā*), signlessness (*animitta*), wishlessness (*apraṇihita*), and nonactivity (*anabhisaṃskāra*), as follows:[25]

oṃ śūnyatā-jñāna-vajra-svabhāvâtmako 'haṃ ||
oṃ animitta-jñāna-vajra-svabhāvâtmako 'haṃ ||
oṃ apraṇihita-jñāna-vajra-svabhāvâtmako 'haṃ ||
oṃ anabhisaṃskāra-jñāna-vajra-svabhāvâtmako 'haṃ ||

oṃ; I consist of the nature of the primordial wisdom vajra of emptiness.
oṃ; I consist of the nature of the primordial wisdom vajra of signlessness.
oṃ; I consist of the nature of the primordial wisdom vajra of wishlessness.
oṃ; I consist of the nature of the primordial wisdom vajra of nonactivity.

Preceding the emptiness mantra the sādhanas often cite a famous verse that also affirms emptiness. Again, like the refuge formula, this is not a mantra. Rather, it is a metrical verse. These are normally chanted by Indian pandits. It goes as follows:[26]

abhāve bhāvanâbhāvo bhāvanā nâiva bhāvanā
iti bhāvo na bhāvaḥ syād bhāvanā nôpalabhyate

When there is no existent thing, there is no meditation. Meditation, too, is not meditation. In this way an existent thing would not be an existent thing. Meditation is not [to be] found.

This verse sounds rather nonsensical. But once we know that it comes from the *Guhyasamāja Tantra*, where it occurs as verse 3 of chapter 2, we can check to see how it is explained in the *Pradīpoddyotana* commentary thereon by Candrakīrti. Here he explains it in this way:[27]

> In the absence of all subjects, the moving and the unmoving, there is no meditation, because there is no object of meditation. "Meditation, too, is not meditation" means: The meditation [taken as] existing, too, is not meditation, because there is no meditation even without [an object of meditation]. In this way an existent thing having [both] existence and nonexistence could not be [since these are contradictory]. Therefore, neither the object of meditation, the meditator, nor meditation are [to be] found. This is the literal meaning.

Candrakīrti then goes on to explain this verse in three more ways, the first of which relates it to the three (not four) doors of liberation: emptiness, signlessness, and wishlessness. He does not discuss the fourth door of liberation, nonactivity, because this one is found in Kālacakra but not in Guhyasamāja, and his commentary is on the latter.

When everything has been dissolved into emptiness, the visualizations of the sādhana proper can begin. These are done from seed-syllables, or *bīja*-mantras. The seed-syllable of the main Kālacakra deity is quite unusual, in that it is a "stacked" syllable rather than a single syllable. It is seven letters written in a stack, one on top of the other. These form a single conjunct consonant cluster, and with the inherent vowel and concluding anusvāra, make the seed-syllable, *hkṣmlvryaṃ*. Obviously, such a *bīja*-mantra cannot be pronounced. So in the translations of the sādhanas the letters it consists of are usually written out in a string, one after the other, adding to each an inherent vowel: *ha-kṣa-ma-la-va-ra-ya*. This allows it to be pronounced, leaving only the question of where in this to put the anusvāra.

The anusvāra in Sanskrit is a dot placed above the stacked syllable. It represents an open nasal, which is transliterated as *ṃ*, even though it does not quite have an *m* sound. It is sometimes written in phoneticized Tibetan as *ng*, as in the seed-syllable *hung*, which is properly transliterated as *hūṃ*, and rhymes with room. But the *ng* sound is no closer to the actual pronunciation than the *m* sound. It should really be somewhere in between the two, a sound that is not found in English. We will here use the transliteration *ṃ*. In the Tibetan texts, like in the Sanskrit texts, it is a dot placed above the stacked syllable. This syllable is often written in the sādhana translations, following the pronunciation of modern Tibetan teachers, as: *haṃ-kṣa-ma-la-va-ra-ya*, where the *ṃ* is put after the first syllable. However, this is not allowable in Sanskrit, where the *ṃ* must be placed after the last syllable, because it is the declensional ending; so: *ha-kṣa-ma-la-va-ra-yaṃ*. As I have observed and noted elsewhere, at least some Tibetans, who have become familiar with Sanskrit now that they are living in India, have adopted this correct pronunciation.[28]

When the letters that make up this stacked *bīja*-mantra are used independently, as they are in the Kālacakra sādhana, they must individually have a declensional ending. So Kālacakra is generated from *haṃ* rather than *ha*, and the wind maṇḍala is generated from *yaṃ* rather than *ya*. The stacked seed-syllable of Kālacakra has not only an anusvāra overhead in the form of a bindu, or dot, but also a visarga in the form of a half-moon under this dot. While the anusvāra is transliterated as *ṃ*, the visarga is transliterated as *ḥ*. It is a hard breathing that echoes the vowel preceding it. Thus, *hoḥ* is pronounced something like *hoho*. It is normally written in Sanskrit much like an English colon, two vertical dots that follow the letter. But in the stacked Kālacakra seed-syllable it is supposed to be represented by the half-moon overhead, under the dot.[29] While six of the seven stacked letters take the anusvāra for their declensional ending when they are used independently, *haṃ*, *maṃ*, *laṃ*, *vaṃ*, *raṃ*, *yaṃ*, the other one takes the visarga for its declensional ending, *kṣaḥ*. These syllables, *haṃ*, etc., should rhyme with the English word "sum." On top of all of these is a flame, representing a tenth soundless sound (*nāda*), thereby making the perfect ten of the Kālacakra mantra.

From emptiness emerge the *bīja*-mantras or seed-syllables, and from these are generated the maṇḍala, i.e., the residence, and the deities who inhabit it. After these are visualized, there follows a key step. The deities whom you have visualized are, at this point, your thought constructions, imagined deities called "pledge beings" (*samaya-sattva*). You now call in the real deities, called "primordial wisdom beings" (*jñāna-sattva*), to merge with and vitalize the imagined deities. You do this with the mantra, *jaḥ hūṃ vaṃ hoḥ*. With the sound *jaḥ* you "invite" (*āvāhana*), or "draw in" (*ākarṣaṇa*) the primordial wisdom beings. For this, an implement that you as Kālacakra hold in one of your twenty-four hands is employed, the aṅkuśa. An aṅkuśa is an elephant goad. The only thing comparable to this found in Western countries is a cattle prod. But an aṅkuśa not only has a point at the end, like a prod, it also has a hook near this pointed end. So the elephant can either be prodded forward with the pointed end, or pulled back with the hook. The use of this hooked goad when inviting the primordial wisdom beings makes the invitation, shall we say, more compelling.

Next the invited primordial wisdom beings or real deities are caused to enter (*praveśana*) the pledge beings or imagined deities with the sound *hūṃ*. For this, another of the implements held in your many hands is employed, the vajra. Then they are bound (*bandhana*) there with the sound *vaṃ*. For this, the rope you hold is employed. Lastly, with the sound *hoḥ* you cause them to be satisfied (*toṣaṇa*) in their new situation. For this, your bell with its pleasing sound is employed. This four-syllable mantra, *jaḥ hūṃ vaṃ hoḥ*, is used throughout Buddhist tantric practice, whenever the primordial wisdom beings are merged with the pledge beings, just as two of the above-cited mantras are used everywhere; namely, the purity mantra, *oṃ svabhāva-śuddhāḥ sarva-dharmāḥ svabhāva-śuddho 'ham*, and the emptiness mantra, *oṃ śūnyatā-jñāna-vajra-svabhāvâtmako 'ham*.

The four syllables, *jaḥ hūṃ vaṃ hoḥ*, are all too often seen in sādhana translations as *jaḥ hūṃ baṃ hoḥ*, where *baṃ* is wrongly written for *vaṃ*. This mistake results from how this mantra is found in the Tibetan sādhanas as transliterated from Sanskrit: *dzaḥ hūṃ baṃ hoḥ*. While most translators know that the Tibetan letter *dz* transliterates the Sanskrit letter *j*, even though there is a Tibetan letter *j*, many do not know that the Tibetan letter *b* very often transliterates the Sanskrit letter *v*, despite the fact that there is a Tibetan letter *v* (or *w*). Thus they correctly write *jaḥ* for *dzaḥ*, but do not recognize that *baṃ* is in fact *vaṃ*.

This problem originated in the Indian province of Bengal, from where so many of the Sanskrit tantra manuscripts that were translated into Tibetan came. There, the Sanskrit letters *b* and *v* are not usually distinguished. The letter *v* is written for both, but is pronounced and transliterated as *b*. This may be seen in the name of the famous Bengali poet, Rabindranath Tagore, where the first part is the Sanskrit word, *ravi*, meaning "sun," not *rabi*. So, when these mantras were transliterated into Tibetan a thousand years ago, the letter *v* was transliterated as *b*. This fact may quickly and easily be ascertained by checking the transliteration of book titles found in the Tibetan Buddhist canon, where we find "badzra" for "vajra," etc. The problem of distinguishing *v* and *b*, whether as written or as pronounced, is well recognized by Bengali Sanskrit pandits such as Benoytosh Bhattacharyya (whose first name is actually Vinayatoṣa), editor of many Sanskrit Buddhist texts including the *Sādhanamālā*. In this collection of sādhanas he distinguishes the Sanskrit letter *b* from *v* in writing (spelling, for example, *bīja* rather than the incorrect *vīja*), and always correctly writes *vaṃ* rather than *baṃ* for this *bīja*-mantra.

A fifth syllable is added to these four seed-syllables in the *Śrī Kālacakra Sādhana*.[30] To the *bīja*-mantras *jaḥ hūṃ vaṃ hoḥ* is added the syllable *hīḥ*. With this syllable the primordial wisdom beings and the pledge beings are made to fuse or become of the "same taste" (*sama-rasīkṛta, sama-rasībhūta*).[31] Lovely words, but what are these primordial wisdom beings that you are supposed to make merge with the pledge beings? What does it mean that the primordial wisdom beings are real deities as opposed to the pledge beings or imagined deities? Certainly Buddhism, like all Indian religions, accepted the existence of real invisible beings known as devas, "shining ones," often translated as gods. Is this what they are? It would seem not.

The deities (*devatā*, literally, "shining one -ness, or -hood") called primordial wisdom beings (*jñāna-sattvas*) are described in the texts as the "purities" (*viśuddhi*)[32] of specific elements of our world. For example, the five Tathāgatas, also called Dhyāni Buddhas, are said to be the purities of the five aggregates (*skandha*) that make up a human being. Their consorts are the purities of the great elements, earth, water, fire, etc. The Kālacakra śaktis are the purities of the vital airs (*prāna*); and so on. As seen above, the jñāna-vajra, or primordial wisdom vajra, is the ultimate or vajra nature of the universe, since it includes the other three vajras, symbolically called body, speech, and mind. Similarly, the jñāna-sattvas, or primordial wisdom beings, are the ultimate purities of the various things that make up the universe.

Understanding what these are helps us to understand the deity called Vajrasattva, the "diamond being," i.e., the ultimate nature of a being. There are the imagined samaya-sattvas, or pledge beings, the "real" jñāna-sattvas, or primordial wisdom beings, and just plain sattvas, ordinary beings such as ourselves. Vajrasattva, as the vajra or ultimate nature of a being, is then, in a certain sense, the ultimate nature of our very selves. But this diamond-nature is that of a Buddha, so Vajrasattva is thought of as the collective purity of the Buddhas.[33] It is this that we are to call upon and identify ourselves with. This is done, as we have now come to expect, with a mantra, the hundred-syllable Vajrasattva mantra, the great mantra of purification.

Over the centuries, used in a land where its language is foreign, errors have crept into this mantra, so that this great mantra of purification is itself now in need of purification. Of course, when recited with faith, this is not to say that it is not effective. But to have the effects that the Tibetan lotsawas of old tried to retain by carefully preserving its sounds, effects it had in old India where it was pronounced correctly and its meaning was accurately understood, its words must be restored to their purity. The correct spelling and meaning of this mantra are:[34]

> oṃ vajrasattva, samayam anupālaya, vajrasattvatvenôpatiṣṭha, dṛḍho me bhava, sutoṣyo me bhava, supoṣyo me bhava, anurakto me bhava, sarva-siddhim me prayaccha, sarva-karmasu ca me cittaṃ śreyaḥ kuru hūṃ, ha ha ha ha hoḥ, bhagavan sarvatathāgata-vajra, mā me muñca, vajrī-bhava mahā-samaya-sattva, āḥ

> *Oṃ*. Vajrasattva, keep [your] pledge. As Vajrasattva, stand near [me]. Be steadfast toward me. Be well pleased with me. Be well fulfilled on account of me. Be attached to me. Grant me all accomplishments; and in all actions make my thought beneficent, *hūṃ*. *Ha ha ha ha hoḥ*. O Blessed One, Diamond-nature of all the Tathāgatas, do not abandon me. Be of diamond-nature, O great pledge being, *āḥ*.

Vajrasattva is a synthesis of the five Tathāgatas, or Dhyāni Buddhas, being their collective ultimate nature. The syllables "ha ha ha ha hoḥ" in this mantra are their seed-syllables. Each of the five has a "family" (*kula*), and the Tathāgata at the head of a family is depicted in the crown of each deity in that family. Kālacakra is crowned with Vajrasattva in the first part of the Kālacakra sādhana, indicating that Kālacakra is here considered to be in Vajrasattva's family; i.e., that Kālacakra is an emanation of Vajrasattva. This means that for this part you as Kālacakra are also identified with Vajrasattva. In the second part, Kālacakra is crowned with Akṣobhya, indicating that Kālacakra is regarded here as being in the family of the Tathāgata Akṣobhya.

The Kālacakra sādhana in its standard form, such as in the *Śrī Kālacakra Sādhana*, has four parts, not counting the circle of protection that precedes these. The second part repeats what was done in the first part, the main difference being the deity in Kālacakra's crown. These two parts of the sādhana involve lengthy visualizations, while the last two parts are brief. So the visualizations that are done in the first part, in which Kālacakra is crowned with Vajrasattva, and repeated in the second part, form the primary portion of the Kālacakra sādhana.

The full Kālacakra sādhana includes a very large number of mantras. These all necessarily come from the great Kālacakra commentary *Vimalaprabhā*, "Immaculate Light." These mantras are more or less corrupt in all existing sādhanas, due largely to copyists' errors. The three known Sanskrit manuscripts of the *Śrī*

Kālacakra Sādhana abound with clerical errors. The good news is that several older Sanskrit manuscripts of the *Vimalaprabhā* exist, including a highly accurate palm-leaf manuscript in Old Bengali script.[35] This is a superb manuscript from near the time of the Tibetan translations. With these and the help of the early Tibetan translations, it is now possible to restore to full accuracy all the mantras of the Kālacakra sādhana. Since the corrected mantras can now be saved as electronic files, they no longer need to be hand copied. This is the step in which most of the errors were introduced, whether it was the copying of an earlier manuscript to a later one, the copying of a manuscript to a woodblock for carving, or the setting up of an edited text into type for printing. The sādhana in which to do this is the *Śrī Kālacakra Sādhana*, because it consists mostly of direct extracts from the *Vimalaprabhā*, already arranged as a sādhana. Once this is done, the mantras in all Kālacakra sādhanas anywhere in use can be corrected on the basis of those found in this sādhana.

Endnotes

1. See: Janice Dean Willis, *The Diamond Light of the Eastern Dawn: A Collection of Tibetan Buddhist Meditations*, New York: Simon and Schuster, 1972. "The Yoga Method of Dorje Sempa," pp. 83-86 (Dorje Sempa is Tibetan for Vajrasattva).

2. See: Dilgo Khyentse Rinpoche, translated and edited by The Padmakara Translation Group, *The Excellent Path to Enlightenment: Oral Teachings on the Root Text of Jamyang Khyentse Wangpo*, Ithaca, New York: Snow Lion Publications, 1996. "Appendix" (the Vajrasattva mantra), pp. 103-104.

3. See: Kalu Rinpoche, *The Gem Ornament of Manifold Oral Instructions, Which Benefits Each and Everyone Appropriate,* San Francisco: KDK Publications, 1986. "Ngondro: Dorje Sempa Meditation," pp. 49-55 (Dorje Sempa is Tibetan for Vajrasattva).

4. For correct pronunciation of Sanskrit, the vowels are the most important. The short "a" is pronounced like English "u" in the word "but." The long "ā" is pronounced like "a" in "father." The short "i" is like in "kit." The long "ī" is pronounced "ee" as in "feet." The short "u" is like in "put," not like in "united." The long "ū" is pronounced "oo" as in "boot." The vowel "ṛ" is kind of like the "ri" in trip, but is trilled. The vowel "ḷ" is kind of like the "le" in "able." The "e" is pronounced like English "ay" as in "day." The "ai" is like the vowel in the word "tie." The "o" is like in "go." The "au" is like the vowel in the word "cow." For consonants, the main things are: The "c" is pronounced "ch." The "th" and "ṭh" are pronounced "ta," and aspirated. They are not like the English "th" sound. The "ś" and "ṣ" are pronounced "sh."

5. That the meanings of the mantras used in the sādhanas were meant to be understood may be seen, for example, by the statement in the *Abhisamayamañjarī of Śubhākara Gupta*, ed. by Samdhong Rinpoche and Vrajvallabh Dwivedi, Sarnath, Varanasi: Central Institute of Higher Tibetan Studies, 1993, p. 5, "having recited '*oṃ śūnyatā-jñāna-vajrasvabhāvâtmako 'ham*' with recollection of the meaning" (*oṃ śūnyatā-jñāna-vajra-svabhāvâtmako 'ham ity arthânusmaraṇenôccārya*).

6. *Kālacakrabhagavatsādhanavidhiḥ*, p. 129. See note 9 below for full bibliographic data.

7. *kāya-vāk-citta-jñāna-viśodhakāni mantra-padāni bhavanti.*

8. *Kālacakrabhagavatsādhanavidhiḥ*, p. 130. See note 9 below for full bibliographic data.

9. This was published as "Kālacakrabhagavatsādhanavidhiḥ of Dharmākaraśānti," in *Dhīḥ: Journal of Rare Buddhist Texts Research Project*, Sarnath, vol. 24, 1997, 127-174. But as pointed out by Yong-hyun Lee, this is actually the *Śrī Kālacakra Sādhana* by Sādhuputra, found in the Tibetan Tengyur (Tohoku no. 1358; Peking no. 2075). According to the colophon in this Tibetan Tengyur translation, which is much earlier than the late Nepalese manuscripts where it is ascribed to Dharmākaraśānti, it was written *for* Dharmākaraśānti, not *by* him. See: *The Niṣpannayogāvalī by Abhayākaragupta: A New Critical Edition of the Sanskrit Text (Revised Edition)*, by Yong-hyun Lee, Seoul: Baegun Press, 2004, p. xii, n. 28. I have used this sādhana since the 1980s, when I obtained microfilms of Sanskrit manuscripts of it from libraries in Nepal and Japan.

10. Although the title *Vimalaprabhā* has now become more widely known in its translation as "Stainless Light," I have preferred the no less accurate "Immaculate Light." This I have adapted from Edward Fitzgerald's "Immaculate Lustre," found in his English translation of Helmut Hoffmann's book, *The Religions of Tibet*, 1961, pp. 129, 162.

11. For the term *devatâhaṃkāra*, see, for example, *Sādhanamālā*, ed. Benoytosh Bhattacharyya, vol. 1, Baroda: Central Library, 1925; Gaekwad's Oriental Series no. 26, p. 258.

12. *Kālacakrabhagavatsādhanavidhiḥ,* p. 130: *tato 'haṃkāraṃ.*

13. *Kālacakrabhagavatsādhanavidhiḥ,* p. 140.

14. *Kālacakrabhagavatsādhanavidhiḥ,* p. 140.

15. *The Buddhist Catechism*, by Henry S. Olcott, 44th ed., 1915, n. to para. 149, citing a letter from Wijesinha Mudaliyar, "This word has been hitherto very inappropriately and erroneously rendered *Refuge* by European Pāli scholars, and thoughtlessly so accepted by native Pāli scholars. Neither Pāli etymology nor Buddhistic philosophy justifies the translation. *Refuge*, in the sense of a *fleeing back or a place of shelter*, is quite foreign to true Buddhism, which insists on every man working out his own emancipation. The root *Sri* in Sanskrit (*Sara* in Pāli) means to move, to go: so that *Saranam* would denote a moving, or he or that which goes before or with another—a Guide or Helper. I construe the passage thus: *Gachchhāmi*, I go, *Buddham*, to Buddha, *Saranam*, as my Guide."

16. By Alexander Berzin, in *Taking the Kalachakra Initiation*, Ithaca: Snow Lion Publications, 1997, pp. 79 ff.

17. *Kālacakrabhagavatsādhanavidhiḥ*, p. 160: *buddhaṃ dharmañ ca saṃghaṃ bhava-bhaya-haraṇaṃ bodhi-sīmnaḥ prayāmi*, "I go to the Buddha, the dharma, and the saṃgha, removing the fears of cyclic existence, until the summit of enlightenment." For a longer version, see: *Sādhanamālā*, vol. 1, pp. 29, 154, 290-291.

18. The generating of bodhicitta is often done in association with the four immeasurables: loving-kindness (*maitrī*), compassion (*karuṇā*), sympathetic joy (*mudita*), and equanimity (*upekṣā*). So the verse or verses recited for this may include these, as is the case in the *Kālacakra Six-Session Guru Yoga* by the Fourteenth Dalai Lama.

19. The three roots of virtue, or wholesome roots (*kuśala-mūla*), are listed in Nāgārjuna's *Dharma-saṃgraha*, 15, as: (1) the generation of *bodhicitta* (*bodhicittotpāda*); (2) the purification of [one's] intentions or motivations (*āśaya-viśuddhi*); and (3) the abandoning of the sense of I and mine (*ahaṃkāra-mamakāra-parityāga*).

20. This mantra has been called the "*śūnyatā-bodhako mantraḥ*," the mantra awakening one to emptiness; see: *Sādhanamālā*, vol. 1, 315.

21. The word "vajra" is regularly defined as "indivisible" (*abhedya*) in the Buddhist tantric literature. For example, Advaya-vajra cites this definition from the *Hevajra Tantra* (1.1.4) in his *Sekatānvaya-saṃgraha* or *Sekatātparyasaṃgraha*, with the words: *abhedyam vajram iti hevajre*. See: *Advayavajrasaṃgraha*, ed. Haraprasad Shastri, Baroda: Oriental Institute, 1927; Gaekwad's Oriental Series no. 40, p. 37. This was reedited in: "Advayavajrasaṃgraha—New Critical Edition and Japanese Translation," ed. Mikkyo-Seiten Kenkyukai (Study Group for the Buddhist Tantric Texts), Part 2, *Annual of the Institute for Comprehensive Studies of Buddhism, Taisho University*, no. 11, March 1989, 231 (114).

22. These four vajras are described in the Kālacakra texts. See, for example, *Vimalaprabhāṭīkā*, vol. 1, ed. Jagannatha Upadhyaya, Sarnath, Varanasi: Central Institute of Higher Tibetan Studies, 1986, p. 45. They are discussed by Vesna Wallace in *The Inner Kālacakratantra: A Buddhist Tantric View of the Individual*, New York: Oxford University Press, 2001, pp. 156-159.

23. Translators are always faced with the question of how to deal with closely related words such as *jñāna* and *prajñā*. The translation "wisdom" for *prajñā* has become widely accepted, as in the "perfection of wisdom" (*prajñā-pāramitā*), although a few translators use "insight" for it instead. But what, then, do we do with *jñāna*, which also means wisdom. Here there is no general consensus among translators. Some prefer "knowledge," its basic meaning in common Sanskrit. But in Buddhism it is a technical term, as was recognized by the early Tibetan translators, and shown by their rendering of it as *ye śes*. In this word, *śes* translates the Sanskrit root *jñā*, "to know," qualified by *ye*, meaning primordial or pristine, or exalted or sublime. Thus, it was understood to mean not just knowledge, but pristine or sublime knowledge; and modern translators often add these qualifying words. Many translators (including myself) prefer "wisdom" over "knowledge" for *jñāna*, even though "know" is linguistically cognate with "*jñā*." In English, you can have knowledge of how to make gunpowder, or how to pick a lock, for example, but this would not be considered wisdom. Some translators have adopted the also linguistically cognate "gnosis" for *jñāna*. This word, however, is little used in English, being primarily a technical term of the now defunct Gnostic sects, and few people know what it means without looking it up in the dictionary. By contrast, *jñāna* is widely used in Sanskrit, and even as a technical term in Buddhism it still retains its well-known meaning of knowledge. Other words that have been used to translate *jñāna* are "cognition" and "awareness," with or without qualifying words such as pristine, and also "intuition." All of these provide helpful insights into the meaning of *jñāna*, but in my opinion unduly restrict its meaning more to aspects of knowledge or wisdom rather than providing the central idea itself. Therefore, to distinguish *jñāna* from *prajñā*, as the Tibetan translators always did, and which has proven so helpful over the last thousand years, I have chosen "primordial wisdom" for *jñāna*. I note that Alan Wallace uses this in his translation of Gen Lamrimpa's book, *Transcending Time: The Kālacakra Six-Session Guru Yoga*, Boston: Wisdom Publications, 1999.

24. The *Jñāna-siddhi* was published in *Two Vajrayāna Works*, ed. Benoytosh Bhattacharyya, Baroda: Oriental Institute, 1929; Gaekwad's Oriental Series no. 44, where these two verses occur on p. 36:

dahyate nâgni-skandhena plāvyate na jalena ca |
bhidyate nahi śastreṇa tīkṣṇenâpi prayatnataḥ || 46 ||

apratiṣṭhaṃ yathâkāśaṃ vyāpi lakṣaṇa-varjitam |
idaṃ tat paramaṃ tattvaṃ vajra-jñānam anuttaram || 47 ||

Even though this Sanskrit edition has been available for more than seventy-five years, there still seems to be no English translation of it. The first of these verses is reminiscent of *Bhagavad-gītā* 2.23: "Weapons do not cut this; fire does not burn it. Water does not wet it; nor does wind dry it."

25. *Kālacakrabhagavatsādhanavidhiḥ*, p. 161.

26. This is found in the *Kālacakrabhagavatsādhanavidhiḥ*, p. 161. It there comes from the *Vimalaprabhā* commentary, chapter 4, verse 5. See: *Vimalaprabhāṭīkā*, vol. 2, ed. Vrajavallabh Dwivedi et al., Sarnath, Varanasi: Central Institute of Higher Tibetan Studies, 1994, 153. But it ultimately comes from the *Guhyasamāja Tantra*, chapter 2, verse 3. Its Tibetan translation in the *Vimalaprabhā*, Derge and Cone eds., with variants from the Narthang and Peking eds. in brackets, is:

dngos po med la bsgom [sgom] pa med
sgom pa sgom pa nyid ma yin
de ltar dngos po dngos min pas [mi 'gyur]
sgom pa dmigs su med pa'o

27. This is in: *Guhyasamājatantrapradīpodyotanaṭīkā-ṣaṭkoṭivyākhyā*, ed. Chintaharan Chakravarti, Patna: Kashi Prasad Jayaswal Research Institute, 1984; Tibetan Sanskrit Works Series no. 25, p. 31. The text found in this edition differs somewhat from the Tibetan translation. My translation is of the Sanskrit, but I have had to correct it in three places with the help of the Tibetan. These are given in brackets below. The two longer bracketed phrases in my translation are based on the differing Tibetan text, which is also given below in full.

sthira-bala-[cala]-sarva-padārthānām abhāve sati bhāvanāyā abhāvaḥ bhāvyâbhāvāt bhāvanā nâiva bhāvanêti | yâpi sato [satī] bhāvanā sā na bhāvanā, vinâpi bhāvanāyā [a]vidyamānatvāt iti | itthaṃ bhāvâbhāva-yukto yo bhāvaḥ sa na syāt | tasmād bhāvyo bhāvako bhāvanā nôpalabhyate | akṣarârthaḥ |

brtan pa dang g.yo ba'i dngos po thams cad kyi ngo bo nyid ni med pa yin na ni sgom pa med pa ste bsgom par bya ba med pa'i phyir ro | bsgom par bya ba bsgom pa min | zhes bya ba ni | gang yod par bsgom pa de yang bsgom pa ma yin te | bsgom par bya ba dang bral bas yod pa ma yin pas so | de ltar zhes pa ni dngos po med pa dang dngos po yod par 'dod pa dang ldan pa gang yin pa de ni dngos po med pa nyid de phyogs gnyi ga dang 'gal lo | de bas na bsgom par bya ba dang sgom pa po dang bsgom pa dmigs su med pa ste yi ge'i don to |

28. "On Kālacakra Sādhana and Social Responsibility," the International Kalachakra Network website, at: http://kalachakranet.org/text_david_reigle_kalacakra_sadhana_social.html:

"The founder and former longtime Director of the Central Institute of Higher Tibetan Studies is Samdhong Rinpoche, currently Prime Minister of the Tibetan Government-in-Exile. Although I knew that Tibetans studying there had to learn Sanskrit pronunciation, it was still a pleasant surprise to me to hear Samdhong Rinpoche pronounce the Kālacakra heart mantra in the Sanskrit fashion. He did this during a break in our 1997 discussions on his ideas of how to have a nonviolent society. When he pronounced the nasal after the last syllable, as is required in Sanskrit, rather than after the first syllable, as is the current practice among Tibetan Lamas, I expressed my surprise. He replied that of course he followed the Sanskrit pronunciation. Why wouldn't he when the original is now available?"

29. *Vimalaprabhāṭīkā*, vol. 1, p. 56: *visargo ardha-candrâkāro*, "*visarga* is in the form of a half-moon."

30. *Kālacakrabhagavatsādhanavidhiḥ*, p. 165.

31. *Vimalaprabhāṭīkā* 4.53, vol. 2, 181:

> evaṃ pañca-prakāraṃ jaḥ-kāreṇâkṛṣṭam, hūṃ-kāreṇa praviṣṭam, vaṃ-kāreṇa baddham, hoḥ-kāreṇa toṣitam, hīḥ-kāreṇa sama-rasīkṛtaṃ |
> vajrâṅkuśena vajreṇa vajra-pāśena vajra-ghaṇṭayā vajra-daṇḍenêti |
> evaṃ jñāna-cakraṃ saṃpūjya pūrvavat samaya-cakraṃ sama-rasībhūtaṃ bhāvayed iti niyamaḥ |

See also: *Vimalaprabhāṭīkā* 3.79, vol. 2, 78-79.

32. *Kālacakra Sādhana and Social Responsibility*, by David Reigle, Santa Fe: Spirit of the Sun Publications, 1996, pp. 42-43: "The primary sources on this are, of course, the *Kālacakra Tantra* and the *Vimalaprabhā* commentary. The symbolism is generally introduced in the commentary by the words, 'Now the purification of . . . is stated' (*idānīṃ . . . viśuddhir ucyate*). Much of it is given in the latter part of the third section (*uddeśa*) of the fourth chapter (*paṭala*) of the *Vimalaprabhā*, 'Generation of the Life and the Deities' (*prāṇa-devatā-utpāda*), verses 95-109. Other references include chapter three, verses 52-55, 160-164, 167-168, etc."

33. See: Lama Thubten Yeshe, *The Tantric Path of Purification: The Yoga Method of Heruka Vajrasattva*, Boston: Wisdom Publications, 1995, pp. 141-142 (2nd ed., 2004, with new title: *Becoming Vajrasattva: The Tantric Path of Purification*): "Who is Heruka Vajrasattva? We consider him to be a manifestation of the unity of fully developed male and female energy, the complete purity of the state of enlightenment. Out of their great compassion and limitless love, the buddhas and bodhisattvas have manifested their collected purity in the archetypal image of Vajrasattva so that we can identify ourselves with him. We have to understand that the qualities of Vajrasattva are already within us. But our realizations, method, and wisdom are limited. They have to be developed through identification with the limitless, pure energy of the archetype."

34. This is from my unfinished article, "The Vajrasattva Mantra: Sanskrit Edition and English Translation," for which I have utilized many Sanskrit and Tibetan sources. For example, I have noted eight occurrences of the Vajrasattva mantra in the *Sādhanamālā*, and these occur seven times in the two old palm-leaf Sanskrit manuscripts that were reproduced in facsimile by Gudrun Bühnemann in the Wiener Studien zur Tibetologie und Buddhismuskunde, vol. 32, 1994. One of the manuscripts came from Bu-ston's Źa lu Monastery in Tibet. These same *Sādhanamālā* occurrences of this mantra are found fourteen times in the Tibetan Tengyur, and in four Tengyur editions. So a fair number of sources have been checked to establish the correct form of this mantra. The most common error in modern books is taking the second occurrence of Vajrasattva as a vocative; that is, as addressing Vajrasattva twice. In fact, this word is Vajrasattvatvena, having the *–tva* suffix, and declined in the third or instrumental case. This declined suffix, literally "by being," means "as being"; thus, "as Vajrasattva." Even though mantras are not normally translated into Tibetan, a few translations were made, and these confirm this word, giving: *rdo rje sems dpa' nyid*, where the *nyid* translates the Sanskrit suffix *-tva*. There are many other errors in modern English translations of this mantra, which translations should be compared with the one given here.

35. This manuscript is found in the library of the Asiatic Society, Calcutta, where it is no. 10766. The usefulness of this manuscript may be seen by the following. Abhayākara-gupta in his *Niṣpannayogāvalī* gives the Kālacakra heart mantra or seed-syllable (*hṛd-bīja*). It is given as *hūṃ* in the 1949 edition by Benoytosh Bhattacharyya, published in the Gaekwad's Oriental Series, no. 109, from Baroda, p. 93. For more than half a century, this was the only edition. Then in the 2004 new critical edition by Yong-hyun Lee (see note 9 above) it is given as *hraṃ* instead (p. 113). The editor adopted this reading on the basis of the printed edition of the *Vimalaprabhāṭīkā* and only a single old palm-leaf manuscript, as against several other later manuscripts and even the two Tibetan translations of the *Niṣpannayogāvalī*. In a footnote on p. xv he notes that "There is a possibility that the editor of the VP misread the reading of the most excellent manuscript *Ca*." This refers to the variant readings given in the *Vimalaprabhāṭīkā*, vol. 2, p. 80, where the manuscript designated *Ca*, the Calcutta manuscript in Old Bengali script that we are discussing, is listed as reading *hūṃ* rather than *hraṃ*. In fact, this most excellent manuscript reads *hraṃ*, as I have verified from a microfilm of it in my possession. Thus, it confirms that the true Kālacakra heart mantra or seed-syllable (*hṛd-bīja*) is *hraṃ*, despite the large number of later sources giving it as *hūṃ*.

–17–

Rendawa and the Question of Kālacakra's Uniqueness

Thupten Jinpa

Preamble

In his autobiographical song, *A Destiny Fulfilled*, when recounting his study of the various Buddhist systems, especially the great systems of tantra, the great Tsongkhapa (1357-1419) writes the following:

> Fourth with respect to the unexcelled [class of tantra],
> I have studied those that are well known to the learned Indian masters—
> The father tantra *Guhyasamāja*, the yogini tantras *Hevajra* and *Saṃvara*,
> Their root tantras, their explanatory tantras, and their condensed tantras—
> As well as the great chariotway so different from others systems,
> The *Kālacakratantra* and its elucidator, the *Stainless Light*.[1]

This idea of the uniqueness of the Kālacakra system is taken up further in Tsongkhapa's later works, such as his *Great Exposition of the Stages of the Secret Mantra* as well as his exposition of the influential Kālacakra text *Stainless Light*, which Khedrup Je (1385-1438) compiled on the basis of notes taken from Tsongkhapa's teachings. In these writings Tsongkhapa not only strives to demonstrate the essential similarity of the *Kālacakratantra* to other, more established tantras of the highest yoga class, such as Guhyasamāja and Cakrasaṃvara, but he also explores in great detail what he perceives to be the unique features of the system. With regard to this second aspect, Tsongkhapa takes great pains to expound these in such a way that these features are totally consonant with the fundamentals of the Mahāyāna tradition, especially its philosophical view of emptiness and dependent origination and its ethical principle of universal compassion. Thus, we see in these writings a self-conscious effort on the part of Tsongkhapa to demonstrate the validity of the system.

Understanding why Tsongkhapa felt the need to demonstrate the validity of the Kālacakra system allows us to appreciate a little-known aspect of the story of this important Buddhist tantra in Tibet. By this I am referring to the qualms raised about the system by a few dissenting voices in Tibet in the midst of what was otherwise an overwhelmingly enthusiastic reception to the tantra. The *Kālacakratantra* came to Tibet in the first half of the eleventh century of the common era when the condensed tantra was translated into Tibetan. This was soon followed by the translation of Puṇḍarīka's voluminous commentary, *Stainless Light,* on the Kālacakra root tantra as well as new translations of the condensed tantra; according to one source, eventually some fourteen different translations were made of the condensed tantra. Over time two main transmissions of the Kālacakra system evolved in Tibet, one known as the "Dro tradition" stemming from the translator Dro Lotsāwa who worked with the Kaśmīri master Somanātha and the second known as the "Ra tradition" stemming from the translator Ra Lotsāwa (1016-98) who worked with the Indian master Samanthaśrī.[2] Of the numerous Tibetan scholars and masters who propagated the Kālacakra system in Tibet, the influential historical work *Blue Annals* credits two figures, the great encylopedist Büton Rinchen Drup (1290-1364) and the Jonang master Dölpopa Sherap Gyaltsen (1292-1361), for making the tantra most widespread in the country. The tantra attracted voluminous commentarial literature across almost all schools of Tibetan tradition, especially the Jonang and Geluk schools.[3]

Most historical writings in Tibetan, including the *Blue Annals*, give the impression that the embracing of the Kālacakra in Tibet was unequivocal. This, however, does not tell the whole story. Already, in the thirteenth century, the noted Kadam master Chomden Rikral (1227-1305) appears to have raised serious questions about the credential of Kālacakra as a legitimate Buddhist tantra. Unfortunately, other than a cursory mention of some of the objections raised by him, today we do not have access to Rikral's own work or any explicit responses to his qualms by others.[4] Undoubtedly, the most famous—or notorious, depending on your perspective—critic of Kālacakra in Tibet was Rendawa Shönu Lodrö (1349-1412), a noted Sakya master who was one of the principal teachers of Tsongkhapa. I first heard of Rendawa's critique of Kālacakra from my own teacher, the late Kyabjé Zemey Rinpoché. This was in response to my sense of unease about some important features of the system, notably the striking similarity in technical vocabulary, especially of the twenty-five categories of reality, with the Sāṃkhya school, as well as the idea of dematerializing the particles within our body through the stacking of drops, "like a powerful mercury consuming the metal nature of a base material and refining it into gold," as a text puts it. In addition, having had the privilege of translating at the Kālacakra initiation conferred by His Holiness the Dalai Lama on several occasions, every time I sat down to recite the sādhana and visualize the maṇḍala, I often felt that there was a certain, deliberate emphasis on elaborate scale, whether in the number of deities in the maṇḍala or in the use of syllables as seeds for the generation of these deities. Rinpoché also told me that although the text of Rendawa's own critique is today almost impossible to find, a succinct rebuttal of his critiques could be found in the exposition of the general meaning of Kālacakra by Taktsang Lotsāwa (b. 1405), the noted critic of Tsongkhapa's

Madhyamaka philosophy. Rinpoché felt that it was important for me to read these exchanges so that I would have a better appreciation of the importance of this system of teaching. To learn that Rendawa raised critical qualms about Kālacakra was intriguing, especially when it is clear that for Tsongkhapa the validity of the system was not an issue at all.

Years went by in the meantime and life moved on; and since the Kālacakra did not figure prominently in my own personal practice, these qualms did not bother me that much. However, everything changed when I had to work on the critical editing of the Tibetan text of Khedrup Norsang Gyatso's (1423-1513) *Ornament of Stainless Light*, which was featured in The Library of Tibetan Classics series on the advice of His Holiness the Dalai Lama. In working on this text, I had to study the system carefully and also to seek out the references to Rendawa where the author attempts to respond to some of the more substantive qualms. Fortunately, by this time Rendawa's text, *A Jewel Garland*, which was the initial open letter that set the debate on the Kālacakra in the open, as well as his own replies to the letter and the responses from other Tibetan masters were published together as part of a collection of texts on Tibetan astronomy.[5] This opened up an opportunity to study Rendawa's qualms on the basis of his own letter as well as the rebuttals it attracted. What follows is a brief analysis of the key qualms raised by Rendawa about Kālacakra. I shall suggest that the serious engagement with these critical points helps us appreciate what makes the Kālacakra system so unique among all the Buddhist tantras of the highest yoga class. In this paper, we shall not have the space or the opportunity to examine the specifics of Rendawa's qualms, including their merits as well as the cogency of the defences offered by his contemporaries and subsequent Tibetan Kālacakra masters. This is a topic that deserves a careful separate study.

Rendawa's qualms

The full title of Rendawa's letter is *A Jewel Garland: A Letter Offered to the Holders of Dharma Pertaining to the Analysis of the Kālacakra*. It is written in verse and runs to ten pages of a standard modern book. In the opening section of the letter, following a standard salutation verse, Rendawa appeals to "the holders of the dharma" to help wash the dirt that stains the wish-granting jewel of the Buddha's teaching with the help of unadulterated scriptures and reasoning, which he likens to the water of the river Ganges. He then goes on to give a brief account of the various categories of teachings which the Buddha gave, how they came to be compiled, and how, following the second council, the four classical Buddhist philosophical schools evolved. Rendawa then establishes one of his central premises: that any system of thought or practice at odds with these four classical philosophical standpoints must lie outside the bounds of Buddhist thought. Having set the stage, the author then opens his critique of the Kālacakra with the remark that in general there exist numerous false texts and spiritual lineages in Tibet and how, even with respect to those that are well known to the learned ones, there exist some that lack reliability. The following verse opens his actual critique of the Kālacakra:

> Although the Kālacakra is renowned as having been composed
> By the powerful [bodhisattvas abiding] on the ten levels,
> When thoroughly analyzed if it is valid or not,
> I do not see it to be acceptable.[6]

According to Rendawa, there is no mention in the Kālacakra root tantra of one of the most important features of the highest yoga class of Buddhist tantra, namely the discussion of EVAM, while the condensed tantra is replete with internal contradictions. Furthermore, there appear to be no authoritative sources for this system of tantra. Given that space prevents us from presenting the entire text of Rendawa's qualms, I shall simply list his key objections. In doing so, I shall follow Taktsang Lotsāwa (b. 1405), who, in his *General Meaning of the Kālacakratantra*, identifies altogether the following thirteen objections raised by Rendawa:[7]

1. Its presentation, on the philosophical level, of a notion of emptiness as a material form that is utterly at odds with any Buddhist philosophical thinking;
2. Its description of sentient beings as fully awakened Buddhas;
3. Its explanation of the worlds of both the container and the contained, including especially the four castes of India, as emerging from the mouth of the Kālacakra deity;
4. Its description of the sexual bliss of emission as the principal cause of cyclic existence;
5. Its presentation of the cosmos is at odds with the Abhidharma account;
6. Its presentation of the inner channels and winds are in contradiction with the other, more established tantras.

Taktsang identifies these six objections as pertaining to the nature of the ground within the threefold basic scheme of ground, path, and result. Of the remaining seven objections, the first four pertain to the path while the latter three relate to the result.

7. Its presentation, on the level of the path, of the empowerments and the commitments are at odds with the other tantras;
8. Its generation stage cannot be a cause for achieving the supreme attainment;
9. Its description of the empty-form of the completion to be the dharmakāya;
10. Its suggestion that one cannot attain Buddhahood in the intermediate state of existence;
11. Its presentation of the body and mind of the resultant state of Buddhahood to be of the same single entity;

12. Its rejection of any materially composed phenomena on the resultant level of Buddhahood; and
13. Its description of the Enjoyment Body to be the nature of speech.

In Rendawa's own letter, much of the attention at the beginning is directed toward demonstrating the influence of non-Buddhist thought on the Kālacakra system. For example, he argues that the opening of the Kālacakra root tantra, with the Kalkī king Sucandra questioning the Buddha about the nature of the twenty-five categories of reality, remains suspicious. He argues that, since it relates to the Sāṃkhya categories, this question pertains to the properties of a nonexistent property-bearer, namely *puruṣa*, so therefore this question should be treated on a par with the fourteen unanswered questions.[8] Similarly, as the root tantra describes the evolution of sentient beings on the basis of the natural physical elements, it propounds a standpoint of the materialist Carvāka school. Since it groups plants in the category of birth as animals, it promotes a Jaina standpoint. As it presents the emergence of the cosmos from "empty particles" it presents a key Vaiśeṣika standpoint. Furthermore, the cosmology presented in the Kālacakra, especially the size of the continents and Mt. Meru, is at odds with the standard Abhidharma system. These objections together appear to follow on Chomden Rikral's principal objection that the *Kālacakratantra* represents a serious adulteration of Buddhist tantra with non-Buddhist elements. Rendawa in fact mentions that Chomden Rikral composed a treatise differentiating the Buddhist and the non-Buddhist elements of the tantra.[9] Finally, Rendawa argues, the statement that the four castes of the human race emerged from the Kālacakra's mouth is no different from the assertion that Brahmā created the world.

In another section, Rendawa critiques the Kālacakra for what he sees as its erroneous reading of the Buddhist schools Vaibhāṣika and Sautrāntika. He particularly singles out the Kālacakra's assertion that the Vaibhāṣika school accepts a notion of an indeterminate, ineffable person and the claim that Sautrāntika rejects the concept of nonobstructive form. In the former case, Rendawa correctly points out that it is the Vātsīputrīyās, not Vaibhāṣikas, which propose the concept of an indeterminate person; while in the latter context, Rendawa points out that Sautrāntika does not reject the notion of nonobstructive form in general. Rendawa also raises an interesting historical question pertaining to the tantra when he refers to a statement in Puṇḍarīka's *Stainless Light* that the root tantra was composed in different languages in different places, including in Tibetan in Tibet! Rendawa argues that if at the time of the composition of *Stainless Light* Buddhism already existed in Tibet, this statement may be tenable; otherwise, this statement should be in the future tense, which it is not. On a practical level, Rendawa levels the charge that it would be impossible to complete the approximation retreat of the entire maṇḍala deities of Kālacakra within the hundred-year human lifespan. Here Rendawa refers to a similar observation made by Butön as well. So if one cannot even accomplish the generation stage, he asks, how can this tantra confer Buddhahood within a single lifetime? He also asserts that the essential points of the six-limbed yoga of the Kālacakra completion stage are in conflict with the Guhyasamāja. Comparing Kālacakra to the more established tantras, such as Guhyasamāja, Hevajra, and Cakrasaṃvara, Rendawa asserts that these tantras were brought to the world by great Mahāsiddhas like Saraha, expounded by Nāgārjuna and his sons, and produced masters who attained freedom on the basis of practicing their essential points. In contrast, in the case of the Kālacakra, he asks:

In your case, who are the authoritative figures that received it?
Who attained freedom on the basis of practicing its essential points?
Since they were not known to the great ones as authorities,
Kālacakrapāda and others are not perfect valid beings.

As for the Kalkī kings of Śambhala and so on,
These are matters to be proven rather than your proof.
Now if your clinging to this [tantra] still does not cease,
For your proof you shall have to swear.
What other evidence can there be?
These are then some of its flaws.
If probed in detail the objections are limitless.[10]

Rendawa closes his letter with a somewhat conciliatory note. He asserts that, regardless of whether the *Kālacakratantra* was composed by the Noble bodhisattvas or not, since many elements of well-uttered insights can be perceived in this tantra, he does not denigrate the system categorically by suggesting that it should never be an entrance for those who seek liberation.

Rendawa's replies to his own qualms

It seems that Rendawa's open letter elicited vigorous rebuttals, some of which appear to have been quite fierce. This is no surprise given that by the mid-fourteenth century Kālacakra had already assumed a central place, not only in Tibetan Buddhist thought and practice in general, but in the intellectual landscape as a whole. One area where Kālacakra's influence was most far-reaching, and in fact seminally defining, is the field of Tibetan astronomy. For example, the Sakya hierarch Phakpa (1235-80) composed in his youth a treatise on the calendral astronomy based on Kālacakra, drawing parity between the Chinese calendar and the Tibetan one.[11] So it is no wonder that most of these rebuttals to Rendawa were penned by noted scholars of Tibetan astronomy. These include Gö Lotsāwa Shönu Pal (1392-1481), the author of the *Blue Annals*, Jangpa Namgyal Draksang (1395-1475), an important student of the prolific Bodong Choklé Namgyal, and the noted Kālacakra scholar Taktsang Lotsāwa. In the first two rebuttals the entire text of Rendawa's letter is cited and responded to point by point, while Taktsang Lotsāwa's is a more pointed response to the key challenges. In addition, we find a short response to Rendawa, specifically on his critique of the Kālacakra cosmology, in the writings of Shākya Chokden (1428-1507).[12] Most probably there were other responses of whose existence we do not know at this point, some of which may have appeared during Rendawa's own lifetime.[13] It is doubtful whether any of the three responses mentioned earlier, which do survive today, appeared before Rendawa's death. Interestingly, Rendawa himself also penned a reply to his own open letter, albeit at the behest of a student.

In his own reply, which is also written in verse and entitled *A Self-addressed Reply to the Letter, A Jewel Garland*, Rendawa opens with the explanation of his motive behind writing the open letter in the first place. He explains that he composed this letter of critical enquiry as a corrective, like straightening out wood that is born crooked, to the proliferation of false discourses which were in vogue in Tibet and which conflicted with an entire host of perfect sūtras and tantras and stemmed from grasping at the literal truth of the Kālacakra and its commentaries. The overall strategy in this self-addressed reply is to argue that all the aspects of the Kālacakra system that are at odds with established Buddhist sūtras and tantras must be recognized as interpretable and thus not taken literally. These include the statement that the sexual bliss of emission is the cause of cyclic existence, which, Rendawa explains, is primarily intended to help appreciate its antidote, the great immutable bliss. Also, the presentation of a cosmology that is consonant with the great Bharata[14] rather than Buddhist Abhidharma is to help sustain the non-Buddhist seers so that, on the basis of a cosmology familiar to them, the truth of the inner elements can be presented to them. Moreover, these non-Buddhists predict that when the face of the earth is overrun by the barbarians, who represent the demi-gods, the powerful Viṣṇu will manifest himself as a Kalkī king and defeat the barbarians; just so, to help sustain the non-Buddhists, there are statements regarding how the Kalkī king Rudracakri will defeat those following the barbarian path, although the true intention refers to the inner process wherein the flow of the twelve winds inside the two side channels are brought to an end through meditative absorptions such as vitality-stopping. Interestingly, Rendawa also argues that, just as in order to help lead non-Buddhists who are attached to the notion of self the Buddha therefore spoke of the presence in all sentient beings of a buddha-essence endowed with all enlightened qualities (the concept of tathāgatagarbhā), with the understanding that the paths of the three vehicles are to be practiced individually by their respective practitioners, so too the *Kālacakratantra* states how the teachings of the three vehicles were compiled by the Disciples, Self-Enlightened Ones, and the bodhisattvas, respectively. Rendawa explains that the reference to the tantra's being taught also in Tibetan is aimed at helping overcome attachment to Sanskrit as a uniquely Buddhist language. In brief, he says, whatever aspects one finds in the Kālacakra system that are in conflict with the sūtras and tantras, the learned ones who rely on the meaning rather than the mere words must seek their intended meaning and demonstrate how the system is free of flaws.

In suggesting that those features of the Kālacakra that are at odds with established sūtras and tantras must be interpreted as having a specific intended purpose, Rendawa is actually following in the footsteps of Abhayākaragupta, a noted Indian

Buddhist author who accepted Kālacakra's authenticity as Buddhist.[15] This approach involves applying the well-known Mahāyāna hermeneutic of distinguishing between the definitive and interpretable meanings of a scripture. The central challenge posed by Rendawa on the lack of authoritative sources for the Kālacakra is taken up quite effectively in Gö Lotsāwa's response, which cites references to Kālacakra found in the explanatory tantra of Guhyasamāja, *Vajramāla*, and a salutation verse in a work by Ghaṇṭapa where the stanza echoes lines from Puṇḍarīka's *Stainless Light* as well as making explicit mention of Śambhala. In addition, Gö Lotsāwa cites how the great Nāropa as well as Abhayākaragupta wrote treatises on the tantra, and how Maitripa's student Sahajavarja cites extensively from Nāropa's work on the tantra.[16]

It seems that much of the debate on the Kālacakra's authenticity revolves around its cosmology. On the one side are those like Abhayākaragupta in India and Rendawa in Tibet for whom the Abhidharma cosmology remains the Buddhist norm and the Kālacakra cosmology must be taken as interpretable. On the other side are those Tibetan Kālacakra enthusiasts like Taktsang and Shākya Chokden for whom the Kālacakra cosmology represents the definitive teaching and the Abhidharma model must be interpreted as having been taught specifically to accommodate those with non-Mahāyāna leanings.[17] Then there are others like Ratnākaraśanti (known also as Śāntipa) in India and Chomden Rikral in Tibet who categorically rejected the system as a genuine Buddhist tantra.[18] Finally, we have those who might be referred to as the syncretists who argue that the Kālacakra cosmology is ultimately not in conflict with the Abhidharma system and that both can be accepted on the literal level. This last group includes Tsongkhapa, Khedrup Je, and the noted authority on Kālacakra and astronomy Khedrup Norsang Gyatso (1423-1513).[19] Norsang Gyatso devotes an entire section of his *Ornament of Stainless Light* to the demonstration of how there exists no contradiction between the two systems of explanation on cosmology.[20]

Judging by its tone and content, it appears that by the time Rendawa came to write his reply to the very qualms he himself raised, he had changed his views on this important Buddhist tantra. Like Abhayākaragupta, he seems to have accepted its authenticity as a genuine Buddhist tantra but took many of its distinctive features as being interpretable with specific purposes behind their presentations.[21] At this point in our historical knowledge, it is difficult to discern what made Rendawa change his mind. Clearly, given the closeness of his relation with Tsongkhapa, who never doubted the authenticity of Kālacakra, we cannot rule out the possibility of Tsongkhapa's being an important influence.

The *Kālacakratantra's* unique features

Although, as noted earlier, Tsongkhapa never alludes to either Rendawa's or Chomden Rikral's critiques of Kālacakra, he appears to have been clearly aware of these objections. For example, when explaining the unique Kālacakra concept of the empty-form, Tsongkhapa takes great pains to underscore the point that this is different from emptiness in the sense of Nāgārjuna's (second century CE) emptiness of intrinsic existence. He distinguishes between two meanings of emptiness in the Kālacakra context, namely emptiness in the sense of emptying of form and emptiness in terms of the absence of intrinsic existence as propounded by Nāgārjuna, especially as interpreted by Candrakīrti (seventh century CE). The first is, Tsongkhapa explains, a means for bringing forth the experience of immutable great bliss while the second is a means for destroying conceptual elaborations in the form of grasping at signs.[22] Of these two, it is the first type of emptiness, the means for engendering great bliss, which remains the extensive focus of the Kālacakra; however, according to Tsongkhapa, its commentarial literature also presents quite extensively, in comparison to other tantras, the emptiness of intrinsic existence in a manner highly consistent with Candrakīrti's explanation.

For Tsongkhapa, one of the unique features of the *Kālacakratantra* is its presentation of the fourth empowerment, the word empowerment. In all other tantras of the highest yoga class, such as Guhyasamāja and Cakrasaṃvara, the fourth empowerment is presented in a hidden manner with the oblique line "The fourth too is similar to this." Instead of explicitly identifying what exactly is the fourth empowerment, these tantras use the third empowerment, the wisdom-knowledge empowerment, as an illustration and then merely state that the fourth is similar to this.[23] In contrast, in the *Kālacakratantra* the fourth empowerment is not only identified explicitly in its own terms, but, more importantly, the tantra itself focuses extensively on its explanation. According to this tantra, the definitive fourth empowerment is identified as the nondual gnosis, which is in turn defined in terms of the nonduality of empty-form and immutable great bliss. Tsongkhapa then goes on to explain how, in the Kālacakra system, the emptiness in the context of the union of bliss and emptiness is in most instances defined in terms of the empty-form. Therefore, it is referred to as "objectified" (*dmigs bcas*), for it is perceived in terms of color and shape, while the immutable bliss represents an awareness that cognizes the suchness of things. Often the latter is described as "unobjectified" (*dmigs med*).[24] In a later section of the same work, Tsongkhapa takes on the challenge of explicating how the dematerializing of the corporeal body does not undermine our ability to experience great bliss and how this idea is different from the Mind Only school's idealism.[25] He also addresses a key objection raised by Rendawa regarding the incoherence of the notion of the Buddha's body and mind being of a single entity. Space prevents us to get into the details of these points.

Perhaps, for Tsongkhapa, the compelling ground for accepting Kālacakra's authenticity as a Buddhist tantra is the history of its interpretation in India, especially by authoritative figures like Abhayākaragupta and, most importantly, Nāropa (circa tenth century CE), whom Tsongkhapa respects deeply. It is also clear that the Indian master Atiśa took Kālacakra as an authoritative Buddhist tantra. Regardless of which standpoint Rendawa finally upheld with respect to Kālacakra, the probing questions he raised appear to have left an enduring mark, at least in the way in which this important Buddhist tantra has been expounded by Tsongkhapa. These questions not only helped to draw attention to the features that are unique to this system, but, and perhaps more importantly, they have caused the Tibetans to appreciate more clearly the essential similarity of this tantra to other well-known tantras of the highest yoga class.

One of the unique features which makes Kālacakra so valuable for studying Buddhist tantra as a whole, at least according to Tsongkhapa, is its explicitness in many areas of explanation. For example, although the practice of correlating specific aspects of the path with the ground, that is, those factors on the ordinary level of existence, lies at the heart of the highest yoga tantra teachings in general, it is Kālacakra where this process of correlation is made most explicit. Effectively, in Kālacakra an intimate correlation is made between the external cosmos and the inner human body such that the human body represents a microcosm of the cosmos. The mechanism by which the outer and the inner worlds are connected is the activity of the winds (*praṇa*). On this model, then, the meditative practice becomes a means for perfecting the inner and outer worlds. These three elements—the outer cosmos, the inner human body, and the meditative practice—are referred to respectively as the "outer Kālacakra," the "inner Kālacakra," and the "alternative Kālacakra." Just as the many aspects of the cosmos that remain implicit in other tantras are made most explicit in the Kālacakra, hence the extensive discussion of astronomy, so similarly many aspects of the inner body, especially the energy channels and vital drops, which remain implicit in the other tantras, are made explicit here. Taktsang Lotsāwa, in fact, argues that the Kālacakra's presentation of the winds, especially the changes observable in the pattern of our breathing in consonance with changes in the passage of the heavenly bodies, is something that he has been able to confirm experientially.[26] He says that, in contrast, he has failed to confirm the explanation of the changes in the breathing pattern explained in other tantra texts despite attempts over a period of months and years. In my own case, I observed that much of the initial unease I felt with Kālacakra was due to a superficial reading of the texts of this system, especially *Stainless Light*. It was finally my reading of the masterful section on the completion stage of Khedrup Norsang Gyatso's *Ornament of Stainless Light* that helped to quell my own qualms. In editing the Tibetan text of that section, often I felt that if I could devote myself to a prolonged intensive meditation retreat, I could actually attain some of the realizations described so wonderfully there.[27]

By way of conclusion, let us briefly reflect on what implications this interesting debate on the Kālacakra in Tibet, and to some extent in India itself, might have for our understanding of the history of Buddhism in India in general and Vajrayāna tradition in particular. There is today a general consensus that Kālacakra may represent the last of the great systems of Buddhist tantra to emerge in India. It could also be argued that, given its detailed astronomy, the root tantra, or at least its commentary *Stainless Light,* must postdate the advent of Islamic culture with its sophisticated astronomy. What is also fascinating is the explicit espousal of some of the influential non-Buddhist technical vocabulary, especially that of the

Sāṃkhya school, which might suggest an interesting cross-fertilization between Buddhist and non-Buddhist tantras in medieval India. For example, we observed how Rendawa saw the myth of Śambhala to be inspired by, if not derived from, the Hindu myth of Viṣṇu's coming to save the world in the form of a Kalkī king. Also since many of the Indian Kālacakra writers appear to have hailed from northern India, there is the question of how this region may have played a significant role in the development and dissemination of Kālacakra in India and Tibet.[28] In following the history of Kālacakra in India, especially in the thirteenth century, we might also be able to shed some new light on the fate of Buddhism in the last stages of its existence in India before its demise.

With respect to its place in Tibetan Buddhism, we already have noted how the Kālacakra was seminal in shaping Tibetan astronomy and, to some extent, general views on cosmology as well. Today, almanacs are produced, solar and lunar eclipses predicted, and summer and winter solstices calculated on the basis of this system of astronomy. For whatever historical reasons, the Kālacakra teachings and practices, and more specifically its empowerment, have come to be hugely popular in the Tibetan tradition, with the ceremony often conducted to a gathering of tens of thousands at a time. I still remember vividly when I first received the empowerment in Dharamsala, India, as a young monk of eleven years old. Perhaps Kālacakra is the only meditation deity belonging to the class of highest yoga tantra whose empowerment is conferred to even an ordinary, illiterate farmer. These large-scale ceremonies, often conducted by the Dalai Lama or the Panchen Lama, have enjoyed a status similar to public blessings rather than an actual initiation into a highest yoga tantra. So, on the general public level, Kālacakra has become the only highest yoga tantra meditation deity having a status somewhat comparable to Avalokiteśvara and Tārā. Furthermore, the Kālacakra myth of the Śambhala kingdom, with its somewhat apocalyptic vision of Śambhala's destruction of the barbarians, exerts a powerful religious appeal to the Tibetan people, for it stands as a reminder that ultimately the forces of good always triumph over those of evil. Today, as Tibetan Buddhism travels to the various parts of the world, especially to the Western world, increasingly people are coming to encounter this fascinating system of Buddhist tantra. Already, His Holiness the Dalai Lama has conducted the Kālacakra empowerment in Australia, Canada, Europe, and several times the United States. In the Tibetan-speaking world, the empowerment still remains the most sought-after religious event in the devout Buddhist's life, hopefully a situation that is likely to remain for a long time to come.

Endnotes

1. *A Destiny Fulfilled* (*rtogs brjod mdun legs ma*), The Collected Works of Tsongkhapa, (Kumbum Edition as scanned by Tibetan Buddhist Resource Center, New York), vol. *kha*, *gsung thor bu* (Miscellaneous Writings), 62 a: 3.

2. For a detailed account of the emergence and transmission of these two lineages of Kālacakra exposition in Tibet, see Gö Shönu Pal's *The Blue Annals*, section 10.

3. In the recently published two-volume catalogue of the old texts discovered at Drepung Monastery, Tibet, *'bras spungs dgon du bzhugs su gsol ba'I dpe rnying dkar chag*, Beijing: Nationalities Press, 2004, vol. 1, it lists some 317 individual texts on Kālacakra that were part of the personal library of the Fifth Dalai Lama. The list includes works on Kālacakra from noted masters from Kadam, Sakya, Kagyü, Jonang, and Geluk, as well as works on Kālacakra astronomy by the Nyingma author Lochen Dharmaśrī.

4. It appears that in India too there were critical questions raised about the authenticity of Kālacakra as a Buddhist tantra, most notably by Ratnākaraśanti, known also as Śāntipa. Rendawa cites a passage from Abhayākaragupta that alludes to the objections raised by authoritative Buddhist masters on how many of Kālacakra's presentations contradict the presentations found in the three vehicles. Rendawa, *A Jewel Garland* (*phrin yig nor bu'I phreng ba*) in *Compendium of Tibetan Astronomy*, (*Bod kyi rtsis rig kun btus chen mo*), vol.1, 285.

5. *Great Compendium of Tibetan Astronomy* (*Bod kyi rtsis rig kun btus chen mo*), vol. 1, Chengdu: Sichuan Minorities Press, 1998.

6. Rendawa, *A Jewel Garland*, in *Great Compendium*, vol.1, 285.

7. Taktsang Lotsāwa, *Thousand Lights of Reasoning: A Rebuttal* (*rtsod lan lung dang rigs pa'i 'od stong*) in *Great Compendium*, vol. 1, 376.

8. The "fourteen unanswered questions" is a list of metaphysical questions, such as "Is the universe finite or infinite," "Is the mind the same as the body in substance?" and so on, all of which the Buddha chose not to answer.

9. Rendawa, *A Jewel Garland*, in *Great Compendium*, vol.1, 286. Rendawa also draws our attention to the fact that the great Sakya patriarch Drakpa Gyaltsen critiqued certain aspects of the Kālacakra pertaining to its presentation of the root tantric precepts. Gö Lotsāwa responds to Drakpa Gyaltsen's specific objections.

10. Ibid., 292.

11. Citing the research of D. Pingree in his "Ravikās in Indian Astronomy and the Kālacakra," *Le Parole e I Marmi. Studi in Onore de Raniero Gnoli nel suo 70th Compleanno*, ed. R. Torella, Serie Orientale Roma, 92, (Roma: Istituto Italiano per l'Africa e l'Oriente, 2001), 655-64, Leonard van der Kuijp remarks that the various computations found in the Kālacakra texts are incomplete, often misleading, and some possibly downright erroneous where their astronomy was concerned. See Leonard van der Kuijp, "The Kālacakra and the Patronage of Tibetan Buddhism by the Mongol Imperial Family," Department of Central Eurasian Studies, Indiana University, 2004, p.12. Since I have no skills in assessing the veracity of the astronomical section of either the condensed tantra or *Stainless Light*, it is difficult to determine if this observation is true. Whatever its truth, I believe that by the fourteenth century and especially by the end of the fifteenth century, with the works of Phugpa Lhundrup Gyatso and Khedrup Norsang Gyatso, Tibetan astronomy appeared to have established its own system of complete calculation.

12. *Repudiation of Objections to the Cosmology Taught in the Kālacakra* (*dus 'lhor las gsungs pa'i 'jig rtenkhams kyi rnam bzhag la rtsod spong*), The Collected Works, vol. *ja*. Although Shākya Chokden does not mention Rendawa by name, he cites from Rendawa's open letter right at the beginning of his repudiation.

13. For example, Jangpa Namgyal Draksang opens his own reply with the observation that many of the responses to Rendawa's open letter composed by great learned ones appeared to be either incomplete, unconnected to the critical issues, or distorted in their explanation of the Kālacakra system. See Jangpa Namgyal Draksang, in *Compendium of Tibetan Astronomy*, vol.1, 327.

14. Khedrup Jé, *Illumination of Reality* (*de nyid snang ba*), The Collected Works, (Kumbum Edition as scanned by Tibetan Buddhist Resource Center, New York,) vol.*ja*, 360 b:4, identifies this "great Bharata" as a lengthy non-Buddhist work of some hundred thousand lines attributed to one Vyasaśri. Most probably this is the well-known Hindu work *Mahābharata*.

15. See, for example, his *Sheaves of Oral Transmission* (*Saṃpuṭatantraṭikā˙nayamañjarı*), Toh 1198, Tengyur, rgyud 'grel, *cha*, chapter 21, p.198b: 6. This section is cited in Khedrup Norsang Gyatso's *Ornament of Stainless Light*, The Library of Tibetan Classics, Boston: Wisdom Publications, 2004, p.149.

16. Gö Lotsāwa Shönu Pal, *Joyful Celebration of Agony-relieving White Water Lilies: A Rebuttal of Objections to the Glorious Kālacakra* (*dpal dus kyi 'khor lo'I rtsod lan ku mu da'I dga' ston*) in *Compendium of Tibetan Astronomy*, vol.1, 300. A similar comment can be found also in his *Blue Annals*, vol.2, 886. (My references here are to the two-volume modern book edition of the Tibetan text reprinted in Sichuan, 1985.)

17. For instance, Shākya Chokden objects on methodological grounds to the very idea of refuting a higher, Mahāyāna treatise on the basis of its conflict with a lower, non-Mahāyāna work. Shākya Chokden, op cit., p. 2a:6.

18. In his monumental work on Kālacakra, *Illumination of Reality* (op cit., 360 a:6 - 67a), Khedrup Je singles out Chomden Rikral's critique of Kālacakra cosmology and responds to these in some detail.

19. For a discussion of these different approaches, see Khedrup Norsang Gyatso, *Ornament of Stainless Light*, The Library of Tibetan Classics, pp.148-50.

20. Ibid., Part I:7, pp. 145-60.

21. There is a text attributed to Rendawa that elucidates the definitive elements of the *Kālacakratantra* entitled *A Precious Light Illuminating the Definitive Meanings of the Glorious Kālacakra* (*dpal dus kyi 'khor lo'I nges don gsal ba'I sgron me*). This text is found also in *Compendium of Tibetan Astrology*, vol.1, 383-428.

22. *A Memorandum on Clear Differentiation of the Difficult Points of Stainless Light* (*stong phrag bcu gnyis pa dri ma med pa'I 'od kyi dka' ba'I gnas rnam par 'byed pa brjed byang*), The Collected Works of Tsongkhapa, vol. *na*, 14 a:1.

23. Ibid., 13 b:4; Tsongkhapa also provides a specific treatment of the nature of the fourth empowerment in Kālacakra in his *Great Exposition of the Stages of the Secret Mantra* (*sngags rim chen mo*), The Collected Works, vol.*ga*, 310 b:6-313 b:6.

24. *Great Exposition of the Stages of the Secret Mantra*, 312 b:2.

25. Ibid., 440 a:5-444 a:5.

26. Taktsang Lotsāwa, op cit., 380.

27. This is Part 5: "Gnosis: The Completion Stage" in the English translation of the work in The Library of Tibetan Classics series.

28. Van der Kuijp, drawing on the biography of Drupthop Ugyenpa (thirteenth century), mentions how the Kālacakra was still studied in Kaśmīr in the thirteenth century and how, interestingly, women too actively participated in these studies. See Leonard van der Kuijp, op cit., p. 24.

III.

Transmission and Transition

–18–

Kālacakra and the Nālandā Tradition: Science, Religion, and Objectivity in Buddhism and the West

Joseph Loizzo, M.D., Ph.D.

The author wishes to thank the editors of *Religion East and West* for permission to reprint portions of the article "Renewing the Nālandā Legacy," from their Fall 2006 issue.

Introduction

In the West, growing interest in Tibetan civilization has focused on the meeting of the Indo-Tibetan sciences and healing arts with Western physics, neuroscience, mind-body medicine, and psychotherapy. As the most modern and complete synthesis of the Indian Buddhist arts and sciences, the *Kālacakratantra,* or *Wheel of Time Process,* offers an ideal entryway for cross-cultural research and practical application. Unfortunately, because we in the West have only recently gained access to Tibet's tantric Buddhism, and since tantric texts and practices were intentionally guarded in symbolism and secrecy, systems like the Wheel of Time have been thus far neglected or misunderstood. While major strides have been made in scholarly translation and study of the tantras,[1] the Kālacakra's intimate ties with the Unexcelled Yoga Tantra (*Anuttarayogatantra*) teachings of Vajrayāna Buddhism have been one rate-limiting step in Western understanding of this rich and complex system. This is especially unfortunate since the *Wheel of Time* is traditionally known as a transparent or extremely clear tantra (*shin tu gsel ba'i rgyud)*, meant to give a clear explication of tantric theory and practice as they relate to physics, biology, psychology, sociology, and associated disciplines.

This chapter addresses three misconceptions I see blocking understanding of the Kālacakra by Western scholars and scientists: (1) that the Kālacakra, as a tantric tradition, is a primarily religious system of mystical symbolism and experience that has little or nothing to do with science either as we know it or as the Buddhists of classical India did; (2) that it is primarily a compendium of prescientific systems of knowledge and expertise regarding the external world, akin to the medieval systems of alchemy, humoral medicine, and astrology received by the modern, scientific West; (3) that it is primarily a compendium of prescientific or religious systems of knowledge and expertise concerning the interior or psychosocial world, akin to the medieval systems of magic or rhetoric, contemplative psychology, and statecraft or politics received by the modern, scientific West.

This chapter aims to expose and dispel these and other misconceptions obscuring our view of the Kālacakra's distinctive approach to the sciences; and hence to help clear the way for its study and application to questions and challenges facing modern science and civilization. The method of the chapter, however, is contextual. Rather than delving into the textual or practical details of the Wheel of Time, I will attempt to locate it within the history of the Indian Buddhist scientific tradition. This involves clarifying the unique role the Wheel of Time played in articulating the final synthesis of the Indian Buddhist scientific tradition at the time of its transplantation into Tibet (eighth to eleventh century CE). In particular, I make three points that I believe help clarify the two faces of this distinctive system: as a scientific version of the Unexcelled Yoga Tantras and as an Unexcelled Tantric version of the Indo-Tibetan sciences. (1) While the *Wheel of Time Process's* Vajrayāna synthesis of science emerged late in the history of Indian Buddhism, its multidisciplinary logic and pedagogic method are consistent with the classical Centrist synthesis of Theravāda and Mahayāna traditions forged at the monastic university of Nālandā from the fifth to seventh century CE. (2) The intent behind its synthesis is to integrate the development of scientific knowledge and social practice with the education of objective, compassionate agents of human knowledge and expertise *via* an alternative or pure science (*antara/akṣara-vidyā*) of self-correction (*buddhiśoddhana*). (3) The utopian social vision of the Wheel of Time is that the future of human civilization on this planet can only be ensured by a global system of universal education in which the mundane arts and sciences are integrated with an extraordinary art and science of human self-correction or self-disarmament. I will conclude with some thoughts about future study.

I. Kālacakra: Time-Capsule of the Nālandā Scientific Tradition

Just outside the capital of ancient Magadha in northern India, the lush suburb of Nālandā was a teaching and retreat site favored by Śakyamūni Buddha, Mahāvīra, and other sages. According to traditional records,[2] by the third Buddhist council it had become the main center of learning for the Mahāsāṃgikā school, a potential precursor of Mahāyāna Buddhism. Developed by the first Indian emperor Aśoka (third century BCE) and by the Mahāyāna champion Nāgārjuna (second century CE), Nālandā became India's first monastic university under the Gupta and post-Gupta dynasties (320-650 CE).[3] It went on to play an international role in the transplanting of Buddhist learning into Central, East, and Southeast Asia.[4] Its role in propagation ensured that after the university was destroyed during the thirteenth century, its traditions survived elsewhere. In Tibet the Nālandā tradition remained largely intact until the mid-twentieth century. So it was that, when Tibet's leading minds fled to India with His Holiness the Dalai Lama, they found themselves on the world stage as a living record of the 2,500-year-old legacy of the world's first university. As the twenty-first century dawns, the living legacy of Nālandā has once again taken root in its native soil and has spread from India around the world.

Though traditionally linked with the southern seat of Mahāsāṃgikā-Mahāyāna learning, i.e., with the Śrīdhānyakaṭaka Stūpa at Amarāvatī where Śakyamūni is said to have revealed it, the Kālacakra tradition is closely intertwined with the scientific version of the Mahāyāna academy that germinated in West and South India, at Takṣaśila and Dhānyakaṭaka, but finally took root and flowered in the Northeast, at Nālandā and its sister colleges. In fact, according to legend, the Buddha was teaching the *Transcendent Wisdom Discourse* (*Prajñāpāramitāsūtra*) only miles from Nālandā, at Vulture Peak, while he sent a magical emanation of the mother-father Kālacakra archetype to Andhra Pradesh in southeast India to teach the *Wheel of Time Process*. While the *Abbreviated* (*Laghu*) *Kālacakratantra* and its commentary, *Stainless Light* (*Vimalaprabhā*), did not emerge in India until the final phase of Nālandā's history (ninth to thirteenth century CE), by the time Kālacakrapāda the Junior built the Kālacakra temple at Nālandā (tenth century CE) its aims and methods were well integrated within the cumulative (Theravāda/Mahāyāna/Vajrayāna) scientific tradition developed at the greatest Mahāyāna university. This integration is prefigured in the iconography surrounding the Wheel of Time.

Revealed in the sacred circle (*maṇḍala*) of Mañjuśrī, the genius behind the Mahāyāna sciences, the divine archetype (*devatā*) Śakyamūni assumed to teach the *Wheel of Time Process* is linked with Avalokiteśvāra, embodiment of the spirit of altruism (*bodhicitta*) guiding all enlightened social agency. As I read this iconography, the Wheel of Time is aimed at the integration of the critical and practical faces of the Mahāyāna that took place at Nālandā from the fifth to the seventh century, and it maps out the integration of the exoteric and esoteric methods of Mahāyāna contemplation that took place there from the eighth to the tenth century. Since it articulates the final integration of the scientific curriculum at Nālandā before its demise, the *Wheel of Time* may be seen as a time-capsule of the Mahāyāna Buddhist academy transplanted into Tibet. Of course, before unpacking this view of the Kālacakra and its approach to Buddhist science, we must first work through some thorny issues of methodology and history that might block our view.

As I said, growing Western interest in Tibetan civilization has focused on the meeting of the Indo-Tibetan sciences and healing arts with Western physics, neuroscience, mind-body medicine, and psychotherapy. This meeting has led inevitably to comparisons, for which three methodologies have been used. Translator-scholars in the Western academy have used the methods of philology, at times enhanced by hermeneutics, comparative philosophy, anthropology, or sociology.[5] Scientists engaged in biomedical research have relied on the empirical methods of neuroscience and other basic sciences, at times enhanced by other disciplines,[6] including philosophy, phenomenology, linguistics, and artificial intelligence. Meanwhile, health practitioners in various clinical settings have preferred the methods of the case study or clinical trial, citing the work of Buddhist scholars and research scientists.[7]

As expected, the findings of comparative studies diverge as widely as these three methods. Scholarly comparisons between the Buddhist tradition and Western science typically cite a shared methodological preference for reason and evidence over authority and revelation, as well as a shared conceptual preference for causal explanation and impersonal description. Research comparisons typically cite physiologic or mechanistic findings that support traditional claims about the effects and mechanisms of meditation. Clinical comparisons typically cite a congruence of psychological theories along with demonstrable health benefits of techniques like meditation. The limits of these three main approaches stem from their narrow scope and ethnocentric choice of method.

Comparing Buddhist and Western views of reason and revelation obscures some key distinctions between these two traditions. Śakyamūni and his heirs critiqued Vedist notions of divine authority and scriptural revelation, while also developing their own critical concepts of valid authority and traditional teaching. While these were restricted to hypothetical matters (*atyāntapokṣa*) beyond ordinary perception and inference, the requirement that empirical and rational demonstrations must be consistent with scriptural statements places Buddhist methodology somewhere between the empirical method of modern science and the analogical method of systematic theology in the West. In Buddhism, authority and tradition are considered to be of human origin (*puruṣeya*) rather than divine origin; they are seen as means of reproducing the results of Buddha's inner experimentation and mastery of mind and body. Thus its methods are aligned with those of modern science. For this reason, I translate the Buddhist term *vidyā* as "science." [8]

In using this translation, however, one must recall that given ethnocentric bias in Western science and scholarship, content-based comparisons typically obscure the key divergence between Indic and Western scientific traditions. That divergence is between a physical science in which mathematics is the privileged language and mechanics the privileged method and a contemplative one in which those roles are played by linguistics and mind/body self-regulation. Although the West developed both types of science, the former has so defined our view of it since Galileo that the latter, found in ancient contemplative science and modern psychosocial science, is either dismissed as pseudo-science or relegated to a proto- or para-scientific status.

While our modern bias is that only Galilean science can yield objective, exact knowledge and reproducible effects, even the most vocal defenders of modern science have had to admit in recent years that objectivity, precision, and efficacy in science are inexorably relative and conventional concepts.[9] Unversed in the latest critical thinking, researchers and clinicians seeking to apologize for the therapeutic logic and qualitative methods of Buddhist science have been caught like their scholarly colleagues in a methodological mismatch. Wanting to show the validity of Buddhist sciences and techniques in accepted terms, they remain bound to the conventional methodology of their respective disciplines. Contrary to their intentions, their attempt to "validate" Buddhist sciences using the mechanistic theories and quantitative measures of the Western physical sciences is at best heuristic and at worst self-defeating.

As for theoretical comparisons, Buddhist thinkers long ago predicted that atoms could be split into smaller particles without limit, and that solar systems were created and destroyed naturally through boundless space and time. The Buddha himself taught that life and mind were not created from nothing by a divine Creator, but that they originated and that they change through impersonal cause and effect depending on nonliving matter and energy. The theory of dependent origination (*pratītya-samutpāda*) at the heart of all Buddhist teaching explains how living beings create and recreate themselves within and across lifetimes through a process of cause and effect (*hetu-phala*), action and reaction (*karma-vipāka*), that shapes the diversity of bodies, minds, and environments, animal, human, and divine. Further, the Buddha insisted that people put his teachings to the test with reason and evidence and use them to repeat his results for themselves, urging his students to make progress in philosophy, science, and medicine.[10]

Though the similarities between Buddhist and Western sciences seem clear, the aims and methods behind them are diverse enough that the intended meaning and use of even the most similar views is often quite different. Unlike Western particle physics, for instance, the intent behind Buddhist physics is that the search for an ultimate structure of matter will never be conclusive. Unlike Western genetics, the intent behind Buddhist biology is that the evolution and development of higher consciousness are the main factors of our health and happiness. And unlike Western empirical method, the intent behind Buddhist scientific method is to ensure that science is of tangible benefit by testing its effects in our own lives and by guiding it with an extraordinary science of self-transcendent honesty, equanimity, and integrity.[11]

As for quantitative measures, however clearly we show that Buddhist meditation has an effect on the brain or on stress, the theories and methods by which this is shown are definitely not those by which the effect is achieved. While such measures may be welcome to all as "proof" that meditation is no culture-bound ritual, they add little or nothing to the qualitative principles and practices by which Buddhist science formulates, replicates, and validates its desired effects. Worse, they run the risk of reinforcing serious cross-cultural misunderstanding by tacitly confirming the bias that modern empirical methods offer the only clear and reliable route to objective, precise, reproducible knowledge. However inclined we are to cling to such measures as more objective, exact, or reliable, in researching qualitative sciences these measures are at best inadequate and at worst confounding. Insisting on them as the gold standards of evaluation or translation of Buddhist science in spite of this betrays both an ethnocentric bias and a serious methodological flaw.[12]

Given our postmodern consensus on science, the modern Western dichotomies of exact versus inexact, objective versus subjective science do not do justice to the divergence between modern Western and traditional Buddhist science. In order to say which type of science is more exact or effective, one would first need to specify a human interest or aim relative to which such questions can be answered.[13] While unpacking the difference in aims assumed by these two traditions would need another paper, let me say that the interests of Buddhist science from the outset are more like the therapeutic, liberative aims of the human sciences sought by Freud and Ricouer than those of our physical sciences.[14]

Like scientific thinkers in the modern West, Buddhist thinkers transgressed the limits placed on human potential by authoritarian religions and rejected theistic ideals of omniscience and omnipotence. But while the West distributed those ideals across human communities over time, conceding that individuals are incapable of objective knowledge and action, Buddhists revised Indian theistic ideals into humanistic ideals of therapeutic omniscience and omni-compassionate social agency. Instead of seeking objectivity by perfecting disembodied, impersonal knowledge and technology, Buddhists saw no surer way to human objectivity than to perfect *humanity itself*.

No appeal to authority, this tradition's commitment to enlightenment is as a reproducible paradigm of what we might call human genius. Anticipating Gadamer,[15] Buddhist science is progressive, not because it discards authority and tradition, but because it insists, one might say democratically, that each and every individual can and should personally reproduce and advance what is best in humanity and human cultural traditions.

The divergence in methods of Western physical sciences and Buddhist mind sciences stems from this divergence in aims. Qualitative, intersubjective methods are preferred because they are appropriate to the humanistic goals of Buddhist science and because they are ideally suited to the mind/body systems in which our self-limitation exists and in which it must be corrected. Recognizing this divergence explains the limits of recent approaches to comparing Western and Buddhist science. Those limits stem from the modern Western prejudice that one can "translate Buddhism" without a serious attempt to translate its experience and practice in one's own mind and life; that one can "validate" meditative techniques by some measure other than valid personal experience and self-transformation; and that one can "study" Buddhist therapies in some way short of learning to heal oneself well enough to help others reproduce the results.[16]

With this overview, I would like next to review the results of my own research and practice in an attempt to arrive at a more accurate and complete translation of the Buddhist sciences in general and the Mahāyāna sciences in particular.

1. Multidisciplinary Science in Buddhism

The first finding of my comparative survey is that, for most of their history, the cultural distance between Western science and the scientific and technical legacy of Nālandā was far less than it is today.[17] The divergence took place in and around the European Renaissance. The Greeks had accepted two types of science: a quantitative or formal logical tradition based on mathematics and physics and traceable to Pythagoras and Aristotle; and a qualitative or contemplative tradition based on linguistics and meditation and traceable to Empedocles and Plato. The Catholic Church controlled both, but actively adopted Platonism, so when Aristotelian Greek culture was revived to challenge its control, moderns privileged mathematics and physics and regarded linguistics and meditation with suspicion. Since then, the relationship between these two paradigms has been inverted to the point that the term "science" is reserved for the quantitative, physical science of Galileo and his heirs.

The history of science is different, however, in the Indo-Tibetan tradition. Among the many reasons for this, three stand out. First, while the Indians were not behind the Greeks either in mathematics or physics, they were far ahead in linguistics and self-regulation. Like Euclid's geometry and Archimedes' physics, Pāṇini's grammar and Patāñjali's yoga provided Indians with linked conceptual and practical systems so elegant and powerful that they became and remained definitive in the analysis and control of nature. So while qualitative science was never imposed by Indian orthodoxy as it was by Roman Catholic tradition, it still became the method of choice for science in the Buddhist academy of India. This qualitative tradition evolved alongside a quantitative alternate tradition like Aristotle's, based on formal logic, math and physics, but this alter-tradition was considered subordinate and elementary. Thus, while the monastic academies of India and the West both preferred the qualitative methods of contemplative science, the Buddhist academy preserved and developed all classical Indian arts and sciences.

This brings us to the second reason for the divergent history of science in Buddhism and the West. Given India's greater stability and tolerance, Indian linguistics and meditation were not restricted to Indian religious elites, but rather were universalized into rational disciplines that supported progressive scientific and spiritual traditions. Comparing the fate of Socrates and his peripatetic academy with that of Śakyamūni and his mendicant community helps gauge the greater tolerance and support Indians gave liberal, scientific education, relative to the Greeks.

In the medieval West, monasticism served in part as a tool of religious and political authority that was able to coopt the progressive academic traditions of Hellenism. In India, Śakyamūni crafted monasticism into a liberative vehicle that let the Buddhist academy play a progressive role in the evolution of both science and religion Though monasticism gave birth to universal education in both civilizations, Mahāyāna universities arose a thousand years earlier than did their Christian counterparts, and they did so as part of India's precocious commitment to liberal, scientific education. This commitment reflected the success of India's Buddhist tradition in engineering a nonviolent, mercantile path for the advancement of science and civilization in Asia.[18]

The third factor that led Western and Buddhist science to diverge was the difference in the aims and interests of their societies. When Constantine chose to adopt Christianity as Rome's official state religion, he set in motion an appropriation of Greek and Hebrew culture meant to stabilize a precarious empire. This lead to the selection of conservative, hierarchical ideas and practices and to the exclusion of progressive, liberative ideas and practices. As a result, progressive and liberative aspects of Hellenistic Christian culture like Aristotle's version of science and the Gnostic contemplative version of Christianity were excluded from Roman Catholic tradition.

Ironically, the European renaissance was equally partial in selecting aspects of Greek and Christian culture to be revived. While Constantine's interest was in peace, Europeans chose an extroverted version of Hellenistic Christian culture friendly to the far West's colonizing ambitions. As a measure of the violence done by this crusading take on Athens and Jerusalem, contrast the London School's motto, "knowledge is power" with the Socratic injunction "know thyself" or gospel verse, "the truth shall set you free." As the youngest and poorest satellites of Eurasia, the far West chose an extroverted, Pythagorean-Aristotelian version of science and civilization to enhance industrial wealth and military power through physical science and technology. Meanwhile, Eurasia's older, richer societies and their satellites kept refining qualitative, contemplative versions meant to sustain and spread mercantile wealth and political tolerance through psychosocial science and technology.

As a result, when satellites like China, Tibet, Mongolia, Korea, and Japan set out to forge an Asian Buddhist renaissance from the ninth through the fifteenth centuries, they could draw on a complete, progressive Buddhist version of Indian science and civilization and had no need to alter it in order to modernize. Because of its late importation of Buddhism and its proximity to Nālandā, Tibet in particular could transplant the scholarly and practical traditions of the university in their entirety, including systematically translating its vast library of classical texts and commentaries. So Tibetans preserved the Nālandā curriculum much as it was at its height, with its integrated use of formal logical methods for basic arts and sciences and qualitative methods for advanced disciplines like hermeneutics, psychology, and self-correction. From the first Buddhist college at Samye (mid-ninth century) to the universities of the Gelukpa renaissance (fifteenth to seventeenth century), this curriculum set the standard shared by all four orders of Tibetan Buddhism.

2. Classical versus Critical Views of Science, East and West

This thumbnail history leads me to the second finding of my basic research: that East-West comparisons must reflect the way science or refined knowledge is actually viewed and used in the Buddhist tradition. If we are to arrive at a comparison of the Western and Buddhist scientific traditions that permits a working translation, it must reflect the critical paradigm of truth and method evolved to support the most advanced levels of the Buddhist curriculum.

Most comparisons of Buddhist and Western science are based on one of two textual reference frames: the basic scientific canons of Buddhagoṣa and Vasubandhu; or the Buddhist logical canon of Dignāga and Dharmakīrti. This choice becomes problematic given Mahāyāna critiques of their realistic theories and formal logical methods, whether from the relativism of Nāgārjuna's Centrist Philosophy (*Mādhyamika*) or from the deconstructive psychology of Asaṅga's Idealism (*Vijñānavāda*).

As these critiques forged a new scientific consensus in India, Buddhist Realism (*Sarvāstivāda*) and Buddhist Logic (*Pramāṇa*) were relegated to the status of heuristic, provisional truth and method. To base a translation of the Buddhist sciences on a realistic version of Buddhist logic or psychology despite the consensus of Mahāyāna thinkers would be conceding too much to modern Western bias. This is especially clear given the culmination of Buddhist sciences in Indo-Tibetan syntheses like the Wheel of Time, where all physical and social sciences were relativized with respect to the ultimate spiritual science of self-correction called alternative or pure science.[19]

Given the findings of my historical survey, I sought a textual reference frame for my comparative study midway between Śakyamūni and Tsong Khapa (1357-1419), within the era in which the Buddhist academy debated between versions of the curriculum based on the methods of Buddhist Realism, Logic, Idealism, and Centrism. I focused on Candrakīrti, the Mahāyāna methodologist *par excellence*, whose view of Centrist method as a qualitative language therapy helped resolve a century-long debate between formal logical syntheses like Empiricist Centrism and psychological syntheses like Idealist Centrism. I was especially interested in contextualizing this debate at Nālandā, where Candrakīrti refined his Dialecticist or Consensualist Centrism *(Prāsaṅgika)* in dialogue with followers of Bhāvaviveka and Dharmapāla, and in debate with language philosopher Candragomin. Fortunately, this took place in the seventh century when Chinese scholars Xuan-zang and Yi-jing were compiling the best records we have of the Mahāyāna academy.

Here I would like to anticipate briefly an objection to my choice of textual and contextual reference frames from the Centrist schools of the Mahāyāna tradition. I have already alluded to the cultural bias Western scholars and scientists have against qualitative methods. A survey of Buddhology since its inception shows one unfortunate result of that bias. Given the commitment modern science has made to realistic theories and formal methods, Western scholars of Buddhism have often aligned Theravāda Buddhist Realism and Logic with empirical science and Mahāyāna Centrism and Idealism with mystical or skeptical religion. This has biased Protestant Buddhology towards the reformation rhetoric of some Theravādins, casting Pāli Buddhism in the role of pure or early Greek Christianity, while Mahāyāna Buddhism is assigned a role analogous to corrupt Catholic tradition.[20] This bias, in turn, sets the stage for a two-pronged objection to my choice of Centrism as a focus of comparison.

The first prong of this objection is itself twofold: first, that the Centrism of Nāgārjuna and his heirs is too skeptical, mystical, or nihilistic to be compatible with science in any form; and, second, that Centrism is a corrupt, revisionist form of Buddhism that mistakes and displaces Śakyamūni's original intent. This objection stands or falls with mystical-skeptical readings of Centrism, readings that have been superseded by recent Indo-Tibetan Buddhist scholarship like Robert Thurman's work on Tsong Khapa. The objection is equally incoherent from a Western standpoint, given the recent turn towards relativistic and constructivist views of science.

As for the second objection, it privileges the realistic theories and methods of Buddhagoṣa, Vasubandhu, or Dignāga based on claims to the purity and priority of Theravāda Buddhism. This objection is anachronistic. The truth is that critical traditions and Nāgārjuna himself preceded these realist figures by centuries; and it is likely that a Mahāsāṃgikā-Mahāyāna version of Buddhism coevolved more or less contemporaneously with the Pāli. Finally, priority claims beg the philosophical and hermeneutic question of which of Buddha's statements, in any canon, are definitive and which version of Buddhist tradition—Vaibhāṣika, Sautrāntika, Cittamātra, or Mādhyamika—gives a definitive account of his ultimate intent.

3. The Complementarity of Buddhist Scientific Traditions

The third finding of my comparative study—the compatibility of Theravāda, Mahāyāna, and Vajrayāna versions of Buddhist science—counters further the objection I have just cited. In contrast to the sectarian tendencies of the Śrī-Lankan reformation, the institutional structure and curriculum of Mahāyāna universities like Nālandā presupposed an inclusive framework more aligned with Buddhist hermeneutics and the cumulative logic of science than with sectarian bias. The Chinese travelers Xuan-zang and Yi-jing both indicate that mastery of the Theravāda threefold canon was considered, along with language proficiency, as an entrance requirement for admission to Nālandā, to be tested by an entrance examination. This, and the Chinese observers' report of secular students at Nālandā, supports the idea that such Mahāyāna institutions set out to provide higher education to build on elementary learning offered by local schools of various Buddhist and non-Buddhist denominations. It is also consistent with the fact that students who entered Nālandā as novice monastics (*śramanera*) would eventually be ordained as *mūlasarvāstivada* monks, effectively becoming Theravādins who may or may not have upheld a complementary Mahāyāna outlook and practice.

A final factor here is the strategy of inclusiveness shared by Theravāda and Mahāyāna pedagogy, expressed in the doctrine of liberative art (*upāyakauśalya*) and the prohibition against rejecting any Buddhist precept or faction. This inclusiveness was reflected in the Mahāyāna hermeneutic strategies of gradualism. The fourfold gradualism expressed in Nāgārjuna's *Jewel Garland (Ratnāvalī)*, for instance, includes three levels of teaching consistent with Theravāda practice and only one consistent with the Mahāyāna. Nāgārjuna's other works support this by aligning his critical theory of two realities with the therapeutic framework of the four noble truths. The first of these realities is that all theories and methods are mere conventions whose truth is relative to the therapeutic aim of freedom of mind and action. Here Nāgārjuna was reiterating a critique of knowledge and expertise basic to all Buddhist arts and sciences, Theravāda and Mahāyāna. Candrakīrti argued that the only coherent Centrist methodology was a dialogical language therapy which empathically assumed others' viewpoints to help them see through reified habits of mind. This helped him bring the Mahāyāna academy back down to its Theravāda foundations, by emphasizing the conventional nature and therapeutic intent of all Buddhist teaching. So the emergence of their Centrist methods as definitive for the Nālandā curriculum defines the Mahāyāna academy by its move to subject the production of scientific knowledge and technical expertise to the human quality control of self-corrective disciplines, based on the therapeutic truth and method of Theravāda, or Hinayāna, tradition.

4. A Multidisciplinary, Human Science of Mind

This brings us to the fourth major finding of my comparative study: the contextual definition of Buddhist science as a multidisciplinary human science. Assuming that the Mahāyāna academy was meant to extend the progressive social role of Theravāda learning into the mainstream of Indian science and civilization, it should be possible to map the Centrist canon and its use onto the context of Nālandā's universal curriculum and mission. In the Western academy, the rise of autonomous disciplines emulating or reacting to the methods of Galilean science has led to a reading of Mahāyāna texts as pure philosophy divorced from science, meditation, and ethics. Yet the logic of the Centrist canon belies this matching, reflecting instead a congruence with the multidisciplinary therapeutic structure of the Theravāda curriculum. To clarify this, I mapped the Centrist canon of Nāgārjuna and Candrakīrti onto the three core disciplines basic to all Buddhist learning. Thus, Nāgārjuna's *Wisdom* (*Mādhyamakakārikā*) and Candrakīrti's *Lucid Exposition* (*Prasannapadā*) elaborate a relativistic theory of knowledge to apply to the discipline of wisdom, while the *Jewel Garland* and *Introduction* (*Mādhyamakāvatāra*) define an altruistic style of social agency to align technical expertise with the discipline of ethics.

In an effort to bridge the gap between Buddhist and Western traditions of Centrist studies, I based my comparative study on texts that highlight the link between the self-corrective approach to knowledge and the altruistic approach to social agency in Centrism. Aligned with the core discipline of meditation, Nāgārjuna's *Reason Sixty (Yuktiṣaṣtika)* and Candrakīriti's *Reason Sixty Commentary* (*Yuktiṣaṣtikavṛtti)* describe how the de-reifying language therapy of Centrist philosophy is put into practice as a self-corrective method of contemplation that in turn fosters the Mahāyāna ethos of enlightened altruism and universal social agency.

Taken together, these meta-disciplines allowed Mahāyāna thinkers to extend the Theravāda curriculum into the Indian mainstream by developing progressive systems of philosophy, meditation, and ethics that provided universal alternatives to the orthodoxy and orthopraxy of India's Vedist elite. Thus, they govern the universalization of the Buddhist arts and sciences in the Mahāyāna academy, with language-therapy universalizing linguistics and logic; self-corrective contemplation universalizing psychology; and altruistic agency universalizing physical science and technology as well as medicine.

Although this strategic alignment of Centrist texts with Theravāda disciplines is not exactly mirrored in Vajrayāna literature, it is likely that the gradual integration of esoteric theory and practice into the mainstream Mahāyāna curriculum was conceived and realized following the strategy of complementarity developed at Nālandā. Since the many controversial questions surrounding the origin of the Buddhist tantras have been recently explored by Christian Wedemeyer[21] and others, I can limit my comments here to questions surrounding the links between the Buddhist Tantras and the sciences. Before exploring this aspect of my findings, so crucial for contextualizing the Wheel of Time, I must briefly recall the common objection to my choice of the critical scientific traditions of Mahāyāna Centrism as a reference frame for studying the Buddhist sciences. Naturally, the objection applies even more strongly when the tantras are taken as representative of the Buddhist sciences. Fortunately, my responses to that objection apply in this case as well. In short, privileging Theravāda Realism and Empiricism over the Centrism and Constructivism assumed in Mahāyāna and Vajrayāna scientific traditions in the belief that the former share the naïve realism and objectivism of the West's modern physical sciences not only betrays an ethnocentric bias about science but also grossly misrepresents the therapeutic, contemplative thrust of the Buddhist scientific tradition in general. Of course, it is even more tempting to apply a reformation-style critique to Vajrayāna traditions than to their Mahāyāna counterparts, as the main charges of revisionism and corruption seem more plausible here. Accordingly, it is all the more crucial that we view Western and non-Western critiques of the Buddhist tantras in light of what we have learned recently about the history of Indian Buddhism from Tibetan scholars and other sources. For instance, Tibetan scholars point out that before Candrakīrti's day, Mahāyāna masters intentionally restricted esoteric teaching and writing, while by Atiśa's (982-1054), the trend was toward integrating Sūtra and Tantra, as they originally were in Mahāyāna scriptures as far back as the *Heart of Transcendent Wisdom Discourse (Prajñāparamitahṛdayasūtra)*. Add to this the fact that the Mahāsāṃgikā canon included a little-known collection of esoteric formulas (*dhāranī-piṭaka*), and the late emergence of the Vajrayāna literature is quite consistent with the claim of Indian tantrikas and Tibetan historians about the origin of the Buddhist tantras. Specifically, it becomes very hard to rule out the possibility that Śakyamūni Buddha personally taught tantras like the *Esoteric Communion Process* (*Guhyasamāja*) or *Wheel of Time Process* to certain disciples whose lineage was preserved within the community that convened at Nālandā, but not within the community that convened at Rājāgṛha.

Although my finding about tantric science in no way hinges on the accuracy of the Tibetan account, I mention it because it provides a modern perspective on the history of the Buddhist tantras that serves as a counterpoint to the conventional wisdom of Western Indology, based on Theravāda Buddhist and modern Vedist sources. Whatever one makes of the early history of the tantras, it seems fairly clear that the more progressive elements within the Indian mainstream, Buddhist and Vedist, began to actively integrate tantric traditions around the time of Candrakīrti.[22] Besides the rising popularity of the tantras, what occurred within the Mahāyāna in general and Nālandā in particular to make this integration possible was the articulation of a system of interpreting, practicing, and teaching the tantras that complemented the Centrist synthesis of Theravāda and Mahāyāna traditions refined by Candrakīrti. According to the Ārya tradition of commentary on the *Esoteric Communion Process*, the esoteric Vajrayāna shared the same pedagogic intent and method as the exoteric Mahāyāna, only offering a more effective contemplative-ethical methodology. In this sense, it fit within the cumulative curriculum of Buddhist arts and sciences as the most advanced way of putting exoteric Centrist philosophy into practice. Thus, it assumes the therapeutic wisdom of Nāgārjuna and Candrakīrti while offering alternate methods of contemplation and ethics to achieve the same goal of compassionate social agency. This complementarity in content is underscored by the historical claim, contested by Western scholars, that the Ārya commentarial tradition was articulated by the same individuals who founded and refined exoteric Centrism, notably Nāgārjuna, Āryadeva, and Candrakīrti.

Whether or not this claim is historically accurate, it reflects the consensus of the Nālandā tradition that Vajrayāna methods could be used at least as well as their Mahāyāna counterparts to universalize the Theravāda curriculum, without diluting its therapeutic efficacy as a system of human self-correction. Whatever we in the West make of this claim, its cogency within the Indo-Tibetan tradition is evident in the historical trend towards greater reliance on tantric forms of organizing and disseminating knowledge and expertise. Besides the integration of tantric methods into the mainstream teaching style of later Indian and Tibetan masters, the two major examples of this trend are the Kālacakra tradition and Tibetan medicine. Unlike Unexcelled Tantras like Cakrasaṃvara and Yamāntaka, which developed after the Ārya tradition explicitly for contemplative-ethical use, these two later systems reflect a broad consensus that the Unexcelled Tantras are preferable for the cultivation of scientific knowledge and expertise as well as spiritual wisdom and compassion.

As a final note before I turn to the West, let me say a few words about the human context of education in Buddhism. Another way in which the Mahāyāna academy extended the therapeutic structure of Theravāda learning was to integrate its vast, content-driven curriculum of text-based classes with an equally intricate process-driven system of human self-correction basic to Buddhist monastic education. This process-driven system included traditions of scholarly tutelage, ethical mentoring, contemplative self-development, and collective self-correction through group confession and debate. This compound pedagogical strategy helps us appreciate the unique context of the Mahāyāna academy and shows how the curricular content and the pedagogic process together fostered an institutional culture of self-corrective ideals and procedures. Such extended dialogical networks constitute a deep procedure of self-correction that complements the logic and method of self-correction central to all Buddhist learning. In the Buddhist scientific tradition, the self-corrective procedures of linguistic self-analysis, contemplative validation of experience, and intersubjective replication of expertise take the place of the depersonalizing procedures of statistical formulation, experimental validation, and inter-laboratory replication that characterize science in the West. Interestingly, the indispensable role of mentoring relationships in the cultivation of objective, responsible agents of human knowledge and expertise is especially clear in Vajrayāna traditions like the Esoteric Communion and Wheel of Time. In the Ārya tradition, the formulation of pedagogic conventions to safeguard the human development of students unprepared for esoteric instruction or practice was key to preserving the complementarity of Theravāda, Mahāyāna, and Vajrayāna curricula. The publication of Candrakīrti's *Extremely Brilliant Lamp* (*Pradīpodyottana*) is seen by Tibetans as pivotal to mainstreaming the tantras because it effectively standardized esoteric instruction in forms observed to this day by all Tibetan schools, although relaxed in the Kālacakra and Tibetan medical traditions.

5. Multidisciplinary Science in the West

The fifth and last finding of my study was to identify a range of contextual matches for Buddhist science in the West today. I have already alluded to the problems faced by researchers and scholars trying to map the Buddhist sciences directly onto the conventional Western physical and social sciences. As for the physical sciences, their extreme objectivism makes them a poor contextual match for the Buddhist sciences. Modern science seeks objective knowledge and mastery of the physical world by divorcing it from any and all personal experience and action, while Buddhist science seeks such knowledge and mastery by eliminating any and all egocentric bias limiting the objectivity of personal experience and action. As a result of this divergence, the basic aims and methods of the Buddhist sciences simply do not map onto those of conventional physical science in the West. While some Western scientists may use the language of systems theory or methodological principles like the uncertainty principle to accommodate the therapeutic aims and intersubjective methods of their Buddhist colleagues, the strain this puts on the consensus of their home disciplines undermines their credibility, limits their ability to translate the intent of Buddhist science, or both. Researchers and clinicians committed to studying the Buddhist mind sciences and healing arts as something more than a curiosity have been making real strides, but they have eventually run up against the limits of Western science and medicine. Those in research disciplines, ranging from physics to psychology, have had to grapple with constraints imposed by a cultural consensus identifying science exclusively with mechanistic theories and quantitative methods. Parallels between Buddhist scientific theories and modern theories in quantum physics, biology, neuroscience, psychology, and medicine have been received as quaint accidents of history, because the language and methods behind Buddhist theories do not conform to modern Western conventions. Even where parallels are supported by current methods, as in neuroscientific studies or clinical trials of meditation, the findings have been taken out of the context in which Buddhist methods are developed, tested, and practiced.

As for the social sciences, scholars, translators, and anthropologists face similar problems trying to map the Buddhist arts and sciences onto the institutional mission and context of the modern Western academy. Because these disciplines have felt obliged to mimic the objectivism of the physical sciences, they seek objective knowledge and expertise about the cultural beliefs, symbols, or products of human societies by divorcing these as much as possible from the personal experience and action of individual human beings. Buddhist science, on the other hand, seeks objective knowledge and expertise about human interaction by eliminating any and all egocentric biases limiting the intersubjectivity of communication and cooperation. As a result of this divergence, the basic aims and methods of the Buddhist sciences simply do not map onto those of conventional social science in the West. Here again, those scholars who try to accommodate the therapeutic aims and intersubjective methods of the Buddhist sciences by citing the insights of hermeneutic phenomenology or methodological principles like participant observation inevitably strain the consensus of their home disciplines in ways that undermine their credibility, limit their ability to translate the intent of Buddhist science, or both.

These difficulties mapping Buddhist sciences onto the Western physical and social sciences are no accident, in my view, but reflect the fragmentation of disciplines caused by the growing divergence between science and religion in the modern West. Deemed necessary to objectivity, the modern fragmentation of knowledge into a hodge-podge of disciplines all divorced from human experience and action is, I believe, neither necessary nor desirable but rather an artifact of the first scientists' need to cede the hearts and minds of Christendom to their Church inquisitors. The fact that Galileo was tolerated while Giordano Bruno was sent to the pyre set a clear double standard for science reminiscent of the Gospel formula, "Render to Ceasar what is Ceasar's and to God what is God's." While the new science of the physical world evolved, the new mind science of Ficino and Bruno went underground, not to resurface until after the European enlightenment, most notably in the new, human science of Nietzsche and Freud. For the first time in the modern West, it appeared that the taboo against studying the life of the mind had been lifted.

Freud envisioned psychotherapy as a complete, multidisciplinary science of mind linked with the related sciences of experimental psychology, brain research, medicine, anthropology, and linguistics as well as humanities disciplines like literature and philosophy. In theory, then, the psychoanalytic institute should provide the best possible match for the multidisciplinary arts and sciences of the Buddhist tradition. Furthermore, it offers a match not just in theory but in practice, since it arrays Western analogues for the Buddhist disciplines around a dialogical practice whose qualitative, intersubjective methods match well with those of mainstream Buddhism. Yet the historic need of psychoanalysis to prove itself against the gold standard of quantitative, objectivist science means that any link with the study of contemplative traditions like Buddhism is controversial at best. Although psychoanalysis is widely considered the modern West's first science of mind, its status as a science has recently come under fire.[23] The main reason for this is that its theories are based on case findings gathered in the process of psychotherapy. Most scientists do not consider psychotherapy a scientific method because it gathers data by intersubjective dialogue in a shared altered state (of "free association") and analyzes it by qualitative description.[24] Hence, more interest in meditative mind science has been shown by researchers in the young field called cognitive science, consciousness studies, or multidisciplinary science of mind.[25] While these researchers are empowered to take an interdisciplinary approach that respects the intersection of philosophy, linguistics, psychology, and neuroscience assumed in the context of Buddhist science, they generally avoid the practice of psychotherapy, especially in the classical form of psychoanalysis. In their efforts to apologize for the therapeutic logic and qualitative methods of Buddhist science, most cognitive scientists feel a need to avoid the controversy over psychotherapy. Instead they attempt to "validate" the Buddhist sciences using the mechanistic theories and quantitative methods of the Western physical sciences. This attempt is at best heuristic and at worst self-defeating, in my view.

The questions here are much like those facing psychotherapy research, where demonstrations in terms of effects on brain or behavior are more or less extraneous to the theories and methods by which therapy works. While I agree with those who would match the Buddhist sciences with the multidisciplinary science of mind in the West, it is with the proviso that the best match is with those controversial forms of mind science that revolve around psychotherapy, including the various psychoanalytic schools.[26] This match assumes that the science of psychotherapy, with its qualitative formulas, state-specific methods, and intersubjective replication of results, is in fact the most appropriate cognitive-practical context for a working translation of Buddhist science, with its therapeutic theories, meditative methods, and intersubjective replication of results.[27] I should add that for such a context match to be rigorous, psychotherapy would not only need to be at the hub of the disciplines involved, it would also need to fully appropriate the knowledge and methods of these disciplines by a critical process which would be like what some call the psychoanalysis of science.[28]

Interestingly, psychoanalysis also provides a match in its deep procedures of self-correction, specifically the role played in psychoanalytic training by the requirements of supervised practice, a training analysis, and ongoing self-analysis. These content and process strategies reflect the choice of the Western psychotherapy tradition to subordinate the production of abstract knowledge and expertise to the replication of objective human agency. It is this close matching of aims and methods that make the multidisciplinary, therapeutic tradition which thinkers like Ricouer call the human sciences the ideal context for translating Buddhist science into the West.

Finally, there is the question of the relationship between Western psychotherapy and the esoteric theory and practice of tantric traditions like the Wheel of Time.

Mainstream psychotherapy has been so dominated by classical psychoanalysis and its recent schools that the full range of psychotherapy is little known in the West, even to professionals. However, if one views the range of psychotherapies as a continuum along the lines of the gradualism of the cumulative Nālandā tradition, it becomes possible to align various Western techniques, which apply a spectrum of insights and arts to a broad range of challenges, with Buddhist analogues. In terms of psychoanalytic approaches, for instance, the aims and means of classical analysis align fairly well with those of Theravāda psychology; those of relational analysis line up well with exoteric Mahāyāna analogues; and those of unconventional analytic approaches align with esoteric Vajrayāna traditions like Kālacakra (see Table 2, below). Assuming the staging system of the Ārya tradition of Unexcelled Tantras, for example, the Jungian methods of active imagery resemble those of the creation stage (*utpattikrama*); the Reichian methods of breath-control and psychosexual disarming resemble those of the ordinary perfection stage (*niṣpaṇṇakrama*); and the Lacanian methods of deconstructing neurotic consciousness and embracing spontaneity resemble those of the great perfection stage (*mahāniṣpaṇṇakrama*) or great seal (*mahāmudrā*). Although this system is modified somewhat in the Wheel of Time, the parallels remain. In what follows I will briefly address common misconceptions about the Kālacakra tradition following its distinctive multidisciplinary framework of outer, inner, and alternative sciences.

II. Kālacakra and the Nālandā Tradition of Multidisciplinary Human Science

1. Outer Kālacakra: Physical Science in the Nālandā Tradition

Much of the interest in the Wheel of Time stems from its unique synthesis of Indian views of the physical world, clear in its influence on Tibet's integration of Eurasian astrophysics, astronomy, and physical chemistry.[29] Yet even a cursory look at its views of the physical world reveals departures from the physics of Buddhist Realism as well as the integration of elements from non-Buddhist systems such as Jaina and Puraṇic cosmology. The Wheel of Time presents physical science in light of the classical Centrist critique of the Realism and Idealism of Buddhist and non-Buddhist schools. Citing the relativity of all knowledge, it explains its unique synthesis of conventional views of the physical world in light of the pedagogic needs of its universal audience.[30] Although all views are ultimately false insofar as they seem to depict a reality independent of constructs of mind or language, some are conventionally true in that they help guide actions that result in health, happiness, peace, or freedom, while others are false even conventionally. A survey of Kālacakra physics helps clarify the outlook and intent behind the view of external reality in this tradition.

The basic theory informing Kālacakra physics derives from the atomic theory of the Analyst (*Vaibhāṣika*) school. The external world is the result of atoms (*paramāṇu*) of earth, water, fire, air, and space that combine and recombine over time as a result of the action (*karma*) of energies (*vāta, vāyu*). This and countless other world-systems (*loka-dhātu*) are created and destroyed without a Creator and provide the inanimate environment for the origination and transformation of living beings, through the combination of the same atoms with the added element of mind or intuition (*jñāna-dhātu*) and the added intentional action (*karma*) and life energy (*prāṇa*) of individuals and groups. Like the physics of the Theravāda schools, this physics has the explicit intent of offering an alternative to creationist views of the origin of the world and life, which Buddhists consider regressive and ineffectual. Further, it has the intent of critiquing Idealism, Buddhist or Vedist, preferring conventions that depict the world as external to mind and life as inexorably dependent on and interactive with inanimate matter and energy. However, unlike the realistic physics of Buddhist Analyst, Vedist Analyst (*Vaiśeṣika*), or Indian Materialist (*Cārvāka*) schools, Kālacakra physics asserts that atoms exist through sheer mutual dependence without intrinsic reality or identity and also implies that matter is devoid of any intrinsic substantiality or objectivity by asserting that all atoms of air, fire, water, and earth originate from atoms of the space element (*akāśa-dhātu*) or space-atoms (*akāśa-paramāṇu*).

The second basic theory of Kālacakra physics expands on the physicalist insight that the bodies of animate beings emerge from the inanimate matter of the world and so tend to mirror the patterns and rhythms of their environment. Expressed in the dictum, "as without, so within," this theory of macrocosm-microcosm nonduality is elegantly formulated in the interweaving of Kālacakra astrophysics and psychobiology. While this interweaving will become clearer in my comments on the inner sciences below, for here suffice it to say that its intent is to help humans develop an objective view of themselves as embedded within the natural world and a responsible view of that world as a dynamic life-space inexorably shaped for better or worse by their every action. This view of outer and inner reality as inseparable harks back to the nondual wisdom of Mahāyāna Idealism and likewise is meant to critique naïve psychosocial constructions of reality and to empower enlightened social agency. Key to this nondual cosmology is the profound insight that the nature of reality can support either saṃsāric misery or nirvāṇic bliss, depending on the mindset and behavior of human beings. Unlike Buddhist Idealism, however, the Wheel of Time supports this macro-micro nondualism with a psychobiology that depicts the depths of the soul not as a subconscious mind (*ālayavijñāna*) but as a subtle body (*sukṣma-śarīra*) in which three levels of consciousness depend on three levels of neural structure and biochemical process.

This brief survey must suffice to address misconceptions of Kālacakra science based on the cultural preconceptions and biases of the modern scientific West. Firstly, since the *Wheel of Time Process* presents a flat-earth cosmology that revolves around the image of Kālacakra as an archetype of enlightened compassion, it is natural for moderns to confuse it with the creationist cosmologies of the medieval West. Although the Wheel of Time assumes the geocentric cosmology of Buddhist Realism, it is at least as critical of naïve geocentrism as modern cosmology in the sense that it assumes multiple worlds extending through infinite space and time. As for creationism, it is in fact a more radical alternative to creationist views than our modern cosmology in that it explicitly rejects the idea of any world system arising from the actions of a single being or from a first cause, such as the "clockwork God" of deism or the remote God of creationist versions of big bang theory. Likewise, while its five-element atomic theory is liable to be misidentified with ancient and medieval Western four-element theory, it anticipates many of the insights of modern physics including the relativity and insubstantiality of matter as well as the dependence of our knowledge of the material world on human faculties and conventions. In fact, behind the deceptively simple, qualitative nature of Kālacakra atomism, there are at least two ways in which it challenges the current consensus of modern physics. By asserting that all matter emerges from space, it predicts that no irreducible substance or structure of matter will ever be found; and by asserting that all material elements are pervaded by a sixth element of truth or intuition (*dharma-dhātu*, *jñāna-dhātu*), it challenges the wisdom of a model of the physical world that accepts the objectivity of insubstantial matter while denying the objectivity of insubstantial consciousness. As for the Wheel of Time's astrophysics, its alignment of the external workings of the cosmos with the inner workings of life and mind are likely to be misidentified with medieval astrology and the "sympathetic magic" of Christian hermeticism. However, its depiction of the interpenetration of the outer and inner worlds is explicitly meant to counter the calculation of predictions or connections supposedly determined by God (*Iśvara*), nature (*prākṛti*), fate (*ṛta*), or chance (*āhetuka*). Rather, it is meant to orient human individuals and societies to an evolutionary view of life and mind as subject to a causality that is continuous with the causality of the physical world; and is also meant to empower them to take full responsibility for understanding and influencing the causality that shapes their lives and the world they share.

Of course, the physical science of the Kālacakra tradition will seem imprecise or dated to those of us schooled in the theories of the modern Western tradition. Nevertheless, it is imperative if we are to understand and learn from the wisdom of the Wheel of Time that we recall what our best scientific and philosophical minds have taught us about science: that its truth and method are inexorably relative to human aims and values. While Kālacakra physics may fall short of Western physics for the purposes of generating nuclear power or navigating the globe or outer space, it may offer a view of the world more useful for the purposes of guiding our everyday lives. Transparent in this respect, the Wheel of Time synthesizes the admittedly provisional science (*kṣara-vidyā*) of classical India for the purpose of modeling a conventional view of the world that will help individuals of all social and cultural backgrounds better understand and care for the world around them. In this sense, it extends and refines the work done by Mahāyāna thinkers in the Nālandā tradition: providing a progressive synthesis of scientific and religious disciplines to advance mainstream culture in India and Indicized Asia. While some of the details may seem quaint to us now, the broad outlook and intent behind its view of the physical world and some of its distinctive insights are surprisingly modern and relevant to the current dilemmas of scientific education in the West.

2. Inner Kālacakra: Life and Mind Science in the Nālandā Tradition

Interest in the Wheel of Time has also been piqued by its unique synthesis of Indian biology, pharmacology, and mind/body medicine, which influenced Tibet's integration of Eurasian medicine.[31] Although rooted in the classical Buddhist scientific tradition, Kālacakra life science is best known for its distinctive formulation of the Unexcelled Yoga Tantras, integrating concepts from the Sāṃkhya, Vaiṣṇava, Jaina, and Śaiva Tantric traditions. The Wheel of Time presents life in light of the contemplative mind and health sciences held in common by all Indian traditions, Buddhist and non-Buddhist. In particular, it reflects the gradual integration of esoteric, contemplative models of mind and body into exoteric sciences like psychology and medicine. As with physical science, the Wheel of Time explains its unique synthesis of conventional views of the inner world in light of the pedagogic needs of its universal audience. A survey of its biology helps clarify the outlook and intent behind the view of life and mind in this tradition.

Among the many complex theories woven into the Wheel of Time's science of life, I will restrict myself to two: its model of human development; and its map of the mind and nervous system. As for the first, Kālacakra biology offers a syncretic view of development that integrates classical Buddhist views of the conception and nature of life with Vedist concepts of the soul's incarnation. The classical Buddhist view of life as originating through the interaction of physical and mental causes across many lives is assumed in the Wheel of Time view of conception as the union of egg and sperm with a mental process that is continuous with prior lives. From this point on, development is described with the help of various non-Buddhist views. The formation of the individual recapitulates the formation of the cosmos through the emergence of physical elements, which in turn give rise to the ten kinds of life energies (*prāṇa*) that support a body of instincts (*vāsanā-śarīra*), adapting the Jaina view. These energies in turn shape the formation of the nervous system with its channels (*nāḍī*), complexes (*cakra*), and drops (*bindu*), supporting the emergence of the remaining aspects of human nature including the life systems (*skandha*), sensory media (*āyatana*), intelligence (*buddhi*), ego-function (*ahaṃkāra*), and mentality (*manas*), adapting the Sāṃkhya view. Finally, Kālacakra describes the development of the ordinary individual in ten life stages, adapting the Vaiṣṇava model of Viṣṇu's ten incarnations (*avatāras*) to depict the way human development recapitulates the evolutionary ascent from more primitive forms of life to higher ones.

The intent behind this syncretic account of human development can be glimpsed through the adaptations that distinguish Kālacakra's distinctive outlook on life. Borrowing the Jaina view of the developmental causality of karma as a subtle material process, the Wheel of Time implicitly critiques Buddhist Realism and Idealism for their reification of mind and mental causation as more or less independent of matter. By restricting this model of developmental causation to the basic, unenlightened life cycle (*saṃsāra*), however, the Wheel of Time critiques the Jaina concept of the soul and its action-patterns as permanent. Likewise, the Kālacakra critiques Buddhist and non-Buddhist Idealism by borrowing the Sāṃkhya model of the involvement of the spirit or person (*puruṣa*) with a material nature (*prakṛti*), while distinguishing its view from Sāṃkhya dualism by asserting the nondualist view that the person is an innate intuition (*sahaja-jñāna*) or blissful omniscience (*sarvajñātā*) actively involved with a nature that is devoid of intrinsic reality (*nihsvabhāva*) and primally luminous (*prakṛti-prabhāsvara*). Finally, the Wheel of Time critiques any nihilistic and materialist reading of Buddhist Centrism or Tantrism by adapting the Vaiṣṇava view of life as a process of spiritual incarnation, while distinguishing its psychobiology from the elitism of Vedist spirituality through identifying Viṣṇu with the innate intuition that makes every mind a vehicle for spiritual evolution throughout the lifespan and across many lives.

The second basic theory that helps clarify the outlook and intent of the Kālacakra science of life is its unique, syncretic view of the mind and nervous system. To clarify the esoteric psychology of the Unexcelled Tantras, the Wheel of Time adapts Vedist concepts from the Śaivite Tantra and Sāṃkhya-Yoga traditions as well as terms and arts from the Buddhist and Vedist systems of Indian medicine. Assuming the esoteric model of mind from Unexcelled Tantras like the *Esoteric Communion Process*, the *Wheel of Time Process* converts it into a psychology suitable for mainstream use by integrating the Sāṃkhya model of three qualities as found within the Śaivite model of four states of mind. Thus, it aligns the coarse, subtle, and extremely subtle levels of mind and nervous system with the qualities of clarity, intensity, and darkness (*sattva, rajas, tamas*), as well as the waking, dream, and deep sleep states. By dividing the extremely subtle level of mind in two, it adds to these a fourth level devoid of the qualities of clarity, intensity, and darkness and associated with the fourth state supporting the bliss and nonduality of sexual orgasm. Finally, the three qualities are also identified with the three humors or aspects (*tridoṣa*) of bodily self-organization defined in Indian medicine, wind, bile, and phlegm (*vāta, pitta, kapha*) as well as their subtle analogues in the central nervous system, the left, right, and central channels (*iḍā, piṅgalā, suṣumnā-nāḍī*), while the four states are identified with the complexes of the central nervous system at the forehead, throat, heart, and navel, and the four kinds of neural drops that originate from those complexes.

As with the Kālacakra view of development, the intent behind its syncretic view of the mind and nervous system may be most readily seen in the ways in which it diverges from its Buddhist and non-Buddhist sources. Rooted in the models of earlier Buddhist tantras, the Wheel of Time maps the mind so as to make its depths seem sensible and accessible to the initiated and uninitiated alike, revealing what prior systems conceal. The introduction of a fourth level of mind, for instance, puts the focus on the most intimate layer of intuitive consciousness linked in the other Unexcelled Tantras with the primary processes of sex and death, and shrouded in secrecy along with the mysterious practices of the great perfection stage. Likewise, Kālacakra's integration of Vedist models of qualities and states of mind help demystify its depths by linking them to the daily experience of cosmological and biological rhythms. Unlike the fourth state in Kaśmiri Śaivism, for instance, in Kālacakra the fourth state refers to the ordinary human orgasm, rather than to an extraordinary spiritual experience. More reminiscent of India's medical systems than its prior Yogic or Tantric traditions, the Wheel of Time's adaptations aim at offering a scientific account of the common condition of everyday life rather than its spiritual transformation through contemplative practice or ethical discipline. Yet unlike Indian medicine, the Wheel of Time emphasizes the innate potential of every human body and mind for self-healing and self-transformation through the control of perception, expression, and breathing. This is conveyed by its designation of the four states and levels of mind as the four bases (*vajras*) of a Buddha's enlightened body, speech, mind, and intuition.

Since the Wheel of Time is an esoteric tradition revolving around a spiritual archetype and ritual initiation into the contemplative life, it is natural for us as moderns to misidentify its inner sciences of life, health, mind, and society with the symbolism and rituals of Western monotheism. Yet the outlook and intent with which it depicts the origin and nature of human life is decidedly scientific and secular, offering a view of life that may be generally described as evolutionary and naturalistic. Where the inner sciences of the Kālacakra tradition adapt the views of India's contemplative traditions, Buddhist and non-Buddhist, it is clearly with a view to describing the human potential for two divergent modes of life: a reactive life driven by self-destructive instincts; or a progressive life based on the sublimation of sexual bliss. Given this intent, its inner science is more akin to the evolutionary psychologies of ancients like Empedocles or moderns like Freud than to the revelatory psychologies of Mediterranean or Indian theism. In fact, I have argued elsewhere[32] that its esoteric map of the mind may be cross-referenced with the Western maps of psychoanalysis and cognitive neuroscience, with the help of meditation research (see Tables 1 and 2). From the standpoint of Buddhology, this involves a retrospective mapping of the main psychologies integrated in the three-vehicle (*triyāna*) synthesis of the gradual path (*patha-krama*) in the Nālandā tradition onto the developmental neuroscience of tantric medicine. Specifically, Theravāda, Mahāyāna, and Vajrayāna psychologies (glossed in Table 1 as "personal," "social," and "process" phases of development), are mapped onto the basic psychobiology of the coarse, subtle, and extremely subtle levels of mind/nervous system. Of course, Kālacakra adds a fourth level, emphasizing the binary nature of the extremely subtle observed in the main division of Nāgārjuna's perfection stage map. In this sense, the Wheel of Time extends and refines the work done by Mahāyāna thinkers in the Nālandā tradition: providing a progressive synthesis of scientific and religious disciplines to advance mainstream culture in India and Asia. While some of the details may seem occult to us now, the broad outlook and intent behind its view of life and mind are surprisingly modern and relevant to the current dilemmas of scientific education in the West.

Practice Phase	Neural Level	Mental Level	Blocks (Drag)	Motive/ Intent	Arousal/ Attention	Skill Level	Insight Level
Personal Care	Coarse/ Cortical	Waking/ Fantasy	Traumatic Cognition	Relief/ Release	Low/ Inclusive	Reflection/ Mindfulness	Analytic/ Gestalt
Social Concern	Subtle/ Limbic	Daydream Dreaming	Traumatic Affect	Care/ Concern	Low/ Exclusive	Alterness/ Effort	Imaginal/ Visceral
Process Integrity	Subtlest/ Core	Sleep/ Orgasm	Stress Instincts	Joy/ Mastery	High/ Integral	Devotion/ Flow	Euphoric/ Ecstatic

Table 1. Simplified Kālacakra Map of Human Psychobiology and Development.

3. Other/Alternative Kālacakra: Contemplative Science in the Nālanda Tradition

Undoubtedly, the greatest interest in the Wheel of Time has focused on its uniquely accessible synthesis of the Indian Buddhist Unexcelled Tantras, especially preserved in the Vajrayāna Buddhism of Tibet. Building on the basic views of the universe and human life presented in the Kālacakra's outer and inner sciences, alternative Kālacakra offers a complete path for the transformation of the human condition from one of compulsive alienation to one of blissful engagement. Here too, it integrates the theories and methods of contemplative science from Buddhist and non-Buddhist, exoteric and esoteric traditions, to provide one of the world's most lucid and scientific systems of mind/body self-transformation. As with its basic outer and inner sciences, the Wheel of Time explains its unique system of alternative science in terms of the pedagogic needs of its universal audience.

The best place to start to understand the outlook and intent behind alternative science in this tradition is to explore its relation to the physical and psychosocial sciences we normally think of as complete in themselves. Assuming the Centrist critique of knowledge and method, the Wheel of Time reverses the objectivist hierarchy of sciences we have come to accept in the modern West. Rather than ranking sciences based on their proximity to a supposedly independent objective reality—physics first, biology second, psychology third, etc.—the Wheel of Time orders knowledge based on the theory of two realities (*dvisatya-vāda*). Since all dualistic knowledge and expertise is relative and conventional, all ordinary science is provisional (*kṣara-vidyā*). Only that knowledge which consists in nondualistic, intuitive openness to the infinitely relative and ungraspable nature of things, outer and inner, is ultimately valid, pure, or unchanging science (*akṣara-vidyā*). Although this critical approach to knowledge and method seems counter to Buddhist Realism and Logic, exoteric Centrists and their Kālacakra peers point out a similar critique in the four noble truth framework of Buddhist teaching as well as the epistemology of Digṅāga and his heirs. Just as the basic science spelled out in the first two noble truths is relative to the third, healing truth of nirvāṇa, so the validity of inference and constructed perception is relative to the deconstructive intuition of direct perception (*pratyakṣa*), especially yogic direct perception (*yogi-pratyakṣa*). In short, no formula of knowledge or practice, however invaluable, can be objective in and of itself; because it is inexorably partial and symbolic, and so must be constantly corrected against the touchstone of purely critical reason and validating personal experience. While we in the West have spent the last centuries learning to tolerate this insight, Mahāyāna Buddhist thinkers were ready long ago to adapt their scientific tradition to this reality. And they did so by developing scientific systems of self-correction effective and universal enough to help individuals and groups reliably cultivate the radical open-mindedness and unbiased concern for the world that make ordinary humans into extraordinary scientists.

The Nālandā tradition of self-correction or mind training (*buddhiśodhana*) preserved in Tibet is often traced back to Śantideva, although its roots are clear in the writings of Nāgārjuna and Candrakīrti. In particular, the *Reason Sixty* and its *Commentary* are known to Tibetan scholars for their focus on the mindset of genuine intuition (*samyak-jñāna*) most receptive to contemplative self-correction. While this focus is most often linked with the rise of exoteric Idealist Centrism (eighth to ninth century CE), a less obvious, esoteric tradition of self-correction leads to three Unexcelled Tantras deeply influenced by the idea of an intuition body (*jñānakaya*) taught in the *Recitation of the Names of Mañjuśrī (Mañjuśrīnāmasaṃīgti)*. Of these three—Guhyamañjuvajra, Yamāntaka, and Kālacakra—Kālacakra is most explicit about how the intuition body, an ecstatic subjectivity innate in all beings, can be quickly developed to help practitioners personally realize the objective reality of all things. Perhaps the best way to appreciate the unique outlook and intent behind the Wheel of Time's contemplative science is to explore the ways it departs from other exoteric and esoteric Mahāyāna systems of self-correction.

Firstly, Kālacakra contemplative science diverges from the exoteric Idealist Centrism developed by Śantarakṣita (c. 740-810) and Kamalaśīla (c. 760-815) by presenting the depth-psychology of intuitive self-correction in terms of the neuroscience of the Unexcelled Yoga Tantras rather than the Idealist theory of a subconscious mind. It also diverges from the other Unexcelled Buddhist Tantras by identifying the intuition body with the fourth state of mind assumed in the Śaivite Tantras, while linking it with the ordinary biology of sexual orgasm. This divergence has a twofold impact. It makes overt the art of sublimating sexual energy and bliss normally kept covert in the final phase of the Unexcelled Tantras called the great perfection stage or great seal practice (*mahāmūdra*). And it also makes that extraordinary art seem more comprehensible and accessible to the initiated and uninitiated alike by depicting it in terms of the ordinary psychophysiology of human sexual experience. This impact is supported by the artful way Kālacakra's contemplative science draws on the complementary theories of its physics and biology. For instance, the theory that life and the world both emerge from a space-element pervaded by an element of intuition (*jñāna-dhātu*) makes it easier for most to conceive of dissolving the subtle matter and energy patterns supporting the ordinary alienated life cycle (*saṃsāra*) and building up in their place the drops of sublimated bliss that sustain the extraordinary, open-hearted release (*nirvāṇa*) of enlightened engagement with the world. Likewise, distinctive concepts like the idea that the central channel is not normally fully blocked, as in other Unexcelled Tantras, but open to the circulation of blissful energy even in nonpractitioners, or that ordinary sexual intercourse does not preclude sublimation practice (*rāga-dharma*), as long as it is motivated by real compassion, have the cumulative effect of encouraging a mainstream audience that they may be capable of this transformational practice. In short, the adaptation of language from enlightened physical and biomedical sciences seem calculated to make contemplative self-correction appear more rational and practical to the increasingly democratic and cosmopolitan community served by Nālandā.

Secondly, the extraordinary outlook and intent of Kālacakra's contemplative science is clear not just in its depiction of the path but also in its distinctive presentation of the result or fruit of that path, the fourfold objectivity or omniscience (*sarvaijñatā*) of Kālacakra. Here, the Wheel of Time's unique fourfold model of mind unfolds as a map of the unexcelled journey or supreme pilgrimage through the nervous system of the individual towards the blissful, nondual mastery of the outer and inner worlds. In particular, objective self-knowledge and artful mastery of the waking, dream, sleep, and orgasmic states transform the practitioner's body, speech, mind, and intuition from their basic conditions to the blissful, omniscient agency of Kālacakra. Thus, the repetitive, traumatic interaction of the outer and inner worlds at these four levels is transformed by four successive stages of contemplation, each of which shifts the atomic energies of the stress instincts that act as demons (*māras*) or obscurations (*avāraṇa*) into a blissful communion of outer and inner, through the nondual realization of the objective physicality of voidness (*śūnyatā-rūpinī*) by the subjective changeless bliss (*akṣara-sukha*) at each level. This constitutes the complete correction (*sarvākārā viśuddhi*) of life in the world that is the four bodies of buddhahood. In particular, the reified waking construct of self and world as intrinsically alien is replaced with the void image (*śūnya-bimba*) of Kālacakra mother-father, representing the blissful interplay of macrocosmic and microcosmic rhythms; the nightmare symbolism of life as a struggle for survival is replaced with the luminous dream of the global community of Kālacakra as a perfectly communicating family of multiracial, multicultural couples all embracing the blissful energy of life; the deluded sleep in which subjectivity and objectivity are mutually obscured from each other is replaced with the numinous absorption in which they commune in their innate freedom from the perplexity of dualistic constructs; and the addictive bliss in which the genetic material of mother and father reproduces stress instincts and their atomic energies is replaced with the changeless bliss in which the male and female spirits of enlightenment (*bodhicitta*), freed from all tainted atomic energies, pervade the spacious physicality of voidness. This fourfold embodiment of blissful omniscience is the full fruition of the primal enlightenment (*ādhibuddha*) innate in all living beings, realized by the mature intuition body of a vajra master (*vajradhara*).

Since the Wheel of Time is an esoteric tradition that culminates in a spiritual science and divine archetype of contemplative living, it is natural for us as moderns to misidentify its path and fruit with the ritual practice and mystical experience of Western monotheism. Yet the outlook and intent with which it teaches the transformation of human life in the world is decidedly humanistic in its aims and scientific in its methods, offering a view of contemplative life that may be generally described as therapeutic and educational. Where the contemplative science of the Kālacakra tradition adapts the models and methods of the Indian Buddhist tradition of self-correction, exoteric and esoteric, it is clearly with a view to describing the human potential for transforming reactive life driven by self-destructive instincts into a progressive life based on the sublimation of sexual bliss. Given this intent, its contemplative science is more akin to the evolutionary psychologies of ancients like Empedocles or moderns like Freud, Jung, and Reich than to the ritual-mystical soteriology of monotheism. The fruit of this path, the individual's correction of self-limiting destructive instincts and sublimation of socially generative sexual instincts, is akin to awakening the civilizing genius of Eros described by Empedocles and in Freud's *Civilization and Its Discontents*. From the standpoint of Buddhology, Kālacakra reconciles the physics of Buddhist Realism with the psychology of Buddhist Idealism by subjecting both to a critical revision guided by Centrist contemplative science. Thus, Buddhist atomism is aligned with the Centrist view of Buddha's insight that matter is void; Buddhist psychology is aligned with the Centrist view of his insight that mind and body coevolve through selfless wisdom and love; and Buddhist contemplative science is revised to better reflect the Centrist view of his omniscience as a blissful openness that accepts the reality of all with unconditional love and care. In short, Kālacakra revises the conventions of Buddhist science to better reflect the ultimate nature of reality Buddha realized in his nirvāṇa, insisting in true Centrist spirit that that luminous, blissful nature is not localized (*apratiṣṭitā*) apart from the world but rather the very nature of this relative matter and mind. In this sense, the Wheel of Time extends and refines the work done by Mahāyāna thinkers in the Nālandā tradition to develop a system of contemplative self-correction that can prepare individuals to guide the advancement of human science and civilization towards a sustainable, global culture of peaceful collaboration. Elsewhere,[33] I have used the similarity between the aims and means of Western psychotherapy and Buddhist mind science to map modern Western and Indo-Tibetan techniques of cultivating nonviolence, compassion, and sublimation (Table 2).

III. The *Wheel of Time*: A Global Vision for Sustainable Science and Education

According to the Kālacakra legend, when Sucandra, ruler of the mythical kingdom of Śambhala, asked Śakyamūni to reveal the *Wheel of Time Process* it was with a global vision of the future of science and civilization in our world. As our world system entered its decadent age (*kāliyuga*), the Universal Monarch (*Cakravartirājā*) sought the former prince's guidance to protect his kingdom, hidden somewhere in the vastness of Central Asia, from the escalating political violence that was already threatening the very survival of Eurasian civilization. In particular, Sucandra sought teachings from the Universal Vehicle (*Mahāyāna*) meant to guide

Cultural Traditions:	**Western Behavioral**	**Western Analytic**	**Indo-Tibetan Buddhist**	**Indian Vedist**
Individual Practices:				
	Relaxation Techniques Autogenic Training Cognitive Therapy	Dynamic Therapy Ego Psychology Classical Analysis	Basic Mindfulness Basic Quiescence Basic Insight	Hatha Yoga TM Stage 1,4 Krishnamurti/ Aurobindo
Social Practices:				
	Family Therapy Dialectical Therapy Couples & Parenting	Object Relations Interpersonal Therapy Existential Therapy	Giving & Taking Exoteric Mind Training Insight & Quiescence	Patanjali Yoga State1-2 Bhakti/Seva Yoga Advaita Vedanta
Process Practices:				
	Hypnotherapy/EMDR Guided Imagery Sex Therapy/ Movement Intimacy Work	Self-Psychology Jungian Analysis Reichian Analysis Lacanian Analysis	Kriya/Carya Tantra Yoga/Unexcelled Yoga Tantra 1 Unexcelled Yoga Tantra 2a Unexcelled Yoga Tantra 2b	Yoga Stage 5 TM Stage 3/Yoga Stage 6 Kundalini Stage 7 Sahaja/Yoga Stage 8

Table 2. Provisional Comparative Map of Cultural Practices of Self-Correction.

whole societies out of the cycle of trauma and violence and into a utopian Pure Land (*Buddha-kṣetra*) of enlightened people and institutions, just as the Kings and Queens of the Kuśana, Śātavāhana, Gupta, and Pāla dynasties of India would in their eras. Further, not content with the exoteric universalist teachings the Buddha gave at Vulture Peak near Nālandā, Sucandra specifically requested the esoteric alternative teachings alluded to in the *Heart Discourse* as the quickest method of realizing transcendent wisdom. In fact, the teachings Śakyamūni revealed as the Wheel of Time articulate a prophetic vision of the not-too-distant future quite unlike that found in most spiritual traditions, including the Mahāyāna Pure Land traditions that became so popular in East Asia. What is unique about the Kālacakra's vision of the role of spiritual wisdom and art in human history is that, in the midst of endangered civilization, it offered a radically progressive alternative to the cultures of prejudice and violence threatening our world to this day, an alternative based on the promise that scientific education and democratic society will spread universally to all the world's diverse cultures and peoples. According to Kālacakra legend, this sustainable alternative tradition profoundly affected the society of Śambhala within the span of just eight generations. By the time of Mañjuśrī Yaśas, the country's first Democratic King (*Kalkī* or *Kūlika-rājā*), education had spread to the point that the caste system could be abolished.

Whatever historical truth there may be to this legend, one thing is clear. The Kālacakra tradition is no idle prophecy, but an eminently reasoned and pragmatic plan for a sustainable global future for humanity, based on a decisive commitment to progressive, democratic forms of science and civilization. While the legend and teaching of the Wheel of Time has seemed to many shrouded in an exotic air of magic and mystery, it is as far from the romantic lore of myth and legend as our own European tradition of enlightenment. This may not be as incredible as it sounds when we consider the fact that, like our enlightenment vision of science and democracy, the Kālacakra vision is grounded in the most mainstream institution of contemplative life: the university. The fact that the emergence of the Wheel of Time preceded our scientific enlightenment by at least a millennium is not so shocking when one considers that the first Indian universities, Takśaśīla, Dhānyakaṭaka, and Nālandā were founded a millennium or more before the first Western universities at Bologna, Paris, and Oxford. More surprising is the fact that the basic elements of the scientific worldview of the Kālacakra anticipate not just the modern physics of Newton or modern biology of Freud, bụt also the postmodern insights of Einstein, Heisenberg, Wittgenstein, and Lacan. As if that were not enough, the timeless contemplative science of the Wheel of Time presents us with the futuristic promise of fully adapting our experience of ourselves and our world to the new realities of quantum physics, neural plasticity, and positive psychology, of which many have not yet heard.

Whether Śambhala is a still-hidden utopia or a global vision shared in a virtual domain, a contemplative scientific community without cultural borders, it is clear that its critical view of reality and its techniques of self-correction are remarkably pertinent to the challenges facing humanity today. In view of the looming problems of terrorism, sectarian violence, ethnic cleansing, inner city violence, and violence in our homes and schools, it is fortunate indeed that the once warlike peoples of Tibet and Mongolia have preserved what may be the world's most accessible and effective system of enlightened self-disarmament.

Faced with the time-warp in which modern science is just catching up with the wisdom of this older tradition, those in the West interested in serious study of the Kālacakra literature, arts, and sciences will need to practice some of the patience the Wheel of Time teaches. For unlike the West's main traditions of religious prophecy, the Kālacakra's scientific futurism embodies a progressive style of cultural agency in which the spirit of universal compassion is active as transcendent tolerance for the blocks that keep alienated individuals and groups attached to prejudice and the repetition of trauma. While we moderns have learned to think of religions as perpetuating superstition and destructive emotions like shame, fear, and hate, in order to learn from the Kālacakra the modern scientific community of the West must begin to face and heal its own reactive bias against things contemplative or spiritual. As I see it, this is the rate-limiting step in recognizing what may be the prime challenge facing scientific civilization today: the need to integrate the psychotherapeutic, contemplative, and ethical disciplines of self-correction modern science and civilization have jettisoned along with the religious traditions and institutions out of which they emerged. This philosophical obstacle has a lot to do with the lack of resolution in certain postmodern debates facing the liberal, scientific academy in the West. These include the debate between the physical and social science communities over objectivity versus cultural relativism; the debate between secularists and traditionalists over the role of science versus religion in education; and the debate between objectivists and pluralists over the possibility of multiple approaches to science and spirituality.

Let me simply say that I believe that these problems were clearly recognized in Buddhist and Vedist thought after Nāgārjuna and resolved at Nālandā by the eighth century. That resolution is reflected in the complementary Buddhist paradigms of embodied objectivity refined by Candrakīrti and Dharmakīrti. The gist of that resolution is to confirm Śakyamūni's critique of the idea of absolute objectivity or omniscience, as well as his insistence that appropriate objectivity or embodied omniscience does ensure that human knowledge and action yield personal freedom and social happiness. Since the objectivity of human knowledge and expertise is no greater than the objectivity of those who employ them, the best way to advance objectivity may be to maximize the natural, social, and cultural processes of self-correction by which individuals and groups become more objective over time.

While modern philosophers of science have had to adapt themselves to this way of thinking in recent years, it is so foreign to the objectivism of modern science that few individuals and fewer communities in the West as yet have been able to make the necessary transition.[34] One voice in the Anglo-American academy that may be a harbinger of the kind of shift needed is legal philosopher Thomas Nagel. I will therefore close with a quote from Nagarjuna's *Reason Sixty*, with an explanatory comment by Candrakīrti, some passages from the *Kālacakratantra*, and finally with some excerpts from Nagel's classic, *The View from Nowhere.*

First, Nāgārjuna:

> Those who insist on a non-relative
> Self or world, Alas!
> They are impoverished by worldviews
> Like absolutism and nihilism.[35]
>
> The great souls are free
> From [self-centered] conflict or bias;
> For they who have no [fixed] position,
> How can there be opposition?[36]
>
> Seeing with their wisdom eye
> That things resemble reflections,
> The great souls do not get caught
> In the thicket of objects.[37]

Here is Candrakīrti's *Commentary*:

> Once the practitioner sees that what the "god" of his consciousness reifies as being existent or non-existent is deceptive and fictive in nature, he sees

> it as uncreated with respect to intrinsic reality and hence definitively understands it. Since the mind thus poised knows [things as] uncreated with intrinsic reality, it is purged of endless [constructs of] things like material elements that are created with such [apparent reality], and hence becomes free of them as a reflected image ceases when the form reflected is removed.[38]

> When freed from egocentric position and opposition by their freedom from [reifying] being as such, those [great souls] with such [purged] intuition will definitely terminate their addictions.[39]

> In the empathic objectivity of the noble, [egocentrically biased minds] seem like children, ignorant of the nature of existence, caught in the trap of the [addictive] world, whatever they do. With an intellectual eye purified by wisdom [however], the noble see objective reality precisely as it is . . . hence, "great souls do not get stuck in the thicket of objects."[40]

Now from the *Kālacakratantra*:

> The individual is like a silkworm, binds himself with conceptualizations, which are the *guṇas* [qualities] present in *prakṛti* [nature]. However, due to the absence of conceptualizations, the individual liberates himself with the mind. Therefore, king, one's own *karma*, present in the *guṇas* of *prakṛti*, causes suffering and happiness.[41]

> A living being, fettered with the psycho-physical aggregates, elements, and sense-faculties, with the fears of the three worlds, with the five faculties of action (*karmendriya*), with the subtle-elements (*tanmatra*), with *karmic* defects, with the mind and its *guṇas*, with the intellect, self-grasping, and the like, roams repeatedly with a subtle state of being within the six states of existence. When a mental state is left behind, one attains the indestructible, supreme state in which one is no longer a living being (*janmin*).[42]

> The body-*vajra* of the Jina, which has all aspects, is inconceivable in terms of sense-objects and sense-faculties. The speech-*vajra* accomplishes Dharma by means of utterances in the hearts of all sentient beings. The mind-*vajra* of the Vajrī, which is the nature of the minds of sentient beings, is present throughout the entire earth. That which, like a pure gem, apprehends phenomena is the gnosis-*vajra*.[43]

Finally, these excerpts from Nagel:

> I shall offer a defense and also a critique of objectivity. Both are necessary in the present climate, for objectivity is both underrated and overrated,

> sometimes by the same persons . . . these errors are connected: they both stem from an insufficiently robust sense of reality and of its independence of any particular form of human understanding.[44]

> What really happens in the pursuit of objectivity is that a certain element of oneself, the impersonal or objective self, which can escape from one's creaturely point of view, is allowed to predominate.[45]

> This involves the idea of an unlimited hypothetical development on the path to self-knowledge and self-criticism, only a small part of which we may actually traverse. We assume that our own advances in objectivity are steps along a path that extends beyond them and beyond all our capacities . . . and can never be completed, short of omniscience.[46]

> Our objectivity is simply a development of our humanity, and doesn't allow us to break free of it; it must serve our humanity and to the extent that it does not we can forget about it.[47]

Of course, the art and science of self-correction, Buddhist or Western, are meant not to displace ordinary science but to advance it, much as alternative science guides the ordinary physical and psychosocial sciences in the Wheel of Time tradition[48] or "extraordinary science" improves "normal science" in Kuhn's vision.[49] The difficulty we postmoderns have understanding this stems from the climate of exclusivity that Nagel describes, a climate whose roots lie in the culture-specific conflict between objectified empirical science and church-controlled contemplative science in the West. Aligned with the therapeutic centrism of Nāgārjuna, Candrakīrti, and the Kālacakra, Nagel envisions the true path of reason today as a middle way between the cultural dead-ends of objectivism and relativism, scientism and antiscientism. Fortunately, the preservation of contemplative traditions like the Wheel of Time suggests he is wrong to assume that "the methods we need to understand ourselves do not yet exist."[50] One of the most precious gifts Tibetan civilization holds for our planet is its living link to this remarkable multidisciplinary science of civilized living, a time-capsule of the liberating arts and sciences of the world's first university at Nālandā.

Endnotes

1. Three recent works on Kālacakra are representative: Wallace, V. A. *The Kālacakratantra: The Chapter on the Individual.* New York: AIBS/Columbia Press, 2004; Wallace, V. A. *The Inner Kālacakratantra.* Oxford: Oxford University Press, 2001; Gyatso, Khedrup Norsang, trans. G. Kilty. *Ornament of Stainless Light.* Boston: Wisdom, 2004.

2. Obermiller, E. *Buston's History of Buddhism in India.* Tokyo: Suzuki, 1975; Chattopadyaya, A. and L. Chimpa. *Taranātha's History of Buddhism.* Simla: Indian Institute of Advanced Studies, 1970.

3. Cf. Loizzo, Joseph. "Candrakīrti and the Moon-Flower of Nālandā: Objectivity and Self-Correction in India's Central Therapeutic Philosophy of Language." University of Michigan: University Microfilm Services, 2001; and Joshi, Lalmani. *Studies of the Buddhistic Culture of India*. Delhi: Motilal Banarsidass, 1980; Stewart, Mary. *The Historical Archeology of Nalanda*. Archeological Survey of India, 1989.

4. Traditional sources for this history are the records of Chinese visiting scholars Xuanzang and Yi-jing: Beal, S. *Su-Yu-Ki: Buddhist Records of the Western World*. London, 1884/1969; Takakusus, J. *A Record of the Buddhist Religion as Practiced in India and the Malay*. Oxford: Oxford, 1896.

5. A good example here is B. Alan Wallace, whose work ranges from traditional Buddhist scholarship to comparisons of Western and Buddhist mind science traditions.

6. See the work of neuroscientist Richard Davidson in Daniel Goleman, *Destructive Emotions*, New York: Bantam, 2003.

7. A key figure here is Jon Kabat-Zinn, as expressed in his book on mindfulness-based stress-reduction, *Full Catastrophe Living*, New York: Bantam, 1998.

8. Palliative-care expert Leslie Blackhall and I review the argument for complementary sciences using the example of Indo-Tibetan Buddhist medicine in Joseph Loizzo and Leslie Blackhall, "Traditional Alternatives as Complementary Sciences: The Challenge of Indo-Tibetan Medicine," *Journal of Alternative and Complementary Medicine*, 1998.

9. Cf. Kitcher, Phillip. *Science, Truth and Democracy*. Oxford: Oxford University Press, 2001.

10. Thurman, Robert A. F. *Tsong Khapa's Speech of Gold: Reason and Enlightenment in the Central Philosophy of Buddhism*. Princeton: Princeton University Press, 1984.

11. This distinction emerges in the fascinating dialogue recorded in Ricard, Mathieu, and Thuan in Trinh Xuan, *The Quantum and the Lotus*, New York: Crown, 2001.

12. Few Western philosophers of science are more attuned to this distinction than French chemist and philosopher Gaston Bachelard. Cf. Tiles, Mary. *Bachelard: Science and Objectivity.* Cambridge: Cambridge University Press, 1984.

13. Although familiar in the West as early as Fichte, this insight was articulated in the later philosophy of Wittgenstein and found its way into Anglo-American philosophy of science *via* his influence on Thomas Kuhn. Cf. Wittgenstein, Ludwig. *Philosophical Investigations*. New York: Macmillan, 1953, and *On Certainty.* New York: Harper, 1970; also Kuhn, Thomas. *The Structure of Scientific Revolutions*. Chicago: University of Chicago Press, 1964.

14. A strong, critical reading of Freud's humanistic approach to science may be found in Patricia Kitcher, *Freud's Dream: A Complete Multidisciplinary Science of Mind,* Cambridge: MIT Press, 1998; while perhaps the most profound defense and use of Freud is in Paul Ricoeur, *Hermeneutics and the Human Sciences,* trans. J. Thompson, Cambridge: Cambridge University Press, 1982.

15. Gadamer, Hans. *Truth and Method.* New York: Seabury Press, 1975.

16. This point was first made by Lama Anagarika Govinda, *The Psychological Attitude of Early Buddhist Philosophy*, New York: Weiser, 1973. For a recent treatment, see John Pickering, ed., *The Authority of Experience*: *Essays on Buddhism and Psychology,* Richmond, Surrey: Curzon, 1997.

17. The continuity between Greek and Indic science parallels the better-known continuity in ancient philosophy. See Thomas McEvilley, *The Shape of Ancient Thought: Comparative Studies in Greek and Indian Philosophies*, New York: Allworth, 2002.

18. Cf. Stanley Tambiah's *World Conqueror and World Renouncer*, Cambridge: Cambridge University Press, 1967.

19. See the chapter on Kālacakra science in Vesna A. Wallace, *The Inner Kālacakratantra*, Oxford: Oxford University Press, 2001.

20. Wedemeyer, Christian. "Vajrayana and its Doubles: The Tantric Works of Āryadeva." University of Michigan: University Microfilm Services, 2000.

21. Ibid.

22. For a discussion of the evidence that this integration was well underway at Nālandā in Candrakīrti's day, see chapter six of my "Candrakīrti and the Moon Flower of Nālandā," University of Michigan: University Microfilm Services, 2001.

23. Cf. Kitcher, Patricia. *Freud's Dream: A Complete Multidicisplinary Science of Mind.* Cambridge: MIT Press, 1998.

24. Loizzo, Joseph. "Intersubjectivity in Wittgenstein and Freud: Other Minds and the Foundations of Psychiatry." *Journal of Theoretical Medicine,* Vol. 18, No. 4, 1997.

25. Varela, Francisco, Evan Thompson, and Katherine Roach. *The Embodied Mind.* Cambridge: MIT Press, 1990.

26. Loizzo, Joseph. "Meditation and Psychotherapy: Stress, Allostasis and Enriched Learning." In *Annual Review of Psychiatry*, American Psychiatric Association, Vol. 19, No. 1, 2000.

27. I have dealt with this in the context of my writings on the philosophy and psychiatry: Loizzo, Joseph: "Guarding Patient Agency." *Philosophy, Psychiatry and Psychology,* Vol. 7, No. 2, 2000; "Intersubjectivity in Wittgenstein and Freud: Other Minds and the Foundations of Psychiatry." *Journal of Theoretical Medicine,* Vol. 18, No. 4, 1997; "Commentary On Insight, Delusion and Belief." *Philosophy, Psychiatry and Psychology*, Vol. 1, No. 4, 1995.

28. This process has deep roots in Continental philosophy of science, beginning with Nietzsche. While most closely associated with phenomenologists like Husserl, Merleau-Ponty, and Ricoeur, it is most clearly articulated in the philosophy of science of Gaston Bachelard. One current Anglo-American heir to this tradition is my colleague, biologist Robert Pollack, founder of the Center for the Study of Science and Religion at Columbia. See also Robert Pollack, *The Missing Moment: How the Unconscious Shapes Modern Science*, Boston: Houghton Mifflin, 1999.

29. This influence is clear in the recent publication of three volumes documenting the linked systems of Tibetan astrophysics, phytochemistry, and Kālacakra contemplation (Rome: Tibet Domani). These are *Tibetan Astro-Science, A Clear Mirror of Tibetan Medicinal Plants,* and *Kalachakra* respectively

30. Vesna Wallace, *The Inner Kālackratantra*, op. cit., 56, n. 2, cites the *Vimalaprabhā* commentary of *Kālacakra*, Ch. I, v. 2.

31. This influence is clear in the recent publication of three volumes documenting the linked systems of Tibetan astrophysics, phytochemistry, and Kālacakra contemplation (Rome: Tibet Domani, 2000).

32. Loizzo, Joseph. "Optimizing Learning and Quality of Life Throughout the Lifespan: A Global Framework for Research and Application." *Annals of New York Academy of Sciences*, forthcoming, Spring, 2007.

33. Ibid.

34. Phillip Kitcher's defense of science is an interesting case in point, showing both the extent to which the objectivity claims of science are being relativized even by its strongest advocates, and the extent to which science remains in the crossfire in the centuries-old struggle between secular and religious versions of Western civilization.

35. *Yuktisastika* (YS), 44. This and the following quotations are my translation of verses and commentary, from *Nāgārjuna's Reason Sixty with Chandrakirti's Commentary: Translated with an introduction and critical editions*, New York: American Institute of Buddhist Studies/Columbia University Press, 2007; hereafter, Loizzo, 2007.

36. YS, 50; Loizzo, 2007.

37. YS, 54; Loizzo, 2007.

38. *Yuktisastikavṛtti* (YSV), ad.k.34; Loizzo, 2007.

39. YSV, ad.k.50; Loizzo, 2007.

40. YSV, ad.k.53; Loizzo, 2007.

41. *Kālacakratantra*, Ch.2, v. 85, as translated and cited by V. A. Wallace, *The Kālacakratantra*, op. cit., 132.

42. *Kālacakratanta*, Ch. 2, v. 95, translated and cited in V. A. Wallace, *The Kālacakratantra*, op. cit., 143.

43. *Kālacakratantra*, Ch. 5, v. 99, translated and cited in V. A. Wallace, *The Inner Kālacakratantra*, op. cit., 156.

44. Nagel, Thomas. *The View from Nowhere*. Oxford: Oxford University Press, 1986, 5; hereafter, Nagel.

45. Nagel, 9.

46. Nagel, 128.

47. Nagel, 221.

48. Wallace, V. A., *The Inner Kālacakra*, op. cit.

49. Kuhn, Thomas. *The Essential Tension*. Chicago: University of Chicago Press, 1977.

50. Nagel, 10.

–19–

Demon Diseases and Tibetan Medicine: The Interface between Religion and Science

Ivette Vargas

The philosopher and environmentalist Max Oelschlaeger, in his *Caring for Creation: An Ecumenical Approach to the Environmental Crisis,* writes, "Religion, more than anything else, confirms for believers their place in a meaningful cosmos, a telos that is an ultimate guide, a reality that legitimates existence."[1] He also notes in regard to the environmental crisis he sees worldwide, "My claim is not that religion alone can solve the environmental crisis but that it has an irreplaceable function in the larger process."[2] When we speak of the Tibetan medical tradition, we must keep in mind that we are also referring to complex religious traditions that are linked with the natural environment. And within this complicated web of interrelationships, we have a healing system transforming itself with the times, adopting new and foreign methods, as it must, and maintaining its foundational, yet contested, identity. There are entities that make up part of this contested identity—spirits, or what others might call reified obstacles or demons as such—which create disharmony within the body and in the environment. For example, early Tibetan chronicles envisioned Lhasa and its surroundings as the domain of a primeval serpent king named Maldrozichen who was held accountable for several floods. In stories surrounding Khri srong lde btsan and Padmasambhava, *klu* are said to govern the four districts of Tibet and were appeased in order to complete the monastery Bsam yas. A variety of *klu* are present in the *Gtsang ma klu 'bum* text and protect the various directions as well as inflict red and gray leprosy (*mdze dmar, mdze skya*).[3] Even among the Sherpas in Nepal, we have the connection of *klu* and pollution of the environment.[4] Finally, small *klu khang* shrines in monasteries, temples, and corners of homes throughout Tibetan areas, and in archaeological sites in Western Tibet, are erected in order to appease and honor *klu* because of their potential to inflict disease and other calamities.[5] Although they are known to protect the Dharma and provide wealth, one wrong move on the environment—pollute a sacred site, cut a tree that is inhabited by a *klu*, or forget to honor a *klu*—could cause a person to be inflicted with dementia, rashes, and even leprosy, or disrupt the environment. Hence, for their good and negative aspects, these spirits form the "embedded ecology of everyday Tibetan life."[6]

But what exactly are these entities? What is their relevance in Tibetan medical texts? Why are illnesses related to these entities still significant categories today for treatment purposes? Do beliefs in these entities reflect a preoccupation about the ecological and medical crisis in modern Tibetan society in the Tibetan Autonomous Region (TAR)? This paper will briefly focus on the role of a specific type of spirit called *klu,* and in general, *gdon*, in the Tibetan medical tradition and how diagnosis and treatment of their illnesses traverse the often tenuous crossroads among religion, politics, and medicine in the modern context. Preliminary textual and some ethnographic work in Lhasa, Tibet, and interviews with physicians from the U.S., Tibet, and Dharamsala, India, from 2004-06 reveal a complex complementary relationship between medical and religious communities.

Klu Identity in Select Buddhist and Bon Texts

What *klu* signifies is, of course, a very complex question, often dependent on religious and historical contexts. What is consistent is that *klu*, or *nāgas*, are considered one of the most ambivalent figures to appear throughout Asian literature. Closely linked with the environment; the monastic, royal, and political institutions; and the well-being of individuals, *klu* as wrathful and protective deities have often been at the center of religious traditions and their transmissions. They were, on the one hand, the Buddha's staunchest adversaries, and on the other, guardians of the Dharma (once they were pacified).[7] *Klu* have been prevalent in Tibetan religious traditions prior to the advent of Buddhism and throughout its transmissions. *Klu* were identified with the well-known *nāgas* from the Indian context perhaps around the time of the eighth century as indicated in the *Abhidharmakośa.*[8]

In Bon po texts like *Bon sgo gsal byed* and the *Gzer mig*, *klu* are classified as both *lha ma yin* (*asura*) and *yi dwags* (*preta*), while in Buddhist texts like the *Abhidharmakośa-bhāṣya,* the two categories of *klu* (*nāga*) such as *nāga rājas* (*nāgādhipataḥ, klu bdag*) and ordinary *nāgas* (*klu phal pa'i ming la*) are classified differently. The first are considered animals (*dud 'gro*) (because of their serpent-like form and their apparitional birth like the *garuda* and the *kinnara*), while the second are considered *pretas.*[9] In the Chinese context, *klu* is often equated with the dragon, *klung*. These theriomorphic snake-human or completely snakelike entities are often believed to inhabit the environment, embodying the forces of nature like trees and water sources as well as inhabiting and possessing humans' bodies or controlling a whole society.

What makes these figures particularly "demonic" is that, in possessing or attacking individuals, they cause diseases that affect sensory perception, nervous system (like in the case of leprosy), common sense (like insanity), and sense of discernment (as discussed in Buddhist and Bon traditions)—in the end, impairing the ability for spiritual advancement. In the *rnam thars* of Dge slong ma Dpal mo, an eleventh-century Buddhist nun, *klu* obstructed her development as a practitioner and even led to her contraction of leprosy. These figures are therefore considered real entities that appear to obstruct practice and biological functions because of karma, some offense, or lack of reverence due to them. They are, however, also conceived of as "psychological" entities in the Buddhist sense (as mental projections based on one's deluded view of reality). Therefore, these texts reflect complex psychological, biological, and environmental concerns.

Klu Identity in Tibetan Medical Texts

In medical texts like the twelfth-century *Rgyud bzhi*, *klu* are subsumed under the larger category of *bgegs* (literally meaning "obstacles"). In Buddhist texts, 84,000 *bgegs* in the sutras are said to correspond to the 84,000 mental defilements. Out of these arises the complex category of *gdon.*[10] *Gdon* includes a pantheon of figures like *asuras, pretas, gandarvas, rakshasas*, or others known as the eight classes (*lha srin sde brgyad*) that include *klu, sa bdag, rgyal po, bdud, mamo, yaksha, lha,* and others coming from Bon and Buddhist traditions.[11] As in religious texts, they retain their theriomorphic and other forms as described earlier. Some, when they are linked with *gdon,* increase their harmful effects on individuals, especially when offended, in the form of a kind of *sgrib* (pollution).

Illness Caused by *Klu* in Medical Texts

In the *Rgyud bzhi,* the descriptions of illnesses caused by *klu* or *gdon (klu nad/gdon nad)* reflect a number of textual sources, one significantly being the well-known Sanskrit medical treatise on *Āyurveda*, the *Aṣṭāṅgahṛdayasaṃhitā* of Vāgbhaṭa and others that seem to have arisen from Tibetan sources.[12] The third and longest of the four parts of the *Rgyud bzhi* is the *Man ngag rgyud* or *Instructional Tantra* whose five chapters, chapters 77 to 81, deal primarily with *gdon nad* (illness caused by spirits), although these diseases are present in other chapters as well.

In the *Rgyud bzhi*, *klu nad* is described as *klu* "possessing," attacking, or inhabiting a human being, controlling his senses due to some poisons (mental obscurations) which they embody or help to agitate. Past karmic relations, low accumulation of virtuous actions, in addition to bad diet that affects the *nyes pas* (humors, that form the three principles of physiologic regulation, *rlung, mkhris pa, bad kan*), provide *gdon/klu* an opportunity to inflict mental and physical harm.

The first chapter describes the connections of these entities to the environment within and outside of the body and their impairment of the senses. Demons are explained in five groups: elemental demons (*'byung po'i gdon*), madness-causing demons (*smyo byed kyi gdon*), epilepsy-causing demons (*brjed*[13] *byed kyi gdon*), planetary-demons (*gza' yi gdon*), and serpent demons (*klu'i gdon*).[14]

Chapters 77 and 81 give a broad view of the effects of *klu* spirits. In chapter 77, *klu* is said to belong to one of the eighteen elemental spirits *('byung po gdon')* that embody both protective qualities and on the negative side, are prone to anger and dangerous behavior (classified as *klu'i gdon)*. The *klu* are also distinguished from the asuras and the pretas which have their own categories and sets of symptoms they inflict. Those affected by *klu'i gdon* or *klu'i nad* exhibit radiant faces, red bloodshot eyes with piercing stares, unclear vision, flickering tongues, blistered skin, unregulated voices, their hearts feel empty, and they sleep backwards with a straight body in the manner of snakes. In chapter 81, there are eighteen different locations for the eighteen types of *klu,* the first being the epidermal and other parts of the body, including the muscles, fat, ligaments, blood, yellow water, bone, and so forth.[15] The onset of *klu'i nad* is often preceded by a dream of a bull or some other animal ready to attack, indicating an offence has been committed.

Chapters 77, 78, and 81 also focus on two major diseases that affect sensory perceptions, dementia and leprosy, thus linking the mind with the skin and to Buddhist philosophical concepts. Because these entities have an undisciplined nature, *klu* manifest in exaggerated ways in the individual—increasing mental obscurations to a near frenzy and obsession or blocking sensations altogether as with neuropathies, rashes, and leprosy.

In chapter 77, the eighteen different *gdon* (demons) appear in the form of figures from the Buddhist and Hindu pantheon and such spiritually advanced figures as gods (*lha*), asuras (*lha min*), *gandharvas* (*dri za*), *Brahmins* (*tshangs pa*), lamas, sages, hungry ghosts (*yi dags*), *nāgas (klu),* and others. Curiously, five listed reflect the negative attributes of beings with advanced spiritual attainments especially lamas, sages, elders, and siddhas such as the lha gdon, lama demon (*bla ma'i gdon*), the sage demon (*drang srong gi gdon*), the respected elder demon (*rgan po'i gdon*), and the accomplishment emanation (*grub pa'i gdon*). The text also emphasizes that these five are known as the five highest elementals and are described as seeds for future insanity, whereas they would otherwise be the seeds for enlightenment. Terms like *'byung po*, these figures, and their enumeration into eighteen and five types, correspond with some basic Buddhist philosophical ideas regarding experience and sensory perception. These analyses are aimed at showing: (1) a relationship between human personality and the external world, and (2) that relationship is in fact a conditioned process or function of consciousness or sense experience. In terms of the elemental demon disease, the demons disrupt an individual's perception of the outside world through a distortion of sensation and a resulting aberrant excessive behavior.[16]

Next, the five *'byung po* that are attributed with future insanity correspond in the Buddhist sense with the five great elements (*'byung ba lnga*): earth, water, fire, air/wind, and space which make up matter. In terms of Tibetan medical ideas, these elements form the three principles of physiologic regulation, the *nyes pa gsum.* Possession or attack by *'byung po'i gdon* results in an imbalance on the physiological and spiritual levels; not only are the *nyes pas* (humors) in disequilibrium but also attainments in spiritual advancement are taken in a negative direction (through excess of one type or another, like the angry *nāgas*, hungry ghosts, and egotistical sages exemplify). Another way of phrasing this is that the person is not possessed by the gods but by a negative force or attachment that causes him to behave in a manner reminiscent of these figures. These demons make people operate in the world of the senses as described by the standard Buddhist mental obscurations (*kleśas, nyong mongs*) and poisons.

According to the brief chapter 78 on *smyo byed kyi gdon*, madness-causing demons distort the senses through the interaction of the emotions and humors (*nyes pas*). For example, arising from *rlung*, one becomes emaciated. Arising from phlegm, one sleeps a lot. Arising from mental distress, one is obsessively thinking of sadness. And finally, the mind is confused and can act in a harmful manner if it arises from poisons or demons. These conditions are said to lead to a confused mind (dementia) which is defined as consciousness staying in the path of the mind.[17] With dementia-causing demons, the path of the mind is blocked and perverted at the crucial center of the heart where all the veins meet. As Terry Clifford makes note in her work, *Tibetan Buddhist Medicine and Psychiatry, gdon* enter the body from the eastern and downward direction which dominates thought and ear consciousness; they come in with confused and agitated thinking and block the path of the mind by staying in the heart center.[18] As in the case of Kaśyapa's story in the Āyurvedic tradition, the actions of individuals cause openings for demons to enter into vital points in the body that eventually afflict the mind and consciousness.[19]

A well-known effect of *klu*, leprosy exemplifies the Tibetan preoccupation with the mind and its link with the skin. In the case of leprosy, the major locus (and most obvious one) of the disease is the skin (the largest sense organ of the body) indicating that the life-extending *rlung* (wind element) is impaired. *Rlung* is the central element that acts as a medium between the mind and the body. The five *rlung* (life-sustaining, ascending, pervasive, fire-like, downward-voiding) are responsible for physical and mental activities, including the clarity of the sense organs and life sustenance. Therefore the condition of the skin (rashes, neuropathies, leprosy) indicates that the demons are creating mental obscurations and impairment of the senses. In the religious context, this reflects a person's inner moral state.[20] In the story of the Buddhist Nun Dge slong ma Dpal mo who contracted leprosy, not only was her practice disrupted but there was a sense of decentralization and disintegration of her mind as well as her connection with the environment and society. She had to appease and transform these entities:

> In the *saga* month
> [at the time of the constellation] *sa ri nam mthongs*,
> the interfering demons were placed in the state of *bodhicitta*.
> [Nun Palmo's] illness, sins, and defilements were purified
> and she saw the truth of the first *bhūmi*.
> On the first day of *sa ga zla ba*,
> she witnessed the countenance of the Holy Tārā

and [Tārā] prophesized,
"Buddha activities of all the Buddhas
of the three times are consolidated in you."
On the eighth day,
she witnessed the majority of the *kriyā* tantra deities
such as five Amoghapaśa deities and so forth.
On the fifteenth day,
she witnessed the countenance of the Eleven-faced One
endowed with a thousand hands
and a thousand eyes and furthermore,
countless Buddhas in all the pores of the body,
the hands also being the quintessence of Buddhahood.
On the eyes on the palms of the hands,
she witnessed a host of tantric deities.
Since the holy one talked about the Dharma,
inconceivable *samādhi* arose in [her].
She saw the truth of the eighth *bhūmi*.
Then moreover she practiced the fasting ritual
for three months more for the sake of all sentient beings.[21]

The leper's skin is therefore a reflection of the broken mind and body. As the medical text indicates, only whole bodies are capable of spiritual cultivation because their minds are intact and their senses are focused.

Demons and the Modern Body Politic

These *klu* and *gdon* diseases have often been encased in social and cultural constructs, also revealing tensions and rivalries. The occurrence of disease also reveals a culture's urgency to retain some semblance of its so-called traditional identity amidst political and economic pressures. There are many times in Tibetan history that point to this. One is the case of smallpox in the royal period when Buddhism was accused of bringing the curse of the disease upon the Tibetan royal court. Matthew Kapstein, in his work *The Tibetan Assimilation of Buddhism: Conversion, Contestation, and Memory*, draws attention to a manuscript found by Pelliot, one of a number of sources which points to a Buddhist persecution that occurred during an outbreak of illness in the eighth century:

> At about the time [during the events in Khotan described earlier in the text] the divine Tsenpo of Tibet and the lord of China formed [the relationship of] nephew and uncle, at which the Chinese princess, too, became the divine Tsenpo's bride. The Chinese princess built one great temple in Tibet and established the provisions. The whole saṃgha went there, whereupon the princess also provided rations. The doctrine of the Mahāyāṇa having

> thus blossomed in Tibet, for a period of twelve years both the saṃgha and ordinary layfolk practiced the doctrine and so were exceedingly happy. But even there Mārā's host became agitated, and Mārạ̄ sent forth the black pox and many other sorts of disease. As for the princess, she died after the black pox appeared at her heart. After that the laity lost faith and said that the occurrence of the black pox and many sorts of disease was an evil due to an arrival in Tibet of the host of the saṃgha. It was ordained that not even one member of the saṃgha be permitted to remain in Tibet. After they were banished, one and all, the entire saṃgha traveled to Gandhārạ in India.[22]

In the modern context, despite the continuing secularization and scientization of Tibetan medicine in the Tibetan Autonomous Region and other areas of China, the diagnosis of diseases as caused by demons (with modification in treatment in urban areas) still remain the same. A diversity of opinions about *klu* and *gdon nad* was shared by physicians, instructors at medical schools, administrators, and lamas in Lhasa, Tibet in 2005-06. As is expected of an increasingly secularized and/or "biomedical" Tibetan environment as the Mentsikhang and the Tibetan Medical College in Lhasa, *gdon* and *klu* diseases are mostly described in empirical and psychological terms, often focused on symptomotology. At the medical college, students are taught that *klu* and *gdon* either do not really exist or are mental projections of some kind (instead of focusing on what the medical texts state and their underlying religious ideas). Therefore training at the college is focused on being "scientific" and secular in its theoretical and practical content; there is either no knowledge and/or interest in incorporating the religious aspects of the Tibetan texts in the curriculum. What students learn about *gdon* and *klu* diseases is that they must treat them physiologically, and not spiritually. This means that they learn how to prescribe certain medicine for symptoms they observe, and this includes a change in diet since the condition is considered a disease which does not concern religion. There is also a contrast with traditional understandings of treating *klu* diseases as discussed in the *Rgyud bzhi* and even Bon po texts like the *Klu 'bum*, which is to treat the *klu* first (since it is the *klu* that is ill), and then to treat the patient. This requires both ritual and medicine. Thus there is a major disjuncture between what is taught at the medical school level, on the one hand, and what is literally stated in the medical texts and believed in many sectors of Tibetan culture.

Informants in Lhasa indicated that there are several ways medical students tackle the ideas about these diseases in their training. One way was talking about these diseases in different ways—as *mdze nad* instead of *klu nad*, for example. In addition, they also refer to these diseases as environmental diseases.[23] This notion, that there is a secularization of the environment, is unlike what Tibetan culture traditionally understands it. As an administrator at the college noted, young Tibetan medical students take pride in thinking that they have inherited an "environmentalist" tradition, a long history of concern about nature.[24] This view, however, is not taken further to the realm of the spiritual, to the nonhuman realm of the hindering spirits who get offended and inflict disease. Thus medical students come out with a superficial sense of their environment and an understanding of *klu* and *gdon nad* at least according to literary *Rgyud bzhi* standards and historical cultural views. But several informants at the medical school noted that it was not harmony with the environment but "harmony with the nonhuman" that we should foster.[25] This, however, cannot be openly discussed in the current political climate. This is reminiscent of a remark given by Dr. Tsering Dorjee from Dharamsala's Mentsikhang, who noted *klu* diseases are not "spiritual" but known to be caused by spirits. This seems to indicate the need to go beyond the discourse of spirituality or religion in the modern Tibetan medical context and think of these beings as actual or "real" entities (and deal with them as such in treatment). In Lhasa, there was also a reticence on the part of some Tibetan physicians, administrators, and medical college professors to talk about *klu* and *gdon nad*, often because the disease was described as a "spiritual disease," and "the Chinese government separated religion from medicine." Often questions directed toward *klu* or *gdon* had to be phrased as "medical questions" and not have any semblance of religion per se. Although texts on *Gdon nad gso ba* were made available to me and were available at the local bookstore in the Barkhor, the content and treatment were not readily discussed in public.

Another reaction encountered during fieldwork was a much more flexible attitude in terms of treatment including religious ideas, to integrate the discourse of religion and medicine as mentioned above. For example, two physicians in two specializations unrelated to *gdon nad* were said to be "experts" in diagnosing and providing some treatment to patients with this disease. In addition, some physicians were even fostering a relationship between institutions like the Mentsikhang and the Klu khang behind the Potala Palace. What was observed was that physicians not only treated patients with suspected *gdon* and *klu* diseases with "conventional" Tibetan and Western biomedicine, but also referred them to the local lama for further "spiritual treatment," i.e., mantra recitation, prayers, and offerings. If patients exhibited mental disturbances, they were also immediately sent to a lama.[26] This is reminiscent of the biography of the elder gyu thog Yon tan Mgon po who received the help of the royal king *nāgas* to heal terrible diseases in the *nāga* realm caused by immoral behavior.[27] According to fieldwork observations at the Klu khang in 2005, numerous patients and others exhibiting symptoms and dream experiences associated with *klu nad* were found requesting prayers from lamas and making offerings. Not only was the klu khang a site of healing or complementary treatment, it also represented a continuity of tradition surrounding beliefs regarding the *klu.* An example closely associated with this behavior related to farmers' visits to the temple. As prior to the 1950s, farmers in the Lhasa valley still bring segments of their fields to the shores of the Klu khang lake in hopes of ensuring good harvests.[28] Both of these actions—physicians referring their patients to the klu khang for "alternative or complementary treatment" and the farmers' visits—represent a continuity of traditional beliefs about the *klu's* connection to the environment.

So what may be called on the surface a "pluralistic or complementary" medical approach regarding *gdon* and *klu* on the part of some physicians was surprising in view of the restrictions concerning religion. Some younger physicians who did not have much knowledge or interest in the religious tradition or its rituals to combat these diseases saw no contradiction whatsoever about sending patients to lamas. For some patients, unlike psychological or psychiatric resources that are readily available and accepted in the West, such "treatment" provided options.

Benefits of *klu nad* in Modern TAR

Overall, based on the observations made in TAR, the benefits of *klu nad* diagnoses are that they maintain traditional associations between medical and religious institutions and an awareness of the environmental conditions. In addition, Tibetan concerns over the demonic nature of *klu* and *gdon nad* were coupled with frustrations about treatments of conditions like increasing infectious diseases as AIDS and HIV (with leprosy still prevalent) and the ecological and cultural crises caused by development projects.

Outside of Lhasa in Qinghai province, *glu rol* rituals might be taken as a parallel case in terms of the recognition of the power of the spirits of the environment and the maintenance of the health of the Tibetan community as a whole.[29] In terms of purification and healing, lay people are invited to bathe in a river beside a sanctuary dedicated to white *klu* who reside there in order for the lay people to recover from skin and eye diseases or mental imbalances.[30] Many who have gone to local physicians also take part in this ceremony. *Klu* are therefore beings to entertain and to appease in the rituals of agriculture, reproduction, order, and health. Thus, what is evident in the modern Tibetan context in China is a practical response to very difficult illness conditions and a continued recognition of maintaining good relations with the environment, using all one's resources, secular and religious, at one's disposal. *Klu* disease therefore reflects a rather complex situation incorporating the psycho-physical, the cultural, and the ecological dimensions.

Even further, the treatment of these diseases also accentuates the current Tibetan medical tradition's way of dealing with challenges within and without. The process of appeasement and negotiation regarding these entities often has to do with the recognition of their negative and uncontrollable aspects as described in the *Rgyu bzhi*, especially their association with creating obstacles in the body and the environment. Strong rituals, often accompanied by prayers, concentrate on appeasing the *klu* by offering whites (curds, milk, and butter),[31] and by burning juniper and equal portions of diverse herbs, peacock feathers, various fruits, snakeskin, gems like white aconite, lavender, urine, and a mixture of scatological substances used alongside Tibetan medicine in order to combat the wrath of the hindering spirits.

Conclusions

In the end, are the *klu* relevant at all in the Tibetan religious and medical contexts today? This study indicates, among other things, that the diseases associated with *klu* are needed as a way of dealing with situations of vulnerability and inferiority. They serve as a reminder of Tibetans' association with an environment that they cannot fully control but of which they must constantly maintain awareness. Another significant issue is that religion is yet to be erased out of Tibetan medical practice, a body of knowledge that is constantly undergoing dissection from diverse parties: religious, political, and medical. What is evident from these few examples is that *klu* cannot be divorced from medical theories, religion, politics, or the environment as a whole (natural, social, and cultural). This creates a dilemma in modern medical practice in TAR where politics, modernization, and Westernization are dictating what is learned and what is practiced. This draws attention to much broader issues of modernity and agency. Ming-Chen M. Lo, in the work *Doctors Within Borders: Profession, Ethnicity, and Modernity in Colonial Taiwan,* draws attention to the case of Taiwan during Japanese occupation of the complex role of agents of modernity and the negotiation between "universalistic narratives of science and the concrete sociopolitical relationships through which science is being delivered, developed, and received."[32] As Lo notes, modernity cannot exist outside of the "culturally specific plans of its deliverers and the culturally specific evaluations of its receivers."[33] Thus there is no modernity that is not localized or a nonrelational process. In terms of the case of *klu nad,* we can see the complex relationships fostered between Tibetan physicians trained in a secularized environment, religious practitioners, and a combination of religious and secular views that permeates the culture, all having a hand in the process of modernity in the medical sense. Even more so, the underlying Tibetan identity is somehow thrust forward through the disease process and its treatment amongst a rapidly changing cultural environment. *Klu nad* therefore expresses underlying tensions and accommodations between the religious and medical dimensions of Tibetan society, a disease that reflects its environment and all that that entails.

Acknowledgments

I am grateful to physicians at the Tibetan Medical College and the Mentsikhang in Lhasa. Textual and fieldwork in 2004-06 was supported by Austin College Richardson Funding. Ethnographic work in Lhasa, Tibet in 2005 was made possible through a generous grant from the Wabash Center for Teaching and Learning. This study is dedicated to my husband, Eric, and my abuela.

Endnotes

1. Max Oelschlaeger, *Caring for Creation: An Ecumenical Approach to the Environmental Crisis* (CT: Yale University Press, 1994): 219. See Sherry Ortner, "The White-Black Ones: The Sherpa View of Human Nature," in J. F. Fisher, ed., *Himayalan Anthropology: The Indo-Tibetan* Interface (The Hague: Mouton, 1978): 263-86.

2. Ibid.

3. Réne De Nebesky-Wojkowitz, *Oracles and Demons of Tibet: The Cult and Iconography of the Tibetan Protective Deities* (Delhi: Book Faith India, 1996): 291.

4. Ortner, "The White-Black Ones," 263-86.

5. Jakob Winkler, "The Rdzogs chen Murals of the Klu Khang in Lhasa," in Henk Blezer, ed., *Religion and Secular Culture in Tibet, Tibetan Studies 2* (Leiden: Brill, 2002): 321-44.

6. V. Nagarajan, "Rituals of Embedded Ecologies: Drawing Kolams, Marrying Trees, and Generating Auspiciousness," in C. K. Chapple and M. E. Tucker, eds., *Hinduism and Ecology: The Intersection of Earth, Sky, and Water* (Reprint, New Delhi: Oxford University Press, 2001): 453-68.

7. In Indian mythology, *nāgas* (Tibetan, *klu*) are the serpent spirits who inhabit what could be labelled as the "underworld," Lanka, or water sources like lakes, rivers, ponds, and trees. In many respects, the Buddhist *nāgaṣ* inherited much of the early Indian Hindu symbolism. In Buddhist cosmology, they are assigned to the lowest level of Mt. Meru with their *garuḍa* (mythical birds) enemies on the level above. See Richard S. Cohen, "Nāga, Yakṣiṇī, Buddha: Local Deities and Local Buddhism at Ajanta," in *History of Religions* 37, no. 4 (May, 1998): 360-400.

8. I thank Geoffrey Samuel for this reference.

9. As these entities, they exhibit hallucinations and fear (pretas) and negative emotions (aggression, anger, and inflict disease and poison) (animals and asuras). In such Bon po texts, these pretas-klu move through space (*mkha' la rgyu ba*), and inhabit the underworld (*gnas na 'dug pa*) accompanied by snakes or water sources (described as *chu bdag klu*). Pretas (like other beings as tsen, gyelpo, shindre, jungpo, mamo, theurang, etc.) in Buddhist texts live their lives in constant terror and hallucination, often afflicted by diseases. As animals according to the Buddhist tradition, klu are constantly tortured by garuda (*khyung*) and kept in their beaks symbolizing the negative emotions, swamped with rains of burning sand, and are stupid, aggressive, and poisonous. As asuras, the Bon po text indicates that klu fall under one of the three classes, one of the eleven che bas who are g-yen of the ground. In Buddhist cosmology, asuras live in constant quarrels and aggression, full of envy toward the gods whose desires are completely taken care of. See Katsumi Mimaki, "A preliminary Comparison of Bonpo and Buddhist Cosmology," in *New Horizons in Bonpo Studies* (Osaka, Japan: National Museum of Ethnology, 2000): 99-101; K. Mimaki and Samten Karmay, "Bon sgo gsal byed, Two Tibetan Manuscripts in Facsimile Edition of a Fourteenth Century Encyclopedia of Bonpo Doxography," in *Bibliotheca Codicum Asiaticorum* 13 (Tokyo: The Centre for East Asian Cultural Studies for Unesco, The Toyo Bunko, 1997).

10. Although according to Tibetan dictionaries, the nominal form is taken to mean "evil spirits or demons," the term itself literally derives from the future tense of the verb *'don* meaning "to cause to come out or come forth, to drive forth"; in modern usage it means "to take out."

11. Geoffrey Samuel, *Civilized Shamans: Buddhism in Tibetan Societies* (Washington, DC: Smithsonian Institution Press, 1993): 161-63.

12. I thank Geoffrey Samuel for directing me to the sources here.

13. Ronald E. Emmerick, "Epilepsy According to the *Rgyud-bźi*," in G. Jan Meulenbeld and Dominik Wujastyk, eds., *Studies on Indian Medical History* (Groningen: Egbert Forsten, 1987): 63-90.

14. *Bdud rtsi snying po yang lag brgyud pa gsang ba man ngag gi rgyud* (Lhasa, Tibet: Bod ljongs mi dmangs pe skrun khang, 2002). See also *Rgyud bzhi: A Reproduction of a Set of Prints from the 18th century Zung-cu-ze blocks from the Collection of Professor Raghu Vira*, reproduction by Orgyan Namgyal (Leh, Ladakh: S. W. Tashigangpa, 1975). See Terry Clifford, *Tibetan Buddhist Medicine and Psychiatry: The Diamond Healing* (Maine: Samuel Weiser, 1984): 179.

15. The major locus of the disease is the skin indicating that the life-extending rlung (wind element) is impaired. Rlung is the central element of the body that acts as a medium between the mind and the body. The five rlung (life-sustaining, ascending, pervasive, fire-like, downward-voiding) are responsible for physical and mental activities including the clarity of the sense organs and sustaining life. Therefore the condition of the skin indicates that the *klu* are creating mental obscurations and impairment of the senses and is a reflection of a broken mind and body. *Bdud rtsi snying po yang lag brgyud pa gsang ba man ngag gi rgyud* (Lhasa, Tibet: Bod ljongs mi dmangs pe skrun khang, 2002): 392-401. See Terry Clifford, *Tibetan Buddhist Medicine and Psychiatry: The Diamond Healing (*Maine: Samuel Weiser, 1984): 179-81.

16. For example, Buddhist philosophy, particularly the Abhidharma, analyzes experience into various elements—physico-psychological combination (*nāmarūpa*), the most basic of these being the five skandhas or aggregates, i.e., form, feeling, perception, mental formation or volition, and consciousness and then the six elements (*cha-dhātu*). The five aggregates and six elements in turn can be analyzed into the eighteen elements, which can be further analyzed into seventy-two elements. Buddhism also utilizes the method of twelve bases/spheres/loci (*āyatana*) of meeting between the six sense-organs and their corresponding objects that are also related to the eighteen elements to refute an eternal self (*ātman).* These are the gateway of sense experience or the ground for bringing about consciousness.

17. According to the *Lapis Lazuli* commentary on the *Rgyud bzhi,* the path of the mind is the normal flowing of the energies of the five skandhas through the five veins of consciousness according to Tantric physiology. See *Bai Dur sNgon po (The Lapis Lazuli Commentary on the Rgyud bzhi) of Sangs-rgyas rGya mtsho,* vol. 3 (Leh: T.Y. Tashigangpa, 1973).

18. Clifford, *Tibetan Buddhist Medicine and Psychiatry: The Diamond Healing* (Maine: Samuel Weiser, 1984).

19. Dominik Wujastyk, *The Roots of Ayurveda: Selections from Sanskrit Medical Texts* (London: Penguin, 2003): 210-38.

20. From the eleventh to thirteenth century, many Tibetan practitioners and teachers contract illnesses (like leprosy) and keep the company of lepers, such as Ras chung pa, Ma gcig Lab sgron (1055-1145), and Chad kha ba Ye shes rdo rje (1102-1176). See Jérôme Edou, *Machig Labdrön and the Foundations of Chöd* (Ithaca, NY: Snow Lion Publications, 1996), 133; a translation of and commentary on 'Chad kha ba's *Blo sbyong don bdun ma'i khrid yig mdor bsdus don bzang bdud rtsi'i snying po* and a brief synopsis of his life are provided by Geshe Kelsang Gyatso, *Universal Compassion: Transforming Your Life Through Love and Compassion* (New York: Tharpa Publications, 2002); Ivette M. Vargas, "Falling to Pieces,

Emerging Whole: Suffering, Illness and Healing Renunciation in the Life of Gelongma Palmo," (Ph.D. diss., Harvard University, 2003); "The Life of dGe slong ma dPal mo: The Experiences of a Leper, Founder of a Fasting Ritual, and Transmitter of Buddhist Teachings on Suffering and Renunciation in Tibetan Religious History," *Journal for the International Association of Buddhist Studies* 24.2 (2001): 157-85.

21. My translation of the Tibetan text: *sa ga sa ri nam mthongs kyi zla ba la bar du gcod pa'i bgegs rnams byang chub kyi sems la bkod/ nad dang sdig sgrib rnams byang ste/ sa dang po'i bden pa mthong/ sa ga zla ba'i tshes gcig la rje btsun sgrol ma'i zhal gzigs te/ dus gsum sangs rgyas thams cad kyi phrin las nyid la 'dus so zhes lung bstan/ tshes brgyad la don zhags lha lnga la sogs kri ya'i lha phal che ba'i zhal gzigs/ bco lnga la zhal bcu gcig pa phyag stong spyan stong dang ldan pa'i zhal gzigs shing/ de yang ba spu'i bu ga thams cad na sangs rgyas dpag tu med pa gnas pa/ phyag rnams kyang sang rgyas kyi ngo bo la/ phyag mthil gyi spyan rnams ni gsang sngags kyi lha tshogs su gzigs/ 'phags pas chos gsungs pas ting nge 'dzin bsam gyis mi khyab pa rgyud la skyes/ sa brgyad pa'i bden pa mthong ngo// de nas yang sems can thams cad kyi don du smyung gnas zla ba gsum mdzad de/*Jo gdan Bsod nams bzang po, *Smyung gnas bla ma brgyud pa'i rnam thar,* blockprint. (Lhasa: Dpal ldan Par khang, n.d.): 6a.6-7a.2.

22. Matthew Kapstein, *The Tibetan Assimilation of Buddhism: Conversion, Contestation, and Memory* (Oxford: Oxford University Press, 2000), 41-42. See also Ronald E. Emmerick, *Tibetan Texts Concerning Khotan* (London: Oxford University Press, 1967), 84-85, lines 57-61. Tibetans themselves in sacred literature also account for the presence of leprosy or illness in general in their vicinity.

23. I thank Dr. Tashi, Dr. Namgyal, and others (I am unable to reveal identities) for this remark.

24. Dr. Tashi and Dr. Tsering from the Mentsikhang.

25. Dr. Tashi noted in September 15, 2006.

26. Tibetan temples like the *klu khang* (short for Rdzong rgyab klu'i pho drang meaning "the water spirit house behind the fortress") in Lhasa are a reminder of the relationship between the religious and medical institutions forged by the *klu*. This structure was built around the time of the Sixth Dalai Lama (Tshangs dbyangs rgya mtsho, 1683-1706?) to appease and honor *klu* because of their potential to create havoc and calamity. *Klu* images abound in this temple, mostly half human and half serpent—one has a serpent head and lower body with a human chest and arms. The two lower floors are dedicated to the *klu*. Some areas depict nāgarājas with a retinue of nāgas; others are holding jewels or other offerings and scepters, mostly emerging or immersed in water, on some pedestal or small temple. The ground floor enshrines a gold-plated image of the nāgarāja, Maldrozichen, whose female partner, *klu mo*, was said to have visited the Fifth Dalai Lama during his meditations. The floor above houses a large gilded statue of Nāgendrarāja, the form taken by Śakyamuni to tame the Nāgas' realm. The surrounding walls of the middle floor depict episodes of Pema Obar, where an earlier form of Padmasambhava reclaims the wish-fulfilling jewel from the Nāgarāja. There are three images of Padmasambhava on the east wall of the top floor that depict him subduing the nāgas. See Winkler, "The Rdzogs chen Murals of the Klu Khang in Lhasa."

27. As in the biography of the elder Gyu thog Yon tan Mgon po, because of immoral actions (not keeping tantric and vinaya vows, women losing their morals, yogis talking nonsense), the protector guardian gods became angry and inflicted diseases like phol-hbras (bubonic plague), swelling of the throat (diphtheria), lumbago, dropsy, ha-la lchog hgyal (falling

disease?), and a fatal disease. It was not until a Tibetan physician—with the help of the royal nāgas—interceded that were they able to heal everyone in the nāga realm. See Ven. Rechung Rinpoche and Jampal Kunzang, *Tibetan Medicine* (Berkeley: University of California Press, 1976): 254.

28. Ian Baker, *The Dalai Lama's Secret Temple: Tantric Wall Paintings from Tibet* (London: Thames and Hudson, 2000): 14.

29. Aside from the blatant Buddhist and Bon po affiliations, rituals like *glu rol* point to the secular qua religious character of *klu* in Tibetan communities. In festivals performed in present-day Reb skong (Ch. Tongren), Huangnan Tibetan Autonomous State, Qinghai Province, sedentary farmers and other laity perform rituals relating to *klu*. Rituals like *klu rtsed* and *lha chu kha*, and worship of *klu mo* reflect a preoccupation with protection of the village from disease, and a need for purification and reproduction, fertility, and prosperity, and order in terms of borders. The focus on reproduction, fertility, and prosperity is evident in the rituals associated with assisting barren women. In *glu rol* festivals, one of the elder male performers possessed by the mountain god puts a wooden image of *klu mo* into the bosom of these women and carries out the ceremony. In *klu rtsed*, there are unmarried girls no older than twenty-five that perform an offering dance (*gar ma*) in slow rhythmic movements said to imitate the movements of the *klu*.

See Sadako Nagano, "Sacrifice and Lha pa in the Glu rol Festival of Reb-skong," in *New Horizons in Bonpo Studies* (Osaka, Japan: National Museum of Ethnology 2000): 567-649. The word, *glu rol*, can be interpreted in two ways since *glu* and *klu* are homonymous. *Glu* means a song, especially one sung only on a mountain. The mountain gods are said to be fond of mountain songs (*ri glu*). *Klu*, on the other hand, stands for dragon. Nagano notes that among these etymologies, *glu* is much more accurate as a general term for this ritual. Next, *rol* means (1) playing a traditional musical instrument, and (2) amusement (*rsted mo*). The word *glu rol* signifies a festival with singing and the playing of musical instruments. This word connotes also a mountain and height, and the play between gods and men.

Klu rol can also be interpreted as "playing with the *klu* deity." *Klu* is an important deity of sedentary farmers, in association with water. In fact, Gling rgyal villagers belonging to the Rnying ma pa perform only *klu rtsed* and worship *klu mo* as well in the *glu rol*. These interpretations reflect an expansion of the worship objects from the main mountain gods to watery deities, *klu*, or the more agricultural development of *glu rol* festivals.

30. Lawrence Epstein and P. Wenbin, "Ritual, Ethnicity, and Generational Identity," in M. C. Goldstein, *Buddhism in Contemporary Tibet* (Berkeley: University of California Press, 1998): 120-38. In terms of order, studies by Epstein and Wenbin point out that in a village called Sog ri, the origins of *glu rol* marks the treaty of Gansu in 822 between Tang China and the Tibetan Empire. *Klu* were invited and celebrated as part of the ritual.

Finally, burning rituals associated with *klu rta* (or *klu gtad*) are used to pacify any evil or disruptive spirits. This ritual is reflected in local practices to the *klu* at shrines in Western Tibet where lay practitioners who dream of being attacked by an animal exhibit skin eruptions and seek the help of lamas who pray over them.

31. Clifford, *Tibetan Buddhist Medicine and Psychiatry,* 180.

32. Ming-Cheng M. Lo, *Doctors Within Borders: Profession, Ethnicity, and Modernity in Colonial Taiwan* (Berkeley: University of California, 2002): 197.

33. Ibid.

Bibliography

Adams, Vincanne. "Particularizing Modernity: Tibetan Medical Theorizing of Women's Health in Lhasa, Tibet. In L. Connor and G. Samuel, eds. *Healing Powers and Modernity: Traditional Medicine, Shamanism, and Science in Asian Societies.* Westport, CT: Bergen and Garvey, 2001.

———. "The Sacred in the Scientific: Ambiguous Practices of Science in Tibetan Medicine." *Cultural Anthropology* 16 (2001): 542-75.

Arnold, David. *Colonizing the Body: State Medicine and Epidemic Disease in Nineteenth-Century India.* Berkeley: University of California, 1993.

Bai Dur sNgon po (The Lapis Lazuli Commentary on the Rgyud bzhi) of Sangs-rgyas rGya mtsho. Vol. 3. Leh: T.Y. Tashigangpa, 1973.

Baker, Ian. *The Dalai Lama's Secret Temple.* London: Thomas and Hudson, 2000.

Bdud rtsi snying po yang lag brgyud pa gsang ba man ngag gi rgyud. Bod ljongs mi dmangs pe skrun khang, 2002.

Chen, Nancy N. *Breathing Spaces: Qigong, Psychiatry, and Healing in China.* New York: Columbia University Press, 2003.

Clifford, Terry. *Tibetan Medicine and Psychiatry: The Diamond Healing.* Maine: Samuel Weiser, 1984.

Cohen, Richard. "Nāga, Yakṣiṇī, Buddha: Local Deities and Local Buddhism at Ajanta." *History of Religions* 37, no. 4 (May, 1998): 360-400.

De Nebesky-Wojkowitz, Réne. *Oracles and Demons of Tibet: The Cult and Iconography of the Tibetan Protective Deities.* Delhi: Book Faith India, 1996.

Donden, Yeshi. *Health Through Balance: An Introduction to Tibetan Medicine.* Ithaca, NY: Snow Lion Publications, 1986.

Dpal-ldan-bkra-shis and Kevin Stuart. "Perilous Novelties: The A-mdo Tibetan klu-rol Festival in Gling-rgyal Village." *Anthropos* 93 (1998): 31-53.

Edou, Jérôme. *Machig Labrön and the Foundations of Chöd.* Ithaca, NY: Snow Lion Publications, 1996.

Emmerick, Ronald E. "A Chapter from the *Rgyud-bźi.*" *Asia Major* 19 (1975): 141-62.

———. "Epilepsy According to the *Rgyud-bźi.*" In G. Jan Meulenbeld and Dominik Wujastyk, eds. *Studies on Indian Medical History.* Groningen: Egbert Forsten, 1987: 63-90.

———. *Tibetan Texts Concerning Khotan.* London: Oxford University Press, 1967.

Epstein, Lawrence, and P. Wenbin. "Ritual, Ethnicity, and Generational Identity." In M. C. Goldstein. *Buddhism in Contemporary Tibet.* Berkeley: University of California Press, 1998: 120-38.

Farkas, Janos, and Tibor Szabo. *The Pictorial World of the Tibeto-Mongolian Demons.* Budapest: Mandala and LibroTrade, 2002.

Freund, P. E. S., M. B. McGuire, and L. S. Podhurst. *Health, Illness, and the Social Body: A Critical Sociology.* Upper Saddle River, NJ: Prentiss Hall, 2003.

Gso rig rgyud bzhi'i dka' 'grel. Bod ljongs mi dmangs dpe skrun khang, 1996.

Gyatso, Janet. "The Authority of Empiricism and the Empiricism of Authority: Medicine and Buddhism in Tibet on the Eve of Modernity." *Comparative Studies of South Asia, Africa and the Middle East* 24.2 (2004): 83-96.

Gyatso, Geshe Kelsang. *Universal Compassion: Transforming Your Life Through Love and Compassion.* New York: Tharpa Publications, 2002.

Gyu thog cha lag bco brgya. Vol 1 and 2. Dolanji: Tibetan Bonpo Monastic Center, 1976.

Janes, Craig. "Buddhism, Science, and Market: The Globalization of Tibetan Medicine." *Anthropology and Medicine* 9, no. 3 (2002) 267-89.

———. "Imagined Lives, Suffering, and the Work of Culture: the Embodied Discourses of Conflict in Modern Tibet." *Medical Anthropology Quarterly* 13 (1999): 391-412.

Jo gdan Bsod nams bzang po, *Smyung gnas bla ma brgyud pa'i rnam thar,* blockprint. Lhasa: Dpal ldan Par khang, n.d.: 6a.6-7a.2.

Kapferer, Bruce. "Mind, Self and Other in Demonic Illness: The Negation and Reconstruction of Self." *American Ethnologist* 6 (1979): 110-33.

Kapstein, Matthew. *The Tibetan Assimilation of Buddhism: Conversion, Contestation, and Memory.* Oxford: Oxford University Press, 2000.

Kelsang, Jhampa. *Ambrosia Heart Tantra.* Dharamsala: Library of Tibetan Works and Archives, 1977.

Kleinman, Arthur. *Patients and Healers in the Context of Culture: An Exploration of the Borderland between Anthropology, Medicine, and Psychiatry*. Berkeley: University of California., 1980.

Leslie, Charles, and Allan Young. *Paths to Asian Medical Knowledge*. Berkeley: University of California., 1992.

Lo, Ming-Cheng M. *Doctors Within Borders: Profession, Ethnicity, and Modernity in Colonial Taiwan.* Berkeley: University of California, 2002.

Martin, Dan. *Unearthing Bon Treasures*. London: Brill, 2001.

Mimaki, Katsumi. "A Preliminary Comparison of Bonpo and Buddhist Cosmology." In *New Horizons in Bonpo Studies*. Osaka, Japan: National Museum of Ethnology, 2000: 89-115.

——— and Samten Karmay. "Bon sgo gsal byed, Two Tibetan Manuscripts in Facsimile Edition of a Fourteenth Century Encyclopedia of Bonpo Doxography." In *Bibliotheca Codicum Asiaticorum* 13. Tokyo: The Centre for East Asian Cultural Studies for Unesco, The Toyo Bunko, 1997.

Nagano, Sadako. "Sacrifice and Lha pa in the Glu rol Festival of Reb-skong." In *New Horizons in Bonpo Studies.* Osaka, Japan: National Museum of Ethnology, 2000: 567-649.

Nagarajan, V. "Rituals of embedded ecologies: Drawing Kolams, Marrying Trees, and Generating Auspiciousness." In C. K. Chapple and M. E. Tucker, eds. *Hinduism and Ecology: The Intersection of Earth, Sky, and Water.* Reprint, New Delhi: Oxford University Press, 2001: 453-68.

Norbu, Namkhai. *Drung, Deu and Bon: Narrations, Symbolic Languages and the Bon Tradition in Ancient Tibet.* Dharamsala, India: Library of Tibetan Works and Archives, 1995.

Oelschlaeger, Max. *Caring for Creation: An Ecumenical Approach to the Environmental Crisis.* New Haven, CT: Yale University Press, 1994.

Ortner, Sherry. "The White-Black Ones: The Sherpa View of Human Nature." In J. F. Fisher, ed. *Himayalan Anthropology: The Indo-Tibetan Interface*. The Hague: Mouton, 1978: 263-86.

Pati, Biswamoy, and Mark Harrison. *Health, Medicine and Empire: Perspectives on Colonial India.* New Delhi: Orient Longman, 2001.

Pordié, Laurent. *The Expression of Religion in Tibetan Medicine: Ideal Conceptions, Contemporary Practices and Political Use*. Pondy Papers in Social Sciences 29. Pondicherry, India: French Institute of Pondicherry, 2003.

Rgyud bzhi'i rnam bshad. Mtsho sngon mi rigs dpe skrun khang, 1999.

Rechung Rinpoche, Ven., and Jampal Kunzang. *Tibetan Medicine.* Berkeley: University of California Press, 1976.

Samuel, Geoffrey. *Civilized Shamans: Buddhism in Tibetan Societies.* Washington: Smithsonian Institution Press, 1993.

———. "Religion, Health and Suffering Among Contemporary Tibetans." In J. R. Hinnells and R. Porter, eds. *Religion, Health and Suffering.* London: Kegan Paul International, 1999: 85-110.

Strickmann, Michel. *Chinese Magical Medicine.* Stanford: Stanford University Press, 2002.

Vāgbhaṭa. *Aṣṭāngahṛdayasaṃhitā.* Wiesbaden: Franz Steiner GMBH, 1965.

Vargas, Ivette M. "Falling to Pieces, Emerging Whole: Suffering, Illness and Healing Renunciation in the Life of Gelongma Palmo." Ph.D. diss., Harvard University, 2003.

———. "The Life of dGe slong ma dPal mo: The Experiences of a Leper, Founder of a Fasting Ritual, and Transmitter of Buddhist Teachings on Suffering and Renunciation in Tibetan Religious History." *Journal for the International Association of Buddhist Studies* 24.2 (2001): 157-85.

Winkler, Jakob. "The Rdzogs chen Murals of the Klu Khang in Lhasa." In Henk Blezer, ed. *Religion and Secular Culture in Tibet, Tibetan Studies 2.* Leiden: Brill, 2002: 321-44.

Wujastyk, Dominik. *The Roots of Ayurveda: Selections from Sanskrit Medical Texts.* London: Penguin, 2003.

–20–

Integrating Modern Neuroscience and Physiology with Indo-Tibetan Yogic Science

William C. Bushell

> Although modern science and the Buddhist contemplative tradition arose out of quite different historical, cultural, and intellectual circumstances, I have found that they have a great deal in common . . . Buddhist practitioners familiar with the workings of the mind have long been aware that it can be transformed through training. What is exciting and new is that scientists have now shown that such mental training can also change the *brain* . . . so that in a real sense the brain we develop reflects the life we lead.[1]
>
> —His Holiness the Dalai Lama

One of the most important initial steps in the program of Indo-Tibetan Highest Yoga Tantra is what is referred to as "overthrowing the tyranny of ordinary appearances," which are a major barrier to obtaining the achievements sought in this yogic system. Normally, all sentient beings are epistemologically—and, consequently, as will be seen, *ontologically*—bound by their erroneous but nevertheless deep-seated convictions of the limited nature of themselves and of reality in general. The antidote to the tyranny of ordinary appearances consists of the initial analytical introduction to their existence and nature, followed by the use of the Highest Yoga Tantra generation stage techniques—i.e., programmatically cultivated, developed, and enhanced multisensory, multimodal *imaginational faculties*—to override, "overthrow" such ordinary appearances. First is the utilization of analytic meditation to "deconstruct" the apparent independent existence, "reality," solidity, etc., of the appearances of the phenomenal world, primarily on an abstract level, followed by the attempt to dissolve, and then finally *actually to replace* ordinary appearances with divine ones, on a more concrete, visceral, experiential level.

In the following analysis we can see that a disparate, somewhat widely distributed, nonunified collection of experimental studies in several subdomains of Western psychology and neuroscience provides us with one kind of basis for understanding the Indo-Tibetan yogic accounts. These studies provide empirical, experimental evidence that individuals may in fact learn, through cognitive-behavioral means involving developed use of multimodal mental imagery and other faculties, to significantly influence neural processes and functions, both of an afferent and efferent nature, in order to transform their experience of the reality of themselves and the world.[2] My own sense is that the Indo-Tibetan tradition has profoundly and radically developed latent faculties, such as those that can be glimpsed in the studies to be described, into a sophisticated and profound *system*, the components of which are articulated, integrated, unified, and highly developed into a kind of "neurotechnology" or "wetware system," to build on Thurman's heuristic (as presented in Thurman 1991), which has powerful transformative potential, as will be described. One analogy that comes to mind—with perhaps some irony—is to the Oriental "invention" (discovery) of gunpowder, which was not exploited, developed, and channeled into the foundation of a world-transformative military machine in the East, as it was in the West. Similarly, although many, but clearly not all, of the properties of mind cultivated in Asian yogic systems have been independently discovered in Western psychology and neuroscience, these have rarely been assembled, integrated, unified, or cultivated into the kinds of yogic systems found in the East, of which the Indo-Tibetan is one of the most advanced.

The common denominator of these studies, which have been conducted in different labs over decades and which involve the full range of sensory modalities, is the demonstration that sensory perceptual functions can be significantly, even dramatically, altered on a fundamental neurophysiological level through cognitive-behavioral means, including the use of mental imagery and induction of highly absorbed states (i.e. "altered states of consciousness" induced through meditation and hypnosis/self-hypnosis). In the present context, Western experimental psychology and neuroscientific studies of meditation and hypnosis/self-hypnosis are considered under one rubric, owing to important neurophysiological, neuroanatomical, and phenomenological similarities between them, the full discussion of which is outside the scope of this essay.[3] Some of the studies to be described have looked explicitly at practitioners of Indo-Tibetan and other forms of Asian meditation techniques, while others have looked at the use of mental imagery and/or hypnotic/self-hypnotic phenomena in Western experimental subjects possessing various levels of ability with respect to these phenomena (e.g., excellent versus ordinary imagers; high versus low hypnotizable subjects).

This analysis focuses on certain key aspects of three phases of Highest Yoga Tantra practice relevant to the overthrowing of ordinary appearances: the voluntary use of meditative techniques to "dissolve" the ordinary sense of self; the substitution of divine for ordinary appearances of self and other (world); and the beginnings of transformation to the "divine" (if nevertheless metaphysically contingent) sense of self, through the further practice of deity yoga and gtummo yoga meditation, with these terms to be described.[4] While there is an appreciable number of variations in these meditations according to different lineages and teachers, and because of a number of other factors, the primary contours of the present description are relevant to many if not most forms of tantric meditation, including the Kālacakra.[5] In the first phase, the practitioner employs analytic meditation on emptiness of self and other to form the foundation for the more experientially-oriented meditation to follow; here one seeks to obtain a *raw feel* sense of selflessness as well as an experience of the dissolution of the solidity of the outside world. In the next phase, one attempts to utilize multimodal mental imagery in close conjunction with states of absorption induced through meditation to create the experience of the reconstitution of self and world (deity yoga, maṇḍala yoga) as divine. In the third phase, the yoga known as gtummo or "inner fire" is practiced, in order to further transform the practitioner on a fundamental level into one who is more capable of achieving the higher goals of the yogic program (see Note 5).

Dissolution of Ordinary Self

Two recent neuroimaging studies of Tibetan meditators specifically engaging in self-dissolution meditation provide neurophysiological results which are consistent with the phenomenological claims of the tradition. In the first study, a single-case electroencephalographic (EEG) study of an advanced, long-term meditator recorded brain activity during four meditation forms, including self-dissolution. According to the investigators:

> Involvement of the right prefrontal cortex in the meditative state of self-dissolution is intriguing in light of recent evidence from functional neuroimaging and human lesion studies indicating an important role of this region in self-consciousness. . . . Right prefrontal activation has been reported during tasks involving self-recognition, autobiographical retrieval, and self-evaluation. . . . Also, lesions to the right fronto-temporal cortex have led in some cases to the experience of cognitive detachment from self . . . , cannabinol-induced depersonalization has been found to be associated with right anterior frontal activation . . . , and comparable results have been reported in psychiatric depersonalization experiences. . . .[6]

In the other study, eight experienced practitioners of Tibetan Buddhist meditation performed similar self-dissolution-style meditation while assayed for brain activity with single photon emission computed tomography (SPECT), demonstrating similar results. In particular, the SPECT revealed alterations in areas of the brain important for the spatial orientation of the self, within the dorsolateral prefrontal cortex. This region is of particular significance in terms of the integration of sensory data into the sense of self and its actual physical sense of "substance" and boundaries with the outside world.[7]

Clearly, these two studies provide neurobiological data which is consistent with the accounts of the phenomenological characterizations of these practices of the Highest Yoga Tantra traditions. Not only is the general sense of self apparently affected by the meditation practice, but in particular the spatial sense of self, in some ways perhaps the most visceral dimension of the experience of self, also appears to be profoundly affected. Moreover, some of the key meditational instructions focus explicitly on the spatial component of the self. According to one translated account of the writings on this topic by Tsongkhapa, one of the major figures in the history of Tibetan Buddhism:

> The special application [in this meditation] is to concentrate on the body from the tip of the head to the soles of the feet, as being utterly empty of material substance, like an empty transparent balloon filled with light. Place the mind firmly and clearly on this image. . . . Here the body is to be envisioned as being entirely without substance. . . .[8]

Substitution of Divine for Ordinary Appearances, Self and Other (Deity and Mandala)

The research to be reviewed here includes studies conducted primarily on the neurophysiological dimension of mental imagery in two main types of subjects, those with unusual abilities to generate vivid mental images (eidetic imagers), and those high in hypnotizability. In fact, it is frequently the case that superior imagers are also high in hypnotizability. Nevertheless, in the present context it is important to point out that, through training and practice, it is possible for individuals to increase both their imagery ability and their hypnotizability—that is, their ability to enter, deepen, and otherwise enhance states of altered consciousness which are often referred to in psychology, neurology, anthropology, and religious studies as trance states.[9] It is for this reason that the Indo-Tibetan yoga tradition emphasizes training and practice in imagery and trance-based, or samādhi, meditation. These studies will, in toto, demonstrate in empirical and experimental terms how, through the utilization of techniques to enhance imagery and trance ability, individuals may actually control sensory-perceptual functioning, and *override*[10] sensations and percepts with voluntary, self-induced mental images, by substituting the latter for the former, in a process consistent with the claims of Indo-Tibetan deity and maṇḍala yoga meditation.

In one of the most impressive of these studies, subjects who were highly proficient in mental imagery or visualization (eidetic imagers) were actually able to control, to a large degree, the most fundamental level of neurosensory response to sensory stimuli (within the experimental setting). Specifically, eidetic imagers instructed "to see" *red* while viewing *green* light flashes, were able to see red despite the presence of green light flashed directly onto the retina, according to electroretinogram (ERG) recordings. The ERG records the light wave form on the retina itself, and each color possesses its own particular wave form. Eidetic imagers were able to *transform the actual retinal response to light*, both in trials to see red when green light was flashed on the retina, and, conversely, in trials to see green when red light was flashed on the retina! Control subjects, individuals not proficient in mental imagery, were not able to do so.[11]

In related studies, the hypnosis researcher David Spiegel of Stanford University instructed highly hypnotizable subjects to perceive an obstruction in the front of the visual stimulus (an object) presented to their eyes. Electrophysiological recordings of the sensory cortex of these highly hypnotizable subjects demonstrated reduction in the fundamental sensory perceptual process when the hypnotically hallucinated obstruction was viewed. In these experiments, it was as if the visual stimulus had disappeared, as in a so-called "negative hallucination." Moreover, the design of the study excluded the possibility that subjects closed or otherwise averted their eyes; control subjects, low hypnotizable subjects, were unable to allow the instructions to cause an obstruction in their visual processing.[12] In another related study conducted by a team of researchers from Harvard, Stanford, and Cornell, highly hypnotizable subjects were instructed "to see" gray when color was presented to their eyes, and to see color when gray was presented, in separate trials, along with normal trials (i.e., see gray during presentation of gray, see color during presentation of color), during positron emission tomography (PET) scanning. The results of this study were in line with the results of these other studies: instructions to see color resulted in activation in the classic color area of the brain (the fusiform area) regardless of the visual stimulus, while conversely, instructions to perceive gray during the presentation of color resulted in *decreased* activation in the fusiform color area of the visual cortex.[13]

Similar results have been found in experimental psychology studies involving the other sensory modalities. A recent study of the sense of hearing found that highly hypnotizable subjects (nonschizophrenic) who reported possessing the ability to hallucinate sounds during hypnosis/self-hypnosis did in fact demonstrate patterns of brain area activation identical to those associated with actual hearing, as assessed by positron emission tomography. When the subjects simply imagined hearing, there was no activation of the central nervous system (CNS) auditory center, nor was there activation in control subjects who did not possess the hypnotic hallucination capacity but who *attempted* to hallucinate while hypnotized.[14]

Somatosensory modalities, or tactile sensation, may also be significantly influenced by imaginational functioning enhanced through cognitive behavioral techniques such as hypnosis and guided imagery. Again, the hypnosis researcher Spiegel demonstrated that highly hypnotizable subjects could block bodily sensations through somatosensory hallucinations as measured by electroencephalographic (event-related potential) means, which control subjects were unable to do. Conversely, these subjects were also capable of intensifying their attention to the somatosensory stimuli, thereby *increasing* somatic sensation (hyperesthesia), as reflected in brain electrophysiological recordings (and see below).[15] More recently, other researchers replicated the results of Spiegel's study, demonstrating that good hypnotic subjects, but not control subjects, could block the effects of painful stimulation to the body by focusing intently on an obstructive image during hypnosis, as measured by the same basic electroencephalographic means.[16] While these two studies focused on cutaneous sensory and nociceptive stimulation, other research has demonstrated that hypnosis and imagery could block *visceral* sensation, such as in the case of pediatric cancer patients who successfully prevented nausea in response to chemotherapy (and see below).[17]

And finally, hypnosis and imagery have been found to produce similar effects with the other sense modalities, both gustatory and olfactory. Good hypnotic subjects have claimed that they could substitute enjoyable tastes for unpleasant ones (e.g., the taste of water for tart or sour flavors), and these claims have in fact been supported by interview data, salivation measures, and other data from experimental psychology studies.[18] Similarly, results of a study investigating the widely claimed hypnotic anosmia phenomenon—exemplified in such stage hypnosis demonstrations as, for example, the hypnotic suggestion to perceive the odor of ammonia as that of a rose—produced electroencephalographic results that were interpreted by investigators as consistent with such claims.[19]

In summary, it can be seen that cognitive-behavioral techniques, based on heightened imagery and absorption ability, can actually override—which includes negating and substituting—sensory-perceptual functioning on a fundamental neurophysiological level across sensory modalities, in line with the claims of Indo-Tibetan Highest Yoga Tantra. While inherent abilities were important in these studies—conducted with excellent hypnotic subjects and excellent, including eidetic, imagers, in comparison to control groups which were not composed of individuals with such inherent abilities—the literature on enhancing hypnotic and imagery ability provides evidence that individuals may nevertheless significantly improve these abilities (see note 9). It can be extrapolated from this data that it would be possible to utilize the abilities revealed by these studies to mobilize them more comprehensively, forcefully, and systematically in order to accomplish the goals of deity and maṇḍala yoga meditation, i.e., to substitute "divine" for ordinary appearances, as one could substitute the imagined sensation and perception of green for red, or color for gray, or an absence for a presence (in visual as well as somatosensory terms), etc., as demonstrated in these experimental studies. The texts on these yogas point out that such techniques initially produce effects that may seem artificial but are nevertheless to be considered, *to be experienced as*, the *similitude* or *approximation* of the sensation, perception, and consciousness of a Buddha. In other words, through imaginational faculties that are highly developed through integrating them with the faculty of intense absorption (trance or samadhi) during repeated meditational practice, one may begin to get a visceral, tangible sense, on a *fundamental sensory-perceptual level,* of how a Buddha experiences the same phenomenal ground of existence in completely opposite ways as do unenlightened beings.

Moreover, these studies suggest that the entire sensorium of humans is amenable to neurosensory modification, which is potentially profound and which may offer—viscerally, palpably, and fundamentally—a sense of the potential for transformation which is compatible with, yet phenomenologically beyond, abstraction and philosophy. In addition, the nature of such meditative states allows for the simultaneous apperception of phenomena as imbued with sensory qualities, whether these are voluntarily or involuntarily "fabricated," while the notion of their ultimate emptiness —the Whiteheadian "fallacy of misplaced concreteness" in Western philosophy of science terms—is maintained.[20] In the next and final section of this essay we shall briefly consider how such neurophysiological potentials for transformation of *afferent* processes may be relevant for transformation of *efferent* neurophysiological potentials as well.

gTummo Yoga and Transformation in Highest Yoga Tantra

In the previous section, evidence was reviewed concerning the use of cognitive-behavioral means (mental imagery, trance induction techniques) to influence the fundamental functioning of afferent neurosensory circuits across sensory modalities, which in turn influence the phenomenological state of the individual. In this section we briefly consider[21] the possibility that individuals may also influence efferent neural functions to create desired changes in the body, centrally and peripherally, specifically in the Highest Yoga Tantra context. In fact, the research team of Benson and colleagues from Harvard found that through the multisensory imagination of warmth in tissues of the body during gtummo meditation, warmth in fact was measurably produced in those tissues (up to 8.3 degrees C in peripheral skin temperature) in three experienced Tibetan gtummo practitioners.[22] This experimental data is consistent with a body of studies demonstrating that subjects in Western experimental research may also increase (and decrease) tissue temperature through the use of hypnosis and mental imagery.[23] Preliminary data suggest that states of focused absorption on multisensory mental images of heat localized to areas of the body influence efferent nerves to dilate the blood vessels to which they are connected, thereby increasing local tissue temperature through increased blood flow.

In fact, one of the phenomena recorded by several observers of gtummo practice is the dramatic demonstration of heat production, as allegedly manifested by the drying of ice-cold wet sheets draped over the body, complete with the rapid, visible evaporation of water vapor ("steaming") from the sheets,[24] as well as the melting of snow around the practitioner.[25] While gtummo meditation texts mention the benefit of this warmth for practitioners living in the cold Himalayan climate, as Thurman points out,[26] this is really a subsidiary purpose of the meditation; the more important function of the meditation is to learn how to control this heat and to direct it into the central channel of the body in order to induce the experience of bliss.

One way to interpret this proposed phenomenon in terms of the present explanatory framework is to understand the heat in the Indo-Tibetan model as, among other things, the heat associated with increased blood flow. In general, increased blood flow leads to increased local tissue temperature, and increased blood flow to the brain, in fact, can be produced through mental imagery of increased warmth directed to the brain. In fact, the same is true for mental imagery which is directed to other tissues and organs of the body, including the deep tissues which have been investigated.[27] In particular, mental imagery of warmth has been found to increase blood flow to the gonads, the spinal column, and abdominal structures, as well as the brain (see Note 27): in short, in the present context, to structures which are found along the axis of the central channel.

Since the winds described in the Highest Yoga Tantra systems can be understood as constructs which include blood flow, metabolically generated heat, and similar physiological processes,[28] the directing of these winds into the central channel and particularly the highest station along the central channel, the crown (*sahasrāra)* cakra, can also be potentially understood in terms of the directing of blood flow, and hence of local, metabolically based *activation*, to organs located along the central axis of the body, including the brain.

Meditation in general is also associated with increased blood flow to the brain, and euphoric or euphoria-like meditation, in particular, is associated with further increased cortical blood flow, as reflected in increased cortical electrical activity.[29] In fact, the study of Benson et al. on the gtummo meditators found fast or beta EEG in both the yogis tested electroencephalographically during the gtummo state, which the yogis claimed to be euphoric or "blissful." In one case, the yogis' metabolism increased during the gtummo state; and in the other, the yogi's metabolism decreased profoundly during the gtummo state, by 45-64%, which is actually within the range of hibernating animals.[30] Both of these metabolic changes may be consistent with the Tibetan yogic claims for the gtummo meditation, however. In the case of the latter yogi, his overall metabolism was reduced while his cerebral metabolism, as reflected in the EEG activation, was *increased.* This could be the case if the winds (or metabolic activation, in one sense) had been *withdrawn* from the periphery—which would result in *reduced* metabolism in the peripheral tissues—and directed to the central channel, where they would then, according to the system, be directed upwards to the sahasrāra cakra and activate a blissful state, associated with *increased* cerebral metabolism. In the case of the other yogi, according to the detailed description of the gtummo process given in the texts, the withdrawal of winds and the directing of them into and up the central channel may also be accompanied by the repeated production and release of heat back into the body. Both phenomena, reduced and increased heat (as in metabolic activation) in the body outside of the central channel, are described as occurring during the course of gtummo practice (such as, for example, in Mullin 1996, pp. 68 and 158). And while several different forms of meditation produce electrocortical activation characterized by euphoric or euphoria-like affective states, it is extremely intriguing to consider that gtummo meditation may represent the voluntary ability to control efferent neural functions in order to produce certain metabolic and psychological effects in the body, as they are described in Highest Yoga Tantra. Future collaborative research, as has been advocated by His Holiness the Dalai Lama and others, might provide further insight into these and other important subjects, including even the subject of the highest goals of Indo-Tibetan yogic practice.

Endnotes

1. His Holiness the Dalai Lama, from the foreword of Begley, Sharon. 2006. *Train Your Mind Change Your Brain.* New York: Ballantine Books.

2. This analysis is offered in the context of the Dalai Lama's suggestion of collaborative endeavors between Indo-Tibetan yogic science and Western neuroscience and physiology, as represented by His comments offered at the recent Society for Neuroscience Meetings in Washington, DC (2005), for example. Afferent functions are those sensory processes that relay incoming information to central processing brain centers, while efferent processes produce behavioral and physiological responses to the incoming stimulation.

3. In-depth discussions of these similarities are found in Grant and Rainville 2005; Cahn and Polich 2006; Bushell 1995: 563ff.; Bushell 2005.

4. The discussion is based primarily on the following sources for the Indo-Tibetan practices: Thurman 1984, 1991, 1995; Cozort 1986; Yeshe, T. 1987, 1998; Gyatso and Hopkins 1989; Powers 1995; Gyatso, T. 1992; Gyatso, K. 1991; Mullin 1991, 1996; Sopa et al. 1985.

5. Although not all forms of meditation and practice for all traditions and lineages are described in the present essay; see sources in note 4 for more comprehensive descriptions.

6. Lehmann et al. 2001: 119. The psychiatric term "depersonalization" refers to an acute experiential sense of the unreality of self. In the present context, I do not believe that the Buddhist sense of unreality of self is psychopathological; however, I believe that the neuroanatomical data is significant in terms of what brain locations are involved with the fundamental sense of self, in an important sense perhaps independently of issues of psychopathology.

7. Newberg et al. 2001; on the neurophysiological basis of the sense of "substance" or "physical presence" of the sense of self, see the most impressive analyses of Antonio Damasio, in particular, for example, Damasio 2003.

8. Mullin 1996: 136.

9. On the association of imagery (including eidetic imagery) with hypnotizability, see Kosslyn et al. 2000; Crawford et al. 1986, and Lynn and Rhue 1986. On the improvability of hypnosis and imagery abilities, see LaBaw 1969; Gfeller et al. 1987; Kunzendorf 1984, and references therein. Some techniques of imagery enhancement are based on hypnotic age-regression techniques, in which aspects of childhood psychology are putatively restored, including eidetic imagery (which is actually found more in children than adults), enhanced suggestibility, enhanced learning ability, as well as the enhanced ability to enter trance-like states of absorption. I believe it is this set of proclivities that is sought in the Kalacakra initiations that are focused on childhood; see Gyatso and Hopkins 1989: 68ff., "Seven initiations in the pattern of childhood." In addition, "sensory deprivation"—or what has now come to be referred to as "restricted environmental stimulation" (REST) has been found to enhance one's ability to experience trance-like states of absorption, as well as vivid imagery (e.g., see Barabasz 1982), and I also believe that this inherent relationship between absorp-

tion, imagery, and "REST" is one of the major reasons for an emphasis on solitary retreat in Tibetan yogic practice, including, in particular, its emphasis in Kālacakra practice (for emphasis on "dark retreat" in Kālacakra practice, see Cozort 1986: 124ff.; also on REST in the ascetico-meditational context in general, see Bushell 1995).

10. Kosslyn et al.'s (2000) term.

11. Kunzendorf 1984.

12. Spiegel 1985, 2003; and see also Lamas and Valle-Inclan 1998.

13. Kosslyn et al. 2000.

14. Szechtman et al. 1998.

15. Spiegel et al. 1989; and see Spiegel 2003.

16. DePascalis and Cacace 2005.

17. Redd and Andrykowski 1982; Dadds et al. 1997.

18. Anbar 2002; Barber et al. 1964; London and Cooper 1969.

19. Barabasz and Lonesdale 1983.

20. In Bushell, in preparation, I review the data on "trance logic"—a kind of logic discovered serendipitously in experimental studies of hypnosis/self-hypnosis, in which subjects in trance can simultaneously maintain two or more disparate positions, without cognitive dissonance, and other relevant topics, including the *complementary* practices of dream yoga. In this context, in dream yoga, the "phenomenal ground" of the dream world is initially experienced as involuntarily fabricated, while after some practice and proficiency, one begins to experience some control over these fabrications. Hence, deity/mandala meditation, and dream yoga, act then in complementary fashion, coming from "opposite" directions on the consciousness continuum from the poles of waking and dreaming, to demonstrate to the practitioner the constructedness and absence of actual solidity, of the referents of perception, whether in dreaming or waking consciousness. Not so incidentally, it should be noted that, based on decades of intensive research, one of the major figures in modern/postmodern neuroscience, Rodolfo Llinas, has concluded that the neurophysiology of waking and dreaming states of consciousness is essentially identical, with the sole exception being that the source of stimulation during dreaming is essentially internal, while the source of stimulation during waking consciousness is essentially external (e.g., Llinas and Ribary 1993; see also LaBerge et al. 1986). On Tibetan dream yoga see Varela et al. 1997; Wangyal 1998.

21. This subject is also discussed in greater detail in Bushell, in preparation.

22. Benson et al. 1982.

23. E.g., see references in Kunzendorf 1984; Barabasz 1982.

24. Benson et al. 1982; David-Neel 1989. Benson et al. filmed the sheet-drying exercise, in which the gtummo-induced evaporation of water vapor was visible.

25. See White 1979.

26. Thurman 1991: 72.

27. See Luthe 1971; Ulrich et al. 1987; Muck-Weymann et al. 1998; review of these and other studies in Bushell, in preparation.

28. E.g.: "The yogas of . . . Highest Yoga Tantra are performed in order to control 'winds,' or vital energies. In Buddhist physiology, the winds are not merely moving air, but are the

vital energies that cause all movement by and within the body, such as muscular movement, the circulation of blood and lymph, . . . and so forth," Cozort 1986: 42.

29. See studies in Das and Gastaut 1955; Banquet 1973; Lutz et al. 2004.

30. Which provides support for the claims emanating from South and Central Asia for centuries, of the ability of advanced yogis to enter hibernation-like states in which bodily functions appear to be profoundly suppressed. A new model assembles considerable physiological data consistent with these accounts, which also have important implications for related claims of the potential for extended longevity in such practitioners; see Bushell and Olivo, in press.

Bibliography

Anbar, R. D. 2002. "You don't like the taste of your medication? So change the taste!" *Clinical Pediatrics* 41(3): 197-99.

Banquet, J. P. 1973. "Spectral analysis of the EEG in meditation." *Electroencephalography and Clinical Neurophysiology* 35: 143-51.

Barabazs, A. 1982. "Restricted environmental stimulation and the enhancement of hypnotizability: Pain, EEG alpha, skin conductance and temperature responses." *International Journal of Clinical and Experimental Hypnosis* 30(2): 147-66.

——— and C. Lonesdale. 1983. "Effects of hypnosis on P300 olfactory-evoked potential amplitudes." *Journal of Abnormal Psychology* 93: 520-23.

Barber, T. X. et al. 1964. "Effects of hypnotic and nonhypnotic suggestions on parotid gland response to gustatory stimuli." *Psychosomatic Medicine* 26: 374-80.

Benson, H. et al. 1982. "Body temperature changes during the practice of g Tum-mo yoga." *Nature* 295(5846): 234-36.

———. 1990. "Three case reports of the metabolic and electroencephalogaphic changes during advanced Buddhist meditation techniques." *Behavioral Medicine* 16(2): 90-95.

Bushell, W. C. 1995. "Psychophysiological and comparative analysis of ascetico-meditational discipline: Toward a new theory of asceticism." In V. I. Wimbush and R. Valantasis, eds. *Asceticism.[Oxford Reference Series].* NY: Oxford University Press.

———. 2001. "Evidence that a specific meditational regimen may induce adult neurogenesis [abstract]." *Developmental Brain Research* 132: A26.

———. 2005a. "Model: Potential cognitive-behavioral stem cell activation in multiple niches [poster]," Stem Cell Biology and Human Disease Conference, Nature Medicine/Salk Institute/USCD, La Jolla, CA.

———. 2005b. "From molecular biology to anti-aging cognitive-behavioral practices: The pioneering research of Walter Pierpaoli on the pineal and bone marrow foreshadows the contemporary revolution stem cell in regenerative biology." *Annals of the New York Academy of Sciences* 1057: 28-49.

———. and E. L. Olivo. In press. Overview, in W. C. Bushell and E. L. Olivo, eds. *Longevity and Optimal Health; Integrating Eastern and Western Perspectives*. Annals of the New York Academy of Sciences.

Cahn, B. R. and J. Polich. 2006. "Meditation states and traits: EEG, ERP, and neuroimaging studies." *Psychological Bulletin* 132(2): 180-211.

Cozort, D. 1986. *Highest Yoga Tantra*. Ithaca, NY: Snow Lion Publications.

Crawford, H. J. et al. 1986. "Eidetic-like imagery in hypnosis: Rare but there." *American Journal of Psychology* 99(4): 527-46.

Dadds, M. R. et al. 1997. "Imagery in human classical conditioning." *Psychological Bulletin* 122(1): 89-103.

Damasio, A. 2003. "Feelings of emotions and the self." *Annals of the New York Academy of Sciences* 1001: 253-61.

Das, N. and H. C. Gastaut. 1955. "Variations de l'activité électrique de cerveau, du cover et des muscles que lettiques au course de la méditation et de l'éxtase yogique." *Electroencephalography and Clinical Neurophysiology* 6: 211-19.

David-Neel, A. 1989. *Magic and Mystery in Tibet*. Calcutta: Rupa and Co.

DePascalis, V. and I. Cacace. 2005. "Pain perception, obstructive imagery, and phase-ordered gamma oscillations." *International Journal of Psychophysiology* 56(2): 157-69.

Gfeller, J. D. et al. 1987. "Enhancing hypnotic susceptibililty: Interpersonal and rapport factors." *Journal of Personality and Social Psychology* 52(3): 586-95.

Grant, J. A. and P. Rainville. 2005. "Hypnosis and meditation: Similar experiential changes and shared brain mechanisms." *Medical Hypotheses* 65(3): 625-26.

Gyatso, K. 1991. *Guide to Dakini Land; A Commentary to the Highest Yoga Tantra Practice of Vajrayogini*. London: Tharpa.

Gyatso, T., H.H. the Dalai Lama. 1992. *The World of Tibetan Buddhism*. Boston: Wisdom Publications.

——— and J. Hopkins. 1989. *Kalachakra Tantra, Rite of Initiation*. Boston: Wisdom Publications.

Kosslyn, S. M. et al. 2000. "Hypnotic visual illusion alters color processing in the brain." *American Journal of Psychiatry* 157(8): 1279-84.

Kunzendorf, R. G. 1984. "Centrifugal effects of eidetic imaging on flash electroretinograms and autonomic responses." *Journal of Mental Imagery* 8(4): 67-76.

LaBerge, S. et al, 1986. "Psychophysiological correlates of the initiation of lucid dreaming." *Sleep Research* 10: 149-56.

Labaw, W. L. 1969. "Assisting adults and children with remedial uses of their trance capability." *Behavioral Neuropsychiatry* 1(9): 24-29.

Lamas, J. R. and F. Valle-Inclan. 1998. "Effects of a negative visual hypnotic hallucination on ERPs and reaction times." *International Journal of Psychophysiology* 29(1): 77-82.

Lehmann, D. et al. 2001. "Brain sources of EEG gamma frequency during volitionally meditation-induced, altered states of consciousness, and experience of the self." *Psychiatry Research, Neuroimaging Section* 108: 111-21.

Llinas, R. and U. Ribary. 1993. "Coherent 40 Hz oscillation characterizes the dream state in humans." *Proceedings of the National Academy of Sciences* 90: 2078-81.

Luthe, W. 1971. "Autogenic training: Method, research, and application in medicine." In Kamiya, J., et al. eds. *Biofeedback and Self-Control*. NY: Aldine.

Lutz, A. et al. 2004. "Long-term meditators self induce high amplitude gamma synchrony during mental practice." *Proceedings of the National Academy of Sciences* 101: 16369-73.

Lynn, S. J. and J. W. Rhue. 1986. "The fantasy-prone person: Hypnosis, imagination, and creativity." *Journal of Personality and Social Psychology* 51(2): 404-8.

Muck-Weymann, M. et al. 1998. "Rhythmical changes of the cutaneous blood flow in the forehead region under the condition of hypnoid relaxation." *Vasa* 27(4): 220-23.

Mullin, Glenn H. 1991. *The Practice of Kalachakra*. Ithaca, NY: Snow Lion Publications.

———. 1996. *Tsongkhapa's Six Yogas of Naropa*. Ithaca, NY: Snow Lion Publications.

Newberg, A. et al. 2001. "The measurement of regional cerebral blood flow during the complex cognitive task of meditation: A preliminary SPECT study." *Psychiatry Research* 106(2): 11-22.

Powers, John. 1995. *An Introduction to Tibetan Buddhism*. Ithaca, NY: Snow Lion Publications.

Redd, W. H. and M. A. Andrykowski. 1982. "Behavioral intervention in cancer treatment: Controlling aversive reactions to chemotherapy." *Journal of Consulting and Clinical Psychology* 50: 1018-29.

Sopa, Geshe et al., eds. 1985. *The Wheel of Time; The Kalachakra in Context*. Madison, WI: Deer Park.

Spiegel, D. 2003. "Negative and positive hypnotic hallucinations: Attending inside and out." *International Journal of Clinical and Experimental Hypnosis* 51(2): 130-46.

——— et al. 1985. "Hypnotic hallucination alters evoked potentials." *Journal of Abnormal Psychology* 94: 249-55.

Szechtman, H. et al. 1998. "Where the imaginal appears real: A positron emission tomography study of auditory hallucinations." *Proceedings of the National Academy of Sciences* 95(4): 1956-60.

Thurman, Robert A. F. 1984. "The balance of transcendence and immanence in Tsong Khapa's presentation of Buddhist spiritual discipline." In J. Duerlinger, ed. *Ultimate Reality and Spiritual Discipline*. NY: New Era (Paragon House).

———. 1991. "Tibetan psychology: Sophisticated software for the human brain." In D. Goleman and Robert A. F. Thurman, eds. *MindScience; An East-West Dialogue* (Proceedings of a Symposium Sponsored by the Mind/Body Medical Institute of Harvard Medical School and Tibet House, US). Boston: Wisdom Publications.

———. 1995. *Essential Tibetan Buddhism.* San Francisco: Harper San Francisco.

Ulrich, P. et al. 1987. "Cerebral blood flow in autogenic training and hypnosis." *Neurosurgery Review* 10(4): 305-7.

Wangyal, T. 1998. *The Tibetan Yogas of Dream and Sleep*. Ithaca, NY: Snow Lion.

White, J. 1979. "The divine fire: Tumo and Kundalini." In J. White, ed. *Kundalini, Evolution and Enlightenment*. Garden City, NY: Anchor.

Yeshe, Lama Thubten. 1987. *Introduction to Tantra: A Vision of Totality*. Boston: Wisdom Publications.

———. 1998. *The Bliss of Inner Fire; Heart Practice of the Six Yogas of Naropa*. Boston: Wisdom Publications.

–21–

Vibrating in Splendor, the Source Experience of Kālacakra's Maṇḍala

Sofia Stril-Rever

The tantric deities of resplendent Kālacakra's maṇḍala
Pervade the myriad world-systems in the ten directions.
They are working at your realization and Enlightenment right now.
Bear in mind that it is thus! Rejoice that you know it is!
Aspirational Prayer by the First Panchen Lama,
Lobsang Choekyi Gyaltsen.[1]

The Great Teaching on Vibrating in Splendor

The Great Teaching on Vibrating in Splendor in the Tantras of the Yoginis and of the Yoga is the title of the first chapter of *The Book of Wisdom* (the fifth volume of the Kālacakratantra[2]). In this chapter, the Buddha expounds a treatise on Kālacakra's maṇḍala,[3] which belongs to the "alternative" cycle of the Kālacakra meditation system—so called because it contains methods to purify the mind. That is why it presents the maṇḍala in its relationships with the subtle body's energies and its vibrating in splendor, from which Kālacakra and all the deities of his retinue emanate.

The Sanskrit word we translate as "vibrating in splendor" is *spharana.* In its literal meaning, it refers to the physical vibration, shaking, or fluttering which is simultaneous with sound vibrating and light radiating.[4] Even though they are much less numerous, one also finds in the same text occurrences of the word *spanda* which means pulsation, shaking, and vibration in the narrow physical sense of expansion, emission, or ejaculation.[5] In the texts of Kashmiri Śaivism, *mahaspanda*[6] is "the great vibration," i.e., the initial emission of life which is the origin of the creation of beings and the world. However, in the context of Kālacakra, *spharana* refers to the source vibration of mantra and clear light "which," according to Mipham Rinpoche, "is thoroughly pure from the origin, the spontaneous radiance of great wisdom, the inner light within each and every phenomenon."[7]

As His Holiness the Dalai Lama teaches, "until you realize that the basic, innate mind of clear light is your true nature, you remain a sentient being; but when you understand your ultimate nature, you become a Buddha."[8] Although clear light tallies with mind's natural state, it does not appear in ordinary states of consciousness because they are darkened by ignorance and obscured by emotions. The *Kālacakratantra* analyzes the nature of those obscurations at the level of life's source motion, i.e., breathing. Each one of our breaths holds immensity within itself and is related to the universe because the very same energy that makes us breathe also sets celestial bodies into motion. In this context, energy is to be understood as some physical magnitude quantified by the calculation of the revolutions of the planets or the number of breaths. However, this physical energy also has its subtle spiritual dimension which is experienced while meditating.

Such subtle energy (or life-breath[9]) manifests itself in two states; one is called "dual" or "polarized," the other "nondual" or "nonpolarized." Dual or polarized states are borne by life-breath's motion in our subtle side-channels,[10] i.e., the right subtle channel which is solar by nature, and the left subtle channel of lunar nature. Those subtle channels are our inner sun and moon. They are related to the dual states of consciousness of discursive thought, to binary logic, and to the mind that clings to a notion of separate and intrinsic reality of the self and phenomena. In its polarized form, energy bears the karmic imprints of ignorance, emotions, and other mental afflictions.

Still, such breaths or winds (which are depicted as the "mount" for samsaric mind) get depolarized naturally six hundred and seventy-five times a day. Indeed, six hundred seventy-five breaths called "wisdom winds" occur daily when life-breath transits through the twelve constellation-petals of the navel's lotus.[11] When each of the twelve transits takes place, the side winds enter the central channel for fifty-six and one-fourth breaths. Wisdom winds tally with nondual, nonconceptual, or unobscured states of consciousness; they bear clear light.

Training in the practice of Kālacakra yogas' meditation aims entirely at intentionally directing the side-winds into the central channel. *The Book of Wisdom* shows how to unite the deities' maṇḍala with the inner maṇḍala of one's breathing cycles: "Every day one must recite the garland of words of the mantras a number of times equal to the number of breathing cycles. For that purpose, it is said that neither the rosary of threaded pearls nor the actual uttering of mantras is necessary. The syllables of the mantras come in and out as one breathes in and out; they form a garland of flowers that circle round both clockwise and in the anticlockwise direction according to the very nature of the motions of the sun and the moon."[12]

Once the mind has been established and purified in the wisdom winds, it purely contemplates its own inner luminosity and relaxes there. At this point of the completion stage, through vibrating in splendor, one reaches the state of suchness of the Great Seal,[13] described by Mipham Rinpoche as "the vibration of the invincible nature of emptiness established in the center, in the very essence of the six chakras, the inherent radiation of the naturally luminous mind."[14]

Kālacakra's maṇḍala is boundless

In *The Great Teaching on Vibrating in Splendor in the Tantras of the Yogini and of the Yoga*, one learns that Kālacakra's maṇḍala is boundless—in the sense of unlimited. Iconography is merely indicative. The sand maṇḍala (or the figurative maṇḍala one can see on thangkas) is just a scheme, a map. It draws up a table for our orientation. The maṇḍala becomes accomplished in the practitioner, at the pace set by his breathing. The maṇḍala is to be breathed. It is to be experienced. It transforms us from within as, through our practice, its boundless wisdom becomes inseparably one with us.

Traditionally, there are seven hundred and twenty-two deities residing in Kālacakra's maṇḍala. They are usually represented by symbols, but some artists have actually painted miniatures of them. However, even that number of seven hundred and twenty-two deities is yet another convention, a concept necessarily limited. Actually, just as the maṇḍala is boundless, so is the number of deities; it is infinite and without limit.

According to Mipham Rinpoche, there are more than one million elementals and hungry spirits in the wheel of air[15]—however, artists only draw the eighty-eight worldly gods and celestial bodies there. The *Niṣpannayogāvalī*, a reference text in iconography,[16] specifies that countless numbers of deities abide in the nooks above the entrance gates of the three maṇḍalas of body, speech, and mind. Yet only the main ones are mentioned following the cardinal and intermediate directions where they abide.

The Great Teaching on Vibrating in Splendor mentions the processions of yoginis, sky dancers, heroines, ladies, and she-messengers[17] emanated from the Ladies of Power (the eight śaktis) seated on the petals of the lotus of Supreme Bliss in the center of the maṇḍala. Those deities are not described; they are said to be "Those Similar to Smoke," "Those Similar to Red Shimmering," or "Those Similar to Mirage."[18] They do not even have names and are merely referred to by the seed-syllable and the color of their lineage. The text mentions the breathing cycles which those deities purify and on which constellation-petal of the inner zodiac in the lotus of the navel one should visualize them. That is all we know about them. It takes a very intimate and accomplished level of realization for them to appear to the practitioner.

The heart of Kālacakra's maṇḍala, the central lotus, is called the "matrix"[19] because the main deities (i.e., Kālacakra father-mother surrounded by the eight Ladies of Power) generate and then send forth copies of themselves in infinite numbers. Their replicas make haste in every direction in order to accomplish the welfare of beings. Therefore the maṇḍala never remains motionless: it evolves and fluctuates, always becoming a new picture which renews us by the motion of its energies and the radiance of its vibrating in splendor. Beginners usually focus on the static appearance of the maṇḍala, but practice teaches one to let oneself get carried away by the impulse of Enlightenment radiating from the core of that figure.

> "On a single atom, there are as many Buddhas as there are atoms in the world."

Kirti Tsenshab Rinpoche brings light to the practice of Kālacakra's inner maṇḍala by saying that "Quite often, in the same place, there are two separate maṇḍalas each with its own seed-syllable. Yet, they do not contradict each other. Remember the line in Samantabhadra's *Prayer of Noble Conduct*: 'On a single atom, there are as many Buddhas as there are atoms in the world.' If one can see countless Buddhas on a single atom, then why not see two different letters in a single maṇḍala? In the same way, at one's navel, Kalagni's maṇḍala and the maṇḍala of the earth refer to the same disk, which simply bears two different names."[20]

The Great Teaching on Vibrating in Splendor also mentions that the same tantric sacred places (*pīṭhasthāna*) may be called different names according to the tantra one reads. It is said that such variations in terminology aim at confounding the inclination to reasoning of those "endowed with sharp minds."[21] Why is that so?

The names of places or seed-syllables varying, the deities of the maṇḍala being numberless (just like the Buddhas on a single atom), all are signs that one needs to go beyond the limits of one's rational mind—that is, if one wants to join in the maṇḍala's dynamics.

In order to realize that the maṇḍala is boundless, one must take a step on the inconceivable side, which is the foundation of the teaching. For instance, in the *Lotus Sutra*, the Buddha tells the assembly of bodhisattvas that the number of years that have elapsed since he has reached Enlightenment is greater than the number of atoms of dust to be found in all the "hundred thousand myriad koti[22] universes." Then the bodhisattvas answer the Buddha by saying that such a number "goes beyond the limit of what thought can fathom."[23]

The unfathomable world faces the world fathomed by reasoning thought.[24] The latter is a world that is bound and full, the object of limits justified by the several branches of knowledge. That world is grasped by a subject who thinks he or she can master it by thought, through a grid of concepts and notions held to be true. Contradictions are set aside by a logic in which something and its opposite cannot be simultaneously valid.

Yet a mind that accepts the unfathomable (or inconceivable) dimension of the boundless world of the Buddhist teachings and the maṇḍala works in quite a different way. Here being logical means inter-being,[25] which enables one to imagine countless universes, for thought now rests in emptiness. In this context, emptiness never means empty in the sense of nothingness but refers to the absence of inherent existence of the self and phenomena. Everything that exists depends on causes and conditions; everything that exists belongs to the evolutionary process of conditioned arising; and within the dimension of emptiness, there is no room left for intellectual speculation. At the level of energy, mind works on the material of existence. It settles down in a state of lucid awareness of the energy of being, which is called "contemplation."

When thought begins to realize emptiness, it can see "on a single atom, as many Buddhas as there are atoms in the universe." Or it can see the whole universe within one grain of rice. Indeed, what is a grain of rice but the result of some uninterrupted cosmic process of germination and ripening bringing together the sky, the elements, and human effort which follow the pace of seasons which rely on the revolutions of the earth, the moon, the sun, and all other celestial bodies? That grain of rice is a whole. It never ends but transforms continuously.

Within the dimension of emptiness, one can also hear a cloud in a bell. When the bell rings, it suggests a cloud bearing rain, which shall fertilize the earth, from which the roots of trees will draw water and nutrients grow, until the cut wood burns in the goldsmith's fireplace to melt the bronze which will be molded into the new bell for the monastery.

The tiny grain of rice and the immaterial tingling of the bell both convey immensity. Within the consciousness of inter-being, there is no limit to time or space. When wisdom contemplates phenomena in their fundamentally interdependent emptiness, it transcends all subject-object duality. The perceiving subject and the perceived object stop existing as independent entities separated from reality, in the way illusion differentiates them for ordinary consciousness.

When one goes beyond duality, one understands that both subject and object, stemming from mind's creative power, embody the natural radiance of primordial wisdom unified in basic inter-being. Such wisdom of the non-two is called *jñana* in Sanskrit, which translates as "fundamental wisdom" or "exalted wisdom." This wisdom is "fundamental" because it is to be found before any distinction is made between the dual instances of a subject and an object through the power of illusion, the source of ignorance and suffering. This wisdom is "exalted" because it dwells beyond such a distinction.

Maitri or genuine Buddha love

To speak about the non-two in Sanskrit, beside *jñana*, one could also use the word *maitri* or "Buddha love." Indeed, etymologically speaking, *maitri* means "to become one," "to unite." Buddha's wisdom is, by essence, one—the wisdom of the non-two. It is also genuine Buddha love, love manifested through becoming one.

What makes it possible to become one is Buddha nature, which abides in each and every sentient being as a latent potential. Buddha nature inside us is also outside us; it is the dimension of our inter-being. *Maitri* (Buddha love) is a field of experiences unified in the profound awareness of being one with everything that is alive. Kālacakra's system ranks foremost in including the cycles of time and integrating historical becoming into its meditative practice.

Meditation on the Wheel of Time stipulates in its ethics of living that we should feel universally responsible to love all living beings in the three times, past, present, and future. For in inter-being, the logical relationship transforms past and future into the karmic experience of a present which reveals the unfolding pattern of reality. We are, right now, the result of what we were before and the cause of what we shall become later.

His Holiness the Dalai Lama gives every Kālacakra initiation for the sake of world peace because the Tantra relates to human destiny. The Dalai Lama even proclaimed that the relationship between the *Kālacakratantra* and Śambhala on the one hand and our humanity on the other shall appear clearly one day in events of world import.[26] The link with the tantric realm is hidden for the time being, but the realm is nonetheless contemporary, as we are reminded at the end of every Kālacakra great initiation. As a matter of fact, when he concludes the ritual, the Dalai Lama says that the initiation was given under the reign of such *Kalkin*-king of Śambhala in the such-and-such year of his reign. As well, Kālacakra's eschatology foretells that in 2424, the Śambhala king to be, Lord of Tears Holding the Wheel,[27] shall establish a golden age of Dharma on earth.

Still, nothing prevents us from living this perfect age to come, right here, right now: the causes and conditions of its birth are already present. Even though they are invisible, they are nonetheless present. Just like a field sown with seeds in winter—the wheat heads of which are hidden within the secret of the seeds buried underground—the hidden kingdom of Śambhala (or the golden age of Dharma) does exist. They are the secret splendor of our Buddha nature. The Dalai Lama says, with a smile, that you cannot buy a plane ticket to Śambhala. However, he adds, you do not really need one. "In fact, one could say that the ticket actually is the good we have made, and that admission will be restricted to those wealthy in merit."[28]

For the tantric realm appears in pure vision. You do not need to leave your body or this universe to reach it. Our egoistic and self-concerned propensities are what prevent us from entering it. Still, they are not an inevitable plague; constant, diligent, and perseverant work, together with the help we get from initiations and teachings, can neutralize them little by little.

Every time you fold up on yourself, failing to conceive of your interrelated place in the universe as a whole, a crack appears in the inter-being's experience. Acting thus keeps us away from the unified field of *maitri*, Buddha love. *Maitri* may be understood as an expanse full of a consciousness which is the realization of genuine Buddha love. Its essence is the splendor of Buddha nature, the essence of the mind of Enlightenment of all beings. The field of *maitri* is unified because there is a continuity of mind at the level of Buddha nature. *Maitri*, Buddha love, spreads from consciousness to consciousness within the wheel of the cycles of existence of the numberless beings. Since there is such a unified love field, the strength of prayers, the power of wishes, and the blessings of the Awakened Ones pervade—spontaneously and without effort—the continuous and universal dimension of Buddha nature. Space and time are no obstacle to them.

"May all sentient beings become a single family through Kālacakratantra's loving-kindness!"

Collectively speaking, within the Śambhala society, the creation of the unified field of Kālacakra's maṇḍala was a victory against pending inner division. The story of the transmission of the *Kālacakratantra* is edifying in that respect: it shows that one must conquer the maṇḍala. One must learn to deserve it by creating auspicious causes and conditions in the human and social contexts where it appears.[29] Yet even in Śambhala, some obstacles threatened the continuity and the integrity of its transmission.

The story of the *Kālacakratantra* gives an account of an identity claim which vented itself when a group wanted to stop practicing Kālacakra as had been established by the first known Śambhala king, Perfect Moon (Sucandra). He had received the Kālacakra initiation directly from Buddha Śakyamuni and subsequently spread it throughout his kingdom. The schism happened under the eighth king, Dazzling.[30] Millions of Brahmins seceded and wanted to resume Vedic cults.

King Dazzling managed to defeat those separatist moves and restored cohesion in the Śambhala society by giving the Kālacakra initiation and teachings to restore the order that had been threatened. Henceforth he was called *kalkin* or "unifier," and, ever since, all Śambhala kings are unifiers. As Dharma Kings, they guarantee order as symbolized by Kālacakra's maṇḍala.

King Dazzling said it was necessary to continue practicing Kālacakra in Śambhala to fight off the current internal danger of schism but also to prevent a pending external threat of invasion by barbarians (i.e., beings who would not practice Dharma[31] and would be radically alien to Kālacakra's maṇḍala).

In the aspirational prayers of Kālacakra's Guru Yoga, those schismatic events at the origin of the lineage of the unifying kings are evoked when mentioning Ravi, the chief of Brahmin separatists, and the lineage of the Wise Ones who repented and resumed Kālacakra's maṇḍala. One also wishes that all sentient beings in the three worlds may become vajra brothers and sisters, a single family reunited in Kālacakra's unified field.

The following lines are taken from the Root Tantra. They emphasize Kālacakra's aptitude as a social peacemaker establishing peace in everybody's heart:

Just as Ravi[32] and the lineage of the Wise Ones accomplished exalted
wisdom by this Tantra,
May all the beings abiding in the three forms of cyclic existence become
a single family through *Kālacakratantra's* loving-kindness!"

The following stanza takes up the wishes of the first *Kalkin*-king, the first unifier, of Śambhala:

Just as the vajra of my mind abides on earth to liberate sentient beings,
May it also abide in the three forms of cyclic existence by the power of
Kālacakra!

May they reach this path and soon enter the palace of vajra jewels,
Those beings who wander unceasingly because of evil friends in the darkness of nontruth and on the path of degeneration![33]

Kālacakra's maṇḍala, an expanse of transparency and reciprocity

The unifying kings of Śambhala are in charge of preserving the unified space ruled by the Kālacakra maṇḍala built in the center of their kingdom. The battlefield traditionally drawn around Śambhala is a reminder of the conflictual reality of past history and a foreteller of wars to come. Iconography translates into symbols the fact that the maṇḍala is a unifying process lying at the core of the tantric realm. For the very same energy, which is the source of destruction and chaos outside the maṇḍala, transforms into a peace-making and mending force inside the maṇḍala. The hand-to-hand fight of men at arms outside the maṇḍala becomes, inside the maṇḍala, the deities' body-to-body embrace. The battlefield is the reverse image of the maṇḍala, of the expanse in which conflicts are sublimed. That reversal is symbolized by the union of antagonistic polarities in the form of the father-mother deities in embrace in the maṇḍala.

The couples of Buddhas, bodhisattvas, and deities illustrate the fusion of fundamentally opposed principles, which become complementary so the Enlightened state may come to life. East embracing West is Infallible Accomplishment embracing The Illuminating Lady.[34] South embracing North is Born of the Jewel embracing The Lady Who is Herself.[35]

Each direction represented by father-mother Buddhas in embrace is also associated with a color; an element, a symbol; a mental affliction and a wisdom with which it interacts. Thus, East is Infallible Accomplishment whose color is black; his essence is the air element and his attribute is the sword; the mental affliction is envy and the wisdom is the All-Accomplishing. Infallible Accomplishment embraces West, The Enlightening Lady, who is yellow; her essence is the earth and her symbol is the wheel; the mental affliction is ignorance and the wisdom is Mirror-like. Opposite energies (air's motion and action vs. earth's stability and passivity), opposite colors (light's yellow vs. darkness' black), the sword that cuts through illusion and the wheel that spreads the doctrine, envy and ignorance, as well as the two Buddha wisdoms pervade each other. The result is an interaction which establishes balance between the principles located in diametrically opposed directions of the maṇḍala. Antagonism is transcended by the symmetry and mutual exchange of the potentials at stake.

Kālacakra's maṇḍala represents order recomposed out of disorder in an expanse of transparency. Transparency should be understood as the quality of fundamental reciprocity within the maṇḍala where nothing remains as an obstacle, nothing opposes anything else, where opposites come together. As a paragon of harmony throughout, from its center to its periphery, the maṇḍala represents the causal hierarchy of the several levels of existence. It is non-set, nonpolarized—it contains a scale of vibrations in tune with our inner maṇḍala, with which it vibrates sympathetically and deeply during the initiation and the meditation practice.

Chögyam Trungpa teaches that this "fundamental" maṇḍala is to be found "beyond time and space. There is neither time nor space because there is no polarity."[36] For the Wheel of Time symbolizes the energetic structure of an instant which gathers the three times (past, present, and future) together in a field of unified love and wisdom. As both the special circumstances of its transmission and the symbolism of its iconography indicate, Kālacakra's maṇḍala is, in the scope of historic becoming, a present that does not pass, the vajra time of Buddha nature.

Mipham Rinpoche teaches that vajra time is not determined by phenomena that are dual by nature. Therefore, it has neither beginning nor end: it does not elapse. And what does not elapse is the essence of "great bliss." Vajra time is "undifferentiated from immutable bliss and emptiness; it is endowed with the supreme aspect of all. Equality of the three times is suchness by nature. It is undivided, universal, and all-encompassing; it is entirely pure subtle semen"[37]—the semen of Buddha nature, the seed of Enlightenment in all beings.

The naked sun of Enlightenment

The creation of Kālacakra's maṇḍala may be experienced as the birth of the sun of one's own Buddha nature. Purple and golden in color, the robes of the monks bent over the four directions of the circle of the maṇḍala suggest the undulations of some spiritual dawn. At the end of a solemn liturgy celebrating the body, speech, and mind of all the Buddhas, the monks' consecrated hands bring the naked sun of Enlightenment into the world. They bring to life the maṇḍala of original splendor, which shines in the heart of every living being. It is the sun of genuine Buddha love, which can tear asunder the night of our sufferings. If we were able to enter Kālacakra's maṇḍala vibrating in splendor, Buddha love would immediately illuminate our lives. We would then see the world in the way which a bodhisattva does.

A bodhisattva is one with all living beings and takes upon himself or herself, effortlessly and unceasingly, the suffering of all beings. In return, he gives them the powerful benefits of his own merits, effortlessly and unceasingly. For the sake of everyone's Enlightenment, a bodhisattva accomplishes Buddha nature's unified whole. And it is vibrating in splendor in the heart of Kālacakra's maṇḍala which carries over *jñana* and *maitri*, Buddha's infinite wisdom and love, to each and every being in each and every world.

"Through his Western mouth, the Prince of Conquerors proclaims . . ."

Vibrating in the splendor of Buddha's nature is vividly described in the beginning of the *Book of Wisdom* in the *Kālacakratantra*. From each mouth of Kālacakra's four faces pours out a vocal symphony, exposing all the words of the world, all the thoughts of the beings of the three times. The four mouths sing what has been said, what is being said, and what is yet to be said:

> Through his Western mouth, the Prince of Conquerors proclaims the *Veda of Anthems*, and through his Northern mouth, he recites the *Veda of Sacrificing Spells.*[38]
> Through his Southern mouth, the *Veda of Songs*, and through his Eastern mouth the *Veda of Magic Spells*[39] of the Hari lineage.
> Through his Eastern mouth, he proclaims *The Kaulas' Tantra,*[40] and through his Western mouth *Garuda's Tantra* and *The Elementals' Tantra.*[41]
> Through his Southern mouth, he voices Śiva's doctrine, and through his mouth which is like a rising sun, he teaches Viśnu's religion. . . . / . . .
> From the cakra in his heart and through his Eastern mouth, vibrating in splendor comes forth; from the cakra at his navel and through his Western mouth also, vibrating in splendor comes forth.
> From his Perfect Enjoyment cakra and through his Southern mouth, from his *unhit cakra*[42] and through his Northern mouth, in all directions, vibrating in splendor comes forth.
> From the centers of his cakras and from all his throats, vibrating in splendor comes forth, and reabsorbing vibrations make the states of existence run through the body,
> As well as beyond the body, throughout all the three worlds, at the pace of the vibrations coming from the several mouths of the sire of Conquerors.[43]

Reciting Kālacakra's mantra, a practice of vibrating in splendor and tong-len

"Vibrating in splendor" refers to a source experience of Kālacakra's maṇḍala which links us up with the root causes of our existence. Those are the energies of the elements and celestial bodies symbolized in the heart of the maṇḍala's deities and alive upon each and every lotus of our subtle body. One can experience reciting Kālacakra's mantra as the practice of vibrating in splendor by associating the sound dimension of each one of its letters together with its own radiance. Kirti Tsenshab Rinpoche[44] invites us to visualize the HŪṂ seed-syllable in the center of our heart lotus, melted together with the seven subscribed syllables that originate from HŪṂ and stand for the elements of the world and Mount Meru. For the Ten Almighty possess all the vibratory structure of the world maṇḍala in their matrices.

The seed-syllables in that sequence are stacked upon each other in the following manner:

HAM is dark blue
KSA is green
MA bears Mount Meru's four colors
LA is yellow
VA is white
RA is red
YA is black.

Dark blue OṂ ĀḤ HŪṂ HOḤ . . . HŪṂ PHAT, the other seed-syllables of the mantra, spin around those letters. Phonetically speaking, the rule is that the *life force* (i.e., the vowel) is elided in subscribed letters. However, Kirti Tsenshab Rinpoche specifies that, in Kālacakra's mantra, one must keep the vowel A, for it symbolizes the emptiness of everything.

Stacking up the seed-syllables leads one to associate mantra recitation with the three-dimensional visualization of the maṇḍala. As a matter of fact, those letters are a reflection of the axial structure of the world maṇḍala according to the cosmology of Kālacakra's maṇḍala, with the elements' disks piled up from the air to the earth, on top of which rests Mount Meru, crowned with the maṇḍala's palace. From the rays of light radiating from each letter, vibrating in splendor comes forth. It is associated with the tong-len practice of purifying the sufferings of each respective realm of existence.

That was how reciting one hundred thousand Kālacakra mantras inspired me with the following song I wrote with great gratitude for Kirti Tsenshab Rinpoche's teachings, the source of all understanding, as far as the insignificant Kalachakra student I am is concerned:

The Song of the Seven Limitless Wishes
within Kālacakra's Mantra

1. Within the embrace of Kālacakra's mantra
May I kiss away all the hatred and anger
That make hell-beings moan under torture!

2. Within the nectar of Kālacakra's mantra
May I soothe the torments of thirst and starvation
That consume hungry ghosts!

3. Within the radiance of Kālacakra's mantra
May I bring light into the darkness of ignorance,
The karma blinding all animals!

4. Within the breath of Kālacakra's mantra
May I blow away all agony from human martyrdom!

5. Within the equanimous joy of Kālacakra's mantra
May I dispel all the envy
Agitating the asuras' restless minds!

6. Within the rapture of Kālacakra's mantra
May I put out the blaze of pride
Atrociously burning out the hearts of all devas!

7. In the bliss-emptiness limitless expanse of Kālacakra's mantra
Shimmering with the resplendent blessing of the Ten Almighty and the celestial Garuda,
Thanks to the peerless loving-kindness of the kings of Śambhala
And the masters who hold the *Kālacakratantra* lineage,
May all the causes of suffering in the six realms cease to exist!

Translation: Philippe Arribet, kindly assisted by Mike Murray.

Endnotes

1. Lobsang Choekyi Gyaltsen quoted in Glenn Mullin, *The Practice of Kalachakra,* Ithaca, Snow Lion, p. 284.

2. *Jñāna Patala* Sanskrit edition of the Rare Buddhist Texts Research Projects, Central Institute for Higher Tibetan Studies, Sarnath, India, 1994, under the guidance of Prof. Samdhong Rinpoche and Prof. Jagannāth Upādhyāya. First chapter translated from Sanskrit into French by S. Stril-Rever, *Tantra de Kalachakra, Le traité du mandala*, Paris, Desclée de Brouwer, 2003.

3. The measures of Kālacakra's maṇḍala were taught according to the secret measures of the world and the human being in *The Book of Initiation*, the third volume of *Kālacakratantra*. Sanskrit edition of the Rare Buddhist Texts Research Projects, Central Institute for Higher Tibetan Studies, Sarnath, India, 1994.

4. David Reigle kindly gave me the following detailed account of possible translation for the word: "The Tibetan translation of *spharana* in the *Vimalaprabhā* is usually *spro ba*, but sometimes *spros pa*. In English it was formerly translated as 'creation,' but this has the Biblical overtones of God creating the world out of nothing. Since this is not the Indian idea, even in Hinduism, translators switched to more literal renderings: emission, emanation, manifestation. The word 'emission' is not used in normal English for anything like creation, so this is probably not a good choice. The English word 'manifestation' is a good translation choice, but it also translates many other Sanskrit words, like *vyakti*, *prapanca*, etc., so it can be a less precise translation of *spharana.* The Tibetan word *spros pa*, which sometimes translates *spharana*, frequently translates *prapanca. Prapanca* is another word that is very hard to translate accurately. K. R. Norman, working with its Pali form, settled

on 'diversification.' Another choice is 'elaboration,' besides 'manifestation.' At the other end of the range of meaning for *spharana*, when it is like *sphurana*, following one of the meanings of the cognate root *sphur*, shine, it is sometimes appropriate to use 'radiating,' as in radiating rays of light." (David Reigle, May 2006)

In the context of Kaśmīr Śaivism, Lilian Silburn freely translates *spharana* as "consciousness." According to her, *spharana* stands for "the vibration which makes something appear to consciousness." See *Maharthamañjari*, tr. L. Silburn, Paris, de Boccard, 1968, p. 118. As a matter of fact, since the term entails the notions of vibration of sound and radiation of light in this particular context, in the French translation my choice has been "vibration en splendeur"—or in English "vibrating in splendor."

5. See the commentary on Stanza 76 in *Tantra de Kalachakra, Le traité du mandala*, S. Stril-Rever, 2003, p. 141.

6. Lilian Silburn freely translates spanda as "primordial act" and writes, for example, that Śiva is "the pure and vibrating act" or shuddhaspanda, equalled to inner reality. See *Maharthamañjari*, op. cit., p. 11.

7. Mipham Rinpoche, *The Vajrasunshiner,* Chapter 4, translated and edited by Phil Lecso for IKN Study Documents. Cf. IKN website http://www.kalachakranet.org.

8. In *L'Initiation de Kalachakra*, S. Stril-Rever, Paris, Desclée de Brouwer, 2001, p. 167.

9. *Prāṇa* in Sanskrit.

10. Cf. exposition of Kālacakra subtle physiology in *Tantra de Kalachakra, Le livre du corps subtil*, translated from Sanskrit into French by Sofia Stril-Rever, Paris, Desclée de Brouwer, 2000.

11. The navel's lotus is related to one's inner zodiac. The twelve petals of its center stand for the constellations prāṇa transits through. Cf. *Tantra de Kalachakra, Le livre du corps subtil*, op. cit., Chapter 2.

12. *Tantra de Kalachakra, Le Traité du mandala,* commentary to Stanza 38, S. Stril-Rever, 2003, pp. 104-112.

13. The Great Seal, or *mahamudra*, is the state of consciousness which perceives reality as it is, in its dimension of emptiness and wisdom.

14. Mipham Rinpoche, *The Vajrasunshiner,* Chapter 4, translated and edited by Phil Lecso for IKN Study Documents. Cf. IKN website http://www.kalachakranet.org.

15. The wheel of air, or the last external circle of elements, is surrounded by the ring of the Buddha's wisdom.

16. B. Bhattacharyya, *Nishpannayogāvali du mahapandita Abhayakaragupta*, Baroda, Oriental Institute, 1972, Gaekwad's Oriental Series, no. 109, 76-85.

17. Or *dakini, vireśvari, nayika,* and *duti* in Sanskrit.

18. Smoke, Red Shimmering, and Mirage are the names of three of the eight Ladies of Power, the Shaktis, seated on the central lotus of the maṇḍala.

19. Or *garbha*, in Sanskrit.

20. Unpublished teaching by Kirti Tsenshab Rinpoche, corrected and edited by Rudy Harderwijk.

21. See commentary to Stanza 35, in *Tantra de Kalachakra, Le Traité du mandala,* S. Stril-Rever, 2003, pp. 90-98.

22. A koti equals ten million.

23. *Le Lotus de la Bonne loi*, Paris, Les Belles-Lettres, 1854, tr. Emile Burnouf, chapitre 15, pp. 191-197.

24. In Sanskrit, the same word refers to both reason and measure (*manas*).

25. A free translation of "interdependence" by Master Thich Nhat Hanh who coins and conjugates *inter-être* in French (inter-be). See *Une Flèche, deux illusions*, ed. Dzambala, 1998, p. 171: "Tu es moi, Je suis toi, Nous inter-sommes. " (You are me, I am you, We inter-are.)

26. His Holiness the Dalai Lama, *Concerning the Kalachakra Initiation in America*, Madison, Deer Park, 1981.

27. Or *Raudrachakrin*, in Sanskrit. See *Tantra de Kalachakra*, S. Stril-Rever, 2000, "Présentation du Chapitre 1."

28. *L'Initiation de Kalachakra*, S. Stril-Rever, 2001, p. 39.

29. The Kālacakra initiation given in Bodhgaya in January 2003 was deemed a victory and His Holiness the Dalai Lama a Victorious one, or *Jina*. As a matter of fact, several groups had decided to prevent the ceremony from taking place and had uttered threats. According to the Dalai Lama, the transmission did take place thanks to the monks who, for the whole month that preceded the event, had been praying to the Protectors every day. This is a reminder that the teachings which brings out the splendor of Buddha nature is always a triumph over the negative forces that oppose it, after the ordeal of an actual fight.

30. Or in Sanskrit, *Yaśas*

31. Those barbarians are called *mleccas* in Sanskrit, literally "those who do not know Sanskrit"—Sanskrit being here the language of Dharma.

32. One of the names of Suryaratha, or Chariot-of-the-Sun, mentioned in the *Homage Prayer to Kālacakra* in the beginning of *The Book of Wisdom*. Suryaratha prompted the Brahmins of Śambhala to leave the kingdom to perform Vedic cults. When he realized his mistake, he led the Brahmins back to Śambhala and begged the king to grant them the Kālacakra initiation and teachings.

33. *Kalachakra, Guide de l'initiation et du Guru Yoga*, Teachings by His Holiness the Dalai Lama and Jhado Tulku Rinpoche, edited by S. Stril-Rever, Paris, Desclée de Brouwer, 2002, pp. 137 and 183.

34. Or in Sanskrit, the father-mother Buddhas Amoghasiddhi and Locana.

35. Or in Sanskrit, the father-mother Buddhas Ratnasambhava and Mamaki.

36. Chögyam Trungpa, *Mandala, un chaos ordonné*, translated by R. Gravel, Paris, Le Seuil, 1994, p. 83.

37. Mipham Rinpoche, *The Vajrasunshiner,* Chapter 1, originally translated by Rime Lodro Waldo and edited by Phil Lecso for IKN Study Documents. Cf. IKN website http://www.kalachakranet.org.

38. Or Rigveda and Yajurveda.

39. Or Samaveda and Atharvaveda.

40. The reference text of the Kaula tantric sect, Bengale, who are adepts of Kundalini yoga.

41. Two subclasses of Śaivist tantras.

42. The heart cakra producing the spontaneous *unhit sound* of its beating.

43. See commentary to Stanzas 49 and 53, in *Tantra de Kalachakra, Le Traité du mandala,* S. Stril-Rever, 2003, p.128 and 130.

44. Unpublished teaching by Kirti Tsenshab Rinpoche, Dharamsala, April 2006.

–22–

The Kālacakra Empowerment as Conducted by Kirti Tsenshab Rinpoche

Ronit Yoeli-Tlalim

Dedicated to the memory of Kirti Tsenshab Rinpoche, a truly great master in his life and death.

The following essay describes the method used by Kirti Tsenshab to conduct the Kālacakra initiation.[1] Kirti Tsenshab (1926-2006) was considered to be one of the highest authorities on the Kālacakra. Following the advice of the Dalai Lama, Kirti Tsenshab gave numerous Kālacakra initiations and teachings on Kālacakra, including to a number of senior lamas and rinpoches, and mostly in the West. He was one of the last masters to conduct the Kālacakra initiation following the Abhayākaragupta tradition. The Abhayākaragupta method is a generic system applicable for all tantras, using a painted mandala as opposed to using a sand mandala for the initiation. From 1987 he performed the Abhayākaragupta version of the Kālacakra initiation more than twenty times.

The following will discuss his method of conducting the Kālacakra initiation[2] together with the relevant sections from the ritual manual used by him, the *'Phreng ba dang kri ya sbrag pa'i dkyil 'khor zhe lnga'i dbang bskur tshul gyi cho ga* by the first lCang skya, lCang skya ngag dbang blo-bzang chos ldan, (1642-1714).[3] This text is a commentary on Abhayākaragupta's *Vajrāvalī* and is one of the main texts on which Kirti Tsenshab based himself when conducting the Kālacakra initiation.[4]

An empowerment—a few general comments

An empowerment (*dbang*/ *dbang bskur*; *abhiśeka*) is a ritual in which a guru confers the authority and ability to practise a certain Vajrayāna method. It is an essential prerequisite for any tantric practice. The rituals conducted are meant to activate various potentials which are inherent in the disciple. These potentials will, eventually, serve to perfect the body, speech, and mind of the disciple. This tantric ritual is often referred to as "initiation," which suggests "the ritualised acceptance of an 'outsider' into a community which reserves to itself certain privileges and responsibilities that are often regarded as secret so far as the outside world is concerned."[5]

The Sanskrit term *abhiśeka* itself means "sprinkling water on the top of the head."[6] There seems to be a connection between the ritualistic and royal aspects of *abhiśeka*.[7] *Abhiśeka* also refers to the tenth Bodhisattva bhūmi, as discussed in the *Mahāvastu*.[8] Other connotations of the term include cleansing, purifying, authorizing, empowering, gaining, lordship, depositing potencies, sprinkling, pouring, casting, and causing possession of a blissful mind.[9]

The Buddhist tantric empowerment rituals display many similarities with the Hindu tantric empowerment rituals (*dīkśā* or *abhiśeka*). Both the actual practices and the overall symbolism resemble each other. In the Hindu ritual, as in the Buddhist, the initiation enacts a type of new birth. This is symbolised by the initial blindfolding, the removal of the blindfold, receiving a new name, and the phased purification. Both in the Hindu and Buddhist ritual the disciple is initiated through water from a vase and is given permission to chant a certain mantra.[10]

The Tibetan translation of the Sanskrit term *abhiśeka* is *dbang* (literally: power). According to Kirti Tsenshab, the term *dbang* refers to two types of power: the power which ripens and the power which liberates. According to him, when one enters the path of Mantrayāna, one receives the "empowerment which ripens." Then when one practises the path, the development stage or the completion stage, one experiences the "empowerment which liberates." The liberation is twofold: from ignorance and from one's defilements. Once one is completely liberated from the defilements, one attains the state of Vajradhara—at that point one has received the complete empowerment.[11]

The Abhayākaragupta tradition

Kirti Tsenshab followed the Abhayākaragupta method of conducting the Kālacakra initiation. The Abhayākaragupta method, based on the *Vajrāvalī,* describes a generic way of conducting initiations regardless of which Tantra class they belong to.

Abhayākaragupta (*'Jig med 'byung gnas sbas pa*) lived during the final decades of the eleventh century and the first quarter of the twelfth century.[12] The *Deb ther sngon po* reports that Abhayākaragupta received Kālacakra teachings from Kālacakrapada the younger and Nāropa. According to other lineage accounts, he was a student of Bodhibadra, of Tsa-mi, and of Kā-so-ri-pa,[13] who was a disciple of Nāropa. Abhayākaragupta became a great master of Kālacakra.[14] The writings of Abhayākaragupta grew very popular in eleventh-century Tibet. Tibetans value Abhayākaragupta's learning to the extent they venerated the Panchen Lamas as his incarnation.[15]

When discussing the background of Abhyākaragupta's tradition, Kirti Tsenshab gave the following account:

> As for the source of this tradition—Abayākaragupta saw Vajrayogini in his dream and it was she who presented him with this way of conducting the initiation. She also told him that it would be better if he wrote the things she had told him, and not her. So unless Vajrayogini herself was wrong, this tradition is correct and true.[16]

Another variant of this episode appears in the *Deb ther sngon po.* It recounts that it was through Vajrayogini's instructions that Abhayākaragupta composed the *Vajrāvalī* as well as two other texts.[17] Accounts of this episode were popular in Tibet.[18]

The primary topic of the *Vajrāvalī* (*dKyil 'khor gyi cho ga rdo rje phreng ba*),[19] composed around 1100 CE,[20] is maṇḍala construction as well as the consecration of a disciple. The importance of the *Vajrāvalī* in Tibet is attested by its many different translations.[21] It describes the construction of the maṇḍalas in extreme detail, sufficient to reconstruct the maṇḍala in the form known to Abhayākaragupta. These include twenty-six maṇḍalas, the last and most detailed being the Kālacakra maṇḍala.[22]

An important difference between the way Kirti Tsenshab conducted the Kālacakra initiation and the way it is performed by the Fourteenth Dalai Lama was Kirti Tsenshab's use of a painted maṇḍala instead of a sand maṇḍala. Kirti Tsenshab identified Abhayākaragupta and his commentators as the source of this tradition.

The *Vajrāvalī*, in the section dealing with drawing the outlines of the different maṇḍalas, contains a separate passage discussing the Kālacakra. In this section Abhayākaragupta says:

> As for the Kālacakra maṇḍala, what is given here, in order to train Nyi-ma-shing-rta [Sūryarata] and others, practices were taught which were different from all other tantras.[23]

Abhayākaragupta, in any case, allows the master to conduct the Kālacakra initiation in whichever way he sees fit:

> Even having taught these different aspirations, there is no contradiction with the rituals of consecration, etc. of other tantras. Do things as you wish.[24]

Abhayākaragupta chooses to disregard the differences of method between the Kālacakra and other consecrations:

> Putting aside the differences of the method of the Kālacakra, I will explain just the drawing of the lines of the maṇḍala.[25]

The invitation to "do things as you wish" refers to performing the initiation in a fourfold structure based on a painted maṇḍala rather than a sand maṇḍala. This differs from the "tantric" way of conducting the Kālacakra initiation which follows Nāropa's description in the *Sekoddeśa*.[26] The Kālacakra initiation based on a sand maṇḍala, as described by Nāropa, is performed by the present Dalai Lama and includes the seven initiations as a child (the seven worldly consecrations), the four higher (extra-worldly), and four "higher than higher" initiations.[27]

While the reference to the Abhayākaragupta tradition was used as the main argument for the use of the painted maṇḍala in Kirti Tsenshab's initiation, he often explained this use in economic terms as well, stating that since he did not have the funds available to the Dalai Lama when he conducted the Kālackara initiation, he used a painted maṇḍala, thus allowing for a much less expensive ritual:

> In the centers I go to, it is not possible to give this elaborate initiation [based on a sand maṇḍala] due to financial constraints, but I give it because the people ask me, and instead of refusing, I give the abbreviated initiation on the basis of a drawn maṇḍala, which hopefully also benefits.[28]

The significance of an initiation

Tibetan masters emphasise the importance of an initiation as an essential prerequisite for performing any type of tantric practice. Its significance is derived from two aspects: first there is the notion of gaining permission from someone who holds authority. The First Dalai Lama, for instance, explains: "Why is it necessary to receive initiation in order to practise the tantras? Just as someone who wishes to undertake a major building project must first obtain permission from the government, the spiritual aspirant wishing to undertake the great task of Vajrayāna yoga must first gain the permission of a qualified lineage master."[29] The other aspect is the attainment of power, without which the various tantric practices would be useless. Again, the First Dalai Lama explains that at the time of an initiation "the master plants the seeds of tantric attainment within the mind of the disciple, and without these seeds our practice of the two stages will be unable to produce the tree, branches, and fruit of enlightenment."[30]

lCang skya includes a long section dealing with the importance of receiving an initiation. He stresses that if one does not receive the initiation—even if one listened to the explanations of the tantra by the lama and perfectly understood its significance—no matter how much one were to practise, there is not only no chance of attaining siddhi, but also both the teacher and the disciple will go to hell. Furthermore, lCang skya emphasises that even if a disciple is a beginner, the attainment of the higher initiations will suffice to practice the completion stage: all that is required as a prerequisite is for the initiation to be correctly bestowed:

> Also, in the *Vajrāvalī* it says: The initiation is the most important thing [in which] all siddhis continually abide [or: is the constant abode of all siddhis]. In order for me to explain the meaning in this way, first you should properly listen. When a student is at the beginning, if the initiation is perfectly bestowed, an intelligent one becomes a worthy vessel at this time, in the yoga of the stages of the Completion Stage. Without the complete initiation, even if the practitioners understand the meaning of the tantra, the teacher and the disciple alike would go to the great unending hell realms.[31]

lCang skya stresses that in order for the student to be allowed to practise both the generation and the completion stages, both the lower (the vase initiations) and the higher initiations (secret, knowledge, and fourth) should be performed. He stresses that the initiations should be conducted not only in full, but also following the right order and by a lama who has received the initiations himself. The retributions mentioned for failing to fulfill these conditions are very harsh, such as going to the hell realms and staying there until the hell realms have been emptied:

> Thus it is taught that to meditate on the two incomparable stages, you need to obtain all the initiations. In particular, the first verse [means that] if the secret initiation is not obtained, [you] are unable to meditate [on the] path of the secret initiation.
>
> The second [verse means that] if the knowledge initiation is not obtained [you] are unable to meditate [on the] path of the knowledge initiation. The fourth [verse means that] if the fourth initiation is not obtained, [you] are unable to meditate [on] the path of the fourth initiation and [if] not having obtained the fourth initiation you call yourself an attainer, lying, and [you] bestow "initiation" on others, [then] as long as the Buddha's teachings survive, [you will] live in hell, and you will stay there until the hell realms themselves are emptied![32]

lCang skya also stresses the power of the initiation to purify the disciples' impurities:

> Also, in this same [text it says]: "Just as poison can be counteracted by mantras, purifying mantras extracting the essence [of the poison], likewise, the initiations purify the disciples' impurities." Thus, the power of the poison to kill and cause illness is counteracted by mantras.
>
> Through the power of the mantras, the poison's [power to] kill and cause illness is purified. In this way, the purified poison has its essences of health and longevity extracted.
>
> Similarly, just as poison can become a medicine for long life and curing illness, so even for ordinary disciples, the initiations will purify their kleśas and defilements and gradually, they will become Buddhas.[33]

lCang skya emphasizes that it is the task of the master to ensure the disciple meets all the requirements for the initiation: bestowing higher initiations only on those who have received lower ones; bestowing the initiation in the correct order; inspiring confidence; and conducting the initiation in an authentic and reliable way.[34] From the point of view of the disciple, lCang skya emphasises his need to listen.[35]

Dealing with the power of the empowerment, lCang skya discusses the enactment of a potential, which is inherent within one's being. He uses the analogy of a collection of guitars, which can turn into music only with a musician who can play them.[36]

At the ritual itself, Kirti Tsenshab did not discuss the importance of receiving the empowerment. In a personal interview, however, Kirti Tsenshab stressed that one should not read any Kālacakra text before one has received the empowerment.

The empowerment is significant also in relationship with the sādhana, which reflects the process and general structure of the empowerment ceremony. During the performance of the sādhanas, the practitioners are meant to reexperience the empowerment. Each of the empowerments has three aspects: the basis (*gzhi*), which is the ritual of the empowerment itself; the path (*lam*), which is the practice in which one should relive the same process which one experienced in the empowerment; and the result (*'bras bu*), which is the ability to achieve the ultimate goal of the practice and interpreted as an empowerment itself.

The process how one *actually* becomes empowered has three aspects: a substance, a mantra, and a meditation. The substance is an object that has been blessed and is used as part of the empowerment, such as a vase or a crown. The mantra is a special mantra that the lama gives at each empowerment. The meditation is the visualization that the disciple should perform according to the instructions of the lama, in parallel with the lama's personal visualization. According to Kirti Tsenshab, it is the visualization that activates the empowerment: if an empowerment is conferred but the disciple does not perform the visualization, then, in effect, one has not received the initiation.

General structure of the initiation

Kirti Tsenshab closely followed the structure of the initiation as described in the *Vajrāvalī* and lCang skya's manual. Consisting of four parts, typical of Anuttara-yoga tantra initiations other than Kālacakra, it comprises a vase initiation, secret initiation, wisdom initiation (also called secret knowledge), and word (also called fourth) initiations. Tāranātha, in his *History of the Kālacakra* (*dPal Dus kyi 'khor lo'i chos bskor gyi byung khungs nyer mkho*), when discussing the method of empowerment of the Anuttara-yoga tantras, says:

> Regarding the Anuttarayoga tantra [the Buddha taught] that at the time of the empowerment [one receives] the vase initiation, the secret initiation, the wisdom initiation, and the fourth initiation.[37]

The *Kālacakratantra* describes two sets of initiations: the seven worldly and the four higher (extra-worldly) consecrations. Mori has suggested that the seven worldly consecrations have their origins in the Yoga tantra class, whereas the extra-worldly part has a structure similar to the four consecrations stipulated in the *Guhyasamājatantra* and other Anuttara-yoga tantras. According to Mori, the Kālacakra consecration system had an important role in the system developed by Abhayākaragupta in the *Vajrāvalī*.[38]

After the four main initiations, Kirti Tsenshab performed various concluding rituals and described the practice duties. The overall structure is similar to that described in lCang skya's manual. It is divided into the following sections:

i. Entering the maṇḍala
ii. The empowerment itself
iii. The rituals with the initiation's supports
iv. The explanations of the meanings of the initiation
v. Methods of ending[39]

Preliminary conditions: who is an appropriate recipient?

The question of who is an appropriate recipient for an Anuttara-yoga tantra initiation has been readdressed by contemporary lamas. The *Kālacakratantra* itself says:

> The novice should [participate] in the flask [empowerment]. The monk [participates] in the empowerment of the secret [place]. He who is called "elder" should [participate] in the higher {third empowerment of wisdom and gnosis} and {he is empowered} in the cause.[40]

lCang skya describes a recipient who is clearly a monk,[41] though he explains that even ordinary disciples can benefit from the initiation, providing it is properly bestowed.

Writing in the early seventies, the Fourteenth Dalai Lama discussed what he considered to be preliminary conditions for receiving initiation. He proposed that one should first take refuge, then a vow of individual emancipation, and then generate the aspirational and practical mind of enlightenment. Only then would one arrive at the point where it is suitable to hear tantra teachings. Commenting on what he regarded as new allowances which he was witnessing, he said:

> In the past, entrance into a mandala and granting initiation were used very carefully, discriminating between the two, but nowadays Tibetans tend to initiate anyone.
>
> Vajradhara set forth a complete system with different levels—those who could just enter a mandala, those who could also receive the water and head-dress initiations, and so forth. When it is done systematically, the lama, prior to granting initiation, analyses the student to determine whether

> he or she can engage in the three trainings [ethics, meditative stabilisation and wisdom] and keep the vows. He allows those who are not qualified but who have great faith to enter a mandala but does not allow initiation.
>
> These systematic restrictions, which when followed make initiation effective and practical, are often not followed nowadays, causing trouble for both lama and initiate.[42]

In preparation for the first Kālacakra initiation in the West the Dalai Lama's view was already modified, at least with regard to the Kālacakra: the minimum requirements to receive the Kālacakra initiation as stated by the Dalai Lama in 1980 were an intense appreciation for and an interest in developing bodhicitta and the concept of emptiness, as well as faith and interest in the Kālacakra. The Dalai Lama also described the basic condition for receiving the initiation as a blessing: "anyone who sincerely appreciates the opportunity."[43] He cited similar conditions ahead of the Kālacakra initiation in Varanasi in 1990. In this initiation he mentioned the prerequisites for any tantric practice to be a firm foundation in the sutrayāna and deep realisation of emptiness.[44]

Another important issue is the gender one. Whilst the texts seem to imply a male practitioner, present-day practitioners are both male and female. Commenting on this point on another occasion, Kirti Tsenshab said:

> The time when the Buddha was in India, at that time there was a difference between the status of men and women. There was a difference in what they were able to achieve because of their status at that time. So the male was seen as superior and the woman was seen as inferior. Often you had in Tibetan the term for woman meaning "lesser born." Now in the present time there is equality between the sexes so men and women can equally accomplish the same things, they are able to develop the same qualities in learning. But some people may feel doubts about that seeing in the texts it describes gaining a male rebirth in order to have all of the conditions to be able to practise and so on. But one should understand that it is something that is related to the conditions during ancient times and not to the present.[45]

The analysis of dreams

The *Vajrāvalī* and lCang skya's manual describe the master as asking the disciple to recount dreams.[46] According to Abhayākaragupta the dream in which one falls from high mountains is a bad omen. Abhayākaragupta suggests chanting mantras of Amṛta kuṇḍalī to protect from this omen.[47]

lCang skya cites many examples of good dreams, such as those where one sees a rising sun or moon; sees the enthronement of a king; obtains a wonderful meal; finds a treasure; meets one's lama or parents or a wise acquaintance; wears beautiful ornamented clothes; flies to the sky, etc. He then gives a number of examples of bad dreams, such as those where one falls off a mountain or a tree; falls into an abyss; rides a monkey, ass, pig, camel, buffalo, or a wild animal; looks towards the south; or travels with the thought of not returning.[48] Also negative are dreams where one is eaten by a crow, dog, or demons; sinks into mud; or sees the sun or moon setting.[49] lCang skya then comments that since dreams have no essence they can be dispelled. This is achieved through the means taught in the teachings of the three cleansings: mantras of Amṛta kuṇḍalī; thinking of the meaning of selflessness; and making peaceful burnt offerings.[50]

Kirti Tsenshab began the initiation with an analysis of dreams.[51] With the large group assembled for the initiation, it was not possible to ask each person for his dreams. Kirti Tsenshab said that there is no reason to worry if one had bad dreams, as dreams are a form of emptiness. In any case, he said, if they were creating obstacles, sacrificial offering (*gtor ma*) could be offered to dispel them.

Motivation and maṇḍala offering

The maṇḍala offering is one of the highest expressions of ritualised devotion towards one's lama.[52] It is understood as a symbolic offering of the entire universe to the lama as a "fee" for the initiation.[53] Kirti Tsenshab propounded a less inclusive definition of what ought to be offered: all of one's possessions and good karma. Interestingly, he also did not specify that any offering should be made to him. Although this difference is slight, it could be interpreted as indicative of a new model of practice which is less centered on a close relationship with a lama.

Commenting on motivation and maṇḍala offering, lCang skya says:

> In order to request entering into the maṇḍala: the lama, indivisible from the main deity, is offered the requested maṇḍala [maṇḍal] offering.[54]

Kirti Tsenshab reminded the disciples that they had taken refuge in the Buddha, Dharma, and Sangha and committed themselves to develop bodhicitta. He emphasised this motivation as necessary for listening to the Kālacakra teachings and for contemplating and meditating on them. Next, he instructed the disciples to make a maṇḍala offering:

> . . . one makes an offering of all one's possessions and good karma with a maṇḍala, making this offering as a request for being able to enter the complete maṇḍala of Kālacakra.[55]

Entering the maṇḍala

Entering the maṇḍala is probably a Buddhist adaptation of an element found in Hindu tantric rituals. As described by Hoens, the Hindu tantric ritual was centered around a hut with four door openings, each to the four points of the compass. The hut represented the universe. A jar was placed in its center, and the main deity was summoned into it. Then the guru led the disciple, whose eyes were blindfolded, several times around the hut before stepping inside. The disciple sat on a special seat, with his face turned to the north-east. At this stage the guru removed the cover of the disciple's eyes and he was shown the jar, representing the main deity. The guru then told him the mantra, which the disciple had to recite daily. Through this rite the śakti of the deity was thought to descend upon the disciple. He then knelt down and threw flowers in the direction of the jar, around which a yantra had been drawn on the ground. The part of the yantra on which the flower fell determined the disciple's iśtadevatā, whose name he would bear.[56]

In lCang skya's manual, entering into the maṇḍala consists of two stages: the first is entering outside the curtain, which is the preliminary preparation; the second is entering inside.[57] Entry into the maṇḍala within the curtain contains three sections:

1. Entering inside, circumambulating, and prostrating;
2. The disciple taking a pledge (placing the disciple in samaya);
3. Bringing down the primordial awareness and performing a recitation of truth.

"Entering into the maṇḍala" consists of two aspects—one is physical, and one is symbolic. lCang skya says: "... although [the disciple] may actually have been placed within the curtain, it is also necessary [for him/her] to meditate on entering into the maṇḍala in meditation."[58] lCang skya then describes how the disciple enters into the maṇḍala[59] and requests the various Buddhas to confer initiation.

Further down, the text gives another example of the parallel physical and meditational elements. Before the section describing the vase initiation, we are told:

> Then the disciple at the eastern side of the maṇḍala should either in actuality or in meditation be established upon a wooden throne above the purified ground, painted with water colours or sand, above which is drawn a various-coloured lotus and a moon disk.[60]

In Kirti Tsenshab's ritual there was no trace of physically entering the maṇḍala—the entire process was only to be visualised.

Receiving the red blindfold and the flower

Bestowal of the blindfold and the flower is described in the *Vajrāvalī*'s "Bestowing the pledge water" (*dam tshig gyi chu sbyin pa'i cho ga*) section. In this section the guru instructs the disciple to bathe, put on red clothes, and cover his eyes with a blindfold.[61]

lCang skya says that the blindfold can be either made of silk or cloth and be either yellow or red. He explains that the eyes are blindfolded to perfect the mind. He further explains that it is inappropriate to see the complete maṇḍala until the master has removed the blindfold, once the flower has been thrown onto the maṇḍala.

The oral instruction is important here since it reveals the use of the blindfold both as a symbolic and real object. lCang skya's description makes it clear that the blindfold is actually tied on the disciple.[62] Kirti Tsenshab explained that the blindfold and the flower represent the garment and adornment of the deities.[63] He explained that the red blindfold symbolises the wisdom that realises emptiness. Explaining its purpose, he said: "This blindfold that we receive is to show that we are still outside of the maṇḍala. We have not entered it yet, so we are not able to see the maṇḍala. We wear this blindfold by placing it on our foreheads."[64]

Kirti Tsenshab explained that the flower symbolizes a garland of flowers, representing all five wisdoms that are received from the maṇḍala. As for the placement of the flower, Kirti Tsenshab said: "One can wear this flower, like wearing a flower garland. One can wear it on one's forehead, behind the ribbon, or on top of the head."[65]

Enquiring about family and aspiration

In the *Vajrāvalī* Abhayākaragupta describes how the guru leads the disciple to the eastern gate of the maṇḍala where the disciple is asked by an assistant, "Who are you?" Abhayākaragupta says that in response to that, the disciple should answer, "I am a fortunate one."

According to lCang skya, the disciple should answer that he is a "fortunate and worthy one," and that his motivation is to seek great bliss. Commenting on this answer, lCang skya says:

> In this reply, as for "fortunate and worthy" [it means that] since [you] are a son of the Victorious One [i.e., a Bodhisattva], you belong to the family of the Mahāyāna, and as for [acquiring] the great bliss, since you [belong to] the vehicle of the secret mantra, you know that you are suitable for entering into the maṇḍala.[66]

In this stage of Kirti Tsenshab's initiation, the disciples were asked to which family they belonged and what their aspiration was. In response they were instructed to answer that their family is a fortunate family, a family of Bodhisattvas who wish to attain the bliss of nirvāṇa. Further, they were told to say that they aspire to practice the stages of the path of the Mantrayāna to the point where they can attain the state of bliss and wisdom. Kirti Tsenshab explained that the reason for this requirement is that only those who are Bodhisattvas and who aspire to the attainment of bliss can receive the empowerment.

Taking vows and pledges

In the two lower tantras, one generally takes refuge as well as the common Mahāyāna precepts. In the Yoga tantras, one also takes on the commitments of the five Buddhas. In Highest Tantra, one takes the fourteen root and eight secondary vows, as well as the precepts unique to the tantra in question.[67]

This structure can be explained in two ways: the emic and the etic. The Tibetan tradition regards the taking of vows and commitments as a gradual path, closely connected with the disciple's level at each stage of his or her development.[68]

A historical explanation can provide an etic perspective. As Snellgrove has explained, the tantric vows are taken only in Anuttara-yoga tantra initiations since the lower tantras represent an earlier development in which tantric practice had not fully developed. Hence, at that time there were no formulated practices and vows that were needed to be taken.[69]

In Kirti Tsenshab's Kālacakra initiation the Bodhisattva vows were followed by the tantric vows. Kirti Tsenshab then summarised the tantric vows into the vows of the five Buddha families. Kirti Tsenshab did not present any of the unique Kālacakra vows.[70] Commenting on this at another occasion, he added:

> When we are dealing with an authorisation ritual (*rjes gnang*) in the Action or Performance Tantra, the vows that are given are only the Bodhisattva vows. When we are dealing with Yoga and Highest Yoga Tantra [initiations], Bodhisattva as well as tantric vows have to be given. Some tantras have some particular, extra vows. When the Kālacakra is given on the basis of the sand maṇḍala, then the particular Kālacakra vows also have to be given. But when empowerment is given on the basis of the printed maṇḍala and the *Vajrāvalī*, which is generic, then only the general tantric vows are given. The specific Kālacakra ones are not given on such an occasion.[71]

Garland consecration

The garland consecration is an important part of the initiation, during which the disciple throws a flower into the maṇḍala. The place where the flower falls determines the Buddha family to which the disciple will belong. It also determines the name that the disciple assumes. The acquisition of a new name is a very important part of initiations in general, since it is one of the elements that signifies a new birth.[72]

The *Vajrāvalī* mentions that if a disciple drops the flower outside the maṇḍala, the guru discontinues the consecration ceremony.[73] Abhayākaragupta then lists various names for male and female practitioners, relating to each Buddha family.

During this part of the initiation, Kirti Tsenshab thought it would be too time-consuming for each participant to cast a flower into the maṇḍala. Hence he asked seven people, representing all participants, to throw a flower onto the maṇḍala. There wasn't really a possibility of cancellation due to inappropriateness.

Vase initiation

Vase initiations (*bum pa'i dbang*) center on a vase, from which the disciple receives sacred water. The vase is then placed on the head of the disciple. Alternatively, water is poured on the disciple's head, or he drinks the water.[74] The vase initiation is conferred in all four tantra classes.[75] The vase empowerment introduces the practitioner to the divine aspects of the five aggregates and confers the power to realize this essence. This is achieved through realising the equivalence between the five aggregates and the five Buddhas.[76] By this process, faults and veils related to the body are dissipated, and the constituents of the personality become the corresponding pure aspects. This empowerment bestows the ability to meditate with one's own body in the form of the deity's body and will ultimately lead the practitioners to achieve the body of emanation.[77]

In Anuttara-yoga tantras, vase initiations are comprised of five,[78] six,[79] or seven primary consecrations.[80] Abhayākaragupta says in the *Vajrāvalī* that the six vase consecrations are called the "Knowledge Consecration" since through them one perfects the ability to counteract ignorance. The disciple who receives these consecrations becomes empowered to hear, perform, and explain the mantras and sādhanas.[81]

According to lCang skya, the vase initiation is comprised of two sections: the ordinary vajra disciple initiation which is divided into water, crown, vajra, bell, and name initiations and the special vajra master initiation.

Kirti Tsenshab's vase initiation followed the structure described by lCang skya. It was divided into two parts: the first part was the general vase initiation, which in turn was divided into five: the water, crown, vajra, bell, and name initiations. The second part was the vajra master vase initiation.[82] The structure of five plus one is significant since Kirti Tsenshab emphasised the symbolism of the number five.

Kirti Tsenshab explained each initiation as corresponding to one of the five Buddhas, purifying one of the five skandhas, transforming one of the five defilements, and resulting in achieving one of the five wisdoms. Kirti Tsenshab then requested the disciples to meditate that it is Kālacakra and the deities of the maṇḍala who actually bestow the initiation upon them and that he, in effect, is acting as their assistant.[83]

The Vajra Master consecration

According to the *Vajrāvalī*, the Vajra Master initiation is given only to those who have taken the vows of the Vajra Master.[84] Once one has received the Vajra Master initiation, one is empowered and required to perform rites of initiation for others as well as to consecrate statues, temples, etc. Prior to the conferral of the Vajra Master consecration, the guru performs the rite of giving the three pledges (*samaya*s). In the vajra pledge, the disciple salutes his master, perceiving him as Vajrasattva, and requests him to bestow the Vajra Master consecration. The guru allows the disciple to hold the vajra in his hand. In the bell pledge, after an exchange of verses between the guru and the disciple, the guru hands the bell to the disciple. In the mudrā pledge, the disciple holds the vajra and bell in a posture of embrace, while visualising Vajrasatva in sexual union with his consort.[85] The disciple then rings the bell. Next, the guru visualises all Tathāgatas and consorts to assemble in the sky and to consecrate the disciple by pouring water on his head. The guru then proclaims that he is granting the disciple the empowerment of all Buddhas and with water inundates him. After this, the guru visualises Akṣobhya sitting on the disciple's head and the other Tathāgatas with their consorts merging into his body. He worships the disciple with flowers and explains the meaning of the maṇḍala and its components once more.[86]

In the section about the bestowal of the three samayas, lCang skya shows how the meditations are linked to the actual experiences of the disciple:

> Meditate on this Dharmadhātu, which is called by the nature of the resultant Vajradhara.
>
> As for the secret meaning, it is called "the great vajra." Since HŪṂ symbolises the [deity's] heart, the "great vajra" [is] the heart vajra of the Buddhas. Meditate on this. This is the significance of the name. Recite: "Primordial awareness inseparable from emptiness, essence of the Victorious One's heart—this is the Secret Vajra." In order to be mindful of this, by grasping the vajra, the essential vajra nature—take hold [of it!]. Reciting this, entrusting [the vajra] into [the student's] right hand, you say, "It is explained as the wisdom song of all the Buddhas. Wishing for Supreme Victorious Enlightenment, you too should always hold [it]!" [i.e., the vajra].
>
> Thinking that the bell proclaims the sound [demonstrating that] all dharmas lack own being, essential nature, ring the bell, taking hold of it with, "This essential nature of the bell!" Recite that. As for the meaning of this verse: The wisdom of suchness of the great enlightenment of all Buddhas is meditated on as emptiness; through its own nature, its various spontaneous melodious sounds demonstrates the dharma to others. So, likewise, this bell also, is the object which is the same as wisdom's melody, symbolising the wisdom which understands emptiness. Therefore [it] symbolises the setting up of the supreme enlightenment of all the Victorious ones, the stainless wisdom meditated on as Emptiness.
>
> So, you too, should continually hold this bell which proclaims the sounds of emptiness and meditate on this wisdom which takes emptiness as its meditation object. To elaborate on this recitation, entrusting the bell into the [student's] left hand, you give the bell samaya. The disciple recites: "The essential nature of existence is pure, [but] the existence of this essen-

> tial nature is misunderstood. This purity in its own being, by the Supreme Being, [i.e., Buddha/Supreme practitioner] brings about the ultimate existence [i.e., nirvāṇa], VAJRA GHANṬA AḤ."[87]

According to Kirti Tsenshab, the Vajra Master initiation purifies the two subtler levels of consciousness. He explained that at the time of death:

> consciousness merges into circle consciousness, which merges into the subtle level of consciousness, which is the *vayu* or the inner air. . . . [The] aggregates other than form merge into consciousness, and consciousness merges into subtler levels of consciousness until it becomes a subtlest union of mind and air. And whatever good actions that one has accumulated, they will rest with that subtler level; and whatever bad actions one has accumulated—that will rest with the level of mind and air. This is what will proceed beyond death, accompanied by one's karma. Then, one's subtle level will obtain the new body—a new aggregate of form—and then will develop within that. . . . So this subtlest level of mind and air—when that is purified, then at the time of the result, that will become the sixth of the Buddha families—that sixth will be Vajrasatva or Vajradhara.[88]

Explaining the subtler levels of consciousness, Kirti Tsenshab gave the following explanation:

> This very subtle level of mind and air can first of all be explained in an example. If you're in a country, you have an electricity power plant and from there the electricity goes to all individual homes. In the individual homes, if everyone turns off their lights, there is no light in their homes, but the power of electricity is still there in the central power plant. So in that way, if there is that subtlest level of mind and air and it obtains a body, an aggregate of form, then can function these three levels of mental arising: the mental activity, identification, and sensation. So just like if you have wire that is connecting the house to the electricity station, then the lights will come on, the same way in the body, the sensation, identification, and mental activity will occur, as will also occur the coarse level of consciousness. These depend upon the subtle level of consciousness, in which are present the potentials of karma, whether it is good or bad: the good karma that will bring an experience of happiness and bad karma that will carry an experience of suffering, those are carried in that subtlest level of mind and air.

Kirti Tsenshab went on to explain that after death the consciousness of the new life arises from that subtlest level of the mind and air. That is why all highest yoga tantras, including Kālacakra, have Vajrasattva at the beginning of the practice. Vajrasattva is the source, the emanation of all Buddha families. For this reason the initiation of the Vajra Master is performed through Vajrasattva or Vajradhara.

Stabilising the vase initiation

At the end of the vase initiation Kirti Tsenshab performed three additional ritual components: the bestowal of the eye ointment, the mirror, and the bow and arrow. He explained that the purpose of these objects is to stabilise the blessing of the vase initiation. Mori has suggested that these rites have their origin in earlier layers of tantra, specifically in the *Mahāvairocanabhisambodhisūtra,* belonging to the *Caryā* tantra class.[89]

Application of eye ointment

The application of the eye ointment (*mig sman*) promotes the acquisition of knowledge and the supernormal powers of the "Divine Eye" (*lha'i mig*). The "Divine Eye" is classified among the supernatural knowledges (*mngon shes*). According to Bentor, the opening of the eye of the disciple may derive from a pretantric ritual of eye opening, which is employed in various contexts.[90] The attainment of the "Divine Eye," which enables one to see all the worlds, belongs to the eight siddhis which are common to both Buddhist and Hindu traditions (*thun mong gi dngos grub brgyad*).[91]

The *Vajrāvalī* describes how the guru uses a golden spoon to smear an ointment made of butter and honey on the eyelids of the disciple. He then recites the same mantra quoted by Tsong-kha-pa.[92]

Kirti Tsenshab referred only to the knowledge aspect of the eye ointment, explaining that the eye ointment symbolises one's vision becoming clearer, dispelling the darkness of ignorance. The application of the eye ointment was only discussed, not actually performed.[93]

The mirror consecration

The *Vajrāvalī* describes the guru holding up a mirror and showing it to the disciple, saying: "All existences, just like reflections in a mirror, are pure and unstained."[94] The guru explains that all phenomena resemble reflections, and the deity Vajrasattva, who rests in the heart of all beings, is the mirror in which they appear. With the performance of this ritual, the disciple should come to the realisation that no entity possesses an intrinsic reality and then would proceed to act with this knowledge for the benefit of all beings.[95]

Kirti Tsenshab explained that the mirror is offered so that one would have a clear perception of reality and would be able to see the empty nature of phenomena. Previously in the initiation, he had used the mirror simile to explain that the disciples imagine the image in the mirror is washed, and thus they are being washed. In the context here, he used the mirror simile to demonstrate the empty nature of phenomena. These two uses of the mirror simile are often alluded to in Buddhist scholastic works.[96] The first is found predominantly in the Yogācāra School.[97] The second, where the mirror is a simile for the emptiness of all phenomena, prevails in Madhyamaka literature.[98] Their significance in the initiation is that they allow a direct *experience* of these two scholastic aspects of the mirror metaphor. Once again, as there were many participants, this rite was not actually performed but imagined by the participants.

Bow and arrow

The *Vajrāvalī* describes how the guru shoots arrows in the various directions in order to remove all obstacles from the disciple's path.[99]

According to Kirti Tsenshab, the bow symbolises the practice of method, and the arrow represents wisdom. By bringing the bow and arrow together, one is able to fire the arrow at the target. In the same way, when there is union of wisdom and method, one will be able to attain the direct perception of emptiness.

Secret initiation

The secret empowerment, as described by Abhayākaragupta, includes an act of sexual yoga.[100] The *Vajrāvalī* states that a ritual feast is to be served. Then the disciple leaves the feast with the girl who will be his consort, goes to the guru, gives the consort to the guru, requests for the secret consecration, and returns to the group outside. Next, the guru performs the devatā yoga of the principal deity of the maṇḍala and performs sexual yoga with the girl. The disciple's face is covered out of fear that he may lose faith. He kneels down and offers a flower. According to the *Vajrāvalī,* the guru then gives the disciple his semen, which the disciple places on his tongue and swallows. The disciple is advised to imagine that the semen is the bodhicitta nectar. After that the consort gives him a "drop of the pollen of all Tathāgatas,"[101] which he should swallow in the same way. The *Vajrāvalī* states that the actual performers should be concealed from the attendants by a curtain.

Much ink has been spilt on the issue whether sexual acts described in tantric texts were intended to be actually performed or whether they are to be understood symbolically.[102]

Kirti Tsenshab made no reference at all to any sexual component. The Fourteenth Dalai Lama, on the other hand, has commented on this point, saying that sexual practices are to be taken symbolically. When conferring the Kālacakra initiation, the Dalai Lama has also mentioned that sexual deeds may actually be performed by those who are of great spiritual attainment. He further noted, however, that in his lifetime he has never met anyone with such degree of accomplishment. Kalu Rinpoche, discussing the secret knowledge empowerment, explained that it is transmitted by wisdom-knowledge (*rig ma*), a young woman painted, for the sake of the ritual, on a small card.

When he discussed the prohibition of sexual acts in the Kālacakra practice, the Dalai Lama referred to the restricts adopted by Atīśa (Jo bo).[103] Atīśa is known in Tibetan historiography as the person who preached against sexual practices and reintroduced celibacy for monks. In his *Lamp for the Path* (*Bodhipathapradīpa*; *Byang chub lam gyi sgron ma*) and his auto-commentary (*Bodhimārgadīpapañjikā*; *Byang chub lam gyi sgron ma'i dka' 'grel*) Atīśa clearly states that the secret initiation and the knowledge wisdom (insight) initiation should not be taken by celibate monks.[104] This position implies that these two initiations involved sexual practices. The basis Atīśa used for his prohibition is the *Kālacakratantra*.[105]

The *Kālackaratantra* indeed warns against taking part in sensual pleasures, since this reveals one's lack of understanding of the true nature of emptiness. It specifies that engagement in sexual practices does not lead to the attainment of primordial wisdom but only to indulgence in sensual pleasures and hence to rebirth in hell.[106]

Kirti Tsenshab informed the disciples that this initiation takes place with blindfolds on, by saying:

> We receive the blessed white substance and the blessed red substance. The white substance from the father and the red substance from the mother. By receiving these we experience bliss such as we have never experienced before and through that we receive the secret empowerment.
>
> . . . by tasting these blessed substances, when receiving them on one's tongue one experiences bliss like one has never experienced before and a bliss which has the nature of primordial emptiness. It is through receiving these blessed substances from Kālacakra and consort that we receive the secret empowerment.

Following this commentary, the disciples were told they could remove their blindfolds. Kirti Tsenshab explained that this empowerment purifies the speech.[107] There was no mention of any sexual element.

Knowledge wisdom initiation

In the *Vajrāvalī* the guru gives the girl with whom he copulated to the disciple.[108] The guru tells the disciple that he should enjoy "true bliss," and the disciple conducts an act of sexual yoga with his consort and experiences the four joys.

In Kirti Tsenshab's empowerment, the disciples were told to visualise themselves as Kālacakra with four faces and twenty-four arms in union with a yellow consort. Then the disciples were told to take their blindfolds off. Kirti Tsenshab explained that the purpose of this initiation is to purify the mind, to enable them to do certain completion stage practises, including Mahāmudrā practice, and to attain the wisdom of Dharmakāya.

Word initiation

The *Vajrāvalī* says on the fourth empowerment:

> [The fourth consecration is] exactly the supreme wisdom, the mind of enlightenment which has sprouted and growing up by the contemplation, truth which has transcended obscurations, its very essence is inconceivability in terms of all dharma, it possesses the nature of great Vajradhara whose true nature is the mahāmudrā which is conjoined with the seven elements.[109]

According to the *Vajrāvalī*, in the fourth empowerment the guru recites an exposition of the nature of the four blisses, featuring quotes from various tantras.[110] The *Vimalaprabhā* points out that unlike other tantras of its class, which equate the fourth initiation with the third, the Kālacakra tradition reveals in full its contents and implications.[111]

Kirti Tsenshab explained that this fourth initiation leads to the attainment of the essence kāya, and thus the four kāyas are realised. Kirti Tsenshab referred to Tsong-kha-pa's *Lam rim chen mo* which explains that the ability to attain all four kāyas is an ability shared by beginners on the path. The union of mind and air exists within every individual, and through the practice of Mantrayāna this very subtle mind and air can be transformed. This transformation happens through the sound of the mantra. First it becomes *saṃbhogakāya*, and then it is transformed into *nirmāṇakāya*. Next, the emptiness of this air and mind becomes the essence *kāya,* and the wisdom that realizes this essence becomes the wisdom *dharmakāya*.[112]

The *Vajrāvalī* describes a number of sections which follow the fourth (word) consecration that were not performed by Kirti Tsenshab. These include the Vow of Consort, the Vow of Vajra, and the Vow of Conduct.[113]

Prophesy/ Permission

In the "Prophesy" section the *Vajrāvalī* describes how the guru adopts the Buddha's prediction posture and prophesies the disciple's liberation. Next he gives him formal permission and encouragement to practise, communicates various rules of discipline, requests and receives his fee, and explains the inner meaning of all the consecrations. In the "Permission" section of the *Vajrāvalī*, the guru is described as giving the disciples a dharma wheel, a conch shell, a sacred text, and a bell.[114]

Kirti Tsenshab explained that following the completion of the four initiations, the bestowal of symbols and prophesy creates an auspicious interdependence between them. The symbols represent the five Buddha families, and the prophesy maintains that in the future one would have the same ability as these five Buddhas. The symbols include the dharma wheel, a conch, a text of the tantra, and a bell. These items were not actually bestowed but were imagined to be given. Kirti Tsenshab explained that the giving of the dharma wheel means that the disciples will be able to benefit beings wherever they go. The conch symbolises the sound that declares emptiness; the text means that the disciples will be able to benefit other beings by teaching the meaning of the mantra, while the bell represents the sound of emptiness.

The practice

Discussing the practice duties required of the participants following the initiations, Kirti Tsenshab recommended that practitioners should recite the mantra of Kālacakra every day in addition to the wishing prayer. He said there is no specific requirement to chant them any certain number of times. Kirti Tsenshab also indicated that it would be beneficial to conduct the six-session guru yoga. Better still would be if one had the opportunity to do a retreat and carry out the practice of the nine-deity Kālachakra together with the Kālachakra six-session guru yoga. Kirti Tsenshab also mentioned that it would be beneficial to accumulate a hundred thousand repetitions of the Kālacakra mantra.

Since his audience was mostly lay practitioners, Kirti Tsenshab explained how one could ease the demands of the practice. For instance, the mantra of bringing down the wisdom as part of the retreat has a long form and a short form. But since, he said, the long form would be too difficult to recite, he recommended reciting the shorter one. After the recitation, one should carry out a Kālacakra fire puja. Again, Kirti Tsenshab conceded that this would be too difficult and he hence recommended doing the fire puja of Vajraḍākinī instead. Kirti Tsenshab said that this practice would suffice to compensate for any error or omissions during the practice.

Kirti Tsenshab also introduced more basic demands with respect to the sādhana. The full Kālacakra sādhana is based on the maṇḍala of body, speech, and mind and includes 634 deities. Kirti Tsenshab said he thought it was not translated into English and even if it were, it would be too difficult to practice. Next he spoke of a middle-sized sādhana which includes only the mind maṇḍala.[115] The sādhana he actually recommended for practice, the nine-deity sādhana,[116] is yet shorter and would be much easier to practice, he said. Of the many versions that exist of the nine-deity sādhana, Kirti Tsenshab recommended the one by Ling Rinpoche.[117] Kirti Tsenshab said that this text would be the best for practice as it is very easy and very short. This text is based on a six-session guru yoga text and adapted to the practice of Kālacakra by Ling Rinpoche (1903-1983), the senior tutor of the Fourteenth Dalai Lama, and the Dalai Lama himself. It represents a system of practice devised by the Fourteenth Dalai Lama and Ling Rinpoche just before the first Kālacakra initiation in the West for those who would not be able to do a full sādhana.[118] In later years the Dalai Lama himself has been paying less attention to this text, and in Graz 2002 he even went as far as *discouraging* any practice of Kālacakra, maintaining that it may even cause damage.[119]

Contemporary empowerments: continuity and change

To conclude this overview, I would like to discuss a number of points which have required a reinterpretation by Kirti Tsenshab and other contemporary lamas. These include the redefinition of secrecy, the move from a personal to group initiations, conducting the initiation for lay practitioners, and the interpretation of various physical aspects of the ritual as symbolic.

Redefinition of secrecy

In the *Vajrāvalī,* keeping the teachings secret is a point which is greatly stressed. It repeats the pledge of secrecy four times[120] and issues fearsome threats for those who fail to do so. lCang skya too includes a terrifying physical description of the punishment of the disciple who reveals the secrets:

> Holding the vajra on the [disciple's] head and ringing the bell, recite: "This vajra samaya of yours—if you speak of this to anyone—your head will be destroyed."
>
> The meaning of the recitation is that the secrets are not to be proclaimed.[121]

Since books with various Kālacakra teachings have been appearing in English and other languages, the restriction of revealing texts only to the initiated has in effect become less plausible. In 1982 Serkong Rinpoche in oral teachings on Kālacakra expressed a pragmatic view on this issue. According to him, one must be skillful and find a middle way between not explaining the teachings at all, and thus face the danger of their dying out, and circulating the teachings too much and thus face the danger of their degeneration.[122]

Through the years the Fourteenth Dalai Lama has adopted a pragmatic stance in this regard, allowing more publications of previously secret teachings. His policy maintains a preference to publicise accurate and authentic teachings rather than to face the proliferation of teachings which are fundamentally wrong. In recent years the Fourteenth Dalai Lama has often made the point that Kālacakra's secrecy is maintained through its profoundness. This argument maintains that the Kālacakra reaches each practitioner in his/her own level. The secret levels can only be understood by practitioners who have profound understanding of the teachings.[123]

The incentive of keeping the teachings secret was presented by Kirti Tsenshab as a matter of speed: keeping the pledge of secrecy will determine how quickly one reaches attainment. Kirti Tsenshab did not specify any active retribution against those who transgress this pledge.

Personal vs. group

Some parts of the ritual suggest that they were performed for one disciple or a small group. Since Kirti Tsenshab performed the initiation for a large group (about fifty people), these parts needed to be adapted. This applied, for instance, to the analysis of dreams; the garland consecration; the mirror consecration; and so forth. Usually, within the group setting, these initiation components were not actually performed but only discussed. Some one-to-one interactions that appear in the *Vajrāvalī* were omitted altogether. For example, the *Vajrāvalī*'s "Entry of the Disciple into the Maṇḍala" section describes the disciple as standing in front of the maṇḍala. The master then asks the disciple about the appearance of the maṇḍala. The disciple, his eyes covered, specifies the colour which he sees while facing the maṇḍala. On this basis the guru assesses the accomplishment (or the prospects for accomplishment) of the disciple.[124] Such one-to-one interactions were excluded from the group initiation.

Monastic vs. lay

The initiation texts cited above assume the practitioner is a monastic disciple and, more specifically, a monastic disciple with a tantric background.[125] lCang skya describes the disciple before entering the maṇḍala as follows:

> Thus [you] sit before your own lama, with calm and disciplined thoughts, being appropriately dressed with the upper garment placed over one shoulder, etc.[126]

After the lama asks the disciple about his background and motivation, he replies that he is a "fortunate and worthy one," that his motivation is to seek the great bliss:

In this reply, as for "fortunate and worthy" (it means that) since (you) are a son of the Victorious One [i.e., a Bodhisattva], you belong to the family of the Mahāyāna and as for [acquiring] the great bliss, since you [belong to] the vehicle of the secret mantra, you know that you are suitable for entering into the maṇḍala.[127]

In Kirti Tsenshab's initiation the majority of participants were lay practitioners. The presence of a lay audience prompted Kirti Tsenshab to allow the initiation to be taken as a blessing. This option accommodated people who did not attend the initiation for its empowerment, but for its blessing. Strictly speaking this option does not appear in the tantric texts, but since participants often request it, lamas have begun to include it in the rite.[128]

The option of taking the initiation as a blessing was raised in several parts of the initiation: when the Bodhisattva vows were taken or in the visualisation processes. Disciples who took the initiation as a blessing could choose not to take the Bodhisattva vows. The option of those taking the initiation as a blessing was also raised when disciples were told to visualise the deity Kālacakra: There were those who wished to receive the entire empowerment and others who only wished to receive the initiation as a blessing. The first were instructed to visualise themselves as Kālacakra. The second were instructed to visualise Kālacakra above their heads.

Kirti Tsenshab, like the Dalai Lama, tended to confer higher initiations to everyone present. Commenting on this, Kirti Tsenshab explained that even though the ones who actually practice the completion stage are very few, he still extends the higher initiations to everyone because "it's not nice to say in the initiation, alright, only you will stay for the completion stage part. So, it is all given to everyone."[129] He further commented:

> It is like in any education: there are the primary levels, then the more advanced, then university, and there too, there are the lower levels and the higher ones. In teaching the Kālacakra it is as if all levels are being taught together at the same time. The Dalai Lama has said that it is good for anyone to attend, even small children, even if they don't understand anything that is being said.[130]

Thus all participants, whether monastic or lay, tantric practitioners or not, receive all types of initiations, the ones for the generation stage as well as the ones for the completion stage. Some take them as real initiations, and others take them as a blessing.

Symbolic vs. physical

Sanderson has argued that almost everything concrete in Vajrayāna empowerments is "non-Buddhist in origin" but "entirely Buddhist in its function."[131] The above description may be seen as a further step in that direction. Kirti Tsenshab's adaptations do away with many of the concrete, physical elements—some of them pre-Buddhist.

In the Kālacakra literature, the emphasis on the symbolic nature of the initiation implements is greater than in the more generic Abhayākaragupta tradition. The first seven Kālacakra initiations propose the visualised implements to be generated in the minds of the disciple and only then employed in the path of the purification. In the four higher initiations it is the disciple's *experience* of emptiness and bliss that serves as the instrument of purification.[132] Compared to the Abhayākaragupta tradition, Kirti Tsenshab's integration of the two systems placed greater emphasis on the meditational aspect.

The interpretation of tantric vows, which often appear to contradict monastic and even lay vows, troubled Buddhist thinkers during the last millennium. Abhyākaragupta proposes that all Buddhist practitioners, whether layperson or monk, may take the tantric vows and receive all consecrations, including those involving sexual intercourse, provided they have achieved realisation of emptiness.[133] Atiśa disagrees, saying that the sexual practices are reserved for married householders, and that monks should receive them in a symbolic or mental form.[134] Others have shifted this contradiction to the hermeneutical plane, introducing new meanings to the terms *neyārtha* and *nītārtha*.[135] The general trend was to modify the ritual to exclude the controversial elements.[136] Kirti Tsenshab's instructions take this one step further: he did not mention sexual practices. In this sense the sexual practices become irrelevant both to married householders and to monks.[137] Other parts of the initiation were also interpreted symbolically. A number of sections which *prima facie* imply a physical component have been left only with the symbolic and meditational aspects of the ritual.

Concluding remarks

Although adhering quite closely not only to the structure of the initiation but also to its various parts as described in the texts, Kirti Tsenshab introduced several significant adaptations to the way he performed the Kālacakra initiation. These adaptations are largely the result of the popularisation of the Kālacakra in exile, both amongst Tibetans and Westerners. It is within this context that the issue of secrecy is redefined and that the rituals and the practices are transformed to fit not only the tantric monastic environment but also to become available to an increasing number of lay practitioners.

While massive initiations of the kind described above are not new and are not specific to the Tibetans' presence in exile, there is a shift in emphasis: whereas Kālacakra in the past was mostly a high practice reserved for monastic tantric practitioners, today it enjoys a broad appeal and has become a form of popular religion.

Displaced in exile and constantly traveling in the West, many prominent lamas have been performing initiations outside the "traditional" monastic context. The new teachings cater to contemporary practitioners, yearning for spiritual bliss but unable to perform the traditional practices. Lay practitioners are allowed to focus on shorter practices or to perform high practices that were previously restricted to the most advanced.

The separation of a teaching from its original context, with its designated temporal flow and space, raises some interesting questions for the future development of initiation ritual. What is the effect of a cyber-cast ritual? Can one be truly initiated through cyberspace? The current position held even by reformist lamas insists that one cannot be initiated through such ritual. But where does the border lie? Large initiations, especially in the West, may involve several spaces and the use of large screens in addition to or sometimes replacing a direct view or a shared space with the lama. What is then the significance of a screened ritual in the same complex in relationship to a cyber-cast one? Perhaps the most substantial question to be observed would be whether these changes in form are also bringing about a change in essence.

Endnotes

1. I would like to thank Edward Henning, Cathy Cantwell, Peter Roberts, and Voula Zarpani for all their help in preparing this material.

2. The account here is mostly based on a ritual conducted in France in October 1999.

3. The common view amongst most Western scholars is that lCang skya Ngag dbang blo bzang is the first lCang skya Khutuktu, since he was the first to hold the title of Khutuktu. The view held by Tibetologists in China, however, is that the title originated from lCang skya, Grags-pa-'od- zer, who was born at the Zhangjia village (Huzhu county, Qinghai province) and passed away in 1641. The word *lCang skya* derives from the Chinese "Zhangjia" (the Zhang family). According to this view, Ngag dbang blo bzang chos ldan became the second lCang skya. On the various lists of previous incarnations of lCang skyas, see Smith, 2001. pp. 145-146. See also Wang, 1995. pp. 40-44.

4. The edition used in this chapter appears in the second volume of lCang skya's collected works (*bKa' 'bum*), appended to the Peking edition of the Tibetan Tripitaka. TTP, Peking edition, text no. 6237, vol. 163.

5. Snellgrove, 1987. p. 213. Snellgrove points out that in Buddhist tantric practice, the term "initiation" is more fitting to translate the Sanskrit *praveśa*, act of entry, especially when referring to the act of entering a maṇḍala.

6. Ōyama, 1961. p. 125.

7. Snellgrove, 1987. p. 234 and Ōyama, 1961.

8. Ōyama, 1961. p. 130.

9. Hopkins, p. 66, in the Fourteenth Dalai Lama and Hopkins, [1985] 1999.

10. On Hindu tantric consecrations, see Hoens, 1965 and Bharati, [1965] 1993. pp. 185-198.

11. Kirti Tsenshab, oral teachings, October 1999. On the Fourteenth Dalai Lama's views on initiations, see the Fourteenth Dalai Lama, 1995. pp. 105-109.

12. On Abhayākaragupta, see: Bühnemann, 1991; Bühnemann, 1992; Chandra, 1977. pp. 1-4; Mori, 1997. Vol. 1, pp. 14-20; Singh, 1968.

13. 'Gos lo gzhon nu dpal. [1949] 1996. pp. 760-761, 795 and 1046.

14. Singh, 1968. p. 183.

15. Mori, 1997. Vol. 1, p. 15.

16. Interview with Kirti Tsenshab, October 2, 1999.

17. 'Gos lo gzhon nu dpal, [1949] 1996. p. 1046.

18. Mori, 1997. Vol. 1. p. 15.

19. TTP, Peking edition. No. 3961. Vol. 80. For a critical edition, see Mori, 1997. Vols. 1 and 2.

20. See Mori, 1997. Vol. 1, pp. 19-20.

21. 'Gos lo gzhon nu dpal, [1949] 1996. p. 1047.

22. Mori, 1997. Vol. 1, pp. 12 and 24.

23. dus kyi 'khor lo'i dkyil 'khor la ni 'dir brjod pa'i rgyud gzhan ma lus par gsungs pa'i cho ga rnams las| nyi ma'i shing rta la sogs pa 'dul ba'i don du bya ba mi mthun par gsungs so|| section 86, in Mori's critical edition of the *Vajrāvalī*. In: Mori, 1997. Vol. 2, p. 322.

24. zhes lhag par mos pa bstan pas rgyud gzhan gyi cho gas kyang rab gnas la sogs pa bya ba mi 'gal te| mngon par 'dod pa sgrub par byed do|| section 86 in Mori's critical edition of the *Vajrāvalī*, ibid.

25. zhes pas dus kyi 'khor lo'i bya ba spos pa dor nas dkyil 'khor gyi thig gdab pa tsam brjod par bya'o|| ibid. See also lCang skya, fol. 207a.

26. See Orofino, 1994; Gnoli and Orofino, 1994.

27. The Fourteenth Dalai Lama does not always perform the four "higher" and four "higher than higher" initiations. This method is described at length in: Fourteenth Dalai Lama and Hopkins, [1985] 1999.

28. Interview with Kirti Tsenshab. Colony and Bianca, 1998.

29. Gendun Drub, 1982. pp. 116-117.

30. Ibid.

31. lCang skya, fol. 171b, lines 6-8.

32. lCang skya, fol. 172a, line 7; 172b, line 1.

33. lCang skya, fol. 172a, lines 2-4.

34. lCang skya, fol. 172b, line 6; 173a, line 3.

35. lCang skya, fol. 171b, line 6; 173a, line 5.

36. lCang skya, fol. 172a, line5: ". . . [even if one has] a collection of guitars and other things [instruments], without a musician it is not suitable to play [them]."

37. See Fendall, 1997. p. 34. As Tāranātha's exposition is given within the general context of the *Kālacakratantra*, it is significant that the method of the seven consecrations as a child is not even mentioned. A plausible explanation for this could be that the seven plus four method was mostly practiced within the *dGe lugs pa*s, whilst the fourfold structure of conducting the Kālacakra was more common amongst the *Jo nang pa*s.

38. Mori, 1997. Vol. 1, pp. 100-101.

39. lCang skya, fol. 171a, line 5.

40. Chap. 3, verse 105. Andresen's translation in: Andresen, 1997.

41. lCang skya, fol. 173a, line 6.

42. The Fourteenth Dalai Lama, Introduction. In Fourteenth Dalai Lama, Tsong-kha-pa, and Hopkins, 1977. p. 77. The Fourteenth Dalai Lama then illustrated the type of trouble which may arise: by giving too many initiations a lama could be causing many to fall from their vows and pledges and thus open their way to hell.

43. The Fourteenth Dalai Lama, 1991 [1985]. p. xix. This text was written in Tibetan by the Fourteenth Dalai Lama in 1980 for the benefit of the participants of the first Kālacakra initiation given in the West, in 1981 in Madison, Wisconsin.

44. The Fourteenth Dalai Lama, Kālacakra initiation, Sarnath, December 29, 1990.

45. Kirti Tsenshab, oral teachings, London, 1996. The gender issue with respect to Vajrayāna initiations in general is one which still needs to be seriously analyzed.

46. In the *Vajrāvalī* the analysis of dreams is described in the "Entry of the Master" (*slob dpon 'jug pa'i cho ga*) section. See Mori, 1997. Vol. 1. p. 92.

47. ri la lhung ba la sogs pas mtshan pa'i rmi lam ngan pa rnams ni 'khyil pa'i sngags kyis bsrungs la| Mori's critical edition. Mori, 1997. Vol. 2. p. 394. On protection from bad dreams with mantras of Amṛta kuṇḍalī, see also Abhayākaragupta's *Abhiśekaprakaraṇa*, Skorupski, trans. 1999. pp. 6-7.

48. Riding these animals and traveling south are common negative signs in Indian dream theory, both Hindu and Buddhist. See Young, 1999. pp. 66 and 209-210, note 64.

49. lCang skya, fol. 170b, line 3; 171a, line 1.

50. Ibid, fol. 171a, lines 1-4.

51. On the significance of dreams in the night before the initiation in Hindu tantric initiations, see Bharati, 1993. p. 196. For an analysis of the place of dreams in Tibetan Buddhism in general, see Young, 1999.

52. See Beyer, 1978. pp. 167-226.

53. See Kongtrul, 1977. pp. 92-105 and Samuel, 1993. pp. 262-263 and 600.

54. lCang skya, fol. 171a, lines 6-7.

55. Kirti Tsenshab, oral teachings, October 1999.

56. See Hoens, 1965. pp. 76-77.

57. lCang skya, fol. 173b, line 1.

58. lCang skya, fol. 175a, lines 1-2.

59. He does not specify here whether he means physically or mentally.

60. lCang skya, fol. 180b, line 6.

61. See Mori, 1997. Vol. 1, p. 92.

62. The blindfold is put on: lCang skya, fol. 173b, lines 4-5. It is taken off: fol. 179b, line 4.

63. In other consecration rites the practitioner puts on the deities' clothes in order to facilitate the visualisation as the deity. These, which are called initiation implements (*dbang rdzas*), seem to have belonged to the initiations of the lower tantras before being adopted by the Anuttara-yoga tantras. See Bentor, 1996. p. 140, note 99. See also Snellgrove, 1987. pp. 233-235.

64. Kirti Tsenshab, oral teaching, October 1999.

65. Kirti Tsenshab, ibid.

66. lCang skya, fol. 174a, line 3.

67. Lati Rinpoche's commentary in Gendun Drub, 1982. p. 124.

68. Dorje, 1991. Dorje describes the vows and commitments according to the rNying-ma school, but with regards to this point, the same can be said about the other schools as well.

69. Snellgrove, 1987. pp. 232-234.

70. There are twenty-five Kālacakra vows, which are mentioned in the *Vimalaprabhā*, chap. 3, verses 93 and 94. The twenty-five Kālacakra vows discuss twenty-five modes of behaviour that are to be guarded against: five ill deeds, five secondary ill-deeds, five killings, five wrong thoughts, and five desires. See Cozort, 1986. pp. 37-38 and Broido [1988] 1993.

71. Kirti Tsenshab, Delhi, 2002.

72. See, for instance, Hoens, 1965. p. 77.

73. Mori, 1997. Vol. 1, p. 94.

74. See Cozort, 1986. pp. 162-163, based on oral teachings given by Tri Rinpoche, July 3, 1980. In Hindu tantric consecrations, the guru also pours water or wine out of a jar onto the disciple. See Hoens, 1965.

75. See Cozort, 1986. p. 34. Tāranātha explains in his *Dpal Dus kyi 'khor lo'i chos bskor gyi byung khungs nyer mkho* that the vase initiation, along with the crown initiation, was taught as part of the Kriyā tantra. In Cārya tantras, mudrā and name initiations were added to those two. In Yoga tantras, initiations included were water, crown, vajra, and bell, as well as name and *vrata* (*brtul zhugs*) empowerments, followed by the *vajrācārya* empowerment and the final support empowerments (*mtha' rten*). See Fendall, 1997. pp. 33-34.

76. See Kalu Rinpoche, 1995. p. 48.

77. Ibid, pp. 53-54.

78. See Sopa [1985] 1991. p. 95. Sopa mentions the same five that were conducted by Kirti Tsenshab: water, crown, vajra, bell, and name.

79. Discussed by bTsong kha pa: *dBang gi don gyi de nyid rab tu gsal ba*, TTP, Peking edition, vol. 160, text no. 6195, fol. 68b, line 6.

80. See Snellgrove, 1987. p. 243.

81. See in Skorupski, 1999. p. 12, note 13.

82. These are in fact the same six consecrations which are discussed by Advayavajra in his discussion of the vase consecration, which are the above *five plus one* as conducted by Kirti Tsenshab: water, crown, vajra, bell, name, and master. See Snellgrove, 1987. p. 229.

83. This point is also mentioned in the *Vajrāvalī*. See Mori, 1997. Vol. 1, p. 94.

84. The following description is based on Sanderson, 1994, and on Mori, 1997. Vol. 1, p. 96.

85. This mudrā is called *jñānamudrā*.

86. Sanderson, 1994. p. 89.

87. lCang skya, fol. 187b, line 3 to fol. 188a, line 4.

88. Kirti Tsenshab, oral teachings, October 1999.

89. Mori, 1997. Vol. 1, p. 101.

90. Bentor, 1996. pp. 33-39 and 287-288.

91. Rigzin, 1986. p. 121; Beyer, [1973] 1978. pp. 252-253.

92. "Just as the lords of medicine removed the blindness of the world, so will the conquerors, oh, son, remove the cataract of ignorance from your eyes." Mori's translation. Mori, 1997. Vol. 1, p. 96-97.

93. See also Hopkins, pp. 127-128 in the Fourteenth Dalai Lama and Hopkins [1985] 1999.

94. Mori, 1997. Vol. 1, p. 97.

95. Sanderson, 1994. p. 89.

96. See Bentor, 1995; Hopkins, pp. 127-128 in the Fourteenth Dalai Lama and Hopkins [1985] 1999; Wayman, 1971 and Wayman, 1974.

97. See Bentor, 1995. For an example of this in Chinese Buddhism, see the description of the initiation given by Ōyama. There the mirror is used for "removing the membrane of ignorance" covering the disciple's mind. Ōyama, 1961. p. 129.

98. See Wayman, 1974 and Bentor, 1995. The same twofold meaning is found in the mirror initiation which constitutes part of the consecration ritual described by Bentor: ". . . phenomena (dharmas) are like reflected images [arising in a mirror] clean, pure, uncontaminated, ungrasped and inexpressible . . . As in a mirror, clear, pure, uncontaminated, myself Rdo-rje-sems-dpa' (Vajrasattva), the essence of all Buddhas, oh son, dwell in your heart . . ." See Bentor, 1996. p. 130.

99. Sanderson, 1994. p. 89. Mori, 1997. Vol. 1, p. 101. See also Panchen Otrol, n.d. p. 71 and the Fourteenth Dalai Lama and Hopkins [1985] 1999. pp. 342.

100. The description of the secret initiation in the *Vajrāvalī* is based on Sanderson 1994, p. 90 and Mori, 1997. Vol. 1, p. 97.

101. Sanderson, 1994. p. 90.

102. The most comprehensive on this topic is still Kværne, 1975.

103. Dalai Lama, oral teachings, Bloomington, 1999.

104. According to Gnoli and Orofino this restriction did not exist before Atīśa's time. Gnoli and Orofino, 1994. p. 81.

105. See verse 64 and 65 of the *Bodhipathapradīpa (Lamp for the Path)*. For two translations of the text see: Davidson, 1995 and Sherburne, 2000. pp. 1-20. For Atīśa's commentary on these two verses see *Byang chub lam gyi sgron ma'i dka' 'grel*, sDe dge 3948, fols. 289a-290a.

106. *Kālacakratantra*, chap. 4, vv. 217-218. See Wallace, 1995. p. 24.

107. Kalu Rinpoche explained, in relation to the secret empowerment, that in the subtle channels of the body a subtle energy circulates that is linked with speech, whose totally pure expression corresponds to the body of perfect experience (*sambhogakāya*). The secret empowerment is conferred in order to achieve this purity. With this empowerment, all impure subtle winds are transformed into pure winds. He further mentioned that in order to undertake this purification, exercises on winds and recitations of mantras are used. Through the secret empowerment, the disciple receives the power to consider all sounds as the deity's mantra. Kalu Rinpoche further explained that this empowerment is transmitted by consecrated alcohol that becomes ambrosia contained in a skullcap, from which the disciple drinks a few drops. He explained that this empowerment purifies faults and veils related to speech, bestows the power to recite the deity's mantra, and allows one to ultimately achieve the body of perfect experience (*sambhogakāya*). Kalu Rinpoche, based on oral teachings given in Samye Ling, March 1983. In Kalu Rinpoche, 1995. pp. 50 and 54.

108. According to Sanderson, he either gives him the same girl, or another who is bound by the pledges and vows, or another who is young and beautiful. See Sanderson, 1994. p. 90.

109. Mori's translation. See Mori, 1997. Vol. 1, p. 98.

110. Sanderson, 1994. p. 90.

111. See V. Wallace, 2001. p. 6.

112. Kalu Rinpoche's explanation to this point is as follows: realising the empty (*stong pa*) nature of mind leads to the *dharmakāya*; realising the clear (*gsal ba*) nature of mind leads to the *sambhogakāya*; realising the unimpeded (*ma 'gags pa*) nature of mind leads to the

nirmanakāya; and realising the three together leads to the *svabhavikāya*. Kalu Rinpoche, Interview, November 4, 1974. In Jamgon Kongtrul, 1977. p. 135. On Kalu Rinpoche's explanation of the fourth initiation, see also Kalu Rinpoche, 1995. p. 52.

113. See Mori, 1997. Vol. 1. p. 98.

114. Ibid.

115. One of these is the *Excellent Vase of Nectars—Condensed Kālacakra Mind Maṇḍala Sādhana* (*dPal dus kyi 'khor lo'i thugs dkyil gyi 'don bsgrigs bdud rtsi'i bum bzang*) by sDe khri Rinpoche 'Jam dbyangs thub bstan nyi ma. In 1987 Kirti Tsenshab gave an oral commentary on this sādhana in Dharamsala. Another (longer) version of the Kālacakra mind maṇḍala sādhana is by the Seventh Dalai Lama (rGyal ba bskal bzang brgya mtsho, 1708-1757) *dPal dus kyi 'khor lo'i thugs dkyil 'khor gyi sgrub dngos grub kun gyi bum bzang* (*Means of Achievement of the Maṇḍala of Exalted Mind of the Glorious Kālacakra: Good Vase of All Feats*.)

116. This sādhana includes *Kālacakra* and its consort, counted as one, surrounded by the eight śaktis.

117. Yong 'dzin gling thub bstan lung rtogs rnam rgyal 'phrin las (1903-1983). The full title of the text is: *Thun drug dang 'brel ba'i dus 'khor bla ma'i rnal 'byor dpag bsam yongs 'du'i snye ma* (*Kālacakra Guru-yoga in Conjunction with Six-session Practice*).

118. See Fourteenth Dalai Lama and Hopkins [1985] 1999. pp. 135; 381-382. In his teachings in the USA Serkong Rinpoche has commented on the difficulty of adapting the Kālacakra's elaborate practice to suit his students. Serkong Rinpoche, 1982.

119. Fourteenth Dalai Lama, Graz, October 21, 2002. Instead the Dalai Lama recommended that participants practice meditating on emptiness and bodhicitta.

120. Mori, 1997. Vol. 1, p. 92.

121 lCang skya, fol. 176b, line 3.

122. Serkong Rinpoche, oral teachings of Kālacakra, Madison, Wisconsin, July 1982.

123. Fourteenth Dalai Lama, preparation for the Kālacakra initiation, Graz, October 19, 2002. A similar point was also made by Matthieu Ricard, 2002.

124. Mori, 1997. Vol. 1, p. 94.

125. The *Vimalaprabhā* has a clear monastic orientation. See Wallace, 2001. p. 129.

126. lCang skya, fol. 173a, lines 5-6.

127. lCang skya, fol. 174a, line 3.

128. Although this phenomenon is not entirely new, it has become more important in exile.

129. Interview with Kirti Tsenshab, October 4, 1999.

130. Ibid.

131. Sanderson, 1994. p. 92.

132. See Wallace, 1995. p. 88.

133. Sanderson, 1994. p. 97.

134. This point was discussed by Sanderson. See ibid.

135. See Broido [1988] 1993.

136. Sanderson, 1994. pp. 97 and 101.

137. As permitted in the *Kriyāsamuccaya*. Initiations of Newar Buddhists omit all sexual elements but do include alcohol, meat, possessions, and the Kapalika accoutrements.

Bibliography

Oral teachings

The Fourteenth Dalai Lama's oral teachings of Kālacakra:
Kālacakra initiation, Sarnath, India, December 1990.
Kālacakra initiation, Bloomington, Indiana, August 1999.
Kālacakra initiation, Graz, Austria, October 2002.
Kirti Tsenshab Rinpoche's oral teachings of Kālacakra:
Kālacakra initiation, Jamyang Buddhist Center, London, June 1996 (translated by Peter Roberts).
Kālacakra initiation, Vajra Yogini Institute, France, October 1999 (translated by Peter Roberts).

Interviews with Kirti Tsenshab:

October 1999 (Lavour); January 2002 (New Delhi).
Serkong Rinpoche, oral teachings of Kālacakra, Madison, Wisconsin, July 1982 (translated by Alexander Berzin).
Matthieu Ricard, talk on Kālacakra, Bodhgaya, India, January 2002.

Tibetan textual (written) sources

Abhayākaragupta. *dKyil 'khor gyi cho ga rdo rje phreng ba. Vajrāvali nāma maṇḍalopāyikā*. Tibetan critical edition in Mori, 1997. pp. 251-447. TTP, Peking edition, text no. 3961.

Atiśa (Jo bo rje) *Byang chub lam gyi sgron ma (Bodhipathapradīpa)* Atiśa. *Byang chub lam gyi sgron ma*. TTP, Peking edition, vol. 103, text no. 5343.

———. *Byang chub lam gyi sgron ma'i dka' 'grel*. TTP, Peking edition. text no. 5344. TTP, sDe dge edition, text no. 3948, Khi 241a-293a4

bTsong kha pa. dBang *gi don gyi de nyid rab tu gsal ba*. TTP, Peking edition, vol. 160, text no. 6195.

lCang skya ngag dbang blo-bzang chos ldan. *'phreng-ba dang kri-ya sbrag-pa'i dkyil-'khor zhe-lnga'i dbang-bskur tshul-gyi cho-ga*. TTP, Peking edition, vol. 163, text no. 6237.

Śrī Kālacakra nāma tantra rāja (Kālacakra laghutantra) mchog gi dang po'i sangs rgyas las byung ba rgyud kyi rgyal po dpal dus kyi 'khor lo). TPP, Peking edition, vol. 1, text no. 4. sDe dge, vol. 16, text no. 362.

Tāranātha. *dPal dus kyi 'khor lo'i chos bskor gyi byung khungs nyer mkho*. Reproduced in Fendall, 1997. (Reproduced from the rTag brtan Phun tshogs gling blocks. Stog Palace Library. Printed: Leh, 1984).

———. *rDo rje'i rnal 'byor gyi 'khrid yig mthong ba don ldan gyi lhan thabs 'od brgya 'bar ba*. Collected works of Tāranātha, vol. 3, pp. 447-805. Stog Palace library edition.

Sources in European languages

Andresen, Jensine. 1997. "Kālacakra: Textual and Ritual Perspectives." Ph.D. thesis, Harvard University.

Bentor, Yael. 1995. "On the Symbolism of the Mirror in Indo-Tibetan Consecration Rituals." *Journal of Indian Philosophy*, vol. 23, pp. 57-71.

———. 1996. *Consecration of Images and Stūpas in Indo-Tibetan Tantric Buddhism*. Leiden: Brill.

Beyer, Stephan. [1973] 1978. *The Cult of Tārā: Magic and Ritual in Tibet.* Berkeley: University of California Press.

Bharati, Agehananda. [1965] 1993. *Tantric Traditions*. Delhi: Hindustan Publishing Corporation.

Broido, Michael M. [1988] 1993. "Killing, Lying, Stealing, and Adultery: A Problem of Interpretation in the Tantras." In Donald Lopez, ed. *Buddhist Hermeneutics*. New Delhi: Motilal Banarsidass. Reprint of Honolulu: University of Hawaii Press, 1988.

Bühnemann, Gudrun. 1991. "Some Remarks on the Author Abhayākaragupta and His Works." In Gudrun Bühnemann and Musashi Tachikawa. *Nispannayogavali: Two Sanskrit Manuscripts from Nepal.* Tokyo: The Centre for East Asian Cultural Studies.

———. 1992. "Some Remarks on the Date of Abhayākaragupta and the Chronology of His Works." *Zeitschrift der Deutschen Morgenländischen Gesellschaft.* Band 142, Heft 1.

Chandra, Lokesh. 1977. *Vajrāvali: A Sanskrit Manuscript from Nepal Containing the Ritual and Delineation of Mandalas* (reproduced). New Delhi: Sata Pitaka Series.

Colony, M., and T. Bianca. 1998. "A Kalachakra Master: Bringing Internal and External Harmony." *Mandala*. Sept.-Dec. 1998. pp. 60-67.

Cozort, Daniel. 1986. *Highest Yoga Tantra: An Introduction to the Esoteric Buddhism of Tibet.* Ithaca, New York: Snow Lion Publications.

Dalai Lama (Fourteenth) bstan 'dzin rgya mtsho. [1985] 1991. "Foreword: Concerning the Kalachakra." In Simon, ed. *The Wheel of Time: The Kalachakra in Context.* Ithaca, New York: Snow Lion Publications, 1991. First published by Deer Park Books, Madison, 1985.

———. 1995. *The World of Tibetan Buddhism: An Overview of Its Philosophy and Practice*. Translated, edited and annotated by Geshe Thubten Jinpa. Boston: Wisdom Publications.

Dalai Lama (Fourteenth) bstan 'dzin rgya mtsho, and Jeffrey Hopkins.[1985] 1999. *Kalachakra Tantra Rite of Initiation for the Stage of Generation: A Commentary on the Text of Kay-drup Ge-leg-bel-sang-bo by Tenzin Gyatso, the Fourteenth Dalai Lama, and the Text Itself.* Translated, edited and introduced by Jeffrey Hopkins. Boston: Wisdom Publications.

Dalai Lama (Fourteenth) bstan 'dzin rgya mtsho, Tsong kha-pa, and Jeffrey Hopkins. 1977. *Tantra in Tibet*. Translated and edited by Jeffrey Hopkins. Ithaca, New York: Snow Lion Publications.

Davidson, Ronald M. 1995. "Atiśa's Lamp for the Path." In Donald Lopez, ed. *Buddhism in Practice.* Princeton: Princeton University Press.

Dorje, Gyurme. 1991. "Interpretation of Commitment and Vow." *The Buddhist Forum*, vol. 2. Tadeusz Skorupski, ed. London: School of Oriental and African Studies.

Fendall, Ramsey. 1997. "Tāranātha's *Dpal Dus kyi 'khor lo'i chos bskor gyi byung khungs nyer mkho* and Its Relation to the Jo-nang-pa School of Tibetan Buddhism." M.A. thesis, Indiana University.

Gendun Drub (First Dalai Lama). 1982. *Bridging the Sutras and the Tantras: A Collection of Ten Minor Works by Gyalwa Gendun Drub, the First Dalai Lama (1391-1474)*. Glenn Mullin, trans. Ithaca, New York: Snow Lion Publications.

Gnoli, R., and G. Orofino. 1994. *Nāropa. L'iniziazione, traduzione e commento della Sekoddeśaṭīkā di Nāropa.* Milano: Adelphi.

'Gos lo gzhon nu dpal. [1949] 1996. *Deb ther sngon po* (Blue Annals). George N. Roerich, trans. Delhi: Motilal Banarsidass.

Hoens, D. J. 1965. "Initiation in Later Hinduism." In C. J. Bleeker, ed. *Initiation*. Leiden: Brill.

Kalu Rinpoche (Kyabje Dorje Chang). 1995. *Secret Buddhism: Vajrayana Practices*. San Francisco, California: Clear Point Press.

Kongtrul, Jamgon. 1977. *The Torch of Certainty*. J. Hanson, trans. Boulder and London: Shambhala.

Kværne, Per. 1975. "On the Concept of Sahaja in Indian Buddhist Tantric Literature." *Temenos*, vol. 11, pp. 88-135.

Mori, Masahide. 1997. "The Vajrāvali of Abhayākaragupta: A Critical Study, Sanskrit Edition of Selected Chapters and Complete Tibetan Version." Ph.D. thesis, School of Oriental and African Studies, University of London.

Orofino, Giacomella. 1994. *Sekoddeśa: A Critical Edition of the Tibetan Translations*. Rome: Istituto Italiano per il Medio ed Estremo Oriente.

Ōyama, Kōjun. 1961. "Abhiśeka." In G. P. Malalasekera, ed. *Encyclopaedia of Buddhism*. Colombo: Government of Ceylon Press, vol. 1, pp. 125-130.

Panchen Otrol Rinpoche. n.d. "The Stages of the Rite of a Tantric Initiation." *Cho Yang*, no. 3, pp. 58-73.

Rigzin, Tsepak. 1986. *Tibetan-English Dictionary of Buddhist Terminology*. Dharamsala: Library of Tibetan Works and Archives.

Samuel, Geoffrey. 1993. *Civilized Shamans: Buddhism in Tibetan Societies*. Washington and London: Smithsonian Institution Press.

Sanderson, A. 1994. "Vajrayāna: Origin and Function." In *Buddhism into the Year 2000*, International Conference Proceedings. Bangkok: Dhammakaya Foundation.

Sherburne, Richard. 2000. *The Complete Works of Atīśa*. New Delhi: Aditya Prakashan.

Singh, Bireshwar Prasad. 1968. "A Tibetan Account of Abhayākaragupta." *Journal of the Bihar Research Society*, vol. 54, parts 1-4.

Skorupski, T. trans. 1999. Abhayākaragupta's *Abhiśekaprakaraṇa.* Unpublished.

Smith, Gene. 2001. *Among Tibetan Texts: History and Literature of the Himalayan Plateau*. Boston: Wisdom Publications.

Snellgrove, David L. 1987. *Indo-Tibetan Buddhism: Indian Buddhists and Their Tibetan Successors*. London: Serindia Publications.

Sopa, Geshe Lhundub. [1985] 1991. "The Kalachakra Tantra Initiation." In Simon, ed. *The Wheel of Time: The Kalachakra in Context*.

Wallace, Vesna A. 1995. "The Inner Kālacakratantra: A Buddhist Tantric View of the Individual." Ph.D. thesis, University of California, Berkeley.

———. 2001. *The Inner Kālacakratantra: A Buddhist Tantric View of the Individual.* Oxford: Oxford University Press.

Wang, Xiangyun. 1995. "Tibetan Buddhism at the Court of the Qing: The Life and Work of lCang-skya Rol-pa'i-rdo-rje (1717-86)." Ph.D. thesis, Harvard University.

Wayman, Alex. 1971. "The Mirror-like Knowledge in Mahāyāna Buddhist Literature." *Asiatische Studien*, vol. 25, pp. 353-363.

———. 1974. "The Mirror as a Pan-Buddhist Metaphor-Simile." *History of Religions*, vol. 13, pp. 251-269.

Young, Serenity. 1999. *Dreaming in the Lotus: Buddhist Dream Narrative, Imagery and Practice.* Boston: Wisdom Publications.

–23–

Dissolution and Emptiness Meditation in the Kālacakra Six-Session Guru Yoga Sādhana

Geshe Drakpa Gelek

All Highest Yoga Tantras, except for Kālacakra, include practices for taking death, bardo, and rebirth into the path. As part of a meditation on emptiness, the practitioner dissolves ordinary appearances similar to the manner of the death process and then purifies it by transforming himself into the Dharmakāya, the Truth Body of a Buddha. Ordinary death is the basis which is to be purified, and the Dharmakāya is the resultant state. Similarly, the practitioner takes bardo into the path, purifying it by transforming himself into the Saṃbhogakāya, the Enjoyment Body of a Buddha, and rebirth into the path, purifying it by transforming himself into the Nirmānakāya, the Emanation Body of a Buddha. The practitioner purifies ordinary death, bardo, and rebirth in order to break free from the cycle of saṃsāra.

Kālacakra sādhanas differ in that the practitioner explicitly takes only death and rebirth into the path by transforming himself into the Dharmakāya and Nirmānakāya. There is no description of a practice involving the bardo state. The bardo state process is considered similar to the process of rebirth and described as part of this process. The Kālacakra practitioner imagines the internal dissolution of his body at the time of death and the internal development of his body at the time of rebirth now in order to be able to do so at the actual time of his death and rebirth. The effectiveness of the practice depends on his understanding of emptiness; the greater his understanding of emptiness, the more effective his practice. For ordinary practitioners this is only a rehearsal for the time of actual death and rebirth. For a yogi, who has realized emptiness directly, it is part of the process of actually becoming Kālacakra. Purifying ordinary death by transforming oneself into the Dharmakāya is one of the most important parts of the Kālacakra Six-Session Guru Yoga sādhana. Practice of this section of the sādhana determines the completeness of the practitioner's generation stage practice.

However, the purification of death is not described at all in the Kālacakra Six-Session Guru Yoga sādhana, and the rebirth process is described briefly.

While these processes are described in more detail in longer sādhanas, such as The Sādhana for the Complete Body, Speech, and Mind Maṇḍala of Bhagavān Kālacakra *by the Seventh Dalai Lama, and in the commentaries, much information is left unstated; and it is still necessary to have instructions directly from a teacher in order to undertake the practice. Geshe Drakpa Gelek is an accomplished yogi who lived for many years in solitary retreat in the mountains above Dharamsala. He has received extensive teachings on Kālacakra from Kālacakra masters, such as His Holiness the Dalai Lama, Kirti Tsenshab Rinpoche, and Jonangpa masters, and he is the Kālacakra teacher at Namgyal Monastery in Dharamsala, India. During a Kalachakra Practice Retreat at Namgyal Monastery in Ithaca, New York in August 2006, Geshe Drakpa gave these teachings on undertaking this practice in accordance with the Kālacakra Six-Session Guru Yoga sādhana.*

By the force of my request,
Through my strong plaintive yearning,
My root guru, great Kalachakra,
Alights on the crown of my head.

Gladly merging with me,
We become of one taste.
All phenomena—causes, effects, natures and actions—
Like an illusion or dream, are, from the start,
Utterly devoid of solid reality. [1]

Before this point in the sādhana the practitioner has cultivated the field of merit, imagining the entire field of the maṇḍala with the principal deity, Kālacakra, and his consort, Viśvamātā, at the center. After the visualization of receiving the empowerments, but before generating oneself as Kālacakra, the practitioner imagines the entire maṇḍala dissolving from the outside in and then into the principal deity at the center. Kālacakra then comes to the crown of the practitioner's head, melts, and dissolves into the practitioner's body, transforming his body fully into light. After merging completely together, the practitioner should feel that he has become one with the deity and his teacher and feel great joy. It is very important that the practitioner's mind becomes one with his root teacher who is inseparable from Kālacakra. Since this feeling can lead the practitioner into feeling some notion of solid existence, he should fall back into a meditation on emptiness.

The light at the heart of the practitioner then becomes fully transformed into the seed syllable *HŪṂ*. The practitioner begins to dissolve himself into the syllable *HŪṂ*, dissolving from the top down and the bottom up. The *HŪṂ* starts to dissolve from the bottom up, and, as this happens, the practitioner experiences the process of death where the bodily elements (water, fire, earth, wind, consciousness, and space) dissolve one after another into each other. As this process takes place, internal signs, such as the smoke-like appearance, the mirage-like appearance, the firefly-like appearance, and the flickering butter lamp appearance are experienced.

The first element that dissolves is the water element. The water element dissolves into the fire element. This takes place as the seed syllable *HŪṂ* starts to dissolve from the bottom up. As the practitioner imagines that the water element starts to dissolve into the fire element, simultaneously a smoke-like appearance arises in the practitioner's mind. The type of smoke-like appearance that is imagined should not be a thick, dark smoke, but rather a light smoke that floats. Suddenly, rays of the sun begin going through it, and the practitioner sees the bluish tint of that appearance of smoke. If you have traveled to India, particularly to Delhi, you may have a clear image of that bluish appearance. It is dirty and misty due to dirt and pollution, and it has a kind of bluish appearance that permeates everything around it.

Next the fire element dissolves into the earth element. As a result, the practitioner develops an image of the mirage-like appearance. This form of a mirage-like appearance is something that is commonly found here in the United States. Just before I landed at the airport in New York City in August, I started to see some mirage-like appearances underneath the airplane. This often happens during the hot weather due to excessive heat. When this kind of appearance happens, the practitioner should think that this is the time when the fire element is dissolving into the earth element.

As the earth element dissolves into the wind element, the practitioner imagines the firefly-like appearance. During this appearance, the practitioner has the idea that now is the time for the earth element to dissolve into the wind element. The appearance of fireflies transforms into lamp-like appearance. The practitioner imagines lighting a butter lamp, and then sees the reflection of the fire, a reddish kind of reflection, somewhere above the butter lamp in the distance. It is during this time that the mind element is actually dissolving into the consciousness element. After these four elements have dissolved into one another, especially when the wind element finally dissolves into the consciousness element, then ordinary consciousness and ordinary appearances have dissolved.

Finally, the consciousness element dissolves into the space element. The type of appearance here is of a pure absence of all those earlier appearances. It is somewhat analogous to the morning during the full moon day, somewhere around the dawn when one may have a pure clarity of space that is purely an absence of all sorts of appearances. It is during this specific appearance of pure vacuity that the consciousness is actually being dissolved into the space element.

> All things in their causes and effects, their natures and their activities, are empty of existing by way of their own characteristics. The water element of my body weakens the fire element. Without fire my earth element dissolves into water. Air dries up the element of water. Air absorbs into consciousness. Consciousness absorbs into space. Thus all dualistic elaborations of the animate and inanimate form from subtle and gross particles disappear,

and I become the entity of the four gateways to liberation, wherein the object emptiness and its gnosis subject become indivisible.[2]

In this particular state when the practitioner has a pure absence of all appearances, a state of pure vacuity, this is the actual time where the most subtle mind dawns. Therefore, this very mind is also termed the Dharmakāya state of death. It is at this specific critical time, if the practitioner has already gained some understanding of emptiness, that he gains a clear insight into emptiness that enables him to actualize the most subtle mind, which is also termed the Dharmakāya during the time of death.

Anyone who takes Kālacakra practice as his main practice in life, when he dies, will go through this process of death and will finally end up at the pure state of vacuity. So, this process of death that the practitioner will actually go through when the time comes for him to die is actually practiced right now while he is still alive. It is almost like he is familiarizing himself with the actual process of death that will take place when he actually dies in the future. This is exactly the time when lamas, after they pass away, sit in a meditative state. So when you hear about lamas being in meditative states of clear light after they die, this is exactly the meditative state they remain in for as long as they desire.

This very appearance of pure vacuity itself is the most subtle form of mind that can manifest during the actual process of death, and it is such a subtle mind manifested at the last moment of life that actually takes emptiness as its primary object. This is how, by taking emptiness as the primary object, one is able to sit in deep meditation. A practitioner should be fully prepared, so that when he reaches this point of his life, he should be able to meditate on emptiness. While you often hear and talk much about this term *emptiness*, this specific meditation is actually making one's self acquainted with this term and the notion of such things, which will be applied at the time of death when you manifest the subtle mind. It is out of such familiarity that the practitioner gains while he is alive the causes that can create the proper conditions, so that at the time when he actually manifests the subtle mind, he can enable that subtle mind to realize emptiness easily.

It is just like a child meeting his mother. The reason why it is almost like a child meeting his mother is because that very subtle mind is extremely clear and pure, and it has the full potential to grasp any object. When the practitioner has such a powerful mind that is clear and pure with the full potential to apprehend any object without effort and has the support of potency that he has already activated when he was alive through the familiarity of such practice, then the practitioner can realize emptiness directly at that particular moment.

For example, when you hear discussion of things at an earlier time of your life, even though you may not remember it clearly, if you were to hear something similar to it later in your life, you could easily connect it to what you heard in the past and relate similar types of stories. This is done only on the basis of ordinary mind, which is extremely weak, especially in terms of apprehension. But if you were to use the subtle mind, the most subtle mind that is manifested during the time of death, then that type of mind with its strength and quality by connecting to what you have experienced in the past can have the fullest power to really remember everything as clearly as possible. This is the reason why the practitioner should acquaint himself more with emptiness right now.

Therefore, when the practitioner practices this part of the sādhana, he should first try to get to that point. Once he has reached the point of manifesting the most subtle mind, he then tries to remain fully focused on the notion of emptiness that he found earlier during analytical meditation. This is the actual practice of taking the Dharmakāya as a means to purify the ordinary death, and it depends on the capacity of the practitioner's mind. He should think that this very mind, the wisdom that realizes emptiness, which he uses for focusing on the emptiness, is in the form of the resultant state of Dharmakāya.

The practitioner imagines strongly that this very wisdom that is now labeled as the Dharmakāya is actually the practitioner himself. He does this in order to develop the pride of thinking that the label of the Dharmakāya that has been applied to his subtle mind is himself. This is how he cultivates the divine pride of being in the state of Dharmakāya.

It is important for the practitioner to be specific with what appears to his mind. Therefore, since he has gone through the earlier dissolution processes, he no longer should have any image of the field of maṇḍala. Nor should he have the image of the seed syllable *HŪṂ*, but only the appearances that arise one after another, the smoke-like, mirage-like, firefly-like, and the flickering butter lamp. These should be specific images that he has in his mind. It is important not to look too deeply into these appearances. Doing so may cause the practitioner to see things as being more solid than they really are. He should not intensify his concentration in seeing these appearances. The essential point to remember is that as he has all these appearances, one after another, to keep these four appearances natural. He should not try to gain more clarity of those appearances. The practitioner should focus on the notion of emptiness based on whatever level of understanding of emptiness he has developed.

Although it may be somewhat difficult to do, because as soon as the appearances arise, you may tend to naturally run after them without any sense of control; but it is only a matter of practice. If you practice enough, then there should come a time when you could actually apply the other means to focus more attention on the notion of emptiness rather than on the appearances. You need to know that your mind has this basic quality which is actually associated with specific experience, and therefore, if you were to train enough you could actually actualize those qualities.

For example, when you have an obsession with something it tends to somehow dominate all forms of experiences. This is how your mind, which is more attached to the object than you like, tends to fall naturally towards that object, and the other objects somehow remain as just mere illusion passing through your mind, one after another. Your entire focus is more or less just on that object that you like the most. Likewise, when you are unhappy to the extent that you can no longer sense what is happening around you, even though you may still have the appearances of what is happening around you, your entire focus is really on the one that you dislike the most. You should understand this and apply it to your practice. You should direct the overall strength of the mind more or less towards the notion of emptiness or the emptiness itself. When the appearances come one after another, you should just let them happen, let them appear naturally to you.

To put it in a simpler form, the practitioner should think that what appears to his mind are these four appearances, but what his mind should ascertain is the actual meaning of emptiness. Therefore, the mode of ascertainment has to be applied to emptiness by retaining the appearance of this series of appearances. Finally, the practitioner will reach a point where even those appearances will start to gradually disappear. He will come to a point that is a mere state of voidness or a state of negation, and nothing appears to his mind. All he experiences is a state of mind that is a pure state of absence of all those earlier appearances. He no longer has any appearances coming to his mind. It is a mere state of absence of those appearances: a state of mere vacuity. It is at this critical moment that the practitioner is introduced to his subtle mind.

When the practitioner reaches this state of absence, because he no longer has any form of appearances, all relative notion of events, such as phenomena, has disappeared. It is due to the negation of all these relative appearances of phenomena that he develops for the first time the cessation of that objective mind that tends to appear as if it exists from its own side. This appearance is ceased for just a moment. At this very critical moment, because the practitioner has the sense of the covering of the objective existence of his mind, he feels overwhelmed or as if he has lost his own consciousness. At this time, he should not analyze at all. For instance, the practitioner may often check during a meditation session to see if he is actually meditating on emptiness or not. But here he should just be, not undertaking any form of analysis. Under such circumstances, he should not be influenced by any form of conceptual thought. Rather he should keep it natural, which is a pure state of absence. Remaining in this state of absence could be considered as a form of stabilization meditation and could be taken as the benefit of a meditation in the Dharmakāya state.

Whether the practitioner meditates on emptiness or whether he meditates on Dharmakāya is very different at this critical point. If he meditates on Dharmakāya, he may soon start to develop a conception of thinking that this very Dharmakāya is actually himself. So, it is very important to keep the focus on emptiness.

Once the practitioner has reached the state of mere absence of all appearances, then he should be in a pure state of negation. He no longer has any sense of subject. There is no notion of subjectivity and objectivity. It is a mere absence of both. This mere state of emptiness is the basis upon which the practitioner will construct the maṇḍala, like an architect preparing a design, and generate himself as Kālacakra. This is the practice of taking the Nirmānakāya into the path in order to purify ordinary rebirth.

Taking the Dharmakāya state as a means to purify ordinary death is one of the most important parts of the practice of the Kālacakra Six-Session Guru Yoga sādhana. Practice of this section of the sādhana determines the completeness of your practice of the generation stage. Therefore, it is helpful to spend more time on this section of the practice. Although this is only a very coarse explanation of taking the Dharmakāya as a means to purify ordinary death, it still should give you some idea of that form of meditation. If you start with this coarse form of meditation, it may help you to gain more subtle levels of realization.

Endnotes

1. *Kalachakra Guru-Yoga in Conjunction with Six-Session Practice: A Cluster of Fruit from an All-Embracing Wish-Granting Tree* (Thun-drug-dang 'brel-ba'i dus-'khor bla-ma'i rnal-'byor dpag-bsam yongs-'du'i snye-ma), by His Holiness the Fourteenth Dalai Lama, bsTan-'dzin rgya-mtsho, versified by Yongdzin Ling Rinpoche (Yongs-'dzin gLing Thub-bstan lung-rtogs rnam-rgyal 'phrin-las), in Alexander Berzin (transl.), *Kalachakra and Other Six-Session Yoga Texts*, Ithaca, NY: Snow Lion, 1998, p. 35.

2. Lobsang Kalsang Gyatso, the Seventh Dalai Lama, *The Oral Transmission of Khedrup: Sadhana for the Complete Body, Speech, and Mind Mandala of Bhagavan Kalacakra*. Translated by Gavin Kilty, 2005, unpublished.

–24–

Essence of the Kālacakra Six-Session Guru Yoga Practice

Jhado Rinpoche, Namgyal Monastery
Geshe Thupten Tashi, Translator

Traditionally, long sādhanas are designed for students beginning a specific tantric practice. A beginning practitioner needs all the details and descriptions of the rituals that a long sādhana provides. Short sādhanas are designed for more advanced practitioners, who are already familiar with the practice and need fewer details in order to undertake an effective practice. Very advanced practitioners can dispense with the written sādhanas altogether and do an essence meditation, which simply consists of doing all the visualizations and meditations of the sādhana.

In the West, students often find the long sādhanas for Highest Yoga Tantra practice overwhelming. This may be caused by a number of reasons. All Highest Yoga Tantra practices are complex, and the student may lack sufficient preparation or experience with tantra to undertake this level of practice. While students may have had the opportunity to receive an initiation, they may not have had the opportunity to receive practice instructions, access to commentaries translated into English, or teachings on the commentaries for the tantra. There may also not be an understanding that they are taking on a practice that will develop gradually over their lifetime, and they become frustrated with not being able to fully understand all aspects of the practice quickly. Limited time for a practice, perhaps an hour or less in the morning, is another issue.

Students may even find the short sādhanas or a simplified practice, such as the Kālacakra Six-Session Guru Yoga, too long and difficult. Out of compassion teachers may respond by giving an essence meditation practice with the thought that doing at least some level of practice is better than doing none, since it may plant the seed for the student to undertake a fuller practice in the future. While this type of practice helps the student to maintain their vows and practice commitments, it is doubtful that such a practice assists the student in developing their practice. It is more likely to be beneficial when used in combination with a short or long sādhana practice and after familiarization with the details of the sādhana.

This article contains the description of a Kālacakra Essence Meditation for Western students given by Jhado Rinpoche of Namgyal Monastery to small groups of students on two occasions: Chicago in 2005 and Amarāvatī in 2006. Rinpoche gave these oral instructions out of compassion for two types of students, those who found the Kālacakra Six-Session Guru Yoga too complex or too long to undertake as a daily practice and those who occasionally needed a shorter practice in order to maintain their vows when their time was limited. However, Rinpoche clearly states that it is better for a serious Kālacakra practitioner to do at least one extensive Kālacakra Six-Session Guru Yoga a day and emphasizes the importance of keeping the commitments made when receiving the initiation.

Why do you need to do this practice every day? When you received the initiation, you took Bodhisattva and Tantric vows. You made a commitment to do the Six-Session Guru Yoga practice six times a day. You also vowed to achieve enlightenment in order to be of benefit to all sentient beings. If you want to be able to achieve enlightenment quickly, then you have to take on more responsibilities and commitments. It will not be possible without hard work.

It would be good to recite at least one extensive Kālacakra Six-Session Guru Yoga sādhana as part of one's daily Six-Session Guru Yoga practice. However, if you lack time to do a full Kālacakra Six-Session Guru Yoga practice with all its visualizations, one can simply meditate on the essence of the practice.

Even though you are very busy and have many responsibilities, it is important to hold the essence of Kālacakra practice in your mind at all times. You need to remain focused on the essential points: refuge, renunciation, bodhicitta, accumulation of merit, and right view. This is what is of benefit. Cultivation of bodhicitta and wisdom realizing emptiness is the main practice, and doing this will allow you to attain the completion stage and then a Buddha's inseparable body and mind.

Refuge

If you really want to practice Kālacakra, it is important to practice refuge and bodhicitta repeatedly every day. This is the most important part of the Kālacakra practice. On this foundation you will be able to practice the generation and completion stages. The common path for both sūtra and tantra is the practice of refuge, renunciation, bodhicitta, and right view. You will do these practices regardless of what tantric system you choose to practice. The recitation is not what is important. Developing internal refuge is the point of what you are trying to do. Focusing on the meaning brings benefits. So, take a little time for this section of the practice; do not hurry.

Bodhicitta and Bodhisattva Vows

It is important to set your motivation for your practice. You need to develop the feeling that today you will follow Śākyamuni Buddha, Kālacakra, your teacher, and the merit field. You vow to undertake the practice of bodhicitta and the practice of the Six Perfections. It is also good to meditate on the Four Immeasurables at this point, since it reinforces your commitment to bodhicitta.

Visualization of the Merit Field

Next you visualize the merit field and invite the Buddhas and Bodhisattvas of the ten directions to come. The Buddhas are always concerned for sentient beings. If you invite them, they will come. Think that from your heart you invite the Buddhas and Bodhisattvas to come. This deep motivation allows you to accumulate merit through the practice of the Seven-Limb Prayer.

Visualize Kālacakra in his simple form with one face and two arms in union with his consort, Viśvamātā, and the entire maṇḍala in which they reside in front of you. It is important to visualize Kālacakra in the nature of your teacher. It is your teacher who is close to you, shows you the path, and brings the Buddha close to you. Śākyamuni Buddha made efforts for three countless eons to achieve Buddhahood, but he only taught until he was eighty. It looks like a contradiction, since he spent so much time achieving Buddhahood, but he only taught for a short time. However for us he is still active because of the kindness of our teacher, who shows us the path. So, in your visualization the deity has the aspect of Kālacakra but is in the nature of your teacher.

Accumulation of Merit

The next section of the practice is the accumulation of merit. Accumulation of merit can be summarized as follows:

- Accumulation—prostrations, offerings, supplicating your teacher to remain, requesting the turning the wheel of dharma, and dedication
- Purification—confession
- Multiplication—rejoicing and dedication

All three are included in the Seven-Limb Prayer. Recitation is not what is important. Rather, contemplate on the meaning of these seven, and you will receive the benefits.

When you make offerings to the merit field, they should include external, internal, secret, and suchness offerings plus a maṇḍala offering. External offerings ripen to allow us to practice the generation stage. Internal offerings plant the seed that ripens into a Buddha's body, secret offerings the seed that ripens into a Buddha's mind, and suchness offerings the seed that ripens into the union of a Buddha's body and mind. Our material offerings are contaminated. The Buddhas are uncontaminated, so contaminated offerings cannot be of use to them. But, if you understand the meaning of your offerings, they become excellent. Your external offering, while in aspect is material things, is an offering in the nature of wisdom. All offerings are in the nature of the wisdom which realizes emptiness; just the aspect changes.

Praise/Rejoicing

Make a supplication to the field of merit asking that you be blessed to attain this state of Kālacakra. Meditate on the qualities of the Buddha's mind, such as power, knowledge, and compassion, and praise them. Aspire to develop these qualities yourself.

Dissolution of Merit Field

Kālacakra, who is the same aspect as your teacher, with joy comes to your crown and dissolves into you. Visualizing Kālacakra at your crown allows you to receive the blessing of Buddha's body, speech, and mind. You feel joy and meditate on emptiness.

Meditation on Emptiness

When you meditate on emptiness, you should ask yourself several questions: How does your teacher dissolve into you? How does your teacher exist? How does Kālacakra exist? How do I exist? Analyze emptiness and realize that everything exists as mere imputation or lacks inherent existence.

At this point you take death into the Dharmakāya path by dissolving your body into emptiness. Why do we do this? We do this so when we are able to undertake the completion stage, we can experience the death process and attain realizations, even though right now we just imagine it. This practice at the completion stage removes obscurations to the omniscient mind and obscurations to liberation. If you practice this now, when you die it will be transformed into virtues, and you will be born in a higher realm. However, this practice is not easy.

Self-generation as Kālacakra

The empty mind transforms itself into Kālacakra. This can be done elaborately or in a simple way.

The simple form:

> On top of an open-petalled lotus are a moon, sun, Rāhu, and Kālāgni discs. In the center of the Kālāgni disc is a blue vajra with a blue HŪṂ. You transform yourself into Kālacakra with one face and two arms holding vajra and bell and embracing the consort, Viśvamātā. It is important to think of the purpose of the vajra, bell, and the union with the consort. These three are the pledges of a Buddha's mind, speech, and body, and they are never separated. If you have time think further on what different parts of the visualization symbolize. Do mantra recitations. Do not dissolve the visualization at the end of your practice.

The elaborate form of self-generation is the process of the five enlightenment pathways. This process is explained in the Kālacakra Six-Session Guru Yoga. It is difficult for beginning practitioners.

Out of emptiness visualize an open-petalled lotus on top of a lion throne. On top of this are moon, sun, Rāhu, and Kālāgni discs. On the Kālāgni disc is a dark blue HŪṂ, which transforms into a dark blue vajra with a small HŪṂ letter in its center. The vajra and HŪṂ transform into Kālacakra with either one face and two arms or four faces and twenty-four arms. This visualization purifies our ordinary rebirth, which has kept us in cyclic existence, and leaves the imprint in the future to attain a Buddha's Form Body. The dissolution of the merit field and subsequent meditation on emptiness purifies ordinary death. It leaves an imprint to attain a Buddha's Wisdom Body in the future. You should then meditate on the emptiness of this visualization.

Ask yourself, how does this Kālacakra exist? The Form Bodies in this visualization look like a rainbow and are in the nature of the path and its result. How does this Kālacakra Form Body relate to the path and our practice? Normally, we have deluded minds, and our body is related to our mind. Our body has many cakras, which are connected to our body and mind. Our deluded mind arises in relation to these. What is the main cause of our deluded mind? The four drops on our four cakras—crown, throat, heart, and navel—are the secondary cause of our delusions. We need to purify our four drops, winds, and channels. The left (white) and right (red) channels and winds that pass through the cakras lead to the arising of our deluded mind. Through meditation we try to cease the winds moving through these two channels and force them into the central channel. Then the winds dissolve in the central channel of the heart cakra, purifying the four drops, so we can attain the four bodies of a Buddha—body, speech, mind, and activity.

Moon, sun, Rāhu, and Kālāgni discs are visualized to purify the defilements of the four drops. The right and left channel winds are purified by visualizing the right leg as red and the left as white. By ceasing the winds in the right and left channels and forcing them to enter the central channel, the clear light mind which realizes emptiness arises. We visualize the body as blue or black for this reason. We visualize Kālacakra in union with his consort, Viśvamātā, to attain the unchangeable supreme bliss of the wisdom mind realizing emptiness. The subject is the wisdom mind and the object emptiness, which are inseparable like water and milk mixed together. The emptiness mind ceases all substances to attain Kālacakra's Empty Form Body. Kālacakra represents unchangeable supreme great bliss wisdom. Viśvamātā represents the Empty Form Body. Both arise from the mind that realizes emptiness. The five elements are purified by the visualization of the five different colors of the fingers. The nature of the Buddha's body, speech, and mind are represented by the three colors on the insides of the fingers.

Why does Kālacakra hold a vajra and bell? The vajra is the pledge of a Buddha's mind and the bell a Buddha's speech. The visualization of yourself as a deity is the pledge of a Buddha's body, speech, and mind.

If we know the symbolism of the visualization, it makes our practice more meaningful. You visualize yourself as Kālacakra embracing your consort. You hold a vajra and bell. This visualization arises from the mind realizing emptiness and this practice. Acknowledge that you, too, can actually attain this.

With this understanding, do the mantra recitations. Do as many as you have time to do.

Dedication

Dedicate the merit you have accumulated by undertaking this practice to achieving enlightenment as Kālacakra in order to be of benefit to all sentient beings. You should also cultivate the intention to keep all your vows. It is important to cultivate the determination to do this daily.

This essence practice can be summarized as follows:

- Take refuge—visualize the refuge merit field
- Meditate on bodhicitta
- Meditate on the Four Immeasurables
- Take the bodhisattva vows
- Visualize the Kālacakra merit field—visualize your guru as Kālacakra with one face and two arms and embracing his consort
- Make offerings to the merit field
    - Outer
    - Inner
    - Secret
    - Suchness
    - Maṇḍala
- Praise/Rejoicing
- Dissolve merit field into self (dissolve guru into self)
- Meditate on emptiness

- Transform into Kālacakra with one face and two arms holding vajra and bell and embracing the consort—it is important to think of the purpose of the vajra, bell, and the consort in union
  - vajra—bodhicitta, represents Buddha's mind
  - bell—wisdom realizing emptiness, object of emptiness, Buddha's speech
  - union with consort—inseparability of Buddha's body and mind
    - Kālacakra—Buddha's body
    - Viśvamātā—Buddha's mind

  Do mantra recitation
- Dedicate virtues and merit for all sentient beings to achieve Buddhahood
- Cultivate intention to keep all vows

–25–

Purifying the Inner and Outer Wheels: Remarks from Venerable Kirti Tsenshab Rinpoche on the Significance of the Kālacakra for Times of Conflict

Venerable Kirti Tsenshab Rinpoche was born in Amdo in 1926 and was recognized at a young age as the reincarnation of the former abbot of Kirti Monastery. After becoming a monk and completing his monastic education at Drepung, where he was debate partner (tsen-shab) with Kirti Rinpoche, he was appointed abbot of Kirti at age thirty-two. Following his flight into exile in 1959, Rinpoche undertook a fifteen-year retreat in the hills above Dharamsala, home of the exiled Dalai Lama. Rinpoche traveled to dozens of countries to teach the Dharma, and he even recently traveled to Antarctica to release blessed water from many water bodies worldwide into the ocean currents, to adjust and balance the fragile environment of the polar caps and to pacify extreme weather patterns.

In July 2006, Rinpoche was in Israel when he was diagnosed with liver cancer. He was evacuated just as a month-long war was erupting and returned to India, where he received care from both modern and traditional Tibetan medical techniques. With treatment from Dr. Yeshe Donden, after it was advised Rinpoche not receive radiation therapy, Rinpoche's health began to improve. Rinpoche was then moved from a hospital to a private home in Delhi. However, it became clear by the end of October that Rinpoche's health was deteriorating, as his weight continued to decrease since he could not take in solid food. His Holiness the Dalai Lama and Lama Zopa Rinpoche both maintained constant contact with Rinpoche's attendants and suggested advice for prayers and practices for his disciples everywhere to assist with his passing. More than one million animals were liberated to this end. Rinpoche maintained meditation on the Kālacakra maṇḍala throughout this period and demonstrated how to practice in the most adverse circumstances. Finally, on December 16, just hours after Lama Tsongkhapa Day, Rinpoche entered final meditation, thukdam. Usually such a high lama will remain in this state for one or two weeks, but Rinpoche remained in thukdam only five days—clearly to allow for a swift return to Dharamsala where his close disciples and the Tibetan refugee community were waiting for him. Rinpoche's body was displayed for three days in his room at Kirti Gompa, where many Western students and Tibetans made offerings. Then on the morning of the twenty-fifth Rinpoche was cremated at a site below the Tibetan Children's Village as monks from Namgyal Monastery performed a Kālacakra fire puja, and monks from the Kirti Gompa performed auspicious prayers.

Ven. Kirti Tsenshab Rinpoche was recognized as one of the leading authorities on Kālacakra and even gave teachings on the *Vimalaprabhā* to His Holiness the Dalai Lama. As Gen Lamrimpa recounts, Rinpoche was the only one outside of Tibet who held the complete oral transmission of the Kālacakra lineage, and His Holiness the Dalai Lama instructed him to pass these instructions to three other masters, which he did. Earlier, Rinpoche had been one of only seven to receive generation and completion stage instructions directly from His Holiness. Therefore even these seemingly simple explanations below carry great weight as they come from one of the great Kālacakra masters of our time.

***Note**: These remarks were originally published in two separate articles in* Mandala Magazine, *as responses to questions posed by Jon Landaw and translated by Ven. Tsenla. The editor wishes to thank Nancy Patton of* Mandala *and Jon Landaw for permission to reprint; Ven. Amy Miller at Tushita Center in Dharamsala for help in securing Rinpoche's permission; and Rinpoche himself for suggesting these be reprinted for this volume. Concluding this piece is the prayer for Rinpoche's swift return, composed by Lama Zopa Rinpoche days after Kirti Tsenshab's passing.*

The term *Kālacakra* means "Wheel of Time." This refers to both the inner Wheel of Time and the outer Wheel of Time. The outer Wheel of Time is the movement of the planets and the other bodies that make up this universe. The inner Wheel of Time refers to the movement of our breath—our inhalation and exhalation—and to the various changes that take place within our own body and mind. The significance of the Kālacakra lies in its purification or positive transformation of both these inner and outer processes of change: our inner mental and physical changes as well as the outer changes that occur in our world.

And when we talk about the inner Wheel of Time, focusing primarily on the movement of the winds as we breathe in and out, because the wind (*prāṇa*) is regarded as the mount of the mind, the changes emphasized here—the purification mainly being talked about—involve the transformation of the mind.

Although the Kālacakra is similar to other tantric practices in that all deity practices involve the purification of these three doors of body, speech, and mind, what is special about Kālacakra is that it is far more intricate and detailed than you would ever imagine knowing the other tantras. To give some sense of this highly detailed system, consider the way in which time is measured. According to the Kālacakra, there are a certain number of breaths that make up one day and night, and then a number of such days in a week, in a month, and in a year. In the inner and outer Kālacakra, the number of meditational deities generated by the practitioner correspond to all these divisions of time.

For example, according to Kālacakra, each month has thirty days, so that there are 360 days in the twelve-month lunar year. As part of the practice of Kālacakra, you visualize a corresponding number of deities located at various points within your body. Just as there is an outer Wheel of Time established upon the sun, the moon, and the various planets, so there is a corresponding inner Wheel of Time established on the basis of the various constituents within your body, visualized as deities.

Also, the *Kālacakratantra* deals with the correspondence between the inner six elements of a being and the outer six elements of the world. If there is a degeneration in the potency of the outer six elements, then there is a degeneration in the six corresponding inner elements as well. These two are interdependent in terms of their increase, decline, and so forth. Everything that is cultivated on the inner basis of our own individual body and mind corresponds to the outer basis of the movement of the planets and so forth.

In the Kālacakra, the aggregates, the elements, and so forth are all explained in groups of six. The six elements it deals with are the five ordinarily listed—earth, water, fire, wind, and space—plus the sixth element known as *yeshe.* Within the Kālacakra system, yeshe—ordinarily translated as "primordial wisdom"—actually refers to the combination of the very subtle wind and the very subtle mind that is mounted on this wind. This combination is energy and consciousness in their most refined form. The inner yeshe is that combination of wind and mind dwelling within the individual; the outer yeshe is the mind-wind combination that pervades all of existence.

The Kālacakra empowerment has great significance in relation to the present time and the current state of people's minds. For example, right now we are living in an age of great external development. At the same time, there is also a similar acute development of the afflictive emotions of attachment, hatred, jealousy, and so forth, in the minds of sentient beings. Our minds are much cleverer, in a negative sense, than they were in past times. Whenever there are conditions of intense change in our outer world, these outer changes usually trigger inner changes as well. The outer changes that will take place in the world, according to Kālacakra, will be so extreme that they will force inner changes to occur. At such times as these, the Kālacakra is particularly relevant.

The Kālacakra texts predict that there will come a time when, after much degeneration and conflict, there will occur what is sometimes called the triumph of the Kingdom of Śambhala. During that time of peace and harmony, the *Kālacakratantra* will flourish. It is for people to cultivate a connection with Kālacakra, thereby enabling them to partake in the benefits of the Kingdom of Śambhala when it is established on Earth, that the Kālacakra empowerment ceremony is often given as a blessing to so many people at a time. Whether we fully participate in the Kālacakra empowerment, simply take it as a blessing, or merely hear about it, we are creating the causes to meet the Kālacakra teachings again when they reemerge with the triumph of Śambhala. It is for that reason that the Kālacakra is given so widely now.

Just as there is an outer Wheel of Time and an inner Wheel of Time, so there is what we can call the outer barbarian and the inner barbarian. After hitting the depths of barbarism and violence, the world will experience a spiritual revival and the reemergence of the *Kālacakratantra*. Under such conditions, those who have established a connection with Kālacakra will have the opportunity of aspiring to these profound teachings. That is the purpose of receiving its blessings now. [Editor's note: there has been significant concern about the historical, "outer" barbarian corresponding to the Muslim invaders of eleventh-century India and what this means to Kālacakra's purported inclusive nature. For more on this topic and possible explanations, please see, and support, Alexander Berzin internet archive: http://www.berzinarchives.com.]

It is very important to keep in mind, when considering such things, that all spiritual paths, whether our own or others, have their own innate goodness. But to hold to one's own tradition in such a way that we become obsessed with it harms not only ourselves but others as well. Of course, it is very good to have interest in and admiration for one's own spiritual path. But we should be more balanced and relaxed in the way we hold onto our path or religion rather than becoming very rigid and dogmatic about it. This is true whether we are talking about outer matters or internal personal matters.

Take, for example, the Buddhism of Tibet where there are four major traditions: the Nyingma, Sakya, Kagyu, and Geluk. His Holiness always points out that when members of any one of these traditions hold onto their point of view in a very obsessive way, then instead of bringing benefit, this attitude only brings about harm. Maintaining the general harmony between the different spiritual paths is very important. To promote one's own path by denigrating other paths is extremely destructive; nothing but harm comes from that kind of mentality. When it comes to spiritual matters, although it is necessary to regard your own spiritual path as something vitally important to yourself, feeling justified in destroying everything else that does not fall into line with your beliefs is completely wrong.

It is natural for people to hold a variety of different viewpoints, whether we are talking about worldly or spiritual matters. If you bring together people holding different political views or proposing different philosophical theories, and if you then debate the pluses and minuses of these different viewpoints in a respectful manner, it is possible for both sides to benefit, to gain greater insight. In the old days, just such types of debate were held between proponents of various Buddhist philosophical positions; these debates were held with the motivation of helping each other out, of enlightening each other. Even though you held to your own theories, you debated in such a manner that you could help increase the intellect, wisdom, and understanding of your debate partner through your insights into the subject matter. That was how it was done. These debates weren't taken to the extreme where, just because you held a different viewpoint from another, that person became someone you wanted to crush. Things didn't go to that extreme. The great learned beings, the pandits, were very open to the views of others; they welcomed these different viewpoints as a way of developing their own insights. The difference in their viewpoints was not taken as a reason to destroy the other person.

Consider the example of the two great Indian masters Candrakīrti and Candragomin. Candrakīrti, a monk, was a follower of the Madhyamaka, or Middle Way, school founded by Nāgārjuna, which propounded what is considered the highest of the Buddhist philosophical views. Candragomin, on the other hand, was a layman who held the view of the Cittamatra, or Mind Only, philosophical school. These two great pandits would often come together and have debates that lasted for days and sometimes even for months! But in these debates there was no violence at all: physically, verbally, or mentally. Within these encounters there was absolutely no thought of aggression. On the contrary, Candrakīrti and Candragomin held each other in the highest esteem.

Candrakīrti was regarded as someone who was under the special guidance of Mañjuśrī, the Buddha of Wisdom, while Candragomin was under the care of Avalokiteśvara, the Buddha of Compassion. Candragomin even possessed a statue of Avalokiteśvara that used to speak to him. On one occasion, Candrakīrti went to where Candragomin was staying while the statue was instructing Candragomin how to answer a question that had come up in debate between the two men. The statue had extended its finger as it emphasized each point and didn't have time to bring its finger back to its normal position before Candrakīrti caught sight of it. Candrakirti then addressed the statue of Arya Avalokiteśvara and said, "If your compassion is truly without discrimination, then you should give advice to *me* as well!" And the statue answered, "No, you are guided by Mañjuśrī, so you don't need my help." As for the statue, it remained as Candrakīrti had spied it, and became known as the "Arya with the Extended Finger."

Ideally, all the spiritual faiths, such as Buddhism, Christianity, Islam, and so forth, should treat each other as Candrakīrti and Candragomin did. Yes, these traditions have their differences, but these differences should help inspire and empower one another. In degenerate times such as this, however, it often doesn't work out like this. People are so deceived in their way of thinking that they feel that, in order to establish their own point of view, they must destroy those who hold differing views. This is extremely unfortunate.

To abandon violence in one's actions of body, speech, and mind is the basis of the spiritual path. Of course, situations may sometimes cause you to engage in behavior you would normally avoid, such as telling a lie in order to save someone whose life is in danger. But other than these exceptions, avoiding violence through the three doors is essential to spiritual development.

There is a story that illustrates the conditions in which is may be necessary to use what could be regarded as a "negative" method to achieve a positive result. At the time of Śākyamuni Buddha there lived a spirit who, in order to feed her five hundred children, was causing a great deal of harm to others. Buddha realized that she had special affection for her youngest child, so he hid this baby from her. The mother grew frantic and searched everywhere for her missing child. After looking through the preta, deva, and human realms with no success, she finally approached Buddha in desperation and begged his help. Buddha said to her, "If you make the commitment not to cause harm anymore, I will find the means of returning your child to you, and my followers will dedicate a portion of their food each day to your family's survival." The mother agreed, the child was returned, and the family was able to survive without anyone being harmed. Buddha's method, though it seemed to cause harm in the beginning, ended up leading to very beneficial results all around.

As already indicated, in any given religion you have people who are fanatics and those who are more open-minded. To hold the view that it is okay to destroy those with whom you disagree is totally contradictory to the teachings of Buddha. The harmony of the different spiritual paths, and the harmony of different secular governments, is very important for the stability of our world. This harmony can only be brought about through peaceful means.

The inner barbarians I mentioned earlier refer to our own poisonous states of mind, and the outer barbarians refer to the inhabitants of those places where conflict and strife, born from these poisonous minds, have become widespread. Much of the imbalance and destruction experienced in our outer world is basically the manifestation of the imbalances and disturbances of sentient beings' inner elements. To find the balance and harmony of the outer elements—for there not to be earthquakes, or floods, or fires, or violent windstorms, etc.—is very much dependent on our finding the balance and harmony of our inner elements; purifying sentient beings internally is the key to establishing the outer balance. The two types of Kālacakra are interdependent: when we purify the inner Kālacakra, the outer one is automatically purified and brought into balance. It cannot be stated too many times that our efforts to bring about this balance must take place in the spirit of harmony, rather than with thoughts of aggression. This is the true spirit behind the teachings of Buddhism in general and the tantra of Kālacakra in particular.

PASSION INVOKING THE BLESSINGS OF THE QUICK RETURN OF THE INCARNATION OF THE GREAT VIRTUOUS FRIEND KIRTI TSENSHAB RINPOCHE

Realm of compassion of all Victorious Ones of the three times,
Compassionate deity playfully manifesting the major and minor marks,
Treasure of compassion, fortunate destiny of the migrators of the Land of Snow:
Please enable the accomplishment of these pure prayers.

Profound, fearless intelligence of pure wisdom,
Eloquent speech of the sublime Dharma
Spreading like a smiling garland of gentle waves,
Treasure filled with a wealthy abundance of instructions,
The virtuous friend, the great ocean:
You are the one I miss from the heart.

Recollecting all qualities of your Holy Body, Speech, and Mind
In distress I single-pointedly request:

Please, our Protector, in all lifetimes,
Never let us slip from the lasso of your compassion.

Alas! Lacking the virtuous friend who is the sole Refuge,
The teachings of the tender Savior, Lama Tsong Khapa, will end.
Migratory beings' happiness will darken like shadows of a setting sun.
Therefore you must come to relieve this sad and urgent plight.

Training over an extensive period of time,
You took responsibility for performing the great activities
Of the Buddha's Teachings as well as those of transmigratory beings
And generated completely the full capacity of the Holy Mind.
Yet do you comprehend the nature of our devastation?

For we, the ignorant thick-skulled ones, are abandoned to a forlorn place
While you enjoy the spheres of bliss and peace!
In this period when five degenerations' faults gather and explode,
It is now especially critical that you adopt the armor of zeal.
Since this is the promise of the Heroic Sons of the Victorious One,
Quickly reveal again the Emanation Body's Holy Face.

Already the time of the Buddha's teachings has reached the end of the five-hundred.
Almost all the Great Holy Beings who could wishfully descend to this world have departed to the Sphere of Peace (Dharmakāya).
We, pitiful fledglings, find ourselves left behind—bereft and alone.

Please recall the commitment generated in your Holy Mind:
To assume responsibility to uphold the Lamp of the teachings of the land of Rongchen (region of Amdo).
Smiling face of the Supreme emanation, the creator of day,
Like the rising sun come quickly without delay.

Not degenerating qualities acquired across lifetime's trainings,
The smile of the white cooling moon of explanation and attainment,
Our only friend who cultivates the Kunu (flower) of the Victorious One's teachings,
May the youthful moon of your unmistaken manifestation immediately appear.

Protectors of the words of the Lamas,
Guardians of the Buddha's teachings,
Special watchers over what has been requested,
Great Victorious Active Heroes

And all Powerful Protectors:
Please impel the unmistaken incarnation to arise.

In short, by the power of the incontrovertible dependent arising
Of the students' fervent faith,
Together with blessings of the Protectors of the Three Sublime Ones,
Like a wish-fulfilling jewel may our prayers without exception
Be instantaneously accomplished.

Colophon

I, the student disciple bearing the name of the incarnated Thashel Kirti, Lozang Tenzin, having heard that at the age of eighty-one the incarnation of the Great Virtuous Friend Tsatrug Geshe Tsang, the Holder of the Lineage of the Near Instruction, the Great Abbot Vajradhara Jetsun Lozang Jigme Damcho Pel Sangpo had seriously ailed and Gone Beyond, felt impelled to compose this requesting prayer entitled *The Persuasive Drum Sound of the Sphere of Great Compassion invoking the blessings of the Quick Return of the incarnation of the great virtuous friend Kirti Tsenshab Rinpoche*. May my incontrovertible pure prayers to the Three Supreme Ones in general and to the Supreme Arya the Great Compassionate One in particular be accomplished as here expressed.

It was written in the village of the Sublime realm of Bodhgaya on the fifteenth of the ninth month 2006.

The most devoted protector, Alak Rinpoche, attendant of Kyabje Kirti Tsenshab Rinpoche whose name is extremely rare to mention and who is the embodiment of and kinder than the Buddhas of the Three Times, and the Translator Voula, who offered him so many years of service, requested me, the Mickey Mouse, Thubten Zopa, to translate this Requesting Prayer. With the help of the Venerable Nun Jane, Venerable Tenzin Namdak, and Ross Moore, I have done so with devotion. Due to the merits may all sentient beings of this world be able to soon see the Smiling Face of the Unmistaken Incarnation, and enjoy again the nectar of Kyabje Rinpoche's teachings, in order to achieve Enlightenment as quickly as possible.

Sera Je Monastery, South India, January 2007.

Resources

NAMGYAL MONASTERY INSTITUTE OF BUDDHIST STUDIES is the North American seat of Namgyal Monastery, the personal monastery of His Holiness the Dalai Lama. Its new temple complex, *Du Khor Choe Ling* (Land of Kālacakra Study and Practice), is expected to be the center for the preservation and transmission of the precious Kālacakra teachings. As a nonsectarian center, Namgyal hosts teachers from all Tibetan lineages and important Western scholars. Each year Namgyal offers two week-long summer retreats, one introductory program for beginners and another, advanced retreat focused on a particular deity or set of teachings. Additionally Namgyal hosts celebrations of all important Tibetan holidays and sponsors Tibetan cultural events. For information please visit the website: http://www.namgyal.org.

THE INTERNATIONAL KALACHAKRA NETWORK (IKN) has its home online at http://www.kalachakranet.org/. It was founded in 1997 to support the practice and study of Kalachakra throughout the world, and has grown into an effective network of groups and individuals in around seventy countries. As a network, there is a looseness of organizational structure, and each person or group in the network is autonomous. To guide the operation of the network, as required from time-to-time, there is an advisory group and within that, a five-person executive who make decisions if these are ever needed. The IKN Memorandum of Intent explains the ethos of the network. It has been signed by Kirti Tsenshab Rinpoche and many translators of Kalachakra materials.

Practitioners of Kalachakra can benefit from the network as follows:

1. News of forthcoming Kalachakra empowerments, teachings, and retreats.
2. Information about Kalachakra traditions and teachers.
3. A very lively online discussion group for "IKN-Initiates."
4. An online repository of Kalachakra practice materials and commentaries, in several languages.
5. Information about Kalachakra Practice Groups which exist in several parts of the world now.
6. Translations of specific practice materials and commentaries sponsored by IKN.

Information about all of the above and much more is available from the website. Several of these are restricted to registered members.

Jonang Foundation is a U.S. nonprofit organization and online educational resource for the Jonang Tibetan Buddhist tradition. Working inside Tibet/China and within the international community, the specific purposes of Jonang Foundation are to uphold and promote greater understanding of the intellectual, creative, and spiritual heritage of the Jonang. Through educational and research-based initiatives, Jonang Foundation works to enhance efforts at preserving Jonang art and literature, educating young students in Tibet/China, translating seminal literary works of the Jonang into Western languages, documenting the Jonang in contemporary contexts, and revivifying the living tradition. To learn more about the programs and the tradition, please visit the website: http://www.jonangfoundation.org.

Contributors

ALEXANDER BERZIN Alexander Berzin is a well-known authority on the Kālacakra tradition, having studied for many years directly with Tsenshab Serkong Rinpoche. Dr. Berzin lived for many years in the Tibetan exile community in Dharamsala and was a founding member of the Translation Bureau of the Library of Tibetan Works and Archives. Among Berzin's many publications are *Taking the Kalachakra Initiation* and *Kalachakra and Other Six-Session Yoga Texts,* both from Snow Lion Publications.

WILLIAM C. BUSHELL Dr. William Bushell recently codirected the conference, "Longevity and Optimal Health: Integrating Eastern and Western Perspectives," with Robert Thurman and His Holiness the Dalai Lama; the proceedings, edited by Bushell, are to be published by the New York Academy of Sciences in May 2007. Bushell is currently collaborating with the scientists who attended that conference on research into possible regenerative and longevity-enhancing effects of Indo-Tibetan meditation and yoga.

GESHE DRAKPA GELEK Geshe la obtained his degree from Drepung Loseling Monastic University in 1991 and spent the next several years teaching there before relocating to Dharamsala in 1997. Since then he has spent most of his time in solitary retreat and served as a teacher at Namgyal Monastery during its annual summer retreat. Geshe la has received extensive personal instructions from His Holiness the Dalai Lama, Ling Rinpoche, Trijang Rinpoche, and Kirti Tsenshab Rinpoche. He is considered to be one of the important Kālacakra scholars of the younger generation and has enormous skill as a teacher of Western students.

DAVID B. GRAY David Gray is Assistant Professor of Religious Studies at Santa Clara University since 2005. He earned his doctorate at Columbia University and has distinguished himself as a scholar of the Cakrasaṃvara tradition, publishing articles in *Journal of Religious History, Numen,* and *History of Religions.* His first book, *The Discourse of Śrī Heruka: A Study and Annotated Translation of the Cakrasaṃvara Tantra* is due to be published by the American Institute for Buddhist Studies/Columbia University Press in 2007.

GEORGIOS T. HALKIAS Georgios Halkias recently received his D.Phil from Oxford University with his dissertation, "Transferring to the Land of Bliss: Among Texts and Practices of Sukhavati in Tibet," studying the canonicity of "Pure Land" doctrinal and ritual developments in Tibet. He has published in *Tibet Journal* and *Eastern Buddhist* and been on the faculty of the Antioch College Buddhist Studies in India program.

URBAN HAMMAR Urban Hammar defended his doctoral thesis, "Studies in the Kālacakra Tantra: A History of the Kālacakra Tantra in Tibet and a Study of the Concept of the Ādibuddha, the Fourth Body of the Buddha, and the Supreme Unchanging," in 2005. He is now working on a text by one of the disciples of Dol-po-pa on the history of *Kālacakra Tantra*. Hammar is affiliated with the Department of History of Religions at Stockholm University and teaches Tibetan at the Department of Oriental Languages.

LAURA HARRINGTON Laura Harrington completed her doctorate in Religion (Buddhist Studies) at Columbia University in 2002 with the dissertation, "A View of Mañjuśrī: Wisdom and Its Crown Prince in Pala-period India." She is a contributing editor of two Kālacakra-related books: *Kalachakra* and *Tibetan Astro-Science*, both published by Tibet Domani. She is presently a Research Associate at Smith College, Department of Religion.

EDWARD HENNING Edward Henning is well known among Kālacakra scholars as the leading expert on Tibetan calendar-making and astronomy. Based in England, Henning is an independent scholar who travels widely and has consulted on many Kālacakra projects, including the translation of *Ornament of Stainless Light.* His own book, *Kālacakra and the Tibetan Calendar,* is due from the American Institute of Buddhist Studies/Columbia University Press in 2007.

JHADO RINPOCHE Jhado Rinpoche served as Abbot of Namgyal Monastery between 1997 and 2004 at the appointment of His Holiness the Dalai Lama. Rinpoche is widely recognized as the leading Tibetan authority on Kālacakra among the younger generation of Gelug scholars. Rinpoche was recognized at the age of three as the sixth incarnation of the abbot of Jhado Monastery and, after fleeing into exile, obtained his Geshe Lharampa degree from Sera Je in 1991. Rinpoche then taught at Namgyal Monastery until being appointed its abbot. Rinpoche now travels widely and is well known for his penetrating insight and warm humor.

THUPTEN JINPA Thupten Jinpa Langri has served as translator to His Holiness the Dalai Lama for many years, but he is an accomplished scholar in his own right. Holder of a geshe degree from Ganden and a doctorate from Cambridge, he is currently president of the Tibetan Classics Institute which publishes important volumes from all aspects of Tibetan thought and culture. He has contributed to or edited many important publications, including *Mind Training: The Great Collection,* and has authored *Self, Reality and Reason in Tibetan Philosophy: Tsongkhapa's Quest for the Middle Way.*

GAVIN KILTY Gavin Kilty spent more than a dozen years in Dharamsala , where he studied at the Institute for Buddhist Dialectics. Since 1984 he has lived in the United Kingdom, where he has been affiliated with Jamyang Buddhist Centre. He has also produced translations for the International Kalachakra Network and is currently translating Desi Sangye Gyatso's *Mirror of Vaidurya* for the Library of Tibetan Classics. Previous publications include the seminal *Ornament of Stainless Light*, the first volume for the Library of Tibetan Classics, and *Splendor of an Autumn Moon: The Devotional Verse of Tsongkhapa.*

KIRTI TSENSHAB RINPOCHE Kirti Tsenshab Rinpoche was one of the most important Kālacakra teachers of our time, traveling the world to disseminate these precious teachings. As the only master to escape Tibet with the complete oral transmission of his lineage, Rinpoche preserved the continuity of the tradition. Rinpoche passed away in December 2006 after a short session with liver cancer. Please see the articles about and by Rinpoche for more information.

PHILLIP LECSO Phillip Lecso has been an important translator for the International Kalachakra Network. For many years, Lecso was Assistant Professor of Medicine at the Medical College of Ohio and published articles on Buddhist attitudes toward biomedical issues. Recently he has had to discontinue these activities due to an aggressive neuromuscular disorder.

JOSEPH LOIZZO Joseph Loizzo M.D., Ph.D. is Assistant Professor of Psychiatry in Complementary and Integrative Medicine, Weill College of Medicine, Cornell University, and Visiting Scholar of Religion, Center for Buddhist Studies, Columbia University. Loizzo is also founder and director of Nalanda Institute for Meditation and Healing in Manhattan. Loizzo's *Nagarjuna's Reason Sixty* (including Candrakirti's commentary) is due to be published by the American Institute of Buddhist Studies/Columbia University Press in 2007.

GIACOMELLA OROFINO Giacomella Orofino is Associate Professor of Indo-Tibetan Religions and Civilizations and Tibetan Language and Literature at the Oriental University of Naples. Orofino has published many articles on Tibetan Buddhism and the Kālacakra tradition specifically. Among these important articles are "On the saḍaṅgayoga and the Realisation of Ultimate Gnosis in the Kālacakratantra," and "Divination with Mirrors: Observations on a Simile Found in the Kālacakra Literature." Her books include *Sacred Tibetan Teachings on Death and Liberation* and *Sekoddeśa: A Critical Edition of the Tibetan Translations.*

DAVID REIGLE David Reigle is a founding member of the International Kalachakra Network and remains on its Executive Team. Reigle is the author of *Kalacakra Sadhana and Social Responsibility* (Santa Fe, 1996). He is working on a critical edition in Sanskrit of the *Śrī Kālacakra Sādhana* by Sadhuputra, along with an English translation.

Francesco Sferra Francesco Sferra is Associate Professor of Sanskrit and Indology at the Oriental University of Naples and a member of the Istituto Italiano per l'Africa e l'Oriente and other professional institutions. Among his main publications are the edition and English translation of the *Saḍaṅgayoga* by Anupamarakṣita with its commentary by Raviśrījñana (Rome 2000) and the new critical edition of the Sanskrit text of the *Sekoddeśaṭika* by Nāropa (Rome 2006). He expects to publish his revised doctoral dissertation with Firenze University Press in 2007.

Miranda Shaw Miranda Shaw is Associate Professor of Religion at the University of Richmond. Shaw's first book, *Passionate Enlightenment*, won both the 1994 James Henry Breasted Prize of the American Historical Association and the 1994 *Tricycle* Prize for Excellence in Buddhist Scholarship. Years of research have resulted in the recent *Buddhist Goddesses of India* and the forthcoming *Buddhist Goddesses of Tibet and Nepal*, both from Princeton University Press.

Michael R. Sheehy Michael R. Sheehy, Ph.D. is the founder and executive director of Jonang Foundation. An author of several articles on Tibetan Buddhism, his research interests include the formulation of *zhentong* (*gzhan stong*) philosophical thinking within contemplative Jonang literature, the history of the sixfold vajrayoga Kalachakra lineage, and the contemporary Jonang tradition. As a researcher and facilitator of projects hosted by Jonang Foundation, he spends his time living in the Tibetan cultural domains of China and in the United States.

Sofia Stril-Rever Sofia Stril-Rever graduated in Indian Studies from Paris University. She received a traditional training from an Indian pandit at the Central Institute of Higher Tibetan Studies in Sarnath and from Tibetan lamas in Dharamsala. A writer and poet, she has authored four books on the Kālacakra tradition, including translations from Sanskrit into French of Chapters Two and Five of the *Stainless Light* (*Vimalaprabhā*). At Paris Kalachakra Center, she is coordinating a Kalachakra practice group.

Ivette Vargas Ivette Vargas is Assistant Professor of Religious Studies at Austin College. Vargas earned her doctorate from Harvard University in 2003 with the dissertation "Falling to pieces, emerging whole: Suffering illness and healing renunciation in the Dge slong ma Dpal mo tradition." She has done extensive fieldwork in Tibet with a focus on the intersection of medicine, healing, and religion and published chapters in *A Communion of Subjects: Animals in Religion, Science, and Ethics* (Columbia University Press 2006) and *Teaching Religion and Healing* (Oxford University Press 2006).

Vesna A. Wallace Vesna Wallace is Associate Professor of Religious Studies at the University of California, Santa Barbara. Wallace is one of the most important scholars of the Kālacakra tradition, having published the monumental overview *The Inner Kalacakratantra: A Buddhist Tantric View of the Individual* and several journal articles. She has also published complete translations of chapters two and four of the root text: *The Kālacakratantra: The Chapter on the Individual Together with the Vimalaprabhā* and *The Chapter on the Sādhana*, which is due to be published in 2007.

GLENN WALLIS Glenn Wallis is Associate Professor of Religion at the University of Georgia, Department of Religion, and is affiliated with The Won Institute of Graduate Studies, Applied Meditation Studies Program. He has published two volumes with Random House, *The Dhammapada* (2004) and *Basic Teachings of the Buddha* (2007), as well as the academic study *Mediating the Power of Buddhas.*

RONIT YOELI-TLALIM Ronit Yoeli-Tlalim wrote her Ph.D. thesis, titled "Contemporary Oral Teachings of the *Kālacakra*: Dialogue between Tradition and Change" at the School of Oriental and African Studies in London. She later worked on a research project on "Islam and Tibet: Cultural Interactions" at the Warburg Institute. She is currently working as a research fellow at the Wellcome Trust Centre for the History of Medicine at University College London (UK), conducting research on early Tibetan medicine.